Selected Writings of Lord Acton

VOLUME III

ESSAYS IN RELIGION, POLITICS, AND MORALITY

Lord Acton

Selected Writings of Lord Acton

VOLUME III

ESSAYS IN RELIGION, POLITICS, AND MORALITY

by
John Emerich Edward Dalberg-Acton
First Baron Acton

edited by J. Rufus Fears

Liberty*Classics*

Indianapolis

The Essays in This Volume, and other editorial additions © 1988 by J. Rufus Fears. All rights reserved. All inquiries should be addressed to Liberty Fund, Inc., 7440 N. Shadeland, Indianapolis, Indiana 46250. This book was manufactured in the United States of America.

Cover art is a reproduction of the painting by Franz von Lenbach at the National Portrait Gallery, London.

Frontispiece photo is from *Lord Acton and His Circle,* published in 1906 by Longmans, Green & Co., New York, New York.

Library of Congress Cataloging in Publication Data

Acton, John Emerich Edward Dalberg-Acton, Baron,
    1834–1902.
    Selected writings of Lord Acton

    Includes bibliographical references and index.
    Contents: v. 1. Essays in the history of liberty.
    1. Liberty—Addresses, essays, lectures.   2. History—
Study and teaching—Addresses, essays, lectures.
3. Historiography—Addresses, essays, lectures.
4. Aphorisms and apothegms—Addresses, essays, lectures.
5. Liberalism—History—19th century—Addresses, essays,
lectures.   I. Fears, J. Rufus.   II. Title.
D15.A25A25   1985   907.2   85-4522

ISBN 0-86597-050-5

ISBN 0-86597-051-3 (pbk.)

10 9 8 7 6 5 4 3 2 1

Contents

SECTION I

Essays in Liberal Catholicism

SECTION II

Acton and the Vatican Council

SECTION III

Perspectives on History, Religion, and Morality

SECTION IV

Selections from the Acton Legacy

Biographical Note

LORD ACTON (1834–1902). Historian and political thinker, John Emerich Edward Dalberg-Acton was one of the most significant figures in the intellectual and political life of Victorian England. A Roman Catholic, he was educated in Munich under the Catholic church historian Ignaz von Döllinger. From 1858 until 1871, through his personality, editorial activities, articles, and reviews, he assumed a major role in the Liberal Catholic movement. Although he was briefly a member of Parliament, his main political influence was exercised as an admirer, friend, and confidant of the Liberal Prime Minister William Gladstone. As Regius Professor of Modern History at Cambridge from 1895 to 1902, Acton was instrumental in transforming the writing of history in England from a form of belles lettres into a rigorously scientific discipline based on the model of German scholarship.

While emphasizing complete objectivity in the pursuit of historical truth, Acton was deeply concerned with the need for moral judgment in history and with the meaning of history. This meaning he found in the concept of human freedom. For Acton, "the idea of liberty is the unity, the only unity of the history of the world, and the one principle of a philosophy of history." Although his planned *History of Liberty* never came to fruition, the lectures, essays, and reviews that he did write are more than sufficient to establish him as a thinker of supreme importance in the intellectual heritage of classical Liberalism. It is an importance of more than historical interest. His powerfully original analysis of the nature of individual and political freedom and of the forces that foster and threaten that freedom speak to the most profound concerns of the late twentieth century.

The Essays in This Volume

Contemporaries confessed themselves puzzled by Lord Acton. They were baffled by his unwillingness to carry out the sustained literary effort involved in writing a book. Even more, his fellow historians, who admired his enormous erudition, were perplexed by the deeper aspects of his philosophy of history, by his unique conception of the history of liberty and by his insistence on judging historical persons and institutions by an absolute code of moral rectitude. Perhaps most of all, his English admirers failed to understand how a man of such decided political Liberalism could be a confirmed Roman Catholic. As the eminent Liberal politician and man of letters John Morley wrote, "[Acton's] union of devoted faith in liberty with devoted faith to the Church of authority was a standing riddle."[1]

Acton was aware of the enigma which his personality and opinions seemed to pose for others, and he claimed to find difficulty in understanding their confusion.[2] To him the matter seemed quite simple. In a letter to Lady Blennerhassett, Acton gave his confession as "a very simple, obvious, and not interesting story." It was the "story of a man who started in life believing himself a sincere Catholic and a sincere Liberal, who therefore renounced everything in Catholicism which was not compatible with Liberty, and everything in Politics which was not compatible with Catholicity."[3]

In other words, Acton did not compartmentalize religion, morality, and politics. For him, true liberty was freedom for the individual to decide his own conscience, to make the moral, ethical, and religious choices he believed to be right. The ultimate duty of the state was to protect the individual's right to conscience. The duty of religion was

[1] John Morley, *Recollections* (New York, 1917), p. 230.
[2] Döllinger III, p. 361.
[3] Acton, *Selected Writings of Lord Acton: Volume III: Essays in Religion, Politics, and Morality*, Fears, ed., p. 657.

to educate that conscience and thus to make men moral beings. This did not mean a dichotomy between private beliefs and public actions. Quite the contrary: we are to judge public figures, political systems, and religions by the degree to which their conduct and actions live up to what Acton believed to be the universally accepted code of moral standards.

His friend Morley called Acton "a passionately interested master of the bonds between moral truth and the action of the political system."[4] Acton himself wrote of spending years searching for men "wise enough to solve the problems that puzzled me, not in religion or politics so much as along the wavy line between the two."[5] He found no easy answers, and he himself does not offer easy solutions. He does offer instruction, and the material in this volume invites the reader to explore with Acton the frontier where religion and morality, politics and history meet.

The first two sections, "Essays in Liberal Catholicism" and "Acton and the Vatican Council" document the most public period of Acton's engagement with central issues of religion and politics in modern society. It was a period that began in 1858 with Acton's first publications in the *Rambler* and concluded in 1874 with a series of four letters to the editor of the London *Times*. It was a time of intensive literary and political activity. It began in confidence and hope and ended in rejection and disillusionment.[6]

---

[4] Morley, *Recollections*, p. 230.

[5] Acton, *Selected Writings* III, p. 663.

[6] Although written before the publication of important collections of Acton's correspondence, Gertrude Himmelfarb, *Lord Acton: A Study in Conscience and Politics* (Chicago, 1952) remains the best biography. David Mathew, *Lord Acton and His Times* (London, 1968) is useful primarily for background material on the personalities and events of the age in which Acton lived. A better biographical treatment, making use of recent Acton scholarship, is Robert Schuettinger, *Lord Acton: Historian of Liberty* (LaSalle, Illinois, 1976). More recent treatments of Acton as a historian include George Watson, *Politics and Literature in Modern Britain* (Totowa, N.J., 1977), pp. 153–172; John Kenyon, *The History Men: The Historical Profession in England since the Renaissance* (London, 1983), pp. 125–143; and M.A. Fitzsimons, *The Past Recaptured* (Notre Dame, 1983), pp. 188–206; Terence Murphy, "Lord Acton and the Question of Moral Judgement in History: The Development of the Position," *Catholic Historical Review* 70(1984), pp. 225–250; and Peter Kaufman, "Unnatural Sympathies? Acton and Döllinger on the Reformation," *Catholic Historical Review* 70(1984), pp. 547–559. J.S. Nurser, *The Reign of Conscience* (New York, 1987) examines a concept central to Acton's political and historical thought.

The following works will serve to guide the interested reader to the issues, personalities, and events central to an understanding of Acton's place amidst the intellectual and

Section I: Essays in Liberal Catholicism

Acton's union of Roman Catholicism and Liberalism was personal and peculiar. It did not lend itself to easy understanding by others, even by friends who were both Catholic and Liberal. It had its origins in the circumstances of birth and family traditions and was stimulated, deepened, and refined by education. His mother saw to it that his early education occurred in Catholic surroundings. Denied admission to Oxford and Cambridge, the young Acton was sent to Munich for university study under the eminent Catholic divine and Church historian Ignaz von Döllinger. The political convictions of his stepfather, Lord Granville, assured that the sixteen-year-old Acton arrived in Munich "primed to the brim with Whig politics." But it was the years with Döllinger which forged Acton's intellectual destiny. From 1850 to 1857, in his most impressionable youth, Acton studied with Döllinger, lived in his home, accompanied him on a series of visits to libraries and archives, and in his company met figures of note in European scholarly and ecclesiastical life.[7]

Döllinger was more than an ecclesiastical historian of depth and originality. He was a figure of major consequence in German Catholic intellectual and even political life. Munich was the center of Catholic Liberalism in Germany, and Döllinger was the leader of this Liberal movement. At its heart was the conviction that the Church must be brought intellectually and politically into the nineteenth century. The methodology and results of modern science and scholarship offered no

political currents of the Catholic Church in the nineteenth century: Josef Altholz, *The Liberal Catholic Movement in England* (London, 1962); Hugh MacDougall, *The Acton–Newman Relationship: The Dilemma of Christian Liberalism* (New York, 1962); Victor Conzemius, "Lord Acton and the First Vatican Council," *Journal of Ecclesiastical History* 20 (1969), pp. 267–294; Damian McElrath (in collaboration with James Holland, Ward White, and Sue Katzman), *Lord Acton: The Decisive Decade* (Louvain, 1970); Frederick Cwiekowski, *The English Bishops and the First Vatican Council* (Louvain, 1971); Walter Arnstein, *Protestant versus Catholic in Mid-Victorian England* (Columbia–London, 1982); Edward Norman, *The English Catholic Church in the Nineteenth Century* (Oxford, 1984). A general study of the Catholic Church in this period is Roger Aubert, *Le Pontificat de Pie IX (1846–1878)*, volume XXI of *Histoire de l'Église depuis les origines jusqu'à nos jours*, A. Fliche and V. Martin, eds., 2nd ed. (Paris, 1963). A useful study in English is E.E.Y. Hales, *Pio Nono* (New York, 1954).

[7] James Holland, *The Education of Lord Acton* (Diss., Catholic University of America, 1968). Almost fifty years later, Acton was still unclear as to why his application to Oxford and Cambridge Colleges had been denied; Acton, *Correspondence*, pp. 157, 256–257.

threat to the doctrines of the Church. On the contrary, Catholic scholarship and the influence of the Church could only profit from the rigorous and unhampered pursuit of scientific truth and from the use of those intellectual tools wielded so skillfully by Protestant thinkers. Indeed, the possession of such tools was essential to the mission of the Church and of critical importance if Catholics were to meet Protestants in equal intellectual debate. Liberal Catholicism thus insisted upon freedom of inquiry and research in the belief that ultimately the truths of religion and science must be compatible. This "harmony of truths" rested on civil as well as intellectual freedom, and the Liberal Catholic movement identified the true Catholic cause with the principles of liberty and independence.[8] The cause of religion was seen as inseparably bound to the cause of freedom and to the ideal of the Church as the guardian of personal and political liberty.[9] The young Acton eloquently summarized the creed of a Liberal Catholic with his statement that "in politics as in science the church need not seek her own ends—she will obtain them if she encourages the pursuit of the ends of science, which are truth—and of the state, which are liberty."[10]

Acton felt called to propagate these ideas among his fellow Catholics in England; to this end he returned from Germany in 1857 and began his association with a series of periodicals that became the primary organs of English Liberal Catholicism. In 1858, along with Richard Simpson, Acton became joint owner and co-editor of the *Rambler*. In 1862 the *Rambler* was transformed into a quarterly periodical with the new name of the *Home and Foreign Review*, but it continued to be owned and edited by Acton and Simpson, and its ideological bent remained the same. In 1867, three years after the demise of the *Home and Foreign Review*, Acton played a major role in launching the *Chronicle*, which appeared weekly between March 30, 1867 and February 15, 1868. A final effort of Liberal Catholic journalism was made in 1869 through the *North British Review*. Like the *Chronicle*, the *North British Review* was avowedly secular in character, but it nonetheless served as the vehicle for Acton's views during the period of the Vatican Council. Having fulfilled this purpose, it came to a natural end in 1871. Although he

---

[8] Altholz, *Liberal Catholic Movement*, p. 52.

[9] See Acton's remarks in his essay "The Count de Montalembert," *Selected Writings* III, pp. 9–11.

[10] Acton, *Selected Writings* III, p. 615.

neither owned nor edited the *Chronicle* or the *North British Review*, Acton was a major force behind them and a frequent contributor.[11]

In his contributions to these four periodicals, we can trace the course of Acton's efforts to use his commitment to Liberalism and his historical knowledge to influence Catholic opinion at a critical moment in the history of the Church. The papacy of Pius IX (1846–1878) had begun in a spirit of accommodation to the forces of Liberalism and nationalism on the Continent. That accommodation was shattered by the very strength of those forces. Nationalism demanded the unification of Italy, a unification which could only mean the absorption of the Papal States and the disappearance of the temporal power of the popes. Liberalism in the form it assumed in Europe, in the policies of men like Cavour, demanded a "state endowed with indefinite powers," a state in which there could be no room for an independent Church.[12] In an age of *Realpolitik*, ideological fervor, and national armies, the survival of the Church as a temporal power became a forlorn hope. By 1870 the annexation of the Papal States by the newly unified Kingdom of Italy was complete. In 1860 major portions of the Pope's territorial possessions in Italy had been lost. In 1870 Italian troops entered Rome. Henceforth the Pope's temporal power would be limited to the Vatican, where Pius IX lived out his days as a self-proclaimed prisoner.

The demise of the territorial aspect of papal power need not have been accompanied by a demise of its spiritual, moral, and even political influence. That at least was the view of Acton and other like-minded Catholic Liberals. As the Reformation had led to renewal within the Catholic Church, so Acton believed that the transformation in political fortunes provided the opportunity for the moral rejuvenation of the Church, which would "stand on its own everlasting foundation, the words of Christ, and not on the gifts of Constantine."[13] The Church must join the vanguard of modern civilization and science in order to shape the forces of the new age. By so doing it would prove true to its mission, erecting a moral bulwark against the demands of an otherwise absolutist and amoral state, creating a security for individual liberty,

---

[11] The history of these periodicals is discussed in more detail in Acton, *Selected Writings* I, pp. xxii–xxiv.

[12] As Acton commented in his essay "Cavour," reprinted in *Selected Writings* I, pp. 434–458; the specific quote is found on p. 441.

[13] Acton, *Selected Writings* III, p. 9.

an irreducible fortress in which men could be free to follow the demands of conscience. To join the Church to the spirit of all that was best in modern civilization, to principles of liberty of conscience, personal dignity, and freedom of inquiry and research, was the response of Liberal Catholics to the political and intellectual crisis of the Church in the nineteenth century.

That was not the response chosen by Pius IX. In 1861 the encyclical *Jamdudum cernimus* denounced modern political doctrines that encouraged non-Catholic religions, permitted freedom to attack the Church in print, and undermined the authority of the Church. On December 8, 1864, he issued the encyclical *Quanta cura* with an attached syllabus listing eighty "principle errors of our times." The last of these denounced as erroneous the view that "the Roman Pontiff can and should reconcile himself to and agree with progress, liberalism, and modern civilisation."

Along with this denunciation of the central tenets of Catholic Liberalism went the conviction that all power in the Church should be exercised through the papal office. It was a tenet fundamental to the political ideas and policy of Ultramontanism. It was this view which triumphed at the Vatican Council of 1869–1870 in the proclamation of papal infallibility: "We teach and define as divinely revealed dogma, that the Roman Pontiff, when he speaks *ex cathedra*, i.e., when, in his character as Pastor and Doctor of all Christians, and in virtue of his supreme apostolic authority, he lays down that a certain doctrine concerning faith or morals is binding upon the universal Church— possesses by the Divine assistance which was promised to him in the person of the blessed Saint Peter, that same infallibility with which the Divine Redeemer thought fit to endow his Church, to define its doctrine with regard to faith and morals; and consequently that these definitions of the Roman Pontiff are irreformable in themselves, and not in consequence of the consent of the Church."

The promulgation of the dogma of papal infallibility represented the culmination of a struggle between Liberals and Ultramontanes to determine the direction of the Church. Neither the designation "Ultramontanism" nor its tendency was new to the nineteenth century. Like its rival, Gallicanism, it hearkened back to central issues in medieval thought and politics. "Ultramontane" described those who looked to Rome for supreme guidance in matters ecclesiastical and political. In the Ultramontane conception of Church and state, the Pope could depose temporal rulers, and his authority over the Church and its bishops was absolute. It was a conception of papal power which encountered the strongest political and intellectual resistance.

Originating in France, Gallicanism insisted that temporal rulers held their power directly from God. It equally maintained that the Church in France had its own traditions of liberties and of administrative control independent from that of Rome. Finally, it believed that the infallible authority of the Church was held jointly by its bishops and the Pope and that the authority of a general Church council was above that of the Pope.

In the nineteenth century, the writings of Joseph de Maistre and others gave a renewed intellectual vigor to Ultramontanism, while its absolutist tendencies were sharped by direct confrontation with Catholic Liberalism. The Liberal believed that the bishops, by virtue of apostolic succession, have an inalienable right to share in the government of the Church. The Ultramontane sought a Church in which power was centralized, a Church ruled by an absolute Pope through the ecclesiastical bureaucracy of the Curia. The Liberal believed that the ends of both Church and state were best served by a Church which was independent of the state, "a free Church in a free State." The Ultramontane joined Church and state in a union in which the Church was the dominant partner, the state serving to carry out its wishes. The Liberal insisted upon freedom of thought and inquiry; the Ultramontane wished rigorously to control thought and research. Freedom of conscience was a fundamental tenet of Catholic Liberalism. To the Ultramontane the belief that there was no salvation outside the Church imposed intolerance of other creeds as a Christian duty.

It was internecine party warfare waged with all the rancor and bitterness of men motivated by deep commitment to intellectual and moral principles and by profound personal antipathy. Among Acton's primary opponents in England were the leaders of the Catholic hierarchy, including Cardinal Wiseman, until his death in 1865, and Cardinal Manning, Wiseman's successor as Archbishop of Westminster.[14] At an early stage, Acton had hoped for the support of John Henry Newman. However, in Acton's opinion Newman was uneasy

---

[14] In this introduction I have tended towards Acton's unflattering and biased view of Wiseman and Manning. For a more balanced perspective, see S. W. Jackman's superb treatment of *Nicholas Wiseman: A Victorian Prelate and His Writings* (Dublin, 1977) and the excellent treatment of both Wiseman and Manning in Norman, *English Catholic Church*, pp. 110–157, 244–286.

with an intellectual position which insisted upon the unfettered search for truth. Certainly, Newman was convinced of the practical necessity of submission to authority. With such a position Acton could have no sympathy, and he would come to speak of his "deep adversion" for this "sophist" and "manipulator of the truth."[15] Both Newman and Manning were converts to Catholicism. So was Richard Simpson, one of the staunchest and most controversial of Catholic Liberals. However, those converts who, like Manning, came under the influence of Cardinal Wiseman formed a particularly strong party of Romanists and were castigated by Acton as "lovers of authority, fearing knowledge much, progress more, freedom most, and essentially unhistoric and unscientific." Moreover, the disharmony in the English Catholic community was made more complicated by very real tensions between these "zealous converts" and members of old Catholic families like Acton.[16] To this was added the tenuous position of Catholics in England. Only with the Catholic Emancipation Act of 1829 were Parliament and most state offices opened to professing Roman Catholics, and in the mid-nineteenth century Catholics remained a small minority, the object of considerable hostility at all levels of English society, an antipathy resulting not only from anti-papal sentiment but also from xenophobia and dislike of the Irish.

The personalities and events of a struggle which consumed sixteen years of Acton's life have long since been laid to rest. However, in the journalistic pieces which Acton wrote in the heat of conflict there was an element which transcended the immediate and which gives to these essays an enduring, indeed an imperishable, quality. That element is truth. Is the human mind to be free to pursue truth wherever it leads, or is to be fettered by authority? Are we to be guided only by our own consciences and the results of our own freely conducted inquiries, or must we accept the dictates of those in authority, of those who, with their own perception of what is in our best interests, tell us what we are free to believe?

For Acton, there could be no ultimate contradiction between the truths of religion and the truths revealed by the free inquiries of science. The Church, by recognizing this and by putting herself in the vanguard of scientific and political progress, would assume her rightful role in modern society. The first six essays in this volume, all published

[15] Paul, pp. 70, 242–243; Acton, *Selected Writings* III, p. 661.
[16] Acton-Simpson III, p. 25.

between 1858 and 1861, represent Acton's efforts to convince fellow Catholics of the truth of this viewpoint. Written in the most positive spirit, these are essays in the creation of a constructive and uniquely Catholic response to the political and intellectual challenges of the modern era, an age in which "political zeal occupies the place made vacant by the decline of religious fervour."[17]

In his review of *Le Progrès par le Christianisme*, Acton pointed to the weaknesses and division of Catholic intellectuals in France, those who resolutely hated and rejected everything which breathed an air of modernism and those who uncritically and without independence of thought accepted and sought to use every current of modern thought, however irreconcilable with fundamental tenets of religious belief. A quite different spirit motivated Charles de Montalembert, the Catholic historian and *bête noir* of French Ultramontanes. With the battle cry of "God and Liberty," Montalembert sought a free Church in a free state, and a society and a Catholicism which would encourage civil as well as intellectual freedom. Montalembert recognized the danger presented to religion by some of the most dominant and characteristic forces of the modern age: democracy and nationalism. In his essays "The Count de Montalembert" and "The Roman Question" Acton defined a distinctly Catholic concept of political authority and liberty and distinguished this sharply from the fundamental and erroneous idea underlying the modern state: "The Catholic notion, defining liberty not as the power of doing what we like, but the right of doing what we ought, denies that general interests can supersede individual rights. It condemns, therefore, the theory of the ancient as well as of the modern state."[18]

Acton believed that there was a philosophy of politics to be derived from a union of this true Catholic concept of liberty with the best principles of the English constitution.[19] His essay "Political Thoughts on the Church" represents the attempt to formulate such a Catholic theory of politics. Published when he was twenty-four and clearly written even to the point of translating quotations, it is an original and provocative contribution to political theory and contains some of the most characteristic elements of Acton's developed philosophy. In it we find that association between liberty and conscience which would

[17] Acton, *Selected Writings* III, p. 17.
[18] Acton, *Selected Writings* III, p. 613.
[19] Acton-Simpson I, p. 6.

lead Acton ultimately to define freedom as "the reign of conscience."[20] Its methodology exemplifies Acton's view that historical knowledge and historical thought are instruments of action, forces that can make the future.[21] It delineates his argument that the idea of liberty is the supreme legacy of the Catholic Middle Ages to the modern era. Above all, "Political Thoughts on the Church" emphasizes and justifies Acton's profound conviction that it is the nature and duty of true religion to transform and to inspire the public as well as the private lives of men.[22]

Thus, it was in its ability to transform the public and private lives of men that Acton saw the supreme purpose of the Church in modern society. He perceived the great danger to personal freedom posed by the ideological assumptions of the modern state, its renunciation of moral foundations and its grounding in the belief that the will of the people was supreme. The modern state possessed the power for a despotism unparalleled in history. Only force could limit such power, and the Church, with its organization, its access to public opinion, and its moral power to cultivate the conscience of its members and thus to educate them for true liberty, represented such a force. Acton hoped that "the principle of resistance to the increasing power of the State over the nation, which is the secret of true liberty, would find among Catholics, in religious as well as political matters, its most determined adherents."[23] His essays "The Catholic Press" and "The Catholic Academy" place Acton's journalistic endeavors for the *Rambler* into this broad context of the Church's mission in the modern world: "It belongs both to [the Church's] character and her interest to require the development of literature and science for the performance of her own great intellectual work, and to promote political liberty because it is the condition of her social action."[24] The Church could not cultivate the moral faculties, it could not educate the intellect, if it shut itself off from truth. If Catholics disarmed themselves intellectually by rejecting the results of modern science, they could never debate, much less convert, their enemies.

Acton's purpose in undertaking the work of the *Rambler* was edu-

---

[20] Acton, *Selected Writings* III, p. 491.

[21] Acton, *Selected Writings* II, pp. 504–505.

[22] Acton, *Selected Writings* III, pp. 11, 22, 28–29.

[23] Acton, *Selected Writings* III, p. 46.

[24] Acton, *Selected Writings* III, pp. 57.

cation: to elevate learning among English Catholics by bringing them into contact with the best books, ideas, and thinkers of Europe. This meant, preeminently, Ignaz von Döllinger;[25] above all, the *Rambler* presented an opportunity for disseminating in England the ideas and opinions of his teacher. Acton's article "Döllinger on the Temporal Power" expounded for an English public Döllinger's views on the most sensitive of Catholic issues. Döllinger's book *Kirche und Kirchen* arose out of lectures given in Munich in April 1861, when major portions of the Papal States in Italy had already been annexed. His motives were of the best; he wished to refute those enemies of the Church who assumed that the demise of the Pope's territorial possessions was a prelude to the dissolution of the Church itself.

Döllinger emphatically stated that temporal power was, given the current state of European politics, the best means to secure the freedom of the papacy; he did not attack the concept of temporal possessions for the Pope. What he did say was that man could not presume to know all, that God in His wisdom might bring about a condition in which, even without temporal possessions, the Holy See would retain its independence and freedom of action, immune to controls by the secular state, and he pointed out that for the first seven centuries of its existence the Church had managed without territorial possessions. He admitted that corruption and abuses had existed in those areas of Italy which until recently the Pope had governed. Above all, Döllinger wanted men to remember that temporal power, its possession or loss, did not affect the essence of the Church's mission.[26]

Like Döllinger, Acton believed that, given the nature of the modern state, the Pope required temporal sovereignty to maintain his freedom of action. He equally believed that such freedom of action was essential, for one of the most important functions of the papacy was to act as an impartial mediator between nations and between churches and governments.[27] His long and detailed analysis of Döllinger's book was, however, more than a colorless restatement of his teacher's views. It also gave Acton the opportunity to develop in an oblique fashion a peculiarly Catholic theory of politics, a theory which argued that the Church preserved in itself the elements by which true liberty, civil as

[25] Döllinger I, p. 128. In a letter of June 27, 1858, Simpson writes to Acton: "I am disposed to accept your dicta as oracles—of Döllinger." Acton-Simpson I, p. 36.

[26] Acton, *Selected Writings* III, pp. 69–77.

[27] Acton, *Selected Writings* III, pp. 77–78, 86, 126.

well as religious, is secured. It was in the nature of Protestantism to subordinate itself to the civil power, to confine the Church within the jurisdiction of the state.[28] The true Catholic principle was to maintain Church and state as separate and distinct entities, exercising mutual checks and salutary influences upon each other and thereby securing liberty and morality, which is the product of faith.[29] Through such a relationship the medieval Church "had bestowed on the English the great elements of their political prosperity—the charter of their liberties, the fusion of the races, and the abolition of villeinage—that is, personal and general freedom, and national unity."[30]

In "Political Thoughts on the Church" and indirectly, in articles like "Döllinger on the Temporal Power," Acton was moving towards a statement of major consequence in the theory of politics: a formulation of the positive and essential role of religion and morality in the modern state, a formulation historically grounded and yet addressed to the needs of the mid-nineteenth century. However, the literary elaboration of this theory was cut off by the increasing need to defend the very existence of Liberal Catholic journalism from attacks by the Catholic hierarchy in England and in Rome.

By the spring of 1861 the threat of censure began to hang over the *Rambler*. Partly to avoid this action and to start afresh, the *Rambler* was renamed the *Home and Foreign Review* and its format was altered to that of a quarterly publication. The last issue of the *Rambler* appeared in May 1862, the first issue of the *Home and Foreign Review* in July 1862. In the interim, Cardinal Barnabò, prefect of the Congregation *de Propaganda Fide*, sent a circular letter to the English bishops, requiring them to issue pastoral letters warning Catholics against a periodical which raised "abstruse questions closely connected with the faith, . . . put forth temerarious and scandalous propositions, . . . [attacked] the temporal authority of the Holy See . . . and the administration of the Papal States, . . . [and] said that Paul III, Paul IV, Pius V preferred temporal emolument to the good of souls."[31]

In the summer of 1862, Archbishop of Westminster Cardinal Wiseman censured the journal, noting that, under either of its names,

---

[28] Acton, *Selected Writings* III, pp. 83–93.
[29] Acton, *Selected Writings* III, pp. 83–86, 89–90.
[30] Acton, *Selected Writings* III, p. 91.
[31] Cited in Edward Cuthbert Butler, *The Life and Times of Bishop Ullathorne* I (London, 1926), p. 322.

it was marked by an absence of reserve or respect in its treatment of persons or things deemed sacred, that it grazed "the very edges of the most perilous abysses of error," and that it had "habitual preference of uncatholic to catholic instincts, tendencies, and motives."[32] In the course of September and October 1861, all but one English bishop had condemned the journal.

In "Cardinal Wiseman and *The Home and Foreign Review*" and "Ultramontanism," Acton and his co-editor Richard Simpson sought to explain and justify their mission as Catholic journalists. Both articles were works of collaboration. Acton supplied the ideas for "Cardinal Wiseman and *The Home and Foreign Review*," but the piece itself was written by Simpson and Thomas Wetherell, a subeditor.[33] "Ultramontanism" was also a collaborative effort, but, according to Simpson, Acton was its primary author.[34]

In commenting upon Cardinal Wiseman's censure, the editors reiterated that the very foundation of their periodical was "a humble faith in the infallible teaching of the Catholic Church, a devotion to her cause which controls every other interest, and an attachment to her authority which no other influence can supplant."[35] However, they also urged an understanding of the nature of journalism and a belief that religion profited most from journalism and literature which worked to achieve their goals independently of the Church. The Church is not alone in possessing ethical and intellectual functions; these are also the prerogatives of science and society: "The political and intellectual orders remain permanently distinct from the spiritual. They follow their own ends, they obey their own laws, and in so doing they support the cause of religion by the discovery of truth and the upholding of right."[36] For Acton, the principles of religion, politics, and science were always and completely in harmony. Their interests, however, could clash. The state must defend the principle of freedom of conscience, even if such freedom were a temptation to heresy or apostasy. Science must proclaim every truth, even those that could undermine faith. "There is no opening for catholics to deny, in the

[32] *Rome and the Catholic Episcopate: Reply of His Eminence Cardinal Wiseman to an Address presented to him by the Clergy Secular and Regular of the Archdiocese of Westminster* (London, 1862), pp. 26–27; cited in Altholz, *Liberal Catholic Movement*, p. 188.

[33] Acton-Simpson III, p. 34.

[34] Acton-Simpson III, p. 73.

[35] Acton, *Selected Writings* III, p. 137.

[36] Acton, *Selected Writings* III, pp. 138–139.

gross, that political science may have absolute principles of right, or intellectual science of truth."[37]

The Cardinal Wiseman essay stands on the frontier where religion, politics, and science meet. The idea of checks and balances is elevated into the sphere of the intellect and spirit. Absolute power corrupts; if science and the state are made subordinate to the Church, she will be corrupted. No less sure is the corruption of a society in which religion and science are made subordinate to the demands and interests of the state. Yet, working to fulfill their ends independently, these three great elements balance and strengthen each other and together promote the cause of truth and progress.

In "Ultramontanism," Acton and Simpson returned to the theme that, for the Christian Church, knowledge is an end in itself, providing the only "atmosphere in which her progress is unwavering and subject to no relapse." To achieve this progress, the Church must always bring herself into harmony with existing ideas and "speak to each age and nation in its own language."[38] The Catholic in the highest sense of the word recognizes and rejoices in this process by which the Church is purged of outworn ideas, opinions that belong to another era and are extraneous to the core beliefs of the Catholic faith. The true Catholic works out "the problems of science or politics on purely scientific and political principles, and then [controls] this process by the doctrine of the Church"; he finds that truth in science, right in politics, and doctrine in Christianity are mutually compatible.[39] Such a Catholic is a true Ultramontane; and by a subtle and refined argument, Acton and Simpson contend that the term "Ultramontane" has been wrongly usurped by that narrow faction which fears the truths of science and politics and thus would constrict and atrophy the natural extension and progress of the Church. The Liberal, as the true believer in the supranational mission of the Church, is the true Ultramontane. In following Acton and Simpson down this slippery path of sophism, one feels a certain sympathy for Wiseman and the concern which such intellectual gymnastics evoked among a conservative hierarchy. Nevertheless, there is nothing sophistic about the integrity of Acton's basic argument, and the essays "Cardinal Wiseman and *The Home and Foreign Review*" and "Ultramontanism" contain the

---

[37] Acton, *Selected Writings* III, pp. 139–140.
[38] Acton, *Selected Writings* III, pp. 149, 192.
[39] Acton, *Selected Writings* III, pp. 193–194.

clearest statement of those intellectual presuppositions which enabled, nay required, Acton to join a commitment to political Liberalism with a devoted adherence to the Catholic faith.

A high watermark of Catholic Liberalism was a congress of Catholic divines and men of letters held in Munich in the fall of 1863. Reporting on "The Munich Congress," Acton saw in this convocation, addressed by Döllinger as its president, hopes for a Catholic revival. He spoke of the dawn of a new era which would infuse vitality into the Catholic Church and vindicate it from the charges that its faith is inimical to freedom and that Catholics acknowledge an authority which can prevent the publication of truth and impose falsehoods.[40]

Instead of the dawn of a new era, Acton witnessed a papal brief, provoked by the congress, effectively denying absolute freedom of inquiry by maintaining that in their scientific researches and opinions Catholic scholars were subject to ecclesiastical authority: "In a word, therefore, the Brief affirms that the common opinions and explanations of Catholic divines ought not to yield to the progress of secular science."[41]

It was this brief which in Acton's opinion made the continuation of the *Home and Foreign Review* pointless, for the whole purpose of the papal rescript was to attack the fundamental principles of that journal. To attempt to continue within the dictates laid down by the brief would be to destroy the character of the journal; to defy the brief would be to ensure condemnation and thus effectively remove any claim by the journal to represent Catholic views and to influence Catholic opinion. In either case, the *Home and Foreign Review* would forfeit the reasons for its existence. Simpson agreed, and with the April issue of 1864, the journal came to its end.[42]

Acton's article "Conflicts with Rome," written for that last issue, explained the reason for the journal's cessation. It was an occasion to reiterate his belief that the truths of religion and science were reconcilable. Heresy was not the fruit of free scientific inquiry. Citing the example of Lamennais and Frohschammer, Acton argued that, instead, heresy grew on the one hand out of a doctrinaire subordination of truth to dogma, or on the other hand out of the complete estrangement of religion from science. Hughes Félicité Robert de Lamennais began

---

[40] Acton, *Selected Writings* III, p. 233.

[41] Acton, *Selected Writings* III, pp. 251–252.

[42] Acton-Simpson III, pp. 185–187.

as a priest, an apostle of Ultramontanism, and an opponent of freedom of inquiry. He ended life out of communion with the Church, a radical republican. Jakob Frohschammer was another priest and philosopher who found himself in opposition to ecclesiastical authority and drew the utterly false conclusion that, because Church authorities are fallible, Church truths are equally fallible. Acton believed in the existence of Christian truths and believed that the Church existed for the sole purpose of preserving those truths: "Whatever authority expresses that knowledge of which she is the keeper must be obeyed. But there is no institution from which this knowledge can be obtained with immediate certainty. A council is not a priori ecumenical; the Holy See is not separately infallible."[43]

As a historian, Acton was convinced that such truths only slowly made progress, resisted all along the way by "hostile habits and traditions" and sullied by unworthy advocates. But as a Catholic he believed that the ultimate victory of these truths was certain. One day the majority of Catholics and ecclesiastical authorities would understand that there must be a fundamental harmony between the truths of revealed religion, the truths of scientific inquiry, and the truths of politics and social justice. Thus "Conflicts with Rome"—and the *Home and Foreign Review*—end on an optimistic note: "The principles which [the journal] has upheld will not die with it, but will find their destined advocates, and triumph in their appointed time. . . . If the spirit of the *Home and Foreign Review* really animates those whose sympathy it enjoyed, neither their principles, nor their confidence, nor their hopes will be shaken by its extinction. It was but a partial and temporary embodiment of an imperishable idea—the faint reflection of a light which still lives and burns in the hearts of the silent thinkers of the Church."[44]

Section II: Acton and the Vatican Council

The air of calm resignation with which Acton closed the *Home and Foreign Review* belied the intense anxiety he felt over developments in the Church. In 1865, Pius IX appointed a commission of cardinals to prepare for the holding of a general council of the Church, the first since the Council of Trent. The formal summons to the council was

---

[43] Acton, *Selected Writings* III, p. 247.
[44] Acton, *Selected Writings* III, pp. 256–259.

issued on June 29, 1868; the council was convened on December 8, 1869. The fifty-one *schemata*, or decrees, proposed for discussion by the convened Fathers did not include the question of papal infallibility. However, from the first, there had been a strong sentiment that the proposed convocation should form the occasion for discussion and proclamation of infallibility as a dogma of the Church. Supported by a large majority of the convened Fathers, Cardinal Manning, the Archbishop of Westminster, was among the leaders of a successful movement to introduce a definition of papal infallibility to the agenda of the council. The movement for definition was encouraged in the most decisive fashion by Pius himself. Throughout the spring and summer of 1870 the issue of papal infallibility was debated with intensity and acrimony. There was a minority of some size, but it was fragmented in the reasons for its opposition. Some opposed papal infallibility for doctrinal reasons, others out of a sense that the proclamation of such a doctrine was inopportune and inexpedient. This tenuously linked party of opposition was quite ineffective, out-maneuvered and overpowered at every step of the way by a determined majority. On July 18, 1870, the doctrine of papal infallibility was promulgated.

In this highly charged political atmosphere and amidst constant caucusing and negotiation, Acton assumed a role of astonishing proportions for a layman. He was a major figure in the movement to prevent promulgation of papal infallibility. In Rome from November 1869 until June 11, 1870, he was intensively engaged in meetings and correspondence. He brought and sought to hold together the most disparate ecclesiastical figures in an effort to forge a tactically sound and intellectually honest opposition. Understanding the use of power well enough to know that truth will not triumph on its own accord, he used his influence with Gladstone in an effort to move the European powers to issue a joint protest to the Vatican strong and clear enough to forestall the promulgation of the decree of infallibility.

Odo Russell, secretary to the English Legation in Italy and in Rome at the time, in writing to Lord Clarendon, the British Foreign Minister, left us the most impressive testimony to Acton's influence during the days of the council:

> The leading bishops of the opposition acknowledge that of all the laymen present in Rome who took an interest in the debates of the Ecumenical Council none will leave a greater name in history than Lord Acton. The

strong ties that now unite the leading theological minds of England, France, Germany, Hungary, and Austria are due to Lord Acton's personal influence, profound knowledge, great talents, and high virtues. Without his personal intervention the bishops of the opposition could scarcely have known each other. Without his knowledge of language and theology the theologians of the various nations represented in the Council could scarcely have understood each other, without his talents as a leader they could not have remained united amongst each other and without his high virtues they could not have accepted and followed the lead of a layman so much younger than any of the Fathers of the Council. The time has not come when the manner in which Lord Acton exercised his all-important influence on the party of opposition can be recounted in detail, but Your Lordship may rest assured that whatever the Liberal Catholic Party achieve in the world after the Council will be mainly due to the influential presence of Lord Acton during the Council in Rome.[45]

Acton had carefully prepared himself for his role in this supreme test of the ideals of Liberal Catholicism. His distinguished aristocratic lineage provided a network of connections reaching into the most rarified strata of continental society and politics. On December 11, 1869, he was raised to the peerage as Baron Acton of Aldenham, and his status as a peer of the realm and his close relationship with Gladstone, who had recently become Prime Minister, further enhanced his social and political importance. As the student and friend of Döllinger he had ties of the closest sort with the members of the opposition drawn from German Liberal circles. Before the council his German estate at Herrnsheim served as the meeting place for major figures in the opposition movement, not only Germans like Hefele, Ketteler, and Döllinger, but also Felix Dupanloup, Bishop of Orléans. To this Acton added his remarkable scholarly abilities. He spoke fluent French, German, and Italian. He had a wide-ranging knowledge of nineteenth-century Catholic scholarship. Even more, he had carefully honed his own critical skills, and from 1864 to 1868 had devoted himself to extensive historical research in the archives of Europe. Among the mass of material studied he devoted particular attention to the documents of the Council of Trent.[46] The proceedings of that

---

[45] Noel Blakiston, ed., *The Roman Question: Extracts from the Despatches of Odo Russell from Rome 1858-1870* (London, 1962), pp. 445-446. Acton's diary of this period has been published by Edmund Campion, ed., *Lord Acton and the First Vatican Council: A Journal* (Sydney, 1975). To the student of Acton's political and historical thought, the journal is neither as interesting nor as informative as might be wished.

[46] Döllinger II, p. 410. In a lecture given at Cambridge some thirty years later, Acton

last ecumenical council could be and were invoked as useful tools in the party strife of the council.

To all these assets Acton brought remarkable courage and energy. He was, of course, not permitted to attend the actual sessions of the council. But incessant meetings with the prelates opposed to infallibility as well as intensive correspondence with Döllinger, Gladstone, and others assured that his days seldom ended before dawn.[47] His detailed reports to Döllinger, who did not attend the council, provided a major source for a series of "Letters from Rome" that reveal the internal politics of the council; these were penned by Döllinger under the name "Quirinus."[48]

Of course, despite the preparation, despite the activity and energy, the movement to prevent promulgation of the doctrine of papal infallibility failed. Acton perceived the failure on two levels. First, the triumph of Ultramontane sentiment at the council was a disappointment. But it was a disappointment which had been foreseen. Second, the aftermath of the council dealt Acton a more crushing blow. Acton believed that those who had been most vocal in their opposition to papal infallibility would continue in opposition, and he awaited their refusal to submit to the doctrine and their public protest of it. But in the "critical hour of decision," they were mute.[49] Acton attempted to organize the minority prelates into an effective movement which would condemn the actions of the council and guide the laity by questioning the validity of its decrees. To this end he sought to collect and publish

---

discussed the archival research he carried out from 1864 to 1868. This talk, "Notes on Archival Researches," was first published in McElrath, pp. 127–140. Owen Chadwick, *Catholicism and History* (Cambridge, 1978), pp. 53–71, discusses Acton's relations with Augustin Theiner, prefect of the Vatican archives and editor of the Acts of the Council of Trent.

[47] Acton's letter of February 17, 1870 to his stepfather, Lord Granville; quoted in McElrath, pp. 84–85.

[48] The character and authorship of these "Letters from Rome" is treated by Victor Conzemius in a series of articles: "Römische Briefe vom Konzil," *Theologische Quartalschrift* 140 (1960), pp. 427–462; "Die Verfasser der 'Römischen Briefe vom Konzil' des 'Quirinus'," *Festschrift Hans Foerster = Freiburger Geschichtsblätter* 52 (1963/64), pp. 229–256; "Die 'Römischen Briefe vom Konzil': Eine Entstehungsgeschichtliche und quellenkritische Untersuchung zum Konzilsjournalismus Ignaz von Döllingers und Lord Actons," *Römische Quartalschrift für christliche Altertumskunde und Kirchengeschichte* 59 (1964), pp. 186–229; 60 (1965), pp. 76–119.

[49] The quote is a translation from the first paragraph of the German text of Acton's *Sendschreiben an einen deutschen Bischof des Vatikanischen Konzils*. This open letter was originally published at Nördlingen in 1870 and is reprinted in McElrath, pp. 228–239.

the speeches and pamphlets originated by members of the minority in the heat of the debates. His efforts met with the coldest reception from those very men who had been "fighting with him in the breach."[50] At the time one prelate had preferred death to acceptance of the decree, and another had called proclamation of papal infallibility "an act of suicide"[51]; now they wished not to be reminded of such words. The Church had spoken, and even those who had been most prominent in their opposition, men like Archbishop Thomas Connolly, professed themselves ready "to bow down like the lowliest and most ignorant layman in the Catholic Church" and to accept a decree which it would be schism to resist.[52] Nothing could justify schism, and these prelates found their motive for submission simply and singly in the "authority of the Catholic Church."[53]

There were, of course, those who did not submit. The Old Catholic Church arose as an institutional statement of this resistance. There were also individuals like Döllinger. In response to a demand for submission from the Archbishop of Munich, Döllinger replied that "as a Christian, as a theologian, as an historian, and as a citizen, I cannot accept this doctrine."[54] Döllinger believed papal infallibility to stand in opposition to the Bible, to the evidence of history, to Church traditions, and to the decrees of general councils; it contradicted the existing relations of Roman Catholics to the state in every nation. Döllinger was excommunicated.

Acton was not excommunicated, nor did he leave the Church or publicly submit. Cardinal Manning did his best to force Acton into submission or excommunication. He regarded Acton as an "intriguer in the dark and the ruin of Gladstone."[55] Men believed him to hate Acton more than any "Protestant or atheist."[56] Acton's letter to the

---

[50] The words are those of Acton's daughter Annie Mary Catherine Georgiana Acton; quoted in McElrath, p. 21.

[51] Acton, *Sendschreiben*, in McElrath, p. 228.

[52] Letter of Connolly to Acton, June 30, 1872; cited in McElrath, p. 205.

[53] The words are those of Peter Richard Kenrick, Archbishop of St. Louis; cited in McElrath, p. 206.

[54] Johann Ignaz von Döllinger, *A Letter Addressed to the Archbishop of Munich* (London, 1881), pp. 22–23.

[55] Letter of Manning to Ullathorne, November 27, 1874; quoted in Shane Leslie, *Henry Edward Manning* (London, 1921), p. 232.

[56] Letter of Granville to Gladstone, November 18, 1870; in Agatha Ramm, ed., *The Political Correspondence of Mr. Gladstone and Lord Granville 1868–1876* I (London, 1952), p. 160.

editor of the *Times* in November 1874 gave Manning the excuse he sought.[57]

Acton's letter was far less inflammatory than much that he had published before the Vatican Council. But Manning now moved against him.[58] Three days after the appearance of Acton's letter to the editor, Manning demanded to know from him whether the letter had any heretical intent and whether he accepted the decrees of the council. Acton assured Manning that he "had no private gloss or personal interpretation for the Vatican Decrees."[59] However, he did not give Manning an explicit statement of submission. In fact, in asking for such a statement, Manning had exceeded his competency. Only Acton's bishop had that authority. This was James Brown, Bishop of Shrewsbury, in whose diocese Acton's seat of Aldenham was located. Despite pressure from Manning, Bishop Brown pronounced himself satisfied with the following declaration by Acton: "To your doubt whether I am a real or a pretended Catholic I must reply that, believing all that the Catholic Church believes, and seeking to occupy myself with no studies that do not help religion, I am, in spite of sins and errors, a true Catholic, and I protest that I have given you no foundation for your doubt. If you speak of the Council because you suppose that I have separated myself in any degree from the Bishops whose friendship I enjoyed in Rome, who opposed the Decrees during the discussion, but accept them now that it is over, you have entirely misapprehended my position. I have yielded obedience to the Apostolic Constitution which embraces those decrees, and I have not transgressed, and certainly do not consciously transgress, obligations imposed under the supreme sanction of the Church. I do not believe that there is a word in my public or private letters that contradicts any Doctrine of the Council; but if there is, it is not my meaning, and I wish to blot it out."[60]

Manning continued to feel that Acton's response was unsatisfactory, and he sent the case to Rome.[61] Ultimately, the matter was allowed to drop. However, Acton's correspondence with Richard Simpson,

[57] Acton's letters to the *Times* are discussed below on pp. 553–554.

[58] Damian McElrath, "An Essay on Acton's Critical Decade," in McElrath, pp. 35–49, discusses Acton's relations with Manning in the aftermath of the council.

[59] Acton, *Correspondence*, p. 153.

[60] Quoted in Leslie, *Manning*, p. 233.

[61] McElrath, p. 46.

If Acton understood the reasons working for such a definition of papal power at the next general council, he was equally clear about the consequences of such a definition. Retroactively, it would invest all legitimate popes with this aura of infallibility. The papal past would haunt the future. On the basis of edicts by past popes, now rendered infallible, every decision by a Protestant judge would be held to be invalid, the priesthood would be exempt from secular allegiance, and the Pope would be held to possess supreme authority over all governments: "A successor of Alexander VI might distribute the new world over again; and the right by which Adrian disposed of Ireland would enable another Pope to barter it for a Concordat with America." Such a proclamation of papal infallibility would destroy any means of discussion with Protestants and put an end to the power of the Church to expand its influence. These consequences are too obvious to be unforeseen, Acton says, but they are willingly borne by those who place the consolidation of power above the propagation of the faith.[69]

In "Essays in Academic Literature," Acton dealt on the personal level with one element of the forces arrayed behind the idea of papal infallibility. Acton's essay was a review of *Essays on Religion and Literature,* edited by Manning and containing articles by such English Catholic authors as E. S. Purcell. Acton laid bare the personal factors behind the support of Rome by men like the Archbishop of Westminster. Manning was a convert to Roman Catholicism. He was, in Acton's unvarnished view, an arriviste, who saw in the support of Rome a means to gain that influence and prestige which he could not otherwise claim and who trimmed his sails accordingly.[70] Manning found it expedient to be an "advocate of the temporal power and the Inquisition, of the Index and the Syllabus." [71] He and the book he edited spoke a party line, the line which Rome wished to hear and one which preferred policy to principle.

For Acton the issue of papal infallibility was quite simply a matter of principle and conscience, and this made it impossible for him to understand or to deal effectively with those who found it easy to subordinate principle and personal conscience to the demands of a dominant party within the Church. To Acton the matter was clear. Papal infallibility was wrong. The critical study of history showed that

---

[69] Acton, *Selected Writings* III, pp. 266–268.

[70] Acton, *Selected Writings* III, p. 271.

[71] Acton, *Selected Writings* III, p. 271.

conviction that the Church could be the force for greatest good and the surest guarantee of true freedom in the modern world. "I am not conscious," he told his friend Sir Mountstuart Grant Duff, "that I have ever in my life held the slightest shadow of a doubt about any dogma of the Catholic Church."[66] Thirty years later he still had not "the slightest difficulty in believing" any doctrine of the Church.[67] As a young man he had sought to consecrate his learning to the service of his Church and to assist efforts to make that Church a supreme force for progress and Liberalism. The Vatican Council had rendered that learning useless and those efforts futile. That for Acton was the tragedy.

However, if such learning and intense engagement failed to sway the institutional Church, it did not fail to produce writings of enduring consequence. The student of Acton and of the Catholic Church in the nineteenth century will turn elsewhere for full documentation of Acton's role in the Vatican Council. Here the goal has been to select the writings of this period which still retain their interest and assume a position of significance within Acton's broader political and historical thought.

The first of these, "The Next General Council" and "Essays in Academic Literature," appeared in the *Chronicle* in 1867.

"The Next General Council" represents Acton's most forceful statement on the meaning of papal infallibility. He has no doubt that the chief purpose of the impending council is to declare the infallibility of the Pope as a doctrine of the Church. To attain this most solemn sanction for the temporal and spiritual absolutism of the Pope is the most cherished aim of the Ultramontane party and of Pius IX himself. The moment has been well chosen. The uneducated mass of Catholics already essentially believes in the infallibility of Christ's vicar on earth. Among "the aristocracy of knowledge" there are strong vested interests working among the episcopate, all tending towards an exaltation of papal prerogative. Not least of these forces is the personal influence of Pius himself, "who has shown a rare power of conciliating and attracting men, who has been made venerable by his misfortune, who has nominated nearly all the cardinals, created many new sees, and instituted bishops in unexampled numbers."[68]

[66] Mountstuart Grant Duff, *Out of the Past* II (London, 1903), p. 195.
[67] Oscar Browning, *Memories of Later Years* (London, 1923), p. 16.
[68] Acton, *Selected Writings* III, pp. 265–266.

If Acton understood the reasons working for such a definition of papal power at the next general council, he was equally clear about the consequences of such a definition. Retroactively, it would invest all legitimate popes with this aura of infallibility. The papal past would haunt the future. On the basis of edicts by past popes, now rendered infallible, every decision by a Protestant judge would be held to be invalid, the priesthood would be exempt from secular allegiance, and the Pope would be held to possess supreme authority over all governments: "A successor of Alexander VI might distribute the new world over again; and the right by which Adrian disposed of Ireland would enable another Pope to barter it for a Concordat with America." Such a proclamation of papal infallibility would destroy any means of discussion with Protestants and put an end to the power of the Church to expand its influence. These consequences are too obvious to be unforeseen, Acton says, but they are willingly borne by those who place the consolidation of power above the propagation of the faith.[69]

In "Essays in Academic Literature," Acton dealt on the personal level with one element of the forces arrayed behind the idea of papal infallibility. Acton's essay was a review of *Essays on Religion and Literature*, edited by Manning and containing articles by such English Catholic authors as E. S. Purcell. Acton laid bare the personal factors behind the support of Rome by men like the Archbishop of Westminster. Manning was a convert to Roman Catholicism. He was, in Acton's unvarnished view, an arriviste, who saw in the support of Rome a means to gain that influence and prestige which he could not otherwise claim and who trimmed his sails accordingly.[70] Manning found it expedient to be an "advocate of the temporal power and the Inquisition, of the Index and the Syllabus." [71] He and the book he edited spoke a party line, the line which Rome wished to hear and one which preferred policy to principle.

For Acton the issue of papal infallibility was quite simply a matter of principle and conscience, and this made it impossible for him to understand or to deal effectively with those who found it easy to subordinate principle and personal conscience to the demands of a dominant party within the Church. To Acton the matter was clear. Papal infallibility was wrong. The critical study of history showed that

[69] Acton, *Selected Writings* III, pp. 266–268.
[70] Acton, *Selected Writings* III, p. 271.
[71] Acton, *Selected Writings* III, p. 271.

editor of the *Times* in November 1874 gave Manning the excuse he sought.[57]

Acton's letter was far less inflammatory than much that he had published before the Vatican Council. But Manning now moved against him.[58] Three days after the appearance of Acton's letter to the editor, Manning demanded to know from him whether the letter had any heretical intent and whether he accepted the decrees of the council. Acton assured Manning that he "had no private gloss or personal interpretation for the Vatican Decrees."[59] However, he did not give Manning an explicit statement of submission. In fact, in asking for such a statement, Manning had exceeded his competency. Only Acton's bishop had that authority. This was James Brown, Bishop of Shrewsbury, in whose diocese Acton's seat of Aldenham was located. Despite pressure from Manning, Bishop Brown pronounced himself satisfied with the following declaration by Acton: "To your doubt whether I am a real or a pretended Catholic I must reply that, believing all that the Catholic Church believes, and seeking to occupy myself with no studies that do not help religion, I am, in spite of sins and errors, a true Catholic, and I protest that I have given you no foundation for your doubt. If you speak of the Council because you suppose that I have separated myself in any degree from the Bishops whose friendship I enjoyed in Rome, who opposed the Decrees during the discussion, but accept them now that it is over, you have entirely misapprehended my position. I have yielded obedience to the Apostolic Constitution which embraces those decrees, and I have not transgressed, and certainly do not consciously transgress, obligations imposed under the supreme sanction of the Church. I do not believe that there is a word in my public or private letters that contradicts any Doctrine of the Council; but if there is, it is not my meaning, and I wish to blot it out."[60]

Manning continued to feel that Acton's response was unsatisfactory, and he sent the case to Rome.[61] Ultimately, the matter was allowed to drop. However, Acton's correspondence with Richard Simpson,

---

[57] Acton's letters to the *Times* are discussed below on pp. 553–554.

[58] Damian McElrath, "An Essay on Acton's Critical Decade," in McElrath, pp. 35–49, discusses Acton's relations with Manning in the aftermath of the council.

[59] Acton, *Correspondence*, p. 153.

[60] Quoted in Leslie, *Manning*, p. 233.

[61] McElrath, p. 46.

Döllinger, Newman, Lady Blennerhassett, and others reveals the enormous time and energy consumed in his efforts to avoid either giving Manning an explicit declaration of acceptance or being excommunicated. It reveals both his belief that he did indeed stand on the verge of excommunication and his intense anxiety over accordingly being cut off from the sacraments of the Church.[62] He succeeded in staying within the Church, but the effect of the council and its aftermath was a shattering experience from which he never really recovered. His daughter Annie believed that the Vatican Council was the supreme crisis in her father's life, and she laid particular stress on his deep disappointment in the failure of the bishops to continue their opposition to the decree of papal infallibility.[63] This distress and psychological battering engendered a sense of isolation and uselessness that surely pertained to the reluctance to write for publication which marked Acton's later years.

The Vatican Council, its preparation, consummation, and aftermath, took from Acton a decade of his life and left him permanently impaired. The modern reader may feel that the real tragedy lay in the fact that Acton devoted such time and energy to a matter of little ultimate import. The dire consequences predicted for the Church did not come to pass. Catholics continued to combine a dutiful allegiance to the secular state with acceptance of the decrees of their faith. Seldom indeed have been the occasions on which subsequent popes have invoked the prerogatives contained in the concept of infallibility.[64]

Such reflections reveal in part the dubious wisdom of hindsight. By no less a figure than Gladstone, papal infallibility had been interpreted as a formidable prospect indeed, one capable of affecting millions of Catholics, who might find themselves torn between loyalty to their Church and loyalty to their nation.[65] But furthermore, such reflections fail to probe the consequences for Acton's deep and unshakeable devotion to the doctrines of the Catholic faith and his profound

[62] Acton, *Correspondence*, pp. 116–118 (Gladstone); McElrath, pp. 112–115, 116–118 (Newman, Blennerhassett); Acton-Simpson III, pp. 318–333; Döllinger III, pp. 129–131, 132–138.

[63] From a manuscript of Annie Acton; quoted in McElrath, pp. 20–21.

[64] Eighty years passed before a Pope invoked the full powers of infallibility ascribed to him by the council: This was Pius XII, and the occasion was the definition on November 1, 1950, of the dogma of the assumption of the Blessed Virgin Mary into heaven.

[65] Norman, *English Catholic Church*, pp. 310–311.

it was wrong. It found sanction neither in scripture nor in the traditions or history of the Church. What is more, it was morally wrong. It was an affront to every canon of political Liberalism and to every standard of morality. It was an attempt to establish a despotism and to assert the popes' superiority "to all human law, civil and ecclesiastical." It was an act of "systematic warfare against freedom of conscience, of science, of speech." [72] It would invest with divine sanction acts of unmitigated immorality by previous popes, including all the cruelty and persecution of the Inquisition.[73]

Acton's article "The Pope and the Council," appearing in the *North British Review* in October 1869, was his most uncompromising published condemnation of the movement towards a definition of papal infallibility. Thomas Wetherell, who had worked closely with Acton on the *Home and Foreign Review* and was now editor of the *North British Review*, regarded it as the most "fiercely polemical" piece that Acton ever wrote.[74] In this review of *Der Papst und das Concil*, which appeared in 1869 and was written by Döllinger under the pseudonym Janus, Acton states in the most absolute terms why the historian and the believer in truth must reject the concept of papal infallibility: "The Christian Fathers not only teach that the Pope is fallible, but deny him the right of deciding dogmatic questions without a Council. In the first four centuries there is no trace of a dogmatic decree proceeding from a Pope. Great controversies were fought and settled without the participation of the Popes; their opinion was sometimes given and rejected by the Church; and no point of doctrine was finally decided by them in the first ten centuries of Christianity. They did not convene the General Councils; they presided over them in two instances only; they did not confirm their acts. Among all the ancient heretics there is not one who was blamed because he had fallen away from the faith of Rome. Great doctrinal errors have been sometimes accepted, and sometimes originated, by Popes; and, when a Pope was condemned for heresy by a General Council, the sentence was admitted without protest by his successors. Several Churches of undisputed orthodoxy held no intercourse with the See of Rome. Those passages of Scripture which are used to prove that he is infallible are not so interpreted by the Fathers. They all, eighteen in number, explain the prayer of Christ

[72] Acton, *Selected Writings* III, p. 280.
[73] Acton, *Selected Writings* III, p. 267.
[74] Ryan, pp. 43, 248.

for Peter, without reference to the Pope. Not one of them believes that the Papacy is the rock on which He built his Church. Every Catholic priest binds himself by oath never to interpret Scripture in contradiction to the Fathers; and if, defying the unanimous testimony of antiquity, he makes these passages authority for papal infallibility, he breaks his oath." [75]

The transformation of the Catholicism of the Fathers into the "Catholicism of the Popes" was, according to Acton, "accomplished by wilful falsehood." What is more, "the whole structure of traditions, laws, and doctrines that support the theory of infallibility, and the practical despotism of the Popes, stands on a basis of fraud." [76] The results of this practical despotism, in Acton's view, have been "the corruption of morality, the aggravation of tyranny, and the fanatical persecution of witchcraft and heresy." [77] For Acton, papal infallibility became a test case in the theory of power. The historical record, he argued, had been perverted and falsified in the interest of power and its consolidation. The consequences of such absolute power were the corruption of the moral and institutional foundations of the Catholic faith.

The Vatican Council had provided the opportunity to check, in decisive fashion, these developments. In the October 1870 issue of the *North British Review*, Acton viewed "The Vatican Council" in retrospection. Such a general council alone possessed sufficient power to check the growth of that papal despotism. The council could have been a force to decentralize power and to alter those forces which had come to dominate the Church since "the Council of Trent impressed on the Church the stamp of an intolerant age, and perpetuated by its decrees the spirit of an austere immorality." [78] Instead, the council had preferred to accept the declarations of authority rather than the proofs of history. It had sanctioned intellectual, spiritual, and political despotism. Indeed, it had become the vehicle for institutionalizing this absolutism. "La tradizione son' io," Pius IX had said: "I am the tradition of the Church." [79] In its very words papal prerogative laid claim to the same absolutism as the monarchy of Louis XIV and its

---

[75] Acton, *Selected Writings* III, p. 283.
[76] Acton, *Selected Writings* III, p. 283.
[77] Acton, *Selected Writings* III, p. 285.
[78] Acton, *Selected Writings* III, p. 291.
[79] Acton, *Selected Writings* III, p. 338.

heir, the modern absolutist state founded on the ideology of democracy. The will to absolute power, as the formative element in the modern papacy, made the modern papacy, for Acton, an immoral force, a sinful force. As the French Revolution perpetrated the most horrifying crimes in the name of democracy, so the papacy committed its sins in the name of religion. Both the modern democratic absolutist state and the modern papacy believe that the end justifies the means, and to secure the desired end the state and the papacy are both willing to use the most evil of methods.[80]

Acton saw in papal absolutism, as it revealed itself in the Vatican Council, "an organized conspiracy to establish a power which would be the most formidable enemy of liberty as well as of science throughout the world." The promulgation of papal infallibility would transform Catholics into "irreconcilable enemies of civil and religious liberty" who would be required to "profess a false system of morality and to repudiate literary and scientific sincerity."[81]

These last, alarming predictions of the consequences of papal infallibility are taken from the letters which Acton wrote to Gladstone during the council, a selection from which is reprinted here. By that time, the warm admiration Acton and Gladstone felt for each other was already well established. They shared a community of intellectual interests, a common political outlook, and a deep sense of confidence in one another.[82] Religion was by no means absent from that wide range of ideas and issues which fascinated a prime minister capable of writing his three-volume *Homer and the Homeric Age*. He was a High Church Anglican with religious leanings close enough to Catholicism to lead his opponents to claim that, in fact, he was a Roman Catholic.[83] No less significantly, his Irish policy gave him a very practical, political reason for concerning himself with developments at the Vatican Council. In 1869 he had succeeded in disestablishing the Protestant Church of Ireland. He was now working to secure the passage of a bill to enhance public aid to higher education in Ireland and for a program of land reform. He feared that these reforms would be dashed

[80] Döllinger III, p. 267.

[81] Acton, *Selected Writings* III, pp. 340, 351.

[82] Ward White, *Acton and Gladstone: Their Friendship and Mutual Influence* (Diss., Catholic University of America, 1973); Owen Chadwick, *Acton and Gladstone, Creighton Lecture in History, 1975* (London, 1976).

[83] Ward White, "Lord Acton and the Governments at the Vatican Council I," in McElrath, p. 149.

upon a parliamentary wave of hostility generated by the promulgation of papal infallibility.[84] Furthermore, in common with other European statesmen, he sincerely feared that the allegiance of Catholics to their own countries would be undermined by the spiritual and temporal prerogatives of an infallible Pope.

For his part, Acton became convinced by January 1, 1870 that only direct intervention by the great powers would effectively forestall the movement to proclaim infallibility. France was the key to any such intervention, for it was the presence of French troops in Rome which alone preserved the Pope's temporal dominion over that city. The French Minister of Foreign Affairs, Count Napoleon Daru, was firmly opposed to the idea of papal infallibility with its implications for subordinating the civil allegiance of Catholics to ecclesiastical control, and he was willing to use the threat of removing French troops from Rome to prevent the council from sanctioning any such alteration in Church–state relations. Gladstone was willing to assist up to a point. He gave Acton his permission to state "in the strongest language you think fit" the British Prime Minister's view that the proclamation of infallibility would have unfavorable repercussions for Catholicism in England.[85] In a second letter to Acton he called Ultramontanism "an anti-social power."[86] The British government also privately made known its displeasure to the Vatican over the directions taken by the council. However, Gladstone and his government did not go to the lengths ultimately requested by Acton.[87] It did not join the other powers in a joint declaration, nor did Britain officially protest against decrees that could affect the allegiance of Catholics as members of civil society. Whatever the personal feelings of Gladstone, his cabinet believed that protest would be ineffective and would do more harm than good to Irish policy by alienating the hierarchy and clergy in Ireland, as well as the Pope.

Gladstone did not effect a political intervention. However, the depth of his concern about the Vatican Council's decisions was revealed in 1874 in his pamphlet *The Vatican Decrees in their Bearing on Civil Allegiance:*

---

[84] White, in McElrath, p. 150.

[85] Acton, *Correspondence*, p. 87.

[86] Acton, *Selected Writings* III, p. 346.

[87] The course and outcome of Acton's efforts to elicit the aid of Gladstone in support of the opposition to papal infallibility is described by Ryan, pp. 260–286, and by White, in McElrath, pp. 143–161.

A Political Expostulation.[88] Gladstone had charged, in Acton's words, that "Catholics obtained Emancipation [in 1829] by declaring that they were in every sense of the term loyal and faithful subjects of the realm, and that Papal Infallibility was not a dogma of their Church. Later events have falsified one declaration, have disturbed the stability of the other; and the problem therefore arises whether the authority which has annulled the profession of faith made by the Catholics would not be competent to change their conceptions of political duty."[89]

It was to answer Gladstone's charge that papal claims to infallibility could infringe upon the civic allegiance of Catholics that Acton wrote the first of his letters to the *Times*. Acton argued that this simply was not likely to occur. There were limits, he maintained, to any authority's ability to enforce unity, and even more importantly, history itself showed the limits to the power of any Pope to persuade men: "The Irish did not shrink from resisting the arms of Henry II, though two popes had given him dominion over them."[90]

To clarify that answer required three subsequent letters to the *Times*; all four letters are published here. The trouble they caused Acton seems out of proportion to the calm, reasoned tone which pervades them. This same reasoned perspective marks Acton's final published comments on the Vatican Council in his review of the first volume of Johann Friedrich's *Geschichte der Vatikanischen Konzils*. It was a calmness which sprang from his conviction that the works of men, even their greatest sins and follies, could not ultimately affect God's plan for mankind. The "guiding, healing hand of God" would assure that the Church and its faith would one day assume again its proper role as guardian and guide of freedom and progress in the social order.[91]

This conviction lay at the heart of a speech (reprinted as "Lord Acton and the Roman Question") which he gave to a lay audience of Catholics and Protestants in Kidderminster in January 1871. Speaking in the aftermath of the Italian occupation of Rome, Acton called upon the great powers of Europe to guarantee the independence of the Holy See. The freedom of the Church and its leader were and must be of fundamental concern to all free states, Catholic and Protestant alike.

---

[88] The context and consequences of Gladstone's pamphlet are described in Arnstein, *Protestant*, pp. 190–196, and in Norman, *English Catholic Church*, pp. 310–311.

[89] Acton, *Selected Writings* III, p. 364.

[90] Acton, *Selected Writings* III, pp. 366–367.

[91] Acton, *Selected Writings* III, p. 392.

We must realize, he said, that "the state cannot forego the aid of religion in preserving social virtue." It is in the interest of the state that "religion should retain the attachment of its followers, and exhort to the utmost its elevating influence upon them." For this very reason, religious instruction is essential in schools. Secular knowledge alone may suffice to protect men against error, but it can never protect them against sin.[92]

Section III:
Perspectives on History, Religion, and Morality

The essays in this section differ markedly from each other in purpose, date of composition, and theme. Central to all three, however, is Acton's concern with the relationship between religion and the moral code of societies and individuals.

"Human Sacrifice" and "Buckle's Philosophy of History" are the writings of the young Acton. Published in 1857, Henry Thomas Buckle's *History of Civilization in England* enjoyed an immediate and remarkable public success. With a great parade of learning, Buckle presented a bold and sweeping interpretation of history, arguing that the scientific historian could deduce from the study of the past fixed laws which determine the actions of men and societies. The book was the subject of intense interest in the year following its publication. Buckle was lionized by English intellectual society, and admiring comments on Buckle's learning and originality came from John Stuart Mill, James Russell Lowell, Charles Darwin, and others. Buckle was at the height of his celebrity when the *Rambler* published a biting two-part review of his *History of Civilization*. Acton saw it as a public duty to expose Buckle as a "mere humbug," the author of a book which was "utterly superficial and obsolete." Acton and Simpson joined forces in the effort. Simpson wrote the essay which appeared under the title "Mr. Buckle's Thesis and Method" in the *Rambler* for July 1858. Acton's article followed in the August issue and it retains its interest as a delightful study in the art of vitriolic reviewing. It has been republished in more than one anthology of Acton's writings, and recent attention

---

[92] Acton, *Selected Writings* III, pp. 355–356.

paid to Buckle by students of Victorian intellectual life has once again directed attention to Acton's review.[93]

More obscure has been the fate of "Human Sacrifice," which appeared in 1863 as a privately printed pamphlet or monograph of forty-seven pages. It has not been reprinted in subsequent collections of Acton's writings, and copies of the original have become extremely rare. That in itself would justify its reprinting here. However, the piece is no mere bibliographic curiosity; it deserves more serious consideration than it has generally received from students of Acton. Its theme, treatment, and the circumstances of composition and publication illuminate the intellectual climate among a certain segment of the leaders of Victorian society as well as Acton's own predispositions and methods of work.

"Human Sacrifice" was orginally intended as an article for the *Home and Foreign Review* and was written at the suggestion of the English historian Lord Stanhope.[94] In 1863, Stanhope had published a volume of *Miscellanies*, bringing together a series of letters and other communications, generally written by others, which Stanhope had collected in the course of his historical researches. This material is arranged in topical chapters and covers a variety of themes: Sir Robert Peel's view of Sir Robert Walpole; the Duke of Wellington's opinion on the comparative military greatness of Napoleon and the Duke of Marlborough; and various opinions on why buff and blue were the colors of the Whig party. The chapters include one entitled "Were Human Sacrifices in use among the Romans?"[95] The chapter grew out of a social breakfast held on December 13, 1847 that was attended by, among others, Peel, Stanhope, and Thomas Babington Macaulay. In the course of conversation, Stanhope mentioned the opinion of the German ecclesiastical historian Johann Gieseler that the Romans of the classical period had offered humans as sacrificial victims. Macaulay was most unconvinced, and there followed a series of letters between him, Stanhope, and Peel. Greek and Latin writers were quoted in the

---

[93] On Buckle, see Giles St. Aubyn, *A Victorian Eminence* (London, 1958); and Kenyon, *History Men*, pp. 108–114. For Acton's view of Buckle as a humbug, see Acton-Simpson I, p. 21.

[94] Acton-Simpson III, p. 73; Döllinger I, p. 295. That it did not appear in the *Home and Foreign Review* was apparently due to the simple fact that Acton did not have it ready in time; see Acton-Simpson III, p. 152.

[95] *Miscellanies*, collected and edited by Earl Stanhope, (London: John Murray, 1863), pp. 112–128.

original and interpreted, all with the result of leaving Peel and Macaulay convinced that no trustworthy sources provided any evidence "on which you could convict the Romans of offering human sacrifices during the classical time of Roman history." Underlying this conviction was the belief that the practice of human sacrifice could not coexist with a "high degree of civilisation and refinement." Peel and Macaulay simply could not imagine Cicero offering up a human victim, and the general silence of the major sources seemed to vindicate their position. Stanhope was less certain that the evidence of Christian writers, late and prejudiced though it might be, could be dismissed, and that human sacrifice and civilization were incompatible.

Stanhope did not forget the debate; and in 1860, partly as a tribute to Macaulay's deep interest in the classics, the letters were printed for private circulation.[96] When *Miscellanies* appeared three years later, Stanhope apparently asked Acton to look further into the matter of human sacrifice. The result was a learned and thoughtful essay in comparative religion, putting the concept of human sacrifice into a broader theoretical framework and amassing a wealth of material drawn from the religions of the ancient Mediterranean, India, the Germanic world, and America. It was among the Aztecs that Acton, following a suggestion by Stanhope, found the clearest indication that human sacrifice was indeed compatible with a high level of civilization, "extraordinary moral energy and fidelity to religious conviction."[97] Acton detailed the inordinate extent to which, in their moral fervor, the Aztecs carried the rite, and the appalling number of victims which they sacrificed to their belief in a concept of universal original sin. He also reminded his readers that "long after the last victim had fallen in honour of the sun-god of the Aztecs, the civilised nations of Christian Europe continued to wage wholesale destruction on a vast scale against persons accused of no crime against the civil order, and not even convicted of the religious guilt which was imputed to them. The parallel phenomenon of trials for witchcraft ought to explain to us the power of superstition to familiarise men with the most inhuman butchery of helpless beings. . . . In England alone, under the Tudors and Stuarts, the victims of this superstition amounted to 30,000."[98]

The modern historian of religion may turn elsewhere for a knowledge

---

[96] Stanhope, *Miscellanies*, pp. 112–113.

[97] Acton, *Selected Writings* III, p. 438; Stanhope, *Miscellanies*, p. 122.

[98] Acton, *Selected Writings* III, p. 442.

of human sacrifice. Nevertheless, the piece retains its value as a remarkable statement of those intellectual interests and presuppositions which give such a unique cast to Acton's intellectual engagement with history and religion. Here is the historian as a moral judge, who collects his evidence objectively and then delivers a moral verdict. Heathen and Christian are judged by the same absolute standard of morality. If human sacrifice is murder, then it is murder whether committed in the name of a pagan sun-god or in the name of purifying the Christian religion. Here too is the historian as a devout and convinced Christian. For Acton, the study of human sacrifice was no mere antiquarian exercise. It was, rather, an attempt to see in full perspective that ultimate human sacrifice and to understand more clearly "the death of that Victim who could alone take away the sins of the world."[99]

Twenty-two years and the Vatican Council separated the author of "Human Sacrifice" from the Acton who reviewed the biography of George Eliot written by her husband, J.W. Cross. Coming at the end of a seven-year hiatus in which he seems to have written nothing for publication, Acton's article on Eliot marked the beginning of a new period of literary activity. In the form of a review, it displays to the fullest that compression of language and ideas which makes the mature Acton at once so difficult yet so stimulating to read. Döllinger called the essay a "masterpiece of its kind" and spoke of the wealth of ideas Acton had compressed into twenty pages. He also complained that such brevity and compression made the essay obscure in parts.[100]

Others apparently felt the same, driving an irritated Acton to explain himself in a letter to Lady Blennerhassett.[101] His standpoint in the essay had been that of a historian, not a literary critic; his concern was not with George Eliot's standing in literature but with her importance as a teacher of morality. As such, Eliot possessed a special, indeed, a unique importance. In her very being she refuted those who asserted that morality is impossible without religion. A complete atheist, she developed and taught a concept of morality equal to anything in religion. This was, Acton believed, a remarkable and seminal achievement in the history of the human mind. At the very time when atheism was becoming the preponderant intellectual disposition of modern man, George Eliot made atheism a powerful moral

---

[99] Acton, *Selected Writings* III, p. 442.
[100] Döllinger III, p. 345.
[101] Acton, *Correspondence*, pp. 288–292.

force and the ethical equivalent of Christianity. She showed that without God and without religion individuals could be taught to uphold and foster the supreme qualities of private and public virtue.

Acton knew George Eliot—that is, Marian Evans Cross—personally and thought her the most brilliant woman in the world.[102] He called her "a consummate expert in the pathology of conscience."[103] The words might have been equally applied to himself; his empathetic portrait of her sprang from the realization that they had shared an intellectual odyssey and that, from very different paths, historian and novelist had reached a common vantage point. Eliot was "the perfect atheist"[104] who showed a devout Catholic that atheism and morality were compatible. Rejecting all habits and influences derived from religion, she had constructed a world view marked by the greatest integrity of conscience and by ethical standards which fulfilled the strictest canon of moral responsibility. "Her teaching was the highest within the resources to which Atheism is restricted, as the teaching of the *Fioretti* [of St. Francis] is the highest within Christian limits." Atheism might fall short of maintaining this standard, but, then, so did Christianity.[105]

Acton's labors on the frontiers of religion and politics convinced him that the worst excesses of immorality were committed out of a willfully perverted sense of religion. Within the context of his discussion of George Eliot, he defined the central problem of Catholicism as the question of "how private virtue and public crime could issue from the same root."[106] The Inquisition and Ultramontanism were the products of men of impeccable private lives and intense religiosity. They were theologically learned and devoted to the Church.[107] It was not possible to excuse their crimes against humanity and human freedom on the grounds of ignorance. "I have never found," Acton said, "that people go wrong from ignorance." They go wrong "from want of conscien-

[102] Döllinger III, p. 200. In this letter of May 19, 1878, Acton speaks of having recently gotten better acquainted with Eliot on a personal level. Acton's admiration for her work grew slowly. In a letter of November 28, 1860, he speaks of never having read her novels (Acton-Simpson II, p. 92). By July 1863, he had recommended that Simpson write on Eliot for the *Home and Foreign Review*, "for there is doctrine as well as art in her" (Acton-Simpson III, p. 116).

[103] Acton, *Selected Writings* III, p. 463.

[104] Acton, *Correspondence*, p. 289.

[105] Acton, *Selected Writings* III, p. 485.

[106] Acton, *Selected Writings* III, p. 483.

[107] Döllinger III, p. 267.

tiousness."[108] With all the instruments of learning, education, and religion at its disposal, the Church had not taught its leading members to be men of conscience. The man of conscience, the man of ethical integrity, believes in an absolute standard of morality: to lie and to murder is at all times and in all places wrong. It cannot be excused for any reason. The Inquisition murdered, the Ultramontane lied and excused murder—all in the name of religion. To Acton this was the ultimate, the unforgivable, the inexcusable wrong. It was also the proof that religion alone was not enough to secure morality. Like the Aztec, the Christian had committed great sins under the impetus of religious fervor.

"It is the part of great men to stand alone," Acton once wrote.[109] Intellectual isolation was the ultimate price of his explorations along the boundaries where religion, politics, and morality meet. He was estranged from his Church, rejecting and abhorring in Catholicism "the godless suppression of morality in favour of dogma, the support of authority through methods that are evil, the corruption of conscience through belief."[110] His final position lacked even the support of his teacher Döllinger. The old comrade in the fight against Ultramontanism could not share the "fiery wine" of Acton's moral absolutism.[111] Döllinger could not rule out the possibility that even Ultramontanes sinned out of ignorance. He was willing to give consideration to extenuating circumstances, to consider Inquisitors and Ultramontanes as men who erred rather than as simple liars and murderers. For seven years, from 1879 to 1886, Acton intensively discussed these issues with Döllinger until, finally, he could only believe that he had misunderstood Döllinger's teachings from the beginning and that the very core of his religious outlook was unacceptable to his teacher.[112] The sense of isolation was compounded by the admiring but baffled response which Döllinger and others gave to his attempt to explain his concept of moral judgment in pieces like "George Eliot's Life" and in the famous review of Mandell Creighton's *History of the Papacy* that Acton published in the *English Historical Review* in 1887.[113] Acton came to feel

[108] Döllinger III, p. 289.
[109] Acton, *Selected Writings* III, p. 653.
[110] Döllinger III, p. 298.
[111] Döllinger III, p. 312.
[112] Döllinger III, p. 352. A selection of Acton's letters and notes relating to the break with Döllinger is given in Acton, *Selected Writings* III, pp. 665–674.
[113] Acton, *Selected Writings* II, pp. 365–377.

himself alone in his essential ethical position, without authorities to cite, without disciples or sympathizers. This intellectual isolation and the sense of futility which it engendered were the primary reasons Acton gave for his unwillingness in later years to write more for publication.

Acton did not change the course of the Catholic Church. He did not convince his peers or posterity that an absolute standard of morality must hold sway in judging the politics of the present or the actions of the past. He did not write that history of liberty which his admirers believed would be the capstone of a life devoted to historical study and thought. What he did accomplish was to leave behind a legacy, in published writings and unpublished notes, of ideas, thoughts, and dispositions which speak with the most compelling immediacy to every concerned citizen of a free society. It is in that legacy that we must search for our own ultimate judgment of Acton and his contribution to the eternal question of the relationship between religion, politics, and morality.

Section IV: Selections from the Acton Legacy

The material in Section IV is not limited to the specific theme of this third volume of Acton's *Selected Writings*. It is rather integral to the edition as a whole. It presents material drawn from Acton's correspondence, from those published writings which have not been chosen for inclusion in this edition, and, for the first time, from a substantial portion of Acton's unpublished notes. Its aim is to supplement the longer essays, presenting in topical arrangement and in often aphoristic form the essence of Acton's legacy to the twentieth century.

Acton's last and happiest years were spent as Regius Professor of Modern History at Cambridge from 1895 until his death in 1902. He left to that university a threefold intellectual legacy.

First there was the inspiration of his teaching and research. He assumed the editorship of the *Cambridge Modern History*, viewing that multivolume work as a bequest of historical knowledge to the twentieth century. This section—and this edition—fittingly ends with Acton's report to the Syndics of the Cambridge University Press on his plans for the work. Perhaps of equal significance was his teaching. He established the concept of "scientific history" at Cambridge and inspired a generation of students to think historically. This inspiration received recognition in the editorial work of John Neville Figgis and Reginald Vere Laurence.[114] After Acton's death, they saw to the publication of his *Lectures on Modern History* and *Lectures on the French Revolution.* They collected his longer published essays into two large volumes, *The History of Freedom and Other Essays* and *Historical Essays and Studies.* They also began to publish his letters, bringing out a single-volume *Lord Acton's Correspondence.* It was through these volumes that Acton assumed his place with "Locke and Jefferson, Humboldt, Mill and Croce among the oracles of the Liberal faith." [115]

The second of Acton's legacies to Cambridge was his library of 60,000 volumes, the product of a lifetime of historical study and research. At the time of Acton's death, the library actually belonged to Andrew Carnegie. Learning that financial difficulties were forcing Acton to sell his library, Carnegie, working with Gladstone, anonymously bought it in 1890 and arranged for Acton to remain in possession of it.[116] When Acton died, Carnegie presented it to John Morley, who then donated it to Cambridge, the entire transaction occurring within four months of Acton's death. The largest single gift of library materials ever given to that university in the seven hundred years of its history, Acton's library has been preserved intact as "the most appropriate monument of . . . one of the most remarkable men of our time, extraordinary in his acquisitions, extraordinary in his compass of mind." [117] To this day, the Acton library retains that special character and unity highlighted by Morley when, in his letter of presentation to the university in October 1902, he described it as "not one of those noble and miscellaneous accumulations that have been gathered by the chances of time and taste in colleges and other places of old

[114] In their introduction to Acton, *Lectures on Modern History*, pp. ix–xix, Figgis and Laurence give a very sympathetic portrait of "Lord Acton as Professor."

[115] G. P. Gooch, *Historical Surveys and Portraits* (New York, 1966), p. 156.

[116] Morley, *Recollections*, pp. 231–235, tells the story of the acquisition of Acton's library by Cambridge. Additional material is added by Chadwick (above, n. 82), pp. 25–28. John Loose, *A Guide to the Acton Papers in the Cambridge University Library* (Ms. Cambridge, 1971), p. 8, gives 70,000 as the number of volumes in Acton's library. Mr. R.P. Carr has communicated to me by letter that 60,000 is a better estimate of the number of books that actually came to Cambrdge in 1902. Many of these were single-bound volumes each containing several individual pamphlets; by 1913, when these had been catalogued and incomplete works had been completed by library purchases, there were some 75,000 catalogue entries. Mr. Carr is preparing a study of the Acton library, and I am deeply grateful to him for sharing his unique knowledge of that collection with me and for suggesting the wording of this paragraph.

[117] Morley, *Recollections*, p. 232.

foundation. It was . . . collected to be the material for a history of Liberty, the emancipation of Conscience from Power, and the gradual substitution of Freedom for Force in the government of men."

Acton's third and, for us, most important legacy was the great collection known as the Acton Papers.[118] These were his working notes, the fruits of a lifetime of reading and thinking about history. They came to Cambridge shortly after Acton's death, partly with the library, partly as the result of purchase from his son. In 1973 the original collection of the Acton working notes was supplemented by the purchase and the moving to Cambridge of the bulk of Acton's correspondence and private papers. The student will search in vain among these papers and working notes for unknown, publishable manuscripts of essays or books written by Acton. The Acton Papers do not contain even a single completed chapter of Acton's planned *History of Liberty*. They are instead great storehouses of materials and ideas for projects planned but never completed, for a history of the Inquisition, for a history of the modern papacy, for a biography of Döllinger, and, above all, for the *History of Liberty*. The working notes consist of notebooks and of index cards placed into black leather boxes. Into these notebooks and onto the index cards Acton supplemented his own thoughts with copiously extracted quotations from books and primary documents. But they served him as more than receptacles for passive knowledge drawn from his prodigious reading. He used them to formulate and to express in private his own ideas on the whole range of history, religion, and politics. In paragraphs and aphoristic sentences of brilliant compression, he distilled the essence of one of the most learned and seminal minds of the nineteenth century.

Acton had a passion to communicate his ideas and knowledge. It came out in his conversation, in the pride he took in his Cambridge lectures, and in his willingness "to give away in half-an-hour the

---

[118] The following brief discussion of the history of the Acton Papers is taken, in part, from the remarks of Loose, *Guide* pp. 8–10. A.E.B. Owen, *University Library, Cambridge, Summary Guide to Accessions of Manuscripts (other than medieval) since 1867* (Cambridge, 1966), pp. 9–10, describes in very short compass the contents of the papers before the acquisition of the bulk of Acton's correspondence and private papers in 1973. Owen divides the contents into four groups: I. Original manuscripts acquired by Acton. II. Transcripts made for Acton, mainly from French and Italian archives. III. Acton's own notes "either on slips (arranged in boxes) or in notebooks." These include some 485 items. Add. Mss. 4937–4956 include material dealing with the history of liberty. IV. Family and personal papers.

substance of an unwritten book." [119] However, as the years passed, he had come to believe that even fervent admirers like Gladstone and well-disposed friends like Döllinger could not really fathom his philosophy of history and his conception of liberty, morality, and conscience. Hence, he did not write books for public consumption. He wrote for himself, entrusting to these notecards the sum of his knowledge and his deepest thoughts about the meaning of history. The value of this material was not recognized until a generation after Acton's death. His editors, Figgis and Laurence, made little use of the initial collection of Acton Papers, which languished in the Cambridge University Library unconsulted and even unsorted until the 1930s and the discovery of Acton by a new generation of historians and political thinkers.[120]

The Victorian Age had been uncomfortable with Acton. But he had a prophetic power for a generation which witnessed the triumph of totalitarianism under the ideological guises of fascism, communism, socialism, and democratic absolutism. Acton opposed totalitarianism in every form. He had warned of the despotism inherent in the dominant forces of democracy, socialism, and nationalism. He prophesied that democracy would end in socialism and that the course of both nationalism and socialism would be marked by the material and moral ruin of Europe. He had understood that in the adherence to an absolute standard of morality and truth lay the only means to prevent the encroachment of forces which could destroy all that was liberal and humane in European society. And he predicted the absolute demands which the modern state in its totality would make upon the conscience of men, subordinating truth and morality to the needs and goals of party and nation.

The rediscovery of Acton began in the 1930s and culminated in the years immediately after the Second World War. In England it was led by Sir Herbert Butterfield, ultimately Acton's successor as Regius Professor at Cambridge. In Germany, both before and after the war, Ulrich Noack sought to interpret Acton's legacy of liberalism and its value for the German experience. In America Gertrude Himmelfarb wrote what remains the best and most sympathetic biographical portrait

---

[119] The quote is from an obituary notice written by F. W. Maitland, *Cambridge Review* (October 16, 1902) and cited in Paul, p. 86.

[120] Writing in 1923, Oscar Browning, *Memories*, p. 17, mentioned Acton's papers at Cambridge and stated, "I never heard of anyone using them. Perhaps their existence is unknown."

of Acton and his mind. All these scholars immersed themselves in the Acton Papers. All came away rightly convinced that "behind the multitude of Acton's reflective notes there is an intellectual system (and a record of the man's achievement) ampler and richer and more imposing than the published writings would suggest." [121]

Acton's notecards are essential for an understanding of the man. More than that, they are of fundamental importance for what they say in and of themselves. With the present edition of Acton's *Selected Writings,* for the first time, a substantial portion of the material from the notecards is being made available to the public. It is only a limited selection from the material to be found in the literally thousands of notecards in the Acton collection. As with the published material chosen for inclusion in this edition, the goal has been to guide the reader to what is most enduring in the political and historical thought of Acton. To publish Acton's notes in their entirety would require numerous volumes. That is certainly not possible here, nor is it certain that such an enterprise would be of any real value. There is much among the notes of interest only to the hardened specialist in Acton. There is also much which is simply of limited value to anyone other than Acton himself. This is obviously true of the extremely large number of cards which are merely quotations and extracts from Acton's reading. It is equally the case with the numerous outlines and lists which Acton was so fond of making: various and differing lists of chapters for the *History of Liberty,* lists of books and authors on a variety of themes, lists which construct the pedigree of an idea, and topical lists, such as that of great political thinkers who made poor politicians.

Our aim in Section IV is to publish a selection from the Acton Papers which will serve to illuminate Acton's thought on those themes which were of central importance to him. Our aim is not to illustrate the Acton Papers. It is rather to provide the reader with additional important material not found in Acton's published writings. For that reason, the simplest and most effective means of presentation has been chosen. The material is presented topically. Moreover, to make the coverage of Acton's thought as complete as possible, the material from the notecards has been supplemented by extracts from Acton's corre-

---

[121] Herbert Butterfield, "Acton: His Training, Methods, and Intellectual System," in A. O. Sarkissian, ed., *Studies in Diplomatic History and Historiography in honour of G. P. Gooch, C. H.* (London, 1961), p. 196.

spondence and from published writings not reprinted in their entirety in this edition.

Acton's correspondence is in itself a source of major importance for documenting central themes and ideas in his philosophy of history and politics. Writing letters served Acton as a vehicle for partially satisfying his desire to communicate his knowledge.[122] He used letters to record events and to clarify his own ideas for himself as well as for the recipient of the letter. Not all of Acton's correspondents were favored with such erudite and candid epistolary expositions of Acton's ideas and feelings. Acton tended instead to direct such revealing letters to a very few people. Preeminent among these was his old teacher Ignaz von Döllinger. From Acton's student days in Munich until Döllinger's death in 1890, pupil and teacher carried out an exchange of letters which remains the best single commentary on Acton's life and thought. The intellectual and political convictions of Acton in the days of the *Rambler* and the *Home and Foreign Review* are richly documented in the correspondence with his co-editor Richard Simpson. His letters to Gladstone tell us much about Acton's unique and very personal brand of Liberalism. Throughout his life there were also female correspondents with whom Acton shared his knowledge and reflections on history, politics, religion, and contemporary society. His wife received such letters, particularly during their engagement and the early years of their marriage. In later life his daughter Mary Elizabeth Anne (Mamy) assumed this role. Even more significant were the letters he wrote to Gladstone's daughter Mary, and to Charlotte Lady Blennerhassett. Mary Gladstone Drew shared her father's deep admiration for Acton. Acton infused her with his own enthusiasm for the planned *History of Liberty*, and she was deeply disappointed by his failure to write that great work. Lady Blennerhassett was, like Gladstone and his daughter, a close friend of Döllinger. Acton and her husband Rowland had been fellow pupils of Döllinger. She was herself a Bavarian aristocrat and a historian of considerable versatility, counting among her publications a three-volume study, *Madame de Stael, her Friends and her Influence in Politics and Literature*.

Lady Blennerhassett and Mary Gladstone were keenly aware of the intellectual treasure which Acton had bestowed upon them with his letters, and both sought in their own way to pass the Acton legacy on

---

[122] Chadwick, *Acton and Gladstone*, pp. 7–17, comments upon this facet of Acton's intellectual character.

to posterity. Lady Blennerhassett planned but did not write a biography of Acton. Mary Gladstone published a selection of his letters to her in 1904. Frank in their appraisal of figures like Cardinal Newman, Acton's letters to Mary Gladstone provoked a storm of controversy in English Catholic circles. To calm that storm, the future Cardinal Gasquet prepared a publication of Acton's letters intended to show the orthodox character of Acton's Catholicism. In the resulting publication, *Lord Acton and His Circle,* material from Acton's correspondence was suppressed, distorted, and arbitrarily and inaccurately presented in order to create an image of Acton as a dutiful son of the Church.[123] By contrast, a frank and honest portrait of Acton did emerge from the volume of his selected correspondence published by his editors Figgis and Laurence in 1917. Despite scholarly defects and inaccuracies, it has been a valuable tool to students of Acton.[124] But it remained incomplete, and a planned second volume, including Acton's correspondence with Döllinger, never appeared. Only sixty years after Acton's death would the valuable material in his correspondence become available to scholars in complete and reliable form. In 1963–1971 the publication of Acton's correspondence with Döllinger appeared in a three-volume edition edited by Victor Conzemius. The correspondence with Richard Simpson appeared in 1971–1975 in a three-volume edition edited by Josef Altholz, Damian McElrath, and James Holland, while correspondence with Newman has been published in *The Letters and Diaries of John Henry Newman,* edited by C. S. Dessain.

Only the briefest selection from the correspondence has been included in Section IV. The aim in making the selection has not been to illustrate the correspondence itself or to serve the biographer of Acton. The goal is simply to provide the reader with additional material from Acton, material which provides insights into key aspects of Acton's thought and which complements, explains, and supplements his published essays. The same rationale lies behind the selection of extracts from Acton's published writings. With the exception of Acton's most famous aphorism on power, none of the material collected in Section

---

[123] Paul, pp. 242, 238, 251. The failings of Gasquet, *Lord Acton and His Circle* (London, 1906), were revealed in specific detail by Aelred Watkins and Herbert Butterfield, "Gasquet and the Acton-Simpson Correspondence," *Cambridge Historical Journal* 10 (1950), pp. 75–105.

[124] Conzemius, in Döllinger I, pp. xviii–xix, briefly notes the defects of the edition of Acton, *Correspondence,* by Figgis and Laurence.

IV is from essays reprinted elsewhere in this edition. The extracts are taken from book reviews and articles which did not merit reprinting in their entirety. Several particularly striking passages from Acton's *Lectures on the French Revolution* and *Lectures on Modern History* have also been chosen for inclusion in Section IV. Not only is the selection of extracts from these briefer reviews and articles fuller than in any previous Acton anthology; it is also the first to be guided by a critical knowledge of Acton's bibliography, and in every instance I have indicated the authority for attributing these anonymous pieces to Acton.[125]

In his unpublished notes as in his correspondence and published writings, Acton's thought processes and literary style lend themselves admirably to a collection of historical reflections arranged in the form of aphorisms. The nineteenth century was an age which cultivated the aphorism. Acton's published and unpublished writings are filled with sentences and paragraphs in which the most profound ideas on freedom and politics are couched in pregnant, pithy, and memorable fashion. Both the conscientious reader and the browser will find in the aphorisms of Section IV the most direct and effective guide to what is timely and enduring in Acton's thought. They will also find revealed aspects and implications of that thought unavailable in any previous Acton collection.

---

[125] Acton, *Selected Writings* I, pp. xxiv–xxvii, discusses the problems which previous Acton bibliographies pose for the editor of his works.

Editor's Note

Volume III concludes the Liberty *Classics* edition of *Selected Writings* of Lord Acton. It is the purpose of this edition to make Acton more accessible to scholars and to the broader public; and in three important respects, it represents an advance over previous collections of Acton's writings.

In the first place, this is the fullest collection of Acton's writings ever published between the covers of a single, uniform edition. Each volume of this edition contains, along with pieces republished in earlier Acton anthologies, significant writings of Acton which have not been reprinted since they originally appeared as unsigned contributions to ephemeral Victorian periodicals and which have consequently long been difficult for the ordinary reader with an interest in Acton to obtain.

Secondly, this is the first collection of Acton's writings to be based upon a full critical knowledge of his bibliography. "The Essays in This Volume" in Volume I (see pp. xxiv–xxvii) describes those scholarly advances which enable us now to attribute securely to Acton significant writings which do not appear in any of the published bibliographies of his works. In cases like Essays 16, 22, and 32–34 of Volume I and Essays 1–4 of Volume II, these represent additions of major consequence for our understanding of Acton's development as a historian and his view of contemporary political events in Europe and America.

Finally, and perhaps most significantly, this is the first collection of Acton's writings to present an extensive selection from his unpublished notes. Deposited after his death in the Cambridge University Library, the Acton Papers, including his notecards and other manuscript materials, contain the fruits of a lifetime of reading and thinking about the meaning of history. They are the private thoughts and reflections of one of the most profound historical minds of the nineteenth century. Scholars have long recognized in these unpublished notes the key to understanding Acton. However, limitations of space, publishing costs, and other considerations have always hindered plans to publish this material. Now, in Volume III of this edition, a significant portion of what is most valuable in Acton's unpublished notes is made available to a broader public.

The quantity of material in the Acton Papers is vast, and any selection from it will invariably reflect the editor's interest. My goal has been to supplement the published writings and thus to provide additional source material for Acton's political and historical thought. As Sir Herbert Butterfield wrote: "Behind the multitude of Acton's reflective notes there is an intellectual system (and a record of the man's achievement) ampler and richer and more imposing than the published writings would suggest."

Editorial comment on these selections from the Acton Papers has been kept to an absolute minimum. Acton was frequently obscure, and I have made no attempt to elucidate him. Beyond the addition of an occasional connective word or phrase, clearly indicated by brackets, the words are Acton's own.

In all three volumes of this edition, the goal is to allow Acton to speak for himself. The essays have been reprinted as they originally appeared, with only minor typographical corrections. Accordingly, apart from the introductory footnote to each essay, giving its provenance and (in the case of unsigned articles and reviews) my sources for attributing the piece to Acton, there are no editorial footnotes in the text. Moreover, and for the same reason, no attempt has been made to translate the numerous foreign language quotations which Acton cited only in the original.

In bringing this edition to a close, it is a pleasure to record the deep debt of gratitude I owe the present Lord Acton. His gracious permission to publish the Acton Papers made the third volume of this edition possible. The interest and enthusiasm he has shown for the project has added a very special personal dimension to the undertaking and has been a chief reward of these editorial labors.

This third volume has profited greatly from the discussion of the participants in two Liberty Fund conferences on Lord Acton. In particular, I wish to thank Walter Arnstein, R.P. Carr, S.W. Jackman, and Edward Norman for reading, commenting upon, and improving "The Essays in This Volume" in Volume III. I also wish to thank Professor Larissa Bonfante of New York University for supervising the review of the foreign language passages in the text for all three volumes.

In this volume it is especially appropriate that I express again my deep appreciation to the Syndics of Cambridge University Library for permission to work with the Acton Papers, for the remarkable efficiency of the Library staff during my period of research in Cambridge, and for their unfailing courtesy and cooperation in all subsequent correspondence. I owe an equal debt of gratitude to the Master and Fellows of Christ's College for the warm hospitality extended me during my stay in Cambridge.

J. Rufus Fears
Boston, Massachusetts

J. Rufus Fears is Professor of Classical Studies at Boston University.

List of Abbreviations

Acton, *Church and State* — Acton, John Emerich Edward Dalberg, First Baron. *Essays on Church and State.* Edited by Douglas Woodruff. London, 1952.

Acton, *Correspondence* — ———. *Selections from the Correspondence of the First Lord Acton.* Edited by John Figgis and Reginald Laurence. London, 1917.

Acton, *Freedom and Power* — ———. *Essays on Freedom and Power.* Edited by Gertrude Himmelfarb. Bonston and Glencoe, Illinois, 1948.

Acton, *Historical Essays* — ———. *Historical Essays and Other Studies.* Edited by John Figgis and Reginald Laurence. London, 1908.

Acton, *History of Freedom* — ———. *The History of Freedom and Other Essays.* Edited by John Figgis and Reginald Laurence. London, 1907.

Acton, *Lectures on French Revolution* — ———. *Lectures on the French Revolution.* Edited by John Figgis and Reginald Laurence. London, 1910.

Acton, *Lectures on Modern History* — ———. *Lectures on Modern History.* Edited by John Figgis and Reginald Laurence. London, 1906.

Acton, *Liberal Interpretation of History* — ———. *Essays in the Liberal Interpretation of History.* Edited by William McNeill. Chicago, 1967.

Acton, *Papal Power* — *Lord Acton on Papal Power.* Edited by H.A. MacDougall. London, 1973.

Acton, *Selected Writings* — *Selected Writings of Lord Acton.* Edited by J. Rufus Fears. Vols. I–III. Indianapolis, 1985–1987.

Acton–Simpson — *The Correspondence of Lord Acton and Richard Simpson.* Edited by Josef Altholz, Damian McElrath, and James Holland. Cambridge, 1971–1975.

Add. Mss. — Acton Papers. Cambridge University Library.

Döllinger — Döllinger, Johann Ignaz von, *Briefwechsel.* Edited by Victor Conzemius. Vols. I–III. Munich, 1963–1971.

McElrath   McElrath, Damian. *Lord Acton: The Decisive Decade
                1864–1874: Essays and Documents. Louvain,
                1970.

Paul   Paul, Herbert, ed. *Letters of Lord Acton to Mary
                Gladstone.* New York and London, 1904.

Ryan   Ryan, Guy. *The Acton Circle, 1864–1871: The 'Chron-
                icle' and the 'North British Review.'* Diss., Uni-
                versity of Notre Dame, 1969.

Shaw   Shaw, W. A. *A Bibliography of the Historical Works
                of Dr. Creighton, late Bishop of London, Dr.
                Stubbs, late Bishop of Oxford, Dr. S. R. Gardiner,
                and the late Lord Acton.* London, 1903.

Wellesley   *The Wellesley Index to Victorian Periodicals, 1824–
                1900.* Edited by Walter Houghton. Toronto
                and London, 1966–1979.

Selected Writings of Lord Acton

VOLUME III

ESSAYS IN RELIGION, POLITICS, AND MORALITY

ESSAYS IN
LIBERAL
CATHOLICISM

[1]
Review of Félix's
Le Progrès par le
Christianisme

These twelve discourses are worthy of the traditions of the place where they were delivered. In no department has the French clergy done so much towards obtaining its proper influence over the intelligent portion of the community as by the eloquence of its preachers. In no other department has the French clergy of the seventeenth century been rivalled by that of the nineteenth. The spirit in which these volumes are composed deserves to be specially noted, for it differs conspicuously—and, in our opinion, much to its advantage—from the tone which generally prevails among the French apologists. There is a party among them who consistently reject and condemn all the ideas and opinions which are at the present day most popular. Accepting nothing which they do not recognise as having originated on what they deem Catholic ground, they refuse to take advantage of the weapons which the progress of the age supplies. In their resolute hatred of whatever bears the mark of novelty or progress, they cover good and evil with the same anathema. Consequently they learn nothing from their opponents; every controversy leaves them where they were, and all their polemical efforts are barren of fruit. They invite attack by perpetually presenting a weak point in the array of the Church's defenders, and condemn themselves as well as others to intellectual sterility. By their dread of enlightenment they keep alive in France that vulgar unbelief which would soon vanish when encountered by serious learning and common sense. In their hands no problems are

Joseph Félix, *Le Progrès par le Christianisme: Conférences de Notre-Dame de Paris*, 2 vols. (Paris: Le Clerc, 1858). This review was published in the *Rambler* n.s. (2d ser.) 10 (July 1858):70–72. Döllinger I, p. 146; Acton-Simpson I, p. 36.

solved, no difficulties cleared away, no progress made in the investigation or application of Catholic truth. In philosophy they assert the impotency of human reason, and they acknowledge the same principle in political and social questions. They insist upon the alliance of the priest and the soldier, in order that by their combined efforts mental as well as political inaction may be enforced. By this means they have estranged all the intellect of the land from the Church they profess to represent. They speak always in a tone either of triumph or contempt, and strive by indignant declamation to disguise their intellectual indolence and their moral cowardice.

Another school, scarcely more original, and in its way almost as exclusive and partial as the one we have described, fully acquiesce in the prevailing doctrines of the day. They endeavour to show that they coincide with the teaching of the Church, properly understood; and they invest with a Catholic sound and colour doctrines any thing but Catholic in their origin. Possessing no independent solution of their own for the great problems of the time, they combat one set of the adversaries of religion with weapons borrowed from another; they draw Catholic conclusions from anti-Catholic premises, and strive by Beelzebub to cast out devils. Whilst the first school construct their political system in harmony with their narrow views of religion and philosophy, the others sometimes overlook in the political dispute the theological difference, and forget, in their zeal against absolutist politicians and infidel philosophers, the antagonism of Protestant Liberalism. English Protestantism, and the pseudo Protestantism affected by some of the literary men in France, meet with no molestation at their hands; and it would haply be hard to say on what grounds a dispute could arise between them.

The character and value of Catholic literature in each country must depend in great part upon the kind of enemy with whom it has to deal. Feeble assailants encourage feebleness in the defence. Ignorance and declamation can elicit no great efforts of learning, and no great moderation of speech. Depth of thought or of knowledge would be wasted on the Epigoni of Voltairianism. The ordinary French infidelity is a very different, and much less improving, adversary than the Protestantism of England, or the scientific Pantheism of Germany. It has neither the moral gravity of the one, nor the intellectual vigour of the other. The unbelief of Catholic countries rarely acts as an incentive to great mental exertion. It neither springs from profound study nor yet leads to it; but is founded generally on mere moral depravity. In Protestant countries it is often founded at least as much upon intellectual superiority. Hatred of the truth produces it in one case; hatred of a particular form of error in the other. Nobody would put Voltaire on the same level with Hegel, or Mazzini with Carlyle. It is not wonderful, then, if the French Catholics have produced little that will be of service in other countries and in other times. They have, nevertheless, succeeded in their generation in making an impression on their own country; and what has been accomplished so far has been chiefly the work of the disciples of Lamennais.

Father Félix, in the pulpit of Notre-Dame, shows no trace of the deficiencies and the disputes of his fellow-Catholics. He is neither a declaimer nor a partisan. A magnanimous boldness, clearness, and sincerity, distinguish his style in grappling with a new and difficult subject: "Donner une direction sûre au mouvement du progrès; ce qui peut nous sauver ce n'est pas le mépris superbe, c'est la solution loyale des questions qu'il nous pose" (vol. i. p. 68). A doctrine which is common enough is eloquently and truly described (vol. i. p. 92): "Le mal dans l'humanité, éternel obstacle à la marche du progrès, s'évanouit comme le rêve des générations et des siècles, sous la marche d'un progrès fatal qui passe en dévorant toutes les vertus et en consacrant tous les crimes; car dans ce système où la brutalité le dispute à l'absurde, le progrès, c'est tout ce qui renverse l'obstacle du présent pour régner dans l'avenir; le progrès, c'est tout ce qui réussit et tout ce qui triomphe; le progrès, c'est toute victoire de ce qui est plus fort sur ce qui est plus faible, c'est la déification de la force, c'est l'apothéose du succès." And this is well contrasted with the notion of progress which is based upon the fall of man: "Progrès difficile, progrès douloureux, condamné à reconquérir par la souffrance cette grandeur qui fut perdue par le plaisir" (vol. i. p. 106). The terms in which he speaks of the state of France are worthy to be remembered: "Messieurs, vous avez peur de quelque chose! Oui, au milieu des merveilles de votre présent et des promesses de votre avenir, une crainte se mêle à toutes vos espérances, et la frayeur est au fond de vos admirations. Qu'est-ce que cela? Quoi! vous avez peur! et de quoi donc? Rien dans le présent et dans le passé peut-il vous apparaître plus fort que notre France en 1856? Vous voici deux fois triomphants, et deux fois glorieux des prodiges de la paix et des miracles de la guerre, entre les conquêtes faites par votre épée et les créations faites par votre génie . . . et vous avez peur? D'où vient dans cette plénitude des ressources cette crainte de la ruine? D'où vient dans tous les enthousiasmes du progrès tant de frayeurs de décadence? Ah! vous avez compris que la puissance matérielle sans la force morale pour la soutenir n'est que la prospérité des corps suspendue sur le vide des âmes. . . . Au jour des suprêmes dangers, rien de ce qui vous fascine ne pourra vous sauver" (vol. i. pp. 218, 219). "Oui, au bout des perfectionnements de toutes vos institutions politiques, administratives et sociales, même les plus puissantes et les mieux concertées, j'affirme qu'une chose est inévitable: la suppression graduelle de la liberté civile; et l'aggravation progressive de la servitude sociale; servitude d'autant plus inévitable qu'elle résulte à la fois du fait de ceux qui obéissent et du fait de ceux qui commandent" (vol. i. p. 314).

[2]
The Count de Montalembert

There was once a time when it was the common belief, both of churchmen and statesmen, that the Church had great need of the State, and that her prosperity was proportioned to the favour she received from it. She was regarded as a useful ornament about the throne of absolute sovereigns; and the pious protection extended to her by Catholic monarchs, such as Philip IV or Lewis XV, was deemed a prodigious security for religion. A prince who expelled the Protestants from his dominions was permitted to beard the Pope. A prince who chiefly proved his orthodoxy by an occasional *auto-da-fé* was, *par excellence*, the Catholic king. In the eyes of most men the fatness of benefices was the measure of the prosperity of the Church. Consequently religion was strong only in the strength of the State; the decline of the monarchy deprived the Church of her chief support; and when the revolution came, she was its first and easiest victim. The result of that old *régime* was, that the king of France was beheaded, and the Pope died in a French prison. In those days people wondered, for it was the first time such things had been. But in the midst of that memorable ruin a lesson was learnt which has borne imperishable fruit. In the times which have succeeded the Church has taken her stand on her own everlasting foundation—on the words of Christ, not on the gifts of Constantine. More than once since then, in different places, she has been stripped of that terrestrial splendour which had proved such a fatal possession; but she has stood her ground in the wreck of those political institutions on which she no longer relied, and alone has saved society. The old position of things has been reversed; and it has been found that it is the State which stands in need of the Church, and that the strength of the Church is her independence. This has been the

Published in the *Rambler* n.s. (2d ser.) 10 (December 1858):421–428. Döllinger I, p. 155; Acton-Simpson I, p. 82.

secret and the moral of that extraordinary revival, which in our own day has rivalled the wonders of the Tridentine age.

All who have been since then the most conspicuous defenders of the Catholic cause, have maintained the principle of liberty and independence. And the truth of it is becoming more manifest in almost every crisis of European affairs. No country, with the exception perhaps of Naples, is Catholic in the old sense of the word. Yet Catholicism, though it has new enemies to deal with, is almost every where stronger than it was before. Those who have not yet understood the teaching of the modern history of the Church, will need some yet sharper lesson to instruct them. Yet it is no secret that there are many such; and the reason of their blindness is not difficult to find. For the independence of the Church brings with it a consequence that is unpalatable to many even among Catholics. A free Church implies a free nation. The absolutism of the State recovers all its oppressiveness where the vast domains of religion are not protected from its control by a Church in which there is no room and no excuse for arbitrary power. He, therefore, that deems he can advocate the cause of religion without advocating at the same time the cause of freedom, is no better than a hypocrite and a traitor.

Of these things France has latterly shown a melancholy but impressive example. Under the monarchy of July the French Catholics were united in their claim of freedom for their schools. Their agreement was such that they adopted the title, which it is always dangerous to allow, of the Catholic party. It was as their acknowledged leader that M. de Montalembert attained his high position among the statesmen and orators of France. But when, after the Revolution, the victory was substantially gained upon the point so long at issue, and a new peril menaced both political and intellectual liberty, it came to light that there had been many among the advocates of the Catholic cause who were not really animated with the Catholic spirit, and who had been looking only for a particular advantage in a contest which involved great principles. They formed themselves into that well-known party which is so great a calamity to religion, and which has done the work of her enemies in obscuring Catholic ideas and disgracing the Catholic name. In the presence of anarchy they sought a remedy in despotism; they opposed modern unbelief with an exploded superstition, and strove to expel the new devil with the old one.

By his constant, timely, and eloquent protests against these tendencies, M. de Montalembert has earned the gratitude and admiration of Catholics in all countries, and has excited in the imperial government that irritation which has at last overflowed. He has with him the hearts of all true friends of religion and of freedom, and of all who are capable of appreciating the loyal and consistent pursuit of a lofty purpose. Above all, he is sure of the sympathy of all Catholics who are inspired with the spirit of their religion; because, even in his panegyric of a Protestant country, his writings are the most faithful expression which Catholic principles have found in France, and because the prosecution of which he is the object is directed against ideas which are inseparably connected with the Catholic faith. This conflict between imperial and Catholic ideas was imminent, in spite of the infatuation on which their delusive alliance is founded, so long as truly Catholic principles continued to be upheld in France. The real significance of the present prosecution is, that only an adaptation of Catholicism can be tolerated; and that consequences that are essential to its integrity, without which it can fulfil but half its mission among men, are to be proscribed by the rigour of the law. Nor was this wanted in order to prove that no friendship could really subsist between the Empire as it is and Catholicism as it ought to be.

For the Emperor has appreciated the political character and importance of the Church about as well as the first Napoleon, who had regicides and apostate monks in his government when he sent for the Pope to crown him. He likes it as a conservative institution, that supplies priests to preach to the people and Bishops to decorate and incense his throne; and many there are who participate in the guilt of feeding this illusion. But it is not in those things which recommend it to the imperial favour that the social power of Catholicity resides. It is not only an institution, but a system of ideas, in which all true principles of policy are rooted, and the guardian of that true liberty which is the privilege of Christian nations. And these ideas it is the duty of Catholics ever to proclaim; and they cannot be put to silence by the interference of police. The Church has to remind princes of their duties, and nations of their rights; and to keep alive the spirit of personal dignity and independence, without which the religious and the political character of men are alike degraded. She is not less afflicted by the immorality of a government than by that of individuals; and that is no position worthy of her in which she exercises no moralising influence upon the State.

We bring the feeble tribute of our admiration and sympathy to Count de Montalembert because we feel that his cause interests all Catholics, and that it is one in which Catholics only can fully sympathise. We do it all the more cordially and sincerely, that we cannot always concur in his manner of upholding our common cause; and that his recent essay reminds us, on more points than one, of differences we have felt before. His writings generally betray the traces of the conflicts in which his ideas have been matured, and of the school in which they were originally formed. They almost invariably assume a controversial form, and appear only for polemical purposes. This is what gives such brilliancy and such earnestness to his eloquence. But, from this very combativeness, it seldom presents a complete and impartial statement of Catholic opinion.

We are almost tempted to question his knowledge of English institutions, when we find him recommending the forms of our government to a nation incapable of its spirit, or comparing them to those of France before 1848: "J'étudie les institutions contemporaines qui ne sont plus les nôtres, mais qui l'ont été" (p. 206). The comparison is neither just nor flattering to ourselves. Between the French and English constitutions there was all the difference that subsists between a republic with the bare forms of monarchy and a monarchy with popular institutions, between a society that proceeds by revolution and a state that proceeds by reform. Our institutions are part and parcel of the nation itself, not a garment that can be imitated by a skilful workman. What they can teach foreign statesmen is, to cling in every political change to the traditions and character of their own people, and to distinguish between the institutions which are accidental and transient and those which are national and unchangeable. The essence of monarchy does not consist in a citizen king, who reigns but does not govern; nor is its true character diminished or imperilled when each order of the state shares the power. Elsewhere we read: "Aujourd'hui tout le monde en Angleterre veut le progrès, et tout le monde aussi le veut sans renier la gloire du passé, sans ébranler les fondations sociales. De toutes les questions qui intéressent aujourd'hui le salut ou l'honneur du pays, il n'y en a pas une seule qui se rattache aux anciennes divisions des Whigs et des Tories" (p. 265). We cannot accept this view of the destruction of the old parties, which amounts to a justification of Radicalism. The Whigs, it is true, have done their part, and have been victorious on all the points which proceeded legitimately from their principles. But parties do not agree because their relative position is no longer the same. The progress of history tends, not to reconcile opinions, but to make the distinction ever greater between them, and to bring out in more naked contrast the antagonism of good and evil. The line between parties, which was once perpendicular, becomes by degrees horizontal. If the quarrels which so long divided our public men are forgotten, it is in presence of the threatening rise of a third party, which is the common enemy of both the others. The passage of Mr. Roebuck's speech on India which Count de Montalembert himself censures points this way; and he might have found a still more significant symptom in the repudiation by the pretended Conservatives of every conservative principle, and their efforts to outbid the popular party in the popular cry. We have pointed this out because it suggests a problem which Catholics will before long be obliged to solve; and because, if we remember rightly, it was one of the things overlooked in the book on the political future of England. In loudly and justly insisting upon the value of liberal institutions, M. de Montalembert seems to us to have sometimes exaggerated the value of the outward forms, in which the substance of liberty does not necessarily reside; and to forget that the absence of the constitutional system does not necessarily imply the absence of that freedom which can exist, and has existed, in other circumstances as well. This would be an injustice to the political influence of the Church, where she can freely exert it, and to the importance, in a merely political point of view, of such a measure, for instance, as the Austrian Concordat. We are persuaded that the Church alone, with her free action secured to her, is the surest safeguard of political liberty where her children are inspired with such ideas as the Count so eloquently proclaims. This somewhat one-sided and excessive partiality, which renders him so indulgent not to England only but to the government of Louis Philippe, and even, if our memory serves us, to the Spanish constitution of 1812, and which led, on a well-known occasion, to a violent and unjust attack on Austria, has given rise in the present instance to a most unfounded arraignment of the colonial policy of Spain. "L'histoire ne crie-t-elle pas d'une voix implacable à l'Espagne, *Caïn, qu'as-tu fait de ton frère?* Qu'a-t-elle fait de ces millions d'Indiens qui peuplaient les îles et le continent du nouveau monde? . . . se sont-ils montrés moins impitoyables que les Anglo-Américains dans le Nord? . . . Que penser des nations orthodoxes, qui, avec de tels apôtres et de tels enseignements, ont dépeuplé la moitié d'un monde? Et quelle société la conquête espagnole a-t-elle substituée à ces races qu'on exterminait au lieu de les civiliser? . . . On y verra ce que la mortelle influence du pouvoir absolu sait faire des colonies catholiques en même temps que de leurs métropoles" (pp. 212, 213). There is something in this habit of proclaiming on all occasions and at all hazards—even of historical truth—hatred of absolute governments, as well as of absolutist principles that unpleasantly reminds us of the perennial abuse of England by which his adversaries try to sustain their cause. To our minds, in a man less chivalrous and honourable, there would be something undignified in the frequent recurrence of this practice. If absolutists among Catholics as well as Protestants refuse to see in history whatever does not suit their system, it surely does not beseem liberal Catholics to use the same arts; and sneers at Protestant England are but imperfectly answered by sneers at despotic Spain. Mr. Helps is referred to in support of the above remarks; to whom we beg leave to oppose the authority of another Protestant writer, of one who has no superior among the political historians of the present day. "From the beginning," says Roscher, in his excellent work on colonisation, "the crown endeavoured to mediate between the conquerors and the conquered, in order to humanise the treatment of the natives. This contest, which the government carried on against the *conquistadores* for the relief of the natives, was often extremely violent, and corresponds exactly with that between the English government and the planters for the protection of negroes, hottentots, &c. . . . It is characteristic of the Spaniards that they commonly unite the terms *descubridores*, *pacificadores*, and *pobladores*; in fact, it was only by them that most of the Indian tribes were introduced to civilised life. . . . Altogether the treatment of the Indians was as gentle as their childishness and the security of the Spanish dominion allowed. . . . Whereas the colonies of the other European nations regularly brought about the extermination of the native barbarians wherever they came into contact with them, the Spaniards succeeded not only in preserving but in converting and partially civilising them. Horrors were indeed committed, such as an unbridled soldiery commit in every war; but only whilst the *conquistadores* remained almost independent of the government at home. . . . Every colonising nation that chooses, may learn of the Spaniards how to proceed with humanity towards the original inhabitants."[1]

[1] Roscher: Kolonien, Kolonialpolitik und Auswanderung, 1856, pp. 146, 147, 149, 151, 153.

It is impossible to reproach M. de Montalembert with the constancy with which he persists in hoping in a hopeless cause, and refuses to recognise the deeper causes which make liberty impossible in France. It is because of his confidence in his own high spirit that he refuses to despair of his country. Yet the reproaches he hurls at the government and its sycophants manifestly touch a vast proportion of his countrymen. The servitude of the whole nation is justified by the servility of the majority. The long duration of a despotism, exercised by a man of no conspicuous virtues and of no conspicuous ability, bespeaks a nation singularly fitted for such a yoke. Against the resistance of moral forces the material force of the imperial bayonets could not permanently prevail:

> Nor stony tower, nor walls of beaten brass,
> Nor airless dungeon, nor strong links of iron,
> Can be retentive to the strength of spirit.

The victims of the imperial despotism are for the most part themselves its instruments. *Tollenda est culpa, ut cesset tyrannorum plaga.*

Yet though the Count's appeal to the better feeling of his countrymen seems likely to meet but a feeble response, the decline of the imperial power is betokened by many familiar signs—by none more significantly than by the folly of the present prosecution. A legal discomfiture would not be more fatal than the moral injury of an ignoble victory over the best remaining elements in France. Nor need we wait for the end to say, that the Emperor, who was hailed as the saviour of society, has signally failed in the mission it was given to him to fulfil. When he is gone, the revolution, for which the only remedy is freedom, will be found to have increased in energy in consequence of his boasted repression. It was of no avail to restore Barabbas to his fetters, without at the same time loosening the bonds of Christ.

With reference to the remarks on the Indian debate, we need not allude to certain minor errors which prove that the mind of the writer was not in India. We will only say, that the memorable despatch of the 7th June receives too little attention; and that it is a manifest injustice to speak, in the face of it, of a change in Lord Canning's Oude policy produced by the remonstrances from home. But, in substance, the Count's views on our Indian empire are indisputably true, and such as cannot be too often or too loudly repeated. He has understood that this semi-Protestant country has the glorious mission of representing in Asia the civilisation of Christianity. The cause of religion will be more truly served by our victories in India than it ever was by the arms of the Crusaders. With the English dominion must stand or fall the hope of converting and civilising Asia; and our troops are fighting the battles of the Pope as much as of the Queen.

Whilst admitting that M. de Montalembert is, in the present instance, the true exponent of a great Catholic principle, and that the Catholic religion is threatened in his person, it was incumbent upon us to specify the points in which his essay less fully and accurately corresponds with our Catholic feelings. They are not new or unexpected to those who have followed his previous career; but at no period of his public life has he stood forward with more honour and universal esteem, as emphatically the champion of the Catholic cause, than at the present moment.

It is a significant coincidence, that whilst the chief organ of Catholic opinion in France is being prosecuted by a despotic government, the first Catholic journal in Germany is undergoing similar treatment at the hands of the Catholic and constitutional government of Bavaria. The *Correspondant* and the *Historischpolitische Blätter* are the most powerful and consistent defenders of ecclesiastical independence, of political liberty, and of freedom of thought. This Protestant country has certainly one great superiority over the so-called Catholic states of the Continent—here at least it is not government interference that will attempt to crush the independence of a Catholic Review.

[3]
Political Thoughts
on the Church

There is, perhaps, no stronger contrast between the revolutionary times in which we live and the Catholic ages, or even the period of the Reformation, than in this: that the influence which religious motives formerly possessed is now in a great measure exercised by political opinions. As the theory of the balance of power was adopted in Europe as a substitute for the influence of religious ideas, incorporated in the power of the Popes, so now political zeal occupies the place made vacant by the decline of religious fervour, and commands to an almost equal extent the enthusiasm of men. It has risen to power at the expense of religion, and by reason of its decline, and naturally regards the dethroned authority with the jealousy of a usurper. This revolution in the relative position of religious and political ideas was the inevitable consequence of the usurpation by the Protestant State of the functions of the Church, and of the supremacy which, in the modern system of government, it has assumed over her. It follows also that the false principles by which religious truth was assailed have been transferred to the political order, and that here, too, Catholics must be prepared to meet them; whilst the objections made to the Church on doctrinal grounds have lost much of their attractiveness and effect, the enmity she provokes on political grounds is more intense. It is the same old enemy with a new face. No reproach is more common, no argument better suited to the temper of these times, than those which are founded on the supposed inferiority or incapacity of the Church in political matters. As her dogma, for instance, is assailed from opposite sides— as she has had to defend the divine nature of Christ against the

Published in the *Rambler* n.s. (2d ser.) 11 (January 1859):30–49. Döllinger I, p. 158; Acton-Simpson I, p. 98. Reprinted in Acton, *History of Freedom*, pp. 188–211.

Ebionites, and His humanity against Docetism, and was attacked both on the plea of excessive rigorism and excessive laxity (Clement Alex., *Stromata*, iii. 5)—so in politics she is arraigned on behalf of the political system of every phase of heresy. She was accused of favouring revolutionary principles in the time of Elizabeth and James I, and of absolutist tendencies under James II and his successors. Since Protestant England has been divided into two great political parties, each of these reproaches has found a permanent voice in one of them. Whilst Tory writers affirm that the Catholic religion is the enemy of all conservatism and stability, the Liberals consider it radically opposed to all true freedom.

> "What are we to think," says the *Edinburgh Review* (vol. ciii. p. 586), "of the penetration or the sincerity of a man who professes to study and admire the liberties of England and the character of her people, but who does not see that English freedom has been nurtured from the earliest times by resistance to Papal authority, and established by the blessing of a reformed religion? That is, under Heaven, the basis of all the rights we possess; and the weight we might otherwise be disposed to concede to M. de Montalembert's opinions on England is materially lessened by the discovery that, after all, he would, if he had the power, place this free country under that spiritual bondage which broods over the empires of Austria or of Spain."

On the other hand, let us hearken to the Protestant eloquence of the *Quarterly Review* (vol. xcii. p. 41):

> Tyranny, fraud, base adulation, total insensibility, not only to the worth of human freedom, but to the majesty of law and the sacredness of public and private right; these are the malignant and deadly features which we see stamped upon the conduct of the Roman hierarchy.

Besides which, we have the valuable opinion of Lord Derby, which no Catholic, we should suppose, east of the Shannon has forgotten, that Catholicism is "religiously corrupt, and politically dangerous." Lord Macaulay tells us that it exclusively promoted the power of the Crown; Ranke, that it favours revolution and regicide. Whilst the Belgian and Sardinian Liberals accuse the Church of being the enemy of constitutional freedom, the celebrated Protestant statesman, Stahl, taunts her with the reproach of being the sole support and pillar of the Belgian constitution. Thus every error pronounces judgment on itself when it attempts to apply its rules to the standard of truth.

Among Catholics the state of opinion on these questions, whether it be considered the result of unavoidable circumstances, or a sign of ingenious accommodation, or a thing to be deplored, affords at least a glaring refutation of the idea that we are united, for good or for evil, in one common political system. The Church is vindicated by her defenders, according to their individual inclinations, from the opposite faults imputed to her; she is lauded, according to circumstances, for the most contradictory merits, and her authority is invoked in exclusive support of very various systems. O'Connell, Count de Montalembert, Father Ventura, proclaim her liberal, constitutional, not to say democratic, character; whilst such writers as Bonald and Father Taparelli associate her with the cause of absolute government. Others there are, too, who deny that the Church has a political tendency or preference of any kind; who assert that she is altogether independent of, and indifferent to, particular political institutions, and, while insensible to their influence, seeks to exercise no sort of influence over them. Each view may be plausibly defended, and the inexhaustible arsenal of history seems to provide impartially instances in corroboration of each. The last opinion can appeal to the example of the Apostles and the early Christians, for whom, in the heathen empire, the only part was unconditional obedience. This is dwelt upon by the early apologists: "Oramus etiam pro imperatoribus, pro ministris eorum et potestatibus, pro statu saeculi, pro rerum quiete, pro mora finis."[1] It has the authority, too, of those who thought with St. Augustine that the State had a sinful origin and character: "Primus fuit terrenae civitatis conditor fratricida."[2] The Liberals, at the same time, are strong in the authority of many scholastic writers, and of many of the older Jesuit divines, of St. Thomas and Suarez, Bellarmine, and Mariana. The absolutists, too, countenanced by Bossuet and the Gallican Church, and quoting amply from the Old Testament, can point triumphantly to the majority of Catholic countries in modern times. All these arguments are at the same time serviceable to our adversaries; and those by which one objection is answered help to fortify another.

The frequent recurrence of this sort of argument which appears to us as treacherous for defence as it is popular as a weapon of attack, shows that no very definite ideas prevail on the subject, and makes it doubtful whether history, which passes sentence on so many theories,

---

[1] Tertullian, *Apologeticum*, 39; see also 30, 32. "We pray also for the emperors, for the ministers of their Government, for the State, for the peace of the world, for the delay of the last day."

[2] *De Civit. Dei*, xv. 5. "The fratricide was the first founder of the secular State."

is altogether consistent with any of these. Nevertheless it is obviously an inquiry of the greatest importance, and one on which controversy can never entirely be set at rest; for the relation of the spiritual and the secular power is, like that of speculation and revelation of religion and nature, one of those problems which remain perpetually open, to receive light from the meditations and experience of all ages, and the complete solution of which is among the objects, and would be the end, of all history.

At a time when the whole system of ecclesiastical government was under discussion, and when the temporal power was beginning to predominate over the Church in France, the greatest theologian of the age made an attempt to apply the principles of secular polity to the Church. According to Gerson (*Opera*, ii. 254), the fundamental forms into which Aristotle divides all government recur in the ecclesiastical system. The royal power is represented in the Papacy, the aristocracy by the college of cardinals, whilst the councils form an ecclesiastical democracy (*timocratia*). Analogous to this is the idea that the constitution of the Church served as the model of the Christian States, and that the notion of representation, for instance, was borrowed from it. But it is not by the analogy of her own forms that the Church has influenced those of the State; for in reality there is none subsisting between them, and Gerson's adoption of a theory of Grecian origin proves that he scarcely understood the spirit of that mediaeval polity which, in his own country especially, was already in its decay. For not only is the whole system of government, whether we consider its origin, its end, or its means absolutely and essentially different, but the temporal notion of power is altogether unknown in the Church. "Ecclesia subjectos non habet ut servos, sed ut filios."[3] Our Lord Himself drew the distinction: "Reges gentium dominantur eorum; et qui potestatem habent super eos, benefici vocantur. Vos autem non sic: sed qui major est in vobis, fiat sicut minor; et qui praedecessor, sicut minor" (Luc. xxii. 25, 26). The supreme authority is not the will of the rulers, but the law of the Church, which binds those who are its administrators as strictly as those who have only to obey it. No human laws were ever devised which could so thoroughly succeed in making the arbitrary exercise of power impossible, as that prodigious system of canon law which is the ripe fruit of the experience and the inspiration of eighteen

---

[3] "The Church reckons her subjects not as her servants but as her children."

hundred years. Nothing can be more remote from the political notions of monarchy than the authority of the Pope. With even less justice can it be said that there is in the Church an element of aristocracy, the essence of which is the possession of hereditary personal privileges. An aristocracy of merit and of office cannot, in a political sense, legitimately bear the name. By baptism all men are equal before the Church. Yet least of all can anything be detected corresponding to the democratic principle, by which all authority resides in the mass of individuals, and which gives to each one equal rights. All authority in the Church is delegated, and recognises no such thing as natural rights.

This confusion of the ideas belonging to different orders has been productive of serious and dangerous errors. Whilst heretics have raised the episcopate to a level with the papacy, the priesthood with the episcopate, the laity with the clergy, impugning successively the primacy, the episcopal authority, and the sacramental character of orders, the application of ideas derived from politics to the system of the Church led to the exaggeration of the papal power in the period immediately preceding the Reformation, to the claim of a permanent aristocratic government by the Council of Basel, and to the democratic extravagance of the Observants in the fourteenth century.

If in the stress of conflicting opinions we seek repose and shelter in the view that the kingdom of God is not of this world; that the Church, belonging to a different order, has no interest in political forms, tolerates them all, and is dangerous to none; if we try to rescue her from the dangers of political controversy by this method of retreat and evasion, we are compelled to admit her inferiority, in point of temporal influence, to every other religious system. Every other religion impresses its image on the society that professes it, and the government always follows the changes of religion. Pantheism and Polytheism, Judaism and Islamism, Protestantism, and even the various Protestant as well as Mahometan sects, call forth corresponding social and political forms. All power is from God, and is exercised by men in His stead. As men's notions are, therefore, in respect to their position towards God, such must their notion of temporal power and obedience also be. The relation of man to man corresponds with his relations to God—most of all his relations towards the direct representative of God.

The view we are discussing is one founded on timidity and a desire of peace. But peace is not a good great enough to be purchased by such sacrifices. We must be prepared to do battle for our religious system in every other sphere as well as in that of doctrine. Theological error affects men's ideas on all other subjects, and we cannot accept in politics the consequences of a system which is hateful to us in its religious aspect. These questions cannot be decided by mere reasoning, but we may obtain some light by inquiring of the experience of history; our only sure guide is the example of the Church itself. "Insolentissima est insania, non modo disputare contra id quod videmus universam ecclesiam credere sed etiam contra id quod videmus eam facere. Fides enim ecclesiae non modo regula est fidei nostrae, sed etiam actiones ipsius actionum nostrarum, consuetudo ipsius consuetudinis quam observare debemus."[4]

The Church which our Lord came to establish had a twofold mission to fulfil. Her system of doctrine, on the one hand, had to be defined and perpetually maintained. But it was also necessary that it should prove itself more than a mere matter of theory—that it should pass into practice, and command the will as well as the intellect of men. It was necessary not only to restore the image of God in man, but to establish the divine order in the world. Religion had to transform the public as well as the private life of nations, to effect a system of public right corresponding with private morality and without which it is imperfect and insecure. It was to exhibit and confirm its victory and to perpetuate its influence by calling into existence, not only works of private virtue, but institutions which are the product of the whole life of nations, and bear an unceasing testimony to their religious senti-ments. The world, instead of being external to the Church, was to be adopted by her and imbued with her ideas. The first, the doctrinal or intellectual part of the work, was chiefly performed in the Roman empire, in the midst of the civilisation of antiquity and of that unparalleled intellectual excitement which followed the presence of Christ on earth. There the faith was prepared for the world whilst the world was not yet ready to receive it. The empire in which was concentrated all the learning and speculation of ancient times was by its intellectual splendour, and in spite, we might even say by reason, of its moral depravity, the fit scene of the intellectual establishment of

---

[4] "It is the maddest insolence, not only to dispute against that which we see the universal Church believing, but also against what we see her doing. For not only is the faith of the Church the rule of our faith, but also her actions of ours, and her customs of that which we ought to observe" (Morinus, *Comment. de Discipl. in administ. Poenitentiae*, Preface).

Christianity. For its moral degradation ensured the most violent antipathy and hostility to the new faith; while the mental cultivation of the age ensured a very thorough and ingenious opposition, and supplied those striking contrasts which were needed for the full discussion and vigorous development of the Christian system. Nowhere else, and at no other period, could such advantages have been found.

But for the other, equally essential part of her work the Church met with an insurmountable obstacle, which even the official conversion of the empire and all the efforts of the Christian emperors could not remove. This obstacle resided not so much in the resistance of paganism as a religion, as in the pagan character of the State. It was from a certain political sagacity chiefly that the Romans, who tolerated all religions,[5] consistently opposed that religion which threatened inevitably to revolutionise a state founded on a heathen basis. It appeared from the first a pernicious superstition ("exitiabilem superstitionem," Tacit. *Annal.* xv. 44), that taught its followers to be bad subjects ("exuere patriam," Tacitus, *Hist.* v. 5), and to be constantly dissatisfied ("quibus praesentia semper tempora cum enormi libertate displicent," Vopiscus, *Vit. Saturn.* 7). This hostility continued in spite of the protestations of every apologist, and of the submissiveness and sincere patriotism of the early Christians. They were so far from recognising what their enemies so vaguely felt, that the empire could not stand in the presence of the new faith, that it was the common belief amongst them, founded perhaps on the words of St. Paul (2 *Thess.* ii. 7)[6] that the Roman empire would last to the end of the world.[7]

The persecution of Julian was caused by the feeling of the danger which menaced the pagan empire from the Christian religion. His hostility was not founded on his attachment to the old religion of Rome, which he did not attempt to save. He endeavoured to replace it by a new system which was to furnish the State with new vigour to withstand the decay of the old paganism and the invasion of Christianity. He felt that the old religious ideas in which the Roman State

---

[5] "Apud vos quodvis colere jus est Deum verum" (Tertullian, *Apolog.* xxiv.).

[6] August, *de Civ. Dei*, xx. 19, 3.

[7] "Christianus nullius est hostis, nedum imperatoris, quem . . . necesse est ut . . . salvum velit cum toto Romano imperio quousque saeculum stabit; tamdiu enim stabit" (Tert. *ad Scapulam*, 2). "Cum caput illud orbis occiderit et ῥύμη esse coeperit, quod Sibyllae fore aiunt, quis dubitet venisse jam finem rebus humanis orbique terrarum?" (Lactantius, *Inst. Div.* vii. 25). "Non prius veniet Christus, quam regni Romani defectio fiat" (Ambrose, *ad ep.* i. *ad Thess.*).

had grown up had lost their power, and that Rome could only be saved by opposing at all hazards the new ideas. He was inspired rather with a political hatred of Christianity than with a religious love of paganism. Consequently Christianity was the only religion he could not tolerate. This was the beginning of the persecution of the Church on principles of liberalism and religious toleration, on the plea of political necessity, by men who felt that the existing forms of the State were incompatible with her progress. It is with the same feeling of patriotic aversion for the Church that Symmachus says (*Epist.* x. 61): "We demand the restoration of that religion which has so long been beneficial to the State ... of that worship which has subdued the universe to our laws, of those sacrifices which repulsed Hannibal from our walls and the Gauls from the Capitol."

Very soon after the time of Constantine it began to appear that the outward conversion of the empire was a boon of doubtful value to religion. "Et postquam ad Christianos principes venerint, potentia quidem et divitiis major sed virtutibus minor facta est," says St. Jerome (in *Vita Malchi*). The zeal with which the emperors applied the secular arm for the promotion of Christianity was felt to be incompatible with its spirit and with its interest as well. "Religion," says Lactantius (*Inst. Div.* v. 19), "is to be defended by exhorting, not by slaying, not by severity, but by patience; not by crime, but by faith: ... *nihil enim est tam voluntarium quam religio.*"[8] "Deus," says St. Hilary of Poitiers ("ad Constantium," *Opp.* i. p. 1221 C), "obsequio non eget necessario, non requirit coactam confessionem."[9] St. Athanasius and St. John Chrysostom protest in like manner against the intemperate proselytism of the day.[10] For the result which followed the general adoption of Christianity threw an unfavourable light on the motives which had caused it. It became evident that the heathen world was incapable of being regenerated, that the weeds were choking the good seed. The corruption increased in the Church to such a degree that the Christians, unable to divest themselves of the Roman notion of the *orbis terrarum*, deemed the end of the world at hand. St. Augustine (*sermo* cv.) rebukes this superstitious fear: "Si non manet civitas quae nos carnaliter genuit, manet quae nos spiritualiter genuit. Numquid (Dominus) dormitando

---

[8] "There is nothing so voluntary as religion."

[9] "God does not want unwilling worship, nor does he require a forced repentance."

[10] Athanas. i. 363 B and 384 C μὴ ἀναγκάζειν ἀλλὰ πείθειν "not compulsion, but persuasion" (Chrysost. ii. 540 A and C).

aedificium suum perdidit, aut non custodiendo hostes admisit? . . . Quid expavescis quia pereunt regna terrena? Ideo tibi coeleste promissum est, ne cum terrenis perires . . . Transient quae fecit ipse Deus; quanto citius quod condidit Romulus . . . Non ergo deficiamus, fratres: finis erit terrenis omnibus regnis."[11] But even some of the fathers themselves were filled with despair at the spectacle of the universal demoralisation: "Totius mundi una vox Christus est . . . Horret animus temporum nostrorum ruinas persequi. . . . Romanus orbis ruit, et tamen cervix nostra erecta non flectitur. . . . Nostris peccatis barbari fortes sunt. Nostris vitiis Romanus superatur exercitus. . . . Nec amputamus causas morbi, ut morbus pariter auferatur. . . . Orbis terrarum ruit, in nobis peccata non ruunt."[12] St. Ambrose announces the end still more confidently: "Verborum coelestium nulli magis quam nos testes sumus, quos mundi finis invenit. . . . Quia in occasu saeculi sumus, praecedunt quaedam aegritudines mundi."[13] Two generations later Salvianus exclaims: "Quid est aliud paene omnis coëtus Christianorum quam sentina vitiorum?"[14] And St. Leo declares, "Quod temporibus nostris auctore diabolo sic vitiata sunt omnia, ut paene nihil sit quod absque idolatria transigatur."[15]

When, early in the fifth century, the dismemberment of the Western empire commenced, it was clear that Christianity had not succeeded in reforming the society and the polity of the ancient world. It had arrested for a time the decline of the empire, but after the Arian separation it could not prevent its fall. The Catholics could not

[11] "If the State of which we are the secular children passes away, that of which we are spiritual children passes not. Has God gone to sleep and let the house be destroyed, or let in the enemy through want of watchfulness? Why fearest thou when earthly kingdoms fall? Heaven is promised thee, that thou mightest not fall with them. The works of God Himself shall pass: how much sooner the works of Romulus! Let us not quail, my brethren; all earthly kingdoms must come to an end."

[12] "The cry of the whole world is 'Christ.' The mind is horrified in reviewing the ruins of our age. The Roman world is falling, and yet our stiff neck is not bent. The barbarians' strength is in our sins; the defeat of the Roman armies in our vices. We will not cut off the occasions of the malady, that the malady may be healed. The world is falling, but in us there is no falling off from sin" (St. Jerome, *ep.* 35, *ad Heliodorum; ep.* 98, *ad Gaudentium*).

[13] "None are better witnesses of the words of heaven than we, on whom the end of the world has come. We assist at the world's setting, and diseases precede its dissolution" (*Expos. Ep. sec. Lucam*, x.).

[14] "What is well-nigh all Christendom but a sink of iniquity?" (*De Gub. Dei*, iii. 9).

[15] "In our age the devil has so defiled everything that scarcely a thing is done without idolatry."

dissociate the interests of the Church and those of the Roman State, and looked with patriotic as well as religious horror at the barbarians by whom the work of destruction was done. They could not see that they had come to build up as well as to destroy, and that they supplied a field for the exercise of all that influence which had failed among the Romans. It was very late before they understood that the world had run but half its course; that a new skin had been prepared to contain the new wine; and that the barbarous tribes were to justify their claim to the double inheritance of the faith and of the power of Rome. There were two principal things which fitted them for their vocation. The Romans had been unable to be the instruments of the social action of Christianity on account of their moral depravity. It was precisely for those virtues in which they were most deficient that their barbarous enemies were distinguished. Salvianus expresses this in the following words (*De Gubern. Dei*, vii. 6): "Miramur si terrae . . . nostrorum omnium a Deo barbaris datae sunt, cum eas quae Romani polluerant fornicatione, nunc mundent barbari castitate?"[16] Whilst thus their habits met half-way the morality of the Christian system, their mythology, which was the very crown and summit of all pagan religions, predisposed them in like manner for its adoption, by predicting its own end, and announcing the advent of a system which was to displace its gods. "It was more than a mere worldly impulse," says a famous northern divine, "that urged the northern nations to wander forth, and to seek, like birds of passage, a milder clime." We cannot, however, say more on the predisposition for Christianity of that race to whose hands its progress seems for ever committed, or on the wonderful facility with which the Teutonic invaders accepted it, whether presented to them in the form of Catholicism or of Arianism.[17] The great marvel in their history, and their chief claim to the dominion of the world, was, that they had preserved so long, in the bleak regions in which the growth of civilisation was in every way retarded, the virtues together with the ignorance of the barbarous State.

    At a time when Arianism was extinct in the empire, it assumed

---

[16] "Do we wonder that God has granted all our lands to the barbarians, when they now purify by their chastity the places which the Romans had polluted with their debauchery?"

[17] Pope Anastasius writes to Clovis: "Sedes Petri in tanta occasione non potest non laetari, cum plenitudinem gentium intuetur ad eam veloci gradu concurrere" (Bouquet, iv. 50).

among the Teutonic tribes the character of a national religion, and added a theological incitement to their animosity against the Romans. The Arian tribes, to whom the work of destruction was committed, did it thoroughly. But they soon found that their own preservation depended on their submission to the Church. Those that persisted in their heresy were extirpated. The Lombards and Visigoths saved themselves by a tardy conversion from the fate with which they were threatened so long, as their religion estranged them from the Roman population, and cut them off from the civilisation of which the Church was already the only guardian. For centuries the pre-eminence in the West belonged to that race which alone became Catholic at once, and never swerved from its orthodoxy. It is a sense of the importance of this fidelity which dictated the well-known preamble of the Salic law: "Gens Francorum inclita, Deo auctore condita, ad Catholicam fidem conversa et immunis ab haeresi," etc.[18]

Then followed the ages which are not unjustly called the Dark Ages, in which were laid the foundations of all the happiness that has been since enjoyed, and of all the greatness that has been achieved, by men. The good seed, from which a new Christian civilisation sprang, was striking root in the ground. Catholicism appeared as the religion of masses. In those times of simple faith there was no opportunity to call forth an Augustine or an Athanasius. It was not an age of conspicuous saints, but sanctity was at no time so general. The holy men of the first centuries shine with an intense brilliancy from the midst of the surrounding corruption. Legions of saints—individually for the most part obscure, because of the atmosphere of light around them—throng the five illiterate centuries, from the close of the great dogmatic controversies to the rise of a new theology and the commencement of new contests with Hildebrand, Anselm, and Bernard. All the manifestations of the Catholic spirit in those days bear a character of vastness and popularity. A single idea—the words of one man—electrified hundreds of thousands. In such a state of the world, the Christian ideas were able to become incarnate, so to speak, in durable forms, and succeeded in animating the political institutions as well as the social life of the nations.

The facility with which the Teutonic ideas of Government shaped themselves to the mould of the new religion, was the second point in

---

[18] "The noble people of the Franks, founded by God, converted to the Catholic faith, and free from heresy."

which that race was so peculiarly adapted for the position it has ever since occupied towards Christianity. They ceased to be barbarians only in becoming Christians. Their political system was in its infancy, and was capable of being developed variously, according to the influences it might undergo. There was no hostile civilisation to break down, no traditions to oppose which were bound up with the recollections of the national greatness. The State is so closely linked with religion, that no nation that has changed its religion has ever survived in its old political form. In Rome it had proved to be impossible to alter the system, which for a thousand years had animated every portion of the State; it was incurably pagan. The conversion of the people and the outward alliance with the Church could not make up for this inconsistency.

But the Teutonic race received the Catholic ideas wholly and without reserve. There was no region into which they failed to penetrate. The nation was collectively Catholic, as well as individually. The union of the Church with the political system of the Germans was so complete, that when Hungary adopted the religion of Rome, it adopted at the same time, as a natural consequence, the institutions of the empire. The ideas of Government which the barbarians carried with them into every land which they conquered were always in substance the same. The *Respublica Christiana* of the Middle Ages, consisting of those States in which the Teutonic element combined with the Catholic system, was governed by nearly the same laws. The mediaeval institutions had this also in common, that they grew up everywhere under the protection and guidance of the Church; and whilst they subsisted in their integrity, her influence in every nation, and that of the Pope over all the nations, attained their utmost height. In proportion as they have since degenerated or disappeared, the political influence of religion has declined. As we have seen that the Church was baffled in the full performance of her mission before Europe was flooded by the great migration, so it may be said that she has never permanently enjoyed her proper position and authority in any country where it did not penetrate. No other political system has yet been devised, which was consistent with the full development and action of Catholic principles, but that which was constructed by the northern barbarians who destroyed the Western empire.

From this it does not seem too much to conclude, that the Catholic religion tends to inspire and transform the public as well as the private life of men; that it is not really master of one without some authority over the other. Consequently, where the State is too powerful by long tradition and custom, or too far gone in corruption, to admit of the influence of religion, it can only prevail by ultimately destroying the political system. This helps us to understand the almost imperceptible progress of Christianity against Mahometanism, and the slowness of its increase in China, where its growth must eventually undermine the whole fabric of government. On the other hand, we know with what ease comparatively savage tribes—as the natives of California and Paraguay—were converted to a religion which first initiated them in civilisation and government. There are countries in which the natural conditions are yet wanting for the kingdom of grace. There is a fulness of time for every nation—a time at which it first becomes capable of receiving the faith.[19] It is not harder to believe that certain political conditions are required to make a nation fit for conversion than that a certain degree of intellectual development is indispensable; that the language, for instance, must have reached a point which that of some nations has not attained before it is capable of conveying the truths of Christianity.

We cannot, therefore, admit that political principles are a matter of utter indifference to the Church. To what sort of principles it is that she inclines may be indicated by a single example. The Christian notion of conscience imperatively demands a corresponding measure of personal liberty. The feeling of duty and responsibility to God is the only arbiter of a Christian's actions. With this no human authority can be permitted to interfere. We are bound to extend to the utmost, and to guard from every encroachment, the sphere in which we can act in obedience to the sole voice of conscience, regardless of any other consideration. The Church cannot tolerate any species of government in which this right is not recognised. She is the irreconcilable enemy of the despotism of the State, whatever its name or its forms may be, and through whatever instruments it may be exercised. Where the State allows the largest amount of this autonomy, the subject enjoys the largest measure of freedom, and the Church the greatest legitimate influence. The republics of antiquity were as incapable as the Oriental despotisms of satisfying the Christian notion of freedom, or even of subsisting with it. The Church has succeeded in producing the kind

---

[19] "Vetati sunt a Spiritu sancto loqui verbum Dei in Asia . . . Tentabant ire in Bithyniam, et non permisit eos spiritus Jesu" (*Acts* xvi. 6, 7).

of liberty she exacts for her children only in those States which she has herself created or transformed. Real freedom has been known in no State that did not pass through her mediaeval action. The history of the Middle Ages is the history of the gradual emancipation of man from every species of servitude, in proportion as the influence of religion became more penetrating and more universal. The Church could never abandon that principle of liberty by which she conquered pagan Rome. The history of the last three centuries exhibits the gradual revival of declining slavery, which appears under new forms of oppression as the authority of religion has decreased. The efforts of deliverance have been violent and reactionary, the progress of dependence sure and inevitable. The political benefits of the mediaeval system have been enjoyed by no nation which is destitute of Teutonic elements. The Slavonic races of the north-east, the Celtic tribes of the north-west, were deprived of them. In the centre of mediaeval civilisation, the republic of Venice, proud of its unmixed descent from the Romans, was untouched by the new blood, and that Christian people failed to obtain a Christian government. Where the influence of the ideas which prevailed in those times has not been felt, the consequence has been the utmost development of extreme principles, such as have doomed Asia for so many ages to perpetual stagnation, and America to endless heedless change. It is a plain fact, that that kind of liberty which the Church everywhere and at all times requires has been attained hitherto only in States of Teutonic origin. We need hardly glance at the importance of this observation in considering the missionary vocation of the English race in the distant regions it has peopled and among the nations it has conquered; for, in spite of its religious apostacy, no other country has preserved so pure that idea of liberty which gave to religion of old its power in Europe, and is still the foundation of the greatness of England. Other nations that have preserved more faithfully their allegiance to the Church have more decidedly broken with those political traditions, without which the action of the Church is fettered.

It is equally clear that, in insisting upon one definite principle in all government, the Church has at no time understood that it could be obtained only by particular political forms. She attends to the substance, not to the form, in politics. At various times she has successively promoted monarchy, aristocracy, and democracy; and at various times she has been betrayed by each. The three fundamental forms of all government are founded on the nature of things. Sovereignty must reside with an individual, or with a minority, or with the majority. But there are seasons and circumstances where one or the other is impossible, where one or the other is necessary; and in a growing nation they cannot always remain in the same relative proportions. Christianity could neither produce nor abolish them. They are all compatible with liberty and religion, and are all liable to diverge into tyranny by the exclusive exaggeration of their principle. It is this exaggeration that has ever been the great danger to religion and to liberty, and the object of constant resistance, the source of constant suffering for the Church.

Christianity introduced no new forms of government, but a new spirit, which totally transformed the old ones. The difference between a Christian and a pagan monarchy, or between a Christian and a rationalist democracy, is as great, politically, as that between a monarchy and a republic. The Government of Athens more nearly resembled that of Persia than that of any Christian republic, however democratic. If political theorists had attended more to the experience of the Christian Ages, the Church and the State would have been spared many calamities. Unfortunately, it has long been the common practice to recur to the authority of the Greeks and the Jews. The example of both was equally dangerous; for in the Jewish as in the Gentile world, political and religious obligations were made to coincide; in both, therefore—in the theocracy of the Jews as the πολιτεία of the Greeks—the State was absolute. Now it is the great object of the Church, by keeping the two spheres permanently distinct—by rendering to Caesar the things that are Caesar's, and to God the things that are God's—to make all absolutism, of whatever kind, impossible.

As no form of government is in itself incompatible with tyranny, either of a person or a principle, nor necessarily inconsistent with liberty, there is no natural hostility or alliance between the Church and any one of them. The same Church which, in the confusion and tumult of the great migrations, restored authority by raising up and anointing kings, held in later times with the aristocracy of the empire, and called into existence the democracies of Italy. In the eighth century she looked to Charlemagne for the reorganisation of society; in the eleventh she relied on the people to carry out the reformation of the clergy. During the first period of the Middle Ages, when social and political order had to be reconstructed out of ruins, the Church everywhere addresses herself to the kings, and seeks to strengthen and to sanctify their power. The royal as well as the imperial dignity received from her their authority and splendour. Whatever her disputes on religious grounds with particular sovereigns, such as Lothar, she had in those ages as yet no contests with the encroachments of monarchical power. Later on in the Middle Ages, on the contrary, when the monarchy had prevailed almost everywhere and had strengthened itself beyond the limits of feudal ideas by the help of the Roman law and of the notions of absolute power derived from the ancients, it stood in continual conflict with the Church. From the time of Gregory VII, all the most distinguished pontiffs were engaged in quarrels with the royal and imperial power, which resulted in the victory of the Church in Germany and her defeat in France. In this resistance to the exaggeration of monarchy, they naturally endeavoured to set barriers to it by promoting popular institutions, as the Italian democracies and the aristocratic republics of Switzerland, and the capitulations which in the thirteenth and fourteenth centuries were imposed on almost every prince. Times had greatly changed when a Pope declared his amazement at a nation which bore in silence the tyranny of their king.[20] In modern times the absolute monarchy in Catholic countries has been, next to the Reformation, the greatest and most formidable enemy of the Church. For here she again lost in great measure her natural influence. In France, Spain, and Germany, by Gallicanism, Josephinism, and the Inquisition, she came to be reduced to a state of dependence, the more fatal and deplorable that the clergy were often instrumental in maintaining it. All these phenomena were simply an adaptation of Catholicism to a political system incompatible with it in its integrity; an artifice to accommodate the Church to the requirements of absolute government, and to furnish absolute princes with a resource which was elsewhere supplied by Protestantism. The consequence has been, that the Church is at this day more free under Protestant than under Catholic governments—in Prussia or England than in France or Piedmont, Naples or Bavaria.

[20] Innocent IV wrote in 1246 to the Sicilians: "In omnem terram vestrae sonus tribulationis exivit . . . multis pro miro vehementi ducentibus, quod pressi tam dirae servitutis opprobrio, et personarum ac rerum gravati multiplici detrimento, neglexeritis habere concilium, per quod vobis, sicut gentibus caeteris, aliqua provenirent solatia libertatis . . . super hoc apud sedem apostolicam vos excusante formidine . . . Cogitate itaque corde vigili, ut a collo vestrae servitutis catena decidat, et universitas vestra in libertatis et quietis gaudio reflorescat; sitque ubertate conspicuum, ita divina favente potentia secura sit libertate decorum" (Raynaldus, *Ann.* ad ann. 1246).

As we have said that the Church commonly allied herself with the political elements which happened to be insufficiently represented, and to temper the predominant principle by encouraging the others, it might seem hardly unfair to conclude that that kind of government in which they are all supposed to be combined—"aequatum et temperatum ex tribus optimis rerum publicarum modis" (Cicero, *Rep.* i. 45)—must be particularly suited to her. Practically—and we are not here pursuing a theory—this is a mere fallacy. If we look at Catholic countries, we find that in Spain and Piedmont the constitution has served only to pillage, oppress, and insult the Church; whilst in Austria, since the empire has been purified in the fiery ordeal of the revolution, she is free, secure, and on the highroad of self-improvement. In constitutional Bavaria she has but little protection against the Crown, or in Belgium against the mob. The royal power is against her in one place, the popular element in the other. Turning to Protestant countries, we find that in Prussia the Church is comparatively free; whilst the more popular Government of Baden has exhibited the most conspicuous instance of oppression which has occurred in our time. The popular Government of Sweden, again, has renewed the refusal of religious toleration at the very time when despotic Russia begins to make a show, at least, of conceding it. In the presence of these facts, it would surely be absurd to assume that the Church must look with favour on the feeble and transitory constitutions with which the revolution has covered half the Continent. It does not actually appear that she has derived greater benefits from them than she may be said to have done from the revolution itself, which in France, for instance in 1818, gave to the Church, at least for a season, that liberty and dignity for which she had struggled in vain during the constitutional period which had preceded.

The political character of our own country bears hardly more resemblance to the Liberal Governments of the Continent—which have copied only what is valueless in our institutions—than to the superstitious despotism of the East, or to the analogous tyranny which in the Far West is mocked with the name of freedom. Here, as elsewhere, the progress of the constitution, which it was the work of the Catholic Ages to build up, on the principles common to all the nations of the Teutonic stock, was interrupted by the attraction which the growth of absolutism abroad excited, and by the Reformation's transferring the ecclesiastical power to the Crown. The Stuarts justified their abuse of

power by the same precepts and the same examples by which the
Puritans justified their resistance to it. The liberty aimed at by the
Levellers was as remote from that which the Middle Ages had handed
down, as the power of the Stuarts from the mediaeval monarchy. The
Revolution of 1688 destroyed one without favouring the other. Unlike
the rebellion against Charles I, that which overthrew his son did not
fall into a contrary extreme. It was a restoration in some sort of the
principles of government, which had been alternately assailed by
absolute monarchy and by a fanatical democracy. But, as it was
directed against the abuse of kingly and ecclesiastical authority, neither
the Crown nor the established Church recovered their ancient position;
and a jealousy of both has ever since subsisted. There can be no
question but that the remnants of the old system of polity—the utter
disappearance of which keeps the rest of Christendom in a state of
continual futile revolution—exist more copiously in this country than
in any other. Instead of the revolutions and the religious wars by
which, in other Protestant countries, Catholics have obtained toleration,
they have obtained it in England by the force of the very principles of
the constitution. "I should think myself inconsistent," says the chief
expounder of our political system, "in not applying my ideas of civil
liberty to religious." And speaking of the relaxation of the penal laws,
he says: "To the great liberality and enlarged sentiments of those who
are the furthest in the world from you in religious tenets, and the
furthest from acting with the party which, it is thought, the greater
part of the Roman Catholics are disposed to espouse, it is that you
owe the whole, or very nearly the whole, of what has been done both
here and in Ireland."[21] The danger which menaces the continuance of
our constitution proceeds simply from the oblivion of those Christian
ideas by which it was originally inspired. It should seem that it is the
religious as well as the political duty of Catholics to endeavour to avert
this peril, and to defend from the attacks of the Radicals and from the
contempt of the Tories the only constitution which bears some
resemblance to those of Catholic times, and the principles which are
almost as completely forgotten in England as they are misunderstood
abroad. If three centuries of Protestantism have not entirely obliterated
the ancient features of our government, if they have not been so
thoroughly barren of political improvements as some of its enemies

[21] Burke's *Works*, i. 391, 404.

would have us believe—there is surely nothing to marvel at, nothing at which we may rejoice. Protestants may well have, in some respects, the same terrestrial superiority over Catholics that the Gentiles had over the people of God. As, at the fall of paganism, the treasures it had produced and accumulated during two thousand years became the spoils of the victor—when the day of reckoning shall come for the great modern apostasy, it will surrender all that it has gathered in its diligent application to the things of this world; and those who have remained in the faith will have into the bargain those products of the Protestant civilisation on which its claims of superiority are founded.

When, therefore, in the political shipwreck of modern Europe, it is asked which political form of party is favoured by the Church, the only answer we can give is, that she is attached to none; but that though indifferent to existing forms, she is attached to a spirit which is nearly extinct. Those who, from a fear of exposing her to political animosity, would deny this, forget that the truth is as strong against political as against religious error, and shut their eyes to the only means by which the political regeneration of the modern world is a possibility. For the Catholic religion alone will not suffice to save it, as it was insufficient to save the ancient world, unless the Catholic idea equally manifests itself in the political order. The Church alone, without influence on the State, is powerless as a security for good government. It is absurd to pretend that at the present day France, or Spain, or Naples, are better governed than England, Holland, or Prussia. A country entirely Protestant may have more Catholic elements in its government than one where the population is wholly Catholic. The State which is Catholic *par excellence* is a by-word for misgovernment, because the orthodoxy and piety of its administrators are deemed a substitute for a better system. The demand for a really Catholic system of government falls with the greatest weight of reproach on the Catholic States.

Yet it is important to remember that in the ages of faith the same unity prevailed in political ideas, and that the civil as well as the religious troubles of our time are in great measure due to the Reformation. It is common to advise Catholics to make up their minds to accept the political doctrines of the day; but it would be more to the purpose to recall the ideas of Catholic times. It is not in the results of the political development of the last three centuries that the Church can place her trust; neither in absolute monarchy, nor in the revolutionary liberalism, nor in the infallible constitutional scheme. She must create anew or revive her former creations, and instil a new life and spirit into those remains of the mediaeval system which will bear the mark of the ages when heresy and unbelief, Roman law, and heathen philosophy, had not obscured the idea of the Christian State. These remains are to be found, in various stages of decay, in every State— with the exception, perhaps, of France—that grew out of the mediaeval civilisation. Above all they will be found in the country which, in the midst of its apostasy, and in spite of so much guilt towards religion, has preserved the Catholic forms in its Church establishment more than any other Protestant nation, and the Catholic spirit in her political institutions more than any Catholic nation. To renew the memory of the times in which this spirit prevailed in Europe, and to preserve the remains of it, to promote the knowledge of what is lost, and the desire of what is most urgently needed— is an important service and an important duty which it behoves us to perform. We are greatly mistaken if these are not reflections which force themselves on every one who carefully observes the political history of the Church in modern Europe.

[4]
The Catholic Press

In the course of last year we twice took occasion to consider our
present duties and position as Catholics in England; and gave utterance
to some thoughts, which we believe had occurred to many besides
ourselves, on questions which nobody can with propriety overlook,
and which nobody can hope to set at rest. An obstacle in the way of
all who wish for agreement on the subject is that whilst every judgment
which we form on our present condition is determined in great measure
by the views we entertain relative to past history, we are no more
agreed about the past than about the present. Where our knowledge
of events is not obscured by time, it is often quite as much distorted
by partiality. We should peradventure be obliged to go back to the
time of the schism and the spoliation of the Church, to get clear of the
debatable land, and obtain firm footing on ground that affords no
matter for Catholics to contest about. Those who look only to the
external apparent effect may consider that such practical discord is a
strange unkindly fruit of the unity of faith, and may argue that an
excessive licence *in dubiis* shows a deficiency either of faith or unity *in
necessariis*. But our differences, however deplorable in their consequences, may readily be explained and excused, if we consider the
causes which produce them. While the Protestant is obliged to cling
to a mendacious tradition on matters of fact to make up for the extreme
divergence of opinions on matters of faith—because such secondary
things, which are of no great consequence to us, are to him of more
vital concern than questions of doctrine—the Catholic is not interested
in maintaining a particular view of the details of history or of natural
science. His religion is no more affected by the detection of a scandal
in the Church than by the discovery of a fossil man, or of an African

Published in the *Rambler* n.s. (2d ser.) 11 (February 1859):73–90. Acton-Simpson I, p.
114. Reprinted in Acton, *Church and State*, pp. 260–278.

tribe whose heads do grow beneath their shoulders. It is not for him that vindications of Catholic times and personages are written. He has no difficulty in admitting the virtues of his adversaries—the humility of Calvin, the temperance of Luther—when they are proved ("quamquam id non meritorium vitae aeternae"); on the contrary, the sin of heresy is so enormous, that a Catholic may be easily indulgent on smaller things. When a man has been guilty of treason and murder it seems both superfluous and spiteful to reproach him with breaking the Sabbath, or cheating his washerwoman. Whilst, therefore, we are content to rely on the laws of historical evidence applied with the utmost rigour, the Protestant must make them bend to the exigencies of his case. His facts must be as false as his theory; he is obliged to be consistent in his perversion of truth.

No true Protestant can surrender the historical assumption on which the Reformation rests—the corruption of the Church in doctrine and discipline during the Middle Ages. If the Popes were justified in condemning heretics, and resisting the temporal power, the Reformation has nothing to stand upon. This is the foundation of all specifically Protestant views of history, and must be held to as firmly as the history of the Apostles. As a real Protestant, he can no more give up one than, as a Christian, the other; so long as his Christianity believes the history of St. Peter, his Protestantism cannot do justice to that of St. Peter's successors.

The really valid excuse for the existing variety of views on our past— from which a similar variety of views on our present must needs follow—is, that our history is very imperfectly known. If it were more thoroughly cleared up—the earlier period from the mists of ignorance, the later from the mists of prejudice—it would then be possible to appeal with effect to the experience of English Catholics as a lesson for their present guidance. The man would render us an incalculable service who displayed the energy, the zeal, and, above all, the courage to bring to light the whole truth concerning both the noble and consoling history of the persecutions, and the less edifying story of our gradual emancipation. It is to illustrate the former that our labours have, by a sort of instinct, been chiefly directed. It would be less easy indeed, but more instructive, to show clearly how, whilst the penal laws were being slowly relaxed, the Catholics dwindled to an insignificant body in the State, weak in numbers, in knowledge, and in zeal; and how, after Milner had seen the dawn of a brighter day, we obtained political consequence through Ireland, and intellectual importance from another source. This would help us to judge the last scene of all—to understand what advantages have been derived from emancipation, especially from the admission of English Catholics into Parliament, and how we have turned to account in literature and education the vast accession of strength which the Oxford Movement sent us; how the old elements have amalgamated with the new, and what has proceeded from their harmonious action.

This last point brings us to a question which has become of serious importance, and for the discussion of which the time seems to have arrived—the condition and prospects of our literature, and of our periodical press in England. Not that we are about to exercise our function of criticism on the writers of books, or to disturb the peaceful enjoyment of their popularity or their dusty repose; our business is with our periodicals; but we may introduce it with one or two general remarks.

If we except certain very elaborate essays in the *Atlantis* there is hardly anything serious or durable in the productions of the Catholic literature of the day. Entertaining books abound; we have history made edifying, science religious, and religion exceedingly attractive— in short, plenty of most unobjectionable reading. But a popular literature cannot stand alone; it must be fed by the overflowings of more serious books. It is incapable of progress or improvement; and, if cultivated to the exclusion of more substantial things, must inevitably degenerate. By itself it is injurious: it encourages people to forget that something else is wanted, and promotes a superficial self-contented way of looking at all things, of despising difficulties, and overlooking the force of objections. It nourishes the delusion that we have only to communicate truths, not to discover them; that our knowledge needs no increase except in the number of those who participate in it. This indifference to real learning is so great that the very meritorious project of a library of translations, which certainly did not begin with books of a very profound character, met with no support. The consequence is, that we have not half a dozen books which will bear critical examination, or which we are not ashamed of before Protestants and foreigners; and we contribute nothing to the literature of the Church. Lingard's *History of England* has been of more use to us than anything that has since been written; it was so far superior to the books that preceded it—to Hume, who could not be trusted, and to Henry, whom nobody could read—that all educated men were obliged to use it, and thus became accustomed to the Catholic statement of the subject. It is to this day a tower of strength to us. Its deficiencies are so notorious, that it is quite the fashion to complain of them; and yet nobody has shown himself able to correct them. A single serious treatise of theology or philosophy or history, if merely as a proof that we have somebody who understands such things, would be of more value than almost all the flimsy publications of Catholic booksellers for the last ten years. Now, though our writers are capable of better things, and though this mode of writing is sanctioned by great examples, and almost imposed on us by circumstances, yet it is our interest and duty to let nothing prevent us from endeavouring to supply its deficiencies.

The great object of our literary efforts ought to be to break down that Protestant tradition which pervades all the literature, serious as well as popular, and enchains all the intellect, of the country; which meets us at every turn, and often forces us into an antagonistic extreme. For, in the absence of a solid literature of our own, we are generally compelled to meet objections by simple negation and contradiction, and by arguing against each particular error on the assumption that the contrary is true. Where there is nothing to fall back upon, no basis of operations, no Catholic literature and traditions of equal weight and standing and consistency to refer to in argument, it is a natural consequence that we should blindly run into extremes, adopt any view and any argument that helps to refute the proposition we are opposing, and have recourse to hasty statements and solutions, which seem safe because they sound well to pious ears, but which really lead to greater difficulties, and expose Catholics to very unpleasant rejoinders. We have a noteworthy example of this in a neighbouring country, where a party of Catholic apologists are for ever answering the falsehoods of an infidel press with statements almost as startling and equally unscrupulous. Perhaps the worst sign of our own imperfection is the want of sensibility to the lessons this spectacle should teach us. We have a Helot perpetually drunk before our eyes, and are hardly moved to a suitable disgust at the hideous sight. Unfortunately there are others upon whom it is not lost, and who know how to avail themselves of it with lamentable effect.

Nothing can be better adapted to raise the character of our literature than the Reviews; and, considering the state of things we have described, it is to them we must chiefly look for improvement: it is for them to point out deficiencies, and to indicate and to promote the remedy.

Last Summer *The Tablet* published a letter, in which the Catholic body was informed that our chief Review could not continue to appear in the state to which it was reduced; and that the editor proposed to resign his charge into other hands, if a successor could be found fitted for the task. This announcement scarcely excited either surprise or regret: it was no secret that the means were wanting for keeping up the character of the Review in the manner desired by its conductors and its readers, and by very many Catholics besides. Not long after, the *Weekly Register* told us that no change had taken place in the management; it is therefore certain that the recent numbers have been prepared under the same auspices which presided over the better days of the Review, when it held among Catholics and Protestants a high and honourable position. Whilst the conductors are still the same, whose competency has been so clearly proved, the public from whom they might expect support has greatly increased, and the addition to the number of writers whose contributions would be extremely valuable has been in proportion still greater. The expectations of the public and the means of satisfying them have risen, yet the Review has declined. Though there is now amongst us an amount of literary ability sufficient, if concentrated, to constitute a first-rate journal, and an educated public quite large enough to support it, yet the writers as well as the readers of the only Catholic Quarterly have fallen off to such an extent that it cannot maintain itself without showing signals of distress. How comes it that, together with such a growth of resources and of legitimate claims, there should be such a diminution of performance? The problem is the more curious, that the deplorable state of things is the consequence of no controversy, of no competition—at least, within the limits of the Catholic body. Whilst the Review has been permitted to censure and attack with impunity, nobody has attacked or desired to injure it; and, what is most remarkable, nobody has profited by its decline. This is the really significant circumstance, that there has been no compensation; it is a dead loss to the Catholics in England. That infidel publication which is the most ably conducted Quarterly in the country, after swallowing up large sums of money for many years, is still unable to subsist without considerable subsidies, and has no difficulty in obtaining them; but an appeal to English Catholics for such assistance as was given to their Review at its commencement seems to have been unsuccessful. Is this apathy to be explained by the hypothesis that Catholics prefer the ability of Protestant organs to the orthodoxy of their own, and are content to read nothing more edifying than the

Edinburgh or *Westminster?* The true explanation, we rather think, will be found in the history of the Review itself.

If we compare our days with the period when it was started, more than twenty years ago, it is obvious that times are so much altered as necessarily to affect the character and aim of a publication which should attempt to be now what it was then, the organ of the English and Irish Catholics. A consciousness of this, by the way, has been shown in the circumstance that a series of articles has appeared with the acknowledged object of modifying and correcting the views of Lingard, one of the early patrons of the Review. But, in reality, it has not adapted itself to the progress of things. Times have changed, and it has not changed with them.

It is, if we mistake not, to that very increase among Catholics, which ought to have enriched the Review, that its decline is to be ascribed. The narrow ground which it was forced to occupy at a time when our literature was in its infancy afforded no space for an increase of range. New ideas and wants arose, which had not been thought of at first, which, as it never enlarged its horizon, it never succeeded in satisfying. Instead of leading, it has fallen behind the march of Catholic thought in England, and has given little aid in keeping pace with it abroad. Not only did many eminent men continue unattached to it, and deprived of encouragement and of an opening for their studies, but it did not always succeed in competing with Protestant periodicals for the services of Catholic writers. Judged by the interests of the Review, this was a serious defect; for the Catholics generally it was a real calamity. This exclusiveness obliged other organs of the Catholic press to occupy the positions which were neglected; and forced them, where opposition was not intended and competition impossible, into a sort of involuntary antagonism. The ideas which were excluded—we will not say proscribed—by the Quarterly, whose voice was too weak to cause an echo, had to obtain a hearing in other places, where a different tone prevailed. It was of more importance to supply its deficiencies than to promote its influence; and the attempt to make up for its exclusive character almost inevitably assumed the appearance of an exclusiveness of another kind.

Thus, in restricting its own sphere, the *Dublin Review* soon looked with an increasing jealousy upon all who did not accept the same limitations; and the elements which were not yet brought into perfect harmony amongst us assumed, in the periodical press, the semblance of discord. This was the more to be regretted, that it was not seriously the case. Differences such as subsist amongst us, founded upon questions of personal influence, and nourished by immaturity of thought and knowledge, though they may have the venom, have neither the permanence nor even the dignity of disputes on principle. But no great question of principle has in our day divided the English Catholics.

Parallel with this increasing deficiency with regard to ourselves, another soon grew up in respect of the Protestant world. The attention of the *Dublin Review* was from the first concentrated upon the Oxford Movement. The party of which the *British Critic* was the mouthpiece was intellectually the most important in the Established Church, and the one with which controversy was most called for and most likely to avail. But since that day great changes have ensued. New schools have risen into importance, already strong in numbers, and far more formidable in point of talent; and all the learning of misbelieving foreigners is made to contribute to their support. The ablest English Quarterly derives its inspiration from Germany, the ablest Weekly from France; and the American Unitarians have a visible influence upon a portion of the Press. With these new adversaries, armed with new and unexpected weapons, the Review has hardly attempted to wage what would certainly be an unequal war. It has not kept pace with the intellectual movement of the country. It has been hampered by its own traditions. It has neglected to draw the attention of its readers to the things which it is most important for them to know, and to inform them of the real secret of the enemy's strength. This omission has led to one most pernicious result. It has encouraged the insane delusion that scientific infidelity is not, like heresy, an antagonist that it behoves Catholics to encounter; that misbelievers and disbelievers must be allowed to fight it out between them, and the dead left to bury their dead; that no danger threatens the Church from that party, and that Catholics have no special duty towards it. People are permitted to imagine that this is no new enemy, that calls for new efforts of polemics or irenics to controvert or to reconcile, and are suffered to indulge the indolent propensity of subsisting on the capital accumulated by their fathers. Why should we be disquieted by the attacks of presumptuous infidels? Is not all this answered in our books? Is not St. Thomas good enough for them, or Bellarmine, or Bossuet, or Butler? What need they more? Did not the Crusaders, with bow and battle-axe, conquer Jerusalem? Wherefore waste gunpowder on miserable Hindoos? Thus an Irishman who has taken a bath in the dogdays considers himself provided with cleanness to last him all the year round. With this supine self-confidence, we have neglected to make the vast advance of European learning available to us; and we consequently find ourselves opposed at a far greater disadvantage to our infidel antagonists now than to the Tractarians eighteen or twenty years ago.

The Catholic public has felt convinced that the most important topics would not be found discussed in its chief literary journal, and that hardly any topics would be found discussed in it by the most competent men. We have enlarged upon these circumstances, not by way of disparagement, but for the purpose of explaining a deficiency which nobody disputes. Before a remedy can be applied the cause of the disease must be ascertained; on the other hand, it is a sign neither of good policy nor self-respect to betray the wants of one's own party without showing at the same time the prospect and the means of relieving them. In this case, the object of our wishes will not be questioned, we apprehend, by any of our readers.

All Catholics would be proud of a Review worthy to uphold their cause and to command the respect and attention of Protestants. We are impatient of that reproach of inferiority which we know to be unjust, but which we must bear so long as a large proportion of the literary power which is amongst us has no opportunity of being employed. We wish the knowledge and ideas of the best men in the Catholic body to be the common property of the whole. We want an organ, which shall speak with the authority both of talent and position, to assist us in our self-improvement and in the perpetual contest with the enemies of the Church. In the knowledge and performance of our social duties it cannot assist us; but in politics and literature it is our only resource. It should keep us informed not only of the progress of Catholic learning, but of the position of the Church in other countries, in order that we might learn by the experience of others, and compare it with our own. A Review has space both to state the facts and to point the moral; and we require its protection against the ignorance, the malignity, and the mendacity of the Protestant press. The spectacle of the comparative prosperity of religion in different countries is full of political instruction as well as religious interest. It shows the Catholics of France paying for an unsafe prosperity a price which goes far to deprive them of all influence and public esteem; in Russia it exhibits the hostility of an inflexible system baffling the apparent benevolence of the imperial family towards the Church; and in Naples it displays despotism producing abuses in religion such as we hardly dare allude to, and such as would scarcely be believed if told even of the Muscovite clergy. Nor do democracies afford a more consoling aspect than absolute governments. In Switzerland the tyranny of a radical majority weighs heavily upon the church; whilst in the United States, exposed to the caprice of a half-civilized population, she is beset with dangers unknown to the Old World. Again, we should observe how in Catholic countries mean governments, by the confiscation of ecclesiastical property, have strengthened religion by diminishing temptation, but have injured the State itself by a revolutionary measure; how, since the Belgian revolution, the Dutch Catholics have obtained a freedom they hardly know how to use, whilst in Belgium they are losing the advantages of their victory, and have escaped a Protestant domination only to become the victims of their liberal allies. Most satisfactory of all perhaps we should find the condition of the church in Prussia, where, in a position nearly resembling our own, the Catholics possess far greater power; and in Austria, where, in laborious conflict with long-cherished customs and with her own traditions, she is acquiring an independence which will transform the empire. With all these things it would be well if we were more familiar, and were more able to follow and sympathize with the contests which are everywhere waging for the freedom and the progress of religion.

If we had been led by the contemplation of the Church in other countries, as well as other times, to draw the inferences to which it irresistibly leads; to understand that democracy is no friend to religion, and that despotism either oppresses or corrupts it; that representative institutions are the protection of the Church in Protestant States, and in Catholic States too frequently her scourge; and that she has more to fear from political than from religious systems—we should possess some criterion of our own by which to judge political affairs, and should have obtained some basis of political principles. If this had not been unfortunately neglected, a sound tone might have been created; we might have learnt to consider more than interests, and a regard might have been kept alive for higher ideas, which is easily lost in the midst of continual strife.

Formerly the Catholics of England were accustomed and content to suffer, when their principles exposed them to terrible penalties. Their resolution was not shaken by the prospect of petty relief; only when a great change approached, and hopes of total emancipation came to be entertained, they accommodated their conduct to circumstances, and sided, contrary to every tradition, with the party which, for no principle, but for purposes of its own, temporarily supported their claims. Hope had more power over us than fear. Since then we have lived from hand to mouth, contemptuous of the morrow. But though the season has arrived when the system of adaptation and the alliance, which would have been ignoble but for the imperiousness of O'Connell, is no longer necessary or excusable, we have yet to learn the wisdom and confidence of a new position. Vices may take the place of virtues in critical moments. There is some general truth in Royer-Collard's panegyric of a famous statesman: "He was ignorant and brutal. These two virtues were the saving of France." But the day comes when these qualities are exhibited with less propriety, and when it is a relief to submit to the habits and precepts of ordinary times. We are, politically, still in a state of transition. If we no longer borrow our doctrines from the system of a party, we are hardly yet conscious of any of our own. Our querulous murmurs, petty skirmishing, and vexatious grievance-hunting, are supported by no consistent plan, by no higher purpose. We have quitted our old ranks, but have not set up a banner of our own, and incur some of the risks of those who have no colour to show. We have our hierarchy, in spite of the law of the land; we ought to acknowledge our principles, in defiance of its prejudices. English Catholics have, indeed, few opportunities of political action, and little occasion of educating themselves for it. But this is precisely the want which it beseems the gravity of a Quarterly Review to supply.

We believe we can discern in that instinctive jealousy with which many Catholics regard the efforts of government to promote education—a jealousy for which we, at least, should be unwilling to admit no deeper cause than that to which it is generally referred—some reason to hope that they will be among the first to understand and to resist the encroachments with which we are threatened in other departments of the State. We alone have something which cannot be sacrificed to its purposes, in which we cannot suffer control. We trust that the principle of resistance to the increasing power of the State over the nation, which is the secret of true liberty, will find amongst Catholics, in political as well as religious matters, its most determined adherents. But it requires more political sagacity and experience than are common in a country where such dangers are new, to detect in the measures of government all the consequences of the principle on which they are based. For the heathen and revolutionary system of compulsion for the public good, of the greatest happiness of the greatest number, by which the whole is distinct from the several parts, and is preferred to them, and by which an abstraction reigns supreme over each individual, has already taken root amongst us. But this is a point on which we shall not learn wisdom from our Protestant contemporaries, and on which it would be well to have a teacher of our own.

Still more do we need a guide, an example, and an authority in literature; and this would be the great purpose which a Review could accomplish. The literary inferiority of Catholics is due to the absence of the will, not of the power to excel. Where they are inferior it is because they do not feel the value and the dignity of the pursuit. The contempt and indifference with which knowledge is often regarded, soon engender aversion and dread. The studies which Catholics neglect are cultivated by others; and if not made to serve the Church, are inevitably used to injure her. Our inferiority is the penalty of our indolence. At the Revolution, as at the Reformation, the literature and science of the day had completely severed themselves from religion. At both periods learning had suddenly advanced, and important discoveries had been made, in which Catholics had had no part. They were almost completely excluded from the intellectual movement of the age; and the hostility of religion and learning, which one party was interested in proclaiming, was foolishly acquiesced in by the other. In the nineteenth century, as in the sixteenth, the lost ground was recovered by the same means—by claiming for the Church the principle of scientific investigation which seemed to threaten her, and binding to her service the force with which she was attacked. This was the great idea expressed by Copernicus in his dedication to Paul III. He knew well, he said, the contempt with which his discoveries would be received by those who play among philosophers the part of drones amongst bees; and if he considered his own comfort, he would communicate them privately, like Pythagoras, to his disciples. But he confidently commits them to the protection of the Pope himself, whose cause they cannot but serve, in spite of the clamour they may at first excite. This was the answer of a great ecclesiastic to the *Epistolae Obscurorum Virorum*, and to the popular scoffs of an illiterate clergy. In the same way, and in the same proud spirit of confidence in the virtue of real science as an auxiliary of true religion, the revival of the nineteenth century has been accomplished. Yet the tradition of those hundred years of the intellectual as well as political degradation of religion, from the time of Fénelon and Noris to Schlegel and de Maistre, has not yet lost all its power. There are many venerable people who still refuse to travel by steam; and there are many who cannot reconcile themselves to the alliance of the Church with that secular science which they have accustomed themselves to consider her foe. The confidence with which the men of science have asserted that religion is opposed to it, has promoted an awe of falsehood and a distrust of the power of truth. The phantom of the eighteenth century pursues many Catholics, and makes them look with suspicion upon the policy which has proved itself the best safeguard of religion.

The necessity of waging this double contest, at once with those who are of little faith and with those who have none at all—with those who for the sake of religion fear science, and with the followers of science who despise religion—is the fruitful cause of so much scandal and vexation in the Church. The devil must be equally gratified with the zeal of either party; for they equally serve his purpose, by confirming the fatal notion of the incompatibility of faith and reason. In reality this pretence of antagonism is on neither side sincere. Solicitude for religion is merely a pretext for opposition to the free course of scientific research, which threatens, not the authority of the Church, but the precarious influence of individuals. The growth of knowledge cannot in the long run be detrimental to religion; but it renders impossible the usurpation of authority by teachers who defend their own false opinions under pretence of defending the faith which they dishonour by their artifices. Such men by their narrow-minded indolence are the advocates of mental lethargy and repression, whether maintained by an inquisition such as ruined the intellectual service of religion in Spain, or by a well-organized police such as has silenced it with the significant applause of a Catholic party in France; and when they find that their influence is lessened because all men are not their dupes, instead of acknowledging that the old conflict of doctrine must be decided by the sword of science, and that the urgency of the case requires them to mend their slovenly ways, they content themselves with denouncing those who, by refusing to share in their dishonest practice, make it the more conspicuous and the more unavailing. They impute to others the evils they themselves have caused, and do not see that the progress of error and unbelief is their own work. Partly afraid of the truth, and partly ashamed of it, they want to shelter their own ignorance by preserving that of others. But religion is not served by denying facts, or by denouncing those who proclaim them. A fire is not put out by a policeman's whistle, nor a thief taken by the cry of "Stop thief!" Truth is not the exclusive possession of the ignorant; the sun does not shine only for the blind. Authority can only condemn error; its vitality is not destroyed until it is refuted.

One of the fruits of this system is mendacity. Ignorance can only be defended by falsehood; every artifice is deemed lawful; a little fraud becomes a necessary ingredient in controversy. Hence means which only the most worthless of her adversaries have the baseness still to use are sometimes pressed into the service of the Church by those who have not the candour or the courage to adopt that method of defence by which alone success is ultimately infallible.

The one thing needful at the present day, when science has made such progress, and has so much perfected its methods as to be far more powerful, whether for friendship or enmity, than ever before in the history of the Church, is to accept it as her necessary and trusty ally. It became hostile to Catholicism only when they had rejected it. Nothing else can save religion from the twin dangers of unbelief and superstition. "Nihil veritas erubescit nisi solummodo abscondi."[1] ("Truth is only ashamed of concealment.") The common reluctance on the part of Catholics to consent to the results of science indicates as much a defect of faith as of knowledge. We are bound to see that the laws of true reasoning and of historical criticism are not tampered with; it is by them only we can know in their reasonableness and their integrity the doctrines which have been revealed and developed in the process of history—"juxta ordinatissimam dispositionem temporum," says the (IV) Council of Lateran. We have to apply to this inquiry only the methods which are developed in the pursuit of other sciences: hence there is something in the progress of all learning with which it is almost sacrilegious, or at least suicidal, to interfere in the name of religion. Nothing can be more insane or more pernicious than to insist on immediate practical advantages, on the premature harmony and conciliation of science and faith. How often has the eagerness and presumption which has based the defence of religion on proofs which

---

[1] Tertullian, *Adversus Valent.*, 3.

later discoveries have exploded covered her with the appearance of ridicule! Those who are too impatient to wait till their wine is fermented are rewarded with a particularly nasty draught. Every branch of learning pursued for the sake of its own conclusions will result in the vindication of religion, and in the discomfiture of those who believe in their antagonism. The progress of knowledge is often more beneficial to the cause of religious truth than any professed apology. The controversial interest which formerly prevailed occupies now a very subordinate place in our literature. The old contrasts are no longer so distinctly marked. Whilst Protestantism has lost much of its dogmatic character, rationalism and infidelity have diverted the attention of disputants, and diminished their asperity. Catholics have sometimes been joined by Protestants in the defence of their common points of belief; sometimes they have found the arguments of infidels a powerful auxiliary against heresy.

When the prevailing mood of infidelity arose, it encountered no visible adversary; neither Kant or Goethe nor Hegel found Catholicism or Protestantism either able to resist or ready to protest. The new schools of philosophy had no occasion for animosity against the Christianity which seemed already gone. Here lies the essential practical difference between the infidelity of the eighteenth century and that of the nineteenth. Voltaire and his school resolved to extirpate religion; and all their writings aimed at this single end; they lied, scoffed and blasphemed; against such adversaries there was nothing to be done, and nothing was done. They were not vulnerable by any weapon of controversy; their spirit was one that can only be exorcized by prayer and fasting. But the modern infidels generally look upon Christianity with the serenity of victors; and their indifference to its claims makes them often willing to recognize its merits. Their position towards it was not that of the pagans, who were still attached to the old mythology; but rather that of the Neoplatonists, such as Porphyry. Those philosophers did not deny that Christianity taught truths, but that it possessed the whole truth; they did not attack its doctrine because it was false, but because it claimed to be divine. In detail they were often full of admiration for it. So there are many amongst our contemporaries who will admit almost anything except the divine character of the Church, and object to nothing in Christianity excepting Christ. Having no religion, and recognizing in history only its human aspect, they highly appreciate all that has been achieved by natural means in the pursuit of a supernatural end. In place of religious zeal, the motive of their life is the desire of scientific truth. Men of this stamp can be answered with no subterfuge; they must be beaten with their own weapons. In encountering them we have a great advantage, which fails us in conflict with Protestant theology. They assail us in the name of science; but they submit to the authority to which they appeal. They are, at least the best of them, sincere in their arguments, without the malice or the guilt of apostasy. Their objections are frequently a sign of their real love of truth; for there are many points on which they are very imperfectly answered by that system of Catholic polemics which has grown up since the Reformation in conflicts with another description of opponent. A fortress proof against battering-ram and catapult needs new defences against Lancaster guns. It has been the great benefit of the rise of the new learned infidelity that it has greatly raised the character and increased the influence of Catholic learning.

The strongest recommendation of true science is the effect it has had in the hands of infidels themselves. When Lingard's *History* appeared, a much better case had been established for the mediaeval Church, and her character and influence had been spoken of abroad by learned men who were not Catholics with more favour than he thought he could manifest, or his readers would accept. It is in history, the branch of learning which has most suffered from the perversions of Protestants, that the principle of impartial inquiry has achieved the greatest results. In the hands of strangers, if not of enemies, it has fought our battles better than we have ever fought them ourselves. If there were no Catholics to use it, the progress of learning would result in the justification of the temporal human part of the history of the Church. All the lies of the Protestants of the sixteenth century are being rapidly refuted by their descendants of the nineteenth. If Catholics only furnish materials for the defence of the Church, there are others who will be sure to use them. A really scientifically learned work, written without any religious interest, helps the truth in spite of its author; whilst a superficial apology will do little or no good, and probably some harm, in spite of the zeal and good intention with which it is written. We have no right to be jealous of an instrument which in the hands of our enemies has turned against them, and forced them like Balaam to bear witness to the truth. The impartiality of scientific research is our surest ally if we adopt it, and if we reject it is sure to cover us with confusion. Its first fruits, the first sign that it has prevailed, will be an intelligent tolerance of error, combined with a consciousness of the limits of our knowledge. We must have confidence in the power of argument and reason to give victory to truth. An error, like a disease, must be brought to a crisis; it must be developed by argument, not smothered. With every undeveloped error, some truth is lost. In order that it may do its part of good in the world, and aid in promoting truth, it must be helped on to its logical results, and made to show itself in all its deformity.

The mere statement of the claims of science, and of its present character, is enough to indicate how far we are from really accepting it, and how great are the services that might now be performed by a Review that kept aloof from none of the intellectual or social problems which occupy the world. In insisting on a high standard of learning and criticism as the great object of a Catholic Quarterly, we have had also our own interest in view; for though our movements are in a more humble sphere, yet we are sensible that so long as this desideratum is not supplied, our efforts must be very imperfect, if not fruitless. We recognize and act upon a principle which is not within the province of a journal such as ours to bring to supremacy. We have no space or opportunity to set up a theory of all that Catholic politics and literature ought to be, or to give sufficient examples of it. This is the privilege of others. We can only give conclusions which we have not always room to prove, and which ought to require no proof, and proceed upon a system which we cannot for ever be explaining and recommending. We are therefore necessarily exposed to perpetual misinterpretation. Nobody will judge us by the criterion which alone we admit, and which we wish to apply to others. In proportion as the *Dublin Review* has fallen short of the position we desire to assign it, our own position has become unnatural and difficult to maintain. When a Review is established answering in some measure to our ideal description, it will be a great benefit to the Catholics in general, but more especially a boon to us; for it will enable us fairly to pursue our proper ends, and occupy our legitimate place: and therefore we need scarcely say how glad we are to hear that a new arrangement is on the point of taking place, and that an infusion of young blood is likely to give new vitality to our old and respected Review. Without any feelings of envy, and renouncing the idea of competition, we shall cordially hail the appearance of a worthy representative of our intellectual culture, and shall anxiously look for the announcement of wider views and an enlarged plan. The great question has hitherto been, not *what* principle shall prevail, but whether principles shall prevail at all. We are not alive to censure in particulars where we know that our fundamental ideas are not admitted. Our premises are denied, it is idle to defend our conclusions. The discussion of a point of learning is superfluous and hopeless where no respect for the freedom and authority of learning exists; all such controversies have generally a very subordinate and contemptible character. In this respect, therefore, we have nothing to modify. But we wish it to be distinctly understood that the *Rambler* is not a theological Review, and that we do not design to treat questions of theology, or to transgress that line which separates secular from religious knowledge. The principle of independent inquiry, within the bounds, and for the promotion, of the Catholic faith, it is our pride and our duty to maintain; the more because the obloquy we thereby incur shows how urgently such advocacy is needed. Speaking for no party ourselves we naturally excite the dislike of all partisans. Doubtless we shall incense many soothing prejudices and contradict many cherished opinions, and shall continue objects of aversion to all who are more attached to persons than to principles, to habits than to ideas. Whoever defies an idol must be prepared for the clamour of its worshippers; nobody who assails folly and error is surprised at being answered by a falsehood or an insult. These, as we well know, besides personal imputations and calumnies which it is infamy to utter, are the fit and natural weapons of many adversaries of the ideas which we defend. But though every human enterprise in which there is no proportion between the trouble and the chance of success is wisely abandoned, it is not so with the higher service to which our efforts are devoted. They are supported by a more powerful encouragement than the immediate prospect of success. Under all circumstances we shall keep in mind the example of forbearance set us by a great and holy man on a very memorable occasion. In that remarkable autobiography, which seems to have been the great obstacle to his canonization, Cardinal Bellarmine relates how he returned good for evil to the Pope, who, after highly applauding his learning, had ended by putting his best work on the Index.[2] The edition of the Vulgate which Sixtus V

---

[2] "Anno 1591, cum Gregorius XIV cogitaret quid agendum esset de Bibliis a Sixto V editis, in quibus erant permulta perperam mutata, non deerant viri graves qui censerent ea Biblia esse publice prohibenda; sed N. (Bellarminus) coram pontifice demonstravit Biblia illa non esse prohibenda, sed esse ita corrigenda, ut salvo honore

had prepared, was found after his death to be so full of faults that some were for prohibiting it altogether. But, in order to save his memory from this indignity, Bellarmine undertook to correct it himself; showing how little he was moved by the intemperate attack of which he had been the object, and exhibiting an instance of generosity and forgiveness of injury which deserves to be remembered.

Sixti V Pontificis Biblia illa emendata proderentur, quod fieret si quam celerrime tollerentur quae male mutata erant, et Biblia recluderentur sub nomine ejusdem, Sixti, et addita, praefatione, qua significaretur, in prima editione Sixti prae festinatione irrepsisse aliqua errata vel typographorum, vel aliorum; et sic N. (Bellarminus) reddidit Sixto Pontifici bona pro malis. Sixtus enim propter illam propositionem de dominio Papae directo in totum orbem posuit controversias ejus in Indice librorum prohibitorum donec corrigerentur: sed ipso mortuo Sacra Rituum Congregatio jussit deleri libro indicis nomen illius. Placuit consilium N. (Bellarmini) Gregorio Pontifici" (*Vita Ven. Card. Rob. Bellarmini, S. J., quam ipsemet scripsit*, p. 22).

[5]
The Catholic Academy

The appearance of this polished and eloquent discourse claims our attention on account both of the distinguished personage whose views on a very important question are expressed in it, and of the occasion and the purpose for which it has been written. From the beginning of the century a Society has existed in Rome, to which for more than thirty years the Cardinal has belonged, and whose labours are dedicated to the illustration and defence of the Catholic and Christian faith. Founded at a period which witnessed the almost unexampled combination of persecution with the prostration of religion, and in which weakness and coldness of faith united with the most bitter animosity to afflict the Church, the Catholic Academy has been one of the instruments of the revival of a better spirit, and has enjoyed the countenance and support of many of the most eminent persons in Rome. The object of its members has been to promote the reconciliation of religion with the advancement of learning, and at the same time to initiate in these studies the educated youth of the city. If we may draw an inference from what we hear and from what we do not hear, it would appear that the last of these objects has been more successfully attained than the former. The good that has been done seems to be principally confined to the society of the capital, and the printed acts of the Academy have not become widely known. So many reasons for this are at once suggested by the circumstances of place and time that have surrounded the institution, that it by no means follows either that the plan is radically defective, or that it would not achieve greater success and wider utility in another sphere.

Dwellers on the outer frontier of Catholicity, surrounded by an atmosphere of unbelief and hatred, and exposed to dangers both of

Published in the *Rambler* n.s. (3d ser.) 5 (September 1861):291–302. Döllinger I, p. 219; Acton-Simpson II, p. 196. Reprinted in Acton, *Church and State*, pp. 279–290.

attack and temptation against which the Church has always endeavoured to protect those who live in the centre of the fold, we might be justified in envying our brethren in the Eternal City an institution which, as a safeguard, we require more than they do, and which we have, in some respects, greater means of using as a weapon for the intellectual support of religion. In no country would there be a better field for its action, or more ample conditions of success, than in England.

The object of the Academy is not controversy; it does not address itself to those who are out of the Church, but seeks to digest and assimilate the results of scientific inquiry, and to maintain the harmony of sacred and secular science. The Catholic body amongst us has especial need of a work of this kind, and possesses the materials for it; and it is one of the greatest misfortunes that no such combination for a definite purpose subsists among its members. It is a consequence of the very advantages of our position, though it detracts from them, that the elements which are united in the Catholic Church in England are of such various derivation that we do not possess even common prejudices, the very lowest symbol of unity; and the bonds of faith and charity are not always powerful enough to secure either the necessary agreement, or the freedom of discussion, or the tolerance of differences enjoined by the well-known Protestant maxim which Catholics have consecrated by attributing it to St. Augustine. The cultivation of literature in a spirit inseparable from Catholicism and on a basis which no Catholic refuses to acknowledge, is perhaps at the present time the only way that could be devised of reconciling, in a higher harmony, divergencies which proceed partly from the contrast of early education and partly from an imperfect and unequal conception of the present position of the world and its works in relation to the Church. It is an enterprise, which, in the beginning, contradicts no opinion, and in the end must reconcile them. When, therefore, Cardinal Wiseman undertook to establish in England a branch of the Roman Accademia, he planted it in a soil prepared to receive it, where it has a vast opportunity of doing good, and in which, if it is only understood, it ought surely to thrive.

The Inaugural Address consists of two parts. The topic of the first portion is the idea that the Church has encouraged and adopted all that was most admirable in the secular movements of different ages, and has enriched herself with the best treasures of the outer world.

Unchanged herself, she received and retained the impression of all that touched her. "Such has been the Church in every age. Whatever is good, whatever virtuous, whatever useful in the world, at every time, she has allowed to leave its seal upon her outward form."[1] There are some considerations suggested by this passage which it is important that the Society to whom it was addressed should not overlook.

In speaking of the temporal action of the Church, or of her success in spiritual things, it behoves us to define and to distinguish, and to eschew generalities which disguise a truism or conceal a fallacy. The divine purpose, which is her essential mission, she can never fail to fulfill; and in pursuing it, she has accomplished innumerable secondary and collateral ends, and while teaching the transitoriness of all earthly things, has conferred immeasurable temporal benefits on mankind. But it is not this that constitutes her proper vocation, and it is not just to dwell on this in supporting her claims to the reverence and gratitude of those who do not believe in her. In comparison with the higher duty she discharges for the world, the encouragement at one time or another of literature or agriculture, of art or of commerce—merits which are primary subjects of consideration in discussing polytheism or Islamism—are altogether insignificant and imperceptible. Nor, if this human point of view is put prominently forward, would it be fair to say that men are under obligation to her for all the things which constitute terrestrial advantages, or that in every thing in which religion can affect civilization, Christianity surpasses every other system in a degree at all proportionate to her intrinsic superiority. In these matters her influence has not been always alike, nor her policy consistent or always in harmony with her nature. It belongs both to her character and her interest to require the development of literature and science for the performance of her own great intellectual work, and to promote political liberty because it is the condition of her social action. There were times when she did both these things, and then a time came when that part of her influence was abandoned to those who were not of her. Then the two great forces, freedom and knowledge, were converted into weapons of assault; they seemed to justify while they avenged the neglect, and, in spite of Protestantism, they prospered better among Protestants than among Catholics. In England the spirit of political liberty, in Germany the spirit of scientific research, overcame

---

[1] p. 20.

the barriers of religious antagonism, and as it were spontaneously did homage to the Church, and protested against their estrangement from her. Human learning has often been an instrument, but not a source, of hostility to religious truth. It has served in spite of great outward difficulties, of a long separation, and of a heavy bribe, and it has acted as a corrosive to all false religions ever since the time when the gods of Greece began to wane before the rising brightness of her philosophy. And this is a character of the present age which we are hardly accustomed to consider, and which we have not used as we might for the advantage of our cause, that learning has acquired an authority before which even religious rancour must give way, and is an ally to the Church that would be more powerful if it was more trusted. So long as its alliance is not claimed by the truth, it is certain to be used against it.

> *Cain.*   I never
> As yet have bowed unto my father's God; . . .
> Why should I bow to thee? . . .
> *Lucifer.*   He who bows not to Him has bowed to me.
> *Cain.*   But I will bend to neither.
> *Lucifer.*   Nevertheless,
> Thou art my worshipper; not worshipping
> Him makes thee mine the same.

The great error of the day, in reference to the position of the Church between science and policy, is that Catholics, men of science, and politicians are inclined to recognize only one authority. In the domain of learning, as well as in civil society, there is an authority distinct from that of the Church, and not derived from it, and we are bound in each sphere to render to Caesar the things that are Caesar's. There can be no conflict of duties or of allegiance between them, except inasmuch as one of them abandons its true purpose, the realization of right in the civil order, and the discovery of truth in the intellectual. Political wrong and scientific error are the only sources of hostility in either department to the Church, and this is met by the restoration of right or of truth, that is, by the advancement of learning or politics. If we neglect this, we are ourselves responsible for disputes and conflicts in which the right may not be on our side, and we shall have no criterion to apply but which we believe to be the interest of religion; forgetful that a true principle is more sacred than the most precious interest, and that the consideration of interests is suspended where the obligation of principles is acknowledged. The danger comes from those who consider only one thing, and take their stand either exclusively on the secular or on the ecclesiastical ground. All that we demand is that science should be true to its own method, and the State to its own principle, and beyond this the interests of religion require no protection.

From the second part of the discourse we learn that this and no other is the spirit in which the English branch of the Academy has been instituted. The Cardinal exhorts its members to follow "without anxiety, but with an unflinching eye, the progress of science." The perversion of learning alone must be resisted and exposed, but the spirit of investigation is to be humbly, joyfully and gratefully accepted; and the day will hereafter come when men will look back with admiration upon its works, and upon the important part it has had in promoting the progress of religion. The rise of this new and mighty power, due in great measure to the lull of religious controversy at a time when Protestantism had lost its vigour, and the Church seemed to be absorbed in her internal troubles, is justly compared to the revival of ancient learning in the fifteenth century. That, too, was a new and powerful element in civilization which might and did accomplish both great evil and great good, and which was viewed by some with confidence, by others with alarm, and by many with satisfaction as a welcome auxiliary against the Church. Then as now, in presence of a somewhat similar phenomenon, the Catholic world resolved itself into three sections. There was a large party, who knew that all the resources of criticism and learning belong to the armoury of the Church, and who greeted in the new discoveries accession to her strength. This was the feeling that for a hundred years uniformly prevailed in Rome; it was shared by the most illustrious prelates of that age, by Ximenes, by Lindanus, by John Dalberg, by Gioberti, and by the two great Cardinals of the House of Borromeo; and the author of this disclosure, whose name is in the foremost rank of those who have combined elegant literature with severer learning, naturally ranges himelf on their side. Then there was a party in which it would be unjust to place Erasmus, because his satire of the clergy that so readily accepted the doctrines and precepts of the Reformation was at least redeemed by his dogmatical opposition to Luther, who, seeing nothing but paganism in antiquity, followed it instead of Christianity, and beheld in the clergy a set of ignorant and selfish conspirators against knowledge.

Such were the authors of the *Epistolae Obscurorum Virorum*, who, although the publication of the first volume preceded by two years the outbreak at Wittenberg, became Protestants for the most part, and whose ridicule of the priesthood was in intention and in reality an insult to the Church. Lastly, there were those whose conduct justified the attacks it drew down on them, who feared and deprecated the introduction of the new studies. But few men of note in the Church shared these views, and it is not probable that they will find favour in the Academy, if the traditions of its inauguration and the spirit of its founder survive in it. Much may be expected from the pursuit of literature by a body of earnest Catholics, who are impressed with the conviction that the harmony of religion with profane learning cannot be made, but may be found; who regard scientific investigation as a suspension rather than an occasion of controversy; and who understand that an important preliminary towards encountering with success the anti-Catholic prejudices of scientific men is the suppression of an unscientific tendency among Catholics. For knowledge, says Thomas à Kempis, has no enemy but the ignorant. "Truth," says John of Salisbury, "becomes obscured as often by the negligence of those who profess it as by the assaults of error."

When Frederick Schlegel concludes his *Philosophy of History* with a chapter on the general restoration as the predominant sign of the age, he touches upon the great point of resemblance between the present time and the period of the Renaissance. For the development of the scientific spirit has proceeded from a revival of forgotten knowledge as comprehensive as that of the fifteenth century, and by the resurrection of a buried world whose influence is as profound and as important for civilization as that of the ancients. The antiquity that was brought to light was partly Christian and partly pagan, but it was a period of civilization deformed by corruption, and of Christianity beset with heresy. The influence of the rivival corresponded to this character. It was in the first place aesthetical rather than practical. We still associate with the word *Renaissance* above all the notion of art. The Humanism of Italy was a study of beauty, of enjoyment, of refinement; what was beautiful was placed before what was true. The bearing of these pursuits on actual life was generally injurious. We need not point for proofs of this to the erotic literature of the fifteenth century, or to the demoralization of the courts; they are most visible in the ideas of politics and of government which were derived from the ancients. The example which the history of their states supplies is only a lesson of false republicanism, generating in its corruption an unlimited despotism. Even the increased insight into the early period of the Church, though it modified and enriched the scholastic teaching, promoted only an archaeological and fragmentary, not a complete, historical study of Christianity. The connection with the immediate past was interrupted, and the continuity of institutions, the genesis and succession of ideas, were completely lost sight of. A time came when the ancients were the only authorities, antiquity the only study, and when the thousand years that separated its restoration from its fall were as little understood as the classic world had been during the supremacy of the barbarians who destroyed it.

The spirit of investigation was rapidly absorbed by the passion of formal elegance. At one moment it appeared as though it would be otherwise, but the first efforts of criticism, eminently characteristic of the times, were not followed up. In the middle of the fifteenth century, Valla wrote a treatise to prove that the Donation of Constantine could not be genuine, and in this he easily succeeded, though it was reserved for our time to ascertain the origin of the forgery which gave Ireland to England, and the Indies to Spain. The result of Valla's skill was merely negative. Finding in the period whose records he had studied no authority for existence of the pontifical state, and certain of the spuriousness of its most famous title-deed, he conceived that the whole fabric of the temporal power was a usurpation, and insisted that it ought to be surrendered. "Men say," he writes, "that the Church is at war with Bologna or Perugia. It is not the Church but the Pope, of his own ambition, that is at war with the towns." But the pope was not alarmed by the Humanists, and Valla obtained promotion at Rome; but here a serious charge was brought against him, and he was denounced to the ecclesiastical authorities for that, puffed up with pride, and abandoning himself to an unseemly and hazardous temerity of statement, he taught that Tarquin the Proud was not the son of Tarquin the First. This was in the early period of the movement. It was not by criticism, but by frivolity and free-thinking, that the classical scholars did harm to religion; their researches were dangerous neither to faith nor to credulity. It was in anticipation of such a change, which did not, however, actually ensue for centuries, that Pius II uttered a cautious saying, which is not in the tone of mediaeval Catholicism: "Christianam fidem, si miraculis non esset approbata, honestate sua recipi debuisse."

That anticipated innovation, which the classic revival failed to introduce, constitutes the essence of the corresponding revival of the nineteenth century. The most comprehensive and penetrating influence, which marks our age, as the Renaissance the age of Medici, and which is the strongest current that counteracts that which set in before the Revolution, is the Restoration of mediaeval learning. Its tendency is in almost every respect exactly contrary to the other revival. The ignorance of the Middle Ages, during the period between the Reformation and the Revolution, amounted to physical blindness. The remains of mediaeval art were not even curiosities. An intelligent traveller could visit Cologne, describe several of the smaller churches, and declare that there was nothing else worth seeing in the place, though the Cathedral towered above the city with that irregular and striking outline which all remember who saw it before the works were commenced for its completion. The great Gothic churches, it has been truly said, had to be discovered again, like Pompeii, after lying hid for ages. The mediaeval world was a palimpsest that had yet to be deciphered. Its history formed no part of education, and it was the great business of governments to obliterate all the traces it had left upon the State. Even in theology those who must faithfully preserve its forms were not likely to study its history. Its languages were extinct among the learned, and no man knew that they possessed a vast treasure of poetry, epic poets who could compare with Dante, and ballads such as in the hands of Percy and of Scott introduced a new era in the literature of England. The poetry of the romantic school, the art of the foreign pre-Raphaelites and the Goths, are the most familiar outward tokens of a revolution immeasurably more profound and more extensive. The mediaeval revival involves a return to continuity in social institutions, to tradition in ideas, and to history in science. The presiding impulse in this pursuit is the opposite of that which guided the Humanists. It is not the charm of beauty or of eloquence, for that is the privilege of antiquity, nor a delight in idle enjoyment, or even the cultivation of the mind; for in these things the Middle Ages have incomparably less to offer. We go back to the Middle Ages in order to know the realities of the past. The poverty of forms, the repulsiveness of style, restrict the inquiry to that which is alone of actual value, the facts of mediaeval life. For the civilization of that age, its ideas, habits, and institutions, possess a direct importance for us who are its descendants and its heirs. Our society is the development of that of the mediaeval chivalry, our civilization is founded on theirs.

Our national instincts and character were moulded by them. Our modern history has been occupied in destroying or modifying what they have left us; it is filled with the contest between mediaeval facts which were no longer understood, and ancient ideas which have no basis in real life. The classical revival was the conquest of an unknown world. The mediaeval revival is a pilgrimage to the homes of our fathers, to the graves of

> The dead but sceptred sovereigns, who still rule
> Our spirits from their urns.

The heroes of the revival of letters went forth in the spirit of adventure, and are of the same type as the men who discovered a new world in the age that had revived the old. Ours is a spirit of reverence and piety, as of men returning after a long migration to places hallowed by the recollections and the traditions of their race.

The aim, then, of these studies is not beauty or pleasure, but truth and instruction. Their method therefore is critical, and their form is historical: for it is less the works of individuals that attract us than the general ideas and deeds of those days. A classical scholar has such a rich literary world before him that he may be anything but a historian. But it is only for the historian that the bulk of mediaeval literature has any attractions. Not only, therefore, does the study of the Middle Ages promote the historical art, and a stricter critical method than the classics, but it has given rise to a totally new feature in the moral sciences, the supremacy of the means over the end. Many problems about which men have disputed and fought naturally resolve themselves when considered as history. Numberless systems and opinions lose their absolute character, and appear in their conditional relative truth when the mode of their formation and the modifying influences of time and place are understood. Ecclesiastical history is filled with conflicts which a knowledge of the history of development would have made superfluous, and in all other branches of learning history is a peacemaker and a destroyer of idols. Until the Middle Ages were reinstated in their proper position, the scientific study of history was in its infancy; for the omission of a large and essential portion of the subject gave the rest a merely antiquarian interest, as a curiosity, not as part of a single and consecutive process to which the present belongs.

Religion has been served by this phase of literature in two ways. The least important is the rehabilitation of the ages of faith by its enthusiastic admirers, like Count de Montalembert and Mr. Digby. What is of far greater consequence is the establishment of those fixed rules, and of that disinterested spirit of investigation, which rigidly exclude the influence of prejudice, interest or passion, pursue not the application of truth so much as its discovery, and apply to moral science something of the patient self-denial and closeness of observation which belong to natural philosophy. If these qualities have been rare till lately in modern times, they were not unknown to an earlier age. Bishop Adelbold of Utrecht begins his life of St. Henry with the following definition of the duties of a historian: "Scriptor veritatem tenere nequit nisi haec quatuor aut potenter devitaverit, aut aliquatenus a mente deposuerit: odium et carnalem dilectationem, invidiam et infernalem adulationem. Odium enim et invidia bene gesta aut omnino tacent, aut dicendo transcurrunt, aut calumniose transmutant. E contra male gesta dicunt, dilatant et amplificant. Carnalis autem affectio et infernalis adulatio, quae male gesta sunt, scientes ignorant et ignorantiam simulantes, veritatem occultant; bene gesta autem, placere quaerentes, spaciose dicunt, et plus justo magnificant. Sic per haec quatuor, aut in bene gestis aut in male gestis veritas evanescit, falsitas superducto colore nitescit. Spiritualis autem dilectio veritatis amica, nec male gesta celat, nec bene gesta pompose dilatat; sciens quia et male gesta saepe prosunt ad correctionem, et bene gesta frequenter obsunt, dum ducuntur in elationem."

We gather from the names that have reached us of the members of the Academy that the moral sciences will be chiefly cultivated, for in the others few of course are really competent, and the interference of amateurs can only lead to a demoralizing shallowness. It will be well if this is so, for those branches of learning are of more vital importance than physical science. They touch religion and morals more directly, and influence more powerfully men of cultivated minds, whilst illiterate persons are more easily struck with the facts and influences of the material world. It is, we presume, only for the facility of illustration, and perhaps from old reminiscences, that so many of the Cardinal's instances are drawn from geology and the physical creation. These sciences are of subordinate utility to religion, even when cultivated in a religious spirit; and when directed against religion, have not the same force as the sciences which are connected with her origin, her history and her doctrine.

Much will depend on the regulations which are to guide the Academy, and on the changes which will become necessary in order to adapt the original rule to new wants. As learning does not flourish even with protection so well as with freedom, no institution without some degree of self-government can retain an enduring vitality. The less it resembles a manufacture, and the more it obtains the character of an organism, the better it will fare. In the constitution of the French Consulate, the majority of the senate was originally appointed by the government, and it then completed its numbers by election. We know not whether this is the plan adopted by the Academy, but we have no doubt that the original list has been drawn up in conformity with the rule which was followed on that occasion. "We put aside," said the Third Consul, "all personal affection in our choice, and considered nothing but the merit, the reputation, and the services of the candidates."

The Academy of the *Lincei*, which is alluded to in the discourse, may supply some useful hints to the new association. Their historian, the Duke of Cezi, tells us that they were different from the philosophers of our day; for they considered religion not only the first of all sciences, but as the only safe basis, the principle and true source of all knowledge—an idea which is better expressed by a writer already quoted: "Quia tam sensus quam ratio humana frequenter errat ad intelligentiam veritatis primum fundamentum locavit in fide."[2] Amongst their rules we applaud the following: "Non minus sedulo et hoc observent ne Lynceorum quemquam aut voce aut calamo perstringant, quorum tamen opiniones, ut amplectantur, non ob id adstringantur, cum cuilibet proprii genii, et ingenii modulo in hujuscemodi disciplinis philosophari, et ad veritatem quam proxime collimare libere linquatur." It is easy to see that the *Lincei* were not the party who were disposed to give up religion and theology for the sake of an elegant Latinity.

The purpose of an Academy has been defined to be to advance learning, whilst the mission of a university is to communicate it. This distinction, founded on the necessity of a fixed and finished matter for the instruction of youth, and of a direct religious control which the growth of science will not bear, did not originally subsist. The first Academy was also the first university, and the name of the spot where Plato lectured on the banks of Cephisus has survived in both. We should think little of a university which did nothing for the enrichment of literature, and produced men, and not books. But it has been usual

[2] *Metalog.*, iv, 41.

for academies to addict themselves more exclusively to their own special function of acquiring, not of distributing knowledge; and it is not one of the least meritorious points in the Society of which we are speaking, that it returns in some manner to the old plan, and proposes to extend to younger men the advantage of witnessing its proceeding and gathering something of its spirit. The majority of the academies which sprung up in every part of Italy, in consequence of the number of universities and the deficiency of public employment, can supply no useful example for the serious and practical design which the Cardinal is endeavouring to realize amongst us. The scheme of Leibniz for the Academy of Berlin, the purpose of which was to advance at the same time the public good, learning and religion ("un point des plus importants serait aussi la propagation de la foi par les sciences"), is the only one with which we are acquainted that combines such exalted ends.

[6]
Döllinger on the Temporal Power

After half a year's delay, Dr. Döllinger has redeemed his promise to publish the text of those lectures which made so profound a sensation in the Catholic world.[1] We are sorry to find that the report which fell into our hands at the time, and from which we gave the account that appeared in our May Number, was both defective and incorrect; and we should further regret that we did not follow the example of those journals which abstained from comment so long as no authentic copy was accessible, if it did not appear that, although the argument of the lecturer was lost, his meaning was not, on the whole, seriously misrepresented. Excepting for the sake of the author, who became the object, and of those who unfortunately made themselves the organs, of so much calumny, it is impossible to lament the existence of the erroneous statements which have caused the present publication. Intending at first to prefix an introduction to the text of his lectures, the Professor has been led on by the gravity of the occasion, the extent of his subject, and the abundance of materials, to compose a book of 700 pages. Written with all the author's perspicuity of style, though without his usual compression; with the exhaustless information which never fails him, but with an economy of quotation suited to the general public for whom it is designed, it betrays the circumstances of its origin. Subjects are sometimes introduced out of their proper place and order; and there are occasional repetitions, which show that he had not at starting fixed the proportions of the different parts of his work. This does not, however, affect the logical sequence of the ideas, or the accuracy of the induction. No other book contains—no other

Published in the *Rambler* n.s. (3d ser.) 6 (November 1861):1–62. Döllinger I, p. 228; Acton-Simpson II, p. 165. Reprinted in Acton, *History of Freedom*, pp. 301–374.
[1] *Kirche und Kirchen*, Munich, 1861 ("Papstum und Kirchenstaat").

writer probably could supply—so comprehensive and so suggestive a description of the state of the Protestant religion, or so impartial an account of the causes which have brought on the crisis of the temporal power.

The *Symbolik* of Möhler was suggested by the beginning of that movement of revival and resuscitation amongst the Protestants, of which Döllinger now surveys the fortunes and the result. The interval of thirty years has greatly altered the position of the Catholic divines towards their antagonists. Möhler had to deal with the ideas of the Reformation, the works of the Reformers, and the teaching of the confessions; he had to answer in the nineteenth century the theology of the sixteenth. The Protestantism for which he wrote was a complete system, antagonistic to the whole of Catholic theology, and he confuted the one by comparing it with the other, dogma for dogma. But that of which Döllinger treats has lost, for the most part, those distinctive doctrines, not by the growth of unbelief, but in consequence of the very efforts which its most zealous and religious professors have made to defend and to redeem it. The contradictions and errors of the Protestant belief were formerly the subject of controversy with its Catholic opponents, but now the controversy is anticipated and prevented by the undisguised admissions of its desponding friends. It stands no longer as a system consistent, complete, satisfying the judgment and commanding the unconditional allegiance of its followers, and fortified at all points against Catholicism; but disorganised as a church, its doctrines in a state of dissolution, despaired of by its divines, strong and compact only in its hostility to Rome, but with no positive principle of unity, no ground of resistance, nothing to have faith in, but the determination to reject authority. This, therefore, is the point which Döllinger takes up. Reducing the chief phenomena of religious and social decline to the one head of failing authority, he founds on the state of Protestantism the apology of the Papacy. He abandons to the Protestant theology the destruction of the Protestant Church, and leaves its divines to confute and abjure its principles in detail, and to arrive by the exhaustion of the modes of error, through a painful but honourable process, at the gates of truth; he meets their arguments simply by a chapter of ecclesiastical history, of which experience teaches them the force; and he opposes to their theories, not the discussions of controversial theology, but the character of a single institution. The opportunity he has taken to do this, the assumed coincidence between the process of dissolution among the Protestants and the process of regeneration in the Court of Rome, is the characteristic peculiarity of the book. Before we proceed to give an analysis of its contents, we will give some extracts from the Preface, which explains the purpose of the whole, and which is alone one of the most important contributions to the religious discussions of the day.

This book arose from two out of four lectures which were delivered in April this year. How I came to discuss the most difficult and complicated question of our time before a very mixed audience, and in a manner widely different from that usually adopted, I deem myself bound to explain. It was my intention, when I was first requested to lecture, only to speak of the present state of religion in general, with a comprehensive view extending over all mankind. It happened, however, that from those circles which had given the impulse to the lectures, the question was frequently put to me, how the position of the Holy See, the partly consummated, partly threatening, loss of its secular power is to be explained. What answer, I was repeatedly asked, is to be given to those out of the Church who point with triumphant scorn to the numerous Episcopal manifestoes, in which the States of the Church are declared essential and necessary to her existence although the events of the last thirty years appear with increasing distinctness to announce their downfall? I had found the hope often expressed in newspapers, books, and periodicals, that after the destruction of the temporal power of the Popes, the Church herself would not escape dissolution. At the same time, I was struck by finding in the memoirs of Chateaubriand that Cardinal Bernetti, Secretary of State to Leo XII, had said, that if he lived long, there was a chance of his beholding the fall of the temporal power of the Papacy. I had also read, in the letter of a well-informed and trustworthy correspondent from Paris, that the Archbishop of Rheims had related on his return from Rome that Pius IX had said to him, "I am under no illusions, the temporal power must fall. Goyon will abandon me; I shall then disband my remaining troops. I shall excommunicate the king when he enters the city; and shall calmly await my death."

I thought already, in April, that I could perceive, what has become still more clear in October, that the enemies of the secular power of the Papacy are determined, united, predominant, and that there is nowhere a protecting power which possesses the will, and at the same time the means, of averting the catastrophe. I considered it therefore probable that an interruption of the temporal dominion would soon ensue—an interruption which, like others before it, would also come to an end, and would be followed by a restoration. I resolved, therefore, to take the opportunity, which the lectures gave me, to prepare the public for the coming events, which already cast their shadows upon us, and thus to prevent the scandals, the doubt, and the offence which must inevitably arise if the States of the Church should pass into other hands, although the pastorals of the Bishops had so energetically asserted that they belonged to the integrity of the Church. I meant, therefore, to say, the Church by her nature can very well exist, and did exist for seven centuries, without the territorial possessions of the Popes; afterwards this possession became necessary, and, in spite of great changes and vicissitudes, has discharged in most cases its function of serving as a foundation for the independence and freedom of the Popes. As long as the present state and arrangement of Europe endures, we can discover no other means to secure to the Holy See its freedom, and with it the confidence of all. But the knowledge and the power of God reach farther than ours, and we must not presume to set bounds to the Divine wisdom and omnipotence, or to say to it, In this way and no other! Should, nevertheless, the threatening consummation ensue, and should the Pope be robbed of his land, one of three eventualities will assuredly come to pass. Either the loss of the State is only temporary, and the territory will revert, after some intervening casualties, either whole or in part to its legitimate sovereign; or Providence will bring about, by ways unknown to us, and combinations which we cannot divine, a state of things in which the object, namely, the independence and free action of the Holy See, will be attained without the means which have hitherto served; or else we are approaching great catastrophes in Europe, the doom of the whole edifice of the present social order—events of which the ruin of the Roman State is only the precursor and the herald.

The reasons for which, of these three possibilities, I think the first the most probable, I have developed in this book. Concerning the second alternative, there is nothing to be said; it is an unknown, and therefore, indescribable, quantity. Only we must retain it against certain over-confident assertions which profess to know the secret things to come, and, trespassing on the divine domain, wish to subject the Future absolutely to the laws of the immediate Past. That the third possibility must also be admitted, few of those who studiously observe the signs of the time will dispute. One of the ablest historians and statesmen—Niebuhr—wrote on the 5th October 1830: "If God does not miraculously aid, a destruction is in store for us such as the Roman world underwent in the middle of the third century—destruction of prosperity, of freedom, of civilisation, and of literature." And we have proceeded much farther on the inclined plane since then. The European Powers have overturned, or have allowed to be overturned, the two pillars of their existence—the principle of legitimacy, and the public law of nations. Those monarchs who have made themselves the slaves of the Revolution, to do its work, are the active agents in the historical drama; the others stand aside as quiet spectators, in expectation of inheriting something, like Prussia and Russia, or bestowing encouragement and assistance, like England; or as passive invalids, like Austria and the sinking empire of Turkey. But the Revolution is a permanent chronic disease, breaking out now in one place, now in another, sometimes seizing several members together. The Pentarchy is dissolved; the Holy Alliance, which, however defective or open to abuse, was one form of political order, is buried; the right of might prevails in Europe. Is it a process of renovation or a process of dissolution in which European society is plunged? I still think the former; but I must, as I have said, admit the possibility of the other alternative. If it occurs, then, when the powers of destruction have done their work, it will be the business of the Church at once to co-operate actively in the reconstruction of social order out of the ruins, both as a connecting civilising power, and as the preserver and dispenser of moral and religious tradition. And thus the Papacy, with or without territory, has its own function and its appointed mission.

These, then, were the ideas from which I started; and it may be supposed that my language concerning the immediate fate of the temporal power of the Pope necessarily sounded ambiguous, that I could not well come with the confidence which is given to other—perhaps more far-sighted—men before my audience, and say, Rely upon it, the States of the Church—the land from Radicofani to Ceperano, from Ravenna to Città Vecchia, shall and must and will invariably remain to the Popes. Heaven and earth shall pass away before the Roman State shall pass away. I could not do this, because I did not at that time believe it, nor do I now; but am only confident that the Holy See will not be permanently deprived of the conditions necessary for the fulfillment of its mission. Thus the substance of my words was this: Let no one lose faith in the Church if the secular principality of the Pope should disappear for a season, or for ever. It is not essence, but accident; not end, but means; it began late; it was formerly something quite different from what it is now. It justly appears to us indispensable, and as long as the existing order lasts in Europe, it must be maintained at any price; or if it is violently interrupted, it must be restored. But a political settlement of Europe is conceivable in which it would be superfluous, and then it would be an oppressive burden. At the same time I wished to defend Pope Pius IX and his government against many accusations, and to point out that the inward infirmities and deficiencies which undeniably exist in the country, by which the State has been reduced to so deplorable a condition of weakness and helplessness, were not attributable to him; that, on the contrary, he has shown, both before and since 1848, the best will to reform; and that by him, and under him, much has been really improved.

The newspaper reports, written down at home from memory, gave but an inaccurate representation of a discourse which did not attempt in the usual way to cut the knot, but which, with buts and ifs, and referring to certain elements in the decision which are generally left out of the calculation, spoke of an uncertain future, and of various possibilities. This was not to be avoided. Any reproduction which was not quite literal must, in spite of the good intentions of the reporter, have given rise to false interpretations. When, therefore, one of the most widely read papers reported the first lecture, without any intentional falsification, but with omissions which altered the sense and the tendency of my words, I immediately proposed to the conductors to print my manuscript; but this offer was declined. In other accounts in the daily press, I was often unable to recognise my ideas; and words were put into my mouth which I had never uttered. And here I will admit that, when I gave the lectures, I did not think that they would be discussed by the press, but expected that, like others of the same kind, they would at most be mentioned in a couple of words, *in futuram oblivionem*. Of the controversy which sprang up at once, in separate works and in newspaper articles, in Germany, France, England, Italy, and even in America, I shall not speak. Much of it I have not read. The writers often did not even ask themselves whether the report which accident put into their hands, and which they carelessly adopted, was at all accurate. But I must refer to an account in one of the most popular English periodicals, because I am there brought into a society to which I do not belong. The author of an article in the July Number of the *Edinburgh Review* . . . appeals to me, misunderstanding the drift of my words, and erroneously believing that I had already published an apology of my orthodoxy. . . . A sharp attack upon me in the *Dublin Review* I know only from extracts in English papers; but I can see from the vehemence with which the writer pronounces himself against liberal institutions, that, even after the appearance of this book, I cannot reckon on coming to an understanding with him. . . .

The excitement which was caused by my lectures, or rather by the accounts of them in the papers, had this advantage, that it brought to light, in a way which to many was unexpected, how widely, how deeply, and how firmly the attachment of the people to the See of St. Peter is rooted. For the sake of this I was glad to accept all the attacks and animosity which fell on me in consequence. But why, it will be asked—and I have been asked innumerable times—why not cut short misunderstandings by the immediate publication of the lectures, which must, as a whole, have been written beforehand? why wait for five months? For this I had two reasons: first, it was not merely a question of misunderstanding. Much of what I had actually said had made an unpleasant impression in many quarters, especially among our optimists. I should, therefore, with my bare statements, have become involved in an agitating discussion in pamphlets and newspapers, and that was not an attractive prospect. The second reason was this: I expected that the further progress of events in Italy, the irresistible logic of facts, would dispose minds to receive certain truths. I hoped that people would learn by degrees, in the school of events, that it is not enough always to be reckoning with the figures "revolution," "secret societies," "Mazzinism," "Atheism," or to estimate things only by the standard supplied by the "Jew of Verona," but that other factors must be admitted into the calculation; for instance, the condition of the Italian clergy, and its position towards the laity. I wished, therefore, to let a few months go by before I came before the public. Whether I judged rightly, the reception of this book will show.

I thoroughly understand those who think it censurable that I should have spoken in detail of situations and facts which are gladly ignored, or touched with a light and hasty hand, and that especially at the present crisis. I myself was restrained for ten years by these considerations, in spite of the feeling which urged me to speak on the question of the Roman government, and it required the circumstances I have described, I may almost say, to compel me to speak publicly on the subject. I beg of these persons to weigh the following points. First, when an author openly exposes a state of things already abundantly discussed in the press, if he draws away the necessarily very transparent covering from the gaping wounds which are not on the Church herself, but on an institution nearly connected with her, and whose infirmities she is made to feel, it may fairly be supposed that he does it, in agreement with the example of earlier friends and great men of the Church, only to show the possibility and the necessity of the cure, in order, so far as in him lies, to weaken the reproach that the defenders of the Church see only the mote in the eyes of others, not the beam in their own, and with narrow-hearted prejudice endeavour to soften, or to dissimulate, or to deny every fact which is or which appears unfavourable to their cause. He does it in order that it may be understood that where the powerlessness of men to effect a cure becomes manifest, God interposes in order to sift on His threshing-floor the chaff from the wheat, and to consume it with the fire of the catastrophes which are only His judgments and remedies. Secondly, I could not, as a historian, present the effects without going back to their causes; and it was therefore my duty, as it is that of every religious inquirer and observer, to try to contribute something to the *Théodicée*. He that undertakes to write on such lofty interests, which nearly affect the weal and woe of the Church, cannot avoid examining and displaying the wisdom and justice of God in the conduct of terrestrial events regarding them. The fate which has overtaken the Roman States must above all be considered in the light of a Divine ordinance for the advantage of the Church. Seen by that light, it assumes the character of a trial, which will continue until the object is attained, and the welfare of the Church so far secured.

It seemed evident to me, that as a new order of things in Europe lies in the design of Providence, the disease, through which for the last half-century the States of the Church unquestionably have passed, might be the transition to a new form. To describe this malady without overlooking or concealing any of the symptoms was, therefore, an undertaking which I could not avoid. The disease has its source in the inward contradiction and discord of the institutions and conditions of the government; for the modern French institutions stand there, without any reconciling qualifications, besides those of the mediaeval hierarchy. Neither of these elements is strong enough to expel the other; and either of them would, if it prevailed alone, be again a form of disease. Yet, in the history of the last few years I recognise symptoms of convalescence, however feeble, obscure, and equivocal its traces may appear. What we behold is not death or hopeless decay, it is a purifying process, painful, consuming, penetrating bone and marrow—such as God inflicts on His chosen persons and institutions. There is abundance of dross, and time is necessary before the gold can come pure out of the furnace. In the course of this process it may happen that the territorial dominion will be interrupted, that the State may be broken up or pass into other hands; but it will revive, though perhaps in another form, and with a different kind of government. In a word, *sanabilibus laboramus malis*—that is what I wished to show; that, I believe, I have shown. Now, and for the last forty years, the condition of the Roman States is the heel of Achilles of the Catholic Church, the standing reproach for adversaries throughout the world, and a stumbling-block for thousands. Not as though the objections, which are founded on the fact of this transitory disturbance and discord in the social and political sphere, possessed any weight in a theological point of view, but it cannot be denied that they are of incalculable influence on the disposition of the world external to the Church.

Whenever a state of disease has appeared in the Church, there has been but one method of cure—that of an awakened, renovated, healthy consciousness and of an enlightened public opinion in the Church. The goodwill of the ecclesiastical rulers and heads has not been able to accomplish the cure, unless sustained by the general sense and conviction of the clergy and of the laity. The healing of the great malady of the sixteenth century, the true internal reformation of the Church, only became possible when people ceased to disguise or to deny the evil, and to pass it by with silence and concealment—when so powerful and irresistible a public opinion had formed itself in the Church, that its commanding influence could no longer be evaded. At the present day, what we want is the whole truth, not merely the perception that the temporal power of the Pope is required by the Church—for that is obvious to everybody, at least out of Italy, and everything has been said that can be said about it; but also the knowledge of the conditions under which this power is possible for the future. The history of the Popes is full of instances where their best intentions were not fulfilled, and their strongest resolutions broke down, because the interests of a firmly compacted class resisted like an impenetrable hedge of thorns. Hadrian VI was fully resolved to set about the reformation in earnest; and yet he achieved virtually nothing, and felt himself, though in possession of supreme power, altogether powerless against the passive resistance of all those who should have been his instruments in the work. Only when public opinion, even in Italy, and in Rome itself, was awakened, purified, and strengthened; when the cry for reform resounded imperatively on every side—then only was it possible for the Popes to overcome the resistance in the inferior spheres, and gradually, and step by step, to open the way for a more healthy state. May, therefore, a powerful, healthy, unanimous public opinion in Catholic Europe come to the aid of Pius IX! . . .

Concerning another part of this book I have a few words to say. I have given a survey of all the Churches and ecclesiastical communities now existing. The obligation of attempting this presented itself to me, because I had to explain both the universal importance of the Papacy as a power for all the world, and the things which it actually performs. This could not be done fully without exhibiting the internal condition of the Churches which have rejected it, and withdrawn from its influence. It is true that the plan increased under my hands, and I endeavoured to give as clear a picture as possible of the development which has accomplished itself in the separated Churches since the Reformation, and through it, in consequence of the views and principles which had been once for all adopted. I have, therefore, admitted into my description no feature which is not, in my opinion, an effect, a result, however remote, of those principles and doctrines. There is doubtless room for discussion in detail upon this point, and there will unavoidably be a decided opposition to this book, if it should be noticed beyond the limits of the Church to which I belong. I hope that there also the justice will be done me of believing that I was far from having any intention of offending; that I have only said what must be said, if we would go to the bottom of these questions; that I had to do with institutions which, because of the dogmas and principles from which they spring, must, like a tree that is nailed to a wall, remain in one position, however unnatural it may be. I am quite ready to admit that, on the opposite side, the men are often better than the system to which they are, or deem themselves, attached; and that, on the contrary, in the Church the individuals are, on the average, inferior in theory and in practice to the system under which they live. . . .

The union of the two religions, which would be socially and politically the salvation of Germany and of Europe, is not possible at present; first because the greater, more active, and more influential portion of the German Protestants do not desire it, for political or religious reasons, in any form or under any practicable conditions. It is impossible, secondly, because negotiations concerning the mode and the conditions of union can no longer be carried on. For this, plenipotentiaries on both sides are required; and these only the Catholic Church is able to appoint, by virtue of her ecclesiastical organisation, not the Protestants. . . .

Nevertheless, theologically, Protestants and Catholics have come nearer each other; for those capital doctrines, those articles with which the Church was to stand or fall, for the sake of which the Reformers declared separation from the Catholic Church to be necessary, are now confuted and given up by Protestant theology, or are retained only nominally, whilst other notions are connected with the words. . . . Protestant theology is at the present day less hostile, so to speak, than the theologians. For whilst theology has levelled the strongest bulwarks and doctrinal barriers which the Reformation had set up to confirm the separation, the divines, instead of viewing favourably the consequent facilities for union, often labour, on the contrary, to conceal the fact, or to provide new points of difference. Many of them probably agree with Stahl of Berlin, who said, shortly before his death, "Far from supposing that the breach of the sixteenth century can be healed, we ought, if it had not already occurred, to make it now." This, however, will not continue; and a future generation, perhaps that which is even now growing up, will rather adopt the recent declaration of Heinrich Leo, "In the Roman Catholic Church a process of purification has taken place since Luther's day; and if the Church had been in the days of Luther what the Roman Catholic Church in Germany actually is at present, it would never have occurred to him to assert his opposition so energetically as to bring about a separation." Those who think thus will then be the right men and the chosen instruments for the acceptable work of the reconciliation of the

Churches, and the true unity of Germany. Upon the day when, on both sides, the conviction shall arise vivid and strong that Christ really desires the unity of His Church, that the division of Christendom, the multiplicity of Churches, is displeasing to God, that he who helps to prolong the situation must answer for it to the Lord—on that day four-fifths of the traditional polemics of the Protestants against the Church will with one blow be set aside, like chaff and rubbish; for four-fifths consist of misunderstandings, logomachies, and wilful falsifications, or relate to personal, and therefore accidental, things, which are utterly insignificant where only principles and dogmas are at stake.

On that day, also, much will be changed on the Catholic side. Thenceforward the character of Luther and the Reformers will no more be dragged forward in the pulpit. The clergy, mindful of the saying, *interficite errores, diligite homines*, will always conduct themselves towards members of other Churches in conformity with the rules of charity, and will therefore assume, in all cases where there are no clear proofs to the contrary, the *bona fides* of opponents. They will never forget that no man is convinced and won over by bitter words and violent attacks, but that every one is rather repelled by them. Warned by the words of the Epistle to the Romans (xiv. 13), they will be more careful than heretofore to give to their separate brethren no scandal, no grounds of accusation against the Church. Accordingly, in popular instruction and in religious life, they will always make the great truths of salvation the centre of all their teaching: they will not treat secondary things in life and doctrine as though they were of the first importance; but, on the contrary, they will keep alive in the people the consciousness that such things are but means to an end, and are only of inferior consequence and subsidiary value.

Until that day shall dawn upon Germany, it is our duty as Catholics, in the words of Cardinal Diepenbrock, "to bear the religious separation in a spirit of penance for guilt incurred in common." We must acknowledge that here also God has caused much good as well as much evil to proceed from the errors of men, from the contests and passions of the sixteenth century; that the anxiety of the German nation to see the intolerable abuses and scandals in the Church removed was fully justified, and sprang from the better qualities of our people, and from their moral indignation at the desecration and corruption of holy things, which were degraded to selfish and hypocritical purposes.

We do not refuse to admit that the great separation, and the storms and sufferings connected with it, was an awful judgment upon Catholic Christendom, which clergy and laity had but too well deserved—a judgment which has had an improving and salutary effect. The great conflict of intellects has purified the European atmosphere, has impelled the human mind on to new courses, and has promoted a rich scientific and literary life. Protestant theology, with its restless spirit of inquiry, has gone along by the side of the Catholic, exciting and awakening, warning and vivifying; and every eminent Catholic divine in Germany will gladly admit that he owes much to the writings of Protestant scholars.

We must also acknowledge that in the Church the rust of abuses and of a mechanical superstition is always forming afresh; that the spiritual in religion is sometimes materialised, and therefore degraded, deformed, and applied to their own loss, by the servants of the Church, through their indolence and want of intelligence, and by the people, through their ignorance. The true spirit of reform must, therefore, never depart from the Church, but must periodically break out with renovating strength, and penetrate the mind and the will of the clergy. In this sense we do not refuse to admit the justice of a call to penance, when it proceeds from those who are not of us—that is, of a warning carefully to examine our religious life and pastoral conduct, and to remedy what is found defective.

At the same time it must not be forgotten that the separation did not ensue in consequence of the abuses of the Church. For the duty and necessity of removing these abuses has always been recognised; and only the difficulty of the thing, the not always unjustifiable fear lest the wheat should be pulled up with the tares, prevented for a time the Reformation, which was accomplished in the Church and through her. Separation on account merely of abuses in ecclesiastical life, when the doctrine is the same, is rejected as criminal by the Protestants as well as by us. It is, therefore, for doctrine's sake that the separation occurred; and the general discontent of the people, the weakening of ecclesiastical authority by the existence of abuses, only facilitated the adoption of the new doctrines. But now on one side some of these defects and evils in the life of the Church have disappeared; the others have greatly diminished since the reforming movement; and on the other side, the principal doctrines for which they separated, and on the truth of which, and their necessity for salvation, the right and duty of secession was based, are given up by Protestant science, deprived of their Scriptural basis by exegesis, or at least made very uncertain by the opposition of the most eminent Protestant divines. Meanwhile we live in hopes, comforting ourselves with the conviction that history, or that process of development in Europe which is being accomplished before our eyes, as well in society and politics as in religion, is the powerful ally of the friends of ecclesiastical union; and we hold out our hands to Christians on the other side for a combined war of resistance against the destructive movements of the age.

There are two circumstances which make us fear that the work will not be received in the spirit in which it is written, and that its object will not immediately be attained. The first of these is the extraordinary effect which was produced by the declaration which the author made on the occasion of the late assembly of the Catholic associations of Germany at Munich. He stated simply, what is understood by every Catholic out of Italy, and intelligible to every reasonable Protestant,

that the freedom of the Church imperatively requires that, in order to
protect the Pope from the perils which menace him, particularly in
our age, he should possess a sovereignty not merely nominal, and that
his right to his dominions is as good as that of all other legitimate
sovereigns. In point of fact, this expression of opinion, which occurs
even in the garbled reports of the lectures, leaves all those questions
on which it is possible for serious and dispassionate men to be divided
entirely open. It does not determine whether there was any excuse for
the disaffection of the Papal subjects; whether the security afforded by
a more extensive dominion is greater than the increased difficulty of
administration under the conditions inherited from the French occupation; whether an organised system of tribute or domains might be
sufficient, in conjunction with a more restricted territory; whether the
actual loss of power is or is not likely to improve a misfortune for
religion. The storm of applause with which these words, simply
expressing that in which all agree, were received, must have suggested
to the speaker that his countrymen in general are unprepared to believe
that one, who has no other aspiration in his life and his works than
the advancement of the Catholic religion, can speak without a reverent
awe of the temporal government, or can witness without dismay its
impending fall. They must have persuaded themselves that not only
the details, but the substance of his lectures had been entirely
misreported, and that his views were as free from novelty as destitute
of offence. It is hard to believe that such persons will be able to
reconcile themselves to the fearless and straightforward spirit in which
the first of Church historians discusses the history of his own age.

Another consideration, almost equally significant with the attitude
of the great mass of Catholics, is the silence of the minority who agree
with Döllinger. Those earnest Catholics who, in their Italian patriotism,
insist on the possibility of reconciling the liberty of the Holy See with
the establishment of an ideal unity, Passaglia, Tosti, the followers of
Gioberti, and the disciples of Rosmini, have not hesitated to utter
openly their honest but most inconceivable persuasion. But on the
German side of the Alps, where no political agitation affects the
religious judgment, or drives men into disputes, those eminent thinkers
who agree with Döllinger are withheld by various considerations from
publishing their views. Sometimes it is the hopelessness of making an
impression, sometimes the grave inconvenience of withstanding the
current of opinion that makes them keep silence; and their silence

leaves those who habitually follow them not only without means of expressing their views, but often without decided views to express. The same influences which deprive Döllinger of the open support of these natural allies will impede the success of his work, until events have outstripped ideas, and until men awake to the discovery that what they refused to anticipate or to prepare for, is already accomplished.

Piety sometimes gives birth to scruples, and faith to superstition, when they are not directed by wisdom and knowledge. One source of the difficulty of which we are speaking is as much a defect of faith as a defect of knowledge. Just as it is difficult for some Catholics to believe that the supreme spiritual authority on earth could ever be in unworthy hands, so they find it hard to reconcile the reverence due to the Vicar of Christ, and the promises made to him, with the acknowledgment of intolerable abuses in his temporal administration. It is a comfort to make the best of the case, to draw conclusions from the exaggerations, the inventions, and the malice of the accusers against the justice of the accusation, and in favour of the accused. It is a temptation to our weakness and to our consciences to defend the Pope as we would defend ourselves—with the same care and zeal, with the same uneasy secret consciousness that there are weak points in the case which can best be concealed by diverting attention from them. What the defence gains in energy it loses in sincerity; the cause of the Church, which is the cause of truth, is mixed up and confused with human elements, and is injured by a degrading alliance. In this way even piety may lead to immorality, and devotion to the Pope may lead away from God.

The position of perpetual antagonism to a spirit which we abhor; the knowledge that the clamour against the temporal power is, in very many instances, inspired by hatred of the spiritual authority; the indignation at the impure motives mixed up with the movement—all these things easily blind Catholics to the fact that our attachment to the Pope as our spiritual Head, our notion that his civil sovereignty is a safeguard of his freedom, are the real motives of our disposition to deny the truth of the accusations made against his government. It is hard to believe that imputations which take the form of insults, and which strike at the Church through the State, are well founded, and to distinguish the design and the occasion from the facts. It is, perhaps, more than we can expect of men, that, after defending the Pope as a sovereign, because he is a pontiff, and adopting against his enemies the policy of unconditional defence, they will consent to adopt a view which corroborates to a great extent the assertions they have combated, and implicitly condemns their tactics. It is natural to oppose one extreme by another; and those who avoid both easily appear to be capitulating with error. The effects of this spirit of opposition are not confined to those who are engaged in resisting the No-popery party in England, or the revolution in Italy. The fate of the temporal power hangs neither on the Italian ministry nor on English influence, but on the decision of the Emperor of the French; and the loudest maintainers of the rights of the Holy See are among that party who have been the most zealous adversaries of the Imperial system. The French Catholics behold in the Roman policy of the emperor a scheme for obtaining over the Church a power of which they would be the first victims. Their religious freedom is in jeopardy while he has the fate of the Pope in his hands. That which is elsewhere simply a manifestation of opinion and a moral influence is in France an active interference and a political power. They alone among Catholic subjects can bring a pressure to bear on him who has had the initiative in the Italian movement. They fear by silence to incur a responsibility for criminal acts. For them it is a season for action, and the time has not yet come when they can speak with judicial impartiality, or with the freedom of history, or determine how far, in the pursuit of his ambitious ends, Napoleon III is the instrument of Providence, or how far, without any merit of his own, he is likely to fulfil the expectations of those who see in him a new Constantine. Whilst they maintain this unequal war, they naturally identify the rights of the Church with her interests; and the wrongs of the Pope are before their eyes so as to eclipse the realities of the Roman government. The most vehement and one-sided of those who have dwelt exclusively on the crimes of the Revolution and the justice of the Papal cause, the Bishop of Orleans for instance, or Count de Montalembert, might without inconsistency, and doubtless would without hesitation, subscribe to almost every word in Döllinger's work; but in the position they have taken they would probably deem such adhesion a great rhetorical error, and fatal to the effect of their own writings. There is, therefore, an allowance to be made, which is by no means a reproach, for the peculiar situation of the Catholics in France.

When Christine of Sweden was observed to gaze long and intently at the statue of Truth in Rome, a court-like prelate observed that this admiration for Truth did her honour, as it was seldom shared by persons in her station. "That," said the Queen, "is because truths are not all made of marble." Men are seldom zealous for an idea in which they do not perceive some reflection of themselves, in which they have not embarked some portion of their individuality, or which they cannot connect with some subjective purpose of their own. It is often more easy to sympathise with a person in whose opposite views we discern a weakness corresponding to our own, than with one who unsympathetically avoids to colour the objectivity of truth, and is guided in his judgment by facts, not by wishes. We endeavoured not many months ago to show how remote the theology of Catholic Germany is in its scientific spirit from that of other countries, and how far asunder are science and policy. The same method applied to the events of our own day must be yet more startling, and for a time we can scarcely anticipate that the author of this work will escape an apparent isolation between the reserve of those who share his views, but are not free to speak, and the foregone conclusions of most of those who have already spoken. But a book which treats of contemporary events in accordance with the signs of the time, not with the aspirations of men, possesses in time itself an invincible auxiliary. When the lesson which this great writer draws from the example of the mediaeval Popes has borne its fruit; when the purpose for which he has written is attained, and the freedom of the Holy See from revolutionary aggression and arbitrary protection is recovered by the heroic determination to abandon that which in the course of events has ceased to be a basis of independence— he will be the first, but no longer the only, proclaimer of new ideas, and he will not have written in vain.

The Christian religion, as it addresses and adapts itself to all mankind, bears towards the varieties of national character a relation of which there was no example in the religions of antiquity, and which heresy repudiates and inevitably seeks to destroy. For heresy, like paganism, is national, and dependent both on the particular disposition of the people and on the government of the State. It is identified with definite local conditions, and moulded by national and political peculiarities. Catholicity alone is universal in its character and mission, and independent of those circumstances by which States are established, and nations are distinguished from each other. Even Rome had not so far extended her limits, nor so thoroughly subjugated and amalgamated the races that obeyed her, as to secure the Church from the natural reaction of national spirit against a religion which claimed a universality beyond even that of the Imperial power. The first and most terrible assault of ethnicism was in Persia, where Christianity appeared as a Roman, and therefore a foreign and a hostile, system. As the Empire gradually declined, and the nationalities, no longer oppressed beneath a vigorous central force, began to revive, the heresies, by a natural affinity, associated themselves with them. The Donatist schism, in which no other country joined, was an attempt of the African people to establish a separate national Church. Later on, the Egyptians adopted the Monophysite heresy as the national faith, which has survived to this day in the Coptic Church. In Armenia similar causes produced like effects.

In the twelfth century—not, as is commonly supposed, in the time of Photius and Cerularius, for religious communion continued to subsist between the Latins and the Greeks at Constantinople till about the time of Innocent III, but after the Crusades had embittered the antagonism between East and West—another great national separation occurred. In the Eastern Empire the communion with Rome was hateful to the two chief authorities. The patriarch was ambitious to extend his own absolute jurisdiction over the whole Empire, the emperor wished to increase that power as the instrument of his own: out of this threefold combination of interests sprang the Byzantine system. It was founded on the ecclesiastical as well as civil despotism of the emperor, and on the exclusive pride of the people in its nationality; that is, on those things which are most essentially opposed to the Catholic spirit, and to the nature of a universal Church. In consequence of the schism, the sovereign became supreme over the canons of the Church and the laws of the State; and to this imperial papacy the Archbishop of Thessalonica, in the beginning of the fifteenth century, justly attributes the ruin and degradation of the Empire. Like the Eastern schism, the schism of the West in the fourteenth century arose from the predominance of national interests in the Church: it proceeded from the endeavour to convert the Holy See into a possession of the French people and a subject of the French crown. Again, not long after, the Hussite revolution sprang from the union of a new doctrine with the old antipathy of the Bohemians for the Germans, which had begun in times when the boundaries of Christianity ran between the two nations, and which led to a strictly national separation, which has not yet exhausted its political effects. Though the Reformation had not its origin in national feelings, yet they became a powerful instrument in the hands of Luther, and ultimately prevailed over the purely theological elements of the movement.

The Lutheran system was looked on by the Germans with patriotic pride as the native fruit, and especial achievement of the genius of their country, and it was adopted out of Germany only by the kindred races of Scandinavia. In every other land to which it has been transplanted by the migrations of this century, Lutheranism appears as eradicated from its congenial soil, loses gradually its distinctive features, and becomes assimilated to the more consolatory system of Geneva. Calvinism exhibited from the first no traces of the influence of national character, and to this it owes its greater extension; whilst in the third form of Protestantism, the Anglican Church, nationality is the predominant characteristic. In whatever country and in whatever form Protestantism has prevailed, it has always carried out the principle of separation and local limitation by seeking to subject itself to the civil power, and to confine the Church within the jurisdiction of the State. It is dependent not so much on national character as on political authority, and has grafted itself rather on the State than on the people. But the institution which Christ founded in order to collect all nations together in one fold under one shepherd, while tolerating and respecting the natural historical distinctions of nations and of States, endeavours to reconcile antagonism, and to smooth away barriers between them, instead of estranging them by artificial differences, and erecting new obstacles to their harmony. The Church can neither submit as a whole to the influence of a particular people, nor impose on one the features or the habits of another; for she is exalted in her catholicity above the differences of race, and above the claims of political power. At once the most firm and the most flexible institution in the world, she is all things to all nations—educating each in her own spirit, without violence to its nature, and assimilating it to herself without prejudice to the originality of its native character. Whilst she thus transforms them, not by reducing them to a uniform type, but by raising them towards a common elevation, she receives from them services in return. Each healthy and vigorous nation that is converted is a dynamic as well as a numerical increase in the resources of the Church, by bringing an accession of new and peculiar qualities, as well as of quantity and numbers. So far from seeking sameness, or flourishing only in one atmosphere, she is enriched and strengthened by all the varieties of national character and intellect. In the mission of the Catholic Church, each nation has its function, which its own position and nature indicate and enable it to fulfil. Thus the extinct nations of antiquity survive in the beneficial action they continue to exert within her, and she still feels and acknowledges the influence of the African or of the Cappadocian mind.

The condition of this immunity from the predominant influence of national and political divisions, and of this indifference to the attachment of particular States and races—the security of unity and universality—consists in the existence of a single, supreme, independent head. The primacy is the bulwark, or rather the corner-stone, of Catholicism; without it, there would be as many churches as there are nations or States. Not one of those who have denounced the Papacy as a usurpation has ever attempted to show that the condition which its absence necessarily involves is theologically desirable, or that it is the will of God. It remains the most radical and conspicuous distinction between the Catholic Church and the sects. Those who attempt to do without it are compelled to argue that there is no earthly office divinely appointed for the government of the Church, and that nobody has received the mission to conduct ecclesiastical affairs, and to preserve the divine order in religion. The several local churches may have an earthly ruler, but for the whole Church of Christ there is no such protection. Christ, therefore, is the only head they acknowledge, and they must necessarily declare separation, isolation, and discord to be a principle and the normal condition of His Church. The rejection of the primacy of St. Peter has driven men on to a slippery course, where all the steps are downwards. The Greeks first proclaimed that they recognised no Pope, that each patriarch ruled over a portion of the Church. The Anglicans rejected both Pope and patriarch, and admitted no ecclesiastical order higher than the Episcopate. Foreign Protestantism refused to tolerate even bishops, or any authority but the parish clergy under the supremacy of the ruler of the land. Then the sects abolished the local jurisdiction of the parish clergy, and retained only preachers. At length the ministry was rejected as an office altogether, and the Quakers made each individual his own prophet, priest, and doctor.

The Papacy, that unique institution, the Crown of the Catholic system, exhibits in its history the constant working of that law which is at the foundation of the life of the Church, the law of continuous organic development. It shared the vicissitudes of the Church, and had its part in everything which influences the course and mode of her existence. In early times it grew in silence and obscurity, its features were rarely and imperfectly distinguishable; but even then the Popes exerted their authority in all directions, and while the wisdom with which it was exercised was often questioned, the right itself was undisputed. So long as the Roman Empire upheld in its strong framework and kept together the Church, which was confined mostly within its bounds, and checked with the stern discipline of a uniform law the manifestations of national and local divergence, the interference of the Holy See was less frequently required, and the reins of Church government did not need to be tightly drawn. When a new order of States emerged from the chaos of the great migration, the Papacy, which alone stood erect amid the ruins of the empire, became the centre of a new system and the moderator of a new code. The long contest with the Germanic empire exhausted the political power both of the empire and of the Papacy, and the position of the Holy See, in the midst of a multitude of equal States, became more difficult and more unfavourable. The Popes were forced to rely on the protection of France, their supremacy over the States was at an end, and the resistance of the nations commenced. The schism, the opposition of the general Councils, the circumstances which plunged the Holy See into the intrigues of Italian politics, and at last the Reformation, hastened the decline of that extensive social and political power, the echoes and reminiscences of which occasioned disaster and repulse whenever an attempt was made to exercise it. Ever since the Tridentine age, the Popes have confined themselves more and more exclusively to the religious domain; and here the Holy See is as powerful and as free at the present day as at any previous period of its history. The perils and the difficulties which surround it arise from temporal concerns—from the state of Italy, and from the possessions of the pontifical dominions.

As the Church advances towards fulness and maturity in her forms, bringing forward her exhaustless resources, and calling into existence a wealth of new elements—societies, corporations, and institutions— so is the need more deeply felt for a powerful supreme guide to keep them all in health and harmony, to direct them in their various spheres, and in their several ways towards the common ends and purposes of all, and thus to provide against decay, variance, and confusion. Such an office the Primacy alone can discharge, and the importance of the Papacy increases as the organisation of the Church is more complete. One of its most important but most delicate duties is to act as an independent, impartial, and dispassionate mediator between the churches and the governments of the different States, and between the conflicting claims and contradictory idiosyncrasies of the various nations. Yet, though the Papacy is so obviously an essential part of a Church whose mission is to all mankind, it is the chosen object of attack both to enemies of Catholicism and to discontented Catholics. Serious and learned men complain of its tyranny, and say that it claims universal dominion, and watches for an opportunity of obtaining it; and yet, in reality, there is no power on earth whose action is restricted by more sacred and irresistible bonds than that of the Holy See. It is only by the closest fidelity to the laws and tradition of the Church that the Popes are able to secure the obedience and the confidence of Catholics. Pius VII, who, by sweeping away the ancient church of France, and depriving thirty-seven protesting bishops of their sees, committed the most arbitrary act ever done by a Pope, has himself described the rules which guided the exercise of his authority:

> The nature and constitution of the Catholic Church impose on the Pope, who is the head of the church, certain limits which he cannot transgress. . . . The Bishops of Rome have never believed that they could tolerate any alteration in those portions of the discipline which are directly ordained by Jesus Christ; or in those which, by their nature, are connected with dogma, or in those which heretics assail in support of their innovations.

The chief points urged against the ambition of Rome are the claim of the deposing Power, according to the theory that all kinds of power are united in the Church, and the protest against the Peace of Westphalia, the basis of the public law and political order of modern Europe. It is enough to cite one of the many authorities which may be cited in refutation of the first objection. Cardinal Antonelli, Prefect of Propaganda, states in his letter to the Irish bishops, 1791, that "the See of Rome has never taught that faith is not to be kept with those of another religion, or that an oath sworn to kings who are separated from the Catholic communion may be broken, or that the Pope is permitted to touch their temporal rights and possessions." The Bull in which Boniface VIII set up the theory of the supremacy of the spiritual over the secular power was retracted soon after his death.

The protest of Innocent X against the Peace of Westphalia is one of the glories of the Papacy. That peace was concluded on an unchristian and tyrannical principle, introduced by the Reformation, that the subjects may be compelled to follow the religion of the ruler. This was very different in principle and in effect from the intolerance of the ages of faith, when prince and people were members of one religion, and all were agreed that no other could be permitted in the State. Every heresy that arose in the Middle Ages involved revolutionary consequences, and would inevitably have overthrown State and society, as well as Church, wherever it prevailed. The Albigenses, who provoked the cruel legislation against heretics, and who were exterminated by fire and sword, were the Socialists of those days. They assailed the fundamental institutions of society, marriage, family, and property, and their triumph would have plunged Europe into the barbarism and licence of pagan times. The principles of the Waldenses and the Lollards were likewise incompatible with European civilisation. In those days the law relating to religion was the same for all. The Pope as well as the king would have lost his crown if he had fallen into heresy. During a thousand years, from the fall of Rome to the appearance of Luther, no Catholic prince ever made an attempt to introduce a new religion into his dominions, or to abandon the old. But the Reformation taught that this was the supreme duty of princes; whilst Luther declared that in matters of faith the individual is above every authority, and that a child could understand the Scriptures better than Popes or Councils, he taught at the same time, with an inconsistency which he never attempted to remove, that it is the duty of the civil power to exterminate popery, to set up the Gospel, and to suppress every other religion.

The result was a despotism such as the world had never seen. It was worse than the Byzantine system; for there no attempt was made to change the faith of the people. The Protestant princes exercised an ecclesiastical authority more arbitrary than the Pope had ever possessed; for the papal authority can only be used to maintain an existing doctrine, whilst theirs was aggressive and wholly unlimited. Possessing the power to command, and to alter in religion, they naturally acquired by degrees a corresponding absolutism in the civil order. The consistories, the office by which the sovereign ruled the Church, were the commencement of bureaucratic centralisation. A great lawyer of those days says, that after the treaties of Westphalia had recognised the territorial supremacy over religion, the business of administration in the German States increased tenfold. Whilst that system remained in its integrity, there could be no peaceful neighbourhood between Catholics and Protestants. From this point of view, the protest of the Pope was entirely justified. So far from having been made in the spirit of the mediaeval authority, which would have been fatal to the work of the Congress, it was never used by any Catholic prince to invalidate the treaties. They took advantage of the law in their own territories to exercise the *jus reformandi*. It was not possible for them to tolerate a body which still refused to tolerate the Catholic religion by the side of its own, which accordingly eradicated it wherever it had the means, and whose theory made the existence of every religion depend on the power and the will of the sovereign. A system which so resolutely denied that two religions could coexist in the same State, put every attempt at mutual toleration out of the question. The Reformation was a great movement against the freedom of conscience—an effort to subject it to a new authority, the arbitrary initiative of a prince who might differ in religion from all his subjects. The extermination of obstinate Catholics was a matter of course; Melanchthon insisted that the Anabaptists should be put to death, and Beza was of opinion that Anti-Trinitarians ought to be executed, even after recantation. But no Lutheran could complain when the secular arm converted him into a Calvinist. "Your conscience is in error," he would say, "but under the circumstances you are not only justified, but compelled, on my own principles, to act as you do."[2]

The resistance of the Catholic Governments to the progress of a religion which announced that it would destroy them as soon as it had the power, was an instinct of self-preservation. No Protestant divine denied or disguised the truth that his party sought the destruction of Catholicism, and would accomplish it whenever they could. The Calvinists, with their usual fearless consistency, held that as civil and ecclesiastical power must be in the same hands, no prince had any right to govern who did not belong to them. Even in the Low Countries,

---

[2] So late as 1791 Pius VI wrote: "Discrimen intercedit inter homines, qui extra gremium Ecclesiae semper fuerunt, quales sunt Infideles atque Judaei, atque inter illos qui se Ecclesiae ipsi per susceptum baptismi sacramentum subjecerunt. Primi enim constringi ad catholicam obedientiam non debent, contra vero alteri sunt cogendi." If this theory had, like that of the Protestants, been put in practice by the Government, it would have furnished the Protestants with an argument precisely similar to that by which the Catholics justified the severity they exercised towards them.

where other sects were free, and the notion of unity abandoned, the Catholics were oppressed.

This new and aggressive intolerance infected even Catholic countries, where there was neither, as in Spain, religious unity to be preserved; nor, as in Austria, a menacing danger to be resisted. For in Spain the persecution of the Protestants might be defended on the mediaeval principle of unity, whilst under Ferdinand II it was provoked in the hereditary dominions by the imminent peril which threatened to dethrone the monarch, and to ruin every faithful Catholic. But in France the Protestant doctrine that every good subject must follow the religion of his king grew out of the intensity of personal absolutism. At the revocation of the Edict of Nantes, the official argument was the will of the sovereign—an argument which in Germany had reigned so triumphantly that a single town, which had ten times changed masters, changed its religion ten times in a century. Bayle justly reproaches the Catholic clergy of France with having permitted, and even approved, a proceeding so directly contrary to the spirit of their religion, and to the wishes of the Pope. A convert, who wrote a book to prove that Huguenots were in conscience bound to obey the royal edict which proscribed their worship, met with applause a hundred years later. This fault of the French clergy was expiated in the blood of their successors.

The excess of evil led to its gradual cure. In England Protestantism lost its vigour after the victory over the Catholic dynasty; religion faded away, and with it that religious zeal which leads to persecution: when the religious antagonism was no longer kept alive by a political controversy, the sense of right and the spirit of freedom which belongs to the Anglo-Saxon race accomplished the work which indifference had begun. In Germany the vitality of the Lutheran theology expired after it had lasted for about two hundred years. The intellectual contradictions and the social consequences of the system had become intolerable to the German mind. Rationalism had begun to prevail, when Frederick II declared that his subjects should work out their salvation in their own way. That generation of men, who looked with contempt on religious zeal, looked with horror on religious persecution. The Catholic Church, which had never taught that princes are supreme over the religion of their subjects, could have no difficulty in going along with public opinion when it disapproved of compulsion in matters of conscience. It was natural that in the new order of things, when

Christendom had lost its unity, and Protestantism its violence, she should revert to the position she occupied of old, when she admitted other religions to equal rights with herself, and when men like St. Ambrose, St. Martin, and St. Leo deprecated the use of violence against heretics. Nevertheless, as the preservation of morality depends on the preservation of faith, both alike are in the interest and within the competence of the State. The Church of her own strength is not strong enough to resist the advance of heresy and unbelief. Those enemies find an auxiliary in the breast of every man whose weakness and whose passions repel him from a Church which imposes such onerous duties on her members. But it is neither possible to define the conditions without which liberty must be fatal to the State, nor the limits beyond which protection and repression become tyrannical, and provoke a reaction more terrible than the indifference of the civil power. The events of the last hundred years have tended in most places to mingle Protestants and Catholics together, and to break down the social and political lines of demarcation between them; and time will show the providential design which has brought about this great change.

These are the subjects treated in the first two chapters on "The Church and the Nations," and on the Papacy in connection with the universality of Catholicism, as contrasted with the national and political dependence of heresy. The two following chapters pursue the topic farther in a general historical retrospect, which increases in interest and importance as it proceeds from the social to the religious purpose and influence of the Papacy, and from the past to the present time. The third chapter, "The Churches and Civil Liberty," examines the effects of Protestantism on civil society. The fourth, entitled "The Churches without a Pope," considers the actual theological and religious fruits of separation from the visible Head of the Church.

The independence of the Church, through that of her Supreme Pontiff, is as nearly connected with political as with religious liberty, since the ecclesiastical system which rejects the Pope logically leads to arbitrary power. Throughout the north of Europe—in Sweden and Denmark, in Mecklenburg and Pomerania, in Prussia, Saxony, and Brunswick—the power which the Reformation gave to the State introduced an unmitigated despotism. Every security was removed which protected the people against the abuse of the sovereign power, and the lower against the oppression of the upper class. The crown became, sooner or later, despotic; the peasantry, by a long series of enactments, extending to the end of the seventeenth century, was reduced to servitude; the population grew scanty, and much of the land went out of cultivation. All this is related by the Protestant historians and divines, not in the tone of reluctant admission, but with patriotic indignation, commensurate with the horrors of the truth. In all these countries Lutheran unity subsisted. If Calvinism had ever succeeded in obtaining an equal predominance in the Netherlands, the power of the House of Orange would have become as despotic as that of the Danish or the Prussian sovereigns. But its triumph was impeded by sects, and by the presence of a large Catholic minority, destitute indeed of political rights or religious freedom, but for that very reason removed from the conflicts of parties, and therefore an element of conservatism, and a natural ally of those who resisted the ambition of the Stadtholders. The absence of religious unity baffled their attempts to establish arbitrary power on the victory of Calvinism, and upheld, in conjunction with the brilliant policy abroad, a portion of the ancient freedom. In Scotland, the other home of pure Calvinism, where intolerance and religious tyranny reached a pitch equalled only among the Puritans in America, the perpetual troubles hindered the settlement of a fixed political system, and the restoration of order after the union with England stripped the Presbyterian system of its exclusive supremacy, and opened the way for tolerance and freedom.

Although the political spirit of Anglicanism was as despotic as that of every other Protestant system, circumstances prevented its full development. The Catholic Church had bestowed on the English the great elements of their political prosperity—the charter of their liberties, the fusion of the races, and the abolition of villeinage—that is, personal and general freedom, and national unity. Hence the people were so thoroughly impregnated with Catholicism that the Reformation was imposed on them by foreign troops in spite of an armed resistance; and the imported manufacture of Geneva remained so strange and foreign to them, that no English divine of the sixteenth century enriched it with a single original idea. The new Church, unlike those of the Continent, was the result of an endeavour to conciliate the Catholic disposition of the people, by preserving as far as possible the externals to which they were attached; whilst the queen—who was a Protestant rather by policy than by conviction—desired no greater change than was necessary for her purpose. But the divines whom she placed at

the head of the new Church were strict Calvinists, and differed from
the Puritans only in their submission to the court. The rapidly declining
Catholic party accepted Anglicanism as the lesser evil; while zealous
Protestants deemed that the outward forms ought to correspond to the
inward substance, and that Calvinistic doctrines required a Calvinistic
constitution. Until the end of the century there was no Anglican
theology; and the attempt to devise a system in harmony with the
peculiar scheme and design of the institution, began with Hooker. The
monarch was absolute master in the Church, which had been established as an instrument of royal influence; and the divines acknowledged
his right by the theory of passive obedience. The consistent section of
the Calvinists was won over, for a time, by the share which the gentry
obtained in the spoils of the Church, and by the welcome concession
of the penal laws against her, until at last they found that they had in
their intolerance been forging chains for themselves. One thing alone,
which our national jurists had recognised in the fifteenth century as
the cause and the sign of our superiority over foreign States—the
exclusion of the Roman code, and the unbroken preservation of the
common law—kept England from sinking beneath a despotism as
oppressive as that of France or Sweden.

As the Anglican Church under James and Charles was the bulwark
of arbitrary power, the popular resistance took the form of ecclesiastical
opposition. The Church continued to be so thoroughly committed to
the principle of unconditional submission to the power from which it
derived its existence, that James II could reckon on this servile spirit
as a means of effecting the subversion of the Establishment; and Defoe
reproached the bishops with having by their flattery led on the king,
whom they abandoned in the moment of his need. The Revolution,
which reduced the royal prerogative, removed the oppressiveness of
the royal supremacy. The Established Church was not emancipated
from the crown, but the Nonconformists were emancipated from the
tyranny of the Established Church. Protestantism, which in the period
of its power dragged down by its servility the liberties of the nation,
did afterwards, in its decay and disorganisation, by the surrender of
its dogmatic as well as of its political principle, promote their recovery
and development. It lost its oppressiveness in proportion as it lost its
strength, and it ceased to be tyrannical when divines had been forced
to give up its fundamental doctrine, and when its unity had been
dissolved by the sects. The revival of those liberties which, in the

Middle Ages, had taken root under the influence of the Church, coincided with the progress of the Protestant sects, and with the decay of the penal laws. The contrast between the political character of those countries in which Protestantism integrally prevailed, and that of those in which it was divided against itself, and could neither establish its system nor work out its consequences, is as strongly marked as the contrast between the politics of Catholic times and those which were introduced by the Reformation. The evil which it wrought in its strength was turned to good by its decline.

Such is the sketch of the effects of the Protestant apostasy in the political order, considered chiefly in relation to the absence of a supreme ecclesiastical authority independent of political control. It would require far more space to exhibit the positive influence of heretical principles on the social foundations of political life; and the picture would not be complete without showing the contrast exhibited by Catholic States, and tracing their passage from the mediaeval system under the influence of the reaction against the Reformation. The third chapter covers only a portion of this extensive subject; but it shows the action of the new mode of ecclesiastical government upon the civil order, and proves that the importance of the Papacy is not confined to its religious sphere. It thus prepares the way for the subject discussed in the fourth chapter—the most comprehensive and elaborate in the book.

Dr. Döllinger begins his survey of the churches that have renounced the Pope with those of the Eastern schism. The Patriarch of Constantinople, whose ecclesiastical authority is enormous, and whose opportunities of extorting money are so great that he is generally deposed at the end of two or three years, in order that many may succeed each other in the enjoyment of such advantages, serves not as a protection, but as an instrument for the oppression of the Christians. The Greek clergy have been the chief means by which the Turks have kept down both the Greek and the Slavonic population, and the Slavs are by degrees throwing off their influence. Submission to the civil power is so natural in communities separated from the Universal Church, that the Greeks look up to the Turkish authorities as arbiters in ecclesiastical matters. When there was a dispute between Greeks and Armenians respecting the mixture of water with the wine in the chalice, the question was referred for decision to the proper quarter, and the Reis Effendi decided that, wine being condemned by the Koran, water alone might be used. Yet to this pusillanimous and degenerate Church belong the future of European Turkey, and the inheritance of the sinking power of the Turks. The vitality of the dominant race is nearly exhausted, and the Christians—on whose pillage they live—exceed them, in increasing proportions, in numbers, prosperity, intelligence, and enterprise.

The Hellenic Church, obeying the general law of schismatical communities, has exchanged the authority of the patriarch for that of the crown, exercised through a synod, which is appointed on the Russian model by the Government. The clergy, disabled for religious purposes by the necessity of providing for their families, have little education and little influence, and have no part in the revival of the Grecian intellect. But the people are attached to their ecclesiastical system, not for religion's sake, for infidelity generally accompanies education, but as the defence of their nationality.

In Russia the Catholic Church is considered heretical because of her teaching on the procession of the Holy Ghost, and schismatical in consequence of the claims of the Pope. In the doctrine of purgatory there is no essential difference; and on this point an understanding could easily be arrived at, if none had an interest in widening the breach. In the seventeenth century, the Russian Church retained so much independence that the Metropolitan of Kiev could hold in check the power of the Czar, and the clergy were the mediators between the people and the nobles or the crown. This influence was swept away by the despotism of Peter the Great; and under Catherine II the property of the Church was annexed to the crown lands, in order, it was said, to relieve the clergy of the burden of administration. Yet even now the Protestant doctrine that the sovereign is supreme in all matters of religion has not penetrated among the Russians. But though the Czar does not possess this authority over the national Church, of which he is a member, the Protestant system has conceded it to him in the Baltic provinces. Not only are all children of mixed marriages between Protestants and schismatics brought up in the religion of the latter, by which the gradual decline of Protestantism is provided for, but conversions to Protestantism, even of Jews, Mohammedans, and heathens, are forbidden; and, in all questions of doctrine or of liturgy, the last appeal is to the emperor. The religious despotism usually associated with the Russian monarchy subsists only for the Protestants.

The Russian Church is dumb; the congregation does not sing, the priest does not preach. The people have no prayer-books, and are therefore confined to the narrow circle of their own religious ideas. Against the cloud of superstition which naturally gathers in a religion of ceremonies, destitute of the means of keeping alive or cultivating the religious sentiments of the people, there is no resource. In spite of the degeneracy of their clergy, which they are unable to feel, the Russians cling with patriotic affection to their Church, and identify its progress and prosperity with the increase of their empire. As it is an exclusively national institution, every war may become a war of religion, and it is the attachment to the Church which creates the longing and the claim to possess the city from which it came. From the Church the empire derives its tendency to expand, and the Czar the hopes of that universal dominion which was promised to him by the Synod of Moscow in 1619, and for which a prayer was then appointed. The schismatical clergy of Eastern Europe are the channel of Russian influence, the pioneers of Russian aggression. The political dependence of the Church corresponds to its political influence; subserviency is the condition of the power it possesses. The certificate of Easter confession and communion is required for every civil act, and is consequently an object of traffic. In like manner, the confessor is bound to betray to the police all the secrets of confession which affect the interest of the Government. In this deplorable state of corruption, servitude, and decay within, and of threatening hostility to Christian civilisation abroad, the Russian Church pays the penalty of its Byzantine descent.

The Established Church and the sects in England furnish few opportunities of treating points which would be new to our readers. Perhaps the most suggestive portion is the description of the effects of Protestantism on the character and condition of the people. The plunder and oppression of the poor has everywhere followed the plunder of the Church, which was the guardian and refuge of the poor. The charity of the Catholic clergy aimed not merely at relieving, but at preventing poverty. It was their object not only to give alms, but to give to the lower orders the means of obtaining a livelihood. The Reformation at once checked alms-giving; so that, Selden says, in places where twenty pounds a year had been distributed formerly, not a handful of meal was given away in his time, for the wedded clergy could not afford it. The confiscation of the lands where thousands had tilled the soil under the shadow of the monastery or the Church, was followed by a new system of cultivation, which deprived the peasants of their homes. The sheep, men said, were the cause of all the woe; and whole towns were pulled down to make room for them. The prelates of the sixteenth century lament the decline of charity since the Catholic times; and a divine attributed the growing selfishness and harshness to the doctrine of justification by faith. The alteration in the condition of the poor was followed by severe enactments against vagrancy; and the Protestant legislature, after creating a proletariate, treated it as a crime. The conversion of Sunday into a Jewish Sabbath cut off the holiday amusements and soured the cheerfulness of the population. Music, singing, and dancing, the favourite relaxation of a contented people, disappeared, and, especially after the war in the Low Countries, drunkenness began to prevail among a nation which in earlier times had been reckoned the most sober of Northern Europe. The institution which introduced these changes has become a State, not a national Church, whose services are more attended by the rich than by the poor.

After describing the various parties in the Anglican system, the decay of its divinity, and the general aversion to theological research, Döllinger concludes that its dissolution is a question of time. No State Church can long subsist in modern society which professes the religion of the minority. Whilst the want of a definite system of doctrine, allowing every clergyman to be the mouthpiece, not of a church, but of a party, drives an increasing portion of the people to join the sects which have a fixed doctrine and allow less independence to their preachers, the great danger which menaces the Church comes from the State itself. The progress of dissent and of democracy in the legislature will make the Church more and more entirely dependent on the will of the majority, and will drive the best men from the communion of a servile establishment. The rise and fortunes of Methodism are related with peculiar predilection by the author, who speaks of John Wesley as the greatest intellect English Protestantism has produced, next to Baxter.

The first characteristic of Scottish Presbyterianism is the absence of a theology. The only considerable divines that have appeared in Scotland since the Reformation, Leighton and Forbes, were prelates of the Episcopal Church. Calvinism was unable to produce a theological literature, in spite of the influence of English writers, of the example of Holland, and of the great natural intelligence of the Scots. "Their theology," says a distinguished Lutheran divine, "possesses no system of Christian ethics." This Döllinger attributes to the strictness with which they have held to the doctrine of imputation, which is incompatible with any system of moral theology. In other countries it was the same; where that doctrine prevailed, there was no ethical system, and where ethics were cultivated, the doctrine was abandoned. For a century after Luther, no moral theology was written in Germany. The first who attempted it, Calixtus, gave up the Lutheran doctrine. The Dutch historians of Calvinism in the Netherlands record, in like manner, that there the dread of a collision with the dogma silenced the teaching of ethics both in literature and at the universities. Accordingly, all the great Protestant moralists were opposed to the Protestant doctrine of justification. In Scotland the intellectual lethargy of churchmen is not confined to the department of ethics; and Presbyterianism only prolongs its existence by suppressing theological writing, and by concealing the contradictions which would otherwise bring down on the clergy the contempt of their flocks.

Whilst Scotland has clung to the original dogma of Calvin, at the price of complete theological stagnation, the Dutch Church has lost its primitive orthodoxy in the progress of theological learning. Not one of the several schools into which the clergy of the Netherlands are divided has remained faithful to the five articles of the synod of Dortrecht, which still command so extensive an allegiance in Great Britain and America. The conservative party, headed by the statesman and historian, Groen van Prinsterer, who holds fast to the theology which is so closely interwoven with the history of his country and with the fortunes of the reigning house, and who invokes the aid of the secular arm in support of pure Calvinism, is not represented at the universities. For all the Dutch divines know that the system cannot be revived without sacrificing the theological activity by which it has been extinguished. The old confessional writings have lost their authority; and the general synod of 1854 decided that, "as it is impossible to reconcile all opinions and wishes, even in the shortest confession, the Church tolerates divergence from the symbolical books." The only unity, says Groen, consists in this, that all the preachers are paid out of the same fund. The bulk of the clergy are Arminians or Socinians. From the spectacle of the Dutch Church, Dr. Döllinger comes to the following result: first, that without a code of doctrine laid down in authoritative confessions of faith, the Church cannot endure; secondly, that the old confessional writings cannot be maintained, and are universally given up; and thirdly, that it is impossible to draw up new ones.

French Protestantism suffered less from the Revolution than the Catholic Church, and was treated with tenderness, and sometimes with favour. The dissolution of Continental Protestantism began in France. Before their expulsion in 1685, the French divines had cast off the yoke of the Dortrecht articles, and in their exile they afterwards promoted the decline of Calvinism in the Netherlands. The old Calvinistic tradition has never been restored, the works of the early writers are forgotten, no new theological literature has arisen, and the influence of Germany has borne no considerable fruit. The evangelical party, or Methodists, as they are called, are accused by the rest of being the cause of their present melancholy state. The rationalism of the *indifférens* generally prevails among the clergy, either in the shape of the naturalism of the eighteenth century (Coquerel), or in the more advanced form of modern criticism, as it is carried out by the faculty of Strasburg, with the aid of German infidelity. Payment by the State and hatred of Catholicism are the only common marks of French Protestant divines. They have no doctrine, no discipline, no symbol, no theology. Nobody can define the principle or the limits of their community.

The Calvinism of Switzerland has been ruined in its doctrine by the progress of theology, and in its constitution by the progress of democracy. In Geneva the Church of Calvin fell in the revolutions of 1841 and 1846. The symbolical books are abolished; the doctrine is based on the Bible; but the right of free inquiry is granted to all; the ruling body consists of laymen. "The faith of our fathers," says Merle d'Aubigné, "counts but a small group of adherents amongst us." In the canton of Vaud, where the whole ecclesiastical power was in the hands of the Government, the yoke of the democracy became insupportable, and the excellent writer, Vinet, seceded with 180 ministers out of 250. The people of Berne are among the most bitter enemies of Catholicism in Europe. Their fanaticism crushed the Sonderbund; but the recoil drove them towards infidelity, and hastened the decrease of devotion and of the influence of the clergy. None of the German Swiss, and few of the French, retain in its purity the system of Calvin. The unbelief of the clergy lays the Church open to the attacks of a Caesaropapistic democracy. A Swiss Protestant divine said recently: "Only a

Church with a Catholic organisation could have maintained itself without a most extraordinary descent of the Holy Spirit against the assaults of Rationalism." "What we want," says another, "in order to have a free Church, is pastors and flocks; dogs and wolves there are in plenty."

In America it is rare to find people who are openly irreligious. Except some of the Germans, all Protestants generally admit the truth of Christianity and the authority of Scripture. But above half of the American population belongs to no particular sect, and performs no religious functions. This is the result of the voluntary principle, of the dominion of the sects, and of the absence of an established Church, to receive each individual from his birth, to adopt him by baptism, and to bring him up in the atmosphere of a religious life. The majority of men will naturally take refuge in indifference and neutrality from the conflict of opinions, and will persuade themselves that where there are so many competitors, none can be the lawful spouse. Yet there is a blessing on everything that is Christian, which can never be entirely effaced or converted into a curse. Whatever the imperfections of the form in which it exists, the errors mixed up with it, or the degrading influence of human passion, Christianity never ceases to work immeasurable social good. But the great theological characteristic of American Protestantism is the absence of the notion of the Church. The prevailing belief is, that in times past there was always a war of opinions and of parties, that there never was one unbroken vessel, and that it is necessary, therefore, to put up with fragments, one of which is nearly as good as another. Sectarianism, it is vaguely supposed, is the normal condition of religion. Now a sect is, by its very nature, instinctively adverse to a scientific theology; it feels that it is short-lived, without a history, and unconnected with the main stream of ecclesiastical progress, and it is inspired with hatred and with contempt for the past, for its teaching and its writings. Practically, sectaries hold that a tradition is the more surely to be rejected the older it is, and the more valuable in proportion to the lateness of its origin. As a consequence of the want of roots in the past, and of the thirst for novelty, the history of those sects which are not sunk in lethargy consists in sudden transitions to opposite extremes. In the religious world ill weeds grow apace; and those communities which strike root, spring up, and extend most rapidly are the least durable and the least respectable. The sects of Europe were transplanted into America: but there the impatience of authority, which is the basis of social and political life, has produced in religion a variety and a multiplicity, of which Europe has no experience.

Whilst these are the fruits of religious liberty and ecclesiastical independence among a people generally educated, the Danish monarchy exhibits unity of faith strictly maintained by keeping the people under the absolute control of the upper class, on whose behalf the Reformation was introduced, and in a state of ignorance corresponding to their oppression. Care was taken that they should not obtain religious instruction, and in the beginning of the eighteenth century the celebrated Bishop Pontoppidan says, "an almost heathen blindness pervades the land." About the same time the Norwegian prelates declared, in a petition to the King of Denmark: "If we except a few children of God, there is only this difference between us and our heathen ancestors, that we bear the name of Christians." The Danish Church has given no signs of life, and has shown no desire for independence since the Reformation; and in return for this submissiveness, the Government suppressed every tendency towards dissent. Things were not altered when the tyranny of the nobles gave way to the tyranny of the crown; but when the revolution of 1848 had given the State a democratic basis, its confessional character was abrogated, and whilst Lutheranism was declared the national religion, conformity was no longer exacted. The king is still the head of the Church, and is the only man in Denmark who must be a Lutheran. No form of ecclesiastical government suitable to the new order of things has yet been devised, and the majority prefer to remain in the present provisional state, subject to the will of a Parliament, not one member of which need belong to the Church which it governs. Among the clergy, those who are not Rationalists follow the lead of Grundtvig. During many years this able man has conducted an incessant resistance against the progress of unbelief and of the German influence, and against the Lutheran system, the royal supremacy, and the parochial constitution. Not unlike the Tractarians, he desires the liberty of establishing a system which shall exclude Lutheranism, Rationalism, and Erastianism; and he has united in his school nearly all who profess positive Christianity in Denmark. In Copenhagen, out of 150,000 inhabitants, only 6000 go regularly to church. In Altona, there is but one church for 45,000 people. In Schleswig the churches are few and empty. "The great evil," says a Schleswig divine, "is not the oppression which falls on the German tongue, but the irreligion and consequent demoralisation which Denmark has imported into Schleswig. A moral and religious tone is the exception, not the rule, among the Danish clergy."

The theological literature of Sweden consists almost entirely of translations from the German. The clergy, by renouncing study, have escaped Rationalism, and remain faithful to the Lutheran system. The king is supreme in spirituals, and the Diet discusses and determines religious questions. The clergy, as one of the estates, has great political influence, but no ecclesiastical independence. No other Protestant clergy possesses equal privileges or less freedom. It is usual for the minister after the sermon to read out a number of trivial local announcements, sometimes half an hour long; and in a late Assembly the majority of the bishops pronounced in favour of retaining this custom, as none but old women and children would come to church for the service alone.

In no other country in Europe is the strict Lutheran system preached but in Sweden. The doctrine is preserved, but religion is dead, and the Church is as silent and as peaceful as the churchyard. The Church is richly endowed; there are great universities, and Swedes are among the foremost in almost every branch of science, but no Swedish writer has ever done anything for religious thought. The example of Denmark and its Rationalist clergy brought home to them the consequences of theological study. In one place the old system has been preserved, like a frail and delicate curiosity, by excluding the air of scientific inquiry, whilst in the other Lutheranism is decomposing under its influence. In Norway, where the clergy have no political representation, religious liberty was established in 1844.

Throughout the north of Europe the helpless decline of Protestantism is betrayed by the numerical disproportion of preachers to the people. Norway, with a population of 1,500,000, thinly scattered over a very large territory, has 485 parishes, with an average of 3600 souls apiece. But the clergy are pluralists, and as many as five parishes are often united under a single incumbent. Holstein has only 192 preachers for an almost exclusively Lutheran population of 544,000. In Schleswig many parishes have been deserted because they were too poor to maintain a clergyman's family. Sometimes there are only two ministers for 13,000 persons. In the Baltic provinces the proportion is one to 4394. In this way the people have to bear the burden of a clergy with families to support.

The most brilliant and important part of this chapter is devoted to the state of Protestantism in the author's native country. He speaks with the greatest authority and effect when he comes near home, describes the opinions of men who have been his rivals in literature, or his adversaries in controversy, and touches on discussions which his own writings have influenced. There is a difference also in the tone. When he speaks of the state of other countries, with which he has made himself acquainted as a traveller, or through the writings of others, he preserves the calmness and objectivity of a historian, and adds few reflections to the simple description of facts. But in approaching the scenes and the thoughts of his own country, the interests and the most immediate occupations of his own life, the familiarity of long experience gives greater confidence, warmth, and vigour to his touch; the historian gives way to the divine, and the narrative sometimes slides into theology. Besides the position of the author, the difference of the subject justifies a change in the treatment. The examination of Protestantism in the rest of the world pointed with monotonous uniformity to a single conclusion. Everywhere there was the same spectacle and the same alternative: either religion sacrificed to the advancement of learning, or learning relinquished for the preservation of religion. Everywhere the same antagonism between intellectual progress and fidelity to the fundamental doctrines of Protestantism: either religion has become stark and stagnant in States which protect unity by the proscription of knowledge, or the progress of thought and inquiry has undermined belief in the Protestant system, and driven its professors from one untenable position to another, or the ascendency of the sectarian spirit has been equally fatal to its dogmatic integrity and to its intellectual development. But in the home of the Reformation a league has been concluded in our time between theology and religion, and many schools of Protestant divines are labouring, with a vast expenditure of ability and learning, to devise, or to restore, with the aid of theological science, a system of positive Christianity. Into this great scene of intellectual exertion and doctrinal confusion the leading adversary of Protestantism in Germany conducts his readers, not without sympathy for the high aims which inspire the movement, but with the almost triumphant security which belongs to a Church possessing an acknowledged authority, a definite organisation, and a system brought down by tradition from the apostolic age. Passing by the schools of infidelity, which have no bearing on the topic of his work, he addresses himself to the believing Protestantism of Germany, and considers its efforts to obtain a position which may enable it to resist unbelief without involving submission to the Church.

The character of Luther separates the German Protestants from those of other countries. His was the master-spirit, in whom his contemporaries beheld the incarnation of the genius of their nation. In the strong lineaments of his character they recognised, in heroic proportions, the reflection of their own; and thus his name has survived, not merely as that of a great man, the mightiest of his age, but as the type of a whole period in the history of the German people, the centre of a new world of ideas, the personification of those religious and ethical opinions which the country followed, and whose influence even their adversaries could not escape. His writings have long ceased to be popular, and are read only as monuments of history; but the memory of his person has not yet grown dim. His name is still a power in his own country, and from its magic the Protestant doctrine derives a portion of its life. In other countries men dislike to be described by the name of the founder of their religious system, but in Germany and Sweden there are thousands who are proud of the name of Lutheran.

The results of his system prevail in the more influential and intelligent classes, and penetrate the mass of the modern literature of Germany. The Reformation had introduced the notion that Christianity was a failure, and had brought far more suffering than blessings on mankind; and the consequences of that movement were not calculated to impress educated men with the belief that things were changed for the better, or that the reformers had achieved the work in which the Apostles were unsuccessful. Thus an atmosphere of unbelief and of contempt for everything Christian gradually arose, and Paganism appeared more cheerful, more human, and more poetical than the repulsive Galilean doctrine of holiness and privation. This spirit still governs the educated class. Christianity is abominated both in life and in literature, even under the form of believing Protestantism.

In Germany theological study and the Lutheran system subsisted for two centuries together. The controversies that arose from time to time developed the theory, but brought out by degrees its inward contradictions. The danger of biblical studies was well understood, and the Scriptures were almost universally excluded from the universities in the seventeenth century; but in the middle of the eighteenth Bengel revived the study of the Bible, and the dissolution of the Lutheran doctrine began. The rise of historical learning hastened the process. Frederic the Great says of himself, that the notion that the history of the Church is a drama, conducted by rogues and hypocrites, at the expense of the deceived masses, was the real cause of his contempt for the Christian religion. The Lutheran theology taught, that after the Apostolic age God withdrew from the Church, and abandoned to the devil the office which, according to the Gospel, was reserved for the Holy Spirit. This diabolical millennium lasted till the appearance of Luther. As soon, therefore, as the reverence for the symbolical books began to wane, the belief in the divine foundation departed with the belief in the divine guidance of the Church, and the root was judged by the stem, the beginning by the continuation. As research went on, unfettered now by the authorities of the sixteenth century, the clergy became Rationalists, and stone after stone of the temple was carried away by its own priests. The infidelity which at the same time flourished in France, did not, on the whole, infect the priesthood. But in Germany it was the divines who destroyed religion, the pastors who impelled their flocks to renounce the Christian faith.

In 1817 the Prussian Union added a new Church to the two original forms of Protestantism. But strict Calvinism is nearly extinct in Germany, and the old Lutheran Church itself has almost disappeared. It subsists, not in any definite reality, but only in the aspirations of certain divines and jurists. The purpose of the union was to bring together, in religious communion, the reigning family of Prussia, which had adopted Calvinism in 1613, and the vast Lutheran majority among the people. It was to be, in the words of the king, a merely ritual union, not an amalgamation of dogmas. In some places there was resistance, which was put down by military execution. Some thousands emigrated to America; but the public press applauded the measures, and there was no general indignation at their severity. The Lutherans justly perceived that the union would promote religious indifference; but at the accession of the late king there came a change; religious faith was once more sought after, believing professors were appointed in almost all the German universities, after the example of Prussia; Jena and Giessen alone continued to be seats of Rationalism. As soon as theology had begun to recover a more religious and Christian character, two very divergent tendencies manifested themselves. Among the disciples of Schleiermacher and of Neander a school of unionists arose who attempted a conciliatory intermediate theology. At the same time a strictly Lutheran theology flourished at the universities of Erlangen, Leipzig, Rostock, and Dorpat, which sought to revive the doctrine of the sixteenth century, clothed in the language of the nineteenth. But for men versed in Scripture theology this was an impossible enterprise, and it was abandoned by the divines to a number of parochial clergymen, who are represented in literature by Rudelbach, and who claim to be the only surviving Protestants whom Luther would acknowledge as his sons and the heirs of his spirit.

The Lutheran divines and scholars formed the new Lutheran party,[3] whose most illustrious lay champion was the celebrated Stahl. They profess the Lutheran doctrine of justification, but reject the notion of the invisible Church and the universal priesthood. Holding to the divine institution of the offices of the Church, in opposition to the view which refers them to the congregation, they are led to assume a sacrament of orders, and to express opinions on ordination, sacraments, and sacrifice, which involve them in the imputation of Puseyism, or even of Catholicism. As they remain for the most part in the State Church, there is an open war between their confessional spirit and the syncretism of the union. In 1857 the Evangelical Alliance met at Berlin in order to strengthen the unionist principles, and to testify against these Pharisees. Baptists, Methodists, and Presbyterians—sects connected by nothing but a common hatred of Catholicism—were greeted by the union divines as bone of their bone, and welcome allies in the contest with an exclusive Lutheranism and with Rome. The confusion in the minds of the people was increased by this spectacle. The union already implied that the dogma of the Lord's Supper, on which Lutherans and Calvinists disagree, was uncertain, and therefore not essential. The alliance of so many denominations added baptism to the list of things about which nothing is positively known. The author of this measure was Bunsen, who was full of the idea of uniting all Protestant sects in a union against the Catholic Church and catholicising tendencies.

For the last fifteen years there has been an active agitation for the improvement of the Church among the Protestant divines. The first question that occupies and divides them is that of Church government and the royal Episcopate, which many deem the chief cause of the ecclesiastical decay. The late King of Prussia, a zealous and enlightened friend of the Protestant Church, declared that "the territorial system

---

[3] The works contained in Clark's library of translations are chiefly of this school.

and the Episcopal authority of the sovereign are of such a nature that either of them would alone be enough to kill the Church if the Church was mortal," and that he longed to be able to abdicate his rights into the hands of the bishops. In other countries, as in Baden, a new system has been devised, which transfers political constitutionalism to the Church, and makes it a community, not of those who believe in Christ, but, in the words of the Government organ, of those who believe in a moral order. Hopes were entertained that the introduction of Synods would be an improvement, and in 1856 and 1857 a beginning was made at Berlin; but it was found that the existence of great evils and disorders in the Church, which had been a secret of the initiated, would be published to the world, and that government by majorities, the ecclesiastical democracy which was Bunsen's ideal, would soon destroy every vestige of Christianity.

In their doctrinal and theological literature resides at the present day the strength and the renown of the Protestants; for a scientific Protestant theology exists only in Germany. The German Protestant Church is emphatically a Church of theologians; they are its only authority, and, through the princes, its supreme rulers. Its founder never really divested himself of the character of a professor, and the Church has never emancipated itself from the lecture-room: it teaches, and then disappears. Its hymns are not real hymns, but versified theological dissertations, or sermons in rhyme. Born of the union of princes with professors, it retains the distinct likeness of both its parents, not altogether harmoniously blended; and when it is accused of worldliness, of paleness of thought, of being a police institution rather than a Church, that is no more than to say that the child cannot deny its parentage.

Theology has become believing in Germany, but it is very far from being orthodox. No writer is true to the literal teaching of the symbolical books, and for a hundred years the pure doctrine of the sixteenth century has never been heard. No German divine could submit to the authority of the early articles and formulas without hypocrisy and violence of his conscience, and yet they have nothing else to appeal to. That the doctrine of justification by faith only is the principal substance of the symbolical writings, the centre of the antagonism against the Catholic Church, all are agreed. The neo-Lutherans proclaim it "the essence and treasure of the Reformation," "the doctrine of which every man must have a clear and vivid comprehension who would know anything of Christianity," "the banner which must be unfurled at least once in every sermon," "the permanent death that gnaws the bones of Catholics," "the standard by which the whole of the Gospel must be interpreted, and every obscure passage explained," and yet this article of a standing or falling Church, on the strength of which Protestants call themselves evangelical, is accepted by scarcely one of their more eminent divines, even among the Lutherans. The progress of biblical studies is too great to admit of a return to the doctrine which has been exploded by the advancement of religious learning. Dr. Döllinger gives a list (p. 430) of the names of the leading theologians, by all of whom it has been abandoned. Yet it was for the sake of this fundamental and essential doctrine that the epistle of St. James was pronounced an epistle of straw, that the Augsburg Confession declared it to have been the belief of St. Augustine, and that when the author of the Confession had for very shame omitted this falsehood in the published edition, the passage was restored after his death. For its sake Luther deliberately altered the sense of several passages in the Bible, especially in the writings of St. Paul. To save this doctrine, which was unknown to all Christian antiquity, the breach was made with all ecclesiastical tradition, and the authority of the dogmatic testimony of the Church in every age was rejected. While the contradiction between the Lutheran doctrine and that of the first centuries was disguised before the laity, it was no secret among the Reformers. Melanchthon confessed to Brenz that in the Augsburg Confession he had lied. Luther admitted that his theory was new, and sought in consequence to destroy the authority of the early Fathers and Councils. Calvin declared that the system was unknown to tradition. All these men and their disciples, and the whole of the Lutheran and Calvinistic theology of the sixteenth and seventeenth centuries, professed to find their doctrine of imputation laid down distinctly in the Bible. The whole modern scientific theology of the Protestants rejects both the doctrine and the Lutheran exegesis of the passages in question. But it is the supreme evangelical principle, that the Scripture is perfectly clear and sufficient on all fundamental points. Yet the point on which this great divergence subsists is a doctrine which is decisive for the existence of the Church, and most important in its practical influence on life. The whole edifice of the Protestant Church and theology reposes therefore on two principles, one material, the other formal—the doctrine of imputation, and the sufficiency of the Bible. But the material principle is given up by exegesis and by dogmatic theology; and as to the formal principle, for the sufficiency of the Bible, or even for the inspiration of the writings of the disciples of the Apostles, not the shadow of a scriptural argument can be adduced. The significance of this great fact is beginning to make its way. "Whilst Rationalism prevailed," says a famous Lutheran divine, "we could impute to its action that our churches were deserted and empty. But now that Christ crucified is everywhere preached, and no serious effect is to be observed, it is necessary to abandon this mistake, and not to conceal from ourselves that preaching is unable to revive religious life."

The religious indifference of the educated classes is the chief security for the existence of the Protestant Church. If they were to take an interest in matters of worship and doctrine, and to inform themselves as to the present relation of theological science to the teaching of the pulpit, the day of discovery and exposure would come, and confidence in the Church would be at an end. The dishonesty of Luther in those very things on which the Reformation depended could not be concealed from them. In Prussia there was a conscientious clergyman who taught his parishioners Greek, and then showed them all the passages, especially in the Epistles of St. Paul, which were intentionally altered in the translation. But one of the Protestant leaders impresses on the clergy the danger of allowing the people to know that which ought to be kept a secret among the learned. At most, he says, it may be necessary to admit that the translation is not perspicuous. The danger of this discovery does not, however, appear to be immediate, for no book is less familiar to the laity than the Bible. "There is scarcely one Christian family in a hundred," says Tholuck, "in which the Holy Scriptures are read." In the midst of this general downfall of Christianity, in spite of the great efforts of Protestants, some take refuge in the phrase of an invisible Church, some in a Church of the future. Whilst there exists a real, living, universal Church, with a settled system and means of salvation, the invisible Church is offered in her stead, wrapped up in the swaddling clothes of rhetoric, like the stone which Rhea gave her husband instead of the child. In a novel of Jean Paul, a Swedish clergyman is advised in the middle of winter to walk about with a bit of orange-sugar in his mouth, in order to realise with all his senses the sunny climes of the south. It requires as much imagination to realise the Church by taking a "spiritual league" into one's mouth.

Another acknowledgment, that the Church has become estranged from the people, and subsists only as a ruin of a past age, is the widely spread hope of a new Pentecost. Eminent theologians speak of it as the only conceivable salvation, though there is no such promise in Scripture, no example in history of a similar desire. They rest their only hope in a miracle, such as has not happened since the Apostles, and thereby confess that, in the normal process of religious life by which Christ has guided His Church till now, their cause is lost. A symptom of the same despair is the rise of chiliastic aspirations, and the belief in the approaching end of the world. To this party belongs the present minister of public worship and education in Berlin. Shortly before his appointment he wrote: "Both Church and State must perish in their earthly forms, that the kingdom of Christ may be set up over all nations, that the bride of the Lamb, the perfect community, the new Jerusalem, may descend from heaven." Not long before this was published another Prussian statesman, Bunsen, had warned his Protestant readers to turn away from false prophets, who announce the end of the world because they have come to the end of their own wisdom.

In the midst of this desperate weakness, although Catholics and Protestants are so mixed up with each other that toleration must soon be universal throughout Germany, the thoughts of the Protestants are yet not turned towards the Catholic Church; they still show a bitter animosity against her, and the reproach of Catholic tendencies has for twenty years been the strongest argument against every attempt to revive religion and worship. The attitude of Protestantism towards Rome, says Stahl, is that of the Borghese gladiator. To soften this spirit of animosity the only possible resource is to make it clear to all Protestants who still hold to Christianity, what their own internal condition is, and what they have come to by their rejection of the unity and the authority which the Catholic Church possesses in the Holy See. Having shown the value of the Papacy by the results which have ensued on its rejection, Döllinger proceeds, with the same truth and impartiality, to trace the events which have injured the influence and diminished the glory and attractiveness of the Holy See, and have converted that which should be the safeguard of its spiritual freedom into a calamity and a dishonour in the eyes of mankind. It seems as though he wished to point out, as the moral to be learnt from the present condition of the religious world, that there is a coincidence in time and in providential purpose between the exhaustion and the despair at which enlightened Protestantism has arrived, from the failure of every attempt to organise a form of church government, to save the people from infidelity, and to reconcile theological knowledge with their religious faith—between this and that great drama which, by destroying the bonds which linked the Church to an untenable system, is preparing the restoration of the Holy See to its former independence, and to its just influence over the minds of men.

The Popes, after obtaining a virtual independence under the Byzantine sceptre, transferred their allegiance to the revived empire of the West. The line between their authority and that of the emperor in Rome was never clearly drawn. It was a security for the freedom and regularity of the election, which was made by the lay as well as ecclesiastical dignitaries of the city, that it should be subject to the imperial ratification; but the remoteness of the emperors, and the inconvenience of delay, caused this rule to be often broken. This prosperous period did not long continue. When the dynasty of Charlemagne came to an end, the Roman clergy had no defence against the nobles, and the Romans did all that men could do to ruin the Papacy. There was little remaining of the state which the Popes had formed in conjunction with the emperors. In the middle of the tenth century the Exarchate and the Pentapolis were in the power of Berengarius, and Rome in the hands of the Senator Alberic. Alberic, understanding that a secular principality could not last long, obtained the election of his son Octavian, who became Pope John XII. Otho the Great, who had restored the empire, and claimed to exercise its old prerogative, deposed the new Pope; and when the Romans elected another, sent him also into exile beyond the Alps. For a whole century after this time there was no trace of freedom of election. Without the emperor, the Popes were in the hands of the Roman factions, and dependence on the emperor was better for the Church than dependence on the nobles. The Popes appointed under the influence of the prelates, who were the ecclesiastical advisers of the Imperial Government, were preferable to the nominees of the Roman chiefs, who had no object or consideration but their own ambition, and were inclined to speculate on the worthlessness of their candidates. During the first half of the eleventh century they recovered their predominance, and the deliverance of the Church came once more from Germany. A succession of German Popes, named by the emperor, opened the way for the permanent reform which is associated with the name of Gregory VII. Up to this period the security of the freedom of the Holy See was the protection of the emperor, and Gregory was the last Pope who asked for the imperial confirmation.

Between the middle of the ninth century and the middle of the eleventh the greater part of the Roman territory had passed into the hands of laymen. Some portions were possessed by the emperor, some by the great Italian families, and the revenues of the Pope were derived from the tribute of his vassals. Sylvester II complains that this was very small, as the possessions of the Church had been given away for very little. Besides the tribute, the vassals owed feudal service to the Pope; but the government was not in his hands, and the imperial suzerainty remained. The great families had obtained from the Popes of their making such extensive grants that there was little remaining, and Otho III tried to make up for it by a new donation. The loss of the patrimonies in Southern Italy established a claim on the Norman conquerors, and they became papal vassals for the kingdom of Sicily. But throughout the twelfth century the Popes had no firm basis of their power in Italy. They were not always masters of Rome, and there was not a single provincial town they could reckon on. Seven Popes in a hundred years sought a refuge in France; two remained at Verona. The donation of Matilda was disputed by the emperors, and brought no material accession of territory, until Innocent III, with his usual energy, secured to the Roman Church the south of Tuscany. He was the first Pope who governed a considerable territory, and became the real founder of the States of the Church. Before him, the Popes had possessions for which they claimed tribute and service, but no State that they administered. Innocent obtained the submission of Benevento and Romagna. He left the towns to govern themselves by their own laws, demanding only military aid in case of need, and a small tribute, which was not always exacted; Viterbo, for instance, paid nothing until the fifteenth century.

The contest with Frederic II stripped the Holy See of most of these acquisitions. In many cases its civil authority was no longer acknowledged; in many it became a mere title of honour, while the real power had passed into the hands of the towns or of the nobles, sometimes into those of the bishops. Rudolph of Habsburg restored all that had been lost, and surrendered the imperial claims. But while the German influence was suspended, the influence of France prevailed over the

Papacy; and during the exile at Avignon the Popes were as helpless as if they had possessed not an acre of their own in Italy. It was during their absence that the Italian Republics fell under the tyrannies, and their dominions were divided among a swarm of petty princes. The famous expedition of Cardinal Albornoz put an end to these disorders. He recovered the territories of the Church, and became, by the Aegidian Constitutions, which survived for ages, the legislator of Romagna. In 1376 eighty towns rose up in the space of three days, declared themselves free, or recalled the princes whom Albornoz had expelled. Before they could be reduced, the schism broke out, and the Church learnt the consequences of the decline of the empire, and the disappearance of its advocacy and protectorate over the Holy See. Boniface IX sold to the republics and the princes, for a sum of money and an annual tribute, the ratification of the rights which they had seized.

The first great epoch in the history of the temporal power after the schism is the election of Eugenius IV. He swore to observe a statute which had been drawn up in conclave, by which all vassals and officers of State were to swear allegiance to the College of Cardinals in conjunction with the Pope. As he also undertook to abandon to the cardinals half the revenue, he shared in fact his authority with them. This was a new form of government, and a great restriction of the papal power; but it did not long endure.

The centrifugal tendency, which broke up Italy into small principalities, had long prevailed, when at last the Popes gave up to it. The first was Sixtus IV, who made one of his nephews lord of Imola, and another of Sinigaglia. Alexander VI subdued all the princes in the States of the Church except the Duke of Montefeltro, and intended to make the whole an hereditary monarchy for his son. But Julius II recovered all these conquests for the Church, added new ones to them, and thus became, after Innocent III, and Albornoz, the third founder of the Roman State. The age which beheld this restoration was marked in almost every country by the establishment of political unity on the ruins of the mediaeval independence, and of monarchical absolutism at the expense of mediaeval freedom. Both of these tendencies asserted themselves in the States of the Church. The liberties of the towns were gradually destroyed. This was accomplished by Clement VII in Ancona, in 1532; by Paul III in Perugia, in 1540. Ravenna, Faenza, Jesi had, under various pretexts, undergone the same fate. By the middle of the sixteenth century all resistance was subdued. In opposition, however, to this centralising policy, the nepotism introduced by Sixtus IV led to dismemberment. Paul III gave Parma and Piacenza to his son Pier Luigi Farnese, and the duchy was lost to the Holy See for good. Paul IV made a similar attempt in favour of his nephew Caraffa, but he was put to death under Pius IV; and this species of nepotism, which subsisted at the expense of the papal territory, came to an end. Pius V forbade, under pain of excommunication, to invest any one with a possession of the Holy See, and this law was extended even to temporary concessions.

In the eighteenth century a time came when the temporal power was a source of weakness, and a weapon by which the courts compelled the Pope to consent to measures he would otherwise never have approved. It was thus that the suppression of the Jesuits was obtained from Clement XIV. Under his successors the world had an opportunity of comparing the times when Popes like Alexander III or Innocent IV governed the Church from their exile, and now, when men of the greatest piety and conscientiousness virtually postponed their duty as head of the Church to their rights as temporal sovereigns, and, like the senators of old, awaited the Gauls upon their throne. There is a lesson not to be forgotten in the contrast between the policy and the fate of the great mediaeval pontiffs, who preserved their liberty by abandoning their dominions, and that of Pius VI and Pius VII, who preferred captivity to flight.

The nepotism of Urban VIII brought on the war of Castro, and in its train increase of debt, of taxes, impoverishment of the State, and the odious union of spiritual with temporal arms, which became a permanent calamity for the Holy See. This attachment to the interest of their families threw great discredit on the Popes, who were dishonoured by the faults, the crimes, and the punishment of their relatives. But since the death of Alexander VIII, in 1691, even that later form of nepotism which aimed at wealth only, not at political power, came to an end, and has never reappeared except in the case of the Braschi. The nepotism of the cardinals and prelates has survived that of the Popes. If the statute of Eugenius IV had remained in force, the College of Cardinals would have formed a wholesome restraint in the temporal government, and the favouritism of the papal relations would have been prevented. But the Popes acted with the absolute power which was in the spirit of the monarchies of that age. When

Paul IV announced to the Sacred College that he had stripped the house of Colonna of its possessions to enrich his nephew, and that he was at war with Spain, they listened in silence, and have been passive ever since. No European sovereignty enjoyed so arbitrary an authority. Under Julius II the towns retained considerable privileges, and looked on their annexation to the Papal State as a deliverance from their former oppressors. Machiavelli and Guicciardini say that the Popes required neither to defend nor to administer their dominions, and that the people were content in the enjoyment of their autonomy. In the course of the sixteenth century the administration was gradually centralised in Rome, and placed in the hands of ecclesiastics. Before 1550 the governors were ordinarily laymen, but the towns themselves preferred to be governed by prelates. By the close of the century the independence of the corporations had disappeared; but the centralisation, though complete, was not vigorous, and practically the towns and the barons, though not free, were not oppressed.

The modern system of government in the Roman States originated with Sixtus V. He introduced stability and regularity in the administration, and checked the growth of nepotism, favouritism, and arbitrary power, by the creation of permanent congregations. In connection with this measure the prelates became the upper class of official persons in the State, and were always expected to be men of fortune. A great burden for the country was the increase of offices, which were created only to be sold. No important duties and no fixed salary were attached to them, and the incumbent had to rely on fees and extortion. In the year 1470 there were 650 places of this kind. In eighty years they had increased to 3500. The theory was, that the money raised by the sale of places saved the people from the imposition of new taxes. Innocent XII, in 1693, put an end to this traffic; but it had continued so long that the ill-effects survived.

There was a great contrast between the ecclesiastical administration, which exhibited a dignified stability, resting on fixed rules and ancient traditions, and the civil government, which was exposed to continual fluctuation by the change of persons, of measures, and of systems; for few Popes continued the plans of their predecessors. The new Pontiff commenced his reign generally with a profound sense of the abuses and of the discontent which prevailed before his elevation, and naturally sought to obtain favour and improvement by opposite measures. In the cultivation of the Roman Campagna, for instance, it was observed that each Pope followed a different system, so that little was accomplished. The persons were almost always changed by the new Pope, so that great offices rarely remained long in the same hands. The Popes themselves were seldom versed in affairs of State, and therefore required the assistance of statesmen of long experience. In the eleventh, twelfth, and thirteenth centuries, when the election was free from outward influence, men were generally chosen who had held under one or two Popes the highest office of state—Gregory VII, Urban II, Gelasius II, Lucius II, Alexander III, Gregory VIII, Gregory IX, Alexander IV. But in modern times it has been the rule that the Secretary of State should not be elected, and that the new Pope should dismiss the heads of the administration. Clement IX was the first who gave up this practice, and retained almost all those who had been employed under his predecessor.

The burdens of the State increased far beyond its resources from the aid which the Popes gave to the Catholic Powers, especially in the Turkish wars. At the beginning of the seventeenth century the debt amounted to 12,242,620 *scudi*, and the interest absorbed three-fourths of the whole income. In 1655 it had risen to 48,000,000 *scudi*. The financial administration was secret, free from the control of public accounts, and the *Tesoriere*, being necessarily a cardinal, was irresponsible. There was no industry in the towns; they remained for the most part small and poor; almost all articles of common use were imported, and the country had little to give in exchange. All the interest of the public debt went to foreign creditors. As early as 1595 the discontent was very great, and so many emigrated, in order to escape the heavy burdens, that Cardinal Sacchetti said, in 1664, that the population was reduced by one-half. In the year 1740 the president De Brosses found the Roman Government the most defective but the mildest in Europe. Becattini, in his panegyrical biography of Pius VI, declares that it was the worst after that of Turkey. There were none of those limitations which in other countries restrained the power of the monarch, no fundamental laws, no coronation oath, no binding decrees of predecessors, no provincial estates, no powerful corporations. But, in reality, this unlimited absolutism was softened by custom, and by great indulgence towards individuals.

When Consalvi adopted the French institutions, he did not understand that an absolute government is intolerable, and must sink under the weight of its responsibility, unless it recognises the restraint of custom and tradition, and of subordinate, but not dependent forces. The unity and uniformity he introduced were destructive. He restored none of the liberties of the towns, and confided the administration to ecclesiastics superficially acquainted with law, and without knowledge of politics or of public economy. In the ecclesiastical States of Germany, the civil and religious departments were separate; and it is as wrong to say that the double position of the head must repeat itself throughout the administration, as to say that a king, because he is the head of the army as well as of the civil government, ought to mix the two spheres throughout the State. It would, in reality, be perfectly possible to separate the political and ecclesiastical authorities.

Leo XII attempted to satisfy the *Zelanti*, the adversaries of Consalvi, by restoring the old system. He abolished the provincial Councils, revived the Inquisition, and subjected official honesty and public morality to a strict espionage. Leo saw the error of Consalvi, but mistook the remedy; and his government was the most unpopular that had been seen for a century. Where the laity are excluded from the higher offices, and the clergy enjoy the monopoly of them, that moral power which modern bureaucracy derives from the corporate spirit, and the feelings of honour which it inspires, cannot subsist. One class becomes demoralised by its privileged position, the other by its limited prospects and insufficient pay. Leo tried to control them by the *congregazione di vigilanza*, which received and examined all charges against official persons; but it was suppressed by his successor.

The famous Memorandum of the Powers, 31st May 1831, recommended the admission of the laity to all secular offices, the restoration of the provincial Councils, and the introduction of elective communal Councils with the power of local government; and finally, a security against the changes incident to an elective sovereignty. The historian Coppi, who was charged to draw up a plan of reform in reply to these demands, relates that the Pope and the majority of the cardinals rejected every serious change, and were resolved to uphold the old principles, and to concede nothing to the lay party, "because, if anything was voluntarily conceded, there would be no right of recalling it afterwards." Two things in particular it was determined not to grant—elective Councils in the towns and provinces, and a lay Council of State beside the Sacred College. In a general way, vague reforms were promised; but the promise was not redeemed. Austria would not tolerate any liberal concessions in Italy which were in contradiction with her own system and her own interests; thus all Italian aspirations for reforms were concentrated in the wish to get rid of the foreign yoke, and Austria never succeeded in forming a party amongst the Italians favourable to her power. Yet Gregory XVI knew that great changes were needed. In 1843 he said:

> The civil administration requires a great reform. I was too old when I was elected; I did not expect to live so long, and had not the courage to begin the undertaking. For whoever begins, must accomplish it. I have now only a few more years to live; perhaps only a few days. After me they will choose a young Pope, whose mission it will be to perform the act, without which it is impossible to go on.

The Austrian occupation caused the Roman Government to be identified with the foreign supremacy, and transferred to it the hatred of the patriots. The disaffection of the subjects of the Pope had deeper motives. Except the clergy, that overshadows all, there are no distinct orders in the society of the Roman State; no country nobility, no wealthy class of peasant proprietors; nothing but the population of the towns, and the degenerate class of patricians. These were generally hostile to the ecclesiastical system. The offices are so distributed, that the clergy govern, and the laity are their instruments. In the principal departments, no amount of services or ability could raise a layman above a certain level, beyond which younger and less competent ecclesiastics were promoted over his head. This subordination, which led to a regular dependence of the lay officials on the prelates, drove the best men away from the service of the State, and disposed the rest to long for a government which should throw open to them the higher prizes of their career. Even the country people, who were never tainted with the ideas of the secret societies, were not always well affected.

It is more difficult for a priest than for a layman to put aside his private views and feelings in the administration of justice. He is the servant and herald of grace, of forgiveness, of indulgence, and easily forgets that in human concerns the law is inexorable, that favour to one is often injury to many or to all, and that he has no right to place his own will above the law. He is still more disqualified for the direction of the police, which, in an absolute State and in troubled times, uses its unlimited power without reference to Christian ideas, leaves unpunished acts which are grievous sins, and punishes others which in a religious point of view are innocent. It is hard for the people to distinguish clearly the priestly character from the action of its bearer in the administration of police. The same indifference to the strict letter of the law, the same confusion between breaches of divine and of human ordinances, led to a practice of arbitrary imprisonment, which contrasts painfully with the natural gentleness of a priestly government. Hundreds of persons were cast into prison without a trial or even an examination; only on suspicion, and kept there more than a year for greater security.

The immunities of the clergy were as unpopular as their power. The laws and decrees of the Pope as a temporal sovereign were not held to be binding on them unless it was expressly said, or was clear from the context, that they were given also in his character of Head of the Church. Ecclesiastics were tried before their own tribunals, and had the right to be more lightly punished than laymen for the same delinquency. Those events in the life of Achilli, which came out at his trial, had not only brought down on him no severe punishment, but did not stand in the way of his promotion. With all these privileges, the bulk of the Roman clergy had little to do; little was expected of them, and their instruction was extremely deficient.

At the end of the pontificate of Gregory XVI the demand for reforms was loud and universal, and men began to perceive that the defects of the civil government were undermining the religious attachment of the people. The conclave which raised Pius IX to the Papal throne was the shortest that had occurred for near three hundred years. The necessity of choosing a Pontiff disposed to understand and to satisfy the pressing requirements of the time, made it important to hasten matters in order to escape the interference of Austria. It was expected that Cardinal Gizzi or Cardinal Mastai would be elected. The latter had been pointed out by Gregory XVI as his fittest successor, and he made Gizzi Secretary of State. The first measure of the new reign, the amnesty, which, as Metternich said, threw open the doors of the house to the professional robbers, was taken not so much as an act of policy, as because the Pope was resolved to undo an accumulation of injustice. The reforms which followed soon made Pius the most popular of Italian princes, and all Catholics rejoiced that the reconciliation of the Papacy with modern freedom was at length accomplished, and that the shadow which had fallen on the priesthood throughout the world was removed with the abuses in the Roman Government. The Constitution was, perhaps, an inevitable though a fatal necessity. "The Holy Father must fall," said his minister, "but at least he will fall with honour."

The preliminary conditions of constitutional life were wanting—habits of self-government in the towns and provinces, security from the vexations of the police, separation of spiritual and temporal jurisdiction. It could not be but that the existence of an elective chamber must give to the lay element a preponderance in the State, whilst in the administration the contrary position was maintained. There could be no peaceful solution of this contradiction, and it is strange that the cardinals, who were unanimously in favour of the statute, should not have seen that it would lead to the destruction of the privileges of the clergy. But in the allocution of 20th April 1849, the Pope declared that he had never intended to alter the character of his government; so that he must have thought the old system of administration by ecclesiastics compatible with the working of the new Constitution. At his return from exile all his advisers were in favour of abrogating all the concessions of the first years of his reign. Balbo and Rosmini visited him at Gaeta, to plead for the Constitution, but they obtained nothing. Pius IX was persuaded that every concession would be a weapon in the hands of the Radicals. A lay *consulta* gave to the laity a share of the supreme government; but the chief offices and the last decision remained, as before, in the hands of the prelates. Municipal reforms were promised. In general the old defects continued, and the old discontent was not conciliated.

It is manifest that Constitutionalism, as it is ordinarily understood, is not a system which can be applied to the States of the Church. It could not be tolerated that a warlike faction, by refusing supplies, should compel the Pope to go to war with a Christian nation, as they sought to compel him to declare war against Austria in 1848. His sovereignty must be real, not merely nominal. It makes no difference whether he is in the power of a foreign State or of a parliamentary majority. But real sovereignty is compatible with a participation of the people in legislation, the autonomy of corporations, a moderate freedom of the press, and the separation of religion and police.

Recent events would induce one to suppose that the enormous power of the press and of public opinion, which it forms and reflects, is not understood in Rome. In 1856 the Inquisitor at Ancona issued an edict, threatening with the heaviest censures all who should omit to denounce the religious or ecclesiastical faults of their neighbours, relatives, or superiors; and in defiance of the general indignation, and of the despondency of those who, for the sake of religion, desired reforms in the States of the Church, the *Civiltà Cattolica* declared that the Inquisitor had done his duty. Such cases as this, and those of Achilli and Mortara, weighed more heavily in the scale in which the Roman State is weighed than a lost battle. Without discussing the cases themselves, it is clear what their influence has been on public opinion, with which it is more important at the present day to treat than with the governments which depend on it. This branch of diplomacy has been unfortunately neglected, and hence the Roman Government cannot rely on lay support.

After describing the evils and disorders of the State, which the Pope so deeply felt that he put his own existence in peril, and inflamed half of Europe with the spirit of radical change in the attempt to remove them, Dr. Döllinger contrasts, with the gloomy picture of decay and failure, the character of the Pontiff who attempted the great work of reform.

> Nevertheless, the administration of Pius IX is wise, benevolent, indulgent, thrifty, attentive to useful institutions and improvements. All that proceeds from Pius IX personally is worthy of a head of the Church—elevated, liberal in the best sense of the term. No sovereign spends less on his court and his own private wants. If all thought and acted as he does, his would be a model State. Both the French and the English envoys affirm that the financial administration had improved, that the value of the land was increasing, agriculture flourishing, and that many symptoms of progress might be observed. Whatever can be expected of a monarch full of affection for his people, and seeking his sole recreation in works of beneficence, Pius richly performs. *Pertransiit benefaciendo*—words used of one far greater—are simply the truth applied to him. In him we can clearly perceive how the Papacy, even as a temporal state, might, so far as the character of the prince is concerned, through judicious elections, be the most admirable of human institutions. A man in the prime of life, after an irreproachable youth and a conscientious discharge of Episcopal duties, is elevated to the highest dignity and to sovereign power. He knows nothing of expensive amusements; he has no other passion but that of doing good, no other ambition but to be beloved by his subjects. His day is divided between prayer and the labours of government; his relaxation is a walk in the garden, a visit to a church, a prison, or a charitable institution. Free from personal desires and from terrestrial bonds, he has no relatives, no favourites to provide for. For him the rights and powers of his office exist only for the sake of its duties. . . . Grievously outraged, injured, rewarded with ingratitude, he has never harboured a thought of revenge, never committed an act of severity, but ever forgiven and ever pardoned. The cup of sweetness and of bitterness, the cup of human favour and of human aversion, he has not only tasted, but emptied to the dregs; he heard them cry "Hosannah!" and soon after

"Crucifige!" The man of his confidence, the first intellectual power of his nation, fell beneath the murderer's knife; the bullet of an insurgent struck down the friend by his side. And yet no feeling of hatred, no breath of anger could ever obscure, even for a moment, the spotless mirror of his soul. Untouched by human folly, unmoved by human malice, he proceeds with a firm and regular step on his way, like the stars of heaven.

Such I have seen the action of this Pope in Rome, such it has been described to me by all, whether near him or afar; and if he now seems to be appointed to pass through all the painful and discouraging experience which can befall a monarch, and to continue to the end the course of a prolonged martyrdom, he resembles in this, as in so many other things, the sixteenth Louis; or rather; to go up higher, he knows that the disciple is not above the Master, and that the pastor of a church, whose Lord and Founder died upon the cross, cannot wonder and cannot refuse that the cross should be laid also upon him (pp. 624–627).

It is a common opinion, that the Pope, as a sovereign, is bound by the common law to the forms and ideas of the Middle Ages; and that in consequence of the progress of society, of the difference between the thirteenth century and the nineteenth, there is an irreconcilable discord between the Papacy and the necessities of civil government. All Catholics are bound to oppose this opinion. Only that which is of Divine institution is unchangeable through all time. But the sovereignty of the Popes is extremely elastic, and has already gone through many forms. No contrast can be stronger than that between the use which the Popes made of their power in the thirteenth or the fifteenth century, and the system of Consalvi. There is no reason, therefore, to doubt, that it will now, after a violent interruption, assume the form best adapted to the character of the age and the requirements of the Italian people. There is nothing chimerical in the vision of a new order of things, in which the election shall fall on men in the prime of their years and their strength; in which the people shall be reconciled to their government by free institutions and a share in the conduct of their own concerns, and the upper classes satisfied by the opening of a suitable career in public affairs. Justice publicly and speedily administered would obtain the confidence of the people; the public service would be sustained by an honourable *esprit de corps*; the chasm between laity and priesthood would be closed by equality in rights and duties; the police would not rely on the help of religion, and religion would no longer drag itself along on the crutches of the police. The integrity of the Papal States would be under the joint guardianship of the Powers, who have guaranteed even the dominions of the Sultan;

and the Pope would have no enemies to fear, and his subjects would be delivered from the burden of military service and of a military budget.

Religious liberty is not, as the enemies of the Holy See declare, and some even of its friends believe, an insurmountable difficulty. Events often cut the knots which appear insoluble to theory. Attempts at proselytising have not hitherto succeeded among the subjects of the Pope; but if it had been otherwise, would it have been possible for the Inquisition to proceed against a Protestant? The agitation that must have ensued would be a welcome opportunity to put an end to what remains of the temporal power. It is true that the advance of Protestantism in Italy would raise up a barrier between the Pope and his subjects; but no such danger is to be apprehended. At the time when the doctrines of the Reformation exercised an almost magical power over mankind, they never took root in Italy beyond a few men of letters; and now that their power of attraction and expansion has long been exhausted, neither Sardinian policy nor English gold will succeed in seducing the Italians to them.

The present position of helpless and humiliating dependence will not long endure. The determination of the Piedmontese Government to annex Rome is not more certain than the determination of the Emperor Napoleon to abrogate the temporal power. Pius IX would enjoy greater security in Turkey than in the hands of a State which combines the tyranny of the Convention, the impudent sophistry of a government of advocates, and the ruthless brutality of military despotism. Rather than trust to Piedmont, may Pius IX remember the example of his greatest predecessors, who, relying on the spiritual might of the Papacy, sought beyond the Alps the freedom which Italy denied to them. The Papacy has beheld the rise and the destruction of many thrones, and will assuredly outlive the kingdom of Italy, and other monarchies besides. It can afford to wait; *patiens quia aeternus*. The Romans need the Pope more than the Pope needs Rome. Above the Catacombs, among the Basilicas, beside the Vatican, there is no place for a tribune or for a king. We shall see what was seen in the fourteenth century: envoys will come from Rome to entreat the Pope to return to his faithful city.

Whilst things continue as they are, the emperor can, by threatening to withdraw his troops, compel the Pope to consent to anything not actually sinful. Such a situation is alarming in the highest degree for other countries. But for the absolute confidence that all men have in the fidelity and conscientiousness of the present Pope, and for the providential circumstance that there is no ecclesiastical complication which the French Government could use for its own ends, it would not be tolerated by the rest of the Catholic world. Sooner or later these conditions of security will disappear, and the interest of the Church demands that before that happens, the peril should be averted, even by a catastrophe.

The hostility of the Italians themselves to the Holy See is the tragic symptom of the present malady. In other ages, when it was assailed, the Italians were on its side, or at least were neutral. Now they require the destruction of the temporal power, either as a necessary sacrifice for the unity and greatness of their country, or as a just consequence of incurable defects. The time will come, however, when they will be reconciled with the Papacy, and with its presence as a Power among them. It was the dependence of the Pope on the Austrian arms, and his identification in popular opinion with the cause of the detested foreigner, that obscured his lofty position as the moral bulwark and protector of the nation. For 1500 years the Holy See was the pivot of Italian history, and the source of the Italian influence in Europe. The nation and the See shared the same fortunes, and grew powerful or feeble together. It was not until the vices of Alexander VI and his predecessors had destroyed the reverence which was the protection of Italy, that she became the prey of the invaders. None of the great Italian historians has failed to see that they would ruin themselves in raising their hands against Rome. The old prophecy of the *Papa Angelico*, of an Angel Pope, who was to rise up to put an end to discord and disorder, and to restore piety and peace and happiness in Italy, was but the significant token of the popular belief that the Papacy and the nation were bound up together, and that one was the guardian of the other. That belief slumbers, now that the idea of unity prevails, whilst the Italians are attempting to put the roof on a building without walls and without foundations, but it will revive again, when centralisation is compelled to yield to federalism, and the road to the practicable has been found in the search after impossibilities.

The tyrannical character of the Piedmontese Government, its contempt for the sanctity of public law, the principles on which it treats the clergy at home, and the manner in which it has trampled on the rights of the Pope and the interests of religion, the perfidy and despotism it exhibits, render it impossible that any securities it may offer to the Pope can possess a real value. Moreover, in the unsettled state of the kingdom, the uncertain succession of parties, and the fluctuation of power, whatever guarantee is proposed by the ministry, there is nobody to guarantee the guarantor. It is a system without liberty and without stability; and the Pope can never be reconciled to it, or become a dweller in the new Italian kingdom.

If he must choose between the position of a subject and of an exile, he is at home in the whole Catholic world, and wherever he goes he will be surrounded by children who will greet him as their father. It may become an inevitable, but it must always be a heroic resolution. The court and the various congregations for the administration of the affairs of the Church are too numerous to be easily moved. In former times the machinery was more simple, and the whole body of the pontifical government could be lodged in a single French monastery. The absence of the Pope from Rome will involve great difficulties and annoyance; but it is a lesser evil than a surrender of principle, which cannot be recalled.

To remove the Holy See to France would, under present circumstances, be an open challenge to a schism, and would afford to all who wish to curtail the papal rights, or to interrupt the communication between the Pope and the several churches, the most welcome pretexts, and it would put arms in the hands of governments that wish to impede the action of his authority within their States.

The conclusion of the book is as follows:

> If the Court of Rome should reside for a time in Germany, the Roman prelates will doubtless be agreeably surprised to discover that our people is able to remain Catholic and religious without the leading-strings of a police, and that its religious sentiments are a better protection to the Church than the episcopal *carceri*, which, thank God, do not exist. They will learn that the Church in Germany is able to maintain herself without the Holy Office; that our bishops, although, or because, they use no physical compulsion, are reverenced like princes by the people, that they are received with triumphal arches, that their arrival in a place is a festival for the inhabitants. They will see how the Church with us rests on the broad, strong, and healthy basis of a well-organised system of pastoral administration and of popular religious instruction. They will perceive that we Catholics have maintained for years the struggle for the deliverance of the Church from the bonds of bureaucracy straightforwardly and without reservation; that we cannot entertain the idea of denying to the Italians what we have claimed for ourselves; and that therefore we are far from thinking that it is anywhere

an advantage to fortify the Church with the authority of the police and with the power of the secular arm. Throughout Germany we have been taught by experience the truth of Fénelon's saying, that the spiritual power must be carefully kept separate from the civil, because their union is pernicious. They will find, further, that the whole of the German clergy is prepared to bless the day when it shall learn that the free sovereignty of the Pope is assured, without sentence of death being still pronounced by ecclesiastics, without priests continuing to discharge the functions of treasury-clerks or police directors, or to conduct the business of the lottery. And, finally, they will convince themselves that all the Catholics of Germany will stand up as one man for the independence of the Holy See, and the legitimate rights of the Pope; but that they are no admirers of a form of government of very recent date, which is, in fact, nothing else than the product of the mechanical polity of Napoleon combined with a clerical administration. And this information will bear good fruit when the hour shall strike for the return, and restitution shall be made . . . .

Meanwhile Pius IX and the men of his Council will "think upon the days of old, and have in their minds the eternal years." They will read the future in the earlier history of the Papacy, which has already seen many an exile and many a restoration. The example of the resolute, courageous Popes of the Middle Ages will light the way. It is no question now of suffering martyrdom, of clinging to the tombs of the Apostles, or of descending into the catacombs; but of quitting the land of bondage, in order to exclaim on a free soil, "Our bonds are broken, and we are free!" For the rest God will provide, and the unceasing gifts and sympathies of the Catholic world. And the parties in Italy, when they have torn and exhausted the land which has become a battle-field; when the sobered and saddened people, tired of the rule of lawyers and of soldiers, has understood the worth of a moral and spiritual authority, then will be the time to think of returning to the Eternal City. In the interval, the things will have disappeared for whose preservation such pains are taken; and then there will be better reason than Consalvi had, in the preface to the *Motu Proprio* of 6th July 1816, to say: "Divine Providence, which so conducts human affairs that out of the greatest calamity innumerable benefits proceed, seems to have intended that the interruption of the papal government should prepare the way for a more perfect form of it."

We have written at a length for which we must apologise to our readers; and yet this is but a meagre sketch of the contents of a book which deals with a very large proportion of the subjects that occupy the thoughts and move the feelings of religious men. We will attempt to sum up in a few words the leading ideas of the author. Addressing a mixed audience, he undertakes to controvert two different interpretations of the events which are being fulfilled in Rome. To the Protestants, who triumph in the expected downfall of the Papacy, he shows the consequences of being without it. To the Catholics, who see in the Roman question a great peril to the Church, he explains how the possession of the temporal sovereignty had become a greater misfortune than its loss for a time would be. From the opposite aspects of the religious camps of our age he endeavours to awaken the misgivings of one party, and to strengthen the confidence of the other. There is an inconsistency between the Protestant system and the progress of modern learning; there is none between the authority of the Holy See and the progress of modern society. The events which are tending to deprive the Pope of his territory are not to be, therefore, deplored, if we consider the preceding causes, because they made this catastrophe inevitable; still less if, looking to the future, we consider the state of Protestantism, because they remove an obstacle to union which is humanly almost insurmountable. In a former work Döllinger exhibited the moral and intellectual exhaustion of Paganism as the prelude to Christianity. In like manner he now confronts the dissolution and spiritual decay of Protestantism with the Papacy. But in order to complete the contrast, and give force to the vindication, it was requisite that the true function and character of the Holy See should not be concealed from the unpractised vision of strangers by the mask of that system of government which has grown up around it in modern times. The importance of this violent disruption of the two authorities consists in the state of religion throughout the world. Its cause lies in the deficiences of the temporal power; its end in the mission of the spiritual.

The interruption of the temporal sovereignty is the only way we can discern in which these deficiences can be remedied and these ends obtained. But this interruption cannot be prolonged. In an age in which the State throughout the Continent is absolute, and tolerates no immunities; when corporations have therefore less freedom than individuals, and the disposition to restrict their action increases in proportion to their power, the Pope cannot be independent as a subject. He must, therefore, be a sovereign, the free ruler of an actual territory, protected by international law and a European guarantee. The restoration consequently is necessary, though not as an immediate consequence of the revolution. In this revolutionary age the protection of the Catholic Powers is required against outward attack. They must also be our security that no disaffection is provoked within; that there shall be no recurrence of the dilemma between the right of insurrection against an arbitrary government and the duty of obedience to the

Pope; and that civil society shall not again be convulsed, nor the pillars of law and order throughout Europe shaken, by a revolution against the Church, of which, in the present instance, the conservative powers share the blame, and have already felt the consequences.

In the earnest and impressive language of the conclusion, in which Döllinger conveys the warnings which all Transalpine Catholicism owes to its Head as an Italian sovereign, it seems to us that something more definite is intended than the expression of the wish, which almost every Catholic feels, to receive the Pope in his own country. The anxiety for his freedom which would be felt if he took refuge in France, would be almost equally justified by his presence in Austria. A residence in an exclusively Catholic country, such as Spain, would be contrary to the whole spirit of this book, and to the moral which it inculcates, that the great significance of the crisis is in the state of German Protestantism. If the position of the Catholics in Germany would supply useful lessons and examples to the Roman court, it is also from the vicinity of the Protestant world that the full benefit can best be drawn from its trials, and that the crimes of the Italians, which have begun as calamities, may be turned to the advantage of the Church. But against such counsels there is a powerful influence at work. Napoleon has declared his determination to sweep away the temporal power. The continuance of the occupation of Rome, and his express prohibition to the Piedmontese government to proceed with the annexation during the life of the present Pope, signify that he calculates on greater advantages in a conclave than from the patient resolution of Pius IX. This policy is supported by the events in Italy in a formidable manner. The more the Piedmontese appear as enemies and persecutors, the more the emperor will appear as the only saviour; and the dread of a prolonged exile in any Catholic country, and of dependence for subsistence on the contributions of the faithful, must exhibit in a fascinating light the enjoyment of the splendid hospitality and powerful protection of France. On these hopes and fears, and on the difficulties which are pressing on the cardinals from the loss of their revenues, the emperor speculates, and persuades himself that he will be master of the next election. On the immovable constancy of her Supreme Pontiff the Catholic Church unconditionally relies; and we are justified in believing that, in an almost unparalleled emergency, he will not tremble before a resolution of which no Pope has given an example since the consolidation of the temporal power.

[7]
Cardinal Wiseman and
The Home and Foreign
Review

Ⅰt is one of the conditions inseparable from a public career to be often misunderstood, and sometimes judged unfairly even when understood the best. No one who has watched the formation of public opinion will be disposed to attribute all the unjust judgments which assail him to the malice of individuals, or to imagine that he can prevent misconceptions or vindicate his good name by words alone. He knows that even where he has committed no errors he must pay tribute to the fallibility of mankind, and that where he is in fault he must also pay tribute to his own. This is a natural law; and the purer a man's conscience is, and the more single his aim, the less eager will he be to evade it, or to defend himself from its penalties.

The man whose career is bound up with that of some school or party will estimate the value of his opponents' censures by the worth which he attributes to the undiscriminating praise of his friends; but he who has devoted himself to the development of principles which will not always bend to the dictates of expediency will have no such short way of dealing with objections. His independence will frequently and inexorably demand the sacrifice of interests to truth—of what is politic to what is right; and, whenever he makes that sacrifice, he will appear a traitor to those whom he is most anxious to serve, while his act will be hailed by those who are farthest from sharing his opinions as a proof of secret sympathy, and harbinger of future alliance. Thus,

Published in *The Home and Foreign Review* 1 (October 1862):501–520. Döllinger I, p. 278; Acton-Simpson III, pp. 34, 62. Acton supplied the ideas for this article; the actual writing was done by Richard Simpson and Thomas Frederick Wetherell. Reprinted in Acton, *History of Freedom*, pp. 436–460.

the censure which he incurs will most often come from those whose views are essentially his own; and the very matter which calls it forth will be that which elicits the applause of adversaries who cannot bring themselves to believe either in the truth of his opinions, in the integrity of his motives, or in the sincerity of his aims.

There are few men living whose career has been more persistently misinterpreted, more bitterly assailed, or more ignorantly judged, than the illustrious person who is the head in England of the Church to which we belong. Cardinal Wiseman has been for many years the chief object of the attacks of those who have desired to injure or degrade our community. He is not only the canonical chief of English Catholics, but his ability, and the devotion of his life to their cause, have made him their best representative and their most powerful champion. No prelate in Christendom is more fully trusted by the Holy See, or exercises a more extensive personal influence, or enjoys so wide a literary renown. Upon him, therefore, intolerance and fanaticism have concentrated their malice. He has had to bear the brunt of that hatred which the holiness of Catholicism inspires in its enemies; and the man who has never been found wanting when the cause of the Church was at stake may boast, with a not unworthy pride, of the indifference with which he has encountered the personal slander of a hostile press.

The Catholics of this country are attached to Cardinal Wiseman by warmer feelings and more personal ties than those of merely ecclesiastical subordination. It has been his privilege to gather the spiritual fruits of the Catholic Emancipation Act; and the history of English Catholicism has been, for a whole generation, bound up with his name. That immense change in the internal condition of the Church in England which distinguishes our days from the time of Milner has grown up under his influence, and has been in great part his work. We owe it to him that we have been brought into closer intercourse with Rome, and into contact with the rest of Europe. By his preaching and his spiritual direction he has transformed the devotions of our people; while his lectures and writings have made Protestants familiar with Catholic ideas, and have given Catholics a deeper insight into their own religion. As a controversialist he influenced the Oxford movement more deeply than any other Catholic. As director of the chief literary organ of Catholics during a quarter of a century he rendered services to our literature, and overcame difficulties, which none are in a better position to appreciate than those who are engaged in a similar work. And as President of Oscott, he acquired the enduring gratitude of hundreds who owed to his guidance the best portion of their training.

These personal relations with English Catholics, which have made him a stranger to none and a benefactor to all, have at the same time given him an authority of peculiar weight amongst them. With less unity of view and tradition than their brethren in other lands, they were accustomed, in common with the rest of Englishmen, to judge more independently and to speak more freely than is often possible in countries more exclusively Catholic. Their minds are not all cast in the same mould, nor their ideas derived from the same stock; but all alike, from bishop to layman, identify their cause with that of the Cardinal, and feel that, in the midst of a hostile people, no diversity of opinion ought to interfere with unity of action, no variety of interest with identity of feeling, no controversy with the universal reverence which is due to the position and character of the Archbishop of Westminster.

In this spirit the Catholic body have received Cardinal Wiseman's latest publication—his "Reply to the Address of his Clergy on his Return from Rome." He speaks in it of the great assemblage of the Episcopate, and of their address to the Holy Father. Among the bishops there present he was the most conspicuous, and he was President of the Commission to which the preparation of their address was intrusted. No account of it, therefore, can be more authentic than that which he is able to give. The reserve imposed by his office, and by the distinguished part he had to bear, has been to some extent neutralised by the necessity of refuting false and exaggerated rumours which were circulated soon after the meeting, and particularly two articles which appeared in *The Patrie* on the 4th and 5th of July, and in which it was stated that the address written by Cardinal Wiseman contained "most violent attacks on all the fundamental principles of modern society."

After replying in detail to the untruths of this newspaper, the Cardinal proceeds as follows:

> With far greater pain I feel compelled to advert to a covert insinuation of the same charges, in a publication avowedly Catholic, and edited in my own diocese, consequently canonically subject to my correction. Should such a misstatement, made under my own eyes, be passed over by me, it might be surmised that it could not be contradicted; and whether chronologically it preceded or followed the French account it evidently becomes my duty

to notice it, as French bishops have considered it theirs to correct the inaccuracies of their native writers.

Otherwise, in a few years, we might find reference made, as to a recognised Catholic authority, for the current and unreproved statement of what occurred at Rome, to *The Home and Foreign Review*. And that in a matter on which reprehension would have been doubly expected, if merited. In its first number the Address, which has, I believe, wonderfully escaped the censure of Protestant and infidel journals, is thus spoken of: "This Address is said to be a compromise between one which took the violent course of recommending that major excommunication should be at once pronounced against the chief enemies of the temporal power by name, and one still more moderate than the present" (*The Home and Foreign Review*, p. 264). Now this very charge about recommending excommunication is the one made by the French paper against my Address. But, leaving to the writer the chance of an error, in this application of his words, I am bound to correct it, to whomever it refers. He speaks of only two addresses: the distinction between them implies severe censure on me. I assure you that neither contained the recommendation or the sentiment alluded to.

My Brethren, I repeat that it pains me to have to contradict the repetition, in my own diocese, of foreign accusations, without the smallest pains taken to verify or disprove them with means at hand. But this can hardly excite surprise in us who know the antecedents of that journal under another name, the absence for years of all reserve or reverence in its treatment of persons or of things deemed sacred, its grazing over the very edges of the most perilous abysses of error, and its habitual preferences of uncatholic to catholic instincts, tendencies, and motives. In uttering these sad thoughts, and entreating you to warn your people, and especially the young, against such dangerous leadership, believe me I am only obeying a higher direction than my own impulses and acting under much more solemn sanctions. Nor shall I stand alone in this unhappily necessary correction.

But let us pass to more cheerful and consoling thoughts. If my connection with the preparation of the Address, from my having held, though unworthy, office in its Committee, enables and authorises me to rebut false charges against it, it has further bestowed upon me the privilege of personal contact with a body of men who justly represented the entire Episcopate, and would have represented it with equal advantage in any other period of the Church. I know not who selected them, nor do I venture to say that many other equal committees of eighteen could not have been extracted from the remainder. I think they might; but I must say that a singular wisdom seemed to me to have presided over the actual, whatever might have been any other possible, choice.

Deliberations more minute, more mutually respectful, more courteous, or at the same time more straightforward and unflinching, could hardly have been carried on. More learning in theology and canon law, more deep religious feeling, a graver sense of the responsibility laid upon the Commission, or a more scrupulous regard to the claims of justice, and no less of mercy, could scarcely have been exhibited. Its spirit was one of mildness, of gentleness, and of reverence to all who rightly claimed it. "Violent courses," invitations to "draw the sword and rush on enemies," or to deal about "the major excommunication by name," I deliberately assure you, were never mentioned, never insinuated, and I think I may say, never thought of by any one in the Council. In the sketches proposed by several there was not a harsh or disrespectful word about any sovereign or government; in anything I ever humbly proposed, there was not a single allusion to "King or Kaiser."

Our duty to the Cardinal and our duty to our readers alike forbid us to pass by these remarks without notice. Silence would imply either that we admitted the charge, or that we disregarded the censure; and each of these suppositions would probably be welcome to the enemies of our common cause, while both of them are, in fact, untrue. The impossibility of silence, however, involves the necessity of our stating the facts on which charges so definite and so formidable have been founded. In doing so, we shall endeavour both to exhibit the true sequence of events, and to explain the origin of the Cardinal's misapprehension; and in this way we shall reply to the charges made against us.

But we must first explicitly declare, as we have already implied, that in the Cardinal's support and approbation of our work we should recognise an aid more valuable to the cause we are engaged in than the utmost support which could be afforded to us by any other person; and that we cannot consider the terms he has used respecting us otherwise than as a misfortune to be profoundly regretted, and a blow which might seriously impair our power to do service to religion.

A Catholic Review which is deprived of the countenance of the ecclesiastical authorities is placed in an abnormal position. A germ of distrust is planted in the ground where the good seed should grow; the support which the suspected organ endeavours to lend to the Church is repudiated by the ecclesiastical rulers; and its influence in Protestant society, as an expositor of Catholic ideas, is in danger of being destroyed, because its exposition of them may be declared unsound and unfair, even when it represents them most faithfully and defends them most successfully. The most devoted efforts of its conductors are liable to be misconstrued, and perversely turned either against the Church or against the *Review* itself; its best works are infected with the suspicion with which it is regarded, and its merits become almost more perilous than its faults.

These considerations could not have been overlooked by the Cardinal when he resolved to take a step which threatened to paralyse one of the few organs of Catholic opinion in England. Yet he took that step. If an enemy had done this, it would have been enough to vindicate ourselves, and to leave the burden of an unjust accusation to be borne by its author. But since it has been done by an ecclesiastical superior, with entire foresight of the grave consequences of the act, it has become necessary for us, in addition, to explain the circumstances by which he was led into a course we have so much reason to deplore, and to show how an erroneous and unjust opinion could arise in the mind of one whom obvious motives would have disposed to make the best use of a publication, the conductors of which are labouring to serve the community he governs, and desired and endeavoured to obtain his sanction for their work. If we were unable to reconcile these two necessities—if we were compelled to choose between a forbearance dishonourable to ourselves, and a refutation injurious to the Cardinal, we should be placed in a painful and almost inextricable difficulty. For a Catholic who defends himself at the expense of an ecclesiastical superior sacrifices that which is generally of more public value than his own fair fame; and an English Catholic who casts back on Cardinal Wiseman the blame unjustly thrown on himself, hurts a reputation which belongs to the whole body, and disgraces the entire community of Catholics. By such a course, a Review which exists only for public objects would stultify its own position and injure its own cause, and *The Home and Foreign Review* has no object to attain, and no views to advance, except objects and views in which the Catholic Church is interested. The ends for which it labours, according to its light and ability, are ends by which the Church cannot but gain; the doctrine it receives, and the authority it obeys, are none other than those which command the acceptance and submission of the Cardinal himself. It desires to enjoy his support; it has no end to gain by opposing him. But we are not in this painful dilemma. We can show that the accusations of the Cardinal are unjust; and, at the same time, we can explain how naturally the suppositions on which they are founded have arisen, by giving a distinct and ample statement of our own principles and position.

The complaint which the Cardinal makes against us contains, substantially, five charges: (1) that we made a misstatement, affirming something historically false to be historically true; (2) that the falsehood consists in the statement that only two addresses were proposed in the Commission—one violent, the other very moderate—and that the address finally adopted was a compromise between these two; (3) that we insinuated that the Cardinal himself was the author of the violent address; (4) that we cast, by implication, a severe censure on that address and its author; and (5) that our narrative was derived from the same sources, and inspired by the same motives, as that given in *The Patrie*—for the Cardinal distinctly connects the two accounts, and quotes passages indifferently from both, in such a way that words which we never used might by a superficial reader be supposed to be ours.

To these charges our reply is as follows: (1) We gave the statement of which the Cardinal complains as a mere rumour current on any good authority at the time of our publication, and we employed every means in our power to test its accuracy, though the only other narratives which had then reached England were, as the Cardinal says (p. 9), too "partial and perverted" to enable us to sift it to the bottom. We stated that a rumour was current, not that its purport was true. (2) We did not speak of "only two addresses" actually submitted to the Commission. We supposed the report to mean, that of the three possible forms of address, two extreme and one mean, each of which actually had partisans in the Commission, the middle or moderate form was the one finally adopted. (3) We had no suspicion that the Cardinal had proposed any violent address at all; we did not know that such a proposal had been, or was about to be, attributed to him; and there was no connection whatever between him and it either in our mind or in our language. (4) We implied no censure either on the course proposed or on its proposer, still less on the Cardinal personally. (5) The articles in *The Patrie* first appeared—and that in France—some days after our Review was in the hands of the public; we know nothing of the authority on which their statements were founded, and we have not the least sympathy either with the politics or the motives of that newspaper.

This reply would be enough for our own defence; but it is right that we should show, on the other side, how it came to pass that the Cardinal was led to subject our words to that construction which we have so much reason to regret. Reading them by the light of his own knowledge, and through the medium of the false reports which afterwards arose with regard to himself, his interpretation of them may easily have appeared both plausible and likely. For there were more draft addresses than one: one was his; the actual address was a compromise between them, and he had been falsely accused of, and severely censured for, proposing violent courses in his address. Knowing this, he was tempted to suspect a covert allusion to himself under our words, and the chronological relation between our own article and those of the *The Patrie* was easily forgotten, or made nugatory by the supposition of their both being derived from the same sources of information.

But this will be made clearer by the following narrative of facts: A Commission was appointed to draw up the address of the bishops; Cardinal Wiseman, its president, proposed a draft address, which was not obnoxious to any of the criticisms made on any other draft, and is, in substance, the basis of the address as it was ultimately settled. It was favourably received by the Commission; but, after some deliberation, its final adoption was postponed.

Subsequently, a prelate who had been absent from the previous discussion presented another draft, not in competition with that proposed by the president, nor as an amendment to it, but simply as a basis for discussion. This second draft was also favourably received; and the Commission, rather out of consideration for the great services and reputation of its author than from any dissatisfaction with the address proposed by the president, resolved to amalgamate the two drafts. All other projects were set aside; and, in particular, two proposals were deliberately rejected. One of these proposals was, to pay a tribute of acknowledgment for the services of the French nation to the Holy See; the other was, to denounce the perfidious and oppressive policy of the Court of Turin in terms which we certainly should not think either exaggerated or undeserved. We have neither right nor inclination to complain of the ardent patriotism which has been exhibited by the illustrious Bishop of Orleans in the two publications he has put forth since his return to his See, or of the indignation which the system prevailing at Turin must excite in every man who in his heart loves the Church, or whose intelligence can appreciate the first principles of government. Whatever may have been the censure proposed, it certainly did not surpass the measure of the offence. Nevertheless, the impolicy of a violent course, which could not fail to cause irritation, and to aggravate the difficulties of the Church, appears to have been fully recognised by the Commission; and we believe that no one was more prompt in exposing the inutility of such a measure than the Cardinal himself. The idea that anything imprudent or aggressive was to be found in his draft is contradicted by all the facts of the case, and has not a shadow of foundation in anything that is contained in the address as adopted.

We need say no more to explain what has been very erroneously called our covert insinuation. From this narrative of facts our statement comes out, no longer as a mere report, but as a substantially accurate summary of events, questioned only on one point—the extent of the censure which was proposed. So that in the account which the Cardinal quoted from our pages there was no substantial statement to correct, as in fact no correction of any definite point but one has been attempted.

How this innocent statement has come to be suspected of a hostile intent, and to be classed with the calumnies of *The Patrie,* is another question. The disposition with which the Cardinal sat in judgment upon our words was founded, not on anything they contained, but, as he declares, on the antecedents of the conductors of *The Home and Foreign Review,* and on the character of a journal which no longer exists. That character he declares to consist in "the absence for years of all reserve or reverence in its treatment of persons or of things deemed sacred, its grazing over the very edges of the most perilous abysses of error, and its habitual preferences of uncatholic to catholic instincts, tendencies, and motives." In publishing this charge, which amounts to a declaration that we hold opinions and display a spirit not compatible with an entire attachment and submission of intellect and will to the doctrine and authority of the Catholic Church, the Cardinal adds, "I am only obeying a higher direction than my own impulses, and acting under much more solemn sanctions. Nor shall I stand alone in this unhappily necessary correction."

There can be little doubt of the nature of the circumstances to which this announcement points. It is said that certain papers or propositions, which the report does not specify, have been extracted from the journal which the Cardinal identifies with this Review, and forwarded to Rome for examination; that the Prefect of Propaganda has characterised these extracts, or some of them, in terms which correspond to the Cardinal's language; and that the English bishops have deliberated whether they should issue similar declarations. We have no reason to doubt that the majority of them share the Cardinal's view, which is also that of a large portion both of the rest of the clergy and also of the laity; and, whatever may be the precise action which has been taken in the matter, it is unquestionable that a very formidable mass of ecclesiastical authority and popular feeling is united against certain principles or opinions which, whether rightly or wrongly, are attributed to us. No one will suppose that an impression so general can be entirely founded on a mistake. Those who admit the bare orthodoxy of our doctrine will, under the circumstances, naturally conclude that in our way of holding or expounding it there must be something new and strange, unfamiliar and bewildering, to those who are accustomed to the prevalent spirit of Catholic literature; something which our fellow-Catholics are not prepared to admit; something which can sufficiently explain misgivings so commonly and so sincerely entertained. Others may perhaps imagine that we are unconsciously drifting away from the Church, or that we only professedly and hypocritically remain with her. But the Catholic critic will not forget that charity is a fruit of our religion, and that his anxiety to do justice to those from whom he must differ ought always to be in equal proportion with his zeal. Relying, then, upon this spirit of fairness, convinced of the sincerity of the opposition we encounter, and in order that there may remain a distinct and intelligible record of the aim to which we dedicate our labours, we proceed to make that declaration which may be justly asked of nameless writers, as a testimony of the purpose which has inspired our undertaking, and an abiding pledge of our consistency.

This Review has been begun on a foundation which its conductors can never abandon without treason to their own convictions, and infidelity to the objects they have publicly avowed. That foundation is a humble faith in the infallible teaching of the Catholic Church, a devotion to her cause which controls every other interest, and an attachment to her authority which no other influence can supplant. If in anything published by us a passage can be found which is contrary to that doctrine, incompatible with that devotion, or disrespectful to that authority, we sincerely retract and lament it. No such passage was ever consciously admitted into the pages either of the late *Rambler* or of this Review. But undoubtedly we may have committed errors in judgment, and admitted errors of fact; such mistakes are unavoidable in secular matters, and no one is exempt from them in spiritual things except by the constant assistance of Divine grace. Our wish and purpose are not to deny faults, but to repair them; to instruct, not to disturb our readers; to take down the barriers which shut out our

Protestant countrymen from the Church, not to raise up division within her pale; and to confirm and deepen, not to weaken, alter, or circumscribe the faith of Catholics.

The most exalted methods of serving religion do not lie in the path of a periodical which addresses a general audience. The appliances of the spiritual life belong to a more retired sphere—that of the priesthood, of the sacraments, of religious offices; that of prayer, meditation, and self-examination. They are profaned by exposure, and choked by the distractions of public affairs. The world cannot be taken into the confidence of our inner life, nor can the discussion of ascetic morality be complicated with the secular questions of the day. To make the attempt would be to usurp and degrade a holier office. The function of the journalist is on another level. He may toil in the same service, but not in the same rank, as the master-workman. His tools are coarser, his method less refined, and if his range is more extended, his influence is less intense. Literature, like government, assists religion, but it does so indirectly, and from without. The ends for which it works are distinct from those of the Church, and yet subsidiary to them; and the more independently each force achieves its own end, the more complete will the ultimate agreement be found, and the more will religion profit. The course of a periodical publication in its relation to the Church is defined by this distinction of ends; its sphere is limited by the difference and inferiority of the means which it employs, while the need for its existence and its independence is vindicated by the necessity there is for the service it performs.

It is the peculiar mission of the Church to be the channel of grace to each soul by her spiritual and pastoral action—she alone has this mission; but it is not her only work. She has also to govern and educate, so far as government and education are needful subsidiaries to her great work of the salvation of souls. By her discipline, her morality, her law, she strives to realise the divine order upon earth; while by her intellectual labour she seeks an even fuller knowledge of the works, the ideas, and the nature of God. But the ethical and intellectual offices of the Church, as distinct from her spiritual office, are not hers exclusively or peculiarly. They were discharged, however imperfectly, before she was founded; and they are discharged still, independently of her, by two other authorities—science and society; the Church cannot perform all these functions by herself, nor, consequently, can she absorb their direction. The political and intellectual orders remain permanently distinct from the spiritual. They follow their own ends, they obey their own laws, and in doing so they support the cause of religion by the discovery of truth and the upholding of right. They render this service by fulfilling their own ends independently and unrestrictedly, not by surrendering them for the sake of spiritual interests. Whatever diverts government and science from their own spheres, or leads religion to usurp their domains, confounds distinct authorities, and imperils not only political right and scientific truths, but also the cause of faith and morals. A government that, for the interests of religion, disregards political right, and a science that, for the sake of protecting faith, wavers and dissembles in the pursuit of knowledge, are instruments at least as well adapted to serve the cause of falsehood as to combat it, and never can be used in furtherance of the truth without that treachery to principle which is a sacrifice too costly to be made for the service of any interest whatever.

Again, the principles of religion, government, and science are in harmony, always and absolutely; but their interests are not. And though all other interests must yield to those of religion, no principle can succumb to any interest. A political law or a scientific truth may be perilous to the morals or the faith of individuals, but it cannot on this ground be resisted by the Church. It may at times be a duty of the State to protect freedom of conscience, yet this freedom may be a temptation to apostasy. A discovery may be made in science which will shake the faith of thousands, yet religion cannot refute it or object to it. The difference in this respect between a true and a false religion is, that one judges all things by the standard of their truth, the other by the touchstone of its own interests. A false religion fears the progress of all truth; a true religion seeks and recognises truth wherever it can be found, and claims the power of regulating and controlling, not the progress, but the dispensation of knowledge. The Church both accepts the truth and prepares the individual to receive it.

The religious world has been long divided upon this great question: Do we find principles in politics and in science? Are their methods so rigorous that we may not bend them, their conclusions so certain that we may not dissemble them, in presence of the more rigorous necessity of the salvation of souls and the more certain truth of the dogmas of faith? This question divides Protestants into rationalists and pietists. The Church solves it in practice, by admitting the truths and the principles in the gross, and by dispensing them in detail as men can bear them. She admits the certainty of the mathematical method, and she uses the historical and critical method in establishing the documents for her own revelation and tradition. Deny this method, and her recognised arguments are destroyed. But the Church cannot and will not deny the validity of the methods upon which she is obliged to depend, not indeed for her existence, but for her demonstration. There is no opening for Catholics to deny, in the gross, that political science may have absolute principles of right, or intellectual science of truth.

During the last hundred years Catholic literature has passed through three phases in relation to this question. At one time, when absolutism and infidelity were in the ascendant, the Church was oppressed by governments and reviled by the people, Catholic writers imitated, and even caricatured the early Christian apologists in endeavouring to represent their system in the light most acceptable to one side or the other, to disguise antagonism, to modify old claims, and to display only that side of their religion which was likely to attract toleration and good will. Nothing which could give offence was allowed to appear. Something of the fulness, if not the truth, of religion was sacrificed for the sake of conciliation. The great Catholic revival of the present century gave birth to an opposite school. The attitude of timidity and concession was succeeded by one of confidence and triumph. Conciliation passed into defiance. The unscrupulous falsehoods of the eighteenth century had thrown suspicion on all that had ever been advanced by the adversaries of religion; and the belief that nothing could be said for the Church gradually died away into the conviction that nothing which was said against her could be true. A school of writers arose strongly imbued with a horror of the calumnies of infidel philosophers and hostile controversialists, and animated by a sovereign desire to revive and fortify the spirit of Catholics. They became literary advocates. Their only object was to accomplish the great work before them; and they were often careless in statement, rhetorical and illogical in argument, too positive to be critical, and too confident to be precise. In this school the present generation of Catholics was educated; to it they owe the ardour of their zeal, the steadfastness of their faith, and their Catholic views of history, politics, and literature. The services of these writers have been very great. They restored the balance, which was leaning terribly against religion, both in politics and letters. They created a Catholic opinion and a great Catholic literature, and they conquered for the Church a very powerful influence in European thought. The word "ultramontane" was revived to designate this school, and that restricted term was made to embrace men as different as De Maistre and Bonald, Lamennais and Montalembert, Balmez and Donoso Cortes, Stolberg and Schlegel, Phillips and Tapparelli.

There are two peculiarities by which we may test this whole group of eminent writers: their identification of Catholicism with some secular cause, such as the interests of a particular political or philosophical system, and the use they make of Protestant authorities. The views which they endeavoured to identify with the cause of the Church, however various, agreed in giving them the air of partisans. Like advocates, they were wont to defend their cause with the ingenuity of those who know that all points are not equally strong, and that nothing can be conceded except what they can defend. They did much for the cause of learning, though they took little interest in what did not immediately serve their turn. In their use of Protestant writers they displayed the same partiality. They estimated a religious adversary, not by his knowledge, but by his concessions; and they took advantage of the progress of historical criticism, not to revise their opinions, but to obtain testimony to their truth. It was characteristic of the school to be eager in citing the favourable passages from Protestant authors, and to be careless of those which were less serviceable for discussion. In the principal writers this tendency was counteracted by character and learning; but in the hands of men less competent or less suspicious of themselves, sore pressed by the necessities of controversy, and too obscure to challenge critical correction, the method became a snare for both the writer and his readers. Thus the very qualities which we condemn in our opponents, as the natural defences of error and the significant emblems of a bad cause, came to taint both our literature and our policy.

Learning has passed on beyond the range of these men's vision. Their greatest strength was in the weakness of their adversaries, and their own faults were eclipsed by the monstrous errors against which they fought. But scientific methods have now been so perfected, and have come to be applied in so cautious and so fair a spirit, that the apologists of the last generation have collapsed before them. Investigations have become so impersonal, so colourless, so free from the prepossessions which distort truth, from predetermined aims and foregone conclusions, that their results can only be met by investigations in which the same methods are yet more completely and conscientiously applied. The sounder scholar is invincible by the brilliant rhetorician, and the eloquence and ingenuity of De Maistre and Schlegel would be of no avail against researches pursued with perfect mastery of science and singleness of purpose. The apologist's armour would be vulnerable at the point where his religion and his science were forced into artificial union. Again, as science widens and deepens, it escapes from the grasp of dilettantism. Such knowledge as existed formerly could be borrowed, or superficially acquired, by men whose lives were not devoted to its pursuit, and subjects as far apart as the controversies of Scripture, history, and physical science might be respectably discussed by a single writer. No such shallow versatility is possible now. The new accuracy and certainty of criticism have made science unattainable except by those who devote themselves systematically to its study. The training of a skilled labourer has become indispensable for the scholar, and science yields its results to none but those who have mastered its methods. Herein consists the distinction between the apologists we have described and that school of writers and thinkers which is now growing up in foreign countries, and on the triumph of which the position of the Church in modern society depends. While she was surrounded with men whose learning was sold to the service of untruth, her defenders naturally adopted the artifices of the advocate, and wrote as if they were pleading for a human cause. It was their concern only to promote those precise kinds and portions of knowledge which would confound an adversary, or support a claim. But learning ceased to be hostile to Christianity when it ceased to be pursued merely as an instrument of controversy—when facts came to be acknowledged, no longer because they were useful, but simply because they were true. Religion had no occasion to rectify the results of learning when irreligion had ceased to pervert them, and the old weapons of controversy became repulsive as soon as they had ceased to be useful.

By this means the authority of political right and of scientific truth has been re-established, and they have become, not tools to be used by religion for her own interests, but conditions which she must observe in her actions and arguments. Within their respective spheres, politics can determine what rights are just, science what truths are certain. There are few political or scientific problems which affect the doctrines of religion, and none of them are hostile to it in their solution. But this is not the difficulty which is usually felt. A political principle or a scientific discovery is more commonly judged, not by its relation to religious truth, but by its bearings on some manifest or probable religious interests. A fact may be true, or a law may be just, and yet it may, under certain conditions, involve some spiritual loss.

And here is the touchstone and the watershed of principles. Some men argue that the object of government is to contribute to the salvation of souls; that certain measures may imperil this end, and that therefore they must be condemned. These men only look to interests; they cannot conceive the duty of sacrificing them to independent political principle or idea. Or, again, they will say, "Here is a scientific discovery calculated to overthrow many traditionary ideas, to undo a prevailing system of theology, to disprove a current interpretation, to cast discredit on eminent authorities, to compel men to revise their most settled opinions, to disturb the foundation on which the faith of others stands." These are sufficient reasons for care in the dispensation of truth; but the men we are describing will go on to say, "This is enough to throw suspicion on the discovery itself; even if it is true, its danger is greater than its value. Let it, therefore, be carefully buried, and let all traces of it be swept away."

A policy like this appears to us both wrong in itself and derogatory to the cause it is employed to serve. It argues either a timid faith which fears the light, or a false morality which would do evil that good might come. How often have Catholics involved themselves in hopeless contradiction, sacrificed principle to opportunity, adapted their theories to their interests, and staggered the world's reliance on their sincerity by subterfuges which entangle the Church in the shifting sands of party warfare, instead of establishing her cause on the solid rock of principles! How often have they clung to some plausible chimera which seemed to serve their cause, and nursed an artificial ignorance where they feared the discoveries of an impertinent curiosity! As ingenious in detraction as in silence and dissimulation, have they not too often answered imputations which they could not disprove with accusations which they could not prove, till the slanders they had invented rivalled in number and intensity the slanders which had been invented against them? For such men principles have had only temporary value and local currency. Whatever force was the strongest in any place and at any time, with that they have sought to ally the cause of religion. They have, with equal zeal, identified her with freedom in one country and with absolutism in another; with conservatism where she had privileges to keep, and with reform where she had oppression to withstand. And for all this, what have they gained? They have betrayed duties more sacred than the privileges for which they fought; they have lied before God and man; they have been divided into fractions by the supposed interests of the Church, when they ought to have been united by her principles and her doctrines; and against themselves they have justified those grave accusations of falsehood, insincerity, indifference to civil rights and contempt for civil authorities which are uttered with such profound injustice against the Church.

The present difficulties of the Church—her internal dissensions and apparent weakness, the alienation of so much intellect, the strong prejudice which keeps many away from her altogether, and makes many who had approached her shrink back—all draw nourishment from this rank soil. The antagonism of hostile doctrines and the enmity of governments count for little in comparison. It is in vain to point to her apostolic tradition, the unbroken unity of her doctrine, her missionary energy, or her triumphs in the region of spiritual life, if we fail to remove the accumulated prejudice which generations of her advocates have thrown up around her. The world can never know and recognise her divine perfection while the pleas of her defenders are scarcely nearer to the truth than the crimes which her enemies impute to her. How can the stranger understand where the children of the kingdom are deceived?

Against this policy a firm and unyielding stand is of supreme necessity. The evil is curable and the loss recoverable by a conscientious adherence to higher principles, and a patient pursuit of truth and right. Political science can place the liberty of the Church on principles so certain and unfailing, that intelligent and disinterested Protestants will accept them; and in every branch of learning with which religion is in any way connected, the progressive discovery of truth will strengthen faith by promoting knowledge and correcting opinion, while it destroys prejudices and superstitions by dissipating the errors on which they are founded. This is a course which conscience must approve in the whole, though against each particular step of it conscience may itself be tempted to revolt. It does not always conduce to immediate advantage; it may lead across dangerous and scandalous ground. A rightful sovereign may exclude the Church from his dominions, or persecute her members. Is she therefore to say that his right is no right, or that all intolerance is necessarily wrong? A newly discovered truth may be a stumbling-block to perplex or to alienate the minds of men. Is she therefore to deny or smother it? By no means. She must in every case do right. She must prefer the law of her own general spirit to the exigencies of immediate external occasion, and leave the issue in the hands of God.

Such is the substance of those principles which shut out *The Home and Foreign Review* from the sympathies of a large portion of the body to which we belong. In common with no small or insignificant section of our fellow-Catholics, we hold that the time has gone by when defects in political or scientific education could be alleged as an excuse for depending upon expediency or mistrusting knowledge; and that the moment has come when the best service that can be done to religion is to be faithful to principle, to uphold the right in politics though it should require an apparent sacrifice, and to seek truth in science though it should involve a possible risk. Modern society has developed no security for freedom, no instrument of progress, no means of arriving at truth, which we look upon with indifference or suspicion. We see no necessary gulf to separate our political or scientific convictions from those of the wisest and most intelligent men who may differ from us in religion. In pursuing those studies in which they can sympathise, starting from principles which they can accept, and using methods which are theirs as well as ours, we shall best attain the objects which alone can be aimed at in a Review—our own instruction, and the conciliation of opponents.

There are two main considerations by which it is necessary that we should be guided in our pursuit of these objects. First, we have to remember that the scientific method is most clearly exhibited and recognised in connection with subjects about which there are no prepossessions to wound, no fears to excite, no interests to threaten. Hence, not only do we exclude from our range all that concerns the ascetic life and the more intimate relations of religion, but we most willingly devote ourselves to the treatment of subjects quite remote from all religious bearing. Secondly, we have to remember that the internal government of the Church belongs to a sphere exclusively ecclesiastical, from the discussion of which we are shut out, not only by motives of propriety and reverence, but also by the necessary absence of any means for forming a judgment. So much ground is fenced off by these two considerations, that a secular sphere alone remains. The character of a scientific Review is determined for it. It cannot enter on the domains of ecclesiastical government or of faith, and neither of them can possibly be affected by its conclusions or its mode of discussion.

In asserting thus absolutely that all truth must render service to religion, we are saying what few perhaps will deny in the abstract, but what many are not prepared to admit in detail. It will be vaguely felt, that views which take so little account of present inconvenience and manifest danger are perilous and novel, though they may seem to spring from a more unquestioning faith, a more absolute confidence in truth, and a more perfect submission to the general laws of morality. There is no articulate theory, and no distinct view, but there is long habit, and there are strong inducements of another kind which support this sentiment.

To understand the certainty of scientific truth, a man must have deeply studied scientific method; to understand the obligation of political principle requires a similar mental discipline. A man who is suddenly introduced from without into a society where this certainty and obligation are currently acknowledged is naturally bewildered. He cannot distinguish between the dubious impressions of his second-hand knowledge and the certainty of that primary direct information which those who possess it have no power to deny. To accept a criterion which may condemn some cherished opinion has hitherto seemed to him a mean surrender and a sacrifice of position. He feels it simple loss to give up an idea; and even if he is prepared to surrender it when compelled by controversy, still he thinks it quite unnecessary and gratuitous to engage voluntarily in researches which may lead to such an issue. To enter thus upon the discussion of questions which have been mixed up with religion, and made to contribute their support to piety, seems to the idle spectator, or to the person who is absorbed in defending religion, a mere useless and troublesome meddling, dictated by the pride of intellectual triumph, or by the moral cowardice which seeks unworthily to propitiate enemies.

Great consideration is due to those whose minds are not prepared for the full light of truth and the grave responsibilities of knowledge; who have not learned to distinguish what is divine from what is human—defined dogma from the atmosphere of opinion which surrounds it—and who honour both with the same awful reverence. Great allowances are also due to those who are constantly labouring to nourish the spark of belief in minds perplexed by difficulties, or darkened by ignorance and prejudice. These men have not always the results of research at command; they have no time to keep abreast with the constant progress of historical and critical science; and the solutions which they are obliged to give are consequently often imperfect, and adapted only to uninstructed and uncultivated minds. Their reasoning cannot be the same as that of the scholar who has to meet error in its most vigorous, refined, and ingenious form. As knowledge advances, it must inevitably happen that they will find some of their hitherto accepted facts contradicted, and some arguments overturned which have done good service. They will find that some statements, which they have adopted under stress of controversy, to remove prejudice and doubt, turn out to be hasty and partial replies to the questions they were meant to answer, and that the true solutions would require more copious explanation than they can give. And thus will be brought home to their minds that, in the topics upon which popular controversy chiefly turns, the conditions of discussion and the resources of arguments are subject to gradual and constant change.

A Review, therefore, which undertakes to investigate political and scientific problems, without any direct subservience to the interests of a party or a cause, but with the belief that such investigation, by its very independence and straightforwardness, must give the most valuable indirect assistance to religion, cannot expect to enjoy at once the favour of those who have grown up in another school of ideas. Men who are occupied in the special functions of ecclesiastical life, where the Church is all-sufficient and requires no extraneous aid, will naturally see at first in the problems of public life, the demands of modern society, and the progress of human learning, nothing but new and unwelcome difficulties—trial and distraction to themselves, temptation and danger to their flocks. In time they will learn that there is a higher and a nobler course for Catholics than one which begins in fear and does not lead to security. They will come to see how vast a service they may render to the Church by vindicating for themselves a place in every movement that promotes the study of God's works and the advancement of mankind. They will remember that, while the office of ecclesiastical authority is to tolerate, to warn, and to guide, that of religious intelligence and zeal is not to leave the great work of intellectual and social civilisation to be the monopoly and privilege of others, but to save it from debasement by giving to it for leaders the children, not the enemies, of the Church. And at length, in the progress of political right and scientific knowledge, in the development of freedom in the State and of truth in literature, they will recognise one of the first among their human duties and the highest of their earthly rewards.

[8]
Ultramontanism

Knowledge is treated by the Christian Church not merely as a means, but much more as an end, because it is the only atmosphere in which her progress is unwavering and subject to no relapse. When in successive ages she defines or surveys anew the system it is her mission to teach, she has always to record some advance upon the past. Though amongst the units of mankind the boundary of her dominion may waver or recede, yet, in the order of truth, she works out a law of inevitable and invariable advance. She must teach all nations; but she has no special promise that any one will listen to her. She must watch over those within her fold, but she knows not whether her vigilance will avail. No divine protection insures her against losses by persecution, dogged unbelief, neglect of her law, or apostasy from her creed; and there is no assurance that the means of grace which she dispenses will effect by degrees the moral improvement of our race, or that sanctity will gain in intensity or in extent as time goes on. There may be diminution in the area of Christendom, and decline in the virtue of Christians. But there must be some exception to the possibility of retrogression, or Christianity would be inferior to Judaism; nay, if stagnation could paralyse every function of the Church of Christ, His works would be less perfect than the works of men. The divine nature of the institution which He founded must therefore be manifest in some element which is secured against loss or deterioration by the assurance of a constant growth. To refuse to the Church this character of progress is to deny the divinity of her Founder; and if we seek it anywhere else than in that order of truth which is subject to the immediate guidance of the Holy Ghost, we are contradicted alike by

Published in *The Home and Foreign Review* 3 (July 1863):162–206. Döllinger I, p. 313; Acton-Simpson III, pp. 73, 75, 76, 113, 155. The article was a collaborative effort by Acton and Richard Simpson. Reprinted in Acton, *Church and State*, pp. 37–85; Acton, *Liberal Interpretation of History*, pp. 160–213.

the holiness of the early ages, and by the most memorable lessons of later religious history.

In this growth the Church does not yield to the action of eternal forces, or simply consent to a change which she cannot impede. Progress is a necessity of her existence, and a law of her nature. She does not passively suffer it, but actively imposes it upon society. Whilst she continually and continuously develops her doctrines, and evolves truth from the inexhaustible tradition of the teaching of our Lord, her action is the ever-present impulse, pattern and guide of society in the formation of law, and in the advancement of learning.

How great is the influence thus exercised by the example of the Church on civil government, and how close is the parallel between her method and the principles of political science, we do not here inquire. Her more direct and necessary action is on human knowledge. For the full exposition of truth is the great object for which the existence of mankind is prolonged on earth. It may be that individual goodness is not greater, or the proportion of the saved larger, than in earlier times; but Almighty God is more fully known, the articles of faith are multiplied, and the certainty of knowledge is increased. This growth in knowledge is not by new revelations or by a continuance of inspiration, but it is a conquest of the Christian mind in its conflict with the phases of untruth. It is earned by exertion; it is not simply given by faith itself. The development of doctrine is essential to the preservation of its purity; hence its preservation implies its development; and the intellectual act which accompanies belief is the agent of the progress of the Church in religious knowledge. In the course of this process she lays under contribution all human learning, which she exacts and sanctifies by using it. As she does not possess at once the fulness of all knowledge, and as her authority leaves many things uncertain, she must rely on other resources for that which is not hers by inheritance; and her demand must necessarily promote the supply of that on which she so much depends. Therefore, by the side of the progressive study of revealed truth a vast intellectual labour continues incessantly, carried on in the presence of authority, on the basis of faith, and within the sphere of unity and charity, in order that all science may become tributary to religion, and that God may be worshipped in the harmony of His words, His works, and His ways.

This duty has been discharged in all ages, except the intervals of corruption and decline, with a zeal commensurate with its importance;

and the bitter anxiety which has accompanied each rising doubt and division has equalled that excited by assaults on the faith itself. For in disputes with a hostile religion there is the certainty of belief to guide, and confidence in authority to sustain the combatant. He confesses himself inferior to the cause; he dares not degrade it by the introduction of personal motives or emotions, or allow it to be desecrated by the conditions of human controversy; and he is not tempted to do so, for neither fear nor doubt mingles with his feelings. But in discussions confined within the sphere of religious unity, which do not directly involve fundamental truths, and where private judgement occupies the place of faith and obedience, the antagonism is necessarily more personal, there is more selfishness in opinion and less assurance of victory, and the purest motives may become tainted by ignorance, interest or pride. Disputes which authority cannot decide are an excitement to those for whom its restraint is irksome, and an indulgence for those who are weary of acquiescing in silent unity. The lines of separation are most distinctly marked because the chasm is less wide.

Hence arise two phenomena which vex the Catholic and perplex the Protestant—the number of parties within the Church, and the heat of their dissensions. It is not always easy for a stranger to reconcile these things with the notion of unity, or for a friend to be sure that they involve no breach of charity; and it is very hard for either to discover, when orthodoxy is disputed and authority necessarily silent, the true exponent of the Catholic idea. As the rise of heresies furnished the text which defined Catholicism to be the most perfect expression of Christianity, so the growth of internal controversy requires some further text to ascertain the purest form of thought on open questions within the Church. For the control of religion extends further than its dogmas; and a view which contradicts no prescribed doctrine may be a more serious symptom of estrangement from the spirit of the Church than some unconscious doctrinal errors. There are certain questions to which the test of orthodoxy does not apply, which yet are more significant than some of those which it decides. The liberty which prevails on doubtful points does not justify a resignation that acquiesces in doubt, and deprecates the efforts by which it may be dispelled. In the absence of the degrees of authority, such points may be settled by scientific inquiry, and an opinion which can never be enforced may claim to be received. Yet, though Catholics may be ready to adopt a criterion which excludes some of those who are in communion with them, they dread what may repel those who are not; and they naturally conceal in the presence of strangers a weapon which they use among themselves. It is impossible that varying parties which cannot agree in a common definition should accept a common term.

Protestant observers have adopted a designation to indicate the esoteric spirit of Catholicism, the real essence of the system they oppose. That designation is Ultramontanism. Unquestionably the significance attached to it has a certain reality and truth which ought to overcome the reluctance to admit the term. Ultramontanism stands in the same relation to Catholicism in matters of opinion as Catholicism to Christianity in matters of faith. It signifies a habit of intellect carrying forward the inquiries and supplementing the work of authority. It implies the legitimate union of religion with science, and the conscious intelligible harmony of Catholicism with the system of secular truth. Its basis is authority, but its domain is liberty, and it reconciles the one with the other. A Catholic may be utterly deficient in human learning, or he may possess it in such a measure as presents no difficulties to his faith, or he may find a ready and universal solution for all such difficulties in an unhesitating sacrifice either of faith or of reason. In no one of these cases, whether he be a good or a bad Catholic, has he any pretensions to the name of Ultramontane. His religion derives no strength or resources from his knowledge, nor does his knowledge find a principle of unity or a guide in his religion. If neither of them has lost anything of its integrity and truth, neither has gained anything from the other. If there is no struggle in his mind, there has also been no combination—no generation of something previously non-existent which neither science alone nor religion alone could have produced. His conscience has obtained no security against the necessity of sacrificing faith to truth or truth to faith, and no impulse to that reflection which recognizes the ultimate unity.

It is plain that Ultramontanism, in this acceptation of the word, can only be a fruit of mature civilization and of a very advanced stage of scientific investigation. Natural science before it was purified by the methods of observation, and historical science before it was regenerated by criticism, consorted better with superstition and error than with religion. But a change took place in their nature at the beginning of this century. There is an interval, as it were, of centuries which divides Cuvier from Buffon, Niebuhr from Gibbon, with a distinctness almost as great as that which separates chemistry from alchemy, astronomy from astrology, history from legend. A similar change ensued in the political system, and established in almost every country the theory and the desire of freedom. In one of the contests arising from this altered condition of society, about a quarter of a century ago, the term Ultramontane began to be applied to those who advocated the rights and principles of the Catholic Church. In one sense the designation was just: in another it was a strange inversion of the meaning which had been hitherto attached to the word.

During the period between the Reformation and the Revolution, Ultramontanism, like Gallicanism, was used as a party term. It designated the strict Roman system as developed by the antagonism of the Gallican theories of the fifteenth century. In comparison with the practice of the Middle Ages, it was a jealousy of liberties, stimulated by an equal jealousy of authority. Such a controversy, raising a false issue on the law and constitution of the Church, could only engage the masters of ecclesiastical learning during an age when history, the touchstone and solvent of extreme systems, was very imperfectly known. At a time when it raged, little had yet been done to illustrate the mediaeval Church, and men were still without the means of solving such historical problems as that of the Donation of Constantine, the spurious Decretals, the story of Pope Joan, and all the various fables which furnished the bases of the rival claims for an almost absolute national independence, and for an arbitrary and universal power. In those days Gallicans and Ultramontanes contended for narrow, extreme, subordinate, we might almost say, uneducated views. The conflict between them was an abatement of the true Catholic spirit, and was lamented by the saints as a disaster for the Church. "Je hais," says St. Francis of Sales, "par inclination naturelle, et, je pense, par inspiration céleste, toutes les contentions et disputes qui se font entre Catholiques, et dont la fin est inutile; encore plus celles dont les effets ne peuvent être que dissensions et différends, surtout en ce temps plein d'esprits disposés aux controverses, aux médisances, aux censures et à la ruine de la charité. Je n'ai pas même trouvé à mon goût certains écrits d'un saint et très-excellent prélat, dans lequels il a touché au pouvoir indirect du Pape sur les princes; non que j'ai jugé s'il a tort ou raison, mais parce qu'en cet age où nous avons tant d'ennemis en dehors, nous ne devons rien émouvoir au dedans du corps de l'Église."

St. Francis also says: "Il est malaisé de dire choses qui n'offensent ceux qui, faisant les bons valets, soit du Pape, soit des princes, ne veulent pas que jamais on s'arrête hors des extremités."[1]

Intellectual indolence conspired with the ignorance of the age to promote these theories. Men were glad to find a formula which saved them the trouble of thinking, and a view which enabled them to shut their eyes. For the defence of a thesis is far easier than the discovery of truth. There is something alarming in the labour of distinguishing and comparing times and places, and of making due allowance for qualifying circumstances and conditions. The followers of a system dreaded lest the knowledge of facts should interfere with the certainty of their opinions, and lest the resistless stream of history should be let in upon their settled and compact conclusions.

The political condition of those times is an important element in the history of the controversy. Gallicanism and Ultramontanism both professed to represent liberty; but they both belonged to an age of absolute power. One system was the instrument by which absolute monarchs extended their power over the Church, whilst by the other the same principle of absolutism was introduced into the Church herself. Both were expedients by which ecclesiastical liberty was curtailed, and authority made superior to law. The source of their vitality and the reason of their existence disappeared when the Revolution put an end to the old society which tolerated, and even approved, the system of arbitrary government. At a later period, under the Restoration, the reverence for law, and the religious aversion for absolute power, which resisted the encroachment of civil government on the liberties of the Church, caused her to maintain, in her own internal system, the authority of law and tradition over the temporary will of her rulers. Instead of Church and State being rivals in absolutism, it came to be understood that both ought to obey their own legislation; while the horror of the lawless epochs they had lately traversed, in the Revolution and the Empire, came to be the predominant influence in the minds of men.

Early in the present century, while Chateaubriand was explaining the charm of religious emotions, and when in Germany the distinction of creeds was all but obliterated by the powerful current of Romanticism, it cannot be said that there were any distinguishable groups of Catholic

---

[1] *Oeuvres*, xi, 406, 401.

opinions. Ecclesiastical literature was at a low ebb, and controversy was almost extinct. There was neither learning, nor leisure, nor definiteness enough to awaken the old discussions. They appeared again when peace and freedom were restored to religion, and literary activity revived, after 1814. In those days the memory of the revolutionary period and its unbelief was very vivid, and the ideas of the Holy Alliance found much favour with thinking Catholics. They dreamed of a league between Church and State, of a renovated loyalty identified with a revived religion, and of a combination between men of goodwill for the restoration of the great interests which had fallen before the common foe. It was hoped that religion might enable the State to protect society against the recurrence of such a catastrophe. There were many who relied for the realization of this scheme (half religious and half political) as much on the Czar as on the Pope. The strong practical purpose by which it was animated is one leading characteristic of the literary movement which followed. Another is, that its writers were chiefly laymen; for the problems of the day were rather social than ecclesiastical, and even theology was treated with a view to the State. Long before the French Revolution the schools of theology had generally declined, and then, for five and twenty years, ecclesiastical studies were almost everywhere suspended. No successors had sprung up to the great scholars who had lived far into the pontificate of Pius VI; and many of the most cultivated priests on the Continent were deeply marked with Rationalism. At the Restoration the clergy, as a body, were not in a condition to take an active part in literature. Their place in the van was supplied by laymen—often recent converts, seldom trained scholars, and all rather inspired by the lessons of recent history than versed in the older details of theological discussion.

The foremost of these men was the Comte de Maistre. During the evil days he had made himself a name by two political pamphlets, written with the power, the eloquence and depth of Burke, with more metaphysical ability than Burke possessed, but without his instinct for political truth, or his anxious attention to the voice of history. In these pamphlets he had laid down some of the most important principles of civil government, and had explained with special success the necessity of aristocracy for the establishment of freedom. His writings had displayed extensive knowledge, earnest faith, a pointed wit, and an almost unexampled union of common sense with love of paradox and passion for extremes. After his return from St. Petersburg, in the first years of the Restoration, he published several works in rapid succession, which have earned for him perhaps the highest place next to Pascal among laymen who have defended religion without the advantage of a theological education.

Society, said M. de Maistre, has been ruined by the want of faith, or by its equivalent in the civil order, the weakness of authority. It is necessary that mankind should be taught the duty of unconditional obedience, the merit of suffering, the sinfulness of self-assertion, the peril of liberty, and the evil of securities against the abuse of power.[2] Tyranny, poverty and slavery are not the faults of society, but the penalties of sin. Monarchy is the only legitimate form of government, because monarchy alone gives the nations a master, and places the sovereign under the restraint of conscience. It is his duty to promote as well as to preserve religion, to suppress error and sinlike crime, and to defend the faith by prescribing knowledge[3] and encouraging superstition.[4]

---

[2] "Il est vrai au fond que les peuples ont des droits, mais non celui de les faire valoir ou d'en punir la violation par la force" (*Correspondance Diplomatique*, ii, 36). "Le dogme catholique, comme tout le monde sait, proscrit tout espèce de révolte sans distinction; et pour défendre ce dogme nos docteurs disent d'assez bonne raisons, philosophiques même, et politiques" (*Du Pape*, p. 161).

[3] "Les inconvénients inévitables de la science, dans tous les pays et dans tous les lieux, sont de rendre l'homme inhabile à la vie active, qui est la vraie vocation de l'homme; de le rendre souverainement orgueilleux, enivré de lui-même, et de ses propres idées, ennemi de toute subordination, frondeur de toute loi et de toute institution, et partisan-né de toute innovation. Elle tend donc nécessairement à tuer l'esprit public et à nuire à la société" (*Quatre Chapitres inédits sur la Russie*, 1859, p. 38). "Restreindre de même la science, de plusieurs manières, savoir ... en supprimant tout enseignement public des connaissances qui peuvent être livrées au goût et au moyens de chaque particulier; comme l'histoire, la géographie, la métaphysique, la morale, la politique, le commerce" (ibid., p. 147). "Il y a dans la science, si elle n'est pas entièrement subordonnée aux dogmes nationaux, quelque chose de caché qui tend à ravaler l'homme, et à le rendre surtout inutile ou mauvais citoyen. ... Il faut subordonner toutes nos connaissances à la religion, croire fermement qu'on étudie en priant; et surtout lorsque nous nous occupons de philosophie rationnelle, ne jamais oublier que toute proposition de métaphysique, qui ne sort pas comme d'elle-même d'un dogme chrétien, n'est et ne peut pas être qu'une coupable extravagance" (*Soirées de St Petersburg*, ii. 221, 223).

[4] "Je crois que la superstition est un ouvrage avancé de la religion qu'il ne faut pas détruire, car il n'est pas bon qu'on puisse venir sans obstacle jusqu'au pied du mur, en mesurer la hauteur et planter les échelles. ... Croyez-vous que les abus d'une chose divine n'aient pas dans la chose même certaines limites naturelles, et que les inconvénients de ces abus puissent jamais égaler le danger d'ébranler la croyance?" (*Soirées de St Petersburg*, ii, 234).

In these writings de Maistre unquestionably relinquished or modified some of his earlier opinions. There was no longer that love of freedom which he had opposed to the violence of the Revolution, or that admiration for England with which he had been inspired by her long resistance to Napoleon.[5] His ideal state had become more centralized, his sovereign more absolute, his nobility less independent, his people less free. The dread of revolutionary despotism had given place to a horror of constitutionalism. This was the current of the hour. But it inspired de Maistre with the theory which is the chief cause of his celebrity, a theory new to the Catholic thinkers of his time. Catholicism, he maintained, inculcates the absolute authority of the sovereign, and forbids resistance even to the gravest wrong.[6] This unity and absolutism of authority spring from the very nature of religion, and are not only necessary for the State, but essential to the Church. Civil society cannot subsist without the maxim that the king can do no wrong. The Church requires the same privilege for the Pope. Absolute infallibility in the one is a corollary of despotism in the other.[7] It is also its remedy. Denying to the people any part in the vindication of right, de Maistre transferred to the Pope alone the whole duty of moderating kings. Thus the argument for the Papal power flowed into two streams from

[5] "On a bien dit: 'Il faut des lois fondamentales, il faut une constitution'. Mais qui les établira, ces lois fondamentales, et qui les fera exécuter? Le corps ou l'individu qui en aurait la force serait souverain. . . . L'Angleterre seule a pu faire quelque chose dans ce genre; mais sa constitution n'a point encore subi l'épreuve du temps. . . . Qu'arrivera-t-il? Je l'ignore; mais quand les choses tourneraient comme je le désire, un example isolé de l'histoire prouverait peu en faveur des monarchies constitutionelles, d'autant que l'expérience universelle est contraire à cet example unique" (*Du Pape*, pp. 159, 160). Ten years earlier he had said: "La constitution est l'ouvrage des circonstances . . . l'unité la plus compliquée et le plus bel équilibre des forces politiques qu'on ait jamais vu dans le monde" (*Essai sur le Principe Générateur des Constitutions Politiques*, p. 16).

[6] "Si l'on veut s'exprimer exactement, il n'y a point de souveraineté limitée; toutes sont absolues et infaillibles, puisque nulle part il n'est permis de dire qu'elles se sont trompées. . . . Elle est toujours et partout absolue, sans que personne ait le droit de lui dire qu'elle est injuste ou trompée" (*Du Pape*, p. 165). "Il faudroit que les souverains protestants eussent perdu le sens pour ne pas apercevoir l'insigne folie qu'ils font, de soutenir une religion qui pose en maxime le jugement particulier et la souveraineté du peuple, contre une autre religion qui soutient que contre notre légitime souverain, fût-il même un Neron, nous n'avons d'autre droit que celui de nous laisser couper la tête en lui disant respectueusement la vérité" (*Correspondance Diplomatique*, ii, 132).

[7] "Il ne peut y avoir de société humaine sans gouvernement, ni de gouvernement sans souveraineté, sans infaillibilité; et ce dernier privilège est si absolument nécessaire, qu'on est forcé de supposer l'infaillibilité, même dans les souverainetés temporelles (où elle n'est pas), sous peine de voir l'association se dissoudre. L'église ne demande rien de plus que les autres souverainetés" (*Du Pape*, p. 147).

one source—the theory of civil absolutism. Reasoning by analogy, the Pope ought to be an arbitrary ruler within the Church; while, by contrast, his power was extended over States, and the security of civil rights was to be sought in the completeness of hierarchical despotism.

Whoever studies the writings of de Maistre will find far more than the memorable theory by which he became the founder of a new school of Ultramontanism. He will find some of the best and wisest things ever written on religion and society—a generous tone, an admirable style of discussion, and the Catholic system presented often in the noblest manner. These qualities have exercised a powerful and salutary influence on all the succeeding schools of Catholic thought; and some who differ most widely from de Maistre on the questions which he made more particularly his own owe much to his writings. But it was only in the course of years, as the publication of eight posthumous volumes defined more clearly and more amply the character of his mind, that men learned to separate the man from his peculiar theory. At first, all the merits of his system and his style served but to give attractiveness and splendour to the theory of the Papal power, which became the symbol of a party, and gave the impulse to an important movement. No distinct view had yet been put forward so positively or so brilliantly; and its influence on contemporaries was extraordinary. It appeared to a large class of persons as the only perfect form of Catholicism. Everything that fell short of it seemed to them treason or surrender. To limit the Holy See in Church or State was to attack religion, and open the door to Jansenism, Protestantism, and infidelity. Inasmuch as authority was especially odious to irreligious Catholics, it became the part of good Catholics to vindicate it with at least a corresponding zeal. All qualification was taken to be opposition, and was deemed to imply a secret aversion.

Since the question raised by de Maistre was one of fact, and not of speculation, its solution was to be found not in theory but in history. For, as the standing object of his school was to establish a prejudice favourable to the supreme authority of the Church in every period, their labour would be in vain if it could be shown that the pontifical power had manifested itself in various degrees in various times, or that there had been serious vicissitudes in its spirit. Here an entrance was found for a personal element new to ecclesiastical literature, which caused the discussion of character to become more prominent than the discussion of principle. Those who defended a particular view of canon law, history, or politics with orthodoxy obliged themselves to treat all objections to this view as blasphemies against religious truth; whatever was inconsistent with the theory was regarded as really equivalent to a denial of the continuity of tradition.[8] Large tracts of history which had formerly involved no theological interest became the arena of controversy; and their adverse and telling facts were only in the brief to be explained away and amplified respectively. De Maistre had given the example of discussing these questions with the arts of advocacy. His rhetorical dexterity enabled him to put wit in the place of argument, to disconcert adversaries by spirited retaliation, or baffle them by ingenuously dissembling or boldly denying whatever might serve their purpose. Many followed him in good faith, fully persuaded that nothing opposed to the theory could be true; but he had other followers who were not in good faith.

The long opposition of science and philosophy to religion had brought their methods into a discredit which the practice of the writers of that time by no means tended to dissipate. Men doubted whether scientific method could be really reconciled to religious truth; and it was felt that so ambiguous a weapon was least unsafe when least used. Men suspected that it was altogether inadequate to give certain demonstration of the truths with which it is conversant,[9] and without the aid of external authority. On this idea a theory was founded which seemed at first to support de Maistre's argument for the Papal authority, though it ended in decided contradiction of it. Lamennais, the author of this new philosophy, taught that no evidence amounts to certain demonstration unless confirmed by the universal consent of the general testimony; and that the organ of this universal reason is the Holy See. This principle, laid down in the second volume of the *Essai sur l'Indifférence*, led necessarily to the rejection of that theory of the absolute authority of the civil power which had furnished de Maistre with the

[8] On February 5, 1820, Lamennais wrote to de Maistre on the publication of his book, *Du Pape:* "En défendant l'autorité du saint-siège, vous défendez celle de l'église, et l'autorité même des souverains, et toute vérité et tout ordre. Vous devez donc compter sur de nombreuses contradictions; mais il est beau de les supporter pour une telle cause. L'opposition des méchants console le cœur de l'homme de bien, il se sent plus séparé d'eux, et dès lors plus près de celui à qui le jugement appartient et à qui restera la victoire."

[9] "Je n'irai point tenter follement d'escaler l'enceinte salutaire dont la sagesse divine nous a environnés; je suis sûr d'être de ce côté sur les terres de la vérité: qui m'assure qu'au-delà (pour ne point faire de supposition plus triste) je ne me trouverai pas sur les domaines de la superstition?" (*Soirées de St Petersburg*, ii, 227).

analogy he used with such effect. If the infallibility of universal opinion is the origin of certainty, it is the source of authority; and the Holy See is therefore exalted over princes as much as over philosophers and thinkers. When, therefore, the French monarchy became odious to the people, and, at the same time, hostile to the Church, Lamennais denied its right, and appealed against it to the people as the source of power, and to the Pope as their organ. This was the spirit of the *Avenir*,[10] and it still largely tinges the political Catholicism of France. The doctrine of the impotence of reason was wrought into a system by Father Ventura, and was adopted by the Traditionalists, who, on the plea of Rationalism, anathematized all the writers who did most honour to the clergy of France. During many years Traditionalism preserved an organ in the journal of the indefatigable M. Bonnetty, until it was condemned, and the claims of reason vindicated both by Pope and Council.[11]

This theory of the vanity of science applied to history made it as uninteresting as an old almanac, and at the same time as arbitrary, unreal and unreliable as the annual prophecy of a new one. It made the teaching of the Church the sole foundation and test of certain knowledge, a criterion alike of the records of history and of the arguments of unbelief. It recognized no means of ascertaining the truth of facts, or the authenticity of documents, sufficiently trustworthy to interfere with theological opinions. It supposed the part of malice and ignorance to be so large, and the powers of unaided reason so minute, that ecclesiastical authority could be the only guide, even in matters

[10] The Abbé Gerbet wrote in the number of February 21, 1831: "L'ordre légal peut cesser de la même manière qu'il a été établi, c'est-à-dire par voie de consentement."

[11] The decree of the Council of Amiens, quoted by Father Gratry, explains better than any description the extremes to which the school had come: "Dum rationalismum impugnant, caveant etiam, ne rationis humanae infirmitatem quasi ad impotentiam reducant. Hominem, rationis exercitio fruentem, hujus facultatis applicatione posse percipere aut etiam demonstrare plures veritates metaphysicas et morales . . . constanti scholarum catholicarum doctrina compertum est. Falsum est, rationem solvendis istis quaestionibus esse omnino impotentem, argumenta quæ proponit nihil certe exhibere et argumentis oppositis ejusdem valoris destrui. Falsum est, hominem has veritates naturaliter admittere non posse, quin prius per actum fidei supernaturalis revelationi divinae credat." The *Congregatio Indici* defined the doctrine of the Church against the Traditionalists in four sentences, of which this is the second: "Ratiocinatio Dei existentiam, animae spiritualitatem, hominis libertatem cum certitudine probare potest. Fides posterior est revelatione, proindeque ad probandam Dei existentiam contra atheum, ad probandam animae rationalis spiritualitatem ac libertatem contra naturalismi ac fatalismi sectatorem allegari convenienter nequit."

foreign to its immediate domain—the next place given to the presumptive authority of the more probable opinion. Otherwise, it was thought, the constant fluctuations of profane science would oblige theology to obey all its movements, and religion would ape the mobility which passion, ignorance, and error impart to literature. Hence it was held impossible to verify the facts of religious history, or to argue from the monuments of tradition. Catholics had no basis of criticism in common with others. Every Protestant was *principia negans*. In all likelihood quite as strong a case might be made out against the Catholic view of the past as in its favour, and no appeal to history was expected to confound adversaries or to confirm belief. The immediate consequence was to set aside historical study as useless or dangerous; and that courageous logician, M. Veuillot, affirmed ignorance to be quite as serviceable as knowledge for the vindication of truth, and urged that no time should be wasted in exchanging the one for the other.

A particular suspicion rested on history, because, as the study of facts, it was less amenable to authority and less controllable by interest than philosophical speculation. In consequence partly of the denial of historical certainty, and partly of the fear of it, the historical study of Dogma in its original sources was abandoned, and the dialectical systematic treatment preferred. Theology became almost entirely scholastic. It was regarded as complete, not susceptible of development, looking backwards and not forwards, more interested in the vindication of authoritative names than in the cultivation of those original studies which are needed for its advance. This movement, which for a time had its centre at Rome, found its most brilliant expression in Father Kleutgen's work on the theology of the old times.

The principle of de Maistre's philosophy which is common to works so discordant in spirit and so dissimilar in execution as the *Essai sur l'Indifférence*, Ventura's *Traditionalism*, and the *Theologie der Vorzeit* of the accomplished Roman Jesuit, has displayed itself in politics as vividly as in theology. The same dread of an outward independent criterion, which causes divines to reject the facts of history, leads canonists, in disputes involving civil questions, to turn from the State to the sole and supreme authority of the Church. Building upon the weakness of human reason and the malice of the outer world, the men of this school arrived at the opinion that, as civil interests are subservient to those of religion, the civil law is necessarily subject to that of the Church. At the same time they could not admit that the interests of the Church might be sacrificed to the letter of her own law. They concluded that no merely political institution, no legislation which is so indirectly connected with the moral law that it can assume various forms in various Christian states, could be permitted to stand in the way of considerations of religious advantage. In canon law, they said, the Holy See can dispense from any obligation which is not of divine right. Why should civil law be more sacred? If the Pope can permit a brother and sister to marry for the sake of expediency, how can any opinion of political right and wrong be allowed to supersede that highest argument? They held, therefore, that no spiritual advantage could be surrendered in obedience to the variable legislation of any local power. Hence arose a system very remote from the servile loyalty of the Gallican Church, a system which assumed on many occasions a liberal and sometimes a revolutionary appearance. But if no civil authority was sacred beyond the limit of religious expediency, no civil rights could enjoy a higher immunity. The Church could make no distinction between political freedom and wrong, but must unite with that cause whose alliance promised most profit. The standard of political duty was held to exist for those only who recognized no higher law; those who did so felt no difficulty in bestowing an equal and consistent admiration for Gregory XVI, rebuking the Archbishop of Paris for his legitimist sympathies, and for Pius IX, supporting the Neapolitan Bourbons. Thus it was made to appear that Catholics are not guided in public life by sentiments which constitute the honour of other men, and that they absolutely repudiate political principle. A feeling of distrust and of contempt was thereby engendered in the minds of governments and nations. The religion which suffered by this conduct was appealed to by one party, and condemned by the other, as countenancing it. Catholic parties did duty for the Church, and eagerly transferred to her the obloquy which they themselves had incurred.

This theory, which has so much affected both theology and politics, has exercised a still deeper influence on the treatment of history; and in this field it has passed more gradually through the successive steps which have led to its complete display. First, it was held, the interests of religion, which are opposed to the study of history, require that precautions should be taken to make it innocuous where it cannot be quite suppressed. If it is lawful to conceal facts or statements, it is equally right to take out their sting when they must be brought forward. It is not truth, but error, which is suppressed by this process, the object of which is to prevent a false impression being made on the minds of men. For the effect of these facts or statements is to prejudice men against the Church, and to lead them to false conclusions concerning her nature. Whatever tends to weaken this adverse impression contributes really to baffle a falsehood and sustain the cause of truth. The statement, however true in its own subordinate place, will only serve to mislead in a higher order of truth, where the consequences may be fatal to the conscience and happiness of those who hear it without any qualification. Words, moreover, often convey to the uninstructed mind ideas contrary to their real significance, and the interpretation of facts is yet more delusive. Put the case of a Protestant sincerely seeking to be instructed, and earnestly inquiring into the spirit and practices of the Church, who perhaps on the very threshold of conversion, when the dogmatic difficulties are over and the longing for the sacraments is awakened, asks if it be true that the spiritual rulers of the Church have been sometimes men of scandalous lives, or whether Catholicism has encouraged or ordained persecution. If he finds the inquiry answered affirmatively in Catholic books, it is probable that he may be disappointed, or even disgusted, and that a few idle sentences of an indiscreet and superficial writer may undo the work of his conversion, and bring ruin to his soul. What end could that writer have in view that would bear comparison with the evil of such a consummation? Nothing obliged him to write at all, still less to write on so delicate a topic, and to handle it without reserve. If his words were true, they still deceived the reader who found in them the evidence of great defects in the Catholic system. The real duty of Catholics is not to gratify an idle curiosity or mere literary vanity, but to bring souls to Christ. The next step is to annul the effect of what has been said and what cannot be unsaid. This may be done in several ways. Reprisals are often successful; for in choosing between rival systems it is natural to compare them. But there are cases in which this argument does not apply, and minds on which it is without effect. Here there may be room for the simple contradiction—a favourite weapon with de Maistre. There have been many forgeries in the world, and it is natural to suspect that they proceed from enemies of truth. If documents on which the Church long relied are proved to be the works of fraud, it may reasonably be assumed that some of those on which her adversaries depend will ultimately meet with the same fate. And if the document is genuine, the writer may have been inspired with bad motives, or his text interpolated, or his information unauthentic. A great deal may be done in this way; and where there is really no room for doubt, it is still unnecessary to say so. For the object is not the discovery of objective truth, but the production of a right belief in a mind. When all is in vain—when the argument by reprisals, and the argument by denial, and the argument by insinuation of motives, or imputation of fraud, and last of all the argument by diversion, have failed, there is the last resource of admitting the fact and defending its righteousness. This may be done in two ways. The most common is to say that the only blame falls on those who shrink from heroic deeds, and judge them by the paltry cowardly standard of a selfish morality.[12] The other is to attribute acts which are hard to justify to the superior insight of those who committed them in the higher interests of religion, and their superiority to the conventional regulations which guide ordinary men. The examples of the Old Testament, the wisdom of the saints, the special illumination which God vouchsafes to those who rule His Church, may be appealed to in support of this argument. It is the duty of the son to cover the shame of his father; and the Catholic owes it to the Church to defend her against every adverse fact as he would defend the honour of his mother. He will not coldly examine the value of testimony, or concede any point because it is hard to meet, or assist with unbiased mind in the discovery of truth before he knows what its bearing may be. Assured that nothing injurious to the Church can be true, he will combat whatever bears an unfavourable semblance with every attainable artifice and weapon. Mindful of the guilt of those who scandalize the weak, or interpose between the waverer and the Church, and fully conscious that a lie may in some cases be the nearest approach to truth, he will allow no adverse statement to pass without contradiction, or without at least an antidote which may remove its danger. For there is but one thing needful; and all facts and all opinions are worthless except to minister to the salvation of men and the promotion of religion.

---

[12] M. de Falloux has shown, in his essay "Le Parti catholique" (*Le Correspondant*, N.S. ii, 192), how this temper carried a party among the Catholics of France to defend the massacre of St Bartholomew and the revocation of the Edict of Nantes. He quotes the following characteristic passage from the *Univers:* "Aujourd'hui, avec les ridicules idées de liberté et de respect des opinions, avec l'opprobre public jeté sur l'inquisition et la crainte de la faire revivre, avec l'absence enfin de foi et de règle dans les consciences, peut-on supposer que les maires soupçonneront qu'ils ont en ce point quelque devoir à remplir?"

Those who traversed unconsciously the course which marks the genesis of these views, and arrived at the extreme we have indicated, were generally sincere at least in the belief that they were defending the cause of religion, and not merely their own interests or opinions; and they succeeded in communicating their belief to Protestants. The enemies of the Church supposed from their example that she could only be defended on the principle that the means are justified by the end; and this identification of her methods with those of a party within her led them to think that in exposing the latter they were tearing down a real outwork of Catholicism. They showed themselves expert in this, without discovering that they were really serving the Church which her own defenders were betraying. But those defenders were not conscious traitors, and honestly thought their own cause that of the Church. Hence they shrank from exposure and danger of scandal, and insisted that Catholics should not show them up, or renounce complicity with their arms, lest the world should lose all confidence in Catholic controversy, and come to believe that a cause so defended cannot be good. And when indignant men vindicated the Church from the suspicion which this conduct had brought upon her, they were accused of introducing discord into the sanctuary, of firing on their own troops, of exhibiting to adversaries the repulsive spectacle of internal discord in a Church whose mark is unity, of bringing sacred things before the incompetent judgement of the outer world. This consideration, and the fear of injuring influences that might be powerful for good, have restrained many from repudiating practices from which their hearts revolted.

The extracts which we are about to give in illustration of this spirit are taken chiefly from books of a popular kind, which have very little authority to lose. We might begin with Damberger's voluminous *History of the Middle Ages*. It would be hard to find in the whole range of Protestant literature since the Centuriators a more monstrous production. But the character of the work is so notorious that, in spite of the real erudition of the author, it has fallen into an obscurity which it is better not to disturb. A far cleverer writer, Wilhelm von Schütz, whose works were much read and admired twenty years ago, will supply us with an example of German aberrations in this direction. In the year 1845 he wrote a tract on the massacre of St. Bartholomew, with a view to vindicate the Catholic cause from that long-standing imputation. He explains the case as follows: the massacre was planned for the purpose of ruining the Catholics, not the Huguenots; and its author was not the Catholic royal family, but the Protestant leader, Henry of Navarre, whose marriage to Margaret of Valois was part of a scheme to betray the Catholic Church and introduce a reactionary policy in favour of the Protestants. His accomplices were pseudo-Catholics acting in the Huguenot interest. The mistake is to suppose that the massacre was a blow aimed at the Huguenots, a conspiracy against them; it was a conspiracy in their favour. . . . The court had sold Catholicism to Protestantism. . . . Attention was to be diverted from the mixed marriage. Therefore the spectacle of a pretended Protestant massacre was instituted in order to deceive the Catholics.[13] In short, it was a got-up thing, perfectly understood by the so-called victims, and a shameful deception on the unfortunate Catholics.

Whilst Schütz in Germany attributes the massacre to the Protestant interest, Rohrbacher in France shows that it proceeded from Protestant principles. His way of defending the Catholics is to lay the blame on Protestant doctrines. Judged by the Reformers' standard, "the massacre was a divine act, which deserves our respect and admiration"; and "Charles IX had a right to do what he did, not only as king but as private individual; and any one may go and do likewise, whenever he has the power and inclination."[14]

The sixteenth century offers many tempting opportunities for manipulations of this kind. Rohrbacher's tone and manner may be gath-

---

[13] "Darin beruht das Missverstehen der Geschichte, dass man sich einbildet die sogenannte Bluthochzeit sei ein Schlag gegen die Hugenotten, eine Verschwörung gegen sie gewesen: es war eine Verschwörung für die Hugenotten. Der Hof hatte den Katholizismus an den Protestantismus verkauft und gab dafür den betrogenen Katholiken ein Feuerwerk, das scheinen sollte einen Schlag gegen die Hugenotten, statt mit Raketen, mit Blut zu feiern. Das Wesentliche lag in dem Katholisch-Protestantischen Beilager. Dies sollte niemand sehen: von ihm wollte man die Blicke abwenden. Deshalb ward das Feuerwerk eines Protestantisch sein sollenden Blutbades abgebrannt, dessen Prasseln die Katholiken zu täuschen die Bestimmung hatte. Die sogenannte Bluthochzeit war eine Anstiftung von Pseudo-Katholiken zu Gunsten einer Katholisch-Hugenottischen Reaktion. Dies geschah nur um die Katholiken zu täuschen und sie glauben zu machen, das, was in hugenottischem Interesse geschahen war, sei zugunsten der Katholiken verübt worden" (*Die aufgehellte Bartholomäusnacht*, pp. 11, 25, 31, 34).

[14] "D'après la croyance des huguenots et de leurs patriarches Luther et Calvin, que Dieu opère en nous le mal comme le bien, c'est une opération divine qui mérite nos respects et notre admiration. D'après le principe fondamental du protestantisme, que chacun n'a d'autre règle ni d'autre juge que soi-même, Charles IX avait droit de faire ce qu'il a fait, non seulement comme roi, mais encore comme particulier; et à chacun il est permis d'en faire autant, dès qu'il en a l'envie et la puissance" (*Histoire Universelle de L'Église*, xxiv, 640).

ered from what he says of Queen Elizabeth. Speaking of her refusal to marry, he says: "L'histoire remarque en effet qu'elle n'a pas eu un mari, mais plus d'un: Lingard en nomme jusqu'à huit."[15] The heading of the paragraph where this occurs, in which the author follows a notorious calumny of Cobbett, runs thus: "La papesse Elizabeth, avec ses maris et ses bâtards, ses emportements et sa tyrannie." Rohrbacher is still more unscrupulous in dealing with the death of Henry III. He was stabbed by a Dominican, and fell crying that he had been murdered by "ce méchant moine." For fear of scandal the historian says not a word of all this. Jacques Clément had only been "educated in a Dominican monastery"; he was carried away by Protestant principles, which justify his act, and Rohrbacher insinuates that he defied the authority of the Pope, and was at heart a Huguenot. So that the reader would never learn that the regicide was a Dominican, but might be led to suppose that he was in fact a crypto-Calvinist.[16]

In comparison with the systematic deceitfulness of Rohrbacher, the arts of Audin appear innocent. He is partial, unjust, and very often ill-informed or misguided, but he is rarely guilty of wilful mendacity. No man is honest who refuses to censure vice in persons of exalted station; but there is after all only a qualified dishonesty in such passages as that on the election of Alexander VI: "In these difficult times a man of the character of Alexander might well be regarded as an instrument of Providence. There is nothing, therefore, but what is quite natural in his election." Audin's irresolute wavering between straightforwardness and falsehood is fairly illustrated by his critical remark on the authority of Burchard: "Nous voudrions bien savoir comment on doit s'en rapporter aveuglément au Protestant, qui s'est chargé de déchiffrer ce journal."[17] He knew perfectly well that MSS. of the Journal abound—there are at least half a dozen at Paris alone—

---

[15] *Histoire Universelle de L'Église*, xxiv, 583.

[16] "Il fut tué la veille par Jacques Clément, né au village de Sorbonne, près de Sense, élevé au couvent des Dominicains de cette ville, et âgé alors de vingt-deux ans. Les assistants le mirent en pièces sur l'heure même. Il s'était porté a ce crime par de prétendues révélations. D'après le principe fondamental du Protestantisme, que chacun n'a de règle et de juge pour sa conscience que soi-même, Clément avait droit de faire ce qu'il a fait. D'après cet autre principe de Calvin et de Luther, que Dieu opère en nous le mal comme le bien, le régicide de Jacques Clément était une action divine. Il est criminel comme Catholique d'avoir agi en Huguenot, pour mettre la main, lui particulier, sur un roi, sur le chef d'une nation, sans le jugement ni l'ordre d'aucun tribunal supérieur à ce roi et à cette nation" (ibid., xxiv, 655).

[17] *Leon X*, i, 157, 304.

and they have often been consulted by historians; but he preferred to take advantage of the badness of the published text to excuse his refusal to avail himself of the authority of the journalist.

M. Nicolas, one of the most popular Catholic writers in France, in a volume written for the purpose of repudiating the co-operation proposed by M. Guizot for the defence of society against the principles of the Revolution, has been obliged to speak of the moral and social influence of the Protestant religion. Wishing to show that Luther encouraged polygamy, he quotes the Reformer's well-known answer to Brück, which, though sufficiently discreditable, is not enough so for M. Nicolas: "Luther lui répondit par cet oracle vraiment delphien: 'Il m'est impossible, en vertu de l'Écriture Sainte, de défendre à qui ce soit de prendre plusieurs femmes en même temps; mais je ne voudrais pas être le premier à introduire cette louable coutume chez les chrétiens.' "[18] Here every word is omitted by which Luther expresses his real sentiment on the matter; another is coolly introduced which converts an expression of dislike and disapproval into a positive recommendation, and the words "nollem primo introduci" are insidiously misinterpreted. Although the passage is well known, we must quote it for the purpose of comparison: "Ego sane fateor, me non posse prohibere, si quis plures vult uxores ducere, nec repugnat Sacris literis; verum tamen apud Christianos id exempli nollem primo introduci, apud quos decet etiam ea intermittere, quae licita sunt, pro vitando scandalo, et pro honestate vitae."[19]

It is recorded that when Papabroch, at the beginning of his long career as a Bollandist, visited Rome, and explained to the Pope the scheme of that great undertaking, Alexander VII expressed delight at hearing that there were methods by which the authentic Lives of the Saints might be distinguished from spurious fabrications. The art of criticism was then just beginning; it soon made progress in the hands of Mabillon, Ruinart, and Tillemont; and, in the perfection it has now attained, it is one of the surest defences of the Catholic system. But to writers of the school we have described its control is naturally unwelcome; for it prevents the arbitrary selection of facts and authorities, interferes with the perfect freedom of speech, and establishes something different from convenience as a test of truth. They therefore reject its laws, not only on principle, but in detail and in practice, and

[18] *Du Protestantisme et de toutes les Hérésies dans leur Rapport avec le Socialisme*, p. 560.

[19] *Luther's Briefe*, ed. de Wette, ii, 459.

deliberately return to the traditions of a period when the means of distinguishing truth from falsehood in ecclesiastical literature did not exist. Dom Guéranger, the learned Abbot of Solesmes, is the most outspoken of these systematic adversaries of modern knowledge. The critical spirit of the close of the seventeenth century, in which the members of the orders took the lead, and in which they were followed by the most learned men among the Jesuits as well as the Jansenists, sprang, he says, from a spirit of party, and belongs legitimately to the infidel Germans. If we would avoid scepticism, we must revise the canons of critical science, and we shall recover much contested literature.[20] On these principles, Dom Guéranger proceeds to rehabilitate many rejected documents and to revive exploded legends, such as the baptism of Constantine by Pope Sylvester. Before long we shall probably hear of writers who defend the authenticity of the Donation of Constantine, and the works of the Areopagite, and who will compensate for their credulity by an equally wilful rejection of authentic works; for the opposite exaggeration of literary scepticism and literary credulity are manifestations of the same reckless spirit.

Dom Guéranger's denial of the principles of science has necessarily conducted him to a position of hostility to all those who understand the manner in which learning serves religion. In particular, he has attacked the most accomplished layman among the French Catholics and the most eminent divine of the French clergy; and he has elicited replies from both. We will quote a passage from that of the Prince de Broglie, because it describes so accurately the method of the school of which Dom Guéranger is perhaps the most learned representative. He had assailed the *History of the Fourth Century* in three articles in the *Univers*, which were the beginning of those *Essays on Naturalism* from which we have already quoted. M. de Broglie says: "In the first and second articles I am a timorous Christian, who, to please the philosophers, attenuates dogmas, dissembles and tones down miracles, loves

---

[20] "On commence à se douter déjà que l'entrainement et l'esprit de parti ont été pour quelque chose dans la rénovation pour ainsi dire complète qui s'opéra, vers la fin du XVIIe siècle, dans la science de l'antiquité ecclésiastique. Les principes critiques qui prévalurent alors, et que les écoles incroyantes de l'Allemagne appliquent de si bon coeur aux évangiles mêmes, ont l'inconvénient de conduire logiquement au pyrrhonisme historique; les esprits sensés se trouvent donc réduits à les soumettre à l'examen; et l'on ne peut nier qu'il n'y ait là un profit tout clair pour la science, en même temps qu'un secours pour la religion et la société, qui ne sauraient s'accommoder du scepticisme" (*Essai sur le Naturalisme Contemporain*, i, 227).

to give to the facts of the Gospel and Church history a natural character and a rational interpretation. In the third, on the contrary, I am transformed into a blind enemy of reason, who denies it even the power of demonstrating the existence of God, and thus falls under the liberal decisions of the Church, so clearly confirmed by a recent document. By turns, I have passed so severe a judgement on the ancient nations as to cast doubts on the goodness of God, and on the other hand, have carried indulgence so far as completely to excuse idolatry. Either I am guilty of the most contrary things, or everything will serve to accuse me."[21]

While the Prince de Broglie treats his assailant with great consideration, the reply of Monseigneur Maret to the attack on his work on the Dignity of Human Reason and the Necessity of Divine Revelation strikes more vigorously home. Dom Guéranger had accused him of asserting the absolute necessity of revelation, and the impotence of the human reason. He was reminded that M. Maret teaches only the moral necessity of revelation, and that these words are in the heading of the chapter which he criticized. To this he replied that he had, indeed, seen the words in the summary, but that he had not paid regard to them, because they were contradicted—not by the text, but—by the title of the book.[22] Monseigneur Maret adds some touches to the description of the methods given by the Prince de Broglie: "I have shown that, in order to avenge some imaginary concessions to a separatist philosophy, and perhaps also unconsciously gratifying the jealousies of party spirit, Dom Guéranger consents to misrepresent, mutilate, and suppress my texts. He makes me say exactly the contrary of what I say; and if his quotation had been entirely faithful, he could

---

[21] "Réponse aux Attaques du R. P. Guéranger," *Questions de Religion et d'Histoire*, ii, 221.

[22] "Quand mon honorable ami M. l'Abbé Hugonin, s'étonnant d'une accusation que rien ne justifie, rappelle à D. Guéranger que je soutiens uniquement la nécessité morale de la révélation, et qu'il a pu lire ces mots dans le sommaire même du chapitre qu'il critique, que répond M. l'Abbé de Solesme? Il a vu en effet, dit-il, ces mots dans le sommaire; mais il n'en a pas tenu compte, parce qu'ils sont contredits par le titre du livre, qui porte, sans correctif, *Nécessité de la Révélation*. Est-il permis à un homme grave, à un religieux, à un prêtre, lorsqu'il s'agit de l'honneur d'un autre prêtre, de recourir à de pareilles échappatoires? Dans presque tous les traités de la religion, ne trouvons-nous pas un chapitre intitulé 'De necessitate revelationis', sans autre explication?" (Lettre de M. l'Abbé Maret, Doyen de la Faculté de Théologie de Paris à Nos Seigneurs les Évêques de France sur les attaques dirigées contre son livre: *Dignité de la Raison Humaine et Nécessité de la Révélation Divine*, par le R. P. D. Guéranger, 1858, p. 15).

not have made himself the accuser of my book. Carried away by controversy, he goes so far as to affirm absolute propositions which, if so stated, would deserve severe censure, and would be reached by pontifical condemnations."[23]

Nothing is more characteristic of the spirit of Dom Guéranger's writing than his repudiation of the liberty of conscience, and his denial of the inclination of the Church to freedom. M. de Broglie had written: "C'est donc avec la liberté et non avec le pouvoir qu'est l'alliance fructueuse et naturelle de l'Église. Elle a été autrefois le plus éclairé des pouvoirs, elle doit être aujourd'hui la plus pure et la plus regulière des libertés." Perhaps this may not be a very philosophical or exact statement; but to Dom Guéranger it appears as an insult to the Church: "De quel droit osez-vous ainsi dégrader celle qui n'a été élevée à la dignité d'Épouse d'un Dieu que pour régner avec lui?"[24] And in asserting the rights of the Church he is careful to assert his enmity to freedom: "Est-ce que par hasard l'Église serait exclue de la liberté, par la raison que l'erreur n'y a pas droit?"[25]

In this matter of the freedom of conscience Father Perrone, the last writer whom we shall cite among the representatives of the unscrupulous school, speaks with much greater judgement. But as a historical question he treats it with as little reverence for the moral obligations of literature as an Orangeman could have shown. Whilst the State punishes open non-conformity, but is compelled to respect concealed dissent, the peculiarity of the penalties imposed by the Church consists in their being directed against the sin of the individual, not against the danger to society; hence they may be incurred by thought as well as by word or deed. The object of the Church is always the conversion of the sinner, whilst that of the State is simply his exclusion or suppression. Therefore it has always been deemed unnatural that capital punishment for heresy should be inflicted by the priesthood; and those who, like de Maistre[26] or Balmez, have defended the Inquisition as a political tribunal in Spain, have denied that persecution

---

[23] ibid., p. 23.

[24] *Essais,* Préface, p. xxxv.

[25] ibid., p. xvii.

[26] "Jamais le prêtre n'éleva d'échafaud; il y monte seulement comme martyr ou consolateur: il ne prêche que miséricorde et clémence; et sur tous les points du globe, il n'a versé d'autre sang que le sien. Voulez-vous de plus connaître, par l'expérience, le véritable esprit sacerdotal sur ce point essentiel? Étudiez-le dans le pays où le prêtre a tenu le sceptre ou le tient encore. . . . Assurément, c'est dans le gouvernement des

ever raged in Rome. Father Perrone boldly denies that the Church proceeded against private opinions, and says that executions for heresy were rare or unknown in Rome.[27]

In his catechism of the Protestant religions he used arguments of the most calumnious kind in order to turn the mind of the people away from it—that the Reformers were men whose private lives were infamous; that Calvin died of a shameful disease, blaspheming and invoking the devil; and that the reform of morals and discipline commonly attributed to the Council of Trent, was proceeding prosperously, and the Church improving daily, when the Reformation interrupted the reform.[28] Such language, if it was not intended to mislead uneducated persons, would read like a satire on the Council of the Lateran.

It would have been easy to quote from the writings of Monseigneur Gaume against the classics passages more striking than these; but his writings belong to a different movement, and the object of his attack is not knowledge in itself, but profane learning. "It is the devil," says Gregory the Great, "who takes away from certain persons the desire of mastering secular sciences, because he knows how much they serve us in religious questions." The *Ver Rongeur* was the prelude to a general attack on the pursuit of all learning that is not purely religious; but writers like Father Ventura and others whom we have quoted went beyond this, and thought that even the things of the Church cannot be the objects of scientific knowledge. There is but one step from the denial of certainty to the denial of truth; and the theory of the applicability of falsehood followed immediately on the theory of the utility of ignorance. By a similar process calumny was grafted on mendacity.

---

pontifes que le véritable esprit du sacerdoce doit se montrer de la manière le moins équivoque" (*Lettres sur l'Inquisition Espagnole*, pp. 18, 21, 22).

[27] "La chiesa non ha mai proceduto contro le opinioni finché queste rimaneano nella conscienza o nel cervello balzano di chi le aveva. In Roma poi o non v'è o apena v'è qualche rarissimo esempio di alcuno messo a morte per sola eresia" (*Catechismo intorno alla Chiesa Cattolica ad uso del Popolo*, pp. 93, 94).

[28] "Già parecchi di essi ai tempi di Lutero erano tolti, ed altri scemati, e la riforma dei costumi e della disciplina si perfezionava oggidì, allorché risorsero quegli uomini ribelli contro la chiesa. Tali sono i corifei del protestantismo, uomini cioè, che a detto di un protestante, erano tutti per la loro malvagità degni del capestro. Calvino per ultimo morì disperato, bestemmiando e invocando il diavolo, di una malattia la più vergognosa, roso dai vermi" (*Catechismo intorno al Protestantismo ad uso del Popolo*, pp. 11, 23).

There are two things which it specially behoves every Catholic engaged in controversy to observe in his treatment of adversaries: that the discussion ought to be a means of converting them from error, instead of repelling them from truth by the fault of its defenders; and that no bitterness or personality should scandalize them by occasions of sin. The course enjoined by the Church is to win over opponents by considerate, gentle, generous, and affectionate treatment, joined to the most uncompromising and relentless exposure of their errors. If gentleness is a duty in the case of those errors against faith which are sinful in themselves, it is even more imperative where the error is a defect of knowledge, which, though indeed it may be a consequence of sin, can hardly be traced to its origin in the will. All Christians must in some measure feel and acknowledge this duty: but Catholics especially can judge of its importance by the horror with which the Church regards the giving of scandal, combined with her doctrine of exclusive salvation. It has been often disregarded in former disputes; but in our time a regular theory has been devised which inverts the law and renounces the Catholic spirit. Two paths appear to have led to this transition. One is the transfer of ecclesiastical language to another sphere. Those who have the sacramental power to bind and to loose, and who administer the ecclesiastical discipline, speak, by virtue of their office, in language of severity and commination even to individuals. It may fall within their province to utter the most solemn maledictions, and they may judge it probable that vehement denunciations will move to repentance those who are not utterly deaf to a voice that unites all the kinds of authority that belong to the father, the judge, and the king. Naturally, and almost imperceptibly, in an age when laymen exerted through the press an influence not less deep, and an authority often more extended, than the bishops themselves, they usurped the same weapons, spoke in the same tone, and affected to deal blows of equal weight. When the most illustrious prelates themselves, like the Bishops of Orleans and Mentz, mingled in the fray and placed themselves on equal terms with adversaries, it very easily happened that some of their privileges were forgotten by those who fought beside as well as against them, and that the thunder was sometimes imitated by those who could not wield the lightning.

Another course was more consciously followed with the same result. Catholics continually see things stated against the Church by educated and even learned men which, they are persuaded, cannot be sincerely believed. They are aware of the malignity of some, and are unable to credit the ignorance in which others persist with regard to Catholic matters. When, therefore, the inventions of men whose trade is lying are repeated by men whose profession is controversy, it is almost impossible to understand that ignorance can assume so closely the guise of wilful calumny. The plea of ignorance may be allowed in the case of Dr. Cumming or Mr. Whalley, but how can it be urged for Baron Bunsen, or M. Michelet, or Mr. Buckle? It is scarcely possible for Catholics to avoid feeling aversion and contempt for men whom they conceive to be wilfully distorting truth; and therefore, instead of confining themselves to the refutation of falsehood, which they are persuaded their opponent does not desire, they endeavour to expose his iniquity. This temper of mind was gradually transferred from controversy with aliens to discussions among Catholics, where there was the new element of insubordination, to which the origins of errors might be attributed. A Catholic might reasonably be supposed to know the religion he had been taught from childhood, and in which he ought to have been more and more confirmed by the practices of piety. If he erred, there was at once a suspicion that he had neglected those practices; or that he was moved by the dislike of obedience to hold what was not held by his teachers; or that he had culpably turned away from the proper guides to hearken to the flattering seductions of hostile parties. In every such dispute a question of morality was directly at issue. Both antagonists could not be equally in harmony with the sentiment of authorities which both acknowledged. In casting off this blame from himself, each necessarily fixed it on the other as a prejudice against his virtue. But where a writer is persuaded that his adversary is persisting in his error insincerely, or from wrong motives, the triumph he seeks is not to convince but to convict him. He desires to produce an effect, not upon him, but upon the audience, which may be impressed by the exposure of the man, while he will be insensible to the confutation of his views. Therefore he strives less for truth than for effect, and abandons the argument in order to pursue the man. He tries to gain every advantage over him; and the best chance he has is to disturb his presence of mind by making him lose his temper. That which will irritate him most is most likely to make him expose himself and give an opening to reply. It would be too long to inquire how many things contributed to promote this habit: in some places, the want of that forbearance which public assemblies often engender between men subject in common to a local special disciplinary system;

in others, the terror which anticipated or the temper which followed great social convulsions; in others, the extreme fierceness or perfidy of an infidel press. It was soon justified by theory; and in practice it seems becoming more general and more vehement.

To these combined causes it is due that a strong and vituperative opposition has been uniformly offered to the progress of Catholic thought. With scarcely one exception, all those who were most eminent in religious science have been denounced, by men not less zealous and devout than themselves, as the corrupters of doctrine and enemies of the Church; and the distance between the two parties was such as to justify a doubt as to their agreement in the same faith or in the same morality. This persecution of those who really advanced religious knowledge is, on the one hand, a natural and direct consequence of that common spirit which manifests itself in different ways in the philosophy of Ventura, the scholasticism of Kleutgen and Clemens, the politics of Donoso Cortés, the polemics of Veuillot, the educational theories of Gaume, and the historical method of Rohrbacher and Guéranger, and, on the other, the most characteristic symptom of the present condition of the Catholic Church. It assailed alike the two greatest thinkers among the Italian clergy, Rosmini and Gioberti, and in a less degree the best of their ecclesiastical historians, whom their knowledge of the Middle Ages prevents from becoming the supporters of things as they are—the Benedictine Tosti, the Oratorian Capecelatro, and the Dominican Marchese. In France it fell on the theoretical defenders of profane learning, like the Bishop of Orleans, and on the first Catholic authorities on theology and metaphysics, Monseigneur Maret and Father Gratry. The two foremost living divines in Germany, Döllinger and Kuhn, were accused in like manner—the one for his treatment of Church history, the other for a dogmatic method which seems heretical to the advocates of the scholastic theology; both alike for their theory of development. The few laymen out of Germany who occupy a rank in Catholic literature approaching that of the ecclesiastical leaders fared scarcely better. The Baron d'Eckstein was held a dreamer and an innovator, indifferent to the Dogma of the Church, for reasons such as in earlier times procured Gerbert and Bacon the reputation of wizards. The Prince de Broglie, while he was attacked by Donoso Cortés with the courteous arms of chivalry for preferring liberty to feudalism, incurred the ruder censures of Dom Guéranger because he recognized in history, besides the action of Providence, the operation of natural and secondary causes. Beyond the Atlantic the spirit is the same. When Dr. Brownson, urged forward by his powerful and independent mind, emancipated himself from the narrow and intolerant school which in the first moments of his conversion he had been taught to consider the legitimate form of Catholic thought, his great services did not protect him from denunciations as violent as those which, in the immaturity of his Catholic ideas, he had heaped on Dr. Newman. These, however, are difficulties in the way of improvement, which eminent men are able to overcome; and it is well that they should confront the obstacles which they alone can ultimately remove.

That which one class of Catholics sought by a sacrifice of truth on behalf of religion, others aimed at by making some scientific opinion the arbiter of doctrine. If there was a deliberate denial of the moral law, there was on the other hand an unconscious surrender of dogmatic truths. The philosophies of Hermes and Günther, Frohschammer's theory of the independence of speculation, and the extreme proposals of ecclesiastical reform made by Hirscher, before he became the adviser and defender of the Archbishop of Freiburg, are instances of such a failure resulting rather from confidence in human reason than from timid solicitude for the safety of God's Church. But the errors of these men proceed from no common principle, and in no wise agree together. The real antithesis to the spurious Ultramontanism that ramified from de Maistre into so many branches is to be found, not in the opposite errors, but in the true course which deflects on neither side.

The rise of the school we have considered depended, first, on the low ebb of scientific knowledge, and on its open hostility to religion, and, secondly, on the absence of any literary co-operation of Catholics with Protestants. Among its leaders there were men of great virtues and talents, and at least one man of genius; but there is not one to whom secular learning is really indebted. As they renounced more and more the results and spirit of modern science, they repelled Protestants, and ended by presenting religion in an aspect which did not entirely attract converts. The want of contact with men who believed in other religions left them in ignorance of real difficulties and of their true solution. To the opposite circumstance of familiarity with non-Catholic science we trace the formation of that Ultramontanism which we have described as the highest intellectual development of the Catholic system.

The prostration of religion on the Continent at the close of the last century was shared by the Protestants in an equal measure. But it was followed by a revived literary activity among them to which there is no parallel in modern history except the Revival of the fifteenth century, to which it bears a real resemblance. For, first, the intellectual movement which proceeded from Weimar to Jena, and Halle, and Heidelberg, and then to other German universities, like that of the Medicean age, obeyed no religious impulse, but was indifferent to doctrine. The Churches were not then either feared for their power or envied for their wealth; and Rationalism ignored, as it had no inducement to assail, them. Secondly, the mental exertion of the period of Goethe, like that of Erasmus, had no definite practical end to attain, no reward to earn but that of literary enjoyment, no mission to fulfil but that of satisfying the thirst for knowledge. Thirdly, the Revival of the nineteenth century, like that of the fifteenth, was distinguished principally by the recovery from oblivion of a forgotten age. But here the analogy is exhausted; for the effect of reviving antiquity was exactly contrary to that of the mediaeval restoration. The learning of the Renaissance was antiquarian. It overleapt a vast interval which it consigned to a complete neglect, in order to resuscitate an extinct society. It set up a remote ideal in all the arts of life, and bent its own civilization to fit the model it had disinterred. Therefore it predominated more in art than in science, because of its luxurious and idle temper, and it was also artificial, unnatural, imitative, and, like all imitators, arbitrary, and in theories of government absolute, and often revolutionary.

The character of the mediaeval Revival which is the distinctive achievement of the age in which we live was not antiquarian but historical. Its study was not of death, but of life—not of a world of ruins, but of that which is our own. Therefore its lesson was a lesson of continuity, not of sudden restoration or servile copying. It taught respect for the past, encouraged patriotic sentiments, and awakened the memory of hereditary rights. The study of national history, literature, and art was one of its most important results. This impulse was strongest in the north of Germany. There the feelings of men towards the Catholic Church were free from bitterness. She had been their companion in misfortune, had suffered under the same tyranny, and had been delivered by the same victories, and nowhere seemed to them formidable or oppressive. As the patriotic feeling carried back these thoughts to the preponderance of their country, the Reformation ceased to be the supreme glory of their nation, and the boundary of their retrospect. They recognized in its system one of the chief elements in their history, one of the most powerful influences over their ideas; but they also recalled a happier period of national greatness, when the princes of the Church were the best and the most beloved rulers of Germany. It was remembered that among the emperors who continued the long struggle with Rome there were many who could not be remembered by Germans with unmixed pride—that Henry IV and Henry VI were men of evil lives, Frederick I a tyrant, and Frederick II an alien; whilst the most devoted protectors of the Church—Charlemagne, St. Henry, Otto the Great, Henry III, and Rudolph of Habsburg—were the greatest of the rulers of the Empire.

Men approached these studies with minds that had been trained in pursuits free from the temptations of party spirit, and from the influence of religious opinions. They came from the study of antiquity, which from the time of Heyne had its home in the schools of Germany; and they applied to the investigation of the mediaeval records the tone and method of classical philology. Other causes contributed to this indifferent rather than impartial temper. The union of the Prussian Protestants had expressed the ruling disregard of dogmatic definitions; and the vague theology which it established could not so heartily oppose Catholicism as a more consistent system. Something must also be attributed to the influence of the Hegelian philosophy on the Rationalists. The pantheism of that school, regarding all things alike as manifestations of the same universal nature, substituted the test of success, and even the order of succession, for the distinction of right and wrong. It was held that all religion is a form of truth, good of its kind; but that the law of life is progress, and the earlier is less perfect than the later. Therefore the advance constituted by Catholicism over the religions of antiquity was explained with the same curious interest as the progress, effected by the Reformation upon the mediaeval Church, or by the Philosophy of the Absolute on dogmatic Protestantism. The question of truth resolved itself into one of fact. Events were studied in their nature rather than in their character; and mankind was allowed to exhibit properties rather than qualities. The action of divine or human will was alike excluded; and accident was denied as well as morality. The Hegelians asserted the unbroken continuity of cause and effect, and held that all the phenomena of history are reasonable and intelligible. There ensued a kind of optimism very conducive to a dispassionate treatment of the past. Then out of the Hegelian philosophy arose the school of infidel and almost atheistic criticism, which ignored the dogmatic differences, and reserved its hardest blows for the foundations of Protestantism.

These causes did not indeed dissipate ignorance and prejudice, but they promoted a critical study of details, and prevented the interference of passion, or interest, or zeal. A school of historians arose who made it their business to write on the Middle Ages as they wrote on the Persian War; who spoke of the Church as they spoke of the Areopagus, and applied to the most obscure moments of her history those tests of credibility and authenticity which had been lavished on Herodotus and Livy. They had nothing of the spirit of panegyrists or accusers; but with all their learning, acuteness, and equity, most of these men were destitute of that faculty or experience which would have enabled them to understand the significance of religion. They understood, better than any Catholic writers before them, the outward action of the ecclesiastical organism, the moral, intellectual, and social influence of the Church; but they knew nothing of her religious character. They betrayed the same incapacity in the study of paganism; and their interpretation of the Hellenic theology was often as superficial as their explanation of Catholic doctrine. The most universal of all modern scholars believed that sacrifice originated in the idea that the gods require food; and the most learned of all writers on mythology explained its rise and power by the artifices of the priesthood.

Catholics were astonished to find that men who wrote with fairness, and often with admiration, of the Church, who made themselves the champions of her maligned or forgotten heroes, who threw a new splendour over the lives of saints, and gave meaning and reality to much that had seemed simply marvellous, cared nothing for the doctrines of the institution they laboriously defended, and repudiated with indignation the proposal to submit to its authority. Subsequently, under the influence of the rising Catholic literature, there were many conversions among the historians, such as Philipps, and Hurter, and Gfrörer; but the great schools of historians who wrote, like Luden and Menzel, under the influence of the War of Independence, the disciples of Eichhorn, who sought after legal antiquities, the pantheistic followers of Hegel, and the disciples of Ranke, who were the critics and commentators of the mediaeval texts, were generally as far as possible from the faith of the Church. But the method they pursued in the investigation of truth prevailed against all hostile inclinations; and the scientific spirit which arose out of the decomposition of Protestantism became in the hands of Catholics the safeguard of religious truth, and the most efficient weapon of controversy.

It is little more than thirty years since a class of writers arose so completely masters of the science of the age that they required to apply no other tests but its methods in order to judge of its results. The name of Ultramontane was given in consequence of their advocacy of the freedom of the Church against the civil power; but the characteristic of their advocacy was, that they spoke not specially for the interests of religion, but on behalf of a general principle which, while it asserted freedom for the Church, extended it likewise to other communities and institutions. Convinced of the efficacy and right of the fundamental precepts of politics, they knew that the Church desires nothing incompatible with them, and can no more require the suspension of political law than of the moral order from which it springs. Pursuing the strict analogy between science and polity, they carried out the same principle in the investigation of philosophy and history. In history, they sought to obtain for the ecclesiastical authority no immunity but that which it would enjoy from the promotion of political rights; and in philosophy, they provided no protection for religious doctrines but in the advancement of scientific truth.

The causes which in Germany gave rise to this school of Catholic apologists did not exist in Italy, and were but partially present in France. The overwhelming authority of de Maistre, and the subtle influence of the theories of Lamennais, were serious obstacles. The want of a severe scientific training was felt by many very accomplished men whose natural place would have been among the defenders of those higher principles. Yet if we compare the tone of the writings of Eckstein and Lenormant, Ozanam, Maret, and de Broglie, with the histories of the Counts Montalembert and Falloux, or with the works of Father Lacordaire, and Monseigneur Dupanloup, the difference between the more scientific and the more brilliant portion of the liberal party among French Catholics is very apparent. But it is due to the general spirit of this school of writers, rather than to the special character of its deeper scholars, that so large a portion of the higher intellects of France, formerly more or less separated from the Church, have during the last few years gradually approached her.[29] The strength

---

[29] Cousin, Villemain, Augustin Thierry, Barrante, and even Guizot.

of this school was necessarily confined to Germany, where its most eminent representatives were the divines Mohler, Döllinger, and Kuhn, the metaphysicians Baader and Molitor, the political writers Görres and Radowitz, and historians such as Movers and Gfrörer. On all the questions on the authority of science and its agreement with religion; of the influence of the Church on the state of intellectual and political liberty; of the propriety of concealment for fear of scandal; the example and the precepts of this Ultramontane school are diametrically opposite to those of the Catholics whose language we have quoted.

The first Catholic theologian who commenced the protest on behalf of Christian science against obscurantism was Gügler of Lucerne, a man not surpassed in knowledge of Scripture and originality of mind by any of those whom we shall have to name. The intensity of the antagonism reveals itself very clearly in the energy of his language, which the present state of literature would not justify. In a lecture against the opponents of a scientific and critical study of Holy Writ, he expresses himself in the following terms: "Timidity is a child of darkness. . . . Wherefore do you complain of us that we investigate the sacred writings? Because, indeed, we are in danger of falling away from the truth; as if truth resided only in unreason, as if the sun's light shone only for the blind! You may be led to unbelieving thoughts quite as easily by merely reading the Scriptures as by a deeper study of them; much more easily, indeed, for error floats upon the surface, while truth lies deep below. If you would be faithful to your cause, you must close these books, and conscientiously abstain from reading them; and this, in fact, is what you really do, and so are secure not only from evil thoughts but from all ideas whatever. At least the lofty freedom of the Christian spirit is far from you, and you labour zealously to reach an opposite extreme. We are to believe the voice of the Church, you say, without seeking to understand; but where do we hear that voice? Not in your mouths certainly, or with the ears of the body; it must be sought for in history and in the written records of the Church. . . . We must examine each document historically, in order to know whether it is the authentic expression of the mind of the Church, without interpolation; only then does faith begin. . . . You endeavour to lull to sleep the spirit of inquiry, to suppress it when it is wakened, to check it in its growth; and by what means? Is it by a great intellectual preponderance and authority which enable you to assume the guardianship of the rest of the world? Far from it; but by ignorance, and by blindly casting suspicion on that which you do not understand. These are your arts, these are your only weapons; and thus you resemble madmen who would extinguish a conflagration, not by work, but by outcry. . . . The universal scorn under which you have fallen is of your own making; for as you will not listen to anything, and understand nothing, men deem that your cause is at an end, and you will seldom find any like ourselves who will honour you with a single word. . . . By your resistance you cast a hideous shadow on Christianity. When the ignorant, who are carried along by the current of the hour, look on you who profess to be true Christians, must they not believe that Christianity is taking darkness under its protection, and making it essential to its own existence? Will they not suppose that Christianity must dread all inquiry, and dare not approach the light? You have betrayed the sanctuary; you are the cause of the decline of faith, because its purity was long ago dimmed in yourselves. . . . Faith is not your motive, for it has no object but truth. . . . Embrace reason and science, become what you ought to be, and your kingdom will rise again from the dead. Give us a protection not only against unbelief, but one equally potent against superstition. It can only be truth, which lies hidden in the depths. To depart but a hair-breadth from it is as bad as to be a hundred miles away. . . . Your disposition is very remote from that love of truth which always asks, True or not true? Your question is, Shall we have it so or not? He that loves the truth has divested himself of all particular inclinations and preferences. He views everything with love or aversion as he finds it true or false. You, on the contrary, care only for externals, and, if the thing were not true, you still would not abandon it. This is the disposition that nailed Christ upon the cross, and made the Jews blind to the dazzling light."[30]

In 1826 the Baron d'Eckstein founded a review, *Le Catholique*, for the purpose of promoting these ideas in France. He pointed out the backwardness of the clergy in learning, and the necessity of a great improvement. The freedom of the press was requisite in order to restore to Catholicism its proper influence. Left without official protection, it would be obliged to look for support in all the sciences, and to furnish itself with new armour. But if the Church of France should make no effort to recover the supremacy of learning, and to master religion intellectually as she practised it in life, she could not resist science and impiety.[31]

---

[30] *Gügler, Rede gegen die Feinde wissenschaftlicher, besonders historisch-kritischer Untersuchung der heiligen Schrift, Nachgelassene Schriften*, i, 75–86.

[31] *Le Catholique*, i, 100; iii, 202; vi, 536; vii, 326. "Nous insistons fortement sur ces

About the same time, Baader was expounding at Munich, in an obscure, unsystematic, and aphoristic style, the most profound philosophy yet attained by Catholic speculation. The understanding requires to be satisfied just as much as the religious feelings of men; we cannot therefore rest contented with faith alone. Faith is the basis of true knowledge, and knowledge the complement of faith; for uninstructed faith is liable to be shaken, but he who has proceeded from faith to knowledge is sure of his belief. Therefore he insisted on the necessary progress of science as the safeguard of religion against unbelief, the only conciliation of authority and liberty, and the only means of protecting the faithful from the burden of a merely external authority which, when it imposes itself on the processes of the understanding instead of confining itself to its own sphere in the will and the reason, becomes as arbitrary as the system of unbelievers.[32] Molitor, the only rival of Baader among the Catholic philosophers of his day, dwells more particularly on the union of faith and knowledge. Science, which seeks to clear up what our consciousness dimly and uncertainly perceives, is the guide through the labyrinth of the feelings, and therefore harmonizes necessarily with faith. Human nature strives after unity with itself; and the union of faith and reason, things equally necessary and important, must be practically attainable at least to a certain extent.[33] "Knowledge," says Dr Döllinger, "is one of the forms, and a necessary portion of morality; and as without an enlightened understanding there can be no real and perfect morality, so also a true and comprehensive knowledge can subsist only in a mind disciplined by morality. . . . It is true that this love of wisdom, often as it is paraded and proclaimed, is as rare as it is precious; for he alone can

points, parce que l'Église est plus que jamais appelée au combat, et que si elle néglige le soin d'unir le savoir aux croyances, toutes les connaissances, toutes les découvertes des hommes tourneraient au profit du mauvais esprit et non à celui de la vérité. À l'avenir rien de ce qui constitue la science ne doit rester étranger à ses principaux défenseurs. Avec la simplicité de la foi on opère la conversion des barbares, et des sauvages; mais c'est avec la science unie a cette divine simplicité, que l'on peut conquérir les peuples vieillis au sein d'une longue civilization. Il ne faut pas craindre les véritables lumières, et redouter de s'en servir, si l'on veut anéantir les fausses" (iii, 204).

[32] Hofmann, *Vorhalle zur spekulativen Lehre F. Baader's*, pp. 20, 31. "Es muss erkannt werden, dass jede neugewonnene Wahrheit keine frühere aufhebt, sondern vielmehr bestätigt, indem sie dieselbe bestimmter entfaltet, und in der Aufzeichnung neue Beziehungen bereichert. . . . Sie müssen zur Erkenntnis kommen, dass eine neue Wahrheit möglich ist, wenn sie nicht in der schon gewonnenen ihre Wurzel hat, dass somit jede neue Wahrheit die alte voraussetzt, und derselben ihr offenbar gewordenes Sein zu verdanken hat" (p. 35).

[33] *Über die Tradition*, ii, 215, 216.

claim to possess it who is willing and able to dedicate himself to Truth with an absolute and unreserved devotion, and to make even the most painful sacrifice in its behalf. This resolute determination ever to seek the truth, the whole truth, and nothing but the truth, is a most difficult and unusual thing; and a man of whom this may be fairly said is not more easy to find than a man who is really determined to fulfil God's will alone." He says more particularly in another passage: "The understanding of ethical matters, or of matters approaching the domain of ethics, cannot be acquired by the operation of the reason alone. Otherwise the clever and the educated would be infinitely superior to the poor and uninstructed even in the knowledge of good and evil. But it is not so, and by an equally wise and equitable law man cannot master with his head what he does not at the same time receive into his heart; and if he hardens his will, he hardens at the same time his understanding against the truth."[34]

Nothing is more striking in the contrasts which the opposite schools present in their treatment of religious opponents than the manner in which they speak of the Reformation. The difference cannot be explained by the national prejudices; for there are many Germans whose language is as sweeping as that of Audin or Perrone. The tone of the greater German writers is very different. Görres speaks as follows: "In truth, it was a great and noble movement in the German people that brought about the Reformation. The Latin nations may condemn it altogether, but we cannot, for it sprang from the inmost spirit of our race, and extended nearly to the same limits. It was the spirit of a lofty moral disgust at every outrage on what is holy, wherever it may appear; of that indignation that is roused by every abuse; of that indestructible love of freedom which is sure always to cast off every yoke that perfidious violence would impose; in a word, the whole mass of salutary qualities which God bestowed on this nation, in order, when need should be, to ward off the corruption to which the warm South so easily inclines."[35]

Möhler says in his *Symbolik:* "Protestantism arose from the opposition to much that was undeniably evil and defective in the Church, and

---

[34] *Irrthum, Zweifel und Wahrheit,* pp. 25, 33, 37. "The real seat of certainty is in the conscience alone. . . . Do not expect that in return, as it were, for your supposed good intentions, a mere superficial acquaintance and dilettante occupation with science and its results will really lead you to truth and supply you with firm convictions."

[35] *Der Katholik,* xv, 279.

this is its merit—a merit not indeed peculiarly its own, since those evils were incessantly attacked, both before and after, on Catholic principles. It sprang partly from hostility to certain scientific representations of dogma, and certain forms of ecclesiastical life, which we may designate by the common term mediaeval, although these, again, had been the object of transforming endeavours, on behalf of the true system of the Church, from the end of the fourteenth century. . . . The Lutheran system will appear more excusable, as it will be shown to have proceeded really from a true Christian zeal, which indeed was, as in most other cases, injudiciously directed."[36] "At the beginning of the sixteenth century," says Döllinger, "a profound disgust at the Papacy of those days, and a not undeserved indignation at the abuses in the Church and the moral depravity of a too wealthy and too numerous clergy, had spread widely over Germany."[37]

It belongs to the nature of this school of divines that their theology is not scholastic. The systematic discussion of doctrines occupies a subordinate place in their method, as it is but one of several modes of ascertaining the teaching of the Church. The historic method, which considers less the covenience of imparting than the means of advancing the knowledge of religious truth, and which proceeds directly to the study of its sources and original records, alone suited their scientific spirit and the necessities of their position; whilst they renounced and condemned the other as barren and obsolete. In his letter to Bautain, Möhler thus describes it: "You have repeatedly and vehemently assailed the scholastic method, which still prevails in the schools of France, as incapable of embracing the boundless substance of the Christian religion, and bringing it to its full development. . . . You attack a form of theological science whose special characteristic I would describe as a love for external demonstration, with a theology that supplies a quantity of proofs, but does not help us to know the thing itself which is to be proved; a theology that never gets through the mass of arguments to the truth itself, and understands better how to hang Christianity round about a man than how to convert him into a Christian. . . . This appears to me your most signal merit."[38] Professor

---

[36] *Symbolik*, pp. 11, 113.

[37] *Kirche und Kirchen*, p. 10.

[38] *Sendschreiben an Bautain, Gesammelte Schriften* ii, 142. Not long before, Eckstein had sketched the state of scholastic theology in France: "Mère céleste des sciences, la théologie n'est enseignée que comme une scholastique stérile dans l'école cartésienne.

Kuhn expresses himself still more strongly in reference to Kleutgen: "If we believe the modern restorers of Scholasticism, the older divines taught with one voice exactly the same doctrine on all the chief points of science which they now proclaim as perfect wisdom and genuine Catholic science. . . . From this wholly unhistorical view of the theology of former days they draw conclusions for the pursuit of theology in our day, which must inevitably injure it; besides which the partisans of this view, by investing their own knowledge and opinions with the authority of the Catholic schools, make their own intellectual work much too easy, and that of others unnecessarily difficult."[39]

The principles of civil and intellectual freedom are maintained by the Ultramontane writers as the necessary condition of that harmony between religion and political as well as moral science which it is their object to obtain. Eckstein deplores, in the first number of his review, that the fear of revolution should have given to the writings of apologists a reactionary taint which was neither requisite nor useful for the maintenance of sound doctrine.[40] He thundered against that monstrous combination of politics and religion which was sought by the inter-vention of a religious police; and he warned the Royalists that a terrible explosion might be the fruit of such mean and secret efforts, and of an impotent oppression exercised by men who, unable to obtain a triumph by open combat, sought it by artifices.[41] A quarter of a century later, Döllinger appealed to the French clergy with a similar warning in favour of liberty: "The Church of France cannot expect that she will be allowed to constitute permanently an exceptional domain of freedom in a state which is not free. . . . She will obtain her just share of the general freedom and will find it not more satisfactory and more secure than if she only forms an exception to the general rule."[42] The Bishop

---

Dans celle de M. Lamennais, elle dégénère en une vaine ostentation de polémique sur l'autorité. Nos aïeux, que nous appelons grossiers, étaient plus avancés que nous dans la science catholique: aujourd'hui un certain parti semble croire que tout a été dit, qu'il n'est plus besoin de penser, d'aimer, de méditer, mais de croire et de s'endormir" (*Le Catholique*, viii, 650).

[39] *Katholische Dogmatik*, i, 916.

[40] *Le Catholique*, i. 9.

[41] *Avant-propos*, pp. 85, 99: "La liberté eût conservé à la religion tout le terrain que les inquisitions lui on fait perdre."

[42] *Betrachtungen über die Kaiserkrönung*, 1853, p. 40. "it is the first principle of the constitutional system that the sovereignty resides, not in the person of the monarch alone, but in the monarch and the people in inseparable unity" (*Debates of the Bavarian Chamber of Deputies*, 1849, i, 432).

of Mentz speaks with the same frankness of the political claims of the Church: "It is perfectly untrue that the Church now claims for her external position all that in former times may have been laid down by a Pontiff when all Christendom revered him as a father. . . . The altered circumstances necessarily require a completely new arrangement of the relations between Church and State. This is what our age is struggling to effect. From the Reformation to the present day it has never been possible to realize it. The recollection of the old Catholic unity survived in men's minds, and they attempted to settle matters in accordance with these recollections in all the lesser states, without reflecting that the old conditions had departed. Thence arose a truly absurd imitation of mediaeval institutions; and that which had been great and legitimate, considered from the point of view of Catholic unity, became, in different circumstances, unnatural and intolerable. Let the world manage its relations with the Church after the manner of the Middle Ages, when by God's mercy it had returned to the unity of religious belief; till then another basis is needed, which I can discover nowhere but in an honest recognition of the freedom of all Christian communities admitted by the State."[43]

The defence of intellectual freedom is founded not on the rights of reason so much as on the duty and on the interests of the Church. The danger to the priest, wrote Eckstein, is less in a momentary oppression than in exaggerated triumph. By every act that does violence to intellect he deludes himself, and the motive is either passionate anger or pure idleness.[44] Neither academies nor universities, but the Church alone can reconcile the unrestricted progress of science with human welfare; the Church, not by acting as she did in the Middle Ages, or by striving, as she strove through the Jesuits, to control the education of European society—for we are neither in the Middle Ages, nor in the sixteenth century—but by employing all the knowledge and reflection of mankind, without putting any impediment in its way.[45] With Görres this was also a favourite theme: "Where will this freedom of speech and writing end? Will not the eternal pillars of religion, law,

---

[43] Ketteler: *Soll die Kirche allein rechtlos sein?* p. 30. In the National Parliament of 1848 he spoke in the same way for the freedom of instruction: "I desire that the unbeliever shall be allowed to bring up his children in unbelief; but it must be lawful for the strictest Catholic to give his children a Catholic education" (*Frankfort Debates*, p. 2183).

[44] *Historisch-politische Blätter*, xi, 578.

[45] ibid., p. 581.

virtue, and society at last be undermined and washed away? Fools! to believe that God has made the enduring order of the universe to depend on your vigilance, and has planted the foundations of the moral world in the blind wit of man! . . . The mind tolerates no tyrants. You can measure off the fields, they bear your limits patiently; but draw your boundary round the flood, divide the air into compartments and districts, contain the fire—how shall you, with your rude instruments shut up ideas and arrest the beams of thought? All that you will gain is, that, by the indignation with which men will be animated at the sight of your violence, the spark that goes forth still and harmless will be transformed into a thunderbolt, and that which would have passed away in a mild electric glow will gather into a destroying tempest."[46]

In an address to King Lewis of Bavaria on his accession which he places in the mouth of the greatest prince of his line, Görres takes care to exhort him faithfully to protect the freedom of thought against the interference of the clergy: "Pride has ever been the rock on which the priesthood has most easily been wrecked. As they are always busy with exalted things . . . and are instituted by God Himself, it may but too easily happen that they will confound His spirit with their own, identify themselves with the sanctity of their vocation, and, instead of obeying the command to govern only by voluntary self-abasement, and to seek their pride in humility, will glory in their office, and extend its functions over a sphere from which by nature it is excluded."[47] The peculiar autonomy of science is accurately defined by Möhler. Science,

---

[46] *Politische Schriften*, v, 166, 135. "Resist the advance of learning, and behold, the genius strikes with his staff, the waters are parted asunder, and the waves stand up like walls on either side; pursue with your hosts, with your warriors and chariots and horses, and the waters shall close over you, and Pharaoh shall be drowned with all his army . . . Go rather and cultivate the new land in the sweat of your brow, and learn to adapt yourself to the altered times. Learn that, in order to govern, wisdom, understanding, ability, and virtue are henceforth required, and make your peace with the coming generation."

[47] *Maximilian der Erste an den König Ludwig von Baiern, Politische Schriften*, v, 256, 241. "While faith, which is internally free and inevitably tends to freedom, is externally bound within the Church . . . knowledge, on the contrary, inasmuch as it acts through conviction, and compels minds by internal force, must be outwardly free, and the interchange of ideas in its special sphere must be arrested and controlled by no unnatural restriction. . . . Be ye, therefore, a Christian prince, at once a pillar of faith and protector of the freedom of the intellect; and let your example put to silence the zealots of both kinds who hold the two things to be incompatible. . . . As deep as thought can penetrate into the nature of things, as high as it can breathe on the summits of the intellectual world, everywhere let its course be kept free by you; and be not frightened if in the ardour of its progress it quits the established paths."

he says, resting on a law of internal necessity which is identical with truth, can arrive at a conscious knowledge of it only by freedom. External bonds produce in literature miserable, superficial, sophistical results. He that has penetrated, by means of original research, to the inmost sanctuary of science, knows how solemn is the reception she gives to her followers—what self-denial, what sacrifice of their own will, and what renunciation of all personal interest she demands—and how she exacts that they shall give themselves up to her own laws.[48]

These extracts must suffice towards the solution of the doubt whether the Church desires the establishment of freedom as the highest phase of civil society, independently of her own interest in it, and of the question of her attitude towards the promotion of learning. But it is necessary to notice briefly an opinion held by some who are either ignorant of the Catholic system or especially hostile to it, that an arbitrary authority exists in the Church which may deny what has been hitherto believed, and may suddenly impose upon the faithful, against their will, doctrines which, while there is no warrant for them in the past, may be in contradiction with the existing and received conclusions of ecclesiastical, or even profane, science. The Ultramontane divines, having regard to this impression, have stated with special care the limited nature of the limits of the Papal authority. Möhler affirms that it was at one time greater than it has since come to be in consequence of the general progress of civilization and knowledge, which rendered its leading-strings insupportable. Rude times, he says, required a strong concentration of power to reform them; and the violence of internal forces called into existence a strong external control. In this way a dictatorship was given to the Pope. But it had no sooner done the work for which it was created than the absolute power was again restricted by the influence of such men as St. Bernard. It is a proof of the efficiency with which the Popes used their power that men grew tired of it so soon. In proportion as intellectual and moral culture improved under it, the temporary form of the Roman supremacy necessarily became intolerable.[49]

Such as it now canonically exists, this authority is described by

[48] *Gesammelte Schriften*, i, 280. "The union of reason and faith must be produced by no external coalition; for nothing is more contrary to reason than the introduction of a foreign authority into its sphere, which is the case where faith is assumed as a postulate; namely, when speculation, unable to proceed farther in its one-sided course, despairing in the power of reason, throws itself violently into the arms of faith" (Molitor, *Über die Tradition*, ii, 215).

[49] *Gesammelte Schriften*, ii, 27.

Döllinger in several places. "You must allow me," he said in the Frankfort Parliament, "to put aside once for all, as entirely groundless, the assertion that the Pope is an absolute ruler in the Catholic Church. . . . No authority is more hampered than his by divers established limitations, and by a legislation descending to the most minute details, which the Pope cannot set aside, and which binds him as much as every other Catholic. If you imagine that there is any room in the Catholic Church for a purely arbitrary power of Pope or bishop, you are greatly mistaken."[50] There is no society in the world whose constitution is more carefully organized, or more exactly regulated, than the Catholic Church. In that Church it is provided that the means of oppression, the tyrannical abuse of entrusted power, shall enjoy the smallest possible scope that is possible among men. Like a vast encompassing net, our ecclesiastical law extends over the whole Church; and none can break through it without abandoning her communion. . . . Blind obedience is neither exacted of the Christian nor conceded by him; and he must reject it as soon as he discerns, or believes that he discerns, something sinful in it. At the same time, he knows that nothing can be proposed to him that is not founded on the immutable order and the laws of the Church."[51]

It is sufficient to appeal to the example of Möhler,[52] Döllinger,[53] and the other principal authors of the school, as a token of their opinion on the propriety of concealing truth for fear of scandal. "Everything must be told," says Gügler, "openly, clearly and without reserve, lest the deceit and suspicion that already surround all the relations of life should penetrate into the temple of science. Here no accommodation, no inherited custom, can be tolerated; whatever checks the free and genuine exhibition of character must be laid aside."[54] Some friends remonstrated with Görres on the manner in which he had spoken of the Popes in his Introduction to Cardinal Diepenbrook's

---

[50] *Debates*, p. 1674.

[51] *Die Freiheit der Kirche*, pp. 18, 19.

[52] *Symbolik*, p. 353; *Neue Untersuchungen*, p. 382.

[53] *Lehrbuch der Kirchengeschichte*, ii, 229, 231, 234.

[54] *Nachgelassene Schriften*, i, 88. "La vérité est dans l'Église; elle possède donc les lumières; elle ne cessera jamais de dominer par la religion et la science; . . . on répétera ce vieux mot de Fontenelle, que toutes les vérités ne sont pas bonnes à dire. C'est une erreur. Il faut les proclamer toutes, si l'on ne veut que l'imposture se serve de la vérité partielle contre la vérité générale, et de la vérité générale contre elle-même" (Eckstein, *Le Catholique*, vii, 326).

Suso. In one of his letters he replies: "They are wrong in wishing truth to be disguised; that is always the worst possible policy, and now most of all. It is dangerous because it is dishonest, and quite unavailing besides. I vote everywhere fearlessly for the pure freshness of truth."[55] This was the maxim with which Möhler inaugurated his lectures on ecclesiastical history: "It is obvious that the student of history must not pervert facts; and one may suppose that Christianity expressly prohibits falsehood. From the Christian point of view most of all, therefore, we are forbidden to be partial, to alter facts, to omit one thing, to be silent on another, or to add any thing which we have not found."[56]

The Catholic is subject to the correction of the Church when he is in contradiction with her truth, not when he stands in the way of her interests. For there is nothing arbitrary or extemporaneous in the authority which she wields; the laws of her government are of general application, ancient, public, and distinctly defined. There is a certain number of ideas which the Christian irrefragably believes, with such a faith as no scientific man thinks of reposing in any of the progressive realizations of inductive science. And he feels that such ideas as the existence of God, the immortality of the soul, and the punishment of sin, can neither be destroyed by knowledge nor impede its acquisition. Not that he thinks these great religious ideas ought to remain in sterile isolation. Like other general principles, each of them is capable of being made the basis of a vast superstructure of doctrine, proceeding from it with logical necessity. The work of this development has been performed by the organic action of the Church, which in the course of centuries has worked out a consistent system of doctrine, altogether free from accidental or arbitrary elements, the inevitable result of the principles of faith reacting upon the strict laws of thought and historical

---

[55] *Gesammelte Briefe,* i, 314. The following are the passages alluded to: "The Popes had become enslaved to their passions; . . . and that very French policy which they had invoked in the House of Anjou, to protect them against the violence of the Germans, was the appointed instrument to heap shame upon their heads, and to forge the fetters, to escape from which they, distrusting God and his divine order, and their own right, had played a senseless game, and had connected themselves with degraded things. The thirst for treasure was soon accompanied by the thirst for power, and the internal government of the Church sank more and more into the principles of the absolute dominion of the spiritual head: . . . a scandal on the side of the spiritual authority that raged irreconcilably, without measure, without dignity, without charity" (*Einleitung,* pp. xxvii, xxix).

[56] *Gesammelte Schriften,* ii, 284.

growth. Every part of this system is equally certain, and, if not equally necessary to be known, yet equally incapable of being denied. No part of it can be destroyed by the progress of knowledge, the last defined dogma no more than the first, no more than the existence of God, or the immortality of the thinking being.

But there is an outward shell of variable opinions constantly forming round this inward core of irreversible dogma, by its contact with human science or philosophy, as a coating of oxide forms round a mass of metal where it comes in contact with the shifting atmosphere. The Church must always put herself in harmony with existing ideas, and speak to each age and nation in its own language. A kind of amalgam between the eternal faith and temporal opinion is thus in constant process of generation, and by it Christians explain to themselves the bearings of their religion, so far as their knowledge allows. No wonder if, morally, this amalgam should be valued by its eternal rather than by its temporary element, and that its ideas should come to be regarded as almost equally sacred with the dogmas on which they are partly built. For they have the prestige of possession in their favour; they have come to be mixed up with social institutions and with philosophical speculation; and they form the outside line of defence in the controversial stronghold of Christendom.

But as opinion changes, as principles become developed, and as habits alter, one element of the amalgam is constantly losing its vitality, and the true dogma is left in an unnatural union with exploded opinion. From time to time a very extensive revision is required, hateful to conservative habits and feelings; a crisis occurs, and a new alliance has to be formed between religion and knowledge, between the Church and society. Every victory thus gained, though in its personal aspect it is a victory of innovators over those who seem to stand in the old paths, and to defend the interests of the unchangeable, is in reality a victory of truth over error, of science over opinion. It is a change not to be deplored but to be accepted with joy. It is a process which, though it has its crises, must be always progressing. There is always some mass or other in the temporary element of the amalgam which is becoming rusty and worn out, and fit only to be thrown aside. And as this purging process is one that involves opinions and feelings nearly conjoined with faith, there will always be an apparent danger, which, however, will at once disappear before the vigour of Catholics who will break the bonds of human tradition, and associate themselves with the progress of their times. The danger is only for those who fail to distinguish the essential from the accidental, and who cling to their religion, not for its substance, but for its appendages. Such men fall away altogether if their own way of explaining dogmas to themselves, and reconciling them with opinions, is cut from them. And even those who see clearly the difference between substance and accident must feel how important it is that their love and allegiance to the Church should be exhibited in those outer spheres where attachment takes the place of faith.

The fear of giving scandal, and the unwillingness to question too closely the limits of authority, are therefore the two motives which make the best-informed Catholics very circumspect in destroying opinions which have become amalgamated with faith. But these motives are misplaced in an age when Catholics can no longer shut themselves out from contact with the world, nor shelter themselves in ignorance. When all opinions are perpetually canvassed in a literature over which no authority and no consideration for others has any control, Catholics cannot help attempting to solve the problems which all the world is discussing. The point is, that while they solve them religiously, they should likewise solve them scientifically; that they should so comprehend them as to satisfy both conscience and reason—conscience, by a solution consistent with the infallible criterion of faith, and reason, by one defensible on grounds quite external to religion.

When a man has really performed this double task—when he has worked out the problem of science or politics, on purely scientific and political principles, and then controlled this process by the doctrine of the Church, and found its results to coincide with that doctrine, then he is an Ultramontane in the real meaning of the term—a Catholic in the highest sense of Catholicism. The Ultramontane is therefore one who makes no parade of his religion; who meets his adversaries on grounds which they understand and acknowledge; who appeals to no extrinsic considerations—benevolence, or force, or interest, or artifice—in order to establish his point; who discusses each topic on its intrinsic merits—answering the critic by a severer criticism, the metaphysician by closer reasoning, the historian by deeper learning, the politician by sounder politics and indifference itself by a purer impartiality. In all these subjects the Ultramontane discovers a point pre-eminently Catholic, but also pre-eminently intellectual and true. He finds that there is a system of metaphysics, and of ethics, singularly agreeable to

Catholicism, but entirely independent of it. Not that this labour is an easy one, or one capable of being brought to a close. Each generation has to carry it forward. None can complete it; for there will always be some progress to be made, some new discoveries to adopt and assimilate, some discord to harmonize, some half-truth which has become an error to lop away. It is a process never to be terminated, till God has finished the work of educating the human race to know Him and to love Him.

But it is a work which no Catholic can deem either impracticable or unnecessary. It is not an idle enterprise: if we seek, we shall find. Religion can be made intelligible if we take the pains to make it so; its proofs may be found, its laws ascertained, and the conscience and reason constrained to acknowledge them. And Catholics are the only persons who can enter on this field of labour with perfect freedom; for they alone have a religion perfectly defined, clearly marked off from all other spheres of thought; they alone therefore can enter these spheres free from all suspicion of doubt, and from all fear of discord between faith and knowledge. If this clear distinction has ever been forgotten by Catholics, defeat was sure to follow, and that defeat was the victory of truth. Authority may put itself in opposition to its own code; but the code is vindicated by the defeat of authority. Thus it was in politics during the drama of the Sicilian Vespers, and in physical science during the opposition to Galileo. Those experiments have taught authority its own bounds, and subjects the limits of obedience; and they have destroyed the last conceivable obstacle to the freedom with which a Catholic can move in the sphere of inductive truth.

[9]
The Munich Congress

The authorized Report[1] of the Congress of Catholic divines and men of letters which was held at Munich three months ago has just been published. Combined with the testimony of several eye-witnesses, it gives us a clear idea of an event beyond measure interesting and suggestive in its details, and destined probably to exercise an almost incalculable influence in the Church. The inaugural address of the president, if it stood alone, would be a work of rare significance; but, in conjunction with the circumstances under which it was delivered, it forms an epoch in the ecclesiastical history of Germany which ought not to be overlooked or undervalued by Catholics in other lands. The circumstances, indeed, from which the Munich conference derives its character present no close analogy with the particular conditions of religion in the rest of Europe. We cannot, by altering the names, apply the narrative or point the allusions to ourselves. The idea would, in that case, have had no practical significance, and the means of realizing it could not have been found out of Germany. But its importance extends beyond national boundaries; and the tree that was planted in the chapter-house of St. Boniface, if in time to come it bears fruit at all, will bear it for the whole of the Catholic world.

The outline of the facts is sufficiently familiar to the public. In the beginning of August a circular was put forth by Dr. Döllinger and two of his friends, inviting the Catholic divines and scholars of Germany to a literary conference, to be opened on the 28th of September. Nearly a hundred professors, authors, and doctors of divinity assembled in the Benedictine monastery at Munich on the appointed day. Some of them were deputed by their bishops; and the assembly contained about

Published in *The Home and Foreign Review* 7 (January 1864):209–244. Döllinger I, p. 326; Acton-Simpson III, p. 155. Reprinted in Acton, *Church and State*, pp. 159–199.

[1] *Verhandlungen der Versammlung katholischer Gelehrten in München vom 28 September bis 1 Oktober 1863*. Regensburg: Manz.

a dozen laymen. During four successive days seven meetings were held, which lasted about three hours each. Several of the speeches were ordered to be printed in the protocol; and two propositions affirming the rights of authority in matters of opinion were adopted after a short discussion. An address of fidelity to the Holy See was unanimously voted: and it was resolved that the meeting should be annually repeated. The proceedings terminated with a dinner in the refectory of the Benedictines, at which the Archbishop of Bamberg and the Bishop of Augsburg gave toasts; and the Pope, by a telegraphic message, bestowed his blessing on the Congress and on the work it had begun. What was the nature of the Congress, and of the work it had begun, we shall endeavour to explain.

In former times theologians were generally held together, as they still are in several countries, by the influence of a uniform system of education, and by fidelity to the traditions of the schools. But no such bond now unites the divines of Germany. Reared in universities which are governed by opposite opinions, and exposed to very different influences according as their lot may be cast in Austria or in Prussia, in Catholic Bavaria or amid the mixed population on the Rhine— sometimes familiar from early youth with the strength and the weakness of Protestant and Rationalist literature, and sometimes brought up in the elaborate seclusion of the seminary or the religious house—they often, according to the curriculum prescribed in certain states, combine a sound knowledge of classics, history, or philosophy, with the special studies of the priesthood, and often, on the other hand, are trained almost exclusively in the theological course. There are instances among the older priests that testify to the success with which, either from religious animosity or from political jealousy, governments have frequently tried to tinge the teaching of the school with uncatholic sentiments; and there are others who bear witness to an extreme reaction against these encroachments. Varying in national character and in mode of speech, disciples of masters whose contending systems have distracted the peace of the Church, they represent different modes of teaching and different schools of thought, the Catholicism of different countries and of different generations. There is no centre of learning in Germany, and no theological headquarters. They have nothing like the Sorbonne, or even like Maynooth; and there is no master among them whose works are the common text-books, or whose name altogether overshadows that of every rival. They have not yet fought out, with their own resources and on their own behalf, the great controversies of modern theology. Whilst some have benefited largely by the results of Protestant science, and others have been influenced by Protestant opinion, many have tried to intrench themselves against both influences behind the systems prevailing in Italy or France. Nearly all the great divisions, therefore, that subsist among the Catholics of other countries have been adopted and naturalized in Germany, in addition to the powerful but discordant action of Protestant learning; and the divines are almost as far as possible from harmony in their tone of thought and in the tendency of their theological views.

The first broad and fundamental distinction among them is one which ramifies into many others, and derives its importance from causes peculiar to the literary character of the German people. This is the distinction between writers of the practical and those of the scientific class. It is the habit of some men to think chiefly of the immediate interests of religion, and to be guided by them in the formation of opinions and the use of knowledge; whilst others consider principally the advancement of learning, with a general assumption that it must contribute to the glory of God. Men of the latter school never shrink from making an admission or concession to Protestants or unbelievers, nor from censuring Catholics, or abandoning and reversing received opinions, if they judge that such a course is demanded by scientific reasons, though they are conscious that the case may be used, and perhaps forcibly used, to prejudice people against the Church. They labour to add to the store of known truths without reference either to the shock which each discovery inflicts on those whose views it contradicts, or to the fear lest the new discovery should be misapplied; and they discard entirely the management and economy of knowledge. This very disregard, however, presupposes the existence of another class of men, whose work it is to adapt and explain the results of science to unprepared minds which would otherwise be puzzled or misled by them, to convert them into instruments of controversy, and to prevent them from being misinterpreted or abused.

Those who are charged with the duty of watching over the purity of the faith are naturally more alive to the importance of this latter function than to the benefit which accrues to religion from the progress of ecclesiastical science. The writers to whom they look for aid in their pastoral office labour not so much to instruct the learned as the ignorant, the prejudiced, and the young—to restore discipline, to defend authority, to refute calumny, and to prevent scandal. The spirit that animates the purely scientific divines, and the principle that guides their researches, often become almost unintelligible to men absorbed in this avocation. It appears to them that there can hardly be anything necessary or profitable to the Church in a kind of literature of which the results are frequently unwelcome, the professors deficient in sympathy with their wants and difficulties, and the immediate effects in some cases demonstrably pernicious. Hence very naturally proceeds jealousy, not only of particular views and certain definite propositions, but of the principle and tenour of a scientific theology. When the test applied to the spirit of a writer is the efficacy of his aid in the defence of religion, in meeting hostile arguments, and in augmenting the polemical resources of Catholics, the most profound theologian is very likely to be found wanting. For the growth of knowledge does not necessarily assist these objects; but it is perpetually bringing to light, or establishing, or repeating conclusions which strew the path of the controversialist with difficulties, or cut two ways, or compel a revision of opinions. A Catholic scholar will often be the first to ascertain a fact unknown to Protestants, and hostile to some view adopted among Catholics; he will disprove some cherished claim or assertion, weaken the force of some popular or conventional argument, and multiply problems as fast as he advances knowledge. The spirit which enables him to do this is widely different from that of the more purely practical and official functions of the priesthood; and it is abhorrent to many persons, even when manifested in questions touching which there is no dispute. An estrangement subsists even without any obvious or material cause of antagonism; and the opposition thus engendered, even when it expresses itself in a vague animosity against the tone and spirit of a school, is not the less profound and real.

There is naturally a close alliance between the episcopate and the divines of the second or practical class—those who, in order to shelter faith, seek to dispense and qualify the truth to the faithful. It generally happens that these men, while they uphold the liberties of the Church, together with the authority of the Holy See, which are essentially inseparable, proceed, with an inconsistency more apparent than real, and not peculiar to the advocates of their cause, to depress intellectual freedom as much as they sustain the rights of the Church. For it is in the learned literature of their country that they see the worst adversary of religion and morality; and therefore even Catholics who help to promote it are obnoxious to them. The obvious way to make it harmless, they conceive, is to bring it as much as possible under the control of ecclesiastical authority. Confident that the Church already possesses scientific systems and conclusions free from danger and error, and equal to any emergencies that may arise, they desire to arrest the uncertain movement of human thought. For this reason the common designation for the school is the Scholastic or the Roman. If the intellectual activity of Catholic Germany is to be brought under subjection to the Roman congregations, it must settle into those systems with which the Roman divines are conversant, and for which, therefore, a direct theological as well as dogmatic influence must be vindicated. The prodigious defects of many German writers, and the violent hostility to Rome which in many shapes survived amongst them until lately, have powerfully contributed to recommend these designs. Their most definite form is a demand that the fixed traditions of theology, as taught by the Jesuits in Rome, shall be made binding on the German Catholics, in order that Rome may not lose all control over their literature. The outward expression of these ideas is a demonstrative zeal for the spiritual and temporal claims of the Holy See, an unqualified reliance on the efficacy of the Index, and a predilection for scholastic theology.

A combination of circumstances has made the city of Mentz the stronghold of these opinions. The Bishop, von Ketteler, one of the most imposing characters in the Catholic episcopate, was raised to the see fifteen years ago, after the nominee of the Chapter had been refused by the Pope. This event, occurring in the midst of the troubles of 1848, violently agitated the public mind in Central Germany; and the University of Giessen, where the rival of the new Bishop was professor of theology, became a hotbed of the sentiments which he was resolved to put down. He accordingly removed the faculty of theology from that university, and reconstructed it under his own eye, and in his own spirit, in the seminary of Mentz. More recently came the obstinate assaults of the Hessian Liberals on the freedom of the Church and the school; and a struggle was engendered by the restrictive measures which were forced on the ministry. In this struggle the Bishop of Mentz, as the champion of religious liberty, became the most unpopular and calumniated person in the country. For him, and for the zealous men who stand with him in the focus of the conflict between the world and the Church, the immediate dangers and the present antagonism are of overwhelming interest. Looking about for the daily means of acting on opinion, in order to sustain an ardent fight against ignorance, violence, and hatred, they find them not in the remoter benefits of science, but in a close adhesion to the Holy See, and in the sympathy they are enabled to acquire in Germany by their writings, and still more by their influence in the annual Catholic assemblies. In this effort many persons have come by degrees to make their own opinions the test of fidelity to the Church they represent,[2] and to look with suspicion on the orthodoxy of those who are at variance with the views which in the midst of strife they themselves have been induced to proclaim. Their organ, the *Katholik*, has allowed itself, at various times, considerable licence in denouncing the chief scholars of Catholic Germany. The Jesuits and the disciples of the schools of Rome constitute the bulk of their adherents; but the views of the party have their most intense expression in the seminary of Mentz—partly because it is placed in the midst of the conflict, and partly because its isolation from the influences of a university deprives it of the natural stimulants to scientific research.

The most serious theological dispute of recent years in Catholic Germany is one in which the organ of the Mentz divines was engaged against the teaching of a still more influential school. Tübingen has possessed for nearly forty years a theological faculty of high repute among Catholics. The professors of this faculty have conducted with great ability the most valuable theological review which, so far as we know, exists in the Church, and have been, since the time of Möhler, strenuous promoters of the patristic theology. The most voluminous of their writers, Hefele, who is generally known as the author of a sophistical defence of the Inquisition in his life of Ximenes, has since the publication of that book obtained a purer fame by his learned history of the Councils. Another of them, Professor Kuhn, is a more definite and original thinker; and his great work on Dogmatic Theology, appearing at long intervals, kindled the controversy. His method is to trace the progress of each dogma through the assaults of heresy, the

---

[2] The following passage, from the last volume of the *Katholik*, shows how boldly this identity is asserted: "Täusche man sich nicht, die Theologie der Orden und der Germaniker (the German college in Rome) ist, unbeschadet der von der Kirche unentschiedenen Controversen, auch die Theologie Rom's und der ganzen katholischen Welt. . . . Der Theologie der Kirche gegenüber eine andere deutsche Wissenschaft statuiren wollen, ist nicht im Geiste der Kirche."

decisions of popes and councils, and the treatises of divines, and then to deal with it speculatively in the light of modern philosophy. By thus adopting the theory of Development, and rejecting the scholastic philosophy, he is directly opposed to the prevailing schools. His theory, though not influenced by that of Dr. Newman, with whose work he was not acquainted, is very similar to it. His application of it is made in such a way as to involve him in almost insurmountable difficulties, and to do nearly as much violence to patristic texts as they suffer from the advocates of mere tradition. He is further open to the imputation of having failed to understand the great defect of modern speculation, since he deserts the old systems not only on the ground of the advance of knowledge, or the impossibility of constructing theology *à priori*, but because of their ruling principle of submission to the authority of the Church. He not only insists on making philosophy independent of theology, without which they cannot aid each other, but he separates them entirely, saying that one has its source in revelation, and the other in reason. This theory of the freedom of science is as extreme in its way as the deliberate hostility which his adversaries display to the progress of knowledge beyond its ancient forms and limits; and a discussion on the subject, which has interested all Catholic Germany, has been carried on for several years between the Tübingen Quarterly and the *Katholik* of Mentz.

A more exaggerated view than that of Kuhn has been maintained by Dr. Frohschammer of Munich, who emancipates philosophy entirely from the control of religion and revelation, and affirms that it cannot be compelled to revise its conclusions, even when they are manifestly at variance with articles of faith. These opinions are confined to a narrow circle of adherents. The philosophy of Günther, which penetrated far more widely, survives, since its condemnation, not as a system, but only as an influence leavening the thought of Germany. Its disciples are no longer distinguished by the special doctrines of the school—for these have in substance been unreservedly abandoned—but rather by an attachment to intellectual freedom, and an anxiety lest the failure of the only system that was adopted in great part of Austria and Germany should prejudice the formation of other philosophies, and lead to the stagnation of speculative activity. The Prussian universities of Breslau and of Bonn, the old home of Hermesianism, betray the influence of this solicitude, and retain some traces of the extinct philosophy. In all these factions, therefore, differing as they do on many questions of detail, the great problem of the day is the definition of the rights of reason and science among Catholics.

The internal dissensions of Catholic scholars not only cause the waste of much valuable power, but seriously injure the authority of the Church. For it is always of the gravest importance that the utterances of supreme authority should be anticipated and supported by a general understanding and agreement among the faithful, so that there may be no temptation to impugn their rightfulness, and error may be intercepted and refuted before it comes into collision with authority. It is the duty of ecclesiastical science to stand between the Church and her assailants, to justify her decrees, to prevent conflict, and to settle theological disputes before they involve danger to faith. In order that this may be accomplished, it is requisite not only that learning should be diligently cultivated, but also that it should mature some degree of unity and harmony of opinion; in other words, it is necessary that the best results of theological science should be generally known, and that there should not be too great an inequality between the proficiency of different schools. When the French clergy were the most learned in Europe, this unity and authority of theology was represented by the Sorbonne; and in times not far distant the same prerogative might become the portion of the divines of Germany, if the superiority of their training were not neutralized by their divisions. It is obvious that, where there is no uniform teaching or close organization, this better understanding and more intimate union can be obtained only by means of conferences, at which opposition may be allayed and misunderstandings removed, which may make the knowledge and the ways of each school familiar to all, and in which personal intercourse may make up for the absence of an enforced unity, and of the sameness that springs from intellectual lethargy.

The idea that an attempt might be successfully made to promote this important result had lately begun to gain strength. Some preliminary negotiations had taken place, we believe, between several divines of southern Germany; and the scheme had been warmly applauded at Vienna by the nuncio, Cardinal De Luca. At the beginning of the summer vacation, a letter signed by Dr. Döllinger, Abbot Kunsburg, and the ecclesiastical historian Alzog of Freiburg, was sent round to the German divines and scholars, proposing the establishment of annual conferences, to be begun at Munich in September. The author of the paper takes the following ground: Unbelief is visibly advancing, and can be arrested only by positive science, which flourishes only in a Catholic soil, and which the Germans, who in their greatest errors have never lost a sincere love of truth, are called on to restore. This has not yet been done, because, in a period of transition like the present age, when many new ways are opened, differences necessarily arise; and the very earnestness of thought and depth of conviction tend to embitter them, so that the ardour of literary enterprise is depressed, and discredit is brought upon Catholics. An exclusive and suspicious censorship would be fatal to the progress of science, which cannot exist in the Church unless it breathes an atmosphere of freedom. Error on particular points is easily set right by the reaction of the general opinion, but intellectual stagnation is a more serious danger. For the conflict in which Catholics are engaged against the enemies of religion demands that all their resources should be combined for mutual support. By the introduction of periodical meetings men would be brought together from a distance. They would exchange their ideas and settle their disputes, or at least learn to carry them on in a spirit of conciliation and religion. Such meetings would afford an opportunity for deliberation on the pressing questions of the day, and the means of combining in great literary undertakings, and associating to give increased power to the Catholic press. The paper declared, in conclusion, that no personal objects should be allowed to assert themselves, but that a purely scientific tone should reign in the meetings; and the bishops were asked to support the scheme.

After the circular of the three divines had been issued an event occurred which made it doubtful whether it would have the intended effect. Time had been wanting to increase the number of subscribers. The document did not even proceed from the faculty of the university; but appeared to be virtually the work of only two professors. The condemnation and contumacy of a priest and professor of Munich, who had been sustained by the government and had obtained much sympathy among the clergy and in the university, had lately brought the place into ambiguous repute. It was at that very moment the scene of the greatest scandal of recent years, and the cradle of the theory, touching the liberty of speculative opinion, which was utterly in contradiction to orthodoxy. To discuss grave theological problems at Munich appeared to many, under the circumstances, like arguing the question of the temporal power at Turin. It was true that the dean of the theological faculty had originated the idea of the Congress, and that, in a series of lectures on the rights and limits of authority, he had publicly repudiated the theories of Frohschammer. But there were other reasons why even Döllinger's illustrious name would not avail to disarm that sort of suspicion which had now been awakened. The magnitude of his services and his capacity is not disputed; but the very qualities which are the secret of his eminence have had their drawbacks, and have been the indirect causes of a resistance to his influence in minds of several descriptions. His rigorous method and inexhaustible resources, and the spirit in which he applies them, are too entirely devoted to the service of truth to be adapted to compromise or dissimulation, or to the necessities of defective knowledge. The weapon so potent against the outward adversaries of the Church retains its force against defects within, and seems in its passage to smite insincerity or treason as well as open enmity. Any writer who uses a dishonest artifice, meets a difficulty with a hasty answer, or ekes out his ignorance with falsehood, would be sensible that he would do well to conceal his act from one whose knowledge of controversy is so extensive, who can never be made an accomplice, and who has a knack of turning all untenable positions occupied by Catholics. Nor is it only his superior learning and honesty, or his resolutions to tolerate no unsound link in the chain of his reasoning, which offends those who in these respects are not free from reproach. His published sentiments on the Roman question differ conspicuously from those of the majority of the episcopate; and his exposure of the defects of the Papal Government has seriously embarrassed its defenders. In a later work, where he related historical events which contradict the theological opinion that the Pope cannot fall into heresy, he has exhibited no solicitude to disguise the facts or to deprecate the consequences; whilst he has shown that certain things which have had an important bearing on the constitution of the Church have taken their origin in illusions or in fraud. Above all, his use of the theory of development innovates far more than that of its other professors on the ordinary teaching of divines. It takes less than this to isolate a priest who is a pioneer of learning, and who publishes many results which he is the first to discover, and many more to which those who accept them dare not give expression.

This antagonism between the overwhelming personal authority of Dr. Döllinger and the reaction against it is a point of high importance, and the real key to the incidents of the Munich Congress. We are the more inclined to give it prominence because it would appear, from many indications, that he himself did not realize the fact when he gave the impulse to the meeting, or even when it was brought rudely home to him by several significant events. In sending forth the circular, he seemed to have forgotten the storm which had burst over his lectures and his book on the Temporal Power, the angry denunciations of which he had been the object, the motives imputed to him, and his breach with a portion of the episcopate. In inviting the sanction of the bishops to an assembly in which he undertook to unite and reconcile the theologians of his country, to moderate their councils, and to guide their resolutions, it was necessary to assume that the breach was healed, that the storm had subsided, and that confidence was reposed in the author of so good a work. And, in the deliberations that followed, Dr. Döllinger insisted so warmly on the need and the possibility of concord, that he seemed to ignore the existence of other than superficial elements of division; he entered so frankly into explanations, and spoke with so much simplicity the matured and intimate convictions of his mind, that one would suppose he thought it possible to remove by arguments the difficulties that might be placed in his way, and reckoned on finding in others a fairness and sincerity equal to his own.

This was the source of a fallacy and unreality that showed itself in the proceedings. It was assumed that Catholics are separated by no broad chasm; that the causes of difference between them are not deeply seated; that charity, piety, and a common purpose in what is most essential would break down all barriers; and that something would actually be done if there was but the will to do it. If all who were there assembled had possessed the clear vision and profound learning of the president, a few brief conferences might have done something towards this end. But the forces that are warring within the Church are not so easily reconciled. The methods and principles of different periods and worlds of thought are contending; ancient and tenacious traditions are suffering transformation; and the truths which are claiming recognition, and the abuses which are struggling for existence, cannot escape the agonies of childbirth or of death. The strict orthodoxy of one body of Catholics is questioned, and the intellectual morality of the other; and when such accusations are exchanged, they cannot both be entirely unfounded. There are none of these elements of contradiction perhaps that will not be absorbed in the progress of knowledge and experience; but they will not depart without a struggle;

and peace can only be the result of a decisive or an exhaustive war. The speediest remedy for the defects, the sorrows, and the scandals of our time will come not from an anxiety to avoid every manifestation of the opposing tendencies, but from a definite and unrelenting exposition and comparison of contending opinions, and from the resolute prosecution of ecclesiastical knowledge. When the Fathers of Trent met in council, under the guidance of the Holy Ghost, they did not quash their differences or silence objections, but let each opinion assert itself manfully, and even rudely, in what may be justly called a trial of strength. Some of the problems which the congress of the German divines will hereafter be invited to solve are even of a more delicate nature than those which were decided at Trent, and will require to be considered with less assistance from tradition or authority, because they belong to those questions in which no general consensus can be established until science leads the way. In the course of these inquiries, before the conclusions of the deepest thinkers become the accepted property of all, even in the select circles of German learning, they will have to do battle for their systems as was done of old, and on a greater occasion, by Canus and Laynez, by Danès and De Martyribus.

Under the influence of the feelings which were afterwards more publicly manifested, the nuncio at Munich, Monsignore Gonella, conveyed to Rome the apprehension which had been created by the unauthorized step of the three divines. He received a reply which he hastened to communicate to the bishops, expressing, it is said, the surprise of the Holy See at a proceeding so unwarranted and pre-sumptuous, and desiring them to take precautions that no evil conse-quences might ensue. This was a very serious affair. By putting the adverse opinion of the Holy See into the balance, not, indeed, in the form of a command, but in the form of an unmistakeable wish, it was made extremely probable that the plan of the Congress might fail. If, on the other hand, it should take place, it had become very difficult to prevent the fact of its occurrence from appearing in the light of a repulse to the authority of Rome, since the nuncio had undertaken to measure his influence with that of the author of the invitation. Fortunately the influence which prevailed was sufficient, not only to overcome this obstacle, but to prevent it from converting the result into a protest or a party demonstration. The effect of the communication from the nuncio, however, is visible in the warnings of those bishops who greeted the scheme most warmly, as well as in the silence of many others. It acted further on the constitution and proceedings of the assembly, for it caused the absence of many whose presence would inevitably have occasioned dissension, and so far diminished the chances of discord while restricting the comprehensive character of the meeting. But the resolution to keep away was not universal among those who shared the uneasiness of the nuncio; and opposite counsels prevailed with some who were not attracted by the ideas of the circular. It was evident that if only those attended who disregarded the objections that had been urged, the danger, whatever it might be, of an injurious issue would be increased. If any ill was to be apprehended, it seemed the fairest course to face it with some counteracting force. Since it was clear that those who hoped well of the Congress would be in a majority over those who feared it, it was important that the minority should be represented, in order to check if they could not control, to denounce if they could not prevent, proceedings which were anticipated with a vague inarticulate alarm. It happened that the convention of the Catholic associations was held at Frankfort in the week preceding the date fixed for the Munich Congress. Several persons, whose ideas were not fully represented by the language of the circular, met and conferred on this occasion, and were confirmed in the resolution of testifying against the tendencies they opposed, at the critical moment which was approaching.

Since the fifteenth century Germany has never beheld so numerous an assembly of her ecclesiastical notables as that which, after hearing High Mass in the Basilica of St. Boniface, on the morning of the 28th of September, adjourned to the neighbouring monastery. Several great schools of learning, however, were not represented. Kuhn, whose appearance might have been the signal for stormy debates, had lately been assailed by the leading periodical of Munich on account of his opposition to the scheme of founding a Catholic university in Germany; and he was in his tents, publishing a reply. His less obnoxious colleague, Hefele, was in Italy; and none of the brilliant Catholic school of Tübingen came. The Austrian Jesuits were also absent. It was not known at first who was there and who had stayed away, for several meetings had been held before a list could be made out. Many a man found himself on that day, for the first time, in the presence of writers whose works had deeply influenced his mind, or whose fame had long excited his curiosity, without knowing their features. It was an interesting moment, therefore, when the names were called over, and each man rose for a moment in answer to his own, in order that the meeting might know him again. About fifty of those who were present had written books which are known and valued by scholars beyond the limits of their country.

Nearly one-third of the members belonged to the diocese of Munich. Among these were several distinguished laymen. One was Ringseis, the most Catholic among the eminent physicians of Germany. Another was Professor Sepp, the sole disciple of the mighty Görres, who is publishing, in an improved form, the voluminous life of Christ which he composed many years ago in reply to Strauss. He is the most ardent and venturesome of the German laity, a brilliant parliamentary speaker, and a very imaginative historian, but rather hasty in council, and not much relied on in literature. He was not a prominent actor in the subsequent proceedings. A third layman, Dr. Jörg, who began in literature as a historical inquirer of the school of Döllinger, but who for ten years has conducted with ability and vigour the *Historisch-politische Blätter*, did not exercise on this occasion an influence commensurate with his just renown as a political writer, and appeared undecided as to the side on which his weight ought to be cast.

Frohschammer, to whom the meeting would have been a welcome arena for the defence of his theories, afterwards affirmed that he had been excluded by order of the archbishop. The fact of the exclusion, as well as of any interference on the part of the archbishop in the affairs of the Congress, had been denied on authority; but there were probably few who regretted that an additional source of discord was not supplied by the presence of a suspended priest, whose writings, in the estimation of nearly the whole assembly, are at variance with dogma. His views on the independence of philosophy were, however, represented by a layman, probably his equal in knowledge, and not so distasteful to his opponents. This was Professor Huber, who has written on the philosophy of the Fathers, and more deeply on Scotus Erigena, and who furnished that report of Döllinger's lectures on the Temporal Power which caused so much sensation three years ago. In his last book he has openly defied the Index; and he is one of those writers whose independence and catholicity of thought are the most visibly affected by the study of Protestant writings. But he spoke gracefully and with moderation; and, having declared that he belonged to the extreme Left of the assembly, he was probably not surprised to find himself on one occasion registering a solitary vote.

He was generally supported by Professor Mayr of Würzburg, a speaker of less prepossessing address, but a philosopher whose methodical precision of thought it was a pleasure to follow, although he did not seem familiar with the problems and motives that occupied the thoughts of his audience. The partisans of the utmost independence of science might have expected more efficient aid from Dr. Schmid of Dillingen, a divine of rising reputation, whose recent volume on the scientific tendencies of Catholic Germany proves him more deeply versed than almost any other man in the several currents of thought that separate the schools. But although he is the only priest who contributes to Frohschammer's review, the *Athenäum*, and appears to occupy nearly the same ground as Kuhn, he observed an obstinate silence, and did nothing for the propagation of his views. Indeed, it is to be regretted that, among so many scholars of high repute, who would have secured a hearing, there were so few who claimed it. The discussion turned much on philosophy and on practical questions, attractive to those who were curious in the movements of parties; but it left untouched great departments of ecclesiastical science. Biblical scholars like Reischl who has translated the Bible into German, Thalhofer who has written on the Psalms, and Schegg of Freising, one of the most prolific and interesting of recent commentators, had no opportunity of using their special accomplishments. The professors of theology at Munich were for the most part inactive, either because they wished to dissociate their faculty from the responsibility of the meeting, or because they thought it sufficiently cared for by their colleagues who had taken the lead. Yet two of the Munich divines, Professor Rietter and Dr. Oischinger, have written on St. Thomas, and well understood the questions which were argued. As much might be said of Dr. Sighart of Freising, the biographer of Albertus Magnus; but the merit of his recent history of art in Bavaria has eclipsed his reputation as a master of the mediaeval philosophy. The last of the silent metaphysicians is Dr. Hayd of Munich, who has lately published an important work on Abelard.

Austria was represented by four of her most distinguished writers— Phillips, Schulte, Werner, and Brunner. The first of these, who is a convert, from the North of Germany, but of English descent, published valuable works on the early constitutional history of England in the time of George IV. Then, having been for many years a most successful lecturer and writer on German jurisprudence, one of the founders of the *Historisch-politische Blätter*, and the most conspicuous layman in the group of Catholic writers that surrounded Görres, and influenced so deeply the mind of Catholic Germany, he was involved in the proscription of the Ultramontane professors in the days of Lola Montez, and has since devoted himself, at Vienna and Salzburg, to the composition of the most elaborate treatise of canon law that the nineteenth century has produced. His name has been, for a quarter of a century, a household word among his Catholic countrymen; and, in spite of a certain deficiency of logic and condensation, and a ponderousness of learned detail that oppresses his ideas, he was, in point of literary reputation, nearly the first man in the assembly. Nevertheless, he seems to have spoken hardly more than once, for his name appears only among the after-dinner speeches. He submitted to the impulse of more ardent men, and figured at one important moment in their wake.

A younger canonist, Schulte of Prague, is a remarkable contrast to his more famous rival. Those who reproach him with writing too much and too hastily, admit that, of all modern works on canon law, his are of most practical utility, and contain the greatest abundance of original thought, though without the immense erudition of Phillips. He spoke often, and nearly always with force and clearness, and acquired far the greatest influence of all the laymen in the assembly. He was one of those who most efficiently supported the president in moderating extremes and keeping the assembly in the course which, by conceding nothing to the exclusive tendencies of particular sections, could alone assure its success in time to come.

A similar influence would probably have been exerted by the most learned of the Austrian priesthood, Professor Werner of St. Pölten; but the death of his bishop summoned him away from Munich. It is probable that many who, on the first day, had seen a small, retiring man sitting awkwardly in a coat that did not seem his own, and apparently scared and humbled by all that surrounded him, were afterwards surprised to hear his honoured name. Unlike other disciples of Günther's sterile school, Dr. Werner has been almost too productive. His moral theology is the most valued that has appeared in German; and his great work on St. Thomas raised his reputation to a level which his book on Suarez and the first volumes of a history of apologetic literature have not sustained. But in the series of histories of the sciences in Germany which was set on foot by the King of Bavaria, and for which the most eminent writers have been chosen, the history of Catholic theology was, at Döllinger's recommendation, entrusted to

Dr. Werner. On the great questions of reason and faith, and of the value of the scholastic divinity, very few were so competent to speak. But, either from weakness or timidity, he could not make himself heard, though he put on paper several propositions, which were read from the chair and adopted in the protocol.

From the first, considerable interest had been exhibited in the project at Vienna, and it was supposed that some of the Viennese theologians, and among others the Jesuit Schrader, Passaglia's former colleague, would have been present. But Vienna is not a theological capital, and was perhaps more fitly represented by a vigorous and courageous journalist, Dr. Brunner, the stalwart adversary of the demoralized rabble that have long predominated in the Austrian press. He contributed, however, rather sense and humour than deep learning to the Munich councils, and sometimes diverted with timely pleasantry the troubled minds of the assembly. In most respects he presented a singular contrast to other men who, like himself, are involved in the pressure and anxiety of popular discussion.

The University of Breslau was represented solely by Dr. Reinkens, a Rhinelander by birth, whose recent investigations have diminished the lustre of the Jesuit schools in the seventeenth century, and who, in an unguarded passage of the work in which this was done, has exasperated the national, or rather the provincial, feelings of the Silesian clergy. An uncommon shrewdness of expression and a thoughtful manner would lead one to believe that he was not likely to write imprudently. A life of St. Hilary by him was already announced, but he has not yet been a productive writer; and the suspicion of an attachment to the doctrines of Günther, which rests on one of the leading professors of the faculty to which he belongs, seems on this occasion to have somewhat impaired his influence. This at least might be gathered from the fate of a proposal which he submitted to the Assembly at the opening of its deliberations. It would be useful, he said, to establish, in addition to the reviews representing the different schools, a central organ which should impartially register the progress of learning, and in which various opinions should be allowed to meet, and, if possible, be reconciled. He proposed that a periodical of this kind should be founded, or that one of those already existing should be enabled to supply the want. The idea was encouraged by Dr. Döllinger, on the ground that it was desirable to be informed of the mere advance of science through some medium coloured by no distinctive opinions, and that an arena open for the discussion of debatable questions might be a means of promoting concord. Nevertheless, all parties united in condemning the plan—some on the ground that the existing reviews were not sufficiently supported, others on the ground that an editor must not promote any views except those which he thinks are right, and others, again, on the ground that even the opposition of contending schools is not to be deprecated, provided they proceed scientifically. The proposition was summarily snuffed out without being put to vote.

The very decided opponent of Dr. Reinkens on this occasion, though generally, it would seem, but little divided from him, was Professor Floss of Bonn, a grave and wary man, and not easily committed to questionable or impractical schemes. He is one of the most indefatigable explorers of manuscript texts, a dry and colourless writer, but a sound critic and a man of facts, as it has been said a German should be. The only collected edition of the writings of Scotus Erigena is due to him. Many of his treatises on mediaeval history possess acknowledged value; and the only thing which hindered him from playing one of the first parts at the meeting was apparently a want of fluency in speaking.

Dr. Hagemann of Hildesheim would have to be referred to the same group as these two historians, if his attainments may be estimated by a book which is not yet published, and his opinions by a single remark with which he took part in the last skirmish with the Mentz divines. He is the author of a history of the Church of Rome during the three first centuries, which was, we believe, already in print, and which is said to be the most valuable treatise on a subject on which many of the most learned Germans have been his rivals; but he exhibited throughout a disappointing taciturnity.

The ecclesiastical historians, animated by the spirit of the great master of Church history, constituted the centre, and were the ruling power in the Congress. The secretary, Father Gams, whose history of the Church in Spain has been noticed in our pages, must be included among them, as well as several other Munich scholars, such as Dr. Pichler, who, after writing a volume on Polybius, has devoted himself to the history of the Eastern Schism, and Dr. Friedrich, whose writings have been chiefly confined to the history of the fifteenth century. For these two men it was evident that the meeting possessed an almost painful interest. They are the junior members of the faculty of theology, and probably find it difficult to counteract the powerful attraction which the theories of Frohschammer exercise over the students. It was therefore important for them to obtain some declaration on the disputed questions, by which the liberty of thought might be so completely vindicated that nothing should remain to justify complaints against the exercise of ecclesiastical authority. Dr. Reusch of Bonn, who in a recent volume of lectures on the cosmogony has walked in the footsteps of Cardinal Wiseman, and who has translated several of his writings, seemed to emulate the good sense and moderation of his colleague Floss. It was understood that he had undertaken the editorship of a theological encyclopaedia, which was one of the literary enterprises most warmly taken up by the assembly.

Without the ballast with which these men steadied the ship it would have been tossed about by the conflicting opinions of others. Dr. Knoodt of Bonn, formerly a strenuous adherent of Günther, placed himself unequivocally on the side of authority, taking the ground that the Church, being infallible, cannot really injure the freedom of science, which is liable to err. This declaration fell very short of that which the adversaries of freedom desired, and in fact avoided the real issue; but yet the attitude assumed by the speaker, who we believe was, with one exception, the only priest present whose works are on the Index, proved at least that the apprehensions for the rights of authority were groundless, and that whatever disputes might arise would be confined to the narrower ground of expedience and formality.

A heavy gray-haired man, deliberate in manner but of fluent speech, was perpetually on his legs, and was heard with much impatience. This was Dr. Eberhard, now the parish priest of a village on the Danube, but many years ago a preacher who gained in the pulpit of the cathedral of Munich successes which remind one of those of the great orators of Notre Dame. He it was who carried among the burghers of the Bavarian capital that new spirit of Catholicism which the persecution of the Archbishop of Cologne had kindled in Germany; and devout people are still named who were among his converts in those days, and were brought by his sermons from indifference to the practice of their religion. In later years he has written on metaphysics, and has joined the *Katholik* in its crusade on behalf of the Index, but without sharing all the fervour or all the opinions of its conductors. In an evil hour he undertook to describe the several schools of thought in Catholic Germany; and the grave and passionless tone of the beginning gave promise at least of an equitable treatment. But the meeting shrank from this self-knowledge. Dr. Heinrich, the editor of the *Katholik*, vehemently interrupted the speaker, whose rude touch threatened to destroy the harmony which had just been painfully established, or at least to dispel the illusion of its existence. The president pronounced this objection perfectly legitimate; and Dr. Eberhard came down to his place with a smile at his own simplicity.

Dr. Michelis, a priest who, in the solitude of a country parish, has risen of late years to great note and influence in Westphalia, was a still more frequent speaker. His distinctly marked opinions were expressed with an ardour that provoked contradiction; and he strode about like a gigantic athlete, interrupting the speeches of his opponents, and disturbing somewhat the decorum and order of the meeting. After writing the cleverest of the refutations of Günther, he published a very elaborate work on Plato, and has ever since been at war with his critics and with those who omitted to notice it. The review which he superintends, *Nature and Revelation*, gives the praiseworthy example of an effort carried on with great constancy to follow the progress of natural science, and to revise the solutions by which, at a less advanced stage of inquiry, it was brought into harmony with religion. Of all the Prussian priests he is the one most regarded and most trusted by that section of the Lutherans which is tending more or less consciously to union with the Church. But among Catholics he appears the most disputatious, and therefore unpopular, of men. He has broken a lance with many of those whom he met on this occasion, and is at open war with the school of Mentz, and with the friends of Günther. Others probably were sometimes annoyed by his vehemence, or angry with his passion for speaking his mind; but his honest and uncompromising spirit enabled him to do much for conciliation, for it was more easy to quarrel with his manner than to refute his opinions.

There was an uncouth person in the meeting, uncourtly and unadorned, little versed in ancient or modern languages, and weighed down as to his literary reputation by the defects of his earlier writings, who is yet the most perspicuous of the German philosophers, and in some respects the most profound. This was Dr. Deutinger, who was dispossessed, like many other professors at Munich, in 1847, and has never been restored; but whose recent works on the history of modern philosophy and on the Gospel of St. John are of the very first merit. His essays on the dispute between Kuhn and Clemens, Kuhn's assailant in the *Katholik*, and in the affair of Frohschammer, foreshadow the solution of the problem of authority and freedom, revelation and reason, to which German theology will inevitably tend. His speech on this subject is, next to the inaugural address, the most valuable thing in the report.

The school of Mentz was led by Canon Moufang, the most eloquent man in the Congress, and by Professor Heinrich, from whom the organ of the party receives its tone. A broad provincial accent disfigures the speaking of the latter; and it seemed more suited to his temper to interrupt or to rise to order than to deliver a set speech. He alone among the assembled divines has the neatness and unction of the French priesthood; and his delicate features and mild expression of countenance are not suggestive of the unyielding energy and bitterness which appear in his writings. He was supported with greater moderation by Professor Hergenröther of Würzburg, the special champion of Roman theology, and author of a vindication of the government of the Holy See, and by his colleague, Dr. Hettinger, who has published a popular apology for the Christian faith, and who once, in the heat of discussion, tried to silence the voice of the laity.

It was to an assembly so composed that Dr. Döllinger, having been elected president, delivered his inaugural address on the history, condition, and duties of Catholic theology. The leading ideas of this address were as follows:

Christian theology owes its origin to the union of Greek philosophy with Hebrew learning at Alexandria, where, contemporaneously with the appearance of the first Christian divines, the last original thinker of antiquity, Plotinus, made the last attempt to supply a pagan substitute for the discarded religion of the people. The child, as it issued from its mother's womb, was deeply tainted with the vices of the parent. The grave dogmatic errors of Origen, the father of Christian science and the founder of the earliest school of theology, served as a warning that the treasure is contained in earthen vessels, and that the intellectual study of religious truth needs the watchful supervision of the Church. A less speculative and more purely biblical school than that of Alexandria afterwards arose at Antioch. While theology remained the almost exclusive possession of these Eastern churches, the dogmatic struggle was chiefly confined to the doctrine of the Person of Christ, to theology, in that narrower sense in which the term *theologus* was applied to St. John and to St. Gregory Nazianzen. Even St. Gregory of Nyssa, the most original of the Greek fathers after Origen, scarcely passed the bounds of that circle of ideas. The doctors of

Latin Europe borrowed their views from the Greeks, and did not go beyond them until St. Augustine, who stands alone among the Western divines, extended the limits of theology, and became the teacher and master of the Latin Church. The Greek theology in the period of its decline shone once more in the works of St. Maximus, and put forth its last great divine in St. John Damascene. During a thousand years since his death it has made no progress, has done nothing for ethics or for the dogmas of grace and redemption, and has been content with the achievements of early times in Scripture and Church history. Excepting the appearance of one divine, who wrote against Proclus, and the deplorable transformation of the doctrine of the Holy Ghost in the contest with the Western Church, it has ever since been stationary.

For five centuries after the great migrations theological science in the West lay in its winter sleep. The Church was busy with the reconstruction of society; and the best writers, such as Paulinus and Alcuin, were only equal to the task of preserving from extinction the knowledge which had come down to them. Controversy was revived for a moment in the ninth century, but died speedily away: and the Neoplatonic philosophy of Scotus Erigena, which stood alone, awakened no interest and exerted no influence.

Modern theology aims at understanding, connecting, and harmonizing the whole system of doctrine, with a completeness and comprehensiveness unknown in the eleven first centuries of the Church. It began with St. Anselm, and has continued ever since, with increasing energy, to strive for the attainment of its end. As theology had begun in the combination of the Platonic philosophy with the dogma at Alexandria, so now, down to the sixteenth century, it was governed by the philosophy of Aristotle. But the scholastic divines were unable to remedy the vices of their starting-point and their method. Their analytical process could not construct a system corresponding to the harmony and wealth of revealed truth; and without the elements of biblical criticism and dogmatic history they possessed only one of the eyes of theology. The one enduring achievement of those times is the creation of a system of ethical science by St. Thomas, albeit on Aristotelian principles.

All the chief nations of Europe laboured together on the scholastic theology, with the same language and method, and without any national distinctions. In Germany a reaction began early in the

fourteenth century, and the ablest divines were attracted by the
unexplored treasures of speculative mysticism. The Areopagitical
writings, not being fully understood, were supposed to be orthodox;
and experience had not yet taught how easily mystic contemplation
glides into theosophic pantheism. The works of Eckart, Tauler, and
their school, will always retain their value, though none but minds
well trained in philosophy and history will be competent to use them.
In the fifteenth century Gerson undertook to reconcile and combine
the mystic with the scholastic method; while Nicholas of Cusa anticipated many of the later discoveries of speculative and historical
theology.

The scholastic theology had been generally abandoned, and a craving
for a method more suited to the nature of Christianity and the wants
of the human mind was strong in Germany when the Reformation
broke out, caused not so much by the defects of theology as by the
evils which its decay had helped to develop in ecclesiastical life. But
the contest which followed had to be fought out on the domain of
doctrine. Here the old scholastic armoury supplied no weapons capable
of defending the Church against her new assailants; and she was
compelled to have recourse to the biblical and historical studies which
had commenced with the Revival. The rupture of the unity of
Christendom, considered in its influence on religious science, proved
highly beneficial; and the idea that Christianity is history, and that in
order to be understood it must be studied in its development, began
to effect a transformation of theology which has not yet attained even
a temporary conclusion. These fruits of the Revival and of the
Reformation did not ripen for Germany. France, Italy, and the
Netherlands could boast of great divines. England gave birth to
Stapleton, the most eminent of all the champions of the Church against
the new doctrines. And throughout the sixteenth century theological
science flourished above all in Spain. But the expulsion of the Protestant
leaven brought on the relapse which shows itself in the uncritical
eclecticism of the later scholastics; and a scientific divinity was finally
extinguished by the Inquisition. After the death of Baronius and
Bellarmine the intellectual decline of Italy made itself felt in her
theology; and her ablest men, such as Sarpi, Galileo, and Campanella,
earned their distinction in other paths. The sceptre had passed to the
clergy of France, who became the creators of patristic theology and
ecclesiastical history, and to whom belongs the praise of having

delivered religion from one of the worst evils of modern times—the immoral and unscientific teaching of the casuists. The rest of Europe did not profit as it might have done by this renovation of ecclesiastical learning; for the French divines, after the example of Duperron, had generally discarded the use of Latin, and by adapting their own tongue to the uses of theology had given their writings rank and influence in the classical literature of their country. The same thing was done, though not so thoroughly, for the English, by Hooker, Bramhall, Baxter, and others. But the Italians have never raised their language to a level with the Latin; Spain has been silent in both languages; and the German has but lately acquired that flexibility and perfection to which it was already rapidly approaching in the fourteenth century.

The introduction of modern languages into purely theological literature was a new Babel for divines; and it would have hindered co-operation, and encouraged national individuality at the expense of Catholicity, if the tendency of recent years had not been to break down the barriers that divide the nations, and to make the intellectual acquisitions of each the common property of all. The actual result, however, gives a great advantage to the Germans, who are more skilled than the Latin races to understand the languages and characters of foreign countries. Before the middle of the eighteenth century the light of theology was eclipsed in France; and the apologists of those days were not able to command the literary popularity of their illustrious predecessors. The university which for six hundred years had been the glory of the French Church perished in the Revolution; and since that catastrophe there has never existed a centre of theology in Christendom invested with the authority of acknowledged learning, nor has theology itself revived in any part of Latin Europe. The works of Balmez exemplify its low condition in Spain, where native history is the only study that appears to thrive. In the age of Benedict XIV many eminent scholars had arisen in Italy, and especially in Rome; but after his pontificate theology rapidly declined. For centuries no important work on Scripture has been written by any Italian divine; and the suppression of the Jesuits deprived the other orders of a rivalry which had been a useful stimulus to exertion. In our generation, the three most gifted members of the Italian priesthood, Rosmini, Gioberti, and Ventura, of whom Balbo prophesied twenty years ago that they would raise the body whose ornaments they were to a high place in the opinion of the world, came into collision with Rome. Two of them died in exile; and the divine who passed for the best of his country has abandoned his former studies. No nation perhaps that experienced the troubles and commotions which have visited Italy in our century could have escaped the same effects.

France has one great advantage in the possession of able and zealous laymen who are efficient advocates of the Catholic cause; and the names of Gerbet, Maret, Lacordaire, Gratry, Bautain, Dupanloup, Ravignan, and Félix prove that there is a school of men among the clergy who understand the wants of their people and their age, and are able to present religion to them in an attractive form. But there are no real divines of the type of Petavius, Bossuet, and Arnauld, because there are no institutions in which theological science can be taught. The seminaries produce excellent priests, but no scholars; and if nothing is done to establish a university, it is to be feared that the French clergy will lose all influence over the male part of the population, and will fall into a social seclusion. It is fortunate for the Germans that they have preserved their universities, and that theology is represented in them; for at length the time has come when the office of carrying onward the torch of ecclesiastical learning has devolved on them. The Greeks and Italians, the Spaniards, the French, and the English, have gone before:

> *Illos primus equis Oriens afflavit anhelis,*
> *Nobis sera rubens accendit lumina Vesper.*

For the Germans the advancement of theology is not only a grave religious duty, it is also a great national necessity. Not only is the exhaustless power of research and love of labour their special intellectual gift, but the curse of the great separation is upon them, and is felt in every moment of their existence. The nation, like Philoctetes, is wasting under this poisoned wound. No political remedies will avail until German theology comes, like the spear of Telephus, to cure the evil it has caused. The unity of Germany is the union of the churches; and that will one day follow as surely as the nation is not decaying but full of life; as surely as the Church possesses the promise that the gates of hell shall not prevail against her.

The Catholic divines can accomplish this reunion upon three conditions. First, they must overcome, with all the means which the progress of the age supplies, all that is really anti-Catholic and an element of separation in the system of their adversaries. Next, they must present the Catholic doctrine in all its organic completeness, and in its connection with religious life, rigidly separating that which is permanent and essential from whatever is accidental, transitory, and foreign. This work is very far from being yet accomplished; and the explanation of the neglect would be a valuable contribution to our self-knowledge. Lastly, theology must give to the Church the property of the magnetic mountain in the fable, that drew to itself all the iron in the ship, so that the ship fell to pieces; it must sift from the admixture of error all the truths in doctrine, history, and society which the separated communities have brought to light, and then frankly accept and claim them as the legitimate though unrecognized property of the one true Church. Catholics cannot pretend that they really desire union until they prove that they desire the means of union, which are humility, charity, and self-denial, honest recognition of what is good and true wherever it is found, and a thorough insight into our own vices, scandals, and defects; and this points out to us the part which falls to theology in the great work of reconciliation. It is theology that gives life and force to the true healthy public opinion in ecclesiastical affairs before which all must bow, even the heads of the Church and those who wield her power. As among the Jews the schools of the prophets existed beside the regular priesthood, so in the Church there is beside the ordinary powers an extraordinary power, and that is public opinion. Through it theological science exercises its legitimate authority, which nothing can permanently resist. For the divine judges things in the Church according to the ideas that are in them, whilst the generality of men judge the idea by the fact which they behold. All reform consists in making every practice and every institution in the Church correspond with its idea.

Germany is henceforward the home of Catholic theology. No nation has cultivated so successfully the sciences which are the eyes of theology, viz. history and philosophy; and no source of information, no criterion of scientific truth which they supply can be neglected. The day has gone by when a man could pass for a good dogmatic divine without a thorough knowledge of exegesis and ecclesiastical history, of the patristic writings, and of the history of philosophy. No German, for instance, could give the name of a theologian to one who was ignorant of Greek, and therefore unable to understand or to explain the Vulgate.

The question as to what constitutes a theologian must be answered according to the age, and its demands upon a scholar, and especially a divine. Though the modern weapons of science may be used for destruction, they cannot be set aside in the work of reconstruction; and the difficulty of theology has not diminished. Time has swept away many bulwarks behind which former generations thought themselves safe. A Protestant may overlook whole centuries, and content himself with a fragment of the Church; but Catholics must know her in the totality of her progress from the beginning to the present day, without any gap in the continuity of her development, or any fault in the harmony of her system; and this is the labour of a life. No effort, therefore, can dam up the current of theology, or force it back into a bed which it has long since overflowed.

It is the privilege of true theology to change all that it touches into gold, and, like the bee, to extract pure honey from poisonous flowers. Error has its salutary influence upon the Church; it is an incentive to progress, and becomes a peril only when theology fails to meet it with a true solution. Every truth that religion professes must at some period be purified and refined in the fire of contradiction. Therefore the test of a genuine theologian is to labour without ceasing, and not to flinch from conclusions that are opposed to favourite opinion and previous judgment. He will not take to flight if the process of reasoning threatens to demolish some truth which he had deemed unassailable, or imitate the savage who trembled during an eclipse for the fate of the sun. He is sure to gain one step in wisdom, if he does not let the occasion slip from him. The Holy Spirit, who teaches the Church, gives to the theologian that light of grace without which his eyes are blind to the things of God, and consumes the chaff of human error slowly but surely. Later generations often have to atone for the faults of short-sighted predecessors; and the example of the schoolmen who, in their disregard for history and their self-sufficient ignorance of the whole Anatolian tradition, powerfully contributed to the fatal breach with the Greek Church, is a warning to leave theology her freedom, and not to elevate her unsettled conclusions prematurely into articles of faith.

Our principle of tradition, the motto *quod semper, quod ubique, quod ab omnibus,* which is written on our banner, has been misunderstood by friends as well as by adversaries. A miser who buries a treasure in a hole, preserves it indeed, and it may remain for centuries without increase or loss; but in that case it will remain also without life or fruit. The doctrine cannot act on the minds and lives of men without undergoing the reaction of their influence. Its force is in its incessant growth. But in the dull and thoughtless hands of a theology that professes to be conservative it can shrink and wither like an old man's body, and in its impotence cease to generate life and light. For the definitions of the Church are only words, which, however accurately chosen, need to be impregnated with thought by the preacher and the divine; and while they may become bright gems in the hands of a true theologian, they may be converted into lustreless pebbles by the manipulations of a rude mechanical mind.

The freedom of the Catholic divine is linked to the authority of the Church, with which he feels himself in harmony even when it does not speak; for he knows that it will always save him from the tyranny of uncertainty and mere opinion, that its utterances will always be a guide to truth, that it can never mislead. Whilst he understands that the progress of knowledge must be for ever breaking down hypothesis and opinion, every difference between his conclusions and the dogma warns him of an error on his part, and not in the teaching of the universal Church. He assumes at once that there was a defect in his process of inquiry; and he at once conscientiously revises the operation, with the certainty that, with more or less exertion, he will discover the seat of his error.

In Germany there is no established theological school or schools; and it is well that it is so, for the ancient chain of theological tradition has been interrupted, the old forms are too decrepit to be repaired, and the moment of transition has arrived, when a new edifice must be reared in their place. Materials already abound, but the building itself is very far from complete; and many works recall those provisional wooden crosses in the churchyards with the inscription "Until the erection of a monument." The new theology must reverse the analytic method of the Middle Ages, and must carry out strictly and fully the principle of historical development. It must be vast enough to comprehend the whole of the past, and to leave room for the future, which will be not less active in the work of dogmatic evolution. It must be universal, like the Church, and like her embrace the past, the present, and the future. It must provide for the future, not by artificially covering and concealing the gaps that remain in the system, but by ascertaining and recognizing their presence, and by rejecting every hasty and arbitrary attempt to invest the opinions of a school with the authority of ecclesiastical doctrines, and to adopt them in the reconstruction of theology as materials similar in nature and equal in value to the universal dogma of the Church. In such matters it must protect the rights of freedom for the present, and refer to the future, when opinion has become permanent and certain, the duty of deciding.

The presence of different systems is not an evil, but an advantage, provided they maintain a scientific character, and each respects the freedom of the other. That freedom is as necessary to science as air to life, and it is a short-sighted and suicidal policy to deny it on the ground of danger to faith. A real dogmatic error against the clear and universal teaching of the Church must be pointed out and retracted; but a purely theological error must be assailed only with the resources of scientific discussion. It is no argument to say that all error is connected with dogmatic error. It would be possible to extract from the *Summa* of St. Thomas a series of propositions which, in their logical consequences, would lead to the most fatal error. The faults of science must be met with the arms of science; for the Church cannot exist without a progressive theology. That in theology it is only through error that truth is attained, is a law which will be as valid in the future as it has been universal in the past.

It is impossible to read this address, which contains the most distinct and pregnant exposition its author has ever made of the spirit of his theology, without perceiving that it challenges discussion on a great variety of points, and controverts many opinions which are by no means universally abandoned. For ourselves, we cannot acquiesce in the justice of totally excluding England from the survey of the theology of the present day, or admit that we have no ecclesiastical writers of the rank of Bautain and Ventura, and no divines who deserve to be placed as models before the educated clergy of Germany. Those, however, are fortunate whose sensitiveness is wounded only by omissions; for the speaker appears to have touched with careful deliberation on all the characteristic faults of Catholics in our time.

Two years ago the author of this address, in his protest against the abuses of the Roman Government, and on behalf of civil rights and freedom, touched merely on the externals of ecclesiastical polity in its contact with the outer world. Now, he penetrates to the very heart of the defects that afflict the Church, to the causes of her injured influence and the source of great spiritual evils. He speaks not for administrative reform, but for the renovation of theology, and the advancement of that which gives religion power against error, for intellectual as well as political liberty. When we consider the position of the speaker, and the influence which the Congress he thus inaugurated will hereafter exercise, we cannot find that any thoughts which reach so far or penetrate so deep have been uttered in our time. Their effect in the Church would depend in great measure on the reception they met with from an audience which has in its hands the formation of theological opinion in a great part of Catholic Germany. They were not spoken as a programme or manifesto representing the thoughts of the meeting, but rather as a topic for discussion and a test for the comparison of views. So far, therefore, the address invited comment; and it would unquestionably have provoked it in any assembly of divines. Those who had come with the design of watching and confronting the speaker, would have been clumsy tacticians if they had extracted from it no opportunity of delivering their protest. There was hardly a paragraph that could pass unquestioned from their point of view. In a paper which was drawn up by Dr. Heinrich, and read on the following day by Canon Moufang, and which was signed by the Würzburg divines, by Phillips, and by three doctors of divinity, exception was taken to several passages.

The remarks on French and Italian learning would probably have been heard with pain by a native of France or Italy. For the former there was nobody to speak; but the criticism on Italian theology threatened to shake the authority of the Roman divines, on whom an important school relies. In order to rescue their reputation and influence, several names recently commemorated in an essay by Dr. Hergenröther were cited, to prove the injustice of the estimate. On this point of literary criticism discussion of course was fruitless. A more serious matter was the vindication of the German clergy from the imputation of indifference to the use of the means by which the reconciliation of Protestants can be effected. This indifference was indignantly repudiated; but here again argument was vain. Dr. Döllinger had defined his meaning to be, that a sincere desire for the accomplishment of an object must manifest itself in a readiness to adopt the necessary means; and it was very easy to show that the language and policy of many Catholics are more repulsive to those beyond the pale of the Church than any of her doctrines. He had said the same thing in *Kirche und Kirchen;* and everybody knows how many impediments obstruct the path of converts, from the ignorance, the imprudence, the want of candour, or the want of discrimination, which is sometimes shown by Catholics.

A graver controversy arose, however, on that passage which asserted the universal law, that the way to truth leads through error. The idea is found, indeed, in every theology since the days of St. Augustine, and is exemplified in every age of the history of the Church. But being coupled in this case with an exhortation to tolerate and forbear, it was probably looked on as tending to invest theological science with functions which have been claimed for ecclesiastical power; and fears were entertained that if the frequency of appeals to the Congregation of the Index were thus checked, the effect of a favourite instrument in discussion might be weakened, and the exercise of the authority of Rome over literature circumscribed. The difficulty of assailing a statement which, as it stood, everybody knew to be true, without betraying the real motive of the objectors, vitiated their argument, and diminished the force of the attack.

Dr. Döllinger, after a brief explanation of what had been misunderstood in his address, speedily took advantage of the false position into which his opponents had fallen; and they, one by one, in a short but sharp debate, in which he was supported by Schulte and Michelis, endeavoured to set themselves right. One admitted that he had in some degree mistaken the drift of the speech; another that he had not heard it, and had given his name on the strength of the report that had been made to him. No understanding was arrived at, however; and the assembly passed on to other matters. But Dr. Döllinger seems to have been determined to expel from the minutes of the proceedings this documentary evidence of existing dissension, and at the last sitting he again brought the question forward. It was necessary to decide on the drawing up of the report, and he began by declaring that he would not permit his address to be published. The objectors, he said, would expect their protest to appear with it, and the effect would be to commemorate and proclaim an impeachment of his theological teaching. Dr. Heinrich, the author of the paper, protested solemnly against this interpretation. He declared on his priestly word that he had intended no imputation on the dogmatic correctness of the president, whose fame he hoped would be handed down as a treasure to the latest ages of the Church in Germany. He had only wished to mark his dissent from certain opinions which either required qualification to be true, or explanation to save them from the danger of being misunderstood. This, however, did not satisfy some of his supporters; and, whilst they contradicted each other, the logic of their antagonist pressed them hard. At last they went out to deliberate; and presently agreed to suppress their protest, and to consent to the publication of the inaugural address in the Acts of the Congress. Then, with a cruel taunt at his discomfited assailants, Dr. Döllinger declared himself satisfied, and explained that he had felt compelled, as a professor of theology, to vindicate his theological good name. At these words the whole assembly rose with one accord to bear testimony to him; and the memorable deliberations closed.

The question of the liberty of human thought, which was introduced by Dr. Döllinger in his address, had from the beginning anxiously occupied the minds of the assembled scholars; and from different motives each party was very desirous that something should be done. The occasion was manifestly the best that could be devised, if not the only one that could be conceived, for a practical effort to reconcile the most momentous difference which subsists in the Catholic body. For where the individual is openly at issue with the supreme authority, or where the limits of power and of liberty are in question, no official decree, and no private argument, can settle the dispute. The voice of authority is not obeyed when its rights are challenged; and a private individual who sets about reforming the Church by the influence of his own word adds at once by his isolation to the force of the adverse opinion. But an assembly of the most learned members of the most learned clergy in Europe would, in approaching the rulers of the Church, be sustained by a prestige not easy to resist, while the men of science would feel its interests safe in their hands. Their appeal for freedom, instead of exciting insubordination and resistance to the decrees of the Holy See, would come as a constitutional remonstrance against dangerous restrictions; while those limits which the most profound scholars and original thinkers were ready to observe could not well be rejected by any who claimed to understand the hierarchy of literary merit.

The assembly was agreed upon a further point beyond the general expedience of some declaration. Whether they wished to preserve authority by restriction, or to promote religion by liberty, they agreed at least in believing that the Holy Spirit protects the Church from falling into dogmatic error, and that human science has no such assurance. If they united in proclaiming in some measure the misgivings that had arisen; and, whilst it was an indispensable preliminary to the future discussion of the rights of intellectual freedom, it would exclude from that discussion opinions which do not stand on the same basis. For men who profess to believe the Catholic teaching have put forward systems in which its indefectibility is virtually denied. It has been said that a proposition at variance with revelation may still be scientifically true; that the universal Church possesses no voice which is the organ of infallibility; that not only is the expression of dogma modified by the initiative of science, but that even its substance is altered in the progress of religious knowledge, and that ecclesiastical authority being liable to error and abuse, its bounds can never be assigned nor its interference admitted in literature. The genesis of these errors in minds more solicitous about the present than studious of the examples of the past is not very difficult to understand. It is conceivable how such conclusions present themselves to men who are conscious of the loss which religion suffers from the enforced stagnation and sterility of Catholic thought, who have watched the blunders in Church government, and seen how school opinions have been identified with the criteria of orthodoxy in an age in which many views once thought essential have become obsolete and ridiculous. If at one time false opinions have been held universally and under pain of censure, and if there is no fixed distinction between open and decided questions, and if an ill use has been sometimes made of the supreme authority in the Church, then, they argue, infallibility does not reside in her. One fallacy runs through all these arguments; but it is a fallacy far more universally prevailing than the conclusions which in this case it supports. It is the confusion between the Church and the authorities in the Church, between matters of faith and matters of opinion, and between development and change. A very slight exaggeration of the theory of Kuhn, that philosophy is as independent of revelation as other secular sciences, joined to that of his extreme opponents who strive to invest the Index with an authority universally binding on the conscience, must result in this attempt to subject even dogma to the authority of science.

On the morning of the second day of the Congress Dr. Michelis demanded that the assembly should pronounce its judgment on the controverted question of the rights of intellectual freedom, or, as he put it, in favour of "the unqualified freedom of scientific investigation."

Authority, he maintained, has nothing to fear, inasmuch as every Catholic thinker knows the criteria of certainty, and admits that his conclusions are not infallible, and does not therefore claim for them an acceptance derogatory to the Church. The proposal was received with general favour; but it was met by Dr. Döllinger with a protest against abstract resolutions on questions of principle. It may be that he did not trust the elements that composed the assembly, or that he thought its future influence might be compromised if it should embark at the very beginning, before its authority was securely established, on questions of so much delicacy, or that the flame of opposition would be fanned by the licence which would be taken in debate. He induced Dr. Michelis to drop two out of his three resolutions, and to refer to a separate committee of philosophers the one which remained, touching the relations of ecclesiastical authority with the freedom of science. The meeting took place that evening, and was attended, among others, by Michelis, Heinrich, Deutinger, Reinkens, Mayr, and Knoodt.

Late that night a report flew over Munich which produced an almost comical sensation. The philosophers, it was said, had adopted certain propositions unanimously, harmony had crowned their labours, and the great struggle between reason and faith was at an end. In a place where the minds of men were perplexed and excited by the theories of Frohschammer, and by the almost unexampled scandal they had caused, it was just possible to forget that the dispute was one of about seven hundred years' standing, and that a thesis on which a dozen professors speedily agreed was not likely to settle it. The sitting of the following morning opened amid much agitation; strangers congratulated each other; and the particulars of the evening discussion were listened to as curiously as the adventures of a jury that has been locked up all night. One gentleman immediately requested that the names of the philosophers should be communicated to the meeting, as he wished to know who were the men to whom he would entertain a life-long gratitude. They are printed accordingly in the report. The two propositions were to the following effect: "1. A close adhesion to revealed truth, as taught in the Catholic Church, is an important and indispensable condition of the progressive development of a true and comprehensive speculation generally, and in particular of victory over the errors that now prevail. 2. It is a matter of conscience for all who stand on the basis of the Catholic faith to submit, in all their scientific investigations, to the dogmatic utterances of the infallible authority of the Church. This submission to authority is not in contradiction to the freedom natural and necessary to science."

The debate which followed was often extremely brilliant. The two propositions were criticized, and were defended with great fairness and discrimination by Dr. Deutinger, and with great earnestness by the Mentz divines, as the basis of a permanent understanding. Dr. Friedrich was dissatisfied because they supplied no weapons against the school of Frohschammer, and Dr. Huber, because they gave him no assistance in his struggle for the liberty of thought. Professor Mayr alone made a serious effort to have them modified; not so much, he said, because they unnecessarily repeat what is to be found in the Catechism, but because they are very vague and indefinite. "I wish," he said, in conclusion, "for propositions that show on the face of them that they are really the work of *men*." Dr. Michelis instantly protested that these propositions showed that they were drawn up by honest fearless men. "On the face of them," cried Mayr, as he sat down—"I said, on the face of them." And people who saw things only on the outside thought his censure just. Not so those who understood the circumstances under which the Congress had assembled, and the peculiar significance of the occasion.

The terms of these propositions show that what had been apprehended was not the assertion of any legitimate freedom within the limits of faith, but an opposition not merely to the undue exercise of authority, but to fundamental doctrines. They were the very least that it was possible for a vigilant orthodoxy to demand. They were what the extremest advocate of intellectual liberty must needs hold if he holds the creed of Catholics. On this basis, therefore, the cause of freedom will henceforth be sustained without that suspicion which has fallen upon it from the faults of treacherous defenders; and its true friends have emphatically testified that it is compatible with the most entire and hearty submission to the doctrines of the Church. They have delivered it from the effects of a disastrous combination with tendencies essentially uncatholic—tendencies which have hitherto found strength in the confusion outwardly existing between the liberty to hold all truths and the liberty to subvert all dogmas. It is the first step which it was necessary to take in the path of intellectual freedom; and the way has been carefully kept open for further progress hereafter. It admits no obstruction from authorities not infallible, or from utterances not dogmatic; and the saving clause at the end of the second proposition renders it impossible to recede in that direction. Inasmuch as dogmatic utterances are very rare, and the authorities which generally intervene in matters of science have no part in infallibility, these propositions implicitly claim for science all the freedom which is demanded in Dr. Döllinger's inaugural address. Both parties, therefore, might with reason be content. The president, who had been averse to any general resolutions, warmly supported them when he heard what they were. He saw the importance of bringing the Congress to so unequivocal an assertion of the rights of authority, and he evidently judged that this prudent measure would give them strength and confidence hereafter to establish more definitely the exact nature of the liberty which science ought to enjoy in the Church. This, he announced, would be the business of the next meeting, which is to be held at Würzburg in September; and the Report adds, that he wished this declaration to be inserted in the minutes. Dr. Huber alone voted against the propositions; and in the *Allgemeine Zeitung* Professor Frohschammer fiercely accused the Congress of having shrunk from the discharge of its duty.

The questions raised by the inaugural address and the discussion on the rights of science were the most important matters which occupied the attention of the Congress. It shows itself in its weakness in the report of a debate raised by a motion of Professor Alzog, that an association of learned men should be formed for the refutation of the current accusations against the Catholic Church. Here we find ourselves at once amid spongy conventionalities. This notion of refuting calumnies is an insidious fallacy, and has done the greatest harm to literature and religion. The worst things are not the calumnies, but the true charges—the scandals concealed, denied, and at last discovered, the abuses, the hypocrisy, the timidity, the uncharitableness and mendacity which, under pretence of a good cause, make men often unscrupulous, and at last almost unable to distinguish between right and wrong. The question how these are to be dealt with in literature would have been better fitted for the consideration of the Congress than those complaints of prejudice and slander which lead Catholics to believe that there is nothing for Protestants to criticize, and that all hostile criticism is insincere. Something might also have been said of the readiness of Catholics to believe evil of their adversaries, and of the example given by some of our apologists of collecting without discrimination all manner of scandals against them. The kind of literary spirit Dr. Alzog's scheme would foster was apparent when Dr. Brunner recommended that a series of histories should be written, treating the English Reformation after Cobbett, and the Spanish Inquisition after Hefele. It would be the destruction of all sound historical research; and, worse still, it would accustom men to look only for what is popular and acceptable in religion, and to lose sight of the consistency of all its truths, and of those awful depths in it from which worldly men recoil. It would make their religion as shallow as their science.

Two subjects were brought forward by the president which were not received with equal favour. One was a motion that the Congress should undertake to consider, at a future meeting, the means of improving the mode of catechetical instruction. Dr. Döllinger affirmed that the manner in which religion is popularly taught in Germany is exceedingly defective, and that the inquiries and suggestions of experienced divines could not fail to be useful in aiding its reform. There was no question, he said, on which all were more completely agreed, and none of more general importance. This idea was opposed, on the ground that it involved an invasion of the province of the episcopate. It was said that the Congress would be taking the initiative, in a practical question, out of the hands of the bishops, and that it ought not to declare that the catechisms used in the several dioceses with the sanction of authority were in urgent need of improvement. The tendency of this opposition was, however, so obvious that it had no effect; and on a division it was supported by only three votes.

The last subject which Dr. Döllinger introduced was the necessity of so extending and modifying the teaching of moral theology as to do justice to the problems of political and economical science. Unfortunately his discourse on this topic, which was greatly admired, is very imperfectly preserved; and it is not clear, from the discussion which followed, that he was entirely understood. He showed that the current theological systems have no solution for the numerous difficulties that arise in the progress of society, and that both in literature and in the cure of souls the clergy are confronted by problems which they have not learned to meet. And yet, both in the principles and in the practical treatment of poor relief, emigration, association, over-population, the Christian religion has its own system, and is able to guide and to assist the inquiries of science. Ignorance of political economy has frequently led to grievous mistakes on the side of the Church—for instance, in the matter of the interest of money; and it is impossible for the canon law to deal with questions of Church property, or the payment of the clergy, without reference to economical laws. Nor is it to be apprehended that the Church will suffer from the recognition of this new influence, or that there will be any inducement to reject or alter the legitimate and independent conclusions of the science. For political economy, at the point of development to which it has now reached, is a powerful aid in the apology of Christianity, and the best exponent of the services performed by the Church to the social progress of mankind. These ideas were carried out and illustrated with a knowledge of the subject, and a mastery of the theories of Malthus, of Hermann, and of Roscher, which showed how little the speaker contemplated that violence should be done to science, or that theology could supply its imperfections. It was therefore rather discouraging to hear a professor allege that it was very important for theology to settle the question of free trade, by which, he said, consciences are often disturbed on the Rhine. The debate on the use of political economy in theology and canon law promised, however, to lead to studies which will help to restore the direct social influence of religion in Germany; and of all the questions discussed in the Congress it was the one which elicited the most hearty and general agreement.

Before the meeting broke up, Dr. Döllinger addressed it in a farewell speech, not, he said, as its president, but as a professor speaking from the experience of a long career. He repeated with impressive earnestness his exhortation to maintain peace and goodwill among Catholics, and to observe in theological discussion the charity and gentleness of which St. Augustine was a pattern in his dispute with St. Jerome. Divinity, he declared, could not flourish if it was pursued with unscientific instruments; and the bitterness of personal attacks, and the habit of denouncing opponents, had already operated in a manner disastrous to Catholic literature in Germany. His last words to the assembly, therefore, were an appeal for unity and concord.

And now, to what is this movement likely to lead? What is the future that may be prognosticated for it from the signs amid which it was ushered into the world? Will the German divines be sustained by the Episcopate in their undertaking to establish that connubium between science and authority which was the parting aspiration of the Bishop of Augsburg? May it be hoped that the clash of hostile sections will be prevented by the authority of a moderator who does equal justice to the rights of the Church and the liberty of science, when Dr.

Döllinger's place shall be vacant? Is there no danger that a crisis may come, when the party that at Munich could muster only eight voices out of eighty will invoke the intervention of Rome against the renewal of conferences which may result in formidable demonstrations against their views? It cannot be denied that this uncertainty exists, and that there is safety only in the continuance of wise and impartial vigilance. The Congress must not be taxed beyond its strength. It must obtain confidence before it attempts reform.

This at least may be with certainty predicted, that the Congress will never swerve from the line which has been traced by the transactions of the first assembly. It can never betray that submission to the dogma of the Church which was proclaimed in the two resolutions; and it can never abandon that earnest care for the rights and interests of science which were impressed upon it by the example and the warnings of the president. These things are its vital principle. By being faithful to this its origin it will have power to infuse a new spirit into the Catholic body, and to create a new and authoritative centre of learning, which shall prevent hereafter the conflict between science and religion. It will enable the Catholic writers of Germany to vindicate the Church from the reproach that faith is inimical to freedom, that we are hampered in our investigations, that we acknowledge a power which may prevent the publicity of truth, or impose untruths on our belief. Then indeed it will mark the dawn of a new era, and will justify the words of the Bishop of Augsburg, that, in giving the impulse to it, Dr. Döllinger has set the crown on the splendid series of his services to the Church.

[10]
Conflicts with Rome

Among the causes which have brought dishonour on the Church in recent years, none have had a more fatal operation than those conflicts with science and literature which have led men to dispute the competence, or the justice, or the wisdom, of her authorities. Rare as such conflicts have been, they have awakened a special hostility which the defenders of Catholicism have not succeeded in allaying. They have induced a suspicion that the Church, in her zeal for the prevention of error, represses that intellectual freedom which is essential to the progress of truth; that she allows an administrative interference with convictions to which she cannot attach the stigma of falsehood; and that she claims a right to restrain the growth of knowledge, to justify an acquiescence in ignorance, to promote error, and even to alter at her arbitrary will the dogmas that are proposed to faith. There are few faults or errors imputed to Catholicism which individual Catholics have not committed or held, and the instances on which these particular accusations are founded have sometimes been supplied by the acts of authority itself. Dishonest controversy loves to confound the personal with the spiritual element in the Church—to ignore the distinction between the sinful agents and the divine institution. And this confusion makes it easy to deny, what otherwise would be too evident to question, that knowledge has a freedom in the Catholic Church which it can find in no other religion; though there, as elsewhere, freedom degenerates unless it has to struggle in its own defence.

Nothing can better illustrate this truth than the actual course of events in the cases of Lamennais and Frohschammer. They are two of the most conspicuous instances in point; and they exemplify the opposite mistakes through which a haze of obscurity has gathered over

Published in the *Home and Foreign Review* 4 (April 1864):667–696. Döllinger I, pp. 339, 347; Acton-Simpson III, pp. 179, 180, 191. Reprinted in Acton, *History of Freedom*, pp. 461–491; Acton, *Freedom and Power*, pp. 269–298.

the true notions of authority and freedom in the Church. The correspondence of Lamennais and the later writings of Frohschammer furnish a revelation which ought to warn all those who, through ignorance, or timidity, or weakness of faith, are tempted to despair of the reconciliation between science and religion, and to acquiesce either in the subordination of one to the other, or in their complete separation and estrangement. Of these alternatives Lamennais chose the first, Frohschammer the second; and the exaggeration of the claims of authority by the one and the extreme assertion of independence by the other have led them, by contrary paths, to nearly the same end.

When Lamennais surveyed the fluctuations of science, the multitude of opinions, the confusion and conflict of theories, he was led to doubt the efficacy of all human tests of truth. Science seemed to him essentially tainted with hopeless uncertainty. In his ignorance of its methods he fancied them incapable of attaining to anything more than a greater or less degree of probability, and powerless to afford a strict demonstration, or to distinguish the deposit of real knowledge amidst the turbid current of opinion. He refused to admit that there is a sphere within which metaphysical philosophy speaks with absolute certainty, or that the landmarks set up by history and natural science may be such as neither authority nor prescription, neither the doctrine of the schools nor the interest of the Church, has the power to disturb or the right to evade. These sciences presented to his eyes a chaos incapable of falling into order and harmony by any internal self-development, and requiring the action of an external director to clear up its darkness and remove its uncertainty. He thought that no research, however rigorous, could make sure of any fragment of knowledge worthy the name. He admitted no certainty but that which relied on the general tradition of mankind, recorded and sanctioned by the infallible judgment of the Holy See. He would have all power committed, and every question referred, to that supreme and universal authority. By its means he would supply all the gaps in the horizon of the human intellect, settle every controversy, solve the problems of science, and regulate the policy of states.

The extreme Ultramontanism which seeks the safeguard of faith in the absolutism of Rome he believed to be the keystone of the Catholic system. In his eyes all who rejected it, the Jesuits among them, were Gallicans; and Gallicanism was the corruption of the Christian idea.[1]

---

[1] Lamennais, *Correspondance*, Nouvelle édition (Paris: Didier).

"If my principles are rejected," he wrote on the 1st of November, 1820, "I see no means of defending religion effectually, no decisive answer to the objections of the unbelievers of our time. How could these principles be favourable to them? they are simply the development of the great Catholic maxim, *quod semper, quod ubique, quod ab omnibus.*" Joubert said of him, with perfect justice, that when he destroyed all the bases of human certainty, in order to retain no foundation but authority, he destroyed authority itself. The confidence which led him to confound the human element with the divine in the Holy See was destined to be tried by the severest of all tests; and his exaggeration of the infallibility of the Pope proved fatal to his religious faith.

In 1831 the Roman Breviary was not to be bought in Paris. We may hence measure the amount of opposition with which Lamennais's endeavours to exalt Rome would be met by the majority of the French bishops and clergy, and by the school of St. Sulpice. For him, on the other hand, no terms were too strong to express his animosity against those who rejected his teaching and thwarted his designs. The bishops he railed at as idiotic devotees, incredibly blind, supernaturally foolish. "The Jesuits," he said, "were *grenadiers de la folie*, and united imbecility with the vilest passions."[2] He fancied that in many dioceses there was a conspiracy to destroy religion, that schism was at hand, and that the resistance of the clergy to his principles threatened to destroy Catholicism in France. Rome, he was sure, would help him in his struggle against her faithless assailants, on behalf of her authority, and in his endeavour to make the clergy refer their disputes to her, so as to receive from the Pope's mouth the infallible oracles of eternal truth.[3] Whatever the Pope might decide, would, he said, be right, for the Pope alone was infallible. Bishops might be sometimes resisted, but the Pope never.[4] It was both absurd and blasphemous even to advise him. "I have read in the *Diario di Roma*," he said, "the advice of M. de Chateaubriand to the Holy Ghost. At any rate, the Holy Ghost is fully warned; and if he makes a mistake this time, it will not be the ambassador's fault."

Three Popes passed away, and still nothing was done against the traitors he was for ever denouncing. This reserve astounded him. Was Rome herself tainted with Gallicanism, and in league with those who had conspired for her destruction? What but a schism could ensue

---

[2] April 12 and June 25, 1830.
[3] Feb. 27, 1831.
[4] March 30, 1831.

from this inexplicable apathy? The silence was a grievous trial to his faith. "Let us shut our eyes," he said, "let us invoke the Holy Spirit, let us collect all the powers of our soul, that our faith may not be shaken."[5] In his perplexity he began to make distinctions between the Pope and the Roman Court. The advisers of the Pope were traitors, dwellers in the outer darkness, blind and deaf; the Pope himself and he alone was infallible, and would never act so as to injure the faith, though meanwhile he was not aware of the real state of things, and was evidently deceived by false reports.[6] A few months later came the necessity for a further distinction between the Pontiff and the Sovereign. If the doctrines of the *Avenir* had caused displeasure at Rome, it was only on political grounds. If the Pope was offended, he was offended not as Vicar of Christ, but as a temporal monarch implicated in the political system of Europe. In his capacity of spiritual head of the Church he could not condemn writers for sacrificing all human and political considerations to the supreme interests of the Church, but must in reality agree with them.[7] As the Polish Revolution brought the political questions into greater prominence, Lamennais became more and more convinced of the wickedness of those who surrounded Gregory XVI, and of the political incompetence of the Pope himself. He described him as weeping and praying, motionless, amidst the darkness which the ambitious, corrupt, and frantic idiots around him were ever striving to thicken.[8] Still he felt secure. When the foundations of the Church were threatened, when an essential doctrine was at stake, though, for the first time in eighteen centuries, the supreme authority might refuse to speak,[9] at least it could not speak out against the truth. In this belief he made his last journey to Rome. Then came his condemnation. The staff on which he leaned with all his weight broke in his hands; the authority he had so grossly exaggerated turned against him, and his faith was left without support. His system supplied no resource for such an emergency. He submitted, not because he was in error, but because Catholics had no right to defend the Church against the supreme will even of an erring Pontiff.[10] He was persuaded that his silence would injure religion, yet he deemed it his duty to be

[5] May 8 and June 15, 1829.
[6] Feb. 8, 1830.
[7] Aug, 15, 1831.
[8] Feb. 10, 1832.
[9] July 6, 1829.
[10] Sept. 15, 1832.

silent and to abandon theology. He had ceased to believe that the Pope could not err, but he still believed that he could not lawfully be disobeyed. In the two years during which he still remained in the Church his faith in her system fell rapidly to pieces. Within two months after the publication of the Encyclical he wrote that the Pope, like the other princes, seemed careful not to omit any blunder that could secure his annihilation.[11] Three weeks afterwards he denounced in the fiercest terms the corruption of Rome. He predicted that the ecclesiastical hierarchy was about to depart with the old monarchies; and, though the Church could not die, he would not undertake to say that she would revive in her old forms.[12] The Pope, he said, had so zealously embraced the cause of antichristian despotism as to sacrifice to it the religion of which he was the chief. He no longer felt it possible to distinguish what was immutable in the external organisation of the Church. He admitted the personal fallibility of the Pope, and declared that, though it was impossible, without Rome, to defend Catholicism successfully, yet nothing could be hoped for from her, and that she seemed to have condemned Catholicism to die.[13] The Pope, he soon afterwards said, was in league with the kings in opposition to the eternal truths of religion, the hierarchy was out of court, and a transformation like that from which the Church and Papacy had sprung was about to bring them both to an end, after eighteen centuries, in Gregory XVI.[14] Before the following year was over he had ceased to be in communion with the Catholic Church.

The fall of Lamennais, however impressive as a warning, is of no great historical importance; for he carried no one with him, and his favourite disciples became the ablest defenders of Catholicism in France. But it exemplifies one of the natural consequences of dissociating secular from religious truth, and denying that they hold in solution all the elements necessary for their reconciliation and union. In more recent times, the same error has led, by a contrary path, to still more lamentable results, and scepticism on the possibility of harmonising reason and faith has once more driven a philosopher into heresy. Between the fall of Lamennais and the conflict with Frohschammer many metaphysical writers among the Catholic clergy had incurred

[11] Oct. 9, 1832.
[12] Jan. 25, 1833.
[13] Feb. 5, 1833.
[14] March 25, 1833.

the censures of Rome. It is enough to cite Bautain in France, Rosmini in Italy, and Günther in Austria. But in these cases no scandal ensued, and the decrees were received with prompt and hearty submission. In the cases of Lamennais and Frohschammer no speculative question was originally at issue, but only the question of authority. A comparison between their theories will explain the similarity in the courses of the two men, and at the same time will account for the contrast between the isolation of Lamennais and the influence of Frohschammer, though the one was the most eloquent writer in France, and the head of a great school, and the other, before the late controversy, was not a writer of much name. This contrast is the more remarkable since religion had not revived in France when the French philosopher wrote, while for the last quarter of a century Bavaria has been distinguished among Catholic nations for the faith of her people. Yet Lamennais was powerless to injure a generation of comparatively ill-instructed Catholics, while Frohschammer, with inferior gifts of persuasion, has won educated followers even in the home of Ultramontanism.

The first obvious explanation of this difficulty is the narrowness of Lamennais's philosophy. At the time of his dispute with the Holy See he had somewhat lost sight of his traditionalist theory; and his attention, concentrated upon politics, was directed to the problem of reconciling religion with liberty—a question with which the best minds in France are still occupied. But how can a view of policy constitute a philosophy? He began by thinking that it was expedient for the Church to obtain the safeguards of freedom, and that she should renounce the losing cause of the old *régime*. But this was no more philosophy than the similar argument which had previously won her to the side of despotism when it was the stronger cause. As Bonald, however, had erected absolute monarchy into a dogma, so Lamennais proceeded to do with freedom. The Church, he said, was on the side of freedom, because it was the just side, not because it was the stronger. As De Maistre had seen the victory of Catholic principles in the Restoration, so Lamennais saw it in the revolution of 1830.

This was obviously too narrow and temporary a basis for a philosophy. The Church is interested, not in the triumph of a principle or a cause which may be dated as that of 1789, or of 1815, or of 1830, but in the triumph of justice and the just cause, whether it be that of the people or of the Crown, of a Catholic party or of its opponents. She admits the tests of public law and political science. When these proclaim the existence of the conditions which justify an insurrection or a war, she cannot condemn that insurrection or that war. She is guided in her judgment on these causes by criteria which are not her own, but are borrowed from departments over which she has no supreme control. This is as true of science as it is of law and politics. Other truths are as certain as those which natural or positive law embraces, and other obligations as imperative as those which regulate the relations of subjects and authorities. The principle which places right above expedience in the political action of the Church has an equal application in history or in astronomy. The Church can no more identify her cause with scientific error than with political wrong. Her interests may be impaired by some measure of political justice, or by the admission of some fact or document. But in neither case can she guard her interests at the cost of denying the truth.

This is the principle which has so much difficulty in obtaining recognition in an age when science is more or less irreligious, and when Catholics more or less neglect its study. Political and intellectual liberty have the same claims and the same conditions in the eyes of the Church. The Catholic judges the measures of governments and the discoveries of science in exactly the same manner. Public law may make it imperative to overthrow a Catholic monarch, like James II, or to uphold a Protestant monarch, like the King of Prussia. The demonstrations of science may oblige us to believe that the earth revolves round the sun, or that the *donation of Constantine* is spurious. The apparent interests of religion have much to say against all this; but religion itself prevents those considerations from prevailing. This has not been seen by those writers who have done most in defence of the principle. They have usually considered it from the standing ground of their own practical aims, and have therefore failed to attain that general view which might have been suggested to them by the pursuit of truth as a whole. French writers have done much for political liberty, and Germans for intellectual liberty; but the defenders of the one cause have generally had so little sympathy with the other, that they have neglected to defend their own on the grounds common to both. There is hardly a Catholic writer who has penetrated to the common source from which they spring. And this is the greatest defect in Catholic literature, even to the present day.

In the majority of those who have afforded the chief examples of this error, and particularly in Lamennais, the weakness of faith which it implies has been united with that looseness of thought which resolves all knowledge into opinion, and fails to appreciate methodical investigation or scientific evidence. But it is less easy to explain how a priest, fortified with the armour of German science, should have failed as completely in the same inquiry. In order to solve the difficulty, we must go back to the time when the theory of Frohschammer arose, and review some of the circumstances out of which it sprang.

For adjusting the relations between science and authority, the method of Rome had long been that of economy and accommodation. In dealing with literature, her paramount consideration was the fear of scandal. Books were forbidden, not merely because their statements were denied, but because they seemed injurious to morals, derogatory to authority, or dangerous to faith. To be so, it was not necessary that they should be untrue. For isolated truths separated from other known truths by an interval of conjecture, in which error might find room to construct its works, may offer perilous occasions to unprepared and unstable minds. The policy was therefore to allow such truths to be put forward only hypothetically, or altogether to suppress them. The latter alternative was especially appropriated to historical investigations, because they contained most elements of danger. In them the progress of knowledge has been for centuries constant, rapid, and sure; every generation has brought to light masses of information previously unknown, the successive publication of which furnished ever new incentives, and more and more ample means of inquiry into ecclesiastical history. This inquiry has gradually laid bare the whole policy and process of ecclesiastical authority, and has removed from the past that veil of mystery wherewith, like all other authorities, it tries to surround the present. The human element in ecclesiastical administration endeavours to keep itself out of sight, and to deny its own existence, in order that it may secure the unquestioning submission which authority naturally desires, and may preserve that halo of infallibility which the twilight of opinion enables it to assume. Now the most severe exposure of the part played by this human element is found in histories which show the undeniable existence of sin, error, or fraud in the high places of the Church. Not, indeed, that any history furnishes, or can furnish, materials for undermining the authority which the dogmas of the Church proclaim to be necessary for her existence. But the true limits of legitimate authority are one thing, and the area which authority may find it expedient to attempt to occupy is another. The interests of the Church are not necessarily identical with those of the ecclesiastical government. A government does not desire its powers to be strictly defined, but the subjects require the line to be drawn with increasing precision. Authority may be protected by its subjects being kept in ignorance of its faults, and by their holding it in superstitious admiration. But religion has no communion with any manner of error: and the conscience can only be injured by such arts, which, in reality, give a far more formidable measure of the influence of the human element in ecclesiastical government than any collection of detached cases of scandal can do. For these arts are simply those of all human governments which possess legislative power, fear attack, deny responsibility, and therefore shrink from scrutiny.

One of the great instruments for preventing historical scrutiny had long been the Index of prohibited books, which was accordingly directed, not against falsehood only, but particularly against certain departments of truth. Through it an effort had been made to keep the knowledge of ecclesiastical history from the faithful, and to give currency to a fabulous and fictitious picture of the progress and action of the Church. The means would have been found quite inadequate to the end, if it had not been for the fact that while society was absorbed by controversy, knowledge was only valued so far as it served a controversial purpose. Every party in those days virtually had its own prohibitive Index, to brand all inconvenient truths with the note of falsehood. No party cared for knowledge that could not be made available for argument. Neutral and ambiguous science had no attractions for men engaged in perpetual combat. Its spirit first won the naturalists, the mathematicians, and the philologists; then it vivified the otherwise aimless erudition of the Benedictines; and at last it was carried into history, to give new life to those sciences which deal with the tradition, the law, and the action of the Church.

The home of this transformation was in the universities of Germany, for there the Catholic teacher was placed in circumstances altogether novel. He had to address men who had every opportunity of becoming familiar with the arguments of the enemies of the Church, and with the discoveries and conclusions of those whose studies were without the bias of any religious object. Whilst he lectured in one room, the next might be occupied by a pantheist, a rationalist, or a Lutheran, descanting on the same topics. When he left the desk his place might be taken by some great original thinker or scholar, who would display all the results of his meditations without regard for their tendency, and without considering what effects they might have on the weak. He was obliged often to draw attention to books lacking the Catholic spirit, but indispensable to the deeper student. Here, therefore, the system of secrecy, economy, and accommodation was rendered impossible by the competition of knowledge, in which the most thorough exposition of the truth was sure of the victory, and the system itself became inapplicable as the scientific spirit penetrated ecclesiastical literature in Germany.

In Rome, however, where the influences of competition were not felt, the reasons of the change could not be understood, nor its benefits experienced; and it was thought absurd that the Germans of the nineteenth century should discard weapons which had been found efficacious with the Germans of the sixteenth. While in Rome it was still held that the truths of science need not be told, and ought not to be told, if, in the judgment of Roman theologians, they were of a nature to offend faith, in Germany Catholics vied with Protestants in publishing matter without being diverted by the consideration whether it might serve or injure their cause in controversy, or whether it was adverse or favourable to the views which it was the object of the Index to protect. But though this great antagonism existed, there was no collision. A moderation was exhibited which contrasted remarkably with the aggressive spirit prevailing in France and Italy. Publications were suffered to pass unnoted in Germany which would have been immediately censured if they had come forth beyond the Alps or the Rhine. In this way a certain laxity grew up side by side with an unmeasured distrust, and German theologians and historians escaped censure.

This toleration gains significance from its contrast to the severity with which Rome smote the German philosophers like Hermes and Günther when they erred. Here, indeed, the case was very different. If Rome had insisted upon suppressing documents, perverting facts, and resisting criticism, she would have been only opposing truth, and opposing it consciously, for fear of its inconveniences. But if she had refrained from denouncing a philosophy which denied creation or the personality of God, she would have failed to assert her own doctrines against her own children who contradicted them. The philosopher cannot claim the same exemption as the historian. God's handwriting exists in history independently of the Church, and no ecclesiastical exigence can alter a fact. The divine lesson has been read, and it is the historian's duty to copy it faithfully without bias and without ulterior views. The Catholic may be sure that as the Church has lived in spite of the fact, she will also survive its publication. But philosophy has to deal with some facts which, although as absolute and objective in themselves, are not and cannot be known to us except through revelation, of which the Church is the organ. A philosophy which requires the alteration of these facts is in patent contradiction against the Church. Both cannot coexist. One must destroy the other.

Two circumstances very naturally arose to disturb this equilibrium. There were divines who wished to extend to Germany the old authority of the Index, and to censure or prohibit books which, though not heretical, contained matter injurious to the reputation of ecclesiastical authority, or contrary to the common opinions of Catholic theologians. On the other hand, there were philosophers of the schools of Hermes and Günther who would not retract the doctrines which the Church condemned. One movement tended to repress even the knowledge of demonstrable truth, and the other aimed at destroying the dogmatic authority of the Holy See. In this way a collision was prepared, which was eventually brought about by the writings of Dr. Frohschammer.

Ten years ago, when he was a very young lecturer on philosophy in the university of Munich, he published a work on the origin of the soul, in which he argued against the theory of pre-existence, and against the common opinion that each soul is created directly by Almighty God, defending the theory of Generationism by the authority of several Fathers, and quoting, among other modern divines, Klee, the author of the most esteemed treatise of dogmatic theology in the German language. It was decided at Rome that his book should be condemned, and he was informed of the intention, in order that he might announce his submission before the publication of the decree.

His position was a difficult one, and it appears to be admitted that his conduct at this stage was not prompted by those opinions on the authority of the Church in which he afterwards took refuge, but must be explained by the known facts of the case. His doctrine had been lately taught in a book generally read and approved. He was convinced that he had at least refuted the opposite theories, and yet it was apparently in behalf of one of these that he was condemned. Whatever errors his book contained, he might fear that an act of submission would seem to imply his acceptance of an opinion he heartily believed to be wrong, and would therefore be an act of treason to truth. The decree conveyed no conviction to his mind. It is only the utterances of an infallible authority that men can believe without argument and explanation, and here was an authority not infallible, giving no reasons, yet claiming a submission of the reason. Dr. Frohschammer found himself in a dilemma. To submit absolutely would either be a virtual acknowledgment of the infallibility of the authority, or a confession that an ecclesiastical decision necessarily bound the mind irrespectively of its truth or justice. In either case he would have contradicted the law of religion and of the Church. To submit, while retaining his own opinion, to a disciplinary decree, in order to preserve peace and avoid scandal, and to make a general acknowledgment that his work contained various ill-considered and equivocal statements which might bear a bad construction—such a conditional submission either would not have been that which the Roman Court desired and intended, or, if made without explicit statement of its meaning, would have been in some measure deceitful and hypocritical. In the first case it would not have been received, in the second case it could not have been made without loss of self-respect. Moreover, as the writer was a public professor, bound to instruct his hearers according to his best knowledge, he could not change his teaching while his opinion remained unchanged. These considerations, and not any desire to defy authority, or introduce new opinions by a process more or less revolutionary, appear to have guided his conduct. At this period it might have been possible to arrive at an understanding, or to obtain satisfactory explanations, if the Roman Court would have told him what points were at issue, what passages in his book were impugned, and what were the grounds for suspecting them. If there was on both sides a peaceful and conciliatory spirit, and a desire to settle the problem, there was certainly a chance of effecting it by a candid interchange of explanations. It was a course which had proved efficacious on other occasions, and in the then recent discussion of Günther's system it had been pursued with great patience and decided success.

Before giving a definite reply, therefore, Dr. Frohschammer asked for information about the incriminated articles. This would have given him an opportunity of seeing his error, and making a submission *in foro interno*. But the request was refused. It was a favour, he was told, sometimes extended to men whose great services to the Church deserved such consideration, but not to one who was hardly known except by the very book which had incurred the censure. This answer instantly aroused a suspicion that the Roman Court was more anxious to assert its authority than to correct an alleged error, or to prevent a scandal. It was well known that the mistrust of German philosophy was very deep at Rome; and it seemed far from impossible that an intention existed to put it under all possible restraint.

This mistrust on the part of the Roman divines was fully equalled, and so far justified, by a corresponding literary contempt on the part of many German Catholic scholars. It is easy to understand the grounds of this feeling. The German writers were engaged in an arduous struggle, in which their antagonists were sustained by intellectual power, solid learning, and deep thought, such as the defenders of the Church in Catholic countries have never had to encounter. In this conflict the Italian divines could render no assistance. They had shown themselves altogether incompetent to cope with modern science. The Germans, therefore, unable to recognise them as auxiliaries, soon ceased to regard them as equals, or as scientific divines at all. Without impeaching their orthodoxy, they learned to look on them as men incapable of understanding and mastering the ideas of a literature so very remote from their own, and to attach no more value to the unreasoned decrees of their organ than to the undefended *ipse dixit* of a theologian of secondary rank. This opinion sprang, not from national prejudice or from the self-appreciation of individuals comparing their own works with those of the Roman divines, but from a general view of the relation of those divines, among whom there are several distinguished Germans, to the literature of Germany. It was thus a corporate feeling, which might be shared even by one who was conscious of his own inferiority, or who had written nothing at all. Such a man, weighing the opinion of the theologians of the Gesù and the Minerva, not in the scale of his own performance, but in that of the great achievements of his age, might well be reluctant to accept their verdict upon them without some aid of argument and explanation.

On the other hand, it appeared that a blow which struck the Catholic scholars of Germany would assure to the victorious congregation of Roman divines an easy supremacy over the writers of all other countries. The case of Dr. Frohschammer might be made to test what degree of control it would be possible to exercise over his countrymen, the only body of writers at whom alarm was felt, and who insisted, more than others, on their freedom. But the suspicion of such a possibility was likely only to confirm him in the idea that he was chosen to be the experimental body on which an important principle was to be decided, and that it was his duty, till his dogmatic error was proved, to resist a questionable encroachment of authority upon the rights of freedom. He therefore refused to make the preliminary submission which was required of him, and allowed the decree to go forth against him in the usual way. Hereupon it was intimated to him—though not by Rome—that he had incurred excommunication. This was the measure which raised the momentous question of the liberties of Catholic science, and gave the impulse to that new theory on the limits of authority with which his name has become associated.

In the civil affairs of mankind it is necessary to assume that the knowledge of the moral code and the traditions of law cannot perish in a Christian nation. Particular authorities may fall into error; decisions may be appealed against; laws may be repealed, but the political conscience of the whole people cannot be irrecoverably lost. The Church possesses the same privilege, but in a much higher degree, for she exists expressly for the purpose of preserving a definite body of truths, the knowledge of which she can never lose. Whatever authority, therefore, expresses that knowledge of which she is the keeper must be obeyed. But there is no institution from which this knowledge can be obtained with immediate certainty. A council is not *à priori* ecumenical; the Holy See is not separately infallible. The one has to await a sanction, the other has repeatedly erred. Every decree, therefore, requires a preliminary examination.

A writer who is censured may, in the first place, yield an external submission, either for the sake of discipline, or because his conviction is too weak to support him against the weight of authority. But if the question at issue is more important than the preservation of peace, and if his conviction is strong, he inquires whether the authority which condemns him utters the voice of the Church. If he finds that it does, he yields to it, or ceases to profess the faith of Catholics. If he finds that it does not, but is only the voice of authority, he owes it to his conscience, and to the supreme claims of truth, to remain constant to that which he believes, in spite of opposition. No authority has power to impose error, and, if it resists the truth, the truth must be upheld until it is admitted. Now the adversaries of Dr. Frohschammer had fallen into the monstrous error of attributing to the congregation of the Index a share in the infallibility of the Church. He was placed in the position of a persecuted man, and the general sympathy was with him. In his defence he proceeded to state his theory of the rights of science, in order to vindicate the Church from the imputation of restricting its freedom. Hitherto his works had been written in defence of a Christian philosophy against materialism and infidelity. Their object had been thoroughly religious, and although he was not deeply read in ecclesiastical literature, and was often loose and incautious in the use of theological terms, his writings had not been wanting in catholicity of spirit; but after his condemnation by Rome he undertook to pull down the power which had dealt the blow, and to make himself safe for the future. In this spirit of personal antagonism he commenced a long series of writings in defence of freedom and in defiance of authority.

The following abstract marks, not so much the outline of his system, as the logical steps which carried him to the point where he passed beyond the limit of Catholicism. Religion, he taught, supplies materials but no criterion for philosophy; philosophy has nothing to rely on, in the last resort, but the unfailing veracity of our nature, which is not corrupt or weak, but normally healthy, and unable to deceive us.[15] There is not greater division or uncertainty in matters of speculation than on questions of faith.[16] If at any time error or doubt should arise, the science possesses in itself the means of correcting or removing it, and no other remedy is efficacious but that which it applies to itself.[17] There can be no free philosophy if we must always remember dogma.[18] Philosophy includes in its sphere all the dogmas of revelation, as well as those of natural religion. It examines by its own independent light the substance of every Christian doctrine, and determines in each case whether it be divine truth.[19] The conclusions and judgments at which it thus arrives must be maintained even when they contradict articles of faith.[20] As we accept the evidence of astronomy in opposition to the once settled opinion of divines, so we should not shrink from the evidence of chemistry if it should be adverse to transubstantiation.[21]

[15] *Naturphilosophie*, p. 115; *Einleitung in die Philosophie*, pp. 40, 54; *Freiheit der Wissenschaft*, pp. 4, 89; *Athenäum*, i, 17.
[16] *Athenäum*, i, 92.
[17] *Freiheit der Wissenschaft*, p. 32.
[18] *Athenäum*, i, 167.
[19] *Einleitung*, pp. 305, 317, 397.
[20] *Athenäum*, i, 208.
[21] *Ibid.* ii, 655.

The Church, on the other hand, examines these conclusions by her standard of faith, and decides whether they can be taught in theology.[22] But she has no means of ascertaining the philosophical truth of an opinion, and cannot convict the philosopher of error. The two domains are as distinct as reason and faith; and we must not identify what we know with what we believe, but must separate the philosopher from his philosophy. The system may be utterly at variance with the whole teaching of Christianity, and yet the philosopher, while he holds it to be philosophically true and certain, may continue to believe all Catholic doctrine, and to perform all the spiritual duties of a layman or a priest. For discord cannot exist between the certain results of scientific investigation and the real doctrines of the Church. Both are true, and there is no conflict of truths. But while the teaching of science is distinct and definite, that of the Church is subject to alteration. Theology is at no time absolutely complete, but always liable to be modified, and cannot, therefore, be made a fixed test of truth.[23] Consequently there is no reason against the union of the Churches. For the liberty of private judgment, which is the formal principle of Protestantism, belongs to Catholics; and there is no actual Catholic dogma which may not lose all that is objectionable to Protestants by the transforming process of development.[24]

The errors of Dr. Frohschammer in these passages are not exclusively his own. He has only drawn certain conclusions from premises which are very commonly received. Nothing is more usual than to confound religious truth with the voice of ecclesiastical authority. Dr. Frohschammer, having fallen into this vulgar mistake, argues that because the authority is fallible the truth must be uncertain. Many Catholics attribute to theological opinions which have prevailed for centuries without reproach a sacredness nearly approaching that which belongs to articles of faith: Dr. Frohschammer extends to defined dogmas the liability to change which belongs to opinions that yet await a final and conclusive investigation. Thousands of zealous men are persuaded that a conflict may arise between defined doctrines of the Church and conclusions which are certain according to all the tests of science: Dr. Frohschammer adopts this view, and argues that none of the decisions of the Church are final, and that consequently in such a case they

[22] *Ibid.* ii, 676.
[23] *Ibid.* ii, 661.
[24] *Wiedervereinigung der Katholiken und Protestanten*, pp. 26, 35.

must give way. Lastly, uninstructed men commonly impute to historical and natural science the uncertainty which is inseparable from pure speculation: Dr. Frohschammer accepts the equality, but claims for metaphysics the same certainty and independence which those sciences possess.

Having begun his course in company with many who have exactly opposite ends in view, Dr. Frohschammer, in a recent tract on the union of the Churches, entirely separates himself from the Catholic Church in his theory of development. He had received the impulse to his new system from the opposition of those whom he considered the advocates of an excessive uniformity and the enemies of progress, and their contradiction has driven him to a point where he entirely sacrifices unity to change. He now affirms that our Lord desired no unity or perfect conformity among His followers, except in morals and charity;[25] that He gave no definite system of doctrine; and that the form which Christian faith may have assumed in a particular age has no validity for all future time but is subject to continual modification.[26] The definitions, he says, which the Church has made from time to time are not to be obstinately adhered to; and the advancement of religious knowledge is obtained by genius, not by learning, and is not regulated by traditions and fixed rules.[27] He maintains that not only the form but the substance varies; that the belief of one age may be not only extended but abandoned in another; and that it is impossible to draw the line which separates immutable dogma from undecided opinions.[28]

The causes which drove Dr. Frohschammer into heresy would scarcely have deserved great attention from the mere merit of the man, for he cannot be acquitted of having, in the first instance, exhibited very superficial notions of theology. Their instructiveness consists in the conspicuous example they afford of the effect of certain errors which at the present day are commonly held and rarely contradicted. When he found himself censured unjustly, as he thought, by the Holy See, it should have been enough for him to believe in his conscience that he was in agreement with the true faith of the Church. He would not then have proceeded to consider the whole Church infected with the liability to err from which her rulers are not exempt, or to degrade the fundamental truths of Christianity to the level of mere school

[25] *Wiedervereinigung*, pp. 8, 10.
[26] *Ibid.* p. 15.
[27] *Ibid.* p. 21.
[28] *Ibid.* pp. 25, 26.

opinions. Authority appeared in his eyes to stand for the whole Church; and therefore, in endeavouring to shield himself from its influence, he abandoned the first principles of the ecclesiastical system. Far from having aided the cause of freedom, his errors have provoked a reaction against it, which must be looked upon with deep anxiety, and of which the first significant symptom remains to be described.

On the 21st of December 1863, the Pope addressed a Brief to the Archbishop of Munich, which was published on the 5th of March. This document explains that the Holy Father had originally been led to suspect the recent Congress of Munich of a tendency similar to that of Frohschammer, and had consequently viewed it with great distrust; but that these feelings were removed by the address which was adopted at the meeting, and by the report of the Archbishop. And he expresses the consolation he has derived from the principles which prevailed in the assembly, and applauds the design of those by whom it was convened. He asked for the opinion of the German prelates, in order to be able to determine whether, in the present circumstances of their Church, it is right that the Congress should be renewed.

Besides the censure of the doctrines of Frohschammer, and the approbation given to the acts of the Munich Congress, the Brief contains passages of deeper and more general import, not directly touching the action of the German divines, but having an important bearing on the position of this *Review*. The substance of these passages is as follows: In the present condition of society the supreme authority in the Church is more than ever necessary, and must not surrender in the smallest degree the exclusive direction of ecclesiastical knowledge. An entire obedience to the decrees of the Holy See and the Roman congregations cannot be inconsistent with the freedom and progress of science. The disposition to find fault with the scholastic theology, and to dispute the conclusions and the method of its teachers, threatens the authority of the Church, because the Church has not only allowed theology to remain for centuries faithful to their system, but has urgently recommended it as the safest bulwark of the faith, and an efficient weapon against her enemies. Catholic writers are not bound only by those decisions of the infallible Church which regard articles of faith. They must also submit to the theological decisions of the Roman congregations, and to the opinions which are commonly received in the schools. And it is wrong, though not heretical, to reject those decisions or opinions.

In a word, therefore, the Brief affirms that the common opinions and explanations of Catholic divines ought not to yield to the progress of secular science, and that the course of theological knowledge ought to be controlled by the decrees of the Index.

There is no doubt that the letter of this document might be interpreted in a sense consistent with the habitual language of the *Home and Foreign Review*. On the one hand, the censure is evidently aimed at that exaggerated claim of independence which would deny to the Pope and the Episcopate any right of interfering in literature, and would transfer the whole weight heretofore belonging to the traditions of the schools of theology to the incomplete, and therefore uncertain, conclusions of modern science. On the other hand, the *Review* has always maintained, in common with all Catholics, that if the one Church has an organ it is through that organ that she must speak; that her authority is not limited to the precise sphere of her infallibility; and that opinions which she has long tolerated or approved, and has for centuries found compatible with the secular as well as religious knowledge of the age, cannot be lightly supplanted by new hypotheses of scientific men, which have not yet had time to prove their consistency with dogmatic truth. But such a plausible accommodation, even if it were honest or dignified, would only disguise and obscure those ideas which it has been the chief object of the *Review* to proclaim. It is, therefore, not only more respectful to the Holy See, but more serviceable to the principles of the *Review* itself, and more in accordance with the spirit in which it has been conducted, to interpret the words of the Pope as they were really meant, than to elude their consequences by subtle distinctions, and to profess a formal adoption of maxims which no man who holds the principles of the *Review* can accept in their intended signification.

One of these maxims is that theological and other opinions long held and allowed in the Church gather truth from time, and an authority in some sort binding from the implied sanction of the Holy See, so that they cannot be rejected without rashness; and that the decrees of the congregation of the Index possess an authority quite independent of the acquirements of the men composing it. This is no new opinion; it is only expressed on the present occasion with unusual solemnity and distinctness. But one of the essential principles of this *Review* consists in a clear recognition, first, of the infinite gulf which in theology separates what is of faith from what is not of faith— revealed dogmas from opinions unconnected with them by logical necessity, and therefore incapable of anything higher than a natural certainty—and next, of the practical difference which exists in ecclesiastical discipline between the acts of infallible authority and those which possess no higher sanction than that of canonical legality. That which is not decided with dogmatic infallibility is for the time susceptible only of a scientific determination, which advances with the progress of science, and becomes absolute only where science has attained its final results. On the one hand, this scientific progress is beneficial, and even necessary, to the Church; on the other, it must inevitably be opposed by the guardians of traditional opinion, to whom, as such, no share in it belongs, and who, by their own acts and those of their predecessors, are committed to views which it menaces or destroys. The same principle which, in certain conjunctures, imposes the duty of surrendering received opinions imposes in equal extent, and under like conditions, the duty of disregarding the fallible authorities that uphold them.

It is the design of the Holy See not, of course, to deny the distinction between dogma and opinion, upon which this duty is founded, but to reduce the practical recognition of it among Catholics to the smallest possible limits. A grave question therefore arises as to the position of a *Review* founded in great part for the purpose of exemplifying this distinction.[29] In considering the solution of this question two circumstances must be borne in mind: first, that the antagonism now so forcibly expressed has always been known and acknowledged; and secondly, that no part of the Brief applies directly to the *Review*. The *Review* was as distinctly opposed to the Roman sentiment before the Brief as since, and it is still as free from censure as before. It was at no time in virtual sympathy with authority on the points in question, and it is not now in formal conflict with authority.

But the definiteness with which the Holy See has pronounced its will, and the fact that it has taken the initiative, seem positively to

---

[29] The prospectus of the *Review* contained these words: "It will abstain from direct theological discussion, as far as external circumstances will allow; and in dealing with those mixed questions into which theology indirectly enters, its aim will be to combine devotion to the Church with discrimination and candour in the treatment of her opponents; to reconcile freedom of inquiry with implicit faith, and to discountenance what is untenable and unreal, without forgetting tenderness due to the weak, or the reverence rightly claimed for what is sacred. Submitting without reserve to infallible authority, it will encourage a habit of manly investigation on subjects of scientific interest."

invite adhesion, and to convey a special warning to all who have expressed opinions contrary to the maxims of the Brief. A periodical which not only has done so, but exists in a measure for the purpose of doing so, cannot with propriety refuse to survey the new position in which it is placed by this important act. For the conduct of a *Review* involves more delicate relations with the government of the Church than the authorship of an isolated book. When opinions which an author defends are rejected at Rome, he either makes his submission, or, if his mind remains unaltered, silently leaves his book to take its chance, and to influence men according to its merits. But such passivity, however right and seemly in the author of a book, is inapplicable to the case of a *Review*. The periodical iteration of rejected propositions would amount to insult and defiance, and would probably provoke more definite measures; and thus the result would be to commit authority yet more irrevocably to an opinion which otherwise might take no deep root, and might yield ultimately to the influence of time. For it is hard to surrender a cause on behalf of which a struggle has been sustained, and spiritual evils have been inflicted. In an isolated book, the author need discuss no more topics than he likes, and any want of agreement with ecclesiastical authority may receive so little prominence as to excite no attention. But a continuous *Review*, which adopted this kind of reserve, would give a negative prominence to the topics it persistently avoided, and by thus keeping before the world the position it occupied would hold out a perpetual invitation to its readers to judge between the Church and itself. Whatever it gained of approbation and assent would be so much lost to the authority and dignity of the Holy See. It could only hope to succeed by trading on the scandal it caused.

But in reality its success could no longer advance the cause of truth. For what is the Holy See in its relation to the masses of Catholics, and where does its strength lie? It is the organ, the mouth, the head of the Church. Its strength consists in its agreement with the general conviction of the faithful. When it expresses the common knowledge and sense of the age, or of a large majority of Catholics, its position is impregnable. The force it derives from this general support makes direct opposition hopeless, and therefore disedifying, tending only to division and promoting reaction rather than reform. The influence by which it is to be moved must be directed first on that which gives its strength, and must pervade the members in order that it may reach the head. While the general sentiment of Catholics is unaltered, the course of the Holy See remains unaltered too. As soon as that sentiment is modified, Rome sympathises with the change. The ecclesiastical government, based upon the public opinion of the Church, and acting through it, cannot separate itself from the mass of the faithful, and keep pace with the progress of the instructed minority. It follows slowly and warily, and sometimes begins by resisting and denouncing what in the end it thoroughly adopts. Hence a direct controversy with Rome holds out the prospect of great evils, and at best a barren and unprofitable victory. The victory that is fruitful springs from that gradual change in the knowledge, the ideas, and the convictions of the Catholic body, which, in due time, overcomes the natural reluctance to forsake a beaten path, and by insensible degrees constrains the mouthpiece of tradition to conform itself to the new atmosphere with which it is surrounded. The slow, silent, indirect action of public opinion bears the Holy See along, without any demoralising conflict or dishonourable capitulation. This action belongs essentially to the graver scientific literature to direct: and the inquiry what form that literature should assume at any given moment involves no question which affects its substance, though it may often involve questions of moral fitness sufficiently decisive for a particular occasion.

It was never pretended that the *Home and Foreign Review* represented the opinions of the majority of Catholics. The Holy See has had their support in maintaining a view of the obligations of Catholic literature very different from the one which has been upheld in these pages; nor could it explicitly abandon that view without taking up a new position in the Church. All that could be hoped for on the other side was silence and forbearance, and for a time they have been conceded. But this is the case no longer. The toleration has now been pointedly withdrawn; and the adversaries of the Roman theory have been challenged with the summons to submit.

If the opinions for which submission is claimed were new, or if the opposition now signalised were one of which there had hitherto been any doubt, a question might have arisen as to the limits of the authority of the Holy See over the conscience, and the necessity or possibility of accepting the view which it propounds. But no problem of this kind has in fact presented itself for consideration. The differences which are now proclaimed have all along been acknowledged to exist; and the conductors of the *Review* are unable to yield their assent to the opinions put forward in the Brief.

In these circumstances there are two courses which it is impossible to take. It would be wrong to abandon principles which have been well considered and are sincerely held, and it would also be wrong to assail the authority which contradicts them. The principles have not ceased to be true, nor the authority to be legitimate, because the two are in contradiction. To submit the intellect and conscience without examining the reasonableness and justice of this decree, or to reject the authority on the ground of its having been abused, would equally be a sin, on one side against morals, on the other against faith. The conscience cannot be relieved by casting on the administrators of ecclesiastical discipline the whole responsibility of preserving religious truth; nor can it be emancipated by a virtual apostasy. For the Church is neither a despotism in which the convictions of the faithful possess no power of expressing themselves and no means of exercising legitimate control, nor is it an organized anarchy where the judicial and administrative powers are destitute of that authority which is conceded to them in civil society—the authority which commands submission even where it cannot impose a conviction of the righteousness of its acts.

No Catholic can contemplate without alarm the evil that would be caused by a Catholic journal persistently labouring to thwart the published will of the Holy See, and continuously defying its authority. The conductors of this *Review* refuse to take upon themselves the responsibility of such a position. And if it were accepted, the *Review* would represent no section of Catholics. But the representative character is as essential to it as the opinions it professes, or the literary resources it commands. There is no lack of periodical publications representing science apart from religion, or religion apart from science. The distinctive feature of the *Home and Foreign Review* has been that it has attempted to exhibit the two in union; and the interest which has been attached to its views proceeded from the fact that they were put forward as essentially Catholic in proportion to their scientific truth, and as expressing more faithfully than even the voice of authority the genuine spirit of the Church in relation to intellect. Its object has been to elucidate the harmony which exists between religion and the established conclusions of secular knowledge, and to exhibit the real amity and sympathy between the methods of science and the methods employed by the Church. That amity and sympathy the enemies of the Church refuse to admit, and her friends have not learned to understand. Long disowned by a large part of our Episcopate, they are now rejected by the Holy See; and the issue is vital to a *Review* which, in ceasing to uphold them, would surrender the whole reason of its existence.

Warned, therefore, by the language of the Brief, I will not provoke ecclesiastical authority to a more explicit repudiation of doctrines which are necessary to secure its influence upon the advance of modern science. I will not challenge a conflict which would only deceive the world into a belief that religion cannot be harmonised with all that is right and true in the progress of the present age. But I will sacrifice the existence of the *Review* to the defence of its principles, in order that I may combine the obedience which is due to legitimate ecclesiastical authority, with an equally conscientious maintenance of the rightful and necessary liberty of thought. A conjuncture like the present does not perplex the conscience of a Catholic; for his obligation to refrain from wounding the peace of the Church is neither more nor less real than that of professing nothing beside or against his convictions. If these duties have not been always understood, at least the *Home and Foreign Review* will not betray them; and the cause it has imperfectly expounded can be more efficiently served in future by means which will neither weaken the position of authority nor depend for their influence on its approval.

If, as I have heard, but now am scarcely anxious to believe, there are those, both in the communion of the Church and out of it, who have found comfort in the existence of this *Review*, and have watched its straight short course with hopeful interest, trusting it as a sign that the knowledge deposited in their minds by study, and transformed by conscience into inviolable convictions, was not only tolerated among Catholics, but might be reasonably held to be of the very essence of their system; who were willing to accept its principles as a possible solution of the difficulties they saw in Catholicism, and were even prepared to make its fate the touchstone of the real spirit of our hierarchy; or who deemed that while it lasted it promised them some immunity from the overwhelming pressure of uniformity, some safeguard against resistance to the growth of knowledge and of freedom, and some protection for themselves, since, however weak its influence as an auxiliary, it would, by its position, encounter the first shock, and so divert from others the censures which they apprehended; who have found a welcome encouragement in its confidence, a satisfaction in its sincerity when they shrank from revealing their own thoughts, or a salutary restraint when its moderation failed to satisfy their ardour; whom, not being Catholics, it has induced to think less hardly of the Church, or, being Catholics, has bound more strongly to her— to all these I would say that the principles it has upheld will not die with it, but will find their destined advocates, and triumph in their appointed time. From the beginning of the Church it has been a law of her nature, that the truths which eventually proved themselves the legitimate products of her doctrine, have had to make their slow way upwards through a phalanx of hostile habits and traditions, and to be rescued, not only from open enemies, but also from friendly hands that were not worthy to defend them. It is right that in every arduous enterprise some one who stakes no influence on the issue should make the first essay, whilst the true champions, like the Triarii of the Roman legions, are behind, and wait, without wavering, until the crisis calls them forward.

And already it seems to have arrived. All that is being done for ecclesiastical learning by the priesthood of the Continent bears testimony to the truths which are now called in question; and every work of real science written by a Catholic adds to their force. The example of great writers aids their cause more powerfully than many theoretical discussions. Indeed, when the principles of the antagonism which divides Catholics have been brought clearly out, the part of theory is accomplished, and most of the work of a *Review* is done. It remains that the principles which have been made intelligible should be translated into practice, and should pass from the arena of discussion into the ethical code of literature. In that shape their efficacy will be acknowledged, and they will cease to be the object of alarm. Those who have been indignant at hearing that their methods are obsolete and their labours vain, will be taught by experience to recognise in the works of another school services to religion more momentous than those which they themselves have aspired to perform; practice will compel the assent which is denied to theory; and men will learn to value in the fruit what the germ did not reveal to them. Therefore it is to the prospect of that development of Catholic learning which is too powerful to be arrested or repressed that I would direct the thoughts of those who are tempted to yield either to a malignant joy or an unjust despondency at the language of the Holy See. If the spirit of the *Home and Foreign Review* really animates those whose sympathy it enjoyed, neither their principles, nor their confidence, nor their hopes will be shaken by its extinction. It was but a partial and temporary embodiment of an imperishable idea—the faint reflection of a light which still lives and burns in the hearts of the silent thinkers of the Church.

ACTON AND THE VATICAN COUNCIL

[11]

The Next General Council

In spite of the ignorant sarcasm and insidious adulation which the announcement has called forth, no attentive observer of recent transactions in Rome can doubt that the design of a General Council is fraught with momentous consequences to the whole of Christendom. Detestation of such assemblies, jealousy of their authority, and fear of their action, have been for three hundred years a constant tradition among the divines of the Papal Court. Nothing can be imagined, says Pallavicino, which would be more perilous; to summon a General Council, except in extreme need, would be tempting God. Writers of this school prophesy that the Church has outgrown General Councils, and that they will be held no more; and De Maistre thinks Hume substantially right when he says that another will not be seen "till the decay of learning and the progress of ignorance shall again fit mankind for these great impostures." But even De Maistre admits that a General Council may be of use in performing things which surpass the force, if not the rights, of the Holy See; and it has long been confidentially whispered, and almost officially proclaimed, that the Pope desires to obtain the most solemn sanction for his spiritual as well as temporal claims. This has been summarily interpreted to mean that the intended Council will be invited to declare the infallibility of the Pope an article of the Catholic faith. All those whose ideas are expressed in the Encyclical and Syllabus of 1864 must wish for such a consummation. Whilst that document conveyed the Papal approbation to a party still struggling for supremacy, the dexterous commentary of the Bishop of Orleans succeeded in dissembling how completely his adversaries had the Pope on their side, and in postponing their triumph. Nothing less than a General Council can enforce a more explicit acquiescence in

Published in the *Chronicle* (13 July 1867):368–370. Döllinger I, p. 499; Ryan, p. 389. Reprinted in Acton, *Papal Power*, pp. 109–118.

263

the ideas of the Encyclical, and deprive the French Catholics who are called Liberals of their temporary respite. It is also the only means of terminating another controversy of much longer standing. From the days of Baronius and Bellarmin, the Roman divines have held that the Pope is infallible whenever he pronounces in his Pontifical character on questions of faith and morals. This opinion has never prevailed in the Church; and the division it has caused, though preserving theology from stagnation, and useful, as Möhler justly holds, as a stimulus to learning, has sometimes been a source of outward weakness to Catholicism. "Deflenda haec controversia," says Fénelon, "quae jam a trecentis annis Cisalpinos et Transalpinos velut alienos fecit." It has been a special anxiety with Pius IX that this question should be finally settled during his pontificate; and he has repeatedly asserted the claim. The proclamation of the dogma of the Immaculate Conception in 1854 was designed as a step in this direction. It was accomplished without the intervention of a Council. But the opinion which was then raised into a dogma of the Church has long passed out of the region of controversy; it has been sanctioned by Popes and confirmed by the Council of Trent, and offers, therefore, no analogy with the present case, and no precedent for the dogmatic acceptance of an opinion which has been generally repudiated by the schools of divinity not under the immediate influence of Rome, and on which no one imagines that the Church is unanimous. The *Civiltà Cattolica*, a journal which is conducted by Jesuits, revised by Dominicans, and corrected at the office of the Cardinal-Secretary, and which commonly expresses the individual sentiments of the Pope, has undertaken to promote the cause. Catholics are invited to bind themselves by a vow to believe and to teach that the decisions of the Pope are infallible, without reference to their confirmation by the Church. In this way it is hoped that such a demonstration may be provoked as shall silence or efface all differences of opinion, and turn the minds of the faithful in the desired direction. Measures are also being taken to induce the bishops to pledge themselves, so that the Papal infallibility may be proclaimed by general consent.

The uneducated mass of Catholics is already disposed to ascribe to the Pope an illimitable power, of which the rude, popular notion of indulgences gives some idea. The faithful do not always heed the reforms of an enlightened theology; and the belief that the Pope might, by one sweeping act, bestow on innumerable souls the immediate enjoyment of eternal happiness has survived the teaching of the school which covered it. Nor is his power to curse deemed less tremendous than his power to bless. Thousands of contemporary Catholics regard excommunication in a very different light from that in which it appeared to the Sicilians or the Venetians of old. They believe that the Pope can virtually close heaven against them, and can diminish almost indefinitely their chances of salvation, by reserving cases, and narrowing the facilities for obtaining forgiveness. They believe that he can make absolution dependent on new conditions—on agreement with his opinions, or on submission to his commands; in fact, that he can impose his own ideas under pain of damnation. It is needless to enquire how far these things are admitted by divines. As Burke says that in states it is prudent not to enquire too curiously into the exact conditions which justify resistance, so it is policy in the clergy not to check the impulse of devotion, or to determine, by a hard line, the prerogative of St. Peter. Now to the masses of mankind it is all but inconceivable that a man can be invested with such awful power who is not overruled in the use of it by the Spirit of God; or that he who holds the keys and controls the fate of men long since dead can yet unconsciously be peopling hell by the abuse of authority on earth, or by false teaching, or by scandalous example. To the untutored multitude the proclamation of Papal infallibility would convey no new impression, and would scarcely be more than the confirmation of an existing belief.

The conviction and confidence of the masses are a sustaining as well as a limiting and checking influence on the action of the Church. Doubtless the faith of the flock is mixed with prejudices and superstitions very unlike the judgments which literary training and experience of controversy produce in the minds of the pastors. A widening chasm separates the aristocracy of knowledge from the democracy of simple faith. Instances of contradiction between current opinion and scientific discovery have multiplied incalculably since Copernicus; and the clergy must tolerate much that it cannot approve. The present moment is well chosen to prevent the resistance of the Episcopate. The storm that has shaken the throne of Pius IX has earned for him an influence over the bishops such as no modern Pontiff has enjoyed. The troubles of his reign have taught him to identify himself with the party which is most eager in exalting his power. The creed of his most strenuous adherents combines the tenets which are dominant amongst the Jesuits with the tenets of the Legitimists; for it is obviously the interest of the political partizans to magnify the sanction under which they act, and the authority which asserts the needfulness of temporal dominion. The fusion is so complete, that any one who denies the Infallibility of the Pope seems to disturb the defence of his earthly power. The whole Episcopate has made the cause of the temporal power its own; and it is calculated that the current which has impelled and united them so far will carry them on still farther. The force with which these reflections press upon the bishops, and prevent the manifestation of independent views, has been shown in significant instances. The Bishop of Orleans was once noted as a disparager of the Roman Government, yet he became in the hour of need its most unqualified advocate. He was one of those who disliked the project of issuing the Syllabus, which was notoriously pointed against his opinions and his friends; yet he defended and justified the published document without any implied reservation. It is supposed, accordingly, that few will be bold enough to revive the Gallican doctrines, or to wrangle concerning the spiritual claims of the Pope, at a moment when all his authority, and the whole moral support of a unanimous episcopate, are being exerted to preserve what remains of a power which he and they have alike pronounced essential. Something also must be allowed for the personal influence of a Pontiff who has shown a rare power of conciliating and attracting men, who has been made venerable by misfortune, who has nominated nearly all the cardinals, created many new sees, and instituted bishops in unexampled numbers. These personal and private influences will have weight when it is remembered that the notion of his infallibility is not the mere official opinion of the Court, but his own specially cherished conviction.

It is more profitable to study the consequences than to estimate the chances of success. A decree proclaiming the Pope infallible would be a confession that the authority of General Councils has been an illusion and a virtual usurpation from the first; so that having come to the knowledge of their own superfluousness, and having directed the Church into the way she ought always to have followed, they could only abolish themselves for the future by an act which would be an act of suicide. It would invest, by its retrospective action, not the Pope and his successors only, but all his legitimate predecessors, with the same immunity. The objects of faith would be so vastly increased by the incorporation of the Bullarium, that the limits would become indistinct by distance. The responsibility for the acts of the buried and repented past would come back at once and for ever, with a crushing weight on the Church. Spectres it has taken ages of sorrowful effort to lay would come forth once more. The Bulls which imposed a belief in the deposing power, the Bulls which prescribed the tortures and kindled the flames of the Inquisition, the Bulls which erected witchcraft into a system and made the extermination of witches a frightful reality, would become as venerable as the decrees of Nicaea, as incontrovertible as the writing of S. Luke. The decisions of every tribunal (by the decretal *Novit*) would be made subject to the revision of the Pope; and the sentences of every Protestant judge (by the Bull *Cum ex apostolatus officio*) would be invalid. The priesthood would be, by Divine right, exempt from all secular allegiance; and the supreme authority over all States would revert to the Holy See—for thus it stands in the Bull *Unam Sanctam*, repeated by Leo X in the Fifth Council of Lateran. Catholics would be bound, by order of Innocent III, to obey all the laws of Deuteronomy. A successor of Alexander VI might distribute the New World over again; and the right by which Adrian disposed of Ireland would enable another Pope to barter it for a Concordat with America, or to exchange Great Britain for a French garrison. The assurances by which the Church has obtained her freedom would be revoked; and the survivor of the Irish bishops who signed the Declaration of 1826 would discover that he had deceived his country by false representations. The Church would take the place of a moon, reflecting passively the light which the Pope receives directly from heaven, but liable to be left in total darkness, sometimes for three years together, during the vacancy of the Holy See, and during much longer periods of schism, when she knows not her rightful head. And as the Pope's decisions would be, not a testimony of the existing faith of the Church, but a result of his own enlightenment by the Holy Ghost, his interpretation and application of Scripture would be also infallible, the dogma could not be separated from the proofs, and the arguments of the mediaeval Bulls would become a norm for theology. The chances of union with the Greeks, the means of discussion with the Protestants, would vanish utterly, and Catholicism would forfeit its expanding power.

Though these results are too obvious to be unforeseen, they will not all be reckoned valid objections. Though the force of argument would be diminished, the power of assertion would increase, and it might even happen that Catholicism would gain a certain temporary attractiveness by the loss of controversial vigour. There are many who long for peace and silence, who are repelled by the existence of so many differences, and shrink from open questions. Those very memories which, on the supposition that Catholics are implicated in the acts of their brethren in former times, would be such convenient weapons for Protestant attack, are revered by the apostles of the Papal Infallibility; and it will not avail to say that it is dangerous to accept such an odious inheritance, and to renounce the better part of what has been urged by the great apologists. Rome has before now insisted on opinions which set a barrier to conversions and supplied a motive for persecution. The preservation of authority is a higher object than the propagation of the faith. The advocates of Roman views are more used to controversy with their fellow Catholics than with Protestants. Their first aspiration is to suppress divisions of opinion within the Church; and this object could not be achieved more effectually than by converting the Vatican into a sort of Catholic Delphi. Two centuries ago the project of affirming the Papal infallibility was very seriously entertained; and Bossuet made the following reply to a letter informing him of the design: "Elle me fait une peinture de l'état présent de la cour de Rome qui me fait trembler. Quoi, Bellarmin y tient lieu de tout, et y fait seul toute la tradition! Où en sommes-nous si cela est, et si le Pape va condamner ce que condamne cet auteur? Jusqu'ici on n'a osé le faire; on n'a osé donner cette atteinte au Concile de Constance, ni aux Papes qui l'ont approuvé. Que répondrons-nous aux hérétiques quand ils nous objecteront ce concile et ses décrets répétés à Bâle avec l'expresse approbation d'Eugène IV, et toutes les autres choses que Rome a faites en confirmation? . . . Faudra-t-il sortir de ces embarras, et se tirer de l'autorité de tous ces décrets, et de tant d'autres décrets anciens et modernes, par des *distinguo* scholastiques, et par les chicanes de Bellarmin? Faudra-t-il dire aussi avec lui et Baronius, que les actes du Concile VI et les lettres de Saint Léon II sont falsifiés? et l'église qui jusqu'ici a fermé la bouche aux hérétiques par des réponses si solides, n'aura-t-elle plus de défense que dans ces pitoyables tergiversations? . . . Je ne puis m'imaginer qu'un Pape si zélé pour la conversion des hérétiques, et pour la réunion des schismatiques, y veuille mettre un obstacle éternel, par une décision telle que celle dont on nous menace. Dieu détournera ce coup." The alarm which these words betray will not be revived by the events that are passing before our eyes. A wrong decree of Innocent XI would have been a grievous trial, such as Catholicism is always exposed to; but there is no fear that a General Council will testify falsely to the faith of the Church.

[12]
Essays in Academic Literature

The volume of Essays by various writers edited by the Archbishop of Westminster is in some danger of being judged unfairly. The name and title of the editor, who is also a contributor, will suggest to many persons the idea of regarding it as the measure of what the English Catholics can do in literature, and of treating its most unguarded propositions as a *reductio ad absurdum* of Catholic opinions. Dr. Newman, in his reply to the *Eirenicon*, warns us that even the best of these writers must not be taken as exponents of Catholicism. Dr. Ward, indeed, though he does not aspire to be an eloquent or genial writer, is immeasurably superior in mental vigour to most of the authorities whom Dr. Newman mentions. It is less, however, a question of ability than of fidelity in retailing views generally entertained. Although the Essayists are not to be estimated according to the value of the testimony they bear to the ideas of the Catholic Church, their work is remarkable in another respect, and possesses its own kind of fidelity and truthfulness. If the responsibility of their teaching does not fall upon the Church, it is fully shared by a large party within it. They do not help to an understanding of the Catholic system, but they supply copious materials for investigating a system that exists within its shadow, and is one of the active forces, and a characteristic symptom, of the age. The representatives of similar opinions on the Continent have not been successful in getting a serious hearing. They lack the restraint of an earnest opposition. They see no difficulties and observe no limits, so that their arguments generally beat the air. They are careless in statement and violent in language, like men who write for a public

Henry Edward Manning, ed., *Essays on Religion and Literature*, 2d ser. (London: Longmans, 1867). This review was published in the *Chronicle* (5 October 1867):664–667. Döllinger I, p. 492; Ryan, p. 390.

269

already convinced, or for a public which has incurred a penal visitation, and is not likely to be influenced by anything less impressive. They display more prejudices than convictions, and defend them with that sort of uneasiness and passion with which men are apt to maintain sentiments they have come by through persuasion or authority, and not through the impersonal coercion of logic. In England the same views meet with every inducement for revision, and with frequent provocation to exact definitions, closer arguments, and outward plausibility, or at least to internal consistency. They are held by men who were not brought up in them, who did not imbibe them before their judgment was formed, and who, whether converts or not, had to break with traditions and early habits in embracing them. Having adopted them deliberately, by process of reasoning, these men must be able to understand the objections, and have an impulse to work their ideas into a system, to subject them to leading principles, to take little for granted, and to fortify every step. Ideas which pervade foreign countries in an amorphous state, or as topics for declamation, or as things good to assert as a matter of course, but above question and proof, are driven by the surrounding Protestantism into shapes and positions that will meet higher requirements on the part of those who accept them, and will furnish a defence against attack.

It has not long been possible to study this kind of opinion to advantage in English writers. The Catholics of the last generation, contemporaries of Milner and Lingard, Doyle and O'Connell, were taught in a different school. They were accustomed to give prominence to that aspect of Catholicism which raised fewest obstacles to emancipation. Like the early Apologists, they denied that there was anything in their doctrines contrary to the policy or the interest of the State; they laboured, often quite sincerely, to rescue their Church from the aversion commonly felt for the interference of Rome, and for the religious policy of Italy and Spain, and sought to reduce indefinitely the Papal influence, and their own solidarity with the Papal acts. The rise at the present day of an opposite school, as anxious to exalt as others had been to depress the claims of Rome, is due to more direct and efficient causes than the increased sense of security, the submissive ardour of converts, or the influence of foreign writers. It is to be ascribed partly to Cardinal Wiseman, and partly to his more energetic successor. In the late Cardinal, who had been reared at Rome, and who probably at no period of his life succeeded in viewing the Papacy objectively, the Roman tendency was spontaneous. In Archbishop Manning it is both a result of conviction and a necessity proceeding from his position. By a special interposition of the Pope he has been raised above prelates several of whom have been bishops longer than he has been a Catholic, and three, if not four of whom had been previously designated for the metropolitan see. The body over which he presides is composed of various and not harmonious elements; and religious orders, with diverse traditions and nearly independent constitutions, are not always easy to control. Cardinal Wiseman, as the author of the hierarchy, and the nominator of almost all the bishops, and by reason of his pre-eminence in controversy and literature, enjoyed a personal authority which, in later years, he neglected to cultivate. His successor, with fewer acquired advantages, has greater enterprise. Not content with a position of ceremonious patronage, he desires to be the tactician as well as the strategist of the English Catholics, to develop and combine their resources, and to bring them under such disciplines as shall exercise a real influence over actions and ideas. Now there is only one force in the Catholic Church that can substantially aid him; and that force is Rome. There is no party but the Roman party. Other opinions, which are discouraged or proscribed at Rome, exist in plenty, but not in groups. There is not only neither combination nor coherence, but no substantial agreement among those who are roughly classified as liberal Catholics—between Tosti and Liverani, Ketteler and Pichler, Gratry and Hyacinthe. If the Archbishop of Westminster had attempted to imitate the example of the Archbishop of Paris, he would not only have been abandoned by Propaganda, but he would have estranged the mass of his own followers. The favour and confidence of Rome are not to be cheaply purchased. Services equal to those which Bossuet rendered to the Church would be more than counterbalanced by an attitude such as Bossuet assumed towards the Pope. Archbishop Manning, in comparatively few years, has converted more Protestants probably than any bishop living; but that would not be enough to make him assured of the sustaining countenance of the Holy See if he failed to promote its interests in the questions which touch it nearly. An advocate of the temporal power and the Inquisition, of the Index and the Syllabus, is worth appreciably more than a controversialist whose energies are spent on the articles of faith. A volume prepared and published under the Archbishop's auspices presents, therefore, a legitimate and favourable opportunity for the study of that class of opinions which Rome prefers. The unity of the book must not be exaggerated. There is no reason to assume that the propositions of each writer are endorsed by all, and differences of degree unquestionably appear. Still the same general character pervades the whole, and may be discerned in the paper which is farthest from the nature of a party manifesto as clearly as in the one which sounds the most defiant note.

The latter distinction belongs to a paper on Church and State, by Mr. E. S. Purcell. We were at first tempted to give the preference to a protracted essay by Mr. Lucas on Christianity in relation to civil society. While Mr. Purcell is rather shabbily dependent on others for his thoughts, his facts, and even his quotations, Mr. Lucas wrestles strenuously with his ideas, and owes each step to himself. There is, moreover, a warm-hearted charity in what he writes. But he gives his readers more of the painfulness of his thinking process than of its results. They follow him up hill, and he neglects to reward their toil. He is an inhospitable host, who sets before his guests wine of his own vintage indeed, but opaque from fermentation. His individuality detracts from his typical value. Casual speculations peculiar to one writer do not assist the representative purpose we are seeking in the volume. Mr. Purcell on the other hand does not pretend to originality, and he brings out with clearness, definiteness, and candour, the ideas of which he is the spokesman. He tells us as follows: The Popes, as Vicegerents of Christ, exercise a supreme sovereignty over all Christian nations. One of the attributes of sovereignty is to execute judgment, and the last punishment of kings is deposition (p. 416). If an heretical prince is elected or succeeds to the throne, the Church has a right to say "I annul the election," or "I forbid the succession" (p. 459). Where, as in uncatholic nations, responsibility is less, authority is less. The Popes refrain from exercising the right out of expediency, because it would not now conduce to the public good; but the right is not forfeited because it is not used (p. 418). If the king violate the divine or ecclesiastical law, he is subject to the penal jurisdiction of the Church (p. 407). But what is in conformity with the Divine will the Church alone can declare (p. 412). And since laws affecting the government and well-being of all Christian peoples are continually issuing from the Church, the civil power is bound both to consult all such laws and to carry them into effect (p. 413). Neither Church nor State, to adopt the words of the German canonist Phillips, has any cognizance of tolerance (p. 403), and every concession in that direction is a sacrifice of principle to necessity. The Church, though having no jurisdiction over the heathen, can call for the destruction of idolatrous temples as an offence against the primeval revelation, and as a hindrance to its divine commission (p. 460).

This spirited language has not often been held before the English public by a Catholic writer. Mr. Purcell's essay signalizes an epoch very different from that of the *Letters to a Prebendary*, when the Catholics always insisted that theirs was not a persecuting Church, and that Pope or prelate could not absolve them from their allegiance to King George. The assertion of loyal and tolerant principles drove them to various shifts, and compelled them to fence awkwardly enough with inconvenient testimonies. The time for these arts has gone by, the *disciplina arcani* is put aside, and there is no longer any fear of letting the world know the least acceptable of their tenets. Mr. Purcell probably has no expectation of converting people to his views, and cannot hope that they will attract any souls towards the Church. He publishes them, crude and unqualified as they are, with all the authority the tacit sanction of the Archbishop can bestow, because he knows that they are also the sentiments of the Pope. The questions on which he speaks with so much frankness and confidence have lately become prominent. The Pope has made a point in the Syllabus, and in the case of Arbues, of insisting on claims and theories which he has no prospect of being able to enforce. It is clear that he does so for the sake of the principle. Persecution and the deposing power are the questions most deeply involved in the antagonism between the Church and the modern State, and those on which the secular triumph seemed most assured. They are points which cannot be formally surrendered without injury to the memory of former Popes, or to some links in the chain of infallibility; and those who defend them discreetly must be welcome to the Holy See. They must be the more welcome because persons of great authority have on these topics shown more ingenuity than candour. The Bishops of Orleans and Mentz, shrinking from the full significance of the Pope's words, endeavoured to attenuate their effect. They sought to dissociate him from his predecessors, or the predecessors from their acts, and denied that he meant really to affirm the principles of the Inquisition. Compared to such apologists, Mr. Purcell appears a mirror in ingenuous honour. His doctrine may be a stumbling-block to some, but it is better that the Church should lose ground than practise concealment. When the Pope speaks to the whole world, it is desirable that he should be understood. That opinions entailing such a price should be published in an age when the Catholic Church possesses both deep scholars and great writers, is less extra-ordinary than the policy of those who explain away the utterances of the moment, and leave unexplained the less ambiguous examples of the past. The theory of intolerance, as Mr. Purcell puts it, enjoys the highest sanction to which, in such matters, Catholics ordinarily look. It has been held, not only by Pius IX, but by a whole catena of Popes before him. It is found in the great divines, in Fathers and Doctors, in the lives and writings of Saints, in the acts of councils, and in the ecclesiastical law. By the exercise of the maxims springing from this theory whole nations were recovered which had been overrun by Arianism, Hussitism, and Protestantism. There is but one country which claims to have put down the doctrines of the Reformation without bloodshed, and that is the country whose name has disappeared from among the States, and threatens to disappear from among nations. It is not surprising that Catholics should prefer the protection of such authorities to the perplexities which attend the opinion that Christianity is in a special manner the religion of toleration. To adopt that opinion they would be compelled, to a great extent, to renounce S. Augustine and S. Thomas, Suarez and Bossuet, and to reject the Encyclicals and the canon law. They would have to deny the infallibility of the Popes and the sanctity of many saints. They would have to hold that the ends of religion do not justify the use of means which are otherwise immoral, and to acknowledge that their faith has been sometimes preserved by means which were suggestions of the devil. All this might be enough to explain why a private Catholic should be content to be silent, and should scruple to contradict ideas to which he supposes that his Church stands committed. It does not explain why he is not content to be silent and to leave to those whom it may concern the responsibility of such assertions. The necessity which urges him to insist on these particular opinions is the point which is really of moment in the present conjuncture.

In this inquisitive age, above all others, reason prepares difficulties for faith. The dangers which surround the use of the intellect have suggested to Dr. Ward the text of a monitory paper in this very volume. A man who relies on the supply of special answers to each of the problems which physical or speculative studies throw from time to time in his way, will waver in his conviction as often as he discovers that the answer he has trusted will not do. More than one conspicuous example has been seen of men who had acquired reputation among Catholics leaving them again, or withdrawing to a position of suspended allegiance. Others who dread the same dilemma readily embrace authority as a refuge from uncertainty. The one authority which can be expected to attend to the settlement of questions as they arise is the Holy See; and its decisions can secure peace only if its voice is accepted as that of the Church. If the Pope expresses no more than the views formed in a particular group of divines, or the result of certain local habits of thought, his answers would not effectually smother differences. If the words of Rome owe their weight to the proofs that sustain them, and make their way by discussion, their success is contingent on the superiority of their interpreters and advocates; and as long as the exponents of Roman views have to contend against the opposition of Catholic theologians and are contra-dicted at home, they are liable to see their authority as representatives of the Church declined by Protestants. It is scarcely possible to elude the necessity which obliges those who desire the increase of the Pope's authority to accept his infallibility, and which connects the belief in his infallibility with the desire to have it recognized as an article with which the Church stands or falls. Of all the acts and words of the Pope those need to be vindicated most which are most likely to be challenged. It becomes a maxim of policy to anticipate his decrees, to proceed as far as possible ahead in the direction which he follows, and to cover his advance. By this path the lines of human reason and evidence are speedily left behind, and men end by exulting in the very things which they are least able to render plausible. The value of the Papal interference is not shown in matters which could be determined without it, but in those which would otherwise be decided in the contrary way. The use of steam is to go against the wind. Men of this class are less zealous to amplify the conquests of human knowledge than to dispute them. Their methods are as unlike those of science as their conclusions. So much is taken for granted that there is no room and no occasion for argument. In the volume before us the following passage occurs: "They deposed, by a right inherent in the Papacy, kings who had forfeited their right to reign over a Christian people. If this right be denied to them, the greatest and holiest of the Popes will be justly exposed to the reproach of having put forward false claims, and of having usurped an authority to which they had no title." In the writer's apprehension this appears to be an argument. His mind has no contact with those which do not perceive its validity.

The practical effect of these tendencies since De Maistre has raised much suspicion against Catholics, and has become the centre of much recent controversy. People who cannot believe that virtue, piety, and honour can co-exist with such habits of thought and speech have set up the vulgar accusation of hypocrisy. The answer is supplied by examples which fall within the observation of most Englishmen. None can be more striking than that of a Frenchman famous in his day, whose career Nisard and Carayon have lately brought into notice. Early in the seventeenth century the most busy and most widely known of the French Jesuits was Garasse. He was the *enfant terrible* of the Society. His outrageous violence, his coarseness and scurrility, his unscrupulous and incautious use of weapons, and the recklessness of his invective, made his name a bye-word among his contemporaries. Those who remember Croker in his prime have a faint idea of Garasse. We are not told that, like S. Augustine and Bellarmine, he ever composed his *Retractationes*; yet, when a pestilence broke out at Poitiers, though it was no part of his immediate duty, he petitioned to be sent to attend the sick, and he perished without abandoning his work of charity down to the last moment. The fact is that in such writings as these essays, the question of sincerity does not properly arise. Men believe in their religion without understanding the connection of each dogma, or knowing all that the theologians have to say for it. To the ardent asserters of the Papal prerogative, a great variety of propositions appear invested with the sanctity that belongs to the objects of faith; many opinions are elevated into the region of indisputable certainty or systematic necessity without becoming clear to the reason, and have to be defended though they cannot be explained, and though the arguments do not appear cogent to those who use them. These advocates accept what they are told, though it may not always be the same. If they turn round and deny that which they have maintained, from no internal reason, but out of deference to authority, they conceive that they are not committing a sin of insincerity, but fulfilling the duty of obedience. Although the *Essays* are written in the tone of a quasi-official advocacy dictated by policy rather than by principle, they are uniformly distinguished by the absence of the inverted ethics and the passionate lying which seem inseparable from the French and Italian polemics of the school. The authors are not even solicitous to be in rigorous conformity with the precepts or the practice of Rome. Mr. Lucas refuses to defend, or to excuse, or even to palliate inhuman cruelties, so that he is at issue with the criminal law which sanctions the use of torture and of fire. Mr. Purcell boldly adopts a proposition directly condemned in the Syllabus; for he says, "The State, whether Christian or heathen, was always charged with the duty of looking after the moral welfare of its subjects." There is no danger of actual collision. When occasion requires, these gentlemen will probably have no more difficulty in accounting for the literal variation than the Count de Falloux in explaining his praise of a free press at Mechlin, or the coadjutor of Geneva in justifying his remarks on the liberty of conscience in reply to the pacific fulminations of Garibaldi. But meanwhile they enjoy their liberty, and seem to do no violence to their opinions.

If Mr. Purcell provides the unadulterated essence, it appears tempered and diluted in Canon Oakeley's essay on *The Mission of the Church in England*. Of all the contributions this is the one which is most agreeable to read, and in which the intention has interfered least with the argument. Its chief defect is in omission. Many of the statements would be quite true if they were a little less bare, and more carefully defined. The way in which they are put often betrays, even in this graceful and unworldly writer, the lurking influence of the disposition which breaks out riotously in others. Either from constitutional sobriety, or from his experience as a priest in some of the least favoured parts of London, Canon Oakeley shares only with reserve the sanguine hope of the conversion of England, which is one of the conditions for the growth of this school. He will not positively contradict the opinion that countries which have renounced Catholicism never returned to it. As a matter of fact, none of the five or six nations which adopted Protestantism in the sixteenth century have abandoned it in the nineteenth; but the examples of States and cities and particular districts are so frequent that the national argument goes for very little. He says of the Catholic Church, "that she alone is the true palladium of civil liberty, by providing in a great central authority, most comprehensive in its aims, most prudent in its counsels, most abundant in its charity, a support of national independence against the encroachments of arbitrary power" (p. 158). The remark is interesting, because the author is aware that the one place where the Church cannot possibly discharge this important function is Rome. It would be true but for its exclusiveness. For though the Church once accomplished this great political office, she has rarely done so since the Reformation. Where sects have multiplied, a certain measure of political liberty has been connected with their success; and the service once rendered by the centre of unity has been continued by the right of private judgment. Again Canon Oakeley urges that a church which embodies the spirit of voluntary self-sacrifice in permanent institutions possesses in them a safeguard against national poverty. It is true that those who adopt a life of privation help the poor, first by their example, and next by diminishing competition and leaving open to those whom it would have excluded the way to comfort and enjoyment. The law which governs the life of the Catholic priest is the most perfect of all the moral checks for the prevention, but not for the cure, of poverty. But the mendicant orders increase the burdens and diminish the resources of the community. They make the struggle for existence more desperate by diverting from those who are poor by necessity the help that would enable them to live. The pressure is not felt until population thickens or food begins to fail; and the mendicant friars are the favourites of the poor until they become their rivals. The idea of S. Francis had not efficacy for all time, but for all times like his own. It was the noblest of the forces acquired by the Church since the Apostolic age; and the revolution which it wrought has had no parallel since the conversion of the civilized world. In the following passage Canon Oakeley is guilty of idle declamation: "What was it which preserved France from falling into apostasy under the tremendous shock of the great Revolution? It was her adherence, as a nation, to the Holy See" (p. 154). The instance is so hopelessly ill-chosen that it is impossible to extract from the words any sense in which they are true. And yet by this infelicitous example the writer is inculcating the important truth that the action of the Church, through her laws and government, is entirely distinct from her action by the truths which she teaches. The equipoise between the national element in the Church and her extra-national head is a security against Byzantinism, which is not to be found in her theological doctrines, her sacraments, or her devotions. Canon Oakeley says that the English Reformation was not promoted by the indignation and despair at the demoralization of the Church which made the Continental Reformers waver in their faith. "It was not, as in some other countries, a hearty, however mistaken, protest against some alleged corruption, but the creation of political circumstances." Little is required to make this a true saying; but as it is, it seems to imply that the writer is not sure that the alleged corruptions really existed. It would be culpable indeed if, in the hope of conciliation, and preferring the sweet to the bitter ways of controversy, he avoided painful topics, and was unwilling to say all the harm he knows of the religions which he combats. But if he refuses to apply the same knife to his own communion, it will be impossible to make men believe in his hatred of sin. In another place he declines to say that Catholic societies are superior in morality to others. There are contrasts in history which would have justified him in taking a higher line. But this is an instance of caution and scruple which forbids an unfavourable interpretation where those qualities appear to be wanting.

[13]
The Pope and the Council

The attempt to establish the infallibility of the Pope by decree of a General Council is a phase of controversy which the internal disputes of the Church of Rome have made almost inevitable. The Catholic opposition in its several forms, national in Italy, scientific in Germany, liberal in France, has uniformly been directed against one or other of the Papal claims. Amongst the Catholics there are numbers who earnestly condemn the despotism of the Popes, their asserted superiority to all human law, civil and ecclesiastical, the exclusiveness with which they profess themselves sole interpreters of the Divine law, their systematic warfare against freedom of conscience, of science, and of speech. These men find the arms of their adversaries effectually strengthened by the Papacy, and their own efforts confounded by reproaches which it justifies; but they seldom acknowledge that the causes of their weakness are in Rome. Sooner or later they almost always renounce or silence their convictions. Rather than definitely contradict the utterances of the Pope, or publicly censure his acts, they devote themselves to force or to veil his meaning. They shrink from a direct antagonism, and refuse to let the cause of the Pope be separated from their own. Their dread of a collision, and their obtrusive submissiveness, encourage the enterprise of those whose desire is to promote the Papal authority. Men who succumb in order to avoid the Index cannot be expected to reject what is proposed as an article of

Ignaz von Döllinger [Janus], *Der Papst und das Concil* (Leipzig: Steinacker, 1869). This review was published in the *North British Review* 51 (October 1869):127–135. Ryan, p. 247. The article was designated as *communicated*, meaning that it did not represent the viewpoint of the *North British Review*. Döllinger was the author of *Der Papst und das Concil*, assisted by Johann Friedrich and Johann Huber. Despite the comments on p. 289, Acton knew when writing the review that Döllinger was Janus. See Acton's letter of October 10, 1869 in Döllinger I, pp. 572–573.

faith. If they will not resist a Roman congregation acting in the name of the Pope, they are not likely to resist an ecumenical council claiming to represent the Church. It is thought at Rome that, by declaring the Pope infallible, the independent action of the liberal party may be arrested, and the troubles of internal discussion averted for the future.

This infallibility is already a received doctrine with a considerable fraction of the Catholics. In the Commission to which the question was submitted at Rome, in preparation for the Council, only one dissentient vote was given. Among the Jesuits it has long prevailed; and the Jesuits being now in power, and recognised exponents of the Pope's own sentiments, the moment is propitious to make their doctrine triumph. For the ideas of the Encyclical and Syllabus of 1864, by which Pius IX desired to remodel society, have not commanded general assent. The mind of Europe moves in other orbits; and nation after nation breaks away from the fetters of the canon law. It is hoped that the Pope's words will be heard with more deference if they are enforced by severer penalties. Obedience or excommunication would be a formidable alternative to the Catholics. The calculation is that it may yet be possible to recover by authority what has not been preserved by reason, and to restore, at one stroke, an influence which is waning, and a spirit that has passed away.

There is no doubt that many of the bishops will be glad if the dogma of infallibility is not submitted to the Council. A book by a French prelate is announced to appear shortly, which proves that the authority and example of Bossuet are not lost upon his countrymen. The German bishops, meeting at Fulda the other day, agreed that it would be better for the Church if the question were not to be raised. The most eminent amongst them has declared his belief that the effect of the proposed decree would be to make all Germany Protestant. Others are not less forcibly impressed with the injury which would be done to the prospects of their Church in Great Britain. They have all combined to issue a pastoral letter, in which they repudiate with indignation the designs imputed to them. But they declare in the same document that no serious differences of opinion disturb the unanimity of the Catholic episcopate. Men who can utter such a thing in Germany must be capable of doing stranger things in Rome.

It will not be easy for the opposition to prevent the decree. In various ways the bishops are already largely committed. Since the revival of Provincial Synods, their acts have been sent to Rome for approval; and many of them have asserted their belief in the Papal infallibility. In 1854 the episcopate allowed the Pope to proclaim a new dogma to the Church. In 1862 they almost unanimously pronounced in favour of the temporal power. In 1864 they accepted the Syllabus. In 1867 they assured the Pope that they were ready to believe whatever he should teach. At that time the intention to summon a General Council, and the purpose of the summons, were no secret; and the bishops knew that their address would not be received if it expressed their obedience in less explicit terms. They will now be required to redeem their pledges. The most sanguine opponent can hardly expect, if the Council meets, that the dogma will not be proposed, or that it will be rejected in principle, or on any higher ground than that of present expediency. Its rejection, so qualified, might easily be represented as implicit acceptance of the principle, leaving the question of time to the judgment of the Pope. It will probably appear that the question of expediency is the only one which will be fairly submitted to be affirmed or negatived by the Council. The managers consider that the doctrine itself is virtually decided, and that only those who believe it are real Catholics. Their object will be gained if the assembled episcopate confirms their opinion by tacit acquiescence, while it determines whether a formal decree is opportune.

No charge is more strenuously repelled by intelligent Catholics than that their faith is subject to be changed at will by the authorities of their Church, and that they may be called upon to believe to-morrow what they deny to-day. Their position in this respect is becoming critical. It is manifestly possible that a Council, at which their episcopate will be more fully assembled than it has been at any former Council, may proclaim that Catholicism must stand or fall with the infallibility of the Pope. They repudiate that doctrine now: will they believe it if the Council should so decide? On the answer to this question, even more than on the deliberations of the bishops at Rome, the future of their cause depends.

An answer to it has at length been given, and given with such force and distinctness that it cannot be forgotten or recalled. A volume has appeared at Leipzig, on the competence of the Council and the infallibility of the Pope, which will complete that revolution in Catholic divinity, and in the conditions of religious controversy, which was begun by Möhler's treatment of the claim to indefectibility, and by Newman's theory of the development of doctrine. The argument of the book, sustained by a portentous chain of evidence, is briefly this: The Christian Fathers not only teach that the Pope is fallible, but deny him the right of deciding dogmatic questions without a Council. In the first four centuries there is no trace of a dogmatic decree proceeding from a Pope. Great controversies were fought out and settled without the participation of the Popes; their opinion was sometimes given and rejected by the Church; and no point of doctrine was finally decided by them in the first ten centuries of Christianity. They did not convene the General Councils; they presided over them in two instances only; they did not confirm their acts. Among all the ancient heretics there is not one who was blamed because he had fallen away from the faith of Rome. Great doctrinal errors have been sometimes accepted, and sometimes originated, by Popes; and, when a Pope was condemned for heresy by a General Council, the sentence was admitted without protest by his successors. Several Churches of undisputed orthodoxy held no intercourse with the See of Rome. Those passages of Scripture which are used to prove that it is infallible, are not so interpreted by the Fathers. They all, eighteen in number, explain the prayer of Christ for Peter, without reference to the Pope. Not one of them believes that the Papacy is the rock on which He built His Church. Every Catholic priest binds himself by oath never to interpret Scripture in contradiction to the Fathers; and if, defying the unanimous testimony of antiquity, he makes these passages authority for Papal infallibility, he breaks his oath.

So far the book only asserts more definitely, and with deeper learning, facts which were already known. The great problem is to explain how it came to pass that the ancient constitution of the Church was swept away, and another system substituted, contrary to it in principle, in spirit, and in action, and by what gradations the present claims arose. The history of this transformation is the great achievement of the book. Each step in the process, prolonged through centuries, is ascertained and accounted for; and nothing is left obscure where the greater part was till now unknown. The passage from the Catholicism of the Fathers to that of the modern Popes was accomplished by wilful falsehood; and the whole structure of traditions, laws, and doctrines that support the theory of infallibility, and the practical despotism of the Popes, stands on a basis of fraud.

The great change began in the middle of the ninth century, with a forgery which struck root so deep that its consequences survive, though it has been discovered and exposed for three centuries. About one hundred decretals of early pontiffs, with acts of Councils and passages from the Fathers, were composed and published in France. The object of their author was to liberate the bishops from the authority of metropolitans and of the civil government, by exalting the power of the Pope, in whom he represented all ecclesiastical authority as concentrated. He placed the final criterion of orthodoxy in the word of the Pope, and taught that Rome would always be true to the faith, and that the acts of Councils were inoperative and invalid without Papal confirmation. The effect was not what he intended. At Rome the ground had long been prepared by interpolations in St. Cyprian, and by the fictitious biographies of early Popes which bear the name of Anastasius; and the advantage supplied by the Frankish prelate was eagerly seized. Nicolas I declared that the originals of these texts were preserved in the Papal archives; and the bishops found themselves reduced to the position of dependants and delegates of the Pope. When Gregory VII undertook to impose his new system of government on the church, he, as well as the able and unscrupulous men who helped him, made all available use of pseudo-Isidore, and added such further fictions and interpolations as the new claims required. These accumulated forgeries, with more of his own making, were inserted by Gratian in the compilation which became the text-book of canon law. The exposure of the devices by which the Gregorian system obtained acceptance, and a spurious code supplanted the authentic law of the Church, is the most brilliant and the newest thing in the volume.

The Councils became passive instruments in the hands of the Pope, and silently registered his decrees at the General Council of Vienne. Clement V stated that he summoned only a few selected prelates, and informed them that whoever dared to speak, without being called on by the Pope, incurred excommunication. The Papal absolutism was practically established when it was forced on the divines by the same arts. A series of forged passages from the Greek Fathers came into existence, by which it appeared that the Pope was recognised as infallible by the Eastern Church in the fourth century. Urban IV communicated them to St. Thomas Aquinas, who constructed the doctrine, as it afterwards flourished, on the proofs thus supplied. He was deceived by the invention of a false tradition; and his great name spread and established the delusion. At length men became aware that the decay of religion and the lamentable evils and abuses in the Church were caused by the usurpations of Rome. At Constance it was proclaimed that the supreme legislative and judicial authority, and the last appeal in matters of faith, belonged to the Council; and thus the belief and discipline of the Church were restored to what they had been before the forgeries began. The decrees were accepted by the Pope and by succeeding Councils; but it was a transitory reform. In the conflict with Protestantism the notion of unbounded power and unfailing orthodoxy was wrought up to the highest pitch at Rome. Cardinal Cajetan called the Church the slave of the Pope. Innocent IV had declared that every priest was bound to obey him, even in unjust things; and Bellarmine asserted that if a Pope should prescribe vice and prohibit virtue, the Church must believe him. "Si autem papa erraret præcipiendo vitia, vel prohibendo virtutes, teneretur Ecclesia credere vitia esse bona et virtutes mala, nisi vellet contra conscientiam peccare." Gregory VII had claimed to inherit the sanctity as well as the faith of Peter; and Innocent X professed that God had made the Scriptures clear to him, and that he felt himself inspired from above. The present volume traces the progress of the theory, and its influence on religion and society, down to the sixteenth century, and shows with careful detail how much it contributed to the schism of the East, to the divisions of Western Christendom, to the corruption of morality, the aggravation of tyranny, and the fanatical persecution of witchcraft and heresy, and how the only hope of Christian union lies in the reformation of those defects which have been introduced by fraud and malice during many ages of credulity and ignorance. If anything can ruin the system which exalts so high the claims and privileges of the Pope, it is such an exposure of the methods and the motives that have reared it.

The author evidently is prepared for the worst. He thinks it conceivable that the Council may err as well as the Pope, and may proclaim as a dogma what is false. The encroachments of the Papacy have left so little independence to the episcopate that the testimony of the bishops is no security for their Church. Their oath of office binds them to preserve and to increase the rights, honours, privileges, and authority of the Pope; they are no longer competent to restrict those rights and authorities, or to resist the proposal to increase them. "Since the time of Gregory VII the Papal power has weighed upon the Councils far more heavily than the imperial influence of old. When the prospect of a General Council was discussed in the sixteenth century, half Europe justly demanded two conditions—that it should not be held at Rome, or even in Italy, and that the bishops should be released from their oath of obedience. The new Council will be held not only in Italy, but at Rome itself. That alone is decisive. It proves that, whatever the course of the Council may be, there is one quality that can never be assigned to it, the quality of true freedom" (p. 448).

That is the reply of men versed in all the knowledge of their Church to the anxious question which has been so often asked; and it is not likely that the Council will produce anything more significant than such a declaration of opinion. Catholicism has never taken up stronger ground. Both among Protestants and Greeks there are men in whose eyes the later forms of Papal domination are the one unpardonable fault of Rome. It has always been objected to the Gallican theology that it gave to the bishops what it took from the Pope, and attributed infallibility to the supreme ecclesiastical authorities. But here it is asserted that grave dogmatic error, imposed by authority and accepted without resistance, may long overcloud the Church; that the Papacy has taught false doctrines, and has made their adoption the test of orthodoxy; that it has excommunicated men who were right, while Rome was wrong; that it has been most potent and active in seducing consciences and leading souls astray; that it has obliterated the divine idea and the patristic doctrine of the Primacy. Understood in this way, and purified from those defects which have proceeded from the arbitrary power usurped by Rome, Catholicism would recover an ample portion of its sway. It will lose at least as much if these detected superstitions are solemnly affirmed. The project has been so long and carefully prepared, and so publicly proclaimed, that the attempt to withdraw it would be ruin. The chronic malady has become acute; and a serious crisis is at hand. Procrastination cannot avert it; and no one can tell whether the ideas of the book which is before us are shared by numbers sufficient to prevail. In the Preface it is stated that they were held by the most eminent men of Catholic Germany in the last generation; and this is true so far as regards their general spirit, their notion of the Church, their practical aspirations, and their moral tone. In this sense the work is the manifesto of a great party, and expresses opinions that are widely spread. But the evidence, the reasoning, the material basis, are in great part new. Many of the investigations were never made before; and the results were not all so clear and so certain as they now are. They are established by many facts which no one knew, and which it was no reproach to be ignorant of; so that the work retains the character of conciliation towards those whose opinions it directly refutes. It constitutes so great an advance in knowledge that it supplies them with some excuse for their errors, and a refuge from the imputation of bad faith.

The author himself has been led by this circumstance into error. It has caused him to underrate the gravity of the charges in which his adversaries are involved. After exposing the fraudulent machinations by which the absolutist theory was set up, he proceeds to assume the sincerity of its advocates. He constantly speaks to the Jesuits, without any qualification, as supporters of the opinions in question. He seems to be utterly unaware that he thereby fixes on the whole Order the stigma of mendacity. It is useless to pretend that, after the progress of learning made known the spurious origin of the documents which are the basis of the modern Roman theory, the theory itself was sincerely believed in by educated men. The power of the modern Popes is retained by the same arts by which it was won. A man is not honest who accepts all the Papal decisions in questions of morality, for they have often been distinctly immoral; or who approves the conduct of the Popes in engrossing power, for it was stained with perfidy and falsehood; or who is ready to alter his convictions at their command, for his conscience is guided by no principle. Such men in reality believe that fair means will not avail to save the Church of Rome. Formerly, in time of great extremity, they betook themselves to persecution: for the same purpose and with the same motives they still practise deceit, and justify it with the name of religion. The Jesuits continue to be identified with these opinions, because Jesuits conduct the journal that chiefly promotes them. But the *Civiltà Cattolica* is the organ of the Vatican, not of the Society; and there is no small number of the Jesuits who heartily deplore its tendency, and are incapable of imitating its intellectual demoralization. In a passage which is quoted in *The Pope and the Council*, a Paris Jesuit has written, "God does not give His blessing to fraud; the false decretals have produced nothing but harm." And it is not just to say that the terms of extreme adulation applied to the Pope came in with the Jesuits. In the fifteenth century an archbishop writes to Alexander VI, "Te alterum in terris Deum semper habebimus" (Petri de Warda Epistolae, 1776, p. 331). It is equally wrong to lay the blame of these things on the recent converts to Rome. In this country at least, most of the able opponents of such views among the Catholics are Oxford men.

A more serious defect in the present work is that, having given so much, it has not given more. It is so rich in thought and matter that it creates a wish to see many questions more amply treated which have been only lightly touched. The author tells us that he hopes for a great reform in the Catholic Church; but he does not describe the reform he desires. He hopes to see the evils remedied that spring from religious absolutism and centralization; but this does not constitute a distinct idea of the Church of the future. It would be interesting to know how far the reforming spirit has penetrated among the enlightened Catholics, and how high they place their ideal. There is a long array of problems which would find their solution, and of abuses which would receive their death-stroke, from the consistent application of the principles laid down in this book. Many of them have arisen in recent times, and have grown out of the system established at Trent. On this later ground the author shows himself reluctant to tread. The fulness of his knowledge, and the firmness of his grasp, attend him down to the sixteenth century; but he scarcely glances at the times that follow. The Council of Trent occupies only two or three pages. Yet no example would be more useful to enforce the lesson he is teaching, or more profitable on the eve of another General Council. The whole system of operations prepared for this occasion is borrowed from the arts that proved so efficacious three centuries ago. And there is one phenomenon which is sure to be repeated. The greatest difficulty of the Legates at Trent was not to resist the pressure of the reforming prelates, but to control the zeal of their own servile followers. They complained that, while the opposition was learned, prudent, and united, the bishops who sustained the policy of Rome compromised it by their obstinacy and the diversity of their views, inasmuch as each endeavoured to excel the others in his anxiety to please the Pope. "Questi ci travagliano non meno che li primi, trovando come facciamo il più delle volte fra loro ostinatione nelle opinioni loro, e diversità, e varietà grande, di modo che quanto è fra li primi di concordia e unione, tanto è discordia e disunione negli secondi, per volersi ciascuno di loro mostrare più affettione l'uno dell' altro alla Sede Apostolica, e al particolare serviggio di N. S. e della Corte; il che quanto noia ci apposti, e quanto disturbo, lassaremo che V. S. Illma, lo consideri per se istessa" (Legates to Borromeo, Jan. 15, 1563).

There is one question of immediate interest to which no answer has yet been given. If the Council were to proclaim the dogma of Papal infallibility, in what sense would those who accept and those who reject it constitute one and the same Church? What bond of unity and test of orthodoxy would remain for them? What doctrinal authority would the Church possess when the Pope had fallen into infallibility? What healing powers are there for such a wound, and by what process of reaction could health be restored? The author avoids these questions. He does not look beyond the immediate issue; and it is probable that, in reality, he feels assured of victory.

For reasons stated in the Preface the authorship of the book is kept secret. The choice of persons capable of writing it cannot be large; and, indeed, the Preface further informs us that it is not the work of one author only. We have disregarded this intimation, because those parts of the volume which have engaged our attention betray a single hand—the hand of one extraordinarily well versed in scholastic divinity and canon law, but not apparently so familiar with the modern history and literature of the Church. There are distinct indications of the school to which he belongs. It is evident that he is a friend of the late Möhler. He censures by name several Catholic writers who have imagined that the false decretals made no change in the constitution of the Church; and of all recent writers, the one whose error on this point is the most flagrant and notorious is Möhler: yet his name is omitted. Möhler compared the preservation of the faith in the Church to the preservation of the language in a nation. This explanation comes very near to the idea of indefectibility, as the author appears to understand it. Möhler, on the other hand, never adopted the theory of Development which has since been naturalized in Germany by Döllinger, in a work which the author quotes. But the theory is entirely ignored throughout his volume. And this, in the judgment of many who most heartily sympathize with the main spirit and purpose of the book, will appear the one point in which it has failed to maintain its position in the very front rank of science.

[14]
The Vatican Council

The intention of Pius IX to convene a General Council became known in the autumn of 1864, shortly before the appearance of the Syllabus. They were the two principal measures which were designed to restore the spiritual and temporal power of the Holy See. When the idea of the Council was first put forward it met with no favour. The French bishops discouraged it; and the French bishops holding the talisman of the occupying army, spoke with authority. Later on, when the position had been altered by the impulse which the Syllabus gave to the ultramontane opinions, they revived the scheme they had first opposed. Those who felt their influence injured by the change persuaded themselves that the Court of Rome was more prudent than some of its partisans, and that the Episcopate was less given to extremes than the priesthood and laity. They conceived the hope that an assembly of bishops would curb the intemperance of a zeal which was largely directed against their own order, and would authentically sanction such an exposition of Catholic ideas as would reconcile the animosity that feeds on things spoken in the heat of controversy, and on the errors of incompetent apologists. They had accepted the Syllabus; but they wished to obtain canonicity for their own interpretation of it. If those who had succeeded in assigning an acceptable meaning to its censures could appear in a body to plead their cause before the Pope, the pretensions which compromised the Church might be permanently repressed.

Published in the *North British Review* 53 (October 1870):183–229. Döllinger II, pp. 455, 456; Ryan, p. 290. Reprinted in Acton, *History of Freedom*, pp. 492–550; Acton, *Freedom and Power*, pp. 299–356; Acton, *Papal Power*, pp. 118–181. A German translation of this article appeared as a monograph: *Zur Geschichte des Vaticanischen Concils* (Munich: M. Riesger'sche Universitäts-Buchhandlung, 1871). The translator was Wilhelm Reischl; see Döllinger II, p. 456. This German translation, but not the original English version, was placed on *The Index of Forbidden Books*; Ryan, p. 293.

Once, during the struggle for the temporal power, the question was pertinently asked, how it was that men so perspicacious and so enlightened as those who were its most conspicuous champions, could bring themselves to justify a system of government which their own principles condemned. The explanation then given was, that they were making a sacrifice which would be compensated hereafter, that those who succoured the Pope in his utmost need were establishing a claim which would make them irresistible in better times, when they should demand great acts of conciliation and reform. It appeared to these men that the time had come to reap the harvest they had arduously sown.

The Council did not originate in the desire to exalt beyond measure the cause of Rome. It was proposed in the interest of moderation; and the Bishop of Orleans was one of those who took the lead in promoting it. The Cardinals were consulted, and pronounced against it. The Pope overruled their resistance. Whatever embarrassments might be in store, and however difficult the enterprise, it was clear that it would evoke a force capable of accomplishing infinite good for religion. It was an instrument of unknown power that inspired little confidence, but awakened vague hopes of relief for the ills of society and the divisions of Christendom. The guardians of immovable traditions, and the leaders of progress in religious knowledge, were not to share in the work. The schism of the East was widened by the angry quarrel between Russia and the Pope; and the letter to the Protestants, whose orders are not recognised at Rome, could not be more than a ceremonious challenge. There was no promise of sympathy in these invitations or in the answers they provoked; but the belief spread to many schools of thought, and was held by Dr. Pusey and by Dean Stanley, by Professor Hase and by M. Guizot, that the auspicious issue of the Council was an object of vital care to all denominations of Christian men.

The Council of Trent impressed on the Church the stamp of an intolerant age, and perpetuated by its decrees the spirit of an austere immorality. The ideas embodied in the Roman Inquisition became characteristic of a system which obeyed expediency by submitting to indefinite modification, but underwent no change of principle. Three centuries have so changed the world that the maxims with which the Church resisted the Reformation have become her weakness and her reproach, and that which arrested her decline now arrests her progress.

To break effectually with that tradition and eradicate its influence, nothing less is required than an authority equal to that by which it was imposed. The Vatican Council was the first sufficient occasion which Catholicism had enjoyed to reform, remodel, and adapt the work of Trent. This idea was present among the motives which caused it to be summoned. It was apparent that two systems which cannot be reconciled were about to contend at the Council; but the extent and force of the reforming spirit were unknown.

Seventeen questions submitted by the Holy See to the bishops in 1867 concerned matters of discipline, the regulation of marriage and education, the policy of encouraging new monastic orders, and the means of making the parochial clergy more dependent on the bishops. They gave no indication of the deeper motives of the time. In the midst of many trivial proposals, the leading objects of reform grew more defined as the time approached, and men became conscious of distinct purposes based on a consistent notion of the Church. They received systematic expression from a Bohemian priest, whose work, *The Reform of the Church in its Head and Members*, is founded on practical experience, not only on literary theory, and is the most important manifesto of these ideas. The author exhorts the Council to restrict centralisation, to reduce the office of the Holy See to the ancient limits of its primacy, to restore to the Episcopate the prerogatives which have been confiscated by Rome, to abolish the temporal government, which is the prop of hierarchical despotism, to revise the matrimonial discipline, to suppress many religious orders and the solemn vows for all, to modify the absolute rule of celibacy for the clergy, to admit the use of the vernacular in the Liturgy, to allow a larger share to the laity in the management of ecclesiastical affairs, to encourage the education of the clergy at universities, and to renounce the claims of mediaeval theocracy, which are fruitful of suspicion between Church and State.

Many Catholics in many countries concurred in great part of this programme; but it was not the symbol of a connected party. Few agreed with the author in all parts of his ideal church, or did not think that he had omitted essential points. Among the inveterate abuses which the Council of Trent failed to extirpate was the very one which gave the first impulse to Lutheranism. The belief is still retained in the superficial Catholicism of Southern Europe that the Pope can release the dead from Purgatory; and money is obtained at Rome on the assurance that every mass said at a particular altar opens heaven to the soul for which it is offered up. On the other hand, the Index of prohibited books is an institution of Tridentine origin, which has become so unwieldy and opprobrious that even men of strong Roman sympathies, like the bishops of Würzburg and St. Pölten, recommended its reform. In France it was thought that the Government would surrender the organic articles, if the rights of the bishops and the clergy were made secure under the canon law, if national and diocesan synods were introduced, and if a proportionate share was given to Catholic countries in the Sacred College and the Roman congregations. The aspiration in which all the advocates of reform seemed to unite was that those customs should be changed which are connected with arbitrary power in the Church. And all the interests threatened by this movement combined in the endeavour to maintain intact the papal prerogative. To proclaim the Pope infallible was their compendious security against hostile States and Churches, against human liberty and authority, against disintegrating tolerance and rationalising science, against error and sin. It became the common refuge of those who shunned what was called the liberal influence in Catholicism.

Pius IX constantly asserted that the desire of obtaining the recognition of papal infallibility was not originally his motive in convoking the Council. He did not require that a privilege which was practically undisputed should be further defined. The bishops, especially those of the minority, were never tired of saying that the Catholic world honoured and obeyed the Pope as it had never done before. Virtually he had exerted all the authority which the dogma could confer on him. In his first important utterance, the Encyclical of November 1846, he announced that he was infallible; and the claim raised no commotion. Later on he applied a more decisive test, and gained a more complete success, when the bishops summoned to Rome, not as a Council but as an audience, received from him an additional article of their faith. But apart from the dogma of infallibility he had a strong desire to establish certain cherished opinions of his own on a basis firm enough to outlast his time. They were collected in the Syllabus, which contained the essence of what he had written during many years, and was an abridgment of the lessons which his life had taught him. He was anxious that they should not be lost. They were part of a coherent system. The Syllabus was not rejected; but its edge was blunted and its points broken by the zeal which was spent in explaining it away; and the Pope feared that it would be contested if he repudiated the soothing interpretations. In private he said that he wished to have no interpreter but himself. While the Jesuit preachers proclaimed that the Syllabus bore the full sanction of infallibility, higher functionaries of the Court pointed out that it was an informal document, without definite official value. Probably the Pope would have been content that these his favourite ideas should be rescued from evasion by being incorporated in the canons of the Council. Papal infallibility was implied rather than included among them. Whilst the authority of his acts was not resisted, he was not eager to disparage his right by exposing the need of a more exact definition. The opinions which Pius IX was anxiously promoting were not the mere fruit of his private meditations; they belonged to the doctrines of a great party, which was busily pursuing its own objects, and had not been always the party of the Pope. In the days of his trouble he had employed an advocate; and the advocate had absorbed the client. During his exile a Jesuit had asked his approbation for a Review, to be conducted by the best talents of the Order, and to be devoted to the papal cause; and he had warmly embraced the idea, less, it should seem, as a prince than as a divine. There were his sovereign rights to maintain; but there was also a doctrinaire interest, there were reminiscences of study as well as practical objects that recommended the project. In these personal views the Pope was not quite consistent. He had made himself the idol of Italian patriots, and of the liberal French Catholics; he had set Theiner to vindicate the suppresser of the Jesuits; and Rosmini, the most enlightened priest in Italy, had been his trusted friend. After his restoration he submitted to other influences; and the writers of the *Civiltà Cattolica*, which followed him to Rome and became his acknowledged organ, acquired power over his mind. These men were not identified with their Order. Their General, Roothan, had disliked the plan of the Review, foreseeing that the Society would be held responsible for writings which it did not approve, and would forfeit the flexibility in adapting itself to the moods of different countries, which is one of the secrets of its prosperity. The Pope arranged the matter by taking the writers under his own protection, and giving to them a sort of exemption and partial immunity under the rule of their Order. They are set apart from other Jesuits; they are assisted and supplied from the literary resources of the Order, and are animated more than any of its other writers by its genuine and characteristic spirit; but they act on their own judgment under the guidance of the

Pope, and are a bodyguard, told off from the army, for the personal protection of the Sovereign. It is their easy function to fuse into one system the interests and ideas of the Pope and those of their Society. The result has been, not to weaken by compromise and accommodation, but to intensify both. The prudence and sagacity which are sustained in the government of the Jesuits by their complicated checks on power, and their consideration for the interests of the Order under many various conditions, do not always restrain men who are partially emancipated from its rigorous discipline and subject to a more capricious rule. They were chosen in their capacity as Jesuits, for the sake of the peculiar spirit which their system develops. The Pope appointed them on account of that devotion to himself which is a quality of the Order, and relieved them from some of the restraints which it imposes. He wished for something more papal than other Jesuits; and he himself became more subject to the Jesuits than other pontiffs. He made them a channel of his influence, and became an instrument of their own.

The Jesuits had continued to gain ground in Rome ever since the Pope's return. They had suffered more than others in the revolution that dethroned him; and they had their reward in the restoration. They had long been held in check by the Dominicans; but the theology of the Dominicans had been discountenanced and their spirit broken in 1854, when a doctrine which they had contested for centuries was proclaimed a dogma of faith. In the strife for the Pope's temporal dominion the Jesuits were most zealous; and they were busy in the preparation and in the defence of the Syllabus. They were connected with every measure for which the Pope most cared; and their divines became the oracles of the Roman congregations. The papal infallibility had been always their favourite doctrine. Its adoption by the Council promised to give to their theology official warrant, and to their Order the supremacy in the Church. They were now in power; and they snatched their opportunity when the Council was convoked.

Efforts to establish this doctrine had been going on for years. The dogmatic decree of 1854 involved it so distinctly that its formal recognition seemed to be only a question of time and zeal. People even said that it was the real object of that decree to create a precedent which should make it impossible afterwards to deny papal infallibility. The Catechisms were altered, or new ones were substituted, in which it was taught. After 1852 the doctrine began to show itself in the Acts of provincial synods, and it was afterwards supposed that the bishops of those provinces were committed to it. One of these synods was held at Cologne; and three surviving members were in the Council at Rome, of whom two were in the minority, and the third had continued in his writings to oppose the doctrine of infallibility, after it had found its way into the Cologne decree. The suspicion that the Acts had been tampered with is suggested by what passed at the synod of Baltimore in 1866. The Archbishop of St. Louis signed the Acts of that synod under protest, and after obtaining a pledge that his protest would be inserted by the apostolic delegate. The pledge was not kept. "I complain," writes the archbishop, "that the promise which had been given was broken. The Acts ought to have been published in their integrity, or not at all."[1] This process was carried on so boldly that men understood what was to come. Protestants foretold that the Catholics would not rest until the Pope was formally declared infallible; and a prelate returning from the meeting of bishops at Rome in 1862 was startled at being asked by a clear-sighted friend whether infallibility had not been brought forward.

It was produced not then, but at the next great meeting, in 1867. The Council had been announced; and the bishops wished to present an address to the Pope. Haynald, Archbishop of Colocza, held the pen, assisted by Franchi, one of the clever Roman prelates, and by some bishops, among whom were the Archbishop of Westminster and the Bishop of Orleans. An attempt was made to get the papal infallibility acknowledged in the address. Several bishops declared that they could not show themselves in their dioceses if they came back without having done anything for that doctrine. They were resisted in a way which made them complain that its very name irritated the French. Haynald refused their demand, but agreed to insert the well-known words of the Council of Florence; and the bishops did not go away empty-handed.

A few days before this attempt was made, the *Civiltà Cattolica* had begun to agitate, by proposing that Catholics should bind themselves to die, if need be, for the truth of the doctrine; and the article was printed on a separate sheet, bearing the papal imprimatur, and distributed widely. The check administered by Haynald and his colleagues brought about a lull in the movement; but the French

---

[1] Fidem mihi datam non servatam fuisse queror. Acta supprimere, aut integra dare oportebat. He says also: Omnia ad nutum delegati Apostolici fiebant.

bishops had taken alarm, and Maret, the most learned of them, set about the preparation of his book.

During the winter of 1868–69 several commissions were created in Rome to make ready the materials for the Council. The dogmatic commission included the Jesuits Perrone, Schrader, and Franzelin. The question of infallibility was proposed to it by Cardoni, Archbishop of Edessa, in a dissertation which, having been revised, was afterwards published, and accepted by the leading Roman divines as an adequate exposition of their case. The dogma was approved unanimously, with the exception of one vote, Alzog of Freiberg being the only dissentient. When the other German divines who were in Rome learned the scheme that was on foot in the Dogmatic Commission, they resolved to protest, but were prevented by some of their colleagues. They gave the alarm in Germany. The intention to proclaim infallibility at the Council was no longer a secret. The first bishop who made the wish public was Fessler of St. Pölten. His language was guarded, and he only prepared his readers for a probable contingency; but he was soon followed by the Bishop of Nîmes, who thought the discussion of the dogma superfluous, and foreshadowed a vote by acclamation. The *Civiltà* on the 6th of February gave utterance to the hope that the Council would not hesitate to proclaim the dogma and confirm the Syllabus in less than a month. Five days later the Pope wrote to some Venetians who had taken a vow to uphold his infallibility, encouraging their noble resolution to defend his supreme authority and all his rights. Until the month of May Cardinal Antonelli's confidential language to diplomatists was that the dogma was to be proclaimed, and that it would encounter no difficulty.

Cardinal Reisach was to have been the President of the Council. As Archbishop of Munich he had allowed himself and his diocese to be governed by the ablest of all the ultramontane divines. During his long residence in Rome he rose to high estimation, because he was reputed to possess the secret, and to have discovered the vanity, of German science. He had amused himself with Christian antiquities; and his friendship for the great explorer De' Rossi brought him for a time under suspicion of liberality. But later he became unrelenting in his ardour for the objects of the *Civiltà*, and regained the confidence of the Pope. The German bishops complained that he betrayed their interest, and that their church had suffered mischief from his paramount influence. But in Rome his easy temper and affable manners made him friends; and the Court knew that there was no cardinal on whom it was so safe to rely.

Fessler, the first bishop who gave the signal of the intended definition, was appointed Secretary. He was esteemed a learned man in Austria, and he was wisely chosen to dispel the suspicion that the conduct of the Council was to be jealously retained in Roman hands, and to prove that there are qualities by which the confidence of the Court could be won by men of a less favoured nation. Besides the President and Secretary, the most conspicuous of the Pope's theological advisers was a German. At the time when Passaglia's reputation was great in Rome, his companion Clement Schrader shared the fame of his solid erudition. When Passaglia fell into disgrace, his friend smote him with reproaches and intimated the belief that he would follow the footsteps of Luther and debauch a nun. Schrader is the most candid and consistent asserter of the papal claims. He does not shrink from the consequences of the persecuting theory; and he has given the most authentic and unvarnished exposition of the Syllabus. He was the first who spoke out openly what others were variously attempting to compromise or to conceal. While the Paris Jesuits got into trouble for extenuating the Roman doctrine, and had to be kept up to the mark by an abbé who reminded them that the Pope, as a physical person, and without co-operation of the Episcopate, is infallible, Schrader proclaimed that his will is supreme even against the joint and several opinions of the bishops.[2]

When the proceedings of the dogmatic commission, the acts of the Pope, and the language of French and Austrian bishops, and of the press serving the interests of Rome, announced that the proclamation of infallibility had ceased to be merely the aspiration of a party and was the object of a design deliberately set on foot by those to whom the preparation and management of the Council pertained, men became aware that an extra-ordinary crisis was impending, and that they needed to make themselves familiar with an unforeseen problem. The sense of its gravity made slow progress. The persuasion was strong among divines that the episcopate would not surrender to a party which was odious to many of them; and politicians were reluctant to believe that schemes were ripening such as Fessler described, schemes intended to alter the relations between Church and State. When the

---

[2] Citra et contra singulorum suffragia, imo praeter et supra omnium vota pontificis solius declarationi atque sententiae validam vim atque irreformabilem adesse potestatem.

entire plan was made public by the *Allgemeine Zeitung* in March 1869, many refused to be convinced.

It happened that a statesman was in office who had occasion to know that the information was accurate. The Prime Minister of Bavaria, Prince Hohenlohe, was the brother of a cardinal; the University of Munich was represented on the Roman commissions by an illustrious scholar; and the news of the thing that was preparing came through trustworthy channels. On the 9th of April Prince Hohenlohe sent out a diplomatic circular on the subject of the Council. He pointed out that it was not called into existence by any purely theological emergency, and that the one dogma which was to be brought before it involved all those claims which cause collisions between Church and State, and threaten the liberty and the security of governments. Of the five Roman Commissions, one was appointed for the express purpose of dealing with the mixed topics common to religion and to politics. Besides infallibility and politics, the Council was to be occupied with the Syllabus, which is in part directed against maxims of State. The avowed purpose of the Council being so largely political, the governments could not remain indifferent to its action; lest they should be driven afterwards to adopt measures which would be hostile, it would be better at once to seek an understanding by friendly means and to obtain assurance that all irritating deliberations should be avoided, and no business touching the State transacted except in presence of its representatives. He proposed that the governments should hold a conference to arrange a plan for the protection of their common interest.

Important measures proposed by small States are subject to suspicion of being prompted by a greater Power. Prince Hohenlohe, as a friend of the Prussian alliance, was supposed to be acting in this matter in concert with Berlin. This good understanding was suspected at Vienna; for the Austrian Chancellor was more conspicuous as an enemy of Prussia than Hohenlohe as a friend. Count Beust traced the influence of Count Bismarck in the Bavarian circular. He replied, on behalf of the Catholic empire of Austria, that there were no grounds to impute political objects to the Council, and that repression and not prevention was the only policy compatible with free institutions. After the refusal of Austria, the idea of a conference was dismissed by the other Powers; and the first of the storm clouds that darkened the horizon of infallibility passed without breaking.

Although united action was abandoned, the idea of sending ambassadors to the Council still offered the most inoffensive and amicable means of preventing the danger of subsequent conflict. Its policy or impolicy was a question to be decided by France. Several bishops, and Cardinal Bonnechose among the rest, urged the Government to resume its ancient privilege, and send a representative. But two powerful parties, united in nothing else, agreed in demanding absolute neutrality. The democracy wished that no impediment should be put in the way of an enterprise which promised to sever the connection of the State with the Church. M. Ollivier set forth this opinion in July 1868, in a speech which was to serve him in his candidature for office; and in the autumn of 1869 it was certain that he would soon be in power. The ministers could not insist on being admitted to the Council, where they were not invited, without making a violent demonstration in a direction they knew would not be followed. The ultramontanes were even more eager than their enemies to exclude an influence that might embarrass their policy. The Archbishop of Paris, by giving the same advice, settled the question. He probably reckoned on his own power of mediating between France and Rome. The French Court long imagined that the dogma would be set aside, and that the mass of the French bishops opposed it. At last they perceived that they were mistaken, and the Emperor said to Cardinal Bonnechose, "You are going to give your signature to decrees already made." He ascertained the names of the bishops who would resist; and it was known that he was anxious for their success. But he was resolved that it should be gained by them, and not by the pressure of his diplomacy at the cost of displeasing the Pope. The Minister of Foreign Affairs and his chief secretary were counted by the Court of Rome among its friends; and the ordinary ambassador started for his post with instructions to conciliate, and to run no risk of a quarrel. He arrived at Rome believing that there would be a speculative conflict between the extremes of Roman and German theology, which would admit of being reconciled by the safer and more sober wisdom of the French bishops, backed by an impartial embassy. His credulity was an encumbrance to the cause which it was his mission and his wish to serve.

In Germany the plan of penetrating the Council with lay influence took a strange form. It was proposed that the German Catholics should be represented by King John of Saxony. As a Catholic and a scholar, who had shown, in his Commentary on Dante, that he had read St. Thomas, and as a prince personally esteemed by the Pope, it was conceived that his presence would be a salutary restraint. It was an impracticable idea; but letters which reached Rome during the winter raised an impression that the King regretted that he could not be there. The opinion of Germany would still have some weight if the North and South, which included more than thirteen millions of Catholics, worked together. It was the policy of Hohenlohe to use this united force, and the ultramontanes learned to regard him as a very formidable antagonist. When their first great triumph, in the election of the Commission on Doctrine, was accomplished, the commentary of a Roman prelate was, "Che colpo per il Principe Hohenlohe!" The Bavarian envoy in Rome did not share the views of his chief, and he was recalled in November. His successor had capacity to carry out the known policy of the prince; but early in the winter the ultramontanes drove Hohenlohe from office, and their victory, though it was exercised with moderation, and was not followed by a total change of policy, neutralised the influence of Bavaria in the Council.

The fall of Hohenlohe and the abstention of France hampered the Federal Government of Northern Germany. For its Catholic subjects, and ultimately in view of the rivalry with France, to retain the friendship of the papacy is a fixed maxim at Berlin. Count Bismarck laid down the rule that Prussia should display no definite purpose in a cause which was not her own, but should studiously keep abreast of the North German bishops. Those bishops neither invoked, nor by their conduct invited, the co-operation of the State; and its influence would have been banished from the Council but for the minister who represented it in Rome. The vicissitudes of a General Council are so far removed from the normal experience of statesmen that they could not well be studied or acted upon from a distance. A government that strictly controlled and dictated the conduct of its envoy was sure to go wrong, and to frustrate action by theory. A government that trusted the advice of its minister present on the spot enjoyed a great advantage. Baron Arnim was favourably situated. A Catholic belonging to any but the ultramontane school would have been less willingly listened to in Rome than a Protestant who was a conservative in politics, and whose regard for the interests of religion was so undamaged by the sectarian taint that he was known to be sincere in the wish that Catholics should have cause to rejoice in the prosperity of their Church. The apathy of Austria and the vacillation of France contributed to his influence, for he enjoyed the confidence of bishops from both countries;

and he was able to guide his own government in its course towards the Council.

The English Government was content to learn more and to speak less than the other Powers at Rome. The usual distrust of the Roman Court towards a liberal ministry in England was increased at the moment by the measure which the Catholics had desired and applauded. It seems improbable to men more solicitous for acquired rights than for general political principle, that Protestant statesmen who disestablished their own Church could feel a very sincere interest in the welfare of another. Ministers so utopian as to give up solid goods for an imaginary righteousness seemed, as practical advisers, open to grave suspicion. Mr. Gladstone was feared as the apostle of those doctrines to which Rome owes many losses. Public opinion in England was not prepared to look on papal infallibility as a matter of national concern, more than other dogmas which make enemies to Catholicism. Even if the Government could have admitted the Prussian maxim of keeping in line with the bishops, it would have accomplished nothing. The English bishops were divided; but the Irish bishops, who are the natural foes of the Fenian plot, were by an immense majority on the ultramontane side. There was almost an ostentation of care on the part of the Government to avoid the appearance of wishing to influence the bishops or the Court of Rome. When at length England publicly concurred in the remonstrances of France, events had happened which showed that the Council was raising up dangers for both Catholic and liberal interests. It was a result so easy to foresee, that the Government had made it clear from the beginning that its extreme reserve was not due to indifference.

The lesser Catholic Powers were almost unrepresented in Rome. The government of the Regent of Spain possessed no moral authority over bishops appointed by the Queen; and the revolution had proved so hostile to the clergy that they were forced to depend on the Pope. Diplomatic relations being interrupted, there was nothing to restrain them from seeking favour by unqualified obedience.

Portugal had appointed the Count de Lavradio ambassador to the Council; but when he found that he was alone he retained only the character of envoy to the Holy See. He had weight with the small group of Portuguese bishops; but he died before he could be of use, and they drifted into submission.

Belgium was governed by M. Frère Orban, one of the most anxious and laborious enemies of the hierarchy, who had no inducement to interfere with an event which justified his enmity, and was, moreover, the unanimous wish of the Belgian Episcopate. When Protestant and Catholic Powers joined in exhorting Rome to moderation, Belgium was left out. Russia was the only Power that treated the Church with actual hostility during the Council, and calculated the advantage to be derived from decrees which would intensify the schism.

Italy was more deeply interested in the events at Rome than any other nation. The hostility of the clergy was felt both in the political and financial difficulties of the kingdom; and the prospect of conciliation would suffer equally from decrees confirming the Roman claims, or from an invidious interposition of the State. Public opinion watched the preparations for the Council with frivolous disdain; but the course to be taken was carefully considered by the Menabrea Cabinet. The laws still subsisted which enabled the State to interfere in religious affairs; and the government was legally entitled to prohibit the attendance of the bishops at the Council, or to recall them from it. The confiscated church property was retained by the State, and the claims of the episcopate were not yet settled. More than one hundred votes on which Rome counted belonged to Italian subjects. The means of applying administrative pressure were therefore great, though diplomatic action was impossible. The Piedmontese wished that the resources of their ecclesiastical jurisprudence should be set in motion. But Minghetti, who had lately joined the Ministry, warmly advocated the opinion that the supreme principle of the liberty of the Church ought to override the remains of the older legislation, in a State consistently free; and, with the disposition of the Italians to confound Catholicism with the hierarchy, the policy of abstention was a triumph of liberality. The idea of Prince Hohenlohe, that religion ought to be maintained in its integrity and not only in its independence, that society is interested in protecting the Church even against herself, and that the enemies of her liberty are ecclesiastical as well as political, could find no favour in Italy. During the session of 1869, Menabrea gave no pledge to Parliament as to the Council; and the bishops who inquired whether they would be allowed to attend it were left unanswered until October. Menabrea then explained in a circular that the right of the bishops to go to the Council proceeded from the liberty of conscience, and was not conceded under the old privileges of the crown, or as a favour that could imply responsibility for what was to be done.

If the Church was molested in her freedom, excuse would be given for resisting the incorporation of Rome. If the Council came to decisions injurious to the safety of States, it would be attributed to the unnatural conditions created by the French occupation, and might be left to the enlightened judgment of Catholics.

It was proposed that the fund realised by the sale of the real property of the religious corporations should be administered for religious purposes by local boards of trustees representing the Catholic population, and that the State should abdicate in their favour its ecclesiastical patronage, and proceed to discharge the unsettled claims of the clergy. So great a change in the plans by which Sella and Rattazzi had impoverished the Church in 1866 and 1867 would, if frankly carried into execution, have encouraged an independent spirit among the Italian bishops; and the reports of the prefects represented about thirty of them as being favourable to conciliation. But the Ministry fell in November, and was succeeded by an administration whose leading members, Lanza and Sella, were enemies of religion. The Court of Rome was relieved from a serious peril.

The only European country whose influence was felt in the attitude of its bishops was one whose government sent out no diplomatists. While the Austrian Chancellor regarded the issue of the Council with a profane and supercilious eye, and so much indifference prevailed at Vienna that it was said that the ambassador at Rome did not read the decrees, and that Count Beust did not read his despatches, the Catholic Statesmen in Hungary were intent on effecting a revolution in the Church. The system which was about to culminate in the proclamation of infallibility, and which tended to absorb all power from the circumference into the centre, and to substitute authority for autonomy, had begun at the lower extremities of the hierarchical scale. The laity, which once had its share in the administration of Church property and in the deliberations of the clergy, had been gradually compelled to give up its rights to the priesthood, the priests to the bishops, and the bishops to the Pope. Hungary undertook to redress the process, and to correct centralised absolutism by self-government. In a memorandum drawn up in April 1848, the bishops imputed the decay of religion to the exclusion of the people from the management of all Church affairs, and proposed that whatever is not purely spiritual should be conducted by mixed boards, including lay representatives elected by the congregations. The war of the revolution and the reaction checked this design; and the Concordat threw things more than ever into clerical hands. The triumph of the liberal party after the peace of Prague revived the movements; and Eötvös called on the bishops to devise means of giving to the laity a share and an interest in religious concerns. The bishops agreed unanimously to the proposal of Deak, that the laity should have the majority in the boards of administration; and the new constitution of the Hungarian Church was adopted by the Catholic Congress on the 17th of October 1869, and approved by the King on the 25th. The ruling idea of this great measure was to make the laity supreme in all that is not liturgy and dogma, in patronage, property, and education; to break down clerical exclusiveness and government control; to deliver the people from the usurpations of the hierarchy, and the Church from the usurpations of the State. It was an attempt to reform the Church by constitutional principles, and to crush ultramontanism by crushing Gallicanism. The Government, which had originated the scheme, was ready to surrender its privileges to the newly-constituted authorities; and the bishops acted in harmony with the ministers and with public opinion. Whilst this good understanding lasted, and while the bishops were engaged in applying the impartial principles of self-government at home, there was a strong security that they would not accept decrees that would undo their work. Infallibility would not only condemn their system, but destroy their position. As the winter advanced the influence of these things became apparent. The ascendency which the Hungarian bishops acquired from the beginning was due to other causes.

The political auspices under which the Council opened were very favourable to the papal cause. The promoters of infallibility were able to coin resources of the enmity which was shown to the Church. The danger which came to them from within was averted. The policy of Hohenlohe, which was afterwards revived by Daru, had been, for a time, completely abandoned by Europe. The battle between the papal and the episcopal principle could come off undisturbed, in closed lists. Political opposition there was none; but the Council had to be governed under the glare of inevitable publicity, with a free press in Europe, and hostile views prevalent in Catholic theology. The causes which made religious science utterly powerless in the strife, and kept it from grappling with the forces arrayed against it, are of deeper import than the issue of the contest itself.

While the voice of the bishops grew louder in praise of the Roman designs, the Bavarian Government consulted the universities, and elicited from the majority of the Munich faculty an opinion that the dogma of infallibility would be attended with serious danger to society. The author of the Bohemian pamphlet affirmed that it had not the conditions which would enable it ever to become the object of a valid definition. Janus compared the primacy, as it was known to the Fathers of the Church, with the ultramontane ideal, and traced the process of transformation through a long series of forgeries. Maret published his book some weeks after Janus and the Reform. It had been revised by several French bishops and divines, and was to serve as a vindication of the Sorbonne and the Gallicans, and as the manifesto of men who were to be present at the Council. It had not the merit of novelty or the fault of innovation, but renewed with as little offence as possible the language of the old French School.[3] While Janus treated infallibility as the critical symptom of an ancient disease, Maret restricted his argument to what was directly involved in the defence of the Gallican position. Janus held that the doctrine was so firmly rooted and so widely supported in the existing constitution of the Church, that much must be modified before a genuine Ecumenical Council could be celebrated. Maret clung to the belief that the real voice of the Church would make itself heard at the Vatican. In direct contradiction with Janus, he kept before him the one practical object, to gain assent by making his views acceptable even to the unlearned.

At the last moment a tract appeared which has been universally attributed to Döllinger, which examined the evidences relied on by the infallibilists, and stated briefly the case against them. It pointed to the inference that their theory is not merely founded on an illogical and uncritical habit, but on unremitting dishonesty in the use of texts. This was coming near the secret of the whole controversy, and the point that made the interference of the Powers appear the only availing resource. For the sentiment on which infallibility is founded could not

---

[3] Nous restons dans les doctrines de Bossuet parce que nous les croyons généralement vraies; nous les défendons parce qu'elles sont attaquées, et qu'un parti puissant veut les faire condamner. Ces doctrines de l'épiscopat français, de l'école de Paris, de notre vieille Sorbonne, se ramènent pour nous à trois propositions, à trois vérités fondamentales: 1° l'Église est une monarchie efficacement tempérée d'aristocracie; 2° la souveraineté spirituelle est essentiellement composée de ces deux éléments quoique le second soit subordonné au premier; 3° le concours de ces éléments est nécessaire pour établir la règle absolue de la foi, c'est-à-dire, pour constituer l'acte par excellence de la souveraineté spirituelle.

be reached by argument, the weapon of human reason, but resided in conclusions transcending evidence, and was the inaccessible postulate rather than a demonstrable consequence of a system of religious faith. The two doctrines opposed, but never met each other. It was as much an instinct of the ultramontane theory to elude the tests of science as to resist the control of States. Its opponents, baffled and perplexed by the serene vitality of a view which was impervious to proof, saw want of principle where there was really a consistent principle, and blamed the ultramontane divines for that which was of the essence of ultramontane divinity. How it came that no appeal to revelation or tradition, to reason or conscience, appeared to have any bearing whatever on the issue, is a mystery which Janus and Maret and Döllinger's reflections left unexplained.

The resources of mediaeval learning were too slender to preserve an authentic record of the growth and settlement of Catholic doctrine. Many writings of the Fathers were interpolated; others were unknown, and spurious matter was accepted in their place. Books bearing venerable names—Clement, Dionysius, Isidore—were forged for the purpose of supplying authorities for opinions that lacked the sanction of antiquity. When detection came, and it was found that fraud had been employed in sustaining doctrines bound up with the peculiar interests of Rome and of the religious Orders, there was an inducement to depreciate the evidences of antiquity, and to silence a voice that bore obnoxious testimony. The notion of tradition underwent a change; it was required to produce what it had not preserved. The Fathers had spoken of the unwritten teaching of the apostles, which was to be sought in the churches they had founded, of esoteric doctrines, and views which must be of apostolic origin because they are universal, of the inspiration of general Councils, and a revelation continued beyond the New Testament. But the Council of Trent resisted the conclusions which this language seemed to countenance, and they were left to be pursued by private speculation. One divine deprecated the vain pretence of arguing from Scripture, by which Luther could not be confuted, and the Catholics were losing ground;[4] and at Trent a speaker averred that Christian doctrine had been so completely determined by the

---

[4] Si hujus doctrinae memores fuissemus, haereticos scilicet non esse infirmandos vel convincendos ex Scripturis, meliore sane loco essent res nostrae; sed dum ostentandi ingenii et eruditionis gratia cum Luthero in certamen descenditur Scripturarum, excitatum est hoc, quod, pro dolor! nunc videmus, incendium (Pighius).

Schoolmen that there was no further need to recur to Scripture. This idea is not extinct, and Perrone uses it to explain the inferiority of Catholics as Biblical critics.[5] If the Bible is inspired, says Peresius, still more must its interpretation be inspired. It must be interpreted variously, says the Cardinal of Cusa, according to necessity; a change in the opinion of the Church implies a change in the will of God.[6] One of the greatest Tridentine divines declares that a doctrine must be true if the Church believes it, without any warrant from Scripture. According to Petavius, the general belief of Catholics at a given time is the work of God, and of higher authority than all antiquity and all the Fathers. Scripture may be silent, and tradition contradictory, but the Church is independent of both. Any doctrine which Catholic divines commonly assert, without proof, to be revealed, must be taken as revealed. The testimony of Rome, as the only remaining apostolic Church, is equivalent to an unbroken chain of tradition.[7] In this way, after Scripture had been subjugated, tradition itself was deposed; and the constant belief of the past yielded to the general conviction of the present. And, as antiquity had given way to universality, universality made way for authority. The Word of God and the authority of the Church came to be declared the two sources of religious knowledge. Divines of this school, after preferring the Church to the Bible, preferred the modern Church to the ancient, and ended by sacrificing both to the Pope. "We have not the authority of Scripture," wrote Prierias in his defence of Indulgences, "but we have the higher authority of the Roman pontiffs."[8] A bishop who had been present at Trent confesses that in matters of faith he would believe a single Pope rather than a thousand Fathers, saints, and doctors.[9] The divine training develops

[5] Catholici non admodum solliciti sunt de critica et hermeneutica biblica. . . . Ipsi, ut verbo dicam, jam habent aedificium absolutum sane ac perfectum, in cujus possessione firme ac secure consistant.

[6] Praxis Ecclesiae uno tempore interpretatur Scripturam uno modo et alio tempore alio modo, nam intellectus currit cum praxi.—Mutato judicio Ecclesiae mutatum est Dei judicium.

[7] Si viri ecclesiastici, sive in concilio oecumenico congregati, sive seorsim scribentes, aliquod dogma vel unamquamque consuetudinem uno ore ac diserte testantur ex traditione divina haberi, sine dubio certum argumentum est, uti ita esse credamus.— Ex testimonio hujus solius Ecclesiae sumi potest certum argumentum ad probandas apostolicas traditiones (Bellarmine).

[8] Veniae sive indulgentiae autoritate Scripturae nobis non innotuere, sed autoritate ecclesiae Romanae Romanorumque Pontificum, quae major est.

[9] Ego, ut ingenue fatear, plus uni summo pontifici crederem, in his, quae fidei mysteria tangunt, quam mille Augustinis, Hieronymis, Gregoriis (Cornelius Mussus).

an orthodox instinct in the Church, which shows itself in the lives of devout but ignorant men more than in the researches of the learned, and teaches authority not to need the help of science, and not to heed its opposition. All the arguments by which theology supports a doctrine may prove to be false, without diminishing the certainty of its truth. The Church has not obtained, and is not bound to sustain it, by proof. She is supreme over fact as over doctrine, as Fénelon argues, because she is the supreme expounder of tradition, which is a chain of facts.[10] Accordingly, the organ of one ultramontane bishop lately declared that infallibility could be defined without arguments; and the Bishop of Nîmes thought that the decision need not be preceded by long and careful discussion. The Dogmatic Commission of the Council proclaims that the existence of tradition has nothing to do with evidence, and that objections taken from history are not valid when contradicted by ecclesiastical decrees.[11] Authority must conquer history.

This inclination to get rid of evidence was specially associated with the doctrine of papal infallibility, because it is necessary that the Popes themselves should not testify against their own claim. They may be declared superior to all other authorities, but not to that of their own see. Their history is not irrelevant to the question of their rights. It could not be disregarded; and the provocation to alter or to deny its testimony was so urgent that men of piety and learning became a prey to the temptation of deceit. When it was discovered in the manuscript of the *Liber Diurnus* that the Popes had for centuries condemned Honorius in their profession of faith, Cardinal Bona, the most eminent man in Rome, advised that the book should be suppressed if the difficulty could not be got over; and it was suppressed accordingly.[12]

---

[10] The two views contradict each other; but they are equally characteristic of the endeavour to emancipate the Church from the obligation of proof. Fénelon says: "Oseroit-on soutenir que l'Église, après avoir mal raisonné sur tous les textes, et les avoir pris à contre-sens, est tout à coup saisie par un enthousiasme aveugle, pour juger bien, en raisonnant mal?" And Möhler: "Die ältesten ökumenischen Synoden führten daher für ihre dogmatischen Beschlüsse nicht einmal bestimmte biblische Stellen an; und die katholischen Theologen lehren mit allgemeiner Übereinstimmung und ganz aus dem Geiste der Kirche heraus, dass selbst die biblische Beweisführung eines für untrüglich gehaltenen Beschlusses nicht untrüglich sei, sondern eben nur das ausgesprochene Dogma selbst."

[11] Cujuscumque ergo scientiae, etiam historiae ecclesiasticae conclusiones, Romanorum Pontificum infallibilitati adversantes, quo manifestius haec ex revelationis fontibus infertur, eo certius veluti totidem errores habendas esse consequitur.

[12] Cum in professione fidei electi pontificis damnetur Honorius Papa, ideo quia pravis

Men guilty of this kind of fraud would justify it by saying that their religion transcends the wisdom of philosophers, and cannot submit to the criticism of historians. If any fact manifestly contradicts a dogma, that is a warning to science to revise the evidence. There must be some defect in the materials or in the method. Pending its discovery, the true believer is constrained humbly but confidently to deny the fact.

The protest of conscience against this fraudulent piety grew loud and strong as the art of criticism became more certain. The use made of it by Catholics in the literature of the present age, and their acceptance of the conditions of scientific controversy, seemed to ecclesiastical authorities a sacrifice of principle. A jealousy arose that ripened into antipathy. Almost every writer who really served Catholicism fell sooner or later under the disgrace or the suspicion of Rome. But its censures had lost efficacy; and it was found that the progress of literature could only be brought under control by an increase of authority. This could be obtained if a general council declared the decisions of the Roman congregations absolute, and the Pope infallible.

The division between the Roman and the Catholic elements in the Church made it hopeless to mediate between them; and it is strange that men who must have regarded each other as insincere Christians or as insincere Catholics, should not have perceived that their meeting in Council was an imposture. It may be that a portion, though only a small portion, of those who failed to attend, stayed away from that motive. But the view proscribed at Rome was not largely represented in the episcopate; and it was doubtful whether it would be manifested at all. The opposition did not spring from it, but maintained itself by reducing to the utmost the distance that separated it from the strictly Roman opinions, and striving to prevent the open conflict of principles. It was composed of ultramontanes in the mask of liberals, and of liberals in the mask of ultramontanes. Therefore the victory or defeat of the minority was not the supreme issue of the Council. Besides and above the definition of infallibility arose the question how far the experience of the actual encounter would open the eyes and search the hearts of the reluctant bishops, and how far their language and their

---

haereticorum assertionibus fomentum impendit, si verba delineata sint vere in autographo, nec ex notis apparere possit, quomodo huic vulneri medelam offert, praestat non divulgari opus.

attitude would contribute to the impulse of future reform. There was a point of view from which the failure of all attempts to avert the result by false issues and foreign intrusion, and the success of the measures which repelled conciliation and brought on an open struggle and an overwhelming triumph, were means to another and a more importunate end.

Two events occurred in the autumn which portended trouble for the winter. On the 6th of September nineteen German bishops, assembled at Fulda, published a pastoral letter in which they affirmed that the whole episcopate was perfectly unanimous, that the Council would neither introduce new dogmas nor invade the civil province, and that the Pope intended its deliberations to be free. The patent and direct meaning of this declaration was that the bishops repudiated the design announced by the *Civiltà* and the *Allgemeine Zeitung*, and it was received at Rome with indignation. But it soon appeared that it was worded with studied ambiguity, to be signed by men of opposite opinions, and to conceal the truth. The Bishop of Mentz read a paper, written by a professor of Würzburg, against the wisdom of raising the question, but expressed his own belief in the dogma of papal infallibility; and when another bishop stated his disbelief in it, the Bishop of Paderborn assured him that Rome would soon strip him of his heretical skin. The majority wished to prevent the definition, if possible, without disputing the doctrine; and they wrote a private letter to the Pope warning him of the danger, and entreating him to desist. Several bishops who had signed the pastoral refused their signatures to the private letter. It caused so much dismay at Rome that its nature was carefully concealed; and a diplomatist was able to report, on the authority of Cardinal Antonelli, that it did not exist.

In the middle of November, the Bishop of Orleans took leave of his diocese in a letter which touched lightly on the learned questions connected with papal infallibility, but described the objections to the definition as of such a kind that they could not be removed. Coming from a prelate who was conspicuous as a champion of the papacy, who had saved the temporal power and justified the Syllabus, this declaration unexpectedly altered the situation at Rome. It was clear that the definition would be opposed, and that the opposition would have the support of illustrious names.

The bishops who began to arrive early in November were received with the assurance that the alarm which had been raised was founded on phantoms. It appeared that nobody had dreamed of defining infallibility, or that if the idea had been entertained at all, it had been abandoned. Cardinals Antonelli, Berardi, and De Luca, and the Secretary Fessler disavowed the *Civiltà*. The ardent indiscretion that was displayed beyond the Alps contrasted strangely with the moderation, the friendly candour, the majestic and impartial wisdom, which were found to reign in the higher sphere of the hierarchy. A bishop, afterwards noted among the opponents of the dogma, wrote home that the idea that infallibility was to be defined was entirely unfounded. It was represented as a mere fancy, got up in Bavarian newspapers, with evil intent; and the Bishop of Sura had been its dupe. The insidious report would have deserved contempt if it had caused a revival of obsolete opinions. It was a challenge to the Council to herald it with such demonstrations, and it unfortunately became difficult to leave it unnoticed. The decision must be left to the bishops. The Holy See could not restrain their legitimate ardour, if they chose to express it; but it would take no initiative. Whatever was done would require to be done with so much moderation as to satisfy everybody, and to avoid the offence of a party triumph. Some suggested that there should be no anathema for those who questioned the doctrine; and one prelate imagined that a formula could be contrived which even Janus could not dispute, and which yet would be found in reality to signify that the Pope is infallible. There was a general assumption that no materials existed for contention among the bishops, and that they stood united against the world.

Cardinal Antonelli openly refrained from connecting himself with the preparation of the Council, and surrounded himself with divines who were not of the ruling party. He had never learned to doubt the dogma itself; but he was keenly alive to the troubles it would bring upon him, and thought that the Pope was preparing a repetition of the difficulties which followed the beginning of his pontificate. He was not trusted as a divine, or consulted on questions of theology; but he was expected to ward off political complications, and he kept the ground with unflinching skill.

The Pope exhorted the diplomatic corps to aid him in allaying the alarm of the infatuated Germans. He assured one diplomatist that the *Civiltà* did not speak in his name. He told another that he would sanction no proposition that could sow dissension among the bishops. He said to a third, "You come to be present at a scene of pacification."

He described his object in summoning the Council to be to obtain a remedy for old abuses and for recent errors. More than once, addressing a group of bishops, he said that he would do nothing to raise disputes among them, and would be content with a declaration in favour of intolerance. He wished of course that Catholicism should have the benefit of toleration in England and Russia, but the principle must be repudiated by a Church holding the doctrine of exclusive salvation. The meaning of this intimation, that persecution would do as a substitute for infallibility, was that the most glaring obstacle to the definition would be removed if the Inquisition was recognised as consistent with Catholicism. Indeed it seemed that infallibility was a means to an end which could be obtained in other ways, and that he would have been satisfied with a decree confirming the twenty-third article of the Syllabus, and declaring that no Pope has ever exceeded the just bounds of his authority in faith, in politics, or in morals.[13]

Most of the bishops had allowed themselves to be reassured, when the Bull *Multiplices inter*, regulating the procedure at the Council, was put into circulation in the first days of December. The Pope assumed to himself the sole initiative in proposing topics, and the exclusive nomination of the officers of the Council. He invited the bishops to bring forward their own proposals, but required that they should submit them first of all to a Commission which was appointed by himself, and consisted half of Italians. If any proposal was allowed to pass by this Commission, it had still to obtain the sanction of the Pope, who could therefore exclude at will any topic, even if the whole Council wished to discuss it. Four elective Commissions were to mediate between the Council and the Pope. When a decree had been discussed and opposed, it was to be referred, together with the amendments, to one of these Commissions, where it was to be reconsidered, with the aid of divines. When it came back from the Commission with corrections and remarks, it was to be put to the vote without further debate. What the Council discussed was to be the work of unknown divines: what it voted was to be the work of a majority in a Commission of twenty-four. It was in the election of these Commissions that the episcopate obtained the chance of influencing the formation of its decrees. But the papal theologians retained their predominance, for they might be

---

[13] That article condemns the following proposition: "Romani Pontifices et Concilia oecumenica a limitibus suae potestati recesserunt, jura Principum usurparunt, atque etiam in rebus fidei et morum definiendis errarunt."

summoned to defend or alter their work in the Commission, from which the bishops who had spoken or proposed amendments were excluded. Practically, the right of initiative was the deciding point. Even if the first regulation had remained in force, the bishops could never have recovered the surprises, and the difficulty of preparing for unforeseen debates. The regulation ultimately broke down under the mistake of allowing the decree to be debated only once, and that in its crude state, as it came from the hands of the divines. The authors of the measure had not contemplated any real discussion. It was so unlike the way in which business was conducted at Trent, where the right of the episcopate was formally asserted, where the envoys were consulted, and the bishops discussed the questions in several groups before the general congregations, that the printed text of the Tridentine Regulation was rigidly suppressed. It was further provided that the reports of the speeches should not be communicated to the bishops; and the strictest secrecy was enjoined on all concerning the business of the Council. The bishops, being under no obligation to observe this rule, were afterwards informed that it bound them under grievous sin.

This important precept did not succeed in excluding the action of public opinion. It could be applied only to the debates; and many bishops spoke with greater energy and freedom before an assembly of their own order than they would have done if their words had been taken down by Protestants, to be quoted against them at home. But printed documents, distributed in seven hundred copies, could not be kept secret. The rule was subject to exceptions which destroyed its efficacy; and the Roman cause was discredited by systematic conceal-ment, and advocacy that abounded in explanation and colour, but abstained from the substance of fact. Documents couched in the usual official language, being dragged into the forbidden light of day, were supposed to reveal dark mysteries. The secrecy of the debates had a bad effect in exaggerating reports and giving wide scope to fancy. Rome was not vividly interested in the discussions; but its cosmopolitan society was thronged with the several adherents of leading bishops, whose partiality compromised their dignity and envenomed their disputes. Everything that was said was repeated, inflated, and distorted. Whoever had a sharp word for an adversary, which could not be spoken in Council, knew of an audience that would enjoy and carry the matter. The battles of the Aula were fought over again, with anecdote, epigram, and fiction. A distinguished courtesy and nobleness of tone prevailed at the beginning. When the Archbishop of Halifax went down to his place on the 28th of December, after delivering the speech which taught the reality of the opposition, the Presidents bowed to him as he passed them. The denunciations of the Roman system by Strossmayer and Darboy were listened to in January without a murmur. Adversaries paid exorbitant compliments to each other, like men whose disagreements were insignificant, and who were one at heart. As the plot thickened, fatigue, excitement, friends who fetched and carried, made the tone more bitter. In February the Bishop of Laval described Dupanloup publicly as the centre of a conspiracy too shameful to be expressed in words, and professed that he would rather die than be associated with such iniquity. One of the minority described his opponents as having disported themselves on a certain occasion like a herd of cattle. By that time the whole temper of the Council had been changed; the Pope himself had gone into the arena; and violence of language and gesture had become an artifice adopted to hasten the end.

When the Council opened, many bishops were bewildered and dispirited by the Bull *Multiplices*. They feared that a struggle could not be averted, as, even if no dogmatic question was raised, their rights were cancelled in a way that would make the Pope absolute in dogma. One of the Cardinals caused him to be informed that the Regulation would be resisted. But Pius IX knew that in all that procession of 750 bishops one idea prevailed. Men whose word is powerful in the centres of civilisation, men who three months before were confronting martyrdom among barbarians, preachers at Notre Dame, professors from Germany, Republicans from Western America, men with every sort of training and every sort of experience, had come together as confident and as eager as the prelates of Rome itself, to hail the Pope infallible. Resistance was improbable, for it was hopeless. It was improbable that bishops who had refused no token of submission for twenty years would now combine to inflict dishonour on the Pope. In their address of 1867 they had confessed that he is the father and teacher of all Christians; that all the things he has spoken were spoken by St. Peter through him; that they would believe and teach all that he believed and taught. In 1854 they had allowed him to proclaim a dogma, which some of them dreaded and some opposed, but to which all submitted when he had decreed without the intervention of a Council. The recent display of opposition did not justify serious alarm. The Fulda bishops feared the consequences in Germany; but they affirmed that all were united, and that there would be no new dogma. They were perfectly informed of all that was being got ready in Rome. The words of their pastoral meant nothing if they did not mean that infallibility was no new dogma, and that all the bishops believed in it. Even the Bishop of Orleans avoided a direct attack on the doctrine, proclaimed his own devotion to the Pope, and promised that the Council would be a scene of concord.[14] It was certain that any real attempt that might be made to prevent the definition could be overwhelmed by the preponderance of those bishops whom the modern constitution of the Church places in dependence on Rome.

The only bishops whose position made them capable of resisting were the Germans and the French; and all that Rome would have to contend with was the modern liberalism and decrepit Gallicanism of France, and the science of Germany. The Gallican school was nearly extinct; it had no footing in other countries, and it was essentially odious to the liberals. The most serious minds of the liberal party were conscious that Rome was as dangerous to ecclesiastical liberty as Paris. But, since the Syllabus made it impossible to pursue the liberal doctrines consistently without collision with Rome, they had ceased to be professed with a robust and earnest confidence, and the party was disorganised. They set up the pretence that the real adversary of their opinions was not the Pope, but a French newspaper; and they fought the King's troops in the King's name. When the Bishop of Orleans made his declaration, they fell back, and left him to mount the breach alone. Montalembert, the most vigorous spirit among them, became isolated from his former friends, and accused them, with increasing vehemence, of being traitors to their principles. During the last disheartening year of his life he turned away from the clergy of his country, which was sunk in Romanism, and felt that the real abode of his opinions was on the Rhine.[15] It was only lately that the ideas of the

---

[14] J'en suis convaincu: à peine aurai-je touché la terre sacrée, à peine aurai-je baisé le tombeau des Apôtres, que je me sentirai dans la paix, hors de la bataille, au sein d'une assemblée présidée par un Père et composée de Frères. Là, tous les bruits expireront, toutes les ingérences téméraires cesseront, toutes les imprudences disparaîtront, les flots et les vents seront apaisés.

[15] Vous admirez sans doute beaucoup l'évêque d'Orléans, mais vous l'admireriez bien plus encore, si vous pouviez vous figurer l'abîme d'idolatrie où est tombé le clergé français. Cela dépasse tout ce que l'on aurait jamais pu l'imaginer aux jours de ma jeunesse, au temps de Frayssinous et de La Mennais. Le pauvre Mgr. Maret, pour avoir

Coblentz address, which had so deeply touched the sympathies of Montalembert, had spread widely in Germany. They had their seat in the universities; and their transit from the interior of lecture-rooms to the outer world was laborious and slow. The invasion of Roman doctrines had given vigour and popularity to those which opposed them, but the growing influence of the universities brought them into direct antagonism with the episcopate. The Austrian bishops were generally beyond its reach, and the German bishops were generally at war with it. In December, one of the most illustrious of them said: "We bishops are absorbed in our work, and are not scholars. We sadly need the help of those that are. It is to be hoped that the Council will raise only such questions as can be dealt with competently by practical experience and common sense." The force that Germany wields in theology was only partially represented in its episcopate.

At the opening of the Council the known opposition consisted of four men. Cardinal Schwarzenberg had not published his opinion, but he made it known as soon as he came to Rome. He brought with him a printed paper, entitled *Desideria patribus Concilii oecumenici proponenda*, in which he adopted the ideas of the divines and canonists who are the teachers of his Bohemian clergy. He entreated the Council not to multiply unnecessary articles of faith, and in particular to abstain from defining papal infallibility, which was beset with difficulties, and would make the foundations of faith to tremble even in the devoutest souls. He pointed out that the Index could not continue on its present footing, and urged that the Church should seek her strength in the cultivation of liberty and learning, not in privilege and coercion; that she should rely on popular institutions, and obtain popular support. He warmly advocated the system of autonomy that was springing up in Hungary.[16]

---

exposé des idées tres modérées dans un langage plein d'urbanité et de charité, est traité publiquement dans les journaux soi-disant religieux d'hérésiarque et d'apostat, par les derniers de nos curés. De tous les mystères que présente en si grand nombre l'histoire de l'Église je n'en connais pas qui égale ou dépasse cette transformation si prompte et si complète de la France Catholique en une basse-cour de *l'anticamera* du Vatican. J'en serais encore plus désesperé qu'humilié, si là, comme partout dans les régions illuminées par la foi, la miséricorde et l'espérance ne se laissaient entrevoir à travers les ténèbres. "C'est du Rhin aujourd'hui que nous vient la lumière." L'Allemagne a été choisie pour opposer une digue à ce torrent de fanatisme servile qui menaçait de tout engloutir (Nov. 7, 1869).

[16] Non solum ea quae ad scholas theologicas pertinent scholis relinquantur, sed etiam doctrinae quae a fidelibus pie tenentur et coluntur, sine gravi causa in codicem dogmatum ne inferantur. In specie ne Concilium declaret vel definiat infallibilitatem Summi

Unlike Schwarzenberg, Dupanloup, and Maret, the Archbishop of Paris had taken no hostile step in reference to the Council, but he was feared the most of all the men expected at Rome. The Pope had refused to make him a cardinal, and had written to him a letter of reproof such as has seldom been received by a bishop. It was felt that he was hostile, not episodically to a single measure, but to the peculiar spirit of this pontificate. He had none of the conventional prejudices and assumed antipathies which are congenial to the hierarchical mind. He was without passion or pathos or affectation; and he had good sense, a perfect temper, and an intolerable wit. It was characteristic of him that he made the Syllabus an occasion to impress moderation on the Pope: "Your blame has power, O Vicar of Jesus Christ; but your blessing is more potent still. God has raised you to the apostolic See between the two halves of this century, that you may absolve the one and inaugurate the other. Be it yours to reconcile reason with faith, liberty with authority, politics with the Church. From the height of that triple majesty with which religion, age, and misfortune adorn you, all that you do and all that you say reaches far, to disconcert or to encourage the nations. Give them from your large priestly heart one word to amnesty the past, to reassure the present, and to open the horizons of the future."

The security into which many unsuspecting bishops had been lulled quickly disappeared; and they understood that they were in presence of a conspiracy which would succeed at once if they did not provide against acclamation, and must succeed at last if they allowed themselves to be caught in the toils of the Bull *Multiplices*. It was necessary to make sure that no decree should be passed without reasonable discussion, and to make a stand against the regulation. The first

---

Pontificis, a doctissimis et prudentissimis fidelibus Sanctae Sedi intime addictis, vehementer optatur. Gravia enim mala exinde oritura timent tum fidelibus tum infidelibus. Fideles enim, qui Primatum magisterii et jurisdictionis in Summo Pontifice ultro agnoscunt, quorum pietas et obedientia erga Sanctam Sedem nullo certe tempore major fuit, corde turbarentur magis quam erigerentur, ac si nunc demum fundamentum Ecclesiae et verae doctrinae stabiliendum sit; infideles vero novam calumniarum et derisionum materiam lucrarentur. Neque desunt, qui ejusmodi definitionem logice impossibilem vocant. . . . Nostris diebus defensio veritatis ac religionis tum praesertim efficax et fructuosa est, si sacerdotes a lege caeterorum civium minus recedunt, sed communibus omnium juribus utuntur, ita ut vis defensionis sit in veritate interna non per tutelam externae exemptionis. . . . Praesertim Ecclesia se scientiarum, quae hominem orant perficiuntque, amicam et patronam exhibeat, probe noscens, omne verum a Deo esse, et profunda ac seria literarum studia opitulari fidei.

congregation, held on the 10th of December, was a scene of confusion; but it appeared that a bishop from the Turkish frontier had risen against the order of proceeding, and that the President had stopped him, saying that this was a matter decided by the Pope, and not submitted to the Council. The bishops perceived that they were in a snare. Some began to think of going home. Others argued that questions of Divine right were affected by the regulation, and that they were bound to stake the existence of the Council upon them. Many were more eager on this point of law than on the point of dogma, and were brought under the influence of the more clear-sighted men, with whom they would not have come in contact through any sympathy on the question of infallibility. The desire of protesting against the violation of privileges was an imperfect bond. The bishops had not yet learned to know each other; and they had so strongly impressed upon their flocks at home the idea that Rome ought to be trusted, that they were going to manifest the unity of the Church and to confound the insinuations of her enemies, that they were not quick to admit all the significance of the facts they found. Nothing vigorous was possible in a body of so loose a texture. The softer materials had to be eliminated, the stronger welded together by severe and constant pressure, before an opposition could be made capable of effective action. They signed protests that were of no effect. They petitioned; they did not resist.

It was seen how much Rome had gained by excluding the ambassadors; for this question of forms and regulations would have admitted the action of diplomacy. The idea of being represented at the Council was revived in France; and a weary negotiation began, which lasted several months, and accomplished nothing but delay. It was not till the policy of intervention had ignominiously failed, and till its failure had left the Roman court to cope with the bishops alone, that the real question was brought on for discussion. And as long as the chance remained that political considerations might keep infallibility out of the Council, the opposition abstained from declaring its real sentiments. Its union was precarious and delusive, but it lasted in this state long enough to enable secondary influences to do much towards supplying the place of principles.

While the protesting bishops were not committed against infallibility, it would have been possible to prevent resistance to the bull from becoming resistance to the dogma. The Bishop of Grenoble, who was reputed a good divine among his countrymen, was sounded in order to discover how far he would go; and it was ascertained that he admitted the doctrine substantially. At the same time, the friends of the Bishop of Orleans were insisting that he had questioned not the dogma but the definition; and Maret, in the defence of his book, declared that he attributed no infallibility to the episcopate apart from the Pope. If the bishops had been consulted separately, without the terror of a decree, it is probable that the number of those who absolutely rejected the doctrine would have been extremely small. There were many who had never thought seriously about it, or imagined that it was true in a pious sense, though not capable of proof in controversy. The possibility of an understanding seemed so near that the archbishop of Westminster, who held the Pope infallible apart from the episcopate, required that the words should be translated into French in the sense of independence, and not of exclusion. An ambiguous formula embodying the view common to both parties, or founded on mutual concession, would have done more for the liberty than the unity of opinion, and would not have strengthened the authority of the Pope. It was resolved to proceed with caution, putting in motion the strong machinery of Rome, and exhausting the advantage of organisation and foreknowledge.

The first act of the Council was to elect the Commission on Dogma. A proposal was made on very high authority that the list should be drawn up so as to represent the different opinions fairly, and to include some of the chief opponents. They would have been subjected to other influences than those which sustain party leaders; they would have been separated from their friends and brought into frequent contact with adversaries; they would have felt the strain of official responsibility; and the opposition would have been decapitated. If these sagacious counsels had been followed, the harvest of July might have been gathered in January, and the reaction that was excited in the long struggle that ensued might have been prevented. Cardinal de Angelis, who ostensibly managed the elections, and was advised by Archbishop Manning, preferred the opposite and more prudent course. He caused a lithographed list to be sent to all the bishops open to influence, from which every name was excluded that was not on the side of infallibility.

Meantime the bishops of several nations selected those among their countrymen whom they recommended as candidates. The Germans and Hungarians, above forty in number, assembled for this purpose under the presidency of Cardinal Schwarzenberg; and their meetings were continued, and became more and more important, as those who did not sympathise with the opposition dropped away. The French were divided into two groups, and met partly at Cardinal Mathieu's, partly at Cardinal Bonnechose's. A fusion was proposed, but was resisted, in the Roman interest, by Bonnechose. He consulted Cardinal Antonelli, and reported that the Pope disliked large meetings of bishops. Moreover, if all the French had met in one place, the opposition would have had the majority, and would have determined the choice of the candidates. They voted separately; and the Bonnechose list was represented to foreign bishops as the united choice of the French episcopate. The Mathieu group believed that this had been done fraudulently, and resolved to make their complaint to the Pope; but Cardinal Mathieu, seeing that a storm was rising, and that he would be called on to be the spokesman of his friends, hurried away to spend Christmas at Besançon. All the votes of his group were thrown away. Even the bishop of Grenoble, who had obtained twenty-nine votes at one meeting, and thirteen at the other, was excluded from the Commission. It was constituted as the managers of the election desired, and the first trial of strength appeared to have annihilated the opposition. The force under entire control of the court could be estimated from the number of votes cast blindly for candidates not put forward by their own countrymen, and unknown to others, who had therefore no recommendation but that of the official list. According to this test Rome could dispose of 550 votes.

The moment of this triumph was chosen for the production of an act already two months old, by which many ancient censures were revoked, and many were renewed. The legislation of the Middle Ages and of the sixteenth century appointed nearly two hundred cases by which excommunication was incurred *ipso facto*, without inquiry or sentence. They had generally fallen into oblivion, or were remembered as instances of former extravagance; but they had not been abrogated, and, as they were in part defensible, they were a trouble to timorous consciences. There was reason to expect that this question, which had often occupied the attention of the bishops, would be brought before the Council; and the demand for a reform could not have been withstood. The difficulty was anticipated by sweeping away as many censures as it was thought safe to abandon, and deciding, independently of the bishops, what must be retained. The Pope reserved to himself alone the faculty of absolving from the sin of harbouring or defending the members of any sect, of causing priests to be tried by secular courts, of violating asylum or alienating the real property of the Church. The prohibition of anonymous writing was restricted to works on theology, and the excommunication hitherto incurred by reading books which are on the Index was confined to readers of heretical books. This Constitution had no other immediate effect than to indicate the prevailing spirit, and to increase the difficulties of the partisans of Rome. The organ of the Archbishop of Cologne justified the last provision by saying, that it does not forbid the works of Jews, for Jews are not heretics; nor the heretical tracts and newspapers, for they are not books; nor listening to heretical books read aloud, for hearing is not reading.

At the same time, the serious work of the Council was begun. A long dogmatic decree was distributed, in which the special theological, biblical, and philosophical opinions of the school now dominant in Rome were proposed for ratification. It was so weak a composition that it was as severely criticised by the Romans as by the foreigners; and there were Germans whose attention was first called to its defects by an Italian cardinal. The disgust with which the text of the first decree was received had not been foreseen. No real discussion had been expected. The Council hall, admirable for occasions of ceremony, was extremely ill adapted for speaking, and nothing would induce the Pope to give it up. A public session was fixed for the 6th of January, and the election of Commissions was to last till Christmas. It was evident that nothing would be ready for the session, unless the decree was accepted without debate, or infallibility adopted by acclamation.

Before the Council had been assembled a fortnight, a store of discontent had accumulated which it would have been easy to avoid. Every act of the Pope, the Bull *Multiplices*, the declaration of censures, the text of the proposed decree, even the announcement that the Council should be dissolved in case of his death, had seemed an injury or an insult to the episcopate. These measures undid the favourable effect of the caution with which the bishops had been received. They did what the dislike of infallibility alone would not have done. They broke the spell of veneration for Pius IX which fascinated the Catholic Episcopate. The jealousy with which he guarded his prerogative in the appointment of officers, and of the great Commission, the pressure during the elections, the prohibition of national meetings, the refusal to hold the debates in a hall where they could be heard, irritated and alarmed many bishops. They suspected that they had been summoned for the very purpose they had indignantly denied, to make the papacy more absolute by abdicating in favour of the official prelature of Rome. Confidence gave way to a great despondency, and a state of feeling was aroused which prepared the way for actual opposition when the time should come.

Before Christmas the Germans and the French were grouped nearly as they remained to the end. After the flight of Cardinal Mathieu, and the refusal of Cardinal Bonnechose to coalesce, the friends of the latter gravitated towards the Roman centre, and the friends of the former held their meetings at the house of the Archbishop of Paris. They became, with the Austro-German meeting under Cardinal Schwarzenberg, the strength and substance of the party that opposed the new dogma; but there was little intercourse between the two, and their exclusive nationality made them useless as a nucleus for the few scattered American, English, and Italian bishops whose sympathies were with them. To meet this object, and to centralise the deliberations, about a dozen of the leading men constituted an international meeting, which included the best talents, but also the most discordant views. They were too little united to act with vigour, and too few to exercise control. Some months later they increased their numbers. They were the brain but not the will of the opposition. Cardinal Rauscher presided. Rome honoured him as the author of the Austrian Concordat; but he feared that infallibility would bring destruction on his work, and he was the most constant, the most copious, and the most emphatic of its opponents.

When the debate opened, on the 28th of December, the idea of proclaiming the dogma by acclamation had not been abandoned. The Archbishop of Paris exacted a promise that it should not be attempted. But he was warned that the promise held good for the first day only, and that there was no engagement for the future. Then he made it known that one hundred bishops were ready, if a surprise was attempted, to depart from Rome, and to carry away the Council, as he said, in the soles of their shoes. The plan of carrying the measure by a sudden resolution was given up, and it was determined to introduce it with a demonstration of overwhelming effect. The debate on the dogmatic decree was begun by Cardinal Rauscher. The Archbishop of St. Louis spoke on the same day so briefly as not to reveal the force and the fire within him. The Archbishop of Halifax concluded a long speech by saying that the proposal laid before the Council was only fit to be put decorously under ground. Much praise was lavished on the bishops who had courage, knowledge, and Latin enough to address the asembled Fathers; and the Council rose instantly in dignity and in esteem when it was seen that there was to be real discussion. On the 30th, Rome was excited by the success of two speakers. One was the Bishop of Grenoble, the other was Strossmayer, the bishop from the Turkish frontier, who had again assailed the regulation, and had again been stopped by the presiding Cardinal. The fame of his spirit and eloquence began to spread over the city and over the world. The ideas that animated these men in their attack on the proposed measure were most clearly shown a few days later in the speech of a Swiss prelate. "What boots it," he exclaimed, "to condemn errors that have been long condemned, and tempt no Catholic? The false beliefs of mankind are beyond the reach of your decrees. The best defence of Catholicism is religious science. Give to the pursuit of sound learning every encouragement and the widest field; and prove by deeds as well as words that the progress of nations in liberty and light is the mission of the Church."[17]

The tempest of criticism was weakly met; and the opponents established at once a superiority in debate. At the end of the first month nothing had been done; and the Session imprudently fixed for the 6th of January had to be filled up with tedious ceremonies. Everybody saw that there had been a great miscalculation. The Council was slipping out of the grasp of the Court, and the regulation was a manifest hindrance to the despatch of business. New resources were required.

[17] Quid enim expedit damnare quae damnata jam sunt, quidve juvat errores proscribere quos novimus jam esse proscriptos? . . . Falsa sophistarum dogmata, veluti cineres a turbine venti evanuerunt, corrupuerunt, fateor, permultos, infecerunt genium saeculi hujus, sed numquid credendum est, corruptionis contagionem non contigisse, si ejusmodi errores decretorum anathemate prostrati fuissent? . . . Pro tuenda et tute servanda religione Catholica praeter gemitus et preces ad Deum aliud medium praesidiumque nobis datum non est nisi Catholica scientia, cum recta fide per omnia concors. Excolitur summopere apud heterodoxos fidei inimica scientia, excolatur ergo oportet et omni opere augeatur apud Catholicos vera scientia, Ecclesiae amica. . . . Obmutescere faciamus ora obtrectantium qui falso nobis imputare non desistunt, Catholicam Ecclesiam opprimere scientiam, et quemcumque liberum cogitandi modum ita cohibere, ut neque scientia, nec ulla alia animi libertas in ea subsistere vel florescere possit. . . . Propterea monstrandum hoc est, et scriptis et factis manifestandum, in Catholica Ecclesia veram pro populis esse libertatem, verum profectum, verum lumen, veramque prosperitatem.

A new president was appointed. Cardinal Reisach had died at the end of December without having been able to take his seat, and Cardinal De Luca had presided in his stead. De Angelis was now put into the place made vacant by the death of Reisach. He had suffered imprisonment at Turin, and the glory of his confessorship was enhanced by his services in the election of the Commissions. He was not suited otherwise to be the moderator of a great assembly; and the effect of his elevation was to dethrone the accomplished and astute De Luca, who had been found deficient in thoroughness, and to throw the management of the Council into the hands of the junior Presidents, Capalti and Bilio. Bilio was a Barnabite monk, innocent of court intrigues, a friend of the most enlightened scholars in Rome, and a favourite of the Pope. Cardinal Capalti had been distinguished as a canonist. Like Cardinal Bilio, he was not reckoned among men of the extreme party; and they were not always in harmony with their colleagues, De Angelis and Bizarri. But they did not waver when the policy they had to execute was not their own.

The first decree was withdrawn, and referred to the Commission on Doctrine. Another, on the duties of the episcopate, was substituted; and that again was followed by others, of which the most important was on the Catechism. While they were being discussed, a petition was prepared, demanding that the infallibility of the Pope should be made the object of a decree. The majority undertook to put a strain on the prudence or the reluctance of the Vatican. Their zeal in the cause was warmer than that of the official advisers. Among those who had the responsibility of conducting the spiritual and temporal government of the Pope, the belief was strong that his infallibility did not need defining, and that the definition could not be obtained without needless obstruction to other papal interests. Several Cardinals were inopportunists at first, and afterwards promoted intermediate and conciliatory proposals. But the business of the Council was not left to the ordinary advisers of the Pope, and they were visibly compelled and driven by those who represented the majority. At times this pressure was no doubt convenient. But there were also times when there was no collusion, and the majority really led the authorities. The initiative was not taken by the great mass whose zeal was stimulated by personal allegiance to the Pope. They added to the momentum, but the impulse came from men who were as independent as the chiefs of the opposition. The great Petition, supported by others pointing to the same end, was kept back for several weeks, and was presented at the end of January

At that time the opposition had attained its full strength, and presented a counter-petition, praying that the question might not be introduced. It was written by Cardinal Rauscher, and was signed, with variations, by 137 bishops. To obtain that number the address avoided the doctrine itself, and spoke only of the difficulty and danger in defining it; so that this, their most imposing act, was a confession of inherent weakness, and a signal to the majority that they might force on the dogmatic discussion. The bishops stood on the negative. They showed no sense of their mission to renovate Catholicism; and it seemed that they would compound for the concession they wanted, by yielding in all other matters, even those which would be a practical substitute for infallibility. That this was not to be, that the forces needed for a great revival were really present, was made manifest by the speech of Strossmayer on the 24th of January, when he demanded the reformation of the Court of Rome, decentralisation in the government of the Church, and decennial Councils. That earnest spirit did not animate the bulk of the party. They were content to leave things as they were, to gain nothing if they lost nothing, to renounce all premature striving for reform if they could succeed in avoiding a doctrine which they were as unwilling to discuss as to define. The words of Ginoulhiac to Strossmayer, "You terrify me with your pitiless logic," expressed the inmost feelings of many who gloried in the grace and the splendour of his eloquence. No words were too strong for them if they prevented the necessity of action, and spared the bishops the distressing prospect of being brought to bay, and having to resist openly the wishes and the claims of Rome.

Infallibility never ceased to overshadow every step of the Council,[18] but it had already given birth to a deeper question. The Church had less to fear from the violence of the majority than from the inertness of their opponents. No proclamation of false doctrines could be so great a disaster as the weakness of faith which would prove that the power of recovery, the vital force of Catholicism, was extinct in the episcopate. It was better to be overcome after openly attesting their belief than to strangle both discussion and definition, and to disperse

[18] Il n'y a au fond qu'une question devenue urgente et inévitable, dont la décision faciliterait le cours et la décision de toutes les autres, dont le retard paralyse tout. Sans cela rien n'est commencé ni même abordable (*Univers*, February 9).

without having uttered a single word that could reinstate the authorities of the Church in the respect of men. The future depended less on the outward struggle between two parties than on the process by which the stronger spirit within the minority leavened the mass. The opposition was as averse to the actual dogmatic discussion among themselves as in the Council. They feared an inquiry which would divide them. At first the bishops who understood and resolutely contemplated their real mission in the Council were exceedingly few. Their influence was strengthened by the force of events, by the incessant pressure of the majority, and by the action of literary opinion.

Early in December the Archbishop of Mechlin brought out a reply to the letter of the Bishop of Orleans, who immediately prepared a rejoinder, but could not obtain permission to print it in Rome. It appeared two months later at Naples. Whilst the minority were under the shock of this prohibition, Gratry published at Paris the first of four letters to the Archbishop of Mechlin, in which the case of Honorius was discussed with so much perspicuity and effect that the profane public was interested, and the pamphlets were read with avidity in Rome. They contained no new research, but they went deep into the causes which divided Catholics. Gratry showed that the Roman theory is still propped by fables which were innocent once, but have become deliberate untruths since the excuse of mediaeval ignorance was dispelled; and he declared that this school of lies was the cause of the weakness of the Church, and called on Catholics to look the scandal in the face, and cast out the religious forgers. His letters did much to clear the ground and to correct the confusion of ideas among the French. The bishop of St. Brieuc wrote that the exposure was an excellent service to religion, for the evil had gone so far that silence would be complicity.[19] Gratry was no sooner approved by one bishop than he was condemned by a great number of others. He had brought home to his countrymen the question whether they could be accomplices of a dishonest system, or would fairly attempt to root it out.

[19] Gratry had written: "Cette apologétique sans franchise est l'une des causes de notre décadence religieuse depuis des siècles. . . . Sommes-nous les prédicateurs du mensonge ou les apôtres de la vérité? Le temps n'est-il pas venu de rejeter avec dégoût les fraudes, les interpolations, et les mutilations que les menteurs et les faussaires, nos plus cruels ennemis, ont pu introduire parmi nous?" The bishop wrote: "Jamais parole plus puissante, inspirée par la conscience et le savoir, n'est arrivée plus à propos que la vôtre. . . . Le mal est tel et le danger si effrayant que le silence deviendrait de la complicité."

While Gratry's letters were disturbing the French, Döllinger published some observations on the petition for infallibility, directing his attack clearly against the doctrine itself. During the excitement that ensued, he answered demonstrations of sympathy by saying that he had only defended the faith which was professed, substantially, by the majority of the episcopate in Germany. These words dropped like an acid on the German bishops. They were writhing to escape the dire necessity of a conflict with the Pope; and it was very painful to them to be called as compurgators by a man who was esteemed the foremost opponent of the Roman system, whose hand was suspected in everything that had been done against it, and who had written many things on the sovereign obligations of truth and faith which seemed an unmerciful satire on the tactics to which they clung. The notion that the bishops were opposing the dogma itself was founded on their address against the regulation; but the petition against the definition of infallibility was so worded as to avoid that inference, and had accordingly obtained nearly twice as many German and Hungarian signatures as the other. The Bishop of Mentz vehemently repudiated the supposition for himself, and invited his colleagues to do the same. Some followed his example, others refused; and it became apparent that the German opposition was divided, and included men who accepted the doctrines of Rome. The precarious alliance between incompatible elements was prevented from breaking up by the next act of the Papal Government.

The defects in the mode of carrying on the business of the Council were admitted on both sides. Two months had been lost; and the demand for a radical change was publicly made in behalf of the minority by a letter communicated to the *Moniteur*. On the 22nd of February a new regulation was introduced, with the avowed purpose of quickening progress. It gave the Presidents power to cut short any speech, and provided that debate might be cut short at any moment when the majority pleased. It also declared that the decrees should be carried by majority—*id decernetur quod majori Patrum numero placuerit*. The policy of leaving the decisive power in the hands of the Council itself had this advantage, that its exercise would not raise the question of liberty and coercion in the same way as the interference of authority. By the Bull *Multiplices*, no bishop could introduce any matter not approved by the Pope. By the new regulation he could not speak on any question before the Council, if the majority chose to close the discussion, or if the Presidents chose to abridge his speech. He could print nothing in Rome, and what was printed elsewhere was liable to be treated as contraband. His written observations on any measure were submitted to the Commission, without any security that they would be made known to the other bishops in their integrity. There was no longer an obstacle to the immediate definition of papal infallibility. The majority was omnipotent.

The minority could not accept this regulation without admitting that the Pope is infallible. Their thesis was, that his decrees are not free from the risk of error unless they express the universal belief of the episcopate. The idea that particular virtue attaches to a certain number of bishops, or that infallibility depends on a few votes more or less, was defended by nobody. If the act of a majority of bishops in the Council, possibly not representing a majority in the Church, is infallible, it derives its infallibility from the Pope. Nobody held that the Pope was bound to proclaim a dogma carried by a majority. The minority contested the principle of the new Regulation, and declared that a dogmatic decree required virtual unanimity. The chief protest was drawn up by a French bishop. Some of the Hungarians added a paragraph asserting that the authority and ecumenicity of the Council depended on the settlement of this question; and they proposed to add that they could not continue to act as though it were legitimate unless this point was given up. The author of the address declined this passage, urging that the time for actual menace was not yet come. From that day the minority agreed in rejecting as invalid any doctrine which should not be passed by unanimous consent. On this point the difference between the thorough and the simulated opposition was effaced, for Ginoulhiac and Ketteler were as positive as Kenrick or Hefele. But it was a point which Rome could not surrender without giving up its whole position. To wait for unanimity was to wait for ever, and to admit that a minority could prevent or nullify the dogmatic action of the papacy was to renounce infallibility. No alternative remained to the opposing bishops but to break up the Council. The most eminent among them accepted this conclusion, and stated it in a paper declaring that the absolute and indisputable law of the Church had been violated by the Regulation allowing articles of faith to be decreed on which the episcopate was not morally unanimous; and that the Council, no longer possessing in the eyes of the bishops and of the world the indispensable condition of liberty and legality, would be inevitably rejected. To avert a public scandal, and to save the honour of the Holy See, it was proposed that some unopposed decrees should be proclaimed in solemn session, and the Council immediately prorogued.

At the end of March a breach seemed unavoidable. The first part of the dogmatic decree had come back from the Commission so profoundly altered that it was generally accepted by the bishops, but with a crudely expressed sentence in the preamble, which was intended to rebuke the notion of the reunion of Protestant Churches. Several bishops looked upon this passage as an uncalled for insult to Protestants, and wished it changed; but there was danger that if they then joined in voting the decree they would commit themselves to the lawfulness of the Regulation against which they had protested. On the 22nd of March Strossmayer raised both questions. He said it was neither just nor charitable to impute the progress of religious error to the Protestants. The germ of modern unbelief existed among the Catholics before the Reformation, and afterwards bore its worst fruits in Catholic countries. Many of the ablest defenders of Christian truth were Protestants, and the day of reconciliation would have come already but for the violence and uncharitableness of the Catholics. These words were greeted with execrations, and the remainder of the speech was delivered in the midst of a furious tumult. At length, when Strossmayer declared that the Council had forfeited its authority by the rule which abolished the necessity of unanimity, the Presidents and the multitude refused to let him go on.[20] On the following day he drew up a protest, declaring

[20] Pace eruditissimorum virorum dictum esto: mihi haecce nec veritati congrua esse videntur, nec caritati. Non veritati; verum quidem est Protestantes gravissimam commisisse culpam, dum spreta et insuperhabita divina Ecclesiae autoritate, aeternas et immutabiles fidei veritates subjectivae rationis judicio et arbitrio subjecissent. Hoc superbiae humanae fomentum gravissimis certe malis, rationalismo, criticismo, etc. occasionem dedit. Ast hoc quoque respectu dici debet, protestantismi ejus qui cum eodem in nexu existit rationalismi germen saeculo xvi. praeextitisse in sic dicto humanismo et classicismo, quem in sanctuario ipso quidam summae auctoritatis viri incauto consilio fovebant et nutriebant; et nisi hoc germen praeextitisset concipi non posset quomodo tam parva scintilla tantum in medio Europae excitare potuisset incendium, ut illud ad hodiernum usque diem restingui non potuerit. Accedit et illud: fidei et religionis, Ecclesiae et omnis auctoritatis contemptum absque ulla cum Protestantismo cognatione et parentela in medio Catholicae gentis saeculo xviii. temporibus Voltairi et encyclopaedistarum enatum fuisse. . . . Quidquid interim sit de rationalismo, puto venerabilem deputationem omnino falli dum texendo genealogiam naturalismi, materialismi, pantheismi, atheismi, etc., omnes omnino hos errores foetus Protestantismi esse asserit. . . . Errores superius enumerati non tantum nobis verum et ipsis Protestantibus horrori sunt et abominationi, ut adeo Ecclesiae et nobis Catholicis in iis oppugnandis et refellendis

that he could not acknowledge the validity of the Council if dogmas were to be decided by a majority,[21] and sent it to the Presidents after it had been approved at the meeting of the Germans, and by bishops of other nations. The preamble was withdrawn, and another was inserted in its place, which had been written in great haste by the German Jesuit Kleutgen, and was received with general applause. Several of the Jesuits obtained credit for the ability and moderation

auxilio sint et adjumento. Ita Leibnitius erat certe vir eruditus et omni sub respectu praestans; vir in dijudicandis Ecclesiae Catholicae institutis aequus; vir in debellandis sui temporis erroribus strenuus; vir in revehenda inter Christianas communitates concordia optime animatus et meritus. [Loud cries of "Oh! Oh!" The President de Angelis rang the bell and said, "Non est hicce locus laudandi Protestantes."] . . . Hos viros quorum magna copia existit in Germania, in Anglia, item et in America septentrionali, magna hominum turba inter Protestantes sequitur, quibus omnibus applicari potest illud magni Augustini: "Errant, sed bona fide errant; haeretici sunt, sed illi nos haereticos tenent. Ipsi errorem non invenerunt, sed a perversis et in errorem inductis parentibus haereditaverunt, parati errorem deponere quamprimum convicti fuerint." [Here there was a long interruption and ringing of the bell, with cries of "Shame! shame!" "Down with the heretic!"] Hi omnes etiamsi non spectent ad Ecclesiae corpus, spectant tamen ad ejus animam, et de muneribus Redemptionis aliquatenus participant. Hi omnes in amore quo erga Iesum Christum Dominum nostrum feruntur, atque in illis positivis veritatibus quas ex fidei naufragio salvarunt, totidem gratiae divinae momenta possident, quibus misericordia Dei utetur, ut eos ad priscam fidem et Ecclesiam reducat, nisi nos exaggerationibus nostris et improvidis charitatis ipsis debitae laesionibus tempus misericordiae divinae elongaverimus. Quantum autem ad charitatem, ei certe contrarium est vulnera aliena alio fine tangere quam ut ipsa sanentur; puto autem hac enumeratione errorum, quibus Protestantismus occasionem dedisset, id non fieri. . . . Decreto, quod in supplementum ordinis interioris nobis nuper communicatum est, statuitur res in Concilio hocce suffragiorum majoritate decidendas fore. Contra hoc principium, quod omnem praecedentium Conciliorum praxim funditus evertit, multi episcopi reclamarunt, quin tamen aliquod responsum obtinuerint. Responsum autem in re tanti momenti dari debuisset clarum, perspicuum et omnis ambiguitatis expers. Hoc ad summas Concilii hujus calamitates spectat, nam hoc certe et praesenti generationi et posteris praebebit ansam dicendi: huic concilio libertatem et veritatem defuisse. Ego ipse convictus sum, aeternam ac immutabilem fidei et traditionis regulam semper fuisse semperque mansuram communem, ad minus moraliter unanimem consensum. Concilium, quod hac regula insuperhabita, fidei et morum dogmata majoritate numerica definire intenderet, juxta meam intimam convictionem eo ipso excideret jure conscientiam orbis Catholici sub sanctione vitae ac mortis aeternae obligandi.

[21] Dum autem ipse die hesterno ex suggestu hanc quaestionem posuissem et verba de consensu unanimi in rebus fidei definiendis necessario protulissem, interruptus fui, mihique inter maximum tumultum et graves comminationes possibilitas sermonis continuandi adempta est. Atque haec gravissima sane circumstantia magis adhuc comprobat necessitatem habendi responsi, quod clarum sit omnisque ambiguitatis expers. Peto itaque humillime, ut hujusmodi responsum in proxima congregatione generali detur. Nisi enim haec fierent anceps haererem an manere possem in Concilio, ubi libertas Episcoporum ita opprimitur, quemadmodum heri in me oppressa fuit, et ubi dogmata fidei definirentur novo et in Ecclesia Dei adjusque inaudito modo.

with which the decree was drawn up. It was no less than a victory over extreme counsels. A unanimous vote was insured for the public session of 24th April; and harmony was restored. But the text proposed originally in the Pope's name had undergone so many changes as to make it appear that his intentions had been thwarted. There was a supplement to the decree, which the bishops had understood would be withdrawn, in order that the festive concord and good feeling might not be disturbed. They were informed at the last moment that it would be put to the vote, as its withdrawal would be a confession of defeat for Rome. The supplement was an admonition that the constitutions and decrees of the Holy See must be observed even when they proscribe opinions not actually heretical.[22] Extraordinary efforts were made in public and in private to prevent any open expression of dissent from this paragraph. The Bishop of Brixen assured his brethren, in the name of the Commission, that it did not refer to questions of doctrine, and they could not dispute the general principle that obedience is due to lawful authority. The converse proposition, that the papal acts have no claim to be obeyed, was obviously untenable. The decree was adopted unanimously. There were some who gave their vote with a heavy heart, conscious of the snare.[23] Strossmayer alone stayed away.

---

[22] Quoniam vero satis non est, haereticam pravitatem devitare, nisi ii quoque errores diligenter fugiantur, qui ad illam plus minusve accedunt, omnes officii monemus, servandi etiam Constitutiones et Decreta quibus pravae eiusmodi opiniones, quae istic diserte non enumerantur, ab hac Sancta Sede proscriptae et prohibitae sunt.

[23] In the speech on infallibility which he prepared, but never delivered, Archbishop Kenrick thus expressed himself: "Inter alia quae mihi stuporem injecerunt dixit Westmonasteriensis, nos additamento facto sub finem Decreti de Fide, tertia Sessione lati, ipsam Pontificiam Infallibilitatem, saltem implicite, jam agnovisse, nec ab ea recedere nunc nobis licere. Si bene intellexerim R^m Relatorem, qui in Congregatione generali hoc additamentum, prius oblatum, deinde abstractum, nobis mirantibus quid rei esset, illud iterum inopinato commendavit—dixit, verbis clarioribus, per illud nullam omnino doctrinam edoceri; sed eam quatuor capitibus ex quibus istud decretum compositum est imponi tanquam eis coronidem convenientem; eamque disciplinarem magis quam doctrinalem characterem habere. Aut deceptus est ipse, si vera dixit Westmonasteriensis; aut nos sciens in errorem induxit, quod de viro tam ingenuo minime supponere licet. Utcumque fuerit, ejus declarationi fidentes, plures suffragia sua isti decreto haud deneganda censuerunt ob istam clausulam; aliis, inter quos egomet, dolos parari metuentibus, et aliorum voluntati hac in re aegre cedentibus. In his omnibus non est mens mea aliquem ex Reverendissimis Patribus malae fidei incusare; quos omnes, ut par est, veneratione debita prosequor. Sed extra concilium adesse dicuntur viri religiosi—forsan et pii—qui maxime in illud influunt; qui calliditati potius quam bonis artibus confisi, rem Ecclesiae in maximum ex quo orta sit discrimen adduxerunt; qui ab initio concilio effecerunt ut in Deputationes conciliares ii soli eligerentur qui

The opposition was at an end. Archbishop Manning afterwards reminded them that by this vote they had implicitly accepted infallibility. They had done even more. They might conceivably contrive to bind and limit dogmatic infallibility with conditions so stringent as to evade many of the objections taken from the examples of history; but, in requiring submission to papal decrees on matters not articles of faith, they were approving that of which they knew the character, they were confirming without let or question a power they saw in daily exercise, they were investing with new authority the existing Bulls, and giving unqualified sanction to the Inquisition and the Index, to the murder of heretics and the deposing of kings. They approved what they were called on to reform, and solemnly blessed with their lips what their hearts knew to be accursed. The Court of Rome became thenceforth reckless in its scorn of the opposition, and proceeded in the belief that there was no protest they would not forget, no principle they would not betray, rather than defy the Pope in his wrath. It was at once determined to bring on the discussion of the dogma of infallibility. At first, when the minority knew that their prayers and their sacrifices had been vain, and that they must rely on their own resources, they took courage in extremity. Rauscher, Schwarzenberg. Hefele, Ketteler, Kenrick, wrote pamphlets, or caused them to be written, against the dogma, and circulated them in the Council. Several English bishops protested that the denial of infallibility by the Catholic episcopate had been an essential condition of emancipation, and that they could not revoke that assurance after it had served their purpose, without being dishonoured in the eyes of their countrymen.[24] The

---

eorum placitis fovere aut noscerentur aut crederentur; qui nonnullorum ex eorum praedecessoribus vestigia prementes in schematibus nobis propositis, et ex eorum officina prodeuntibus, nihil magis cordi habuisse videntur quam Episcopalem auctoritatem deprimere, Pontificiam autem extollere; et verborum ambagibus incautos decipere velle videntur, dum alia ab aliis in eorum explicationem dicantur. Isti grave hoc incendium in Ecclesia excitarunt, et in illud insufflare non desinunt, scriptis eorum, pietatis speciem prae se ferentibus sed veritate ejus vacuis, in populos spargentibus.

[24] The author of the protest afterwards gave the substance of his argument as follows: "Episcopi et theologi publice a Parlamento interrogati fuerunt, utrum Catholici Angliae tenerent Papam posse definitiones relativas ad fidem et mores populis imponere absque omni consensu expresso vel tacito Ecclesiae. Omnes Episcopi et theologi responderunt Catholicos hoc non tenere. Hisce responsionibus confisum Parlamentum Angliae Catholicos admisit ad participationem jurium civilium. Quis Protestantibus persuadebit Catholicos contra honorem et bonam fidem non agere, qui quando agebatur de iuribus sibi acquirendis publice professi sunt ad fidem Catholicam non pertinere doctrinam

Archbishop of St. Louis, admitting the force of the argument, derived from the fact that a dogma was promulgated in 1854 which had long been disputed and denied, confessed that he could not prove the Immaculate Conception to be really an article of faith.[25]

An incident occurred in June which showed that the experience of the Council was working a change in the fundamental convictions of the bishops. Döllinger had written in March that an article of faith required not only to be approved and accepted unanimously by the Council, but that the bishops united with the Pope are not infallible, and that the ecumenicity of their acts must be acknowledged and ratified by the whole Church. Father Hötzl, a Franciscan friar, having published a pamphlet in defence of this proposition, was summoned to Rome, and required to sign a paper declaring that the confirmation of a Council by the Pope alone makes it ecumenical. He put his case into the hands of German bishops who were eminent in the opposition, asking first their opinion on the proposed declaration, and secondly, their advice on his own conduct. The bishops whom he consulted replied that they believed the declaration to be erroneous; but they added that they had only lately arrived at the conviction, and had been shocked at first by Döllinger's doctrine. They could not require him to suffer the consequences of being condemned at Rome as a rebellious friar and obstinate heretic for a view which they themselves had doubted only three months before. He followed the advice, but he perceived that his advisers had considerately betrayed him.

When the observations on infallibility which the bishops had sent in to the Commission appeared in print it seemed that the minority had burnt their ships. They affirmed that the dogma would put an end to the conversion of Protestants, that it would drive devout men out of the Church and make Catholicism indefensible in controversy, that it would give governments apparent reason to doubt the fidelity of Catholics, and would give new authority to the theory of persecution and of the deposing power. They testified that it was unknown in

---

infallibilitatis Romani Pontificis, statim autem ac obtinuerint quod volebant, a professione publice facta recedunt et contrarium affirmant?''

[25] Archbishop Kenrick's remarkable statement is not reproduced accurately in his pamphlet *De Pontificia infallibilitate*. It is given in full in the last pages of the *Observatione*, and is abridged in his *Concio habenda sed non habita*, where he concludes: "Eam fidei doctrinam esse neganti, non video quomodo responderi possit, cum objiceret Ecclesiam errorem contra fidem divinitus revelatam diu tolerare non potuisse, quin, aut quod ad fidei depositum pertineret non scivisse, aut errorem manifestum tolerasse videretur."

many parts of the Church, and was denied by the Fathers, so that neither perpetuity nor universality could be pleaded in its favour; and they declared it an absurd contradiction, founded on ignoble deceit, and incapable of being made an article of faith by Pope or Council.[26] One bishop protested that he would die rather than proclaim it. Another thought it would be an act of suicide for the Church.

What was said, during the two months' debate, by men perpetually liable to be interrupted by a majority acting less from conviction than by command,[27] could be of no practical account, and served for protest, not for persuasion. Apart from the immediate purpose of the discussion, two speeches were memorable—that of Archbishop Conolly of Halifax, for the uncompromising clearness with which he appealed to Scripture

[26] Certissimum ipsi esse fore ut infallibilitate ista dogmatice definita, in dioecesi sua, in qua ne vestigium quidem traditionis de infallibilitate S. P. hucusque inveniatur, et in aliis regionibus multi, et quidem non solum minoris, sed etiam optimae notae, a fide deficiant.—Si edatur, omnis progressus conversionum in Provinciis Foederatis Americae funditus extinguetur. Episcopi et sacerdotes in disputationibus cum Protestantibus quid respondere possent non haberent.—Per eiusmodi definitionem a catholicis, inter quos haud pauci iique optimi reditus redditur difficilis, imo impossibilis.—Qui Concilii decretis obsequi vellent, invenient se maximis in difficultatibus versari. Gubernia civilia eos tanquam subditos minus fidos, haud sine verisimilitudinis specie, habebunt. Hostes Ecclesiae eos lacessere non verebuntur, nunc eis objicientes errores quos Pontifices aut docuisse, aut sua agendi ratione probasse, dicuntur et risu excipient responsa quae sola afferri possint.—Eo ipso definitur in globo quidquid per diplomata apostolica huc usque definitum est . . . Poterit, admissa tali definitione, statuere de dominio, temporali, de eius mensura, de potestate deponendi reges, de usu coercendi haereticos.—Doctrina de Infallibilitate Romani Pontificis nec in Scriptura Sacra, nec in traditione ecclesiastica fundata mihi videtur. Immo contrariam, ni fallor, Christiana antiquitas tenuit doctrinam.—Modus dicendi Schematis supponit existere in Ecclesia duplicem infallibilitatem, ipsius Ecclesiae et Romani Pontificis, quod est absurdum et inauditum.—Subterfugiis quibus theologi non pauci in Honorii causa usi sunt, derisui me exponerem. Sophismata adhibere et munere episcopali et natura rei, quae in timore Domini pertractanda est, indignum mihi videtur.—Plerique textus quibus eam comprobant etiam melioris notae theologi, quos Ultramontanos vocant, mutilati sunt, falsificati, interpolati, circumtruncati, spurii, in sensum alienum detorti.—Asserere audeo eam sententiam, ut in schemate jacet, non esse fidei doctrinam, nec talem devenire posse per quamcumque definitionem etiam conciliarem.

[27] This, at least, was the discouraging impression of Archbishop Kenrick: Semper contigit ut Patres surgendo assensum sententiae deputationis praebuerint. Primo quidem die suffragiorum, cum quaestio esset de tertia parte primae emendationis, nondum adhibita indicatione a subsecretario, deinde semper facta, plures surrexerunt adeo ut necesse foret numerum surgentium capere, ut constaret de suffragiis. Magna deinde confusio exorta est, et ista emendatio, quamvis majore forsan numero sic accepta, in crastinum diem dilata est. Postero die R^{ms} Relator ex ambone Patres monuit, deputationem emendationem istam admittere nolle. Omnes fere eam rejiciendam surgendo statim dixerunt.

and repudiated all dogmas extracted from the speculations of divines, and not distinctly founded on the recorded Word of God,[28] and that of Archbishop Darboy, who foretold that a decree which increased authority without increasing power, and claimed for one man, whose infallibility was only now defined, the obedience which the world refused to the whole Episcopate, whose right had been unquestioned in the Church for 1800 years, would raise up new hatred and new suspicion, weaken the influence of religion over society, and wreak swift ruin on the temporal power.[29]

The general debate had lasted three weeks, and forty-nine bishops

[28] Quodcumque Dominus Noster non dixerit etiam si metaphysice aut physice certissimum nunquam basis esse poterit dogmatis divinae fidei. Fides enim per auditum, auditus autem non per scientiam sed per verba Christi. . . . Non ipsa verba S. Scripturae igitur, sed genuinus sensus, sive litteralis, sive metaphoricus, prout in mente Dei revelantis fuit, atque ab Ecclesiae patribus semper atque ubique concorditer expositus, et quem nos omnes juramento sequi abstringimur, hic tantummodo sensus Vera Dei revelatio dicendus est. . . . Tota antiquitas silet vel contraria est. . . . Verbum Dei volo et hoc solum, quaeso et quidem indubitatum, ut dogma fiat.

[29] Hanc de infallibilitate his conditionibus ortam et isto modo introductam aggredi et definire non possumus, ut arbitror, quin eo ipso tristem viam sternamus tum cavillationibus impiorum, tum etiam objectionibus moralem hujus Concilii auctoritatem minuentibus. Et hoc quidem eo magis cavendum est, quod jam prostent et pervulgentur scripta et acta quae vim ejus et rationem labefactare attentant; ita ut nedum animos sedare queat et quae pacis sunt afferre, e contra nova dissensionis et discordiarum semina inter Christianos spargere videatur. . . . Porro, quod in tantis Ecclesiae angustiis laboranti mundo remedium affertur? Iis omnibus qui ab humero indocili excutiunt onera antiquitus imposita, et consuetudine Patrum veneranda, novum ideoque grave et odiosum onus imponi postulant schematis auctores. Eos omnes qui infirmae fidei sunt novo et non satis opportuno dogmate quasi obruunt, doctrina scilicet hucusque nondum definita, praesentis discussionis vulnere nonnihil sauciata, et a Concilio cujus libertatem minus aequo apparere plurimi autumant et dicunt pronuntianda. . . . Mundus aut aeger est aut perit, non quod ignorat veritatem vel veritatis doctores, sed quod ab ea refugit eamque sibi non vult imperari. Igitur, si eam respuit, quum a toto docentis Ecclesiae corpore, id est ab 800 episcopis per totum orbem sparsis et simul cum S. Pontifice infallibilibus praedicatur, quanto magis quum ab unico Doctore infallibili, et quidem ut tali recenter declarato praedicabitur? Ex altera parte, ut valeat et efficaciter agat auctoritas necesse est non tantum eam affirmari, sed insuper admitti. . . . Syllabus totam Europam pervasit at cui malo mederi potuit etiam ubi tanquam oraculum infallibile susceptus est? Duo tantum restabant regna in quibus religio florebat, non de facto tantum, sed et de jure dominans: Austria scilicet et Hispania. Atqui in his duobus regnis ruit iste Catholicus ordo, quamvis ab infallibili auctoritate commendatus, imo forsan saltem in Austria eo praecise quod ab hac commendatus. Audeamus igitur res uti sunt considerare. Nedum Sanctissimi Pontificis independens infallibilitas praejudicia et objectiones destruat quae permultos a fide avertunt, ea potius arguit et aggravat. . . . Nemo non videt si politicae gnarus, quae semina dissensionum schema nostrum contineat et quibus periculis exponatur ipsa temporalis Sanctae sedis potestas.

were still to speak, when it was brought to a close by an abrupt division on the 3rd of June. For twenty-four hours the indignation of the minority was strong. It was the last decisive opportunity for them to reject the legitimacy of the Council. There were some who had despaired of it from the beginning, and held that the Bull *Multiplices* deprived it of legal validity. But it had not been possible to make a stand at a time when no man knew whether he could trust his neighbour, and when there was fair ground to hope that the worst rules would be relaxed. When the second regulation, interpreted according to the interruptors of Strossmayer, claimed the right of proclaiming dogmas which part of the Episcopate did not believe, it became doubtful whether the bishops could continue to sit without implicit submission. They restricted themselves to a protest, thinking that it was sufficient to meet words with words, and that it would be time to act when the new principle was actually applied. By the vote of the 3rd of June the obnoxious regulation was enforced in a way evidently injurious to the minority and their cause. The chiefs of the opposition were now convinced of the invalidity of the Council, and advised that they should all abstain from speaking, and attend at St. Peter's only to negative by their vote the decree which they disapproved. In this way they thought that the claim to ecumenicity would be abolished without breach or violence. The greater number were averse to so vigorous a demonstration; and Hefele threw the great weight of his authority into their scale. He contended that they would be worse than their word if they proceeded to extremities on this occasion. They had announced that they would do it only to prevent the promulgation of a dogma which was opposed. If that were done the Council would be revolutionary and tyrannical; and they ought to keep their strongest measure in reserve for that last contingency. The principle of unanimity was fundamental. It admitted no ambiguity, and was so clear, simple, and decisive, that there was no risk in fixing on it. The Archbishops of Paris, Milan, Halifax, the Bishops of Djakovar, Orleans, Marseilles, and most of the Hungarians, yielded to these arguments, and accepted the policy of less strenuous colleagues, while retaining the opinion that the Council was of no authority. But there were some who deemed it unworthy and inconsistent to attend an assembly which they had ceased to respect.

The debate on the several paragraphs lasted till the beginning of July, and the decree passed at length with eighty-eight dissentient votes. It was made known that the infallibility of the Pope would be promulgated in solemn session on the 18th, and that all who were present would be required to sign an act of submission. Some bishops of the minority thereupon proposed that they should all attend, repeat their vote, and refuse their signature. They exhorted their brethren to set a conspicuous example of courage and fidelity, as the Catholic world would not remain true to the faith if the bishops were believed to have faltered. But it was certain that there were men amongst them who would renounce their belief rather than incur the penalty of excommunication, who preferred authority to proof, and accepted the Pope's declaration, "La tradizione son'io." It was resolved by a small majority that the opposition should renew its negative vote in writing, and should leave Rome in a body before the session. Some of the most conscientious and resolute adversaries of the dogma advised this course. Looking to the immediate future, they were persuaded that an irresistible reaction was at hand, and that the decrees of the Vatican Council would fade away and be dissolved by a power mightier than the Episcopate and a process less perilous than schism. Their disbelief in the validity of its work was so profound that they were convinced that it would perish without violence, and they resolved to spare the Pope and themselves the indignity of a rupture. Their last manifesto, *La dernière Heure*, is an appeal for patience, an exhortation to rely on the guiding, healing hand of God.[30] They deemed that they had assigned the course which was to save the Church, by teaching the Catholics to reject a Council which was neither legitimate in constitution, free in action, nor unanimous in doctrine, but to observe moderation in contesting an authority over which great catastrophes impend. They conceived that it would thus be possible to save the peace and unity of the Church without sacrifice of faith and reason.

---

[30] Espérons que l'excès du mal provoquera le retour du bien. Ce Concile n'aura eu qu'un heureux résultat, celui d'en appeler un autre, réuni dans la liberté. . . . Le Concile du Vatican demeurera stérile, comme tout ce qui n'est pas éclos sous le souffle de l'Esprit Saint. Cependant il aura révélé non seulement jusqu'à quel point l'absolutisme peut abuser des meilleures institutions et des meilleurs instincts, mais aussi ce que vaut encore le droit, alors même qu'il n'a plus que le petit nombre pour le défendre. . . . Si la multitude passe quand même nous lui prédisons qu'elle n'ira pas loin. Les Spartiates, qui étaient tombés aux Thermopyles pour défendre les terres de la liberté, avaient preparé au flot impitoyable du despotisme la défaite de Salamis.

[15]

The Vatican Council:
Correspondence with
William Ewart Gladstone

Rome, January 1, 1870

My dear Mr. Gladstone,

The events at Paris, coincident with the change in the position of things at Rome, suggest a possibility of exercising some influence on the progress of the Council. Each step taken by the Roman Court has added to the danger and increased the need for prudent and intelligent action on the part of the States.

The Regulations which were the first document issued, assumed to the Pope the right of making decrees and defining dogmas, and left to the Council only the function of approving. It has not even a right to propose questions for its own consideration, as nothing can be submitted to the Council without the permission of a Committee representing the Pope. Only eighteen French bishops signed a remonstrance against these arrangements.

On the 30th of December a bishop, Strossmayer, objected to the title of a decree, and to the formula which excluded the Episcopate from all real share in the defining authority, and he was stopped by one of the presiding Cardinals, Capalti, on the ground that this point had been settled by the Regulations. He passed to another topic and the other bishops submitted in silence.

The position therefore is this, that the Pope alone proposes decrees, that he can refuse his sanction to any act of the Council, that the

Published in Acton, *Correspondence*, pp. 89–113. With the exception of the letter of 1 March 1870, the correspondence between Acton and Gladstone—of which this is a selection—is reprinted in McElrath, pp. 166–182.

Council cannot prevent, invalidate, or rescind, any act of his. This is now no longer merely a claim of the Roman Court: it has been accepted and implicitly acknowledged by the Council. The sole legislative authority has been abandoned to the Pope. It includes the right of issuing dogmatic decrees, and involves the possession of all the infallibility which the Church claims.

This is not distinct or final, but it is an important step towards the intended dogma, and an indication of the amount of resisting power among the bishops.

The second manifestation of policy was the Constitution reciting the excommunications directed against the spirit of civilised governments. It is nothing less than a revival of the Bull *In Coena Domini*, which was dropped by Ganganelli when he suppressed the Jesuits, and which naturally appears again, now that the Jesuits are in power. Everything is done to mollify foreign Powers and especially France, on the ground that States having a Concordat are exempt from these censures, which is utterly untrue and cannot be said officially.

The Irish bishops wish to have the Constitution modified in this particular, that they shall have authority to absolve in all the reserved cases; by which, in fact, they would accept the principle and incur the complicity. They will hardly protest, as it is not submitted to the Council, but is an independent, sovereign act of the Papacy.

Thirdly, a paper was distributed, containing censures upon a great number of opinions. It anathematises those who deny several of the fundamental doctrines of Christianity, but it includes a condemnation of secular science. It declares that human science cannot be independent of divine Revelation, and explains this by saying that science has no certainty and no authority apart from that of the Church and her organs. It follows that the opinions received and approved here may lawfully be supported by censures against any disturbing conclusions of historical or physical science.

This would revive the action of the Index in its extreme form, not only against opinions, but against mathematical discoveries and historical documents.

In these three papers the papal absolutism reveals itself completely, in its hostility to the rights of the Church, of the State, and of the intellect. We have to meet an organised conspiracy to establish a power which would be the most formidable enemy of liberty as well as of science throughout the world.

It can only be met and defeated through the Episcopate, and the Episcopate is exceedingly helpless.

There is indeed a considerable minority opposed to the Papal Infallibility, and to the other enormous claims of Rome, and its numbers have been increasing up to the present time. There are even signs of organisation. An international committee has been appointed, consisting of the most enlightened bishops of France, Germany, and America. They have concerted a plan of action in case of an attempt to proclaim the Dogma by acclamation; and they have brought their numbers to something like two hundred. The two first discussions, on Tuesday and Thursday, were entirely occupied by speakers of this party. To the surprise of everybody several Italians were amongst them. I have before me now the notes made for Menabrea on the character and probable opinions of the Italian bishops, and they are not entirely unfavourable.

It is not likely that the opposition will add further to its numbers. The disintegrating influences will soon begin to tell. The most ardent opponents feel their helplessness, and look for encouragement to the laity. The Constitution, containing so many political censures, awakened hopes that the Governments at home would be roused from their apathy and that the opposition would have something to fall back upon. This idea has begun to show itself lately in several unexpected quarters. It was expressed to me by one of the most conspicuous and moderate of the Prussian prelates. These men find themselves abandoned to the wiles and threats of Rome. All that hope and fear can do will be done to break down their resistance, and it is sustained by no human inducements whatever. I know that one of those who showed courage and vigour in the opening debate, on the 28th, has since complained that he is left to his fate, that he is a ruined man.

The result of the first two days of discussion has been to make it certain and notorious that the elements of a real and sincere opposition exist, an opposition which is worth supporting, which is almost sure to prevail if it is supported, and almost sure to be crushed if it is not. The position is therefore essentially altered, since Hohenlohe's proposal fell to the ground, and the policy of indifference was adopted by the Powers.

That policy was adopted by other States in consequence of the determination of the French Government to take no part, and to send no ambassador. Prussia, Bavaria, Portugal, and, I presume, other

States, waited to follow the example of France. The Emperor put himself in communication with the bishops who were likely to exercise influence at the Council, even with some who are unfriendly to the Empire, such as Dupanloup, and showed them clearly what his hopes and wishes were. Maret saw him also, and was at one time confident that an ambassador would be sent. But the Prince de la Tour d'Auvergne, advised by M. Armand, late Secretary at Rome, and a strong partisan, appears to have prevented it. M. Ollivier is a man of another stamp. He has seriously studied religious questions, and entertains views on the old French Church, and the Concordat which destroyed it, which he will very probably keep secret for some time. But his views on the Roman question are known, and he has lately confided to Nigra his sentiments regarding the French occupation. It will certainly not be his own wish to follow in this respect the line of his predecessors. He will have the support of at least half the French Episcopate if he abandons it. At this moment Dupanloup relies on about forty, of near seventy who are in Rome. When the crisis comes there will not be quite so many. But it may come in such a shape that Darboy, Dupanloup, and their friends will have to look for the aid which the State alone can give. The idea of proclaiming the Pope infallible by acclamation is not given up, and if the Roman party attempts to carry it by a mere vote and to crush the minority, few bishops will dare to risk a schism. They will know that they can protest without fear of isolation and schism, if they are backed by their Government. The ablest and most popular of the French bishops will meet the new minister half-way if he gives them the least encouragement. I know that they have been considering what their position would be if they had to leave the Council, with a public protest.

The States, at present, are exerting little or no influence. The Austro-Hungarian Episcopate, indeed, is nearly united, but not by reason of any advice from the ambassador, who has little weight, or from Beust, who seems to have no ideas about the Council, either from ignorance of Catholic matters or from natural levity. Spain is unrepresented at Rome. The Prussian Minister is a Protestant, and on that account, probably, the few Prussian bishops do not bestow their confidence on him. One of them has admitted this to me, and both Baron Arnim and other members of the Legation have spoken of it to me with much regret and annoyance. During the summer Arnim advised Bismarck to send an ambassador to the Council, and he is still strongly of the same opinion, although he would be, to some extent, eclipsed. The experience of the last few weeks has confirmed his original idea. It would certainly be satisfactory to him and to his Government, which fully entered into his view in the summer, if the example of France made it possible to send an ambassador for Germany. As Bavaria would unite in accrediting the same ambassador, there would even be a slight point gained in the existence of one representative for all extra-Austrian Germany. Count Lavradio arrived with credentials as ambassador for the Council, but he put them in his pocket, and declared himself only a Minister when he found what the other Powers have done. Spain, of course, will be guided by the consideration whether it would or would not be convenient to reopen its embassy here under cover of the Council.

The question will be a very anxious one for Italy. Menabrea was not prepared with any definite plan of action for the Council. The new Ministers, Lanza and Sella, are both impatient of Church questions, and have never attended to the Roman difficulty. It is left entirely to the Foreign Secretary, Visconti Venosta. He has already arranged with Lanza that he shall be free to use what means he can to assist the better portion of the bishops. Their property is still in the hands of the Government, and their position is very trying and unsettled. Arrangements will be made for regulating their affairs as speedily and as favourably as possible, giving the preference to those who best deserve it. There is even some idea of giving back the unsold property of the Church, to be administered by lay trustees. But this is a legislative, not an administrative question, and cannot be undertaken without interference of Parliament. I don't even know what Visconti thinks of the plan. It has much occupied his Segretario Generale, Albert Blanc. But I know that Visconti is alive to the importance of doing something for the Council. Lavradio has charge of Italian interests here, and the Pope has said something to him of his wish to reopen negotiations on ecclesiastical questions. If they send an envoy for the Council, the probable failure or at least delay of his negotiations with the Vatican would not so much matter. By sending him for the Council they would avoid the affront or awkwardness of having no Nuncio in return. And, in appearance, the mission would have a conciliatory effect, and might be a step towards an understanding. There will be a great difficulty about the title of the sovereign to be represented; but that alone will hardly prevent the sending of an Italian ambassador.

It is the French, not the Italian, whom they will be afraid of at

Rome. The change of Ministry has already caused much alarm, though the ambassador Banneville declares that there will be no change of policy. I am told, confidentially, that nobody would do better, or would be less distasteful than Rouher. If the new Ministry makes some general profession of an intention to bring about the recall of the French troops, the presence of Rouher would have a positively reassuring effect upon the Court as well as the Council. Indeed any ambassador to the Council would be a new security, for the time. Yet I can imagine that a time may come when Dupanloup himself will look for the departure of the French as the way to save the Church.

My very gloomy view of the prospects which are before us is not the effect of a momentary change for the worse. On the contrary, the opposition are jubilant to-day. Cardinal Rauscher, who was supposed to be thoroughly Roman, has circulated a paper against Papal Infallibility, and led the attack on Tuesday. He was supported by Italian prelates. Two whole days have been entirely occupied with speeches against the decrees proposed in the name of the Pope, and there are still eighteen speakers to be heard on both sides of the same question. Time has been gained for the preparation of a paper which the bishops have asked me to obtain from Germany, and which they think will be decisive. The arrival of Hefele, the new bishop of Rottenburg, with whom no Roman divine will bear comparison for a moment, is expected daily, and the bravest of the bishops, the Croatian, Strossmayer, has made a very great impression by his eloquence. I live almost entirely with the opposition, and seeing and hearing what I do, and knowing the bishops as I have learned to know them before and since coming here, I am bound to say that I do not believe that the means of preventing the worst excess exist within the Council. In the case of almost every bishop it would be possible to point out the way in which his position may be forced or turned. The only invincible opponent is the man who is prepared, in extremity, to defy excommunication, that is, who is as sure of the fallibility of the Pope as of revealed truth. Excepting Strossmayer and perhaps Hefele, I don't know of such a man among the bishops; and some of the strongest admit that they will accept what they do not succeed in preventing. It is to give these men strength and courage that the help of the State is needed. The time seems to have arrived when the counsel of England, or of other Powers speaking in concert with England, would effect the necessary change in the policy of France. I understand that the

Emperor hesitated, and was alarmed at finding that some prelates deemed hostile to the Empire—Bonnechose, for instance—recommended the sending of an extra-ordinary envoy, while some of his own friends gave opposite advice. Lavalette, I am told, was not favourable to the proposal. If anything is done it would probably be better that it should be done at Paris, or at least not through Lavalette alone.

I now hear that the international Committee has been dissolved by the Pope, as savouring of clubs and revolution; and that the Regulations will be made stricter, so as to take away all liberty of speech.

If you do not altogether reject the idea even of indirect action, the time has unmistakably arrived when it is most likely to take effect.— I remain, yours very sincerely,

Acton

[Postscript:] Necessary precautions have delayed this letter till to-day, the 4th. Twenty-five Germans have protested, like the French, and no addition to the Regulations has yet been made public. On the third day of debate the opposition continued to speak, and an Eastern Patriarch pronounced against all innovation, in the name of the Oriental Christians.

Hawarden Castle, Chester, January 8, '70

My dear Lord Acton,

I take the opportunity of a messenger from the Foreign Office to write a few lines.

My answer to your appeal was written on the instant, and I stated that which first occurred to me, namely, the additional difficulties which the rampancy of Ultramontanism would put in the way of our passing measures of public Education which should be equitable and not otherwise than favourable to religion.

But in truth this was only a specimen. There is the Land Bill to be settled, and there are the wings of the Church Bill: one the measure relating to Loans for Building, the other having reference to the Ecclesiastical Titles Act. Even the first will be further poisoned, and either or both of the two last may become the subject of fierce and distracting controversy so as to impede our winding up the great chapter of account between the State and not the Roman Church or Priesthood but the people of Ireland.

The truth is that Ultramontanism is an anti-social power, and never has it more undisguisedly assumed that character than in the Syllabus.

Of all the Prelates at Rome none have a finer opportunity, to none is a more crucial test now applied, than to those of the United States. For if there, where there is nothing of covenant, of restraint, or of equivalents between the Church and the State, the propositions of the Syllabus are still to have the countenance of the Episcopate, it becomes really a little difficult to maintain in argument the civil right of such persons to toleration, however conclusive is the argument of policy in favour of granting it.

I can hardly bring myself to speculate or care on what particular day the foregone conclusion is to be finally adopted. My grief is sincere and deep, but it is at the whole thing, so ruinous in its consequences as they concern Faith.

In my view the size of the minority, though important, is not nearly so important as the question whether there will be a minority at all. Whatever its numbers, if formed of good men, it will be a nucleus for the future, and will have an immense moral force even at the present moment, a moral force sufficient perhaps to avert much of the mischief which the acts of the majority would naturally entail. For this I shall watch with intense interest.—Believe me, most sincerely yours,

W. E. Gladstone

Rome, February 16, 1870

My dear Mr. Gladstone,

The opinion which I expressed to you many weeks ago, that the opposition would prevail with aid from the European Powers, and would fail without it, has been adopted by the leading bishops of the party. I am writing now not only with their knowledge, but at their express and most urgent request, renewed several times during the last week. It is better that I should mention no names; but Lord Granville will easily remember one bishop with whom I have long been on intimate terms.

The habit of exercising absolute authority, and the habit of submitting to it, have reached such a point in the Catholic Church that the prophecy in the last pages of *Janus* is very nearly realised. There is very little hope that the Council, left to itself, will have sufficient vigour and consistency to resist the pressure of the Court. There is a determined minority, but it is so small that it will be overwhelmed if it stands alone. It carries with it a considerable group of undecided, perplexed, and ignorant men, who will resist only up to a certain point. They are impressed with the discouraging belief that the Governments abandon them, and that public opinion, except in part of Germany, is indifferent to their struggle. Rome is determined to carry things to extremity, and it is certain that many of the opposing bishops are prepared to yield before coming to extremity. Efforts are being made by them to check the demonstrations which Döllinger has provoked, and the action of France has hardly been perceptible.

The question of Infallibility will be brought forward shortly. Yesterday and to-day French bishops urged that it should be introduced immediately, as it was the only question they were brought here to decide.

The language of the French Government has been clear enough, but its effect has been weakened by the Nuncio at Paris, by the ambassador here, and by the belief that there is no understanding between France and Italy as to the settlement of the Roman question.

Two days ago a definite message was sent by the Emperor to Cardinal Antonelli, in which the Emperor declared that he could not afford to have a schism in France where all the *employé* class, all the literary class, and even the Faubourg St. Germain are against the Infallibility of the Pope. He added that it would dissolve all the engagements existing between France and Rome. They are unmoved by these threats, because they expect to obtain an apparent unanimity among the bishops, and they think that if the bishops yield the rest will follow.

Hitherto, it appears, the French Government have shared this opinion. Seeing at the head of the opposition men notorious as defenders of the Syllabus and agitators against the recall of the French troops, they must have suspected that they would not resist to the uttermost the proposal to sanction and dogmatise propositions which scarcely go further than the Syllabus, and that they would not support the Emperor in a course of action adverse to the temporal power. That such a man as the Bishop of Orleans should be really willing to sacrifice the Roman State, which he has so warmly defended, out of aversion for the ideas of the Syllabus, which he has defended not less warmly, implies so vast a change that they might reasonably hesitate.

But the change has really occurred, and the proof will be in the hands of the French Government before this reaches you. I have induced the bishop alluded to at the beginning of my letter to commit himself explicitly, and I forwarded yesterday to M. Daru a paper drawn up under the bishop's eye exposing the anti-social character and the political danger of the *Schema de Ecclesia*. The bishop says quite truly that it only requires to be understood in order to rouse the indignation and anger of every Government in Europe. For the Canons which have been published are the most innocent part of the *Schema*. It makes civil legislation on all points of contract, marriage, education, clerical immunities, mortmain, even on many questions of taxation and Common Law, subject to the legislation of the Church, which would be simply the arbitrary will of the Pope. Most assuredly no man accepting such a code could be a loyal subject, or fit for the enjoyment of political privileges. In this sense the French bishops have written to the French Government, and that is what they ask me to write to you.

They see no human remedy for this peril other than the intervention of the Powers.

They say that as long as the question at issue was Infallibility, which is a question of dogmatic theology and only indirectly dangerous to society, the abstention of the Governments might be justified. But it is not now the only question, and the *Schema de Ecclesia*, to be followed by a yet extremer *Schema de Romano Pontifice*, proves what the object, what the consequence of exalting the attributes of the Papacy would be for the civilised world. They therefore desire, through me, to make a direct appeal to the Government of the Queen. They believe that you cannot have read the extracts published by the German press without understanding as they do the purport and the peril of the measures proposed to the Council by the Pope. They believe that you are in a position to act in the matter without offending susceptibilities. They do not wish to give to their appeal the undue form of actual suggestions. But I can say that the idea in their minds is that England should urge the Great Powers to take united action, in the shape of a joint—or identical—note upon the subject of the new *Schema*, and of the Dogma which would include it. Of course this implies the hope that a new settlement will be come to with Italy, as to the temporal power—a settlement which cannot well be entirely contingent on the result of the Council.

I have the best reason to believe that Prussia would be willing to join in such a step as this; though the co-operation of Bavaria might not now be obtainable. Austria has been, as far as its Government is concerned, an impediment to our cause. The Emperor Napoleon would have great influence on the Court of Vienna, and they would only have to be invited to support their own Episcopate.

The thing could probably be done by means of a good understanding between England and France; more especially as France does not profess to wish that you should act directly on the Court of Rome.

The Archbishop of Paris is not one of those who are in the secret of this appeal. His relations with the Emperor prevented me from consulting him upon it. Whatever may be his political sentiments in the matter, I am able to say positively that, in the interest of the Council, he substantially agrees.—I remain, dear Mr. Gladstone, very faithfully yours,

Acton

11 Carlton House Terrace, S.W., March 1, '70

My dear Lord Acton,

I have waited for an opportunity to answer by messenger your letter of the 16th. Immediately on its arrival I sent it to Lord Clarendon. He has had every desire to forward your views though with little hope of effecting any considerable result. In truth I am myself sorrowfully conscious that it is in our power to do little or nothing with advantage beyond taking care that the principal Governments are aware of our general view, and our repugnance to the meditated proceedings, so that they may call on us for any aid we can give in case of such. However, Lord Clarendon has gone beyond this and has conveyed to the German Courts the kind of intimation you wished. But Bismarck apprehends positive mischief from his taking a forward position, and the King of Bavaria is, I suppose, disabled by the overthrow of Hohenlohe. He (B.) points to the attitude of Austria as indecisive, and I understand him to say the only thing to be done is to exhort the Austrian bishops to work with their German brethren, and that as far as Prussia is concerned they may rely upon being thoroughly supported by the Government on their return home. As respects France, you know we have done the little that in us lay.

I never read a more extraordinary letter than that of Newman to Bishop Ullathorne, which doubtless you have seen: admirable in its strength, strange in its weakness, incomparable in speculation, tame and emasculated in action.

Apprehending that fear will be the governing agent in determining the issue at Rome, I can only desire, as I do from my heart, that the fears of the majority may be more violent than those of the minority. A great courage, I suppose, may win, on that side. Nothing else can.— Ever yours sincerely,

W. E. Gladstone

Rome, March 10, 1870

My dear Mr. Gladstone,

You have already seen, by the production of the decree of Infallibility on Sunday, that the position of things has altered in Rome.

The Pope has at last openly identified himself with the extreme party, at the very moment when France is beginning to use sterner language, and the minority is protesting against the Regulations in terms that threaten the authority and the Ecumenicity of the Council. The change was sudden, and probably the deciding motive was the desire to be beforehand with the Germans, whose protest was expected to be more threatening than the one which the French presented on Friday. But there was also the publication of Daru's letters in the *Times* of Thursday, and the fact that the Pope had shown a disposition to accept a formula proposed by the archbishops of Rouen and Algiers, and others of the Centre.

If you have seen the French protest—I sent it on Sunday to the *Perseveranza,* and I suppose it has been copied in the other papers— you will understand how flagrant an insult to the minority is the proposal of the new Dogma at such a moment and in such a form.

In Chapters VIII and IX the Protest affirms the principle that no Dogma can be proclaimed which does not command a moral unanimity among the bishops representing churches. The Germans have added, at the end of VIII, where those words occur, a very significant passage, which I can only communicate to you in strict confidence: *Haec conditio pro Concilio Vaticano eo magis urgenda esse videtur, quum ad ferenda suffragia tot patres admissi sunt de quibus non constat evidenter, utrum jure tantum ecclesiastico, an etiam jure divino ipsis votum decisivum competat.* It is obvious that, if the office of the bishops in Council is to bear testimony to the faith of their respective flocks and to the tradition of their several churches, the numerous bishops made out of Roman Monsignori, who have no jurisdiction and no flock, are a foreign as well as an arbitrary element in the Council.

The last paragraph of IX, where the bishops say that the claim to make dogmas in spite of the minority endangers the authority, liberty, and Ecumenicity of the Council, was inserted by me. These two passages supply materials for further action, in reply to the invitation to discuss the new decree. I have proposed a declaration in which the bishops would say that they cannot admit this topic for discussion until the doubts they have just expressed as to the authority and legitimacy of the Council, in the eyes of the world and of posterity, are removed by an explicit explanation of the points which are ambiguous in the new Regulation.

There is no immediate prospect that this measure will be adopted. The minority are in great confusion and uncertainty, and disposed to rely on external help.

There is no doubt, I think, that the issuing of the proposed decree puts the Governments in a position more favourable for action. The prerogative of inerrancy or infallibility in all questions of morals, that is, in all questions of conscience, gives to the Pope the ultimate control over the actions of Catholics, in politics and in society. We know also, from the *Schema de Ecclesia,* in favour of what principles and of what interests that supreme and arbitrary power will be exerted. The Catholics will be bound, not only by the will of future Popes, but by that of former Popes, so far as it has been solemnly declared. They will not be at liberty to reject the deposing power, or the system of the Inquisition, or any other criminal practice or idea which has been established under penalty of excommunication. They at once become irreconcilable enemies of civil and religious liberty. They will have to profess a false system of morality, and to repudiate literary and scientific sincerity. They will be as dangerous to civilised society in the school as in the State.

Divine truth cannot long be bound up peaceably with blasphemous error, and the healthy forces in the Church will end by casting off the disease. But there would be a disastrous interval and a formidable struggle. We know something of the vitality of religious error. Rome taught for four centuries and more that no Catholic could be saved who denied that heretics ought to be put to death.

The proposed decree makes the Infallibility of the Pope embrace everything to which the Infallibility of the Church extends. But in the twenty-one Canons *de Ecclesia* the Church is declared infallible in all matters that are necessary to the preservation of the faith. The Infallibility of the Pope would therefore be unconditional and unlimited, as he alone would have to decide what is necessary for the preservation of the faith. My letter has just been interrupted by a visit from the most learned prelate in Rome, Hefele, bishop of Rottenburg. He says distinctly that the Pope would have no limits to his Infallibility, and therefore to his authority, but such as he might choose to set himself.

There was no exaggeration in that which I wrote to you last December of the political dangers involved in this insane enterprise. Its bearings on English affairs, and on some of the measures which you have in hand, especially its consequences for the conflict against sin and unbelief, are incalculable. I am convinced that you see this as clearly as if you had passed the winter here, and I only wish that you might deem it consistent with policy and duty to speak a word of warning in Parliament, or in a letter that might be published, such as would sound the alarm far and wide.

I hope we shall yet succeed in preserving the Church from this great calamity. But the papacy itself cannot cast off the guilt and the penalty or recover the moral authority it enjoyed before.—I remain, my dear Mr. Gladstone, ever faithfully yours,

Acton

[Postscript:] I am obliged to mark this letter *private* both on account of the quotation from the Protest, and of the mention of Hefele.

Rome, March 20

My dear Mr. Gladstone,

It appears to be ascertained that the ambassadors will be refused. Meanwhile M. de Banneville has gone to plead his own cause at Paris; and Bismarck has telegraphed that he has never opposed the joint action of the Powers, as nothing of the kind has been proposed, so that Arnim has seen the Bishop of Orleans and has despatched a courier urging his Government to take a more active part.

The French Government, having accomplished nothing hitherto beyond giving the minority some hope of future aid, will have to make up its mind decidedly on the line to take, and it will be a good opportunity to bring neighbourly influence to bear.

The Powers have a distinct claim upon France, as France is responsible for all the evil that the Council may do. Since the *Schema de Ecclesia* and the Decree *de Infallibilitate Pontificis* were published, there can be no uncertainty as to the designs of Rome. We know that it seeks to be made absolute over the consciences of men, and we know for what civil purposes it will employ its power.

The danger which thus threatens religion and society is made possible by the French occupation, and would be impossible without it. The French Ministry do not profess to be indifferent to the consequences, or to deny the danger for which they are responsible. It threatens other countries quite as seriously as France, and they have good ground for remonstrance and a perfect right to insist in the strongest way that such troubles should not be caused by a Power professing to be liberal and friendly.

The religious pretext for the occupation cannot be urged at a time when it is indirectly producing effects injurious to religion, and is continued only on account of the interest which France has in dividing Italy. The liberal Ministry of Ollivier and Daru are preparing grave internal difficulties for England and Germany in order to keep up difficulties of another kind for the Italians.

If they do not send an ambassador, they have no other security to offer to Europe, except the recall of the troops. To give up the Concordat and all the system of the French Church would be, at least for the time, an injury rather than a benefit to religion, and a blow struck not so much at the Pope as at the Episcopate.

It is easy to show that the financial embarrassment of Italy is increased by the Roman question. It excludes the conservative element from political life, and makes it a merit with great part of the population to resist the law. The Government is driven to the resource of confiscating Church property by the Roman difficulty itself. The religious houses are suppressed, the schools of divinity reduced, the priesthood almost starved, because France is determined to keep the Pope on his despotic throne. It is a policy which degrades the Italian Government in the eyes of the nation, nurses the revolutionary passion, and hinders the independence of the country, and which can no longer be defended on the score of religious liberty. The French protectorate has become as injurious to Catholicism as to the Italian State, and it is about to prove as pernicious to other countries as it is to Italy.

I find one part of the Episcopate busily trying to find sophisms that will justify persecution, despotism, regicide, and the other things to which the Church is committed if the Popes are infallible; and I find others anxiously awaiting the active intervention of the European Powers. Both seem to me to suggest the same moral.

All the Governments that dislike to act now, and look forward to some mode of self-protection after the Dogma is adopted, must prefer that the necessity should be averted, that the Definition should be prevented before it involves them in struggles and disputes at home.

If it is true that Count Daru is nearly alone in the Ministry in the view he takes of the Council, it will be impossible for him to stand the refusal of his ambassador. His resignation would greatly weaken the Ministry. Probably he will either insist, or seek some alternative.—I remain, yours very sincerely,

Acton

[16]
Lord Acton on the
Roman Question

Ladies and Gentlemen:

It is really gratifying to attend a meeting where neighbours of different religions unite in promoting the interests of one religious body, for I venture to say that the presence of protestants in this room is not only generous and charitable, but wise and patriotic. . . . Since the country has undertaken the great work of educating the people, so much of sectarian jealousy and rivalry has been awakened that I heartily rejoice over this instance of cordial co-operation. . . . For the time has come, later in this than in other countries, but it has come at last, when society has become conscious that it is responsible for much guilt and suffering by resting content with a state of things which degrades whole classes by making it almost impossible for them to educate the souls of their children. . . . This is a most important and salutary change, but it imposes new burdens on us. There is a widely spread opinion that the state is interested only in giving moral instruction, and that if morality can be imparted without reference to creeds, the force of dogmatic conviction will be undermined, and sectarianism will be gradually extinguished. No opinion, I think, can be more erroneous or impolitic. The security against the blindness and violence of religious passion is not indifference but charity. . . . Most of the intolerance that disturbs and disgraces Christendom comes much less from excess of zeal or intensity of faith than from the want of it, from the weakness that comes from ignorance and doubt-ignorance of truth, doubt of the providence of God. . . . When a man meets opposition with uproar

Report of a speech by Acton, given at a Catholic soirée at the music hall in Kidderminster (Worcestershire) in January 1871. Published in the *Kidderminster Shuttle*, 4 February 1871. Reprinted in McElrath, pp. 240–245. Ellipses mark applause by the audience.

355

and bullying it generally happens that he knows he cannot meet it with the patient serenity of conviction. Indeed, the state cannot forego the aid of religion in preserving social virtue. It is its interest that religion should retain the attachment of its followers, and exhort to the utmost its elevating influence upon them. Knowledge alone may protect men against error, but it cannot against sin. One of the great tests of moral character is fidelity to religious conviction, because it is a duty exposed to much temptation, and enforced and supported by no human penalty. Therefore it is just that when we make efforts to supply the necessary religious instruction in our schools, all men should acknowledge that we are fulfilling a duty to society as well as to the church, and accomplishing a public work which no other machinery could do as well. . . . I do not for a moment attribute, or wish that I could attribute this friendly interest in our proceedings, this decay of the old spirit of antagonism to a feeling of indifference. But I do believe that some of the barriers which separated us from our countrymen are gradually falling, and that catholics will continue to be more trusted as they are better understood. . . . For many years the world has been moving in a direction which led to this result. The ancient connection of catholicism with the powers of the world, with state patronage and political privilege, is fast falling asunder all over Europe. All that was invidious in the position of the church, all that excited jealousy, or envy, or fear is rapidly disappearing. . . . The concordat is abolished in Austria; the separation of church and state is being carried out in Spain and Italy, and catholic Germany has been united under a protestant sceptre. . . . In particular cases it may be that religion has undergone a loss. It is commonly said, for instance, that the introduction of the voluntary system into France would lead to the extinction of the church in parts of the country. But so far as the effect of this almost universal change is felt amongst ourselves, I think it has been to our advantage. The influence of religion is deeper and more pure where it imposes sacrifices than where it is supported by endowments and dignities, and it is better that men should take their notion of catholicism from countries where its priests are devoted missionaries among the humble poor than where they enjoy the benefits of an established church. . . . There has been till now an uneasy contrast between the two. Catholicism associated with authority and catholicism associated with liberty have not always been in apparent harmony with each other. We have had to bear responsibility for ideas as far as possible from those in which we live. We were accused of inconsistency and insincerity. People said that we claimed liberty for ourselves where we were weak, and denied it where we were strong; that our liberality was only provisional—an expedient to be adopted or abandoned as it suited our purpose; that we were liberal from interest, but illiberal and intolerant in principle. And when these accusations were indignantly denied, people pointed to countries where the whole spirit of the people was different to ours. . . . But the instances on which these reproaches were founded have vanished away, and the time is not distant when the universal rule will be that liberty alone will be the true safeguard of the church. I do not of course underrate the causes of the division of Christendom, but I am sure that one of the chief social and political obstacles to the prosperity of our religion has been the fact that we were involved, or supposed to be implicated, in a system not our own and not congenial to us, by the absolutism of foreign countries and the advantage we were supposed to derive from it. For we live in a country where the idea of religious liberty is so strong that it makes and unmakes governments, and that the most vigorous current of popular favour known in our time was that which carried to power statesmen pledged to disestablish protestantism in Ireland. . . . I hope that current will not slacken, but will carry us over the shallows of prejudice which ignorance has made. I say ignorance, because it is not the reality of catholicism, but a false image and phantom of it, against which the public feeling and opinion are so easily roused. What we want is to be known to live, as it were, in a glass house, so that there may be no opportunity for confusion or misunderstanding. Do what we will we shall never overcome the antagonism between the church and the world. We shall always continue to be encountered by men in whom passion is too strong for principle, who are too intent on their objects to be particular in their choice of means, and who think that sin is better than justice if it can serve their religion and injure ours. That sort of fanaticism is natural to degenerate man, and is not the exclusive badge of any one denomination. But this is what we can do. We can make it plain that our claims are founded on principles which all true men acknowledge—that we seek for nothing partial and nothing exclusive; that we have no antagonism on public matters with any class of honest, sincere, and consistently liberal protestants. . . . If this were not the truth, if we were sailing under false colours, or putting any disguise on our real sentiments, then we should not be meeting here in amicable assembly to-day. I cannot exemplify what I have been saying better than by the resolution I am about to propose. I wish to call on your sympathy in the cause of the Pope at a time when his position, always a cause of solicitude to catholics, has become a matter of European interest. Every statesman perceives how important it is, not only that the Pope should be independent, but that the world should be convinced and satisfied of his independence. For the last four months it has been a daily question whether he would not declare that to remain longer in Rome in the present condition of things, with a rebellious people and a shattered throne, was incompatible with the performance of his duties as head of the church on earth. And his bitterest religious and political enemies are conscious that Pius IX, in his 8oth year, at the close of the longest and most unfortunate pontificate on record, going forth once more to eat the bread of exile and to die in a strange land, would afford a spectacle that would rouse the feelings of many millions of men, and would agitate Europe with an inevitable reaction. . . . Perhaps if he had fled at the first moment when he lost the corruptible crown of earthly monarchy, the consequences would have been less evident, and the effect less immediate, because men would have said only one thing was then at stake, and that, the least of his attributes, the temporal sovereignty alone. But he did not fly at the moment of danger. . . . He remained in the midst of the people he had ceased to govern, and became a witness of the revolution that overthrew not only his power but the whole of the system on which his power was founded. By his patience under this long and anxious trial he has stored up a new kind of power, which was unknown in more prosperous days. He has tried the experiment of living on at Rome under the altered conditions, and if he now declares that the attempt has proved a failure, that the position instead of mending has become intolerable, that the promised securities which were to be given in exchange for the patrimony of the church have been tested by experience and found wanting, he will depart from Rome, not only on account of his temporal sovereignty, but on account of his spiritual liberty, and for an order of things which is divine. . . . That will be a protest of tenfold force. It will reach further even than the sympathies of catholics, because, if the government and constitution of catholicism should be paralysed the whole civilised world would feel the shock. He would stand, not in the thankless character of a deposed sovereign appealing for the means of recovering his throne, but as the vicar of the King of Peace calling on all men to vindicate the sanctity of the moral law, in order that the reign of force may not become universal and perpetual, and that a religious authority may be able to maintain itself in the midst of our civilisation, not by violence and the tax of blood, but by the reverence of one-half of Christendom and the respect of the other. . . . If the Pope should fly from Rome on these grounds, it will be a serious blow to the Italian kingdom, and it is very much for the interest of Europe that so dangerous a crisis should be averted. Although these seem obvious considerations there are some people who refuse to see their force, and who are angry because an English man-of-war has been held at the disposal of the Pope, and because the Government has declared that the liberty of the papacy is an object to which England may be totally indifferent, and which is of no moment. But the liberty of the Pope is part of the liberty of the church, and the loss of that liberty is a danger to the state and to the peace of the world. . . . I will mention only two points that bear on this question. It is certain that the catholic world will never rest content if the Pope is unable to discharge his spiritual functions without impediment, or without the suspicion of undue influence. It is perfectly conceivable that a foreign power, taking advantage of this uneasy and agitated feeling, might attempt to restore the Pope by force of arms. Nothing can protect Europe from the danger of a new conflagration but some sincere and intelligent solution that will allay the alarm, and can only be brought about under the sanction of the European Powers. For this great question will be solved by violence if it is not settled by the pressure of opinion. But besides this, there is the home question. The Pope can determine the choice of every catholic bishop in the dominions of the queen—that is, some 45 bishops in the mother country, and a still greater number in the colonies. It is of the first importance to the empire that all these appointments should be made on purely religious grounds, and that the Pope, who controls them, should not even seem to be involved in the influence or political purposes of some foreign power whose interest it may be to raise up trouble to the British Government. Those who deny that England is concerned in the independence of the Pope therefore proclaim their indifference to the choice of our bishops, for instance, in Ireland. They believe that by allowing the papacy to fall under oppression, either the unity or the liberty of the church will suffer—that the links of our hierarchy will be weakened, or that we shall fall once more under the distrust and the odium of the times that are happily gone by. At any rate these manifestations of opinion are a proof that the charity which is the essence of liberality, that the love of religious liberty which is the proof and condition of civil liberty, have still great obstacles to overcome amongst us. I cannot better exemplify what I have been saying than by the resolution I have to submit to this meeting: "That it is the true policy of free states to protect the liberty of the Holy See, irrespective of Treaty obligations, and to secure its independence of national and political influences." If this were a political meeting I should have something to say about the way in which these supreme objects can be attained; about various projects which have been officially or confidentially put forward; about the position taken by the several European Powers with regard to this question in the last half-year. But I must not presume to trespass on the debateable ground of politics, but will confine myself to those issues of principle on which I am persuaded you are already unanimous. The resolution calls on the powers to provide for the independence of the Holy See. The Pope himself cannot do it, for he is not in a position either to fight or to negotiate. . . . As Europe is now constituted, no army that he could raise would avail for his protection, and it is necessary to rely on the stronger forces of opinion, and to obtain international securities. The resolution does not distinguish between Protestant and Catholic countries, because the distinction is entirely irrelevant. No difference of religion can justify men in being blind to the difference between what is right and wrong in policy. In some respects Protestant States are more interested in the matter than Catholic. Catholic Governments generally have the Church patronage, and other means of acting on opinion, whilst in Protestant countries the Catholics are more directly under the influence of Rome, and far more directly under the influence of ecclesiastical motives. Excepting Belgium, there is no country where the pressure of Catholic agitation would be more severely felt than in Prussia, and in this empire. Moreover, such significant events as the disestablishment of the Irish Church, which, it must be remembered, was the act of the liberal Protestants of this country, show that the time has gone by when states could be guided by motives of sectarian interest—least of all, by sectarian hatred. The resolution speaks of free states only. For this is, strictly, a question of liberty. Despotism such as prevails in Russia could only by a momentary inconsistency sustain a cause which is

sanctified by the sacred rights of conscience. There is no valid ground
on which the freedom of the Pope can be claimed except that on which
every Christian can claim that his religion shall be free. The resolution
demands not only freedom, but independence of national and political
influences, for there are other dangers to provide against besides actual
depression. Spiritual authority has often shown itself capable of resisting
threats and violence, and the cases are rare where open enemies have
exercised any control over the government of the church. But it is not
always so easy to guard against more subtle influences. Even the
hospitality and protection of governments may become an embarrassment, for they are seldom quite disinterested. Therefore not only no
refuge the Pope could seek in France, or Spain, or Germany, could
really appease the vigilant anxiety of catholics; but whereas many
people think that a complete reconciliation between the Papacy and
the Italian people would accomplish the solution, I can conceive no
terms of such an understanding as can be expected now, that would
not contain the germ of dangers more formidable than those we have
now to face. . . . I fear the insidious concessions of Italian statesmen
more than the batteries of Italian armies. I believe that Pius IX, in
refusing to be won by the enormous bribes with which the Italian
Government is tempting him, is serving in the truest sense the interests
both of Italy and of the catholic church. . . . The confidence which is
felt in the universality of the papacy would be compromised if the
duty of protecting it should become the permanent and exclusive
privilege of any single country. Lastly, we say that the independence
of the papacy is not to be made contingent on the force of any existing
stipulations of public law. It is not to stand or fall with the provisions
of the Treaty of Vienna. For forty years Europe has been steadily
employed in demolishing the whole fabric which that Treaty had set
up. It has become the poorest of all securities for dynastic rights, and
it was never any security for popular rights. The independence of the
Holy See is not a dynastic, but a popular question. It is not bound up
with the stability of thrones and the perpetuity of reigning families,
but with the inalienable rights of conscience, which are the sacred
foundation of all public liberties. . . . The Congress of Vienna proceeded
throughout on principles which have been justly repudiated by mankind. It held that absolute governments are legitimate, and that nations
may be distributed and divided without regard to their traditions,
their interest, or their consent. Its spirit was directly contrary to those

ideas to which alone we can appeal as Englishmen, and as men who would do to others as we would be done by. But indeed no voluntary contract can be commensurate with the sanctity of the cause I am pleading. A treaty is a temporary expedient, depending on conditions which are liable to change, and seldom efficacious beyond a single generation. Religious liberty is not an occasional product of transient combinations; it is not an expedient, but one of the chief objects for which civil society exists, because liberty is the medium of religious truth. . . . Therefore it is with hope and confidence that I ask your assent to this proposition, which appears to me to embody in fair terms the union of catholic and of liberal sentiments. We desire that the spiritual power of catholicism be maintained in the majesty of its unity and freedom not by perishable institutions and fragile enactments of public law, but by virtue of those principles which are the glory of our civilization and the special pride of our race. We wish it secured by no momentary combinations of policy, but by the recognized, the unchanging, the eternal interests and duties of mankind. And we fearlessly and consistently claim the support of our countrymen for a cause which concerns all Christendom, in the name of a principle which is their own.

[17]
Letters to the Editor
of the *Times*

Sir,

May I ask you to publish the enclosed preliminary reply to Mr. Gladstone's public Expostulation?

> Your obedient servant,
> Acton

Athenaeum, November 8

Dear Mr. Gladstone,

I will not anticipate by a single word the course which those who are immediately concerned may adopt in answer to your challenge. But there are points which I think you have overlooked, and which may be raised most fitly by those who are least responsible. The question of policy and opportuneness I leave for others to discuss with you. Speaking in the open daylight, from my own point of view, as a Roman Catholic born in the 19th century, I cannot object that facts which are of a nature to influence the belief of men should be brought completely to their knowledge. Concealment is unworthy of those things which are Divine and holy in religion, and in those things which are human and profane publicity has value as a check.

I understand your argument to be substantially as follows: The Catholics obtained Emancipation by declaring that they were in every sense of the term loyal and faithful subjects of the realm, and that

---

Four letters to the editor written in response to William Ewart Gladstone's *The Vatican Decrees in their Bearing on Civil Allegiance: A Political Expostulation* (London: J. Murray, 1874). Reprinted in Acton, *Correspondence*, pp. 119–144; McElrath, pp. 246–261.

Papal Infallibility was not a dogma of their Church. Later events having falsified one declaration, have disturbed the stability of the other; and the problem therefore arises whether the authority which has annulled the profession of faith made by the Catholics would not be competent to change their conceptions of political duty.

This is a question that may be fairly asked, and it was long since made familiar to the Catholics by the language of their own Bishops. One of them has put it in the following terms: "How shall we persuade the Protestants that we are not acting in defiance of honour and good faith, if, having declared that Infallibility was not an article of our faith while we were contending for our rights, we should, now that we have got what we wanted, withdraw from our public declaration and affirm the contrary?" The case is, *primâ facie,* a strong one, and it would be still more serious if the whole structure of our liberties and our toleration was founded on the declarations given by the English and Irish Bishops some years before the Relief Act. Those documents, interesting and significant as they are, are unknown to the Constitution. What is known, and what was for a generation part of the law of the country, is something more solemn and substantial than a series of unproved assertions—namely, the oath in which the political essence of those declarations was concentrated. That was the security which Parliament required; that was the pledge by which we were bound; and it binds us no more. The Legislature, judging that what was sufficient for Republicans was sufficient for Catholics, abolished the oath, for the best reasons, some time before the disestablishment of the Irish Church. If there is no longer a special bond for the loyalty of Catholics, the fact is due to the deliberate judgment of the House of Commons. After having surrendered the only real Constitutional security there seems scarcely reason to lament the depreciation of a less substantial guarantee, which was very indirectly connected with the action of Parliament, and was virtually superseded by the oath.

The doctrines against which you are contending did not begin with the Vatican Council. At the time when the Catholic oath was repealed the Pope had the same right and power to excommunicate those who denied his authority to depose Princes that he possesses now. The writers most esteemed at Rome held that doctrine as an article of faith; a modern Pontiff had affirmed that it cannot be abandoned without taint of heresy, and that those who questioned and restricted his authority in temporal matters were worse than those who rejected it in spirituals, and accordingly men suffered death for this cause as others did for blasphemy and Atheism. The recent decrees have neither increased the penalty nor made it more easy to inflict.

That is the true answer to your appeal. Your indictment would be more just if it was more complete. If you pursue the inquiry further, you will find graver matter than all you have enumerated, established by higher and more ancient authority than a meeting of Bishops half-a-century ago. And then I think you will admit that your Catholic countrymen cannot fairly be called on to account for every particle of a system which has never come before them in its integrity, or for opinions whose existence among divines they would be exceedingly reluctant to believe.

I will explain my meaning by an example: A Pope who lived in Catholic times, and who is famous in history as the author of the first Crusade, decided that it is no murder to kill excommunicated persons. This rule was incorporated in the Canon Law. In the revision of the Code, which took place in the 16th century, and produced a whole volume of corrections, the passage was allowed to stand. It appears in every reprint of the "Corpus Juris." It has been for 700 years and continues to be part of the ecclesiastical law. Far from having been a dead letter, it obtained a new application in the days of the Inquisition, and one of the later Popes has declared that the murder of a Protestant is so good a deed that it atones, and more than atones, for the murder of a Catholic. Again, the greatest legislator of the Mediaeval Church laid down this proposition, that allegiance must not be kept with heretical Princes—*cum ei qui Deo fidem non servat fides servanda non sit.* This principle was adopted by a celebrated Council, and is confirmed by St. Thomas Aquinas, the oracle of the schools. The Syllabus which you cite has assuredly not acquired greater authority in the Church than the Canon Law and the Lateran Decrees, than Innocent the Third and St. Thomas. Yet these things were as well known when the oath was repealed as they are now. But it was felt that, whatever might be the letter of Canons and the spirit of the Ecclesiastical Laws, the Catholic people of this country might be honourably trusted.

But I will pass from the letter to the spirit which is moving men at the present day. It belongs peculiarly to the character of a genuine Ultramontane not only to guide his life by the example of canonized Saints, but to receive with reverence and submission the words of Popes. Now Pius V, the only Pope who has been proclaimed a Saint for many centuries, having deprived Elizabeth, commissioned an assassin to take her life; and his next successor, on learning that the Protestants were being massacred in France, pronounced the action glorious and holy, but comparatively barren of results; and implored the King during two months, by his Nuncio and his Legate, to carry the work on to the bitter end until every Huguenot had recanted or perished. It is hard to believe that these things can excite in the bosom of the most fervent Ultramontane that sort of admiration or assent that displays itself in action. If they do not, then it cannot be truly said that Catholics forfeit their moral freedom, or place their duty at the mercy of another.

There is waste of power by friction even in well-constructed machines, and no machinery can enforce that degree of unity and harmony which you apprehend. Little fellowship or confidence is possible between a man who recognizes the common principles of morality as we find them in the overwhelming mass of the writers of our Church and one who, on learning that the murder of a Protestant Sovereign has been inculcated by a saint, or the slaughter of Protestant subjects approved by a Pope, sets himself to find a new interpretation for the Decalogue. There is little to apprehend from combinations between men divided by such a gulf as this, or from the unity of a body composed of such antagonistic materials. But where there is not union of an active or aggressive kind, there may be unity in defence; and it is possible, in making provision against the one, to promote and to confirm the other.

There has been, and I believe there is still, some exaggeration in the idea men form of the agreement in thought and deed which authority can accomplish. As far as decrees, censures, and persecution could commit the Court of Rome, it was committed to the denial of the Copernican system. Nevertheless, the history of astronomy shows a whole catena of distinguished Jesuits; and, a century ago, a Spaniard who thought himself bound to adopt the Ptolemaic theory was laughed at by the Roman divines. The submission of Fénelon, which Protestants and Catholics have so often celebrated, is another instance to my point. When his book was condemned Fénelon publicly accepted the judgment as the voice of God. He declared that he adhered to the decree absolutely and without a shadow of reserve, and there were no bounds to his submission. In private he wrote that his opinions were perfectly orthodox and remained unchanged, that his opponents were in the wrong, and that Rome was getting religion into peril.

It is not the unpropitious times only, but the very nature of things, that protect Catholicism from the consequences of some theories that have grown up within it. The Irish did not shrink from resisting the arms of Henry II, though two Popes had given him dominion over them. They fought against William III although the Pope had given him efficient support in his expedition. Even James II, when he could not get a mitre for Petre, reminded Innocent that people could be very good Catholics and yet do without Rome. Philip II was excommunicated and deprived, but he despatched his army against Rome with the full concurrence of the Spanish divines.

That opinions likely to injure our position as loyal subjects of a Protestant Sovereign, as citizens of a free State, as members of a community divided in religion, have flourished at various times, and in various degrees, that they can claim high sanction, that they are often uttered in the exasperation of controversy, and are most strongly urged at a time when there is no possibility of putting them into practice—this all men must concede. But I affirm that, in the fiercest conflict of the Reformation, when the rulers of the Church had almost lost heart in the struggle for existence, and exhausted every resource of their authority, both political and spiritual, the bulk of the English Catholics retained the spirit of a better time. You do not, I am glad to say, deny that this continues to be true. But you think that we ought to be compelled to demonstrate one of two things—that the Pope cannot, by virtue of powers asserted by the late Council, make a claim which he was perfectly able to make by virtue of powers asserted for him before; or that he would be resisted if he did. The first is superfluous. The second is not capable of receiving a written demonstration. Therefore, neither of the alternatives you propose to the Catholics of this country opens to us a way of escaping from the reproach we have incurred. Whether there is more truth in your misgivings or in my confidence the event will show, I hope, at no distant time.

I remain sincerely yours,
Acton

Sir,

Many persons have called on me, both in public and in private, to furnish the means of testing certain statements made by me in a letter of November 8 to Mr. Gladstone. Those statements are easy to verify. But I comply with their appeal in order to repel the charge that the facts were invented for a theory, or that a faithful narrative of undogmatic history could involve contradiction with the teaching or authority of the Church whose communion is dearer to me than life.

In my endeavour to show that the safety of the State is not affected by the Vatican decrees I affirmed that they assign to the Papacy no power over temporal concerns greater than that which it had claimed and exercised before, and that the causes which heretofore deprived those claims of practical effect continue to operate now. The instance I chose was the deposing power which was renounced by the Catholic oath, and which most assuredly was present neither in the language nor in the mind of the Council. The facts I alluded to are these: King James I, whose sympathies were strong on the side of ecclesiastical tradition, and whose Queen was a Catholic, repeatedly manifested a desire to be reconciled with Rome. He lived in the incessant terror of plots; and he proposed, through the French Ambassador, to favour the English Catholics and to recognize the Primacy of the Holy See on condition that the Pope would renounce the power of deposing Kings. His overtures were rejected. Paul V was willing to discourage conspiracies; but he replied that to surrender his temporal authority would be to incur the reproach of heresy. The French Ambassador writes from Rome, August 19, 1609: "Il me dit ne le pouvoir faire sans être taché d'hérésie" (*Notices et Extraits des Manuscrits*, VII, 310; Goujet, *Pontificat de Paul V*, I, 309). Cardinal Bellarmine relates that his Controversies were put on the Index by Sixtus V, not for denying this power, for he vehemently asserts it, but for denying the direct and universal dominion of the Popes over the whole world. "Sixtus enim, propter illam propositionem de dominio Papae directo in totum orbem, posuit Controversias ejus in Indice Librorum Prohibitorum, donec corrigerentur; sed ipso mortuo Sacra Rituum Congregatio jussit deleri ex libro Indicis nomen illius" (*Vita Card. Bellarmini*, 22). Baronius proclaims it heresy to deny that the ecclesiastical power enjoys, by Divine institution, the right of judging in the temporal affairs of men (*Analecta juris pontificii*, 1860, p. 281). And Suarez, writing against James in 1613, holds that the deposing power is an article of faith: "Propositio haec, Papa potestatem habet ad deponendos Reges haereticos et pertinaces, suove regno in rebus ad salutem animae pertinentibus perniciosos, inter dogmata fidei tenenda et credenda est" (*Defensio*

Fidei Catholicae, 742). At that time the Venetian divines were attacking the doctrine which attributed to the Popes political authority beyond their own dominions. Paul's biographer, Bzovius, calls the theory of these writers *omnium perniciosissima haeresis,* and the Pope himself said that their books were worse than Calvin's (*Notices et Extraits,* VII, 305). About a century later, an Italian divine, replying to Bossuet, affirmed that there is no foothold for Catholicism if the Popes have erred for many centuries on such a point as this (Bianchi, *Potestà della Chiesa,* I, 20).

The attitude of James I towards Rome is to be seen in Beaumont's despatch of July 23, 1603, in those of La Boderie, June 21, 1606, and July 1, 1609, and of Puisieux, July 22, 1609; in Gondomar's despatch of February 18, 1621; in a report of the journey of the Archbishop of Embrun to England in 1624; in the letters of the Tuscan agent, Lotti, and in a joint letter of James and Andrewes which is among the epistles of Casaubon (Mercier de Lacombe, *Henri IV,* p. 490; Siri, *Memorie,* I, 239; La Boderie, *Ambassades,* I, 130; IV, 387; Gardiner's *Spanish Marriage,* I, 406; *Mémoires particuliers,* III, 224; *Istoria del Granducato,* V, 194; *Casauboni Epistolae,* p. 389, and his *Ephemerides,* p. 807). There were proselytes less likely than James I and Bishop Andrewes. I have seen in the library of St. Mark a letter from the Nuncio Rossetti, dated Ghent, July 19, 1641, in which he states that Archbishop Ussher applied to be received into the Catholic Church, and to be allowed to end his days at Rome, with a pension from the bounty of the Pope.

It was my object to show that the principle of imputing to the Catholics whatever may seem to be involved constructively or potentially in the Vatican decrees, and throwing on us the burden of disproof, would lead to extravagant consequences; and I drew attention to the acts of two famous Pontiffs of the Middle Ages, Urban II and Innocent III. Urban lays down the rule that it is no murder to kill excommunicated persons, provided it be done from religious zeal only, and not from an inferior motive. "Non enim eos homicidas arbitramur, quod adversus excommunicatos zelo Catholicae matris ardentes, eorum quoslibet trucidasse contigerit" (*Urbani II. Epistolae,* ed. Migne, 122). The words are copied by Ivo of Chartres (X, 54), and by Gratian in the second part of his "Decretum" (causa 23, quaestio 5, cap. 57). This may fairly be taken to be one of those passages of which Roger Bacon says that much of Gratian's jurisprudence was already obsolete. But it stands in the revised edition to which Gregory XIII prefixed the injunction that nothing should ever be omitted; and the gloss gives the following paraphrase: "Non putamus eos esse homicidas qui zelo justitiae eos occiderunt." The spirit of the rule survived in the sixteenth century. Several citizens of Lucca, having imbibed Protestant opinions, fled into foreign countries. The Government of the Republic, acting under pressure from Rome, made a law that if any man should kill one of these refugees his reward should be 300 crowns; that, if he had been outlawed for previous crimes his outlawry should be reversed; and that, if he was not in trouble himself, he might transfer his pardon to another who needed it (*Archivio Storico Italiano*, X, app. 177). The date of the decree is January 9, 1562. On the 20th Pius IV replied. He congratulated the Republic on this wise and pious law, esteeming, he said, that nothing could do greater honour to God, provided it was diligently executed: "Legimus pia laudabilaque decreta. . . . Gavisi admodum sumus tam pie et sapienter haec apud vos acta et constituta fuisse. . . . Nec vero quicquam fieri potuisse judicamus, vel ad tuendum Dei honorem sanctius, vel ad conservandam vestrae patriae salutem prudentius. . . . Hortamur vos, et ceteros qui in isto munere vobis successuri sunt, ut diligenter ea servanda et exequenda curetis" (p. 178).

In the Bull *Rem crudelem audivimus* of March 10, 1208, Innocent III deprives and proscribes the Count of Toulouse in these words: "Cum juxta sanctorum patrum canonicas sanctiones, ei qui Deo fidem non servat fides servanda non sit, a communione fidelium segregato, utpote qui vitandus est potius quam fovendus, omnes qui dicto comiti fidelitatis seu societatis aut federis hujuscemodi juramento tenentur, auctoritate apostolica denuntient ab eo interim absolutos, et cuilibet Catholico viro licere, salvo jure domini principalis, non solum persequi personam ejusdem, verum etiam occupare ac detinere terram ipsius" (Teulet, *Trésor des Chartes*, I, 316). In the same Pontificate the Fourth Lateran Council determined that the Pope might depose any Prince who neglected the duty of exterminating heresy, and might bestow his State on others (Harduin, *Concilia*, VII, 19). The same canon reappears in the *Decretale* of Gregory IX (lib. IV, tit. 7, cap. 13): and St. Thomas Aquinas declares that the loss of all claim to political allegiance is incurred by the fact of excommunication (*Summa*, 1853, III, 51).

I have been asked whether I meant to hold Innocent III responsible for the maxim that faith must not be kept with heretics. He was speaking undoubtedly of the fidelity which is paid to princes, but the principle applied with equal force the other way, and was liable to be construed in a wider sense. In the days of the Council of Constance,

Ferdinand of Aragon employed the same words to induce the Emperor to disregard the safeconduct he had given to Hus, *"quoniam non est frangere fidem ei qui Deo fidem frangit"* (Palacky, *Documenta Joannis Hus*, p. 540). A decree embodying this maxim, which is found among the Acts of the Council, is not authentic. But the theory remained. When Henry of Valois swore to respect the liberty of conscience in Poland, the Cardinal Penitentiary informed him that it would be a grievous sin to observe his oath, but that, if it was taken with the intention of breaking it, his guilt would be less. "Minor fuit offensio, ubi mens ea praestandi, quae petebantur defuit" (*Hosii Opera*, II, 367). At this time it was the common opinion of divines that a private person need not keep faith with a heretic, "ob tanti hujus criminis pravitatem, communis doctorum sententia recepta est, fidem a privato praestitam haereticis servandam neutiquam esse" (De Roias, *Opus Tripartitum*, III, 55).

In order to establish my point that a gulf divides the extreme opinions from the common sentiment of Catholics, I spoke of the conspiracy of Ridolfi and of the Massacre of St. Bartholomew. It would seem that a thoroughly consistent and unflinching partisan of those extremes must regard the slaughter of Protestants with feelings akin to favour if the act obtained the approval of the supreme authority, and could hardly look with horror on the murder of a Queen if it was sanctioned by a Saint. On the other hand, it would not be easy to point to a single English writer at the present day, whom the prestige of canonization and authority has inclined to applaud such deeds.

Queen Elizabeth had reigned ten years, and had nearly accomplished the suppression of the Catholic religion in England, when Pius V declared that she had forfeited her Crown, and forbade her subjects to obey her. The first insurrection failed, as the bulk of Catholics pleaded that the Papal orders had not been brought to their knowledge. Many copies of the Bull had been delivered to Ridolfi, a Florentine, who was the secret agent of the Pope (*Acta Sanctorum Maii*, I, 661). By means of this man a new conspiracy was set on foot, and Ridolfi went to Rome to explain the details to the Pope and to seek his aid. Pius earnestly recommended the matter to the King of Spain, assuring him that it was most important for religion. At Madrid Ridolfi was supported by the Nuncio Castagna, and he produced credentials which left no room to doubt that he spoke the real mind of the Pope, and presented truly the business on which he was sent. For Pius had accredited him in the the following terms:

"Has literas nostras Majestati tuae reddet dilectus filius Robertus

Rodolphus, qui, adjuvante Deo, nonnulla ei praesens praesenti prae-
terea exponet, ad honorem ejusdem omnipotentis Dei reique publicae
Christianae, non parum pertinentia utilitatem: super quibus ut ipsi,
sine ulla hesitatione majestas tua fidem habeat vehementer illam in
Domino requirimus ac rogamus a qua pro eximia sua in Deum pietate
illud majorem in modum petimus, ut rem ipsam de qua cum majestate
tua acturus est, animo ac voluntate suscipiens quidquid ad eam
conficiendam opus atque auxilii afferre se posse judicaverit, id sibi
faciendum esse existimet."

When Ridolfi had exposed his commission it became apparent that
it resolved itself into little more than a plot for murdering Elizabeth.
We read in the report of the deliberations of the Council: "Ridolfi
aseguró que los Catolicos de Inglaterra estaban resueltos a apoderarse
de la Reina Isabel y matarla" (*Memorias de la Academia de la Historia,*
VII, 361). Feria, who received the first communications from Ridolfi,
says that the whole question was, how to get the Queen killed without
open war. "La empresa se ha de hacer de la persona de la reina de
Inglaterra, que hecho esto es acavado toto. . . . Conviene atender a
despachar a la reina. . . . Conviene no venir a rotura." Another
councillor, Velasco, describes the death of Elizabeth as the real object,
"El verdadero effecto es la muerte." Philip himself wrote to Alva on
the 14th of July, 1571: "Il dit que le moment le plus favorable à
l'exécution de l'entreprise serait le mois d'Août ou de Septembre; que
la reine Élizabeth quittant alors Londres, pour aller à ses maisons de
campagne, ce serait une occasion de se saisir de sa personne, et de la
tuer. . . . Le Saint Père, à qui Ridolfi a rendu compte de tout, a écrit
au Roi et lui a fait dire, par son Nonce, l'Archevêque de Rossano,
qu'il envisage cette affaire comme étant de la plus haute importance
pour le service de Dieu." The man who finally undertook to do the
deed was Ciappin Vitelli. The letter of Pius V, and the remarks of
Feria and Velasco are printed from the archives of Simancas, in
Mignet's *Marie Stuart,* appendix K.; and the letter of Philip to the Duke
of Alva is calendared by M. Gachard, *Correspondance de Philippe II,* II,
185.

In common with many of those who have raised objections to my
letter, I was long tempted to doubt the accuracy of this story on two
grounds—because it seemed inconsistent with the many virtues of
Pius, and because it ought to have been an obstacle to his canonization.
Neither of these objections is valid. The first allows too little for the

influence of the Inquisition, over which Pius presided in the years of its greatest activity, on the minds of humane and charitable men. Pius V declared that he was willing to spare a culprit guilty of a hundred murders rather than a single notorious heretic (*Legazioni di Serristori*, 443). His Roman panegyrist relates that he caused men to be kidnapped in foreign countries that they might be brought to trial and punishment at Rome (*Catena, Via di Pio V*, p. 158). He assured the King of France that he must not spare the Huguenots, because of their offences against God (*Pii Quinti Epistolae*, p. 163). He declared that a Pope who should permit the least grace to be shown to heretics would sin against faith, and would thus become subject to the judgment of men (*Catena*, p. 325). He required that they should be pursued until they were all destroyed: "ad internecionem usque . . . donec, deletis omnibus, exinde nobilissimo isti regno pristinus Catholicae religionis cultus . . . restituatur" (*Pii Quinti Epistolae*, p. 155). It was a cruel mercy, he said, to spare the impious: "nihil est enim ea pietate misericordiaque crudelius, quae in impios et ultima supplicia meritos confertur" (p. 242). He appears to allude to a theory which was current, that it is a mercy to heretics to shorten their opportunities of sin: "expedit eos citius tollere e medio, ne gravius postea damnentur" (Lancelottus, *Haereticum Quare*, p. 579). A declared heretic was considered a public enemy whom any private person might rob or kill. "Si infidelitatis peccatum est notorium, et judices dissimulant, tunc quidem a privatis occidi possunt haeretici" (Stephanus, Episc. Oriolanus, *De Bello Sacro*, 146; Jacobus Septimancensis, *Institutiones Catholicae*, 166). Nothing in the character or the position of Elizabeth exempted her from the rigorous application of these maxims. In the judgment of the entire Catholic world, she was a bastard and a usurper, and she was by far the most ingenious, the most powerful and the most successful oppressor of the Church then living. If the summary punishment of contumacy could ever be justified, it was reasonable to apply it to her.

Sovereignty was no protection, for it had been forfeited by the Papal sentence; and the common belief was that the Pope may lawfully ordain that condemned princes be put to death. John of Salisbury, the divine who obtained from the English Pope Ireland as a gift to the Norman kings, introduced the theory of tyrannicide into Christian theology; and it became generally popular under the presumed but not undisputed authority of Saint Thomas. Long after the death of Pius the Fifth it continued to be taught by the most renowned divines—

by Gregory of Valentia, for instance, and Suarez. The language of Suarez is explicit: "Post sententiam latam omnino privatur regno, ita ut non possit justo titulo illud possidere; ergo ex tunc poterit tanquam omnino tyrannus tractari, et consequenter a quocunque privato poterit interfici" (*Defensio*, 721). In a work on moral theology, which was widely popular, and which was printed after the middle of the last century, we still find the maxim that a person lying under the ban of the Pope may be killed in any place. "Bannitus autem a Papa potest occidi ubique" (Zacharia, *Theologia Moralis*, I, 260).

The case of Tyrrell, in the time of Gregory XIII, resembles that of Ridolfi, but Mr. Froude gives, I think, good reason to doubt the evidence on which it rests. But the lawfulness of similar actions was scarcely doubted. On the 13th of January, 1591, the Nuncio at Paris reports that a young friar had applied to him for permission to murder Henry IV. The Nuncio replied that he would know whether the spirit that impelled him was from above by taking the opinion of the Pope on his design; at the same time he wrote to Rome that the man seemed to him really inspired. The letter is in the Chigi Library. An extract is printed in the *North British Review*, LI, 672.

One piece of evidence exists, which has never, I think, been employed in this inquiry. A petition from Ridolfi to Pope Gregory is extant at Rome in which he describes his services and his claims, but does not say that the plot was aimed against the life of the Queen. This circumstance appears to me to throw not a featherweight into either scale. But, if it is cited at all, it can only be cited to exonerate the memory of the Pope.

Having stated that Gregory XIII approved the massacre of Saint Bartholomew, but complained that too little had been done, I have been assured by a Doctor, and former Professor, of Divinity, who has devoted twenty years to these researches, that this is a hackneyed story which the veriest bigot is ashamed to repeat. I submit to the later and better judgment of my correspondent the facts which I am about to prove. When Gregory was informed that the Huguenots were being slain over the whole of France, he sent word to the King that this was better news than a hundred battles of Lepanto. On the 11th of September the Ambassador, Ferrals, wrote as follows to Charles the Ninth: "Après quelques autres discours qu'il me feist sur le contentement que luy et le collège des Cardinaux avoient receu de ladicte exécution faicte et des nouvelles qui journellement arrivoient en ceste cour de semblables exécutions que l'on a faicte et font encore en plusieurs villes de vostre royaume qui, à dire la vérité, sont les nouvelles les plus agréables que je pense qu'on eust sceu apporter en ceste ville, sadicte Saincteté pour fin me commanda de vous escrire que cest évènement luy a esté cent fois plus agréable que cinquante victoires semblables à celle que ceulx de la ligue obtindrent l'année passée contre le Turcq, ne voulant oublier vous dire, Sire, les commandemens estroictz qu'il nous feist à tous, mesmement aux françois d'en faire feu de joye, et qui ne l'eust faict eust mal senty de la foy." The Pope proclaimed a Jubilee, principally to thank God for this great mercy, and to pray that the King might have constancy to pursue to the end the pious work he had begun. This Bill has not, I think, been reprinted. I take the words from one of the original placards distributed in Rome from the press of the Apostolic Chamber. "Nos ipsi statim hoc audito una cum venerabilibus fratribus nostris S.R.E. Cardinalibus, in templo Sancti Marci quas maximas potuimus omnipotenti Deo Gratias egimus, et ut pro sua immensa bonitate Regem ipsum in persequendo tam pio salutarique consillio conservare et custodire, viresque ei ad Regnum antea religiosissimum a pestilentissimis haeresibus omnino expurgandum, et ad pristinum Catholicae religionis cultum redigendum ac restituendum subministrare dignetur, ex toto corde, totaque mente nostra precari et obsecrare. . . . Pro felici Christianissimi Regis contra haereticos successu gratias agant ipsumque orent, ut quae idem Rex auctore Domino facienda cognovit, ipso operante implere valeat." A rumour gradually spread to the effect that the slaughter, far from being an act of religion, had been provoked by the detection of a Protestant conspiracy. The Nuncio Salviati informed the Pope that this was an utter falsehood, too ridiculous to be believed. "Cela n'en demeurera pas moins faux en tous points, et ce seroit une honte pour quiconque est à même de connaître quelque chose aux affaires de ce monde de le croire." (Despatch of September 2. The letters of Salviati are preserved in Paris in copies made by Chateaubriand, and I am quoting his translation of them.) There were signs of intermission, and Gregory required the Nuncio to insist on the utter extirpation of the heretics. "Je lui fis part de la très-grande consolation qu'avaient procurée au Saint Père les succès obtenus dans ce royaume par une grâce singulière de Dieu, accordée la Chrétienté sous son pontificat. Je fis connaître le désir qu'avait sa Sainteté de voir pour la plus grande gloire de Dieu, et le plus grand bien de la France, tous les hérétiques extirpés du royaume, et j'ajoutai que dans cette vue le Saint Père estimait très à propos que l'on révoquat l'édit de pacification." Salviati wrote this on the 22nd of September. On the 11th of October he says: "Le Saint Père, ai-je dit, en éprouve une joie infinie, et a ressenti une grande consolation d'apprendre que sa Majesté m'avait commandé d'écrire qu'elle esperait qu'avant peu la France n'aurait plus de Huguenots." Cardinal Orsini, having been despatched as Legate from Rome with extraordinary solemnity to congratulate Charles and to support the exhortations of Salviati, describes, on the 19th of December, his audience with the King. Orsini assured him that he had surpassed, by this action, the glory of all his forefathers, but he pressed him to fulfil his promise that not a single Huguenot should be left alive on the soil of France:

"Se si riguardava all'objetto della gloria, non potendo niun fatto de' suoi antecessori, se rettamente si giudicava, agguagliarsi al glorioso et veramente incomparabil fatto di sua Maestà, in liberar, con tanta prudentia et pietà in un giorno solo il suo regno da cotanta diabolica peste. . . . Esortai . . . che non essendo servitio ne di Dio ne di sua Maestà, lasciar fargli nuovo piede a questa maladetta setta, volesse applicare tutto il suo pensiero et tutte le forze sue per istirparla affatto, recandosi a memoria quello che ella haveva fatto scrivere a sua santità da Monsignor il Nuntio, che infra pochi giorni non sarebbe più un ugonotto in tutto il suo regno." (This letter may be found in the Egerton Manuscripts, 2,077, and in the Paris Library, Mss. Ital., 1,272.)

This language is the expression of a spirit that has not passed entirely away, though it is no longer to be feared. Some months after the event the Cardinal of Lorraine, haranguing the King in the name of the assembled clergy of France, declared that he had eclipsed all preceding monarchs, not by the massacre only, but by the holy deceit with which he had laid his plans (*Procès-Verbaux des Assemblées du Clergé*, I, Appendix, 28). A writer of our day, distinguished by his valuable publications on the history of the Jesuits, describes the discourse in which these words occur as a favourable specimen of the tone that becomes a bishop. He compares it advantageously with the obsequious rhetoric of Bossuet, and he designates the speaker as a saintly and illustrious prelate whose memory will ever be dear to Catholics (*Documents inédits concernant la Compagnie de Jésus*, XXII, p. 63–67).

From the midst of the applauding Cardinals one voice was raised in protest. Montalto, who was destined, as Sixtus V, to stand in the foremost rank among Kings and Pontiffs, and who was a true type of the Catholic revival in its grandeur and its strength, entreated the Pope to prohibit rejoicings which would convince the world that the Church was thirsting for blood. It was an act in keeping with the character of Sixtus, as an unsparing censor of preceding Popes. In spite of his deadly feud with Elizabeth he shares so little in the feelings of Pius against her, that he spoke of her as the ablest ruler of her time, and commended her example to the King of France, for the plausible legality with which she achieved the ruin of Mary Stuart. He went so far as to say that Clement VII had upheld the marriage of Henry VIII with Catherine from a sordid motive, whereas it was a sinful and invalid union which Rome had no right to tolerate.

I affirmed that the apprehension of civil danger from the Vatican Council overlooks the infinite subtlety and inconsistency with which men practically elude the yoke of official uniformity in matters of opinion. I used the obvious illustration that astronomy flourished at Rome in spite of the condemnation of Copernicus and Galileo; and I stated that Fénelon, while earning admiration for his humility under censure, had retained his former views unchanged. "The Archbishop of Cambrai," said Bossuet, "is very sensible of his humiliation, and not at all of his error." In his celebrated pastoral letter of the 9th of April, 1699, Fénelon used these words: "Nous adhérons à ce bref, mes chers frères, tant pour le texte du livre que pour les 23 propositions, simplement, absolument, et sans ombre de restriction. . . . A Dieu ne plaie qu'il soit jamais parlé de nous, si ce n'est pour se souvenir qu'un pasteur a cru devoir être plus docile que la dernière brebis du troupeau, et qu'il n'a mis aucune borne à sa soumission." Three weeks later, on the 1st of May, he writes to a friend: "Je n'admettrai rien d'ambigu ni sur la pureté de mes opinions en tout temps, ni sur l'orthodoxie de la doctrine que j'ai soutenue. . . . Si les gens de bien ne se réveillent à Rome, la foi est en grand péril." These passages, as well as the others to which I made allusion, will be found among the letters at the beginning of the tenth volume of Fénelon's works.

Lastly, in support of my contention that the policy of Rome in modern times has seldom prevailed, even with the most zealous Kings and the most Catholic nations, against their own ideas of political interest, I pointed to the resistance of the Irish, and to the attitude of Philip II and James II towards the Holy See. The quarrel between

Philip and the Caraffas, and the Opinion of Melchior Cano touching a war with the Pope may be studied in books as common as those which tell how Adrian invested Henry with the emerald ring which was the symbol of his lordship over Ireland. That William of Orange secured the sanction of the Pope for his expedition in 1688 was a circumstance already known to Carte. We now learn that the Emperor wavered long between hatred of Louis XIV and alarm for Catholicism in England; but that Innocent XI removed his scruples by assuring him that the Government of James II was inspired not by religion but by France (Droysen, *Friedrich I*, p. 42). For James, though advised by Jesuits, did not live on cordial terms with Rome. Just then, indeed, the bonds that attached the Society to the Papacy had been somewhat relaxed. Innocent had set himself against the system of ethics taught in most of their schools, and he reproached them with having degenerated from their old fidelity to the Holy See. The General of the Jesuits, Gonzales, in his evidence for the beatification of Innocent (No. 180), reports his sentiments in these words: "Quod Societas Jesu hoc tempore videretur oblita sui primitivi spiritus, quo eam S. Ignatius instituerat ad defensionem Apostolicae sedis, pro qua quondam tanta cum laude se gessisse ejus filii, quorum degeneres viderentur qui hoc tempore viverent, dum tam alte tacebant, quando nunquam major adesset necessitas loquendi." The Jesuits on their side would not undertake to defend the Roman theory against Gallican Articles of 1682, which, in France, they afterwards brought themselves at last to adopt. (Declaration of the 19th of December, 1761, *Procés-Verbaux*, VIII, app. 349.) In these circumstances Innocent persistently refused the prayer of James to make Father Petre either a Bishop or a Cardinal. Petre threatened vengeance, and James was induced to write a curt and angry letter warning Innocent that Catholics could contrive to live without the Court of Rome:

"Li Giesuiti havevano inteso cosí male le repulse di Sua Santità, di quale natura elle si fussero, che hebbero efficacia di persuadere a Sua Maestà che era tempo ormai di mostrarne a Sua Santità qualche risentimento; e proposero a Sua Maestà la richiamata del suo ministro da Roma, la discacciata del di lui Nuntio d'Inghilterra, come che attribuiscano a questo l'obbietioni tutte e l'esclusive, che vengano da Sua Santità. Ma fu resoluto in fine, e messo in esequtione, che scrivesse a Sua Santità la Maestà del Rè una secca e compendiosissima lettera, con la quale rimostrasse al Papa la Maestà Sua che non era piú il vescovato, ma che era il cardinalato che si pretendeva al presente, concludendo finalmente, che si poteva bene esser Cattolico Romano e passarsi della Corte di Roma."

This passage from a despatch of the Florentine Envoy, Terriesi, was printed by Madame de Campana in her work on the later Stuarts (II, 148). The King's letter is not extant; but Terriesi had the information from Petre, of whom he says: "Cadde in seguito a raccontarmi quanto ho di sopra descritto." This I take from the Florence Transcripts at the British Museum, Additional Manuscripts 25, 375. There also will be found recorded, in a despatch of January 12, 1688, the words of the Jesuit speaking of the Pope.

I know that there are some whose feelings of reverence and love are, unhappily, wounded by what I have said. I entreat them to remember how little would be gained if all that came within the scope of my argument could be swept out of existence—to ask themselves seriously the question whether the laws of the Inquisition are or are not a scandal and a sorrow to their souls. It would be well if men had never fallen into the temptation of suppressing truth and encouraging error for the better security of religion. Our Church stands, and our faith should stand, not on the virtues of men, but on the surer ground of an institution and a guidance that are divine. Therefore I rest unshaken in the belief that nothing which the inmost depths of history shall disclose in time to come can ever bring to Catholics just cause of shame or fear. I should dishonour and betray the Church if I entertained a suspicion that the evidence of religion could be weakened or the authority of Councils sapped by a knowledge of the facts with which I have been dealing, or of others which are not less grievous or less certain because they remain untold.

I am, Sir, your obedient servant,

Aldenham, Nov. 21   Acton

Sir, The Bishop of Nottingham thinks that I have misrepresented Pope Urban II and Suarez. I hope not. But, if I have, I will endeavour promptly and fully to repair the wrong.

And, first of all, it is true that the words I transcribed from Suarez do not contain the definite and final statement of his opinion. I ought to have taken that from the paragraph of which the Bishop has quoted a part. Suarez states his own conclusion, a few lines lower than the point where the Bishop's extract ends, in the following words: "Recte dixit Soto-licet Rex in solo regimine tyrannus non possit a quolibet interfici, *Lata vero sententia quisque* (inquit) *potest institui executionis minister.* Eodemque modo si Papa Regem deponat, ab illis tantum poterit expelli, vel interfici, quibus ipse id commiserit."

It may be thought that there is little practical difference between the two propositions that a king deprived by the Pope may be murdered by anybody, and that he may be murdered only by persons commissioned by the Pope to do it; and for my purpose, which was to show that participation in Ridolfi's conspiracy would be no bar to canonization, they are of equal effect. But, for Suarez, there was probably this important distinction—that the former might have brought him under the decree of Constance against Tyrannicide, a decree which the General of the Jesuits had pressed on the attention of the Society after the assassination of Henry IV. This difficulty might be avoided by making the lawfulness of the murder depend on the commission given by the Pope.

While I wish to make this correction in the most explicit way, I regret that I cannot profit by the Bishop's other criticism. Urban II says positively that he deems the killing of excommunicated persons no murder if done from religious zeal only. But he wishes a penance to be imposed, in case there may have been any intrusion of an inferior motive. It would be hardly possible to say more definitely that though there may be murder in one case there is no murder in the other.

It may be worth while to mention that the page I referred to in Droysen is 47, not 42; and that in citing Bianchi I have given not the page, but the chapter, as the argument in question runs through several pages.

I remain, Sir, your obedient servant,

Athenaeum, Nov. 29   Acton

Sir, One whose distinguished position and character give him the strongest claim to be heard has expressed to me his belief that "the charge of equivocation brought by" me "against Fénelon cannot be sustained." In support of my contention that the agreement in thought and deed attainable among Catholics is not of a kind which justifies the apprehension of danger to the State, I described Fénelon as earning credit by his humility under censure while he retained his former views. I said, He "publicly accepted the judgment as the voice of God. He declared that he adhered to the decree absolutely, and without a shadow of reserve, and there were no bounds to his submission. In private he wrote that his opinions were perfectly orthodox and remained unchanged, that his opponents were in the wrong, and that Rome was getting religion into peril." The doubt entertained by my correspondent may apply either to my account of the Archbishop's public acts or of his private thoughts; I will therefore give the authority for both.

Fénelon explained his personal sentiments in a letter of the 9th of October, 1699:

"J'ai toujours soutenu que je n'avois jamais cru aucune des erreurs en question. Le Pape n'a condamné aucun des points de ma vraie doctrine, amplement éclaircie dans mes défenses. Il a seulement condamné les expressions de mon livre avec le sens qu'elles présentent naturellement, et que je n'ai jamais eu en vue. Dire que je me suis retracté, ce seroit faire entendre que j'ai avoué avoir eu des erreurs, et ce seroit me faire une injustice."

On the 3d of April in the same year he wrote:

"Je n'ai jamais pensé les erreurs qu'ils m'imputent. Je puis bien, par docilité pour le Pape, condamner mon livre comme exprimant ce que je n'avois pas cru exprimer, mais je ne puis trahir ma conscience, pour ne noircir lâchement moi-même sur des erreurs que je ne pensai jamais."

On the 17th he describes himself as "un archevêque innocent, soumis, qui a défendu l'ancienne doctrine sur la charité contre une nouveauté dangereuse." He says on the 3d of May: "Ne voit-on pas que je ne puis en conscience confesser des erreurs que je n'ai jamais pensées?." And on the 24th of April, speaking of his opponents, he says: "Ils n'ont rien de décidé sur le fond de la doctrine." He continued to think that they, not he, were theologically in the wrong, and that Rome encouraged them. He wrote, on the 17th of April, that it was felt that all honest men thought him right and Bossuet wrong—"que tous les honnêtes gens me plaignent, et trouvent que j'avois raison, et M. de Meaux tort dans notre controverse." On the 3d of April he wrote: "Si Rome ne veut point rendre témoignage à la pureté de la doctrine que j'ai soutenue, et qui est tout ce que j'ai eu dans l'esprit, ils font encore plus de tort à cette doctrine qu'à moi." On the 24th of April: "Le parti est d'une telle hauteur qu'ils entrainent tout. Rome a donné des armes à des esprits bien violens." He writes on the 1st of

May to his agent at Rome: "Il faut tâcher d'éviter les surprises dans une cour où tout est si incertain, et où la cabale ennemie est si puissante." And again, on the 15th: "Vous connoissez l'esprit de mes parties et vous ne savez que trop par expérience combien ils sont accrédités dans la cour ou vous êtes."

That is Fénelon's avowal of his opinions. I proceed to the account he gives of his submission.

On the 28th of April he wrote: "Ma soumission sera, moyennant la grâce de Dieu, aussi constante qu'elle est absolue, et accompagnée de la plus sincère docilité pour le Saint-Siège." On the 8th of May: "On peut juger par là combien mon mandement est d'un exemple décisif pour la pleine soumission à l'Église Romaine." In his letter to Innocent XII, of the 4th of April, he said: "Libellum cum XXIII. propositionibus excerptis, simpliciter, absolute, et absque ulla vel restrictionis umbra condemnabo—Nulla erit distinctionis umbra levissima, qua Decretum eludi possit, aut tantula excusatio unquam adhibeatur." It was, he declared, the most perfect submission a Bishop could make (April 3).

I know nothing in my remarks on Fénelon which these extracts, added to those which I have already given, leave unproved. In matters of history it is well to abstain from hazarding unnecessary judgments. I have not expended an adjective on Suarez, and have imputed nothing worse than subtleties to Fénelon. The reproach of equivocation, which I have not adopted, was made by his adversaries: "ils disent que ma soumission si fastueuse est courte, sèche, contrainte, superbe, purement extérieure et apparente; mais que j'aurois dû reconnoitre mes erreurs évidentes dans tout mon livre" (May 15). The agents of his accusers have recorded their impression as follows:

"On croyoit qu'il ne songeroit plus qu'a réparer le scandale qu'il avoit causé à l'Église par une rétractation publique de ses erreurs, mais on n'y trouva rien d'approchant, tout y paroissoit sec et plein de paroles vagues, qui pouvoient n'exprimer qu'une soumission extérieure et forcée" (*Relation du Quiétisme*, II, 278). "Au lieu d'en être édifié, j'en fus scandalisé au dernier point. Il ne me fut pas difficile d'en découvrir tout l'orgueil et tout le venin. On voit bien par là ce qu'on doit penser de la soumission, qu'il n'est plus permis de croire sincère, et qui ne peut être que forcée" (Abbé Bossuet to his uncle, May 5).

Bossuet, though he expressed himself with greater dignity, thought the pastoral evasive:

"M. de Cambray ne se plaint que de la correction, en évitant d'avouer sa faute. On est encore plus étonné que, très-sensible à son humiliation, il ne le paroisse en aucune sorte à son erreur, ni au malheur qu'il a eu de la vouloir répandre. Il dira, quand il lui plaira, qu'il n'a point avoué d'erreur.—Encore qu'il ne puisse pas se servir du prétexte de l'ignorance, il n'en manquera jamais" (May 25, April 19).

Of Fénelon's explanations he said (May 25),

"Si elles sont justes, si elles conviennent au livre, le Saint Père a mal condamné le livre *in sensu obvio, ex connexione sententiarum*, &c. Il ne faut que brûler le bref? C'est le Saint Siège et son décret qu'on attaque, et non pas nous."

This was the general impression. Fénelon himself gave no public intimation that, as has been said, it was his grammar and not his theology that he condemned. Neither the decree nor the pastoral distinguished the doctrine of the author from the text of his book, and the people who read the condemnation, qualified by no saving clause, could hardly fail to suppose that the censure and the submission implied that Fénelon had been in error.

"Ce qui est certain c'est que les uns n'osent plus parler d'amour de pure bienveillance, et que les autres supposent tout ouvertement qu'il est condamné dans mon livre. Aussi disent-ils qu'il ne s'agit pas de mes expressions, mais de ma doctrine, qui est, disent-ils, condamnée, en sorte que je dois l'abjurer" (April 24).

Although Fénelon knew that this belief prevailed he let it pass; and the motives of the reserve which brought him exaggerated credit for humility under censure continue to be variously interpreted.

But in dealing with his own suffragans and with the Court of Rome he took care to explain that he deemed his orthodoxy unimpeached, and he even endeavoured to have it formally acknowledged. It would go against his conscience, he declared, to renounce his real opinions:

"Tout le repos de ma vie roule sur l'acceptation de cette soumission, faute de quoi nous tomberions dans une persécution sur un formulaire captieux, qui nous mèneroit à d'affreuses extrémités."

He speaks with alarm of "le danger d'un formulaire qui allât à me faire souscrire, contre ma conscience, la condamnation de *sensus ab auctore intentus*" (April 4, 17).

Fénelon's position was understood at Rome. His friends wished to have his real sentiments expressly excluded from the condemnation of his book, and his opponents wished that he should be required to retract them. But neither party prevailed. The Pope appears to have hoped that he would recognize his errors, but admitted afterwards that he was not convinced of having erred. He said to the Abbé Bossuet, "qu'il falloit espérer que l'Archevêque de Cambrai reconnoitroit ses erreurs et s'humilieroit." Three weeks later, when he had received Fénelon's answer to the Decree, he said, "qu'il voyoit très-bien qu'il n'étoit pas persuadé d'avoir erré" (April 14, May 5). Bossuet himself was of [the] opinion that although the submission was illusory it ought to be accepted.

It is open to man to decline his harsh interpretation, and to prefer the milder judgment shown in the tolerant acquiescence of Rome. If I adopted the worst view of Fénelon's conduct I should detract materially from the effect with which his example shows the difficulty of forcing upon men an iron rule of uniformity. To imagine that British institutions are secure because ecclesiastical authority may be evaded by those who choose to equivocate, or that conscience can be sheltered by duplicity, would be the part, of an idiot. But it is a valid and relevant illustration of my argument to note that a famous controversy which raged for years between the ablest prelates in the Church, setting in motion all the influence of France and all the resources of Rome, and occupying for many months the anxious thought of the Pope and his cardinals, a controversy which was decided by the unqualified triumph of one party and the defeat of the other, ended by leaving the feud unquenched, and each side persistent in maintaining the orthodoxy of its own exclusive opinion.

I remain, Sir, your obedient servant,
Acton

Aldenham, Dec. 9

[18]
Review of Friedrich's
Geschichte des Vatikanischen Konzils

Professor Friedrich, whose personal memorials of Rome in 1870 have been widely read, has commenced a comprehensive history of the Vatican Council, moved by much new testimony to disregard the axiom that great transactions seldom find their historian until the generation engaged in them is beyond the reach of praise and blame. The part now published does not display the promised matter, as it comes no farther than the autumn of 1869. It is, in fact, a studied exposition of the growth of Ultramontanism, glancing rapidly at the times before the Revolution, but describing in full detail how the revival of the Ultramontane theory formed a phase of the Legitimist reaction; how Lamennais brought strength to it from the opposite quarter; how and by what tactics, it battled with the Gallicans, until it gained possession of the Papacy after the restoration of Pius IX.

Although the volume extends to 800 pages, it is written from a point of view which leaves social and political problems out of sight; and the author prefers the strictly theological aspects of the subject before him. Ultramontanism, coupled with the highest principles, or the broadest liberality, appears under his tests, as Ultramontanism still; and it is treated as essentially a question between Popes and bishops, between the nations at large and the nation beyond the Alps. To make liberty the central and deciding issue would have robbed the book of its argument and its climax, as the improvement is manifest since the days when the error that springs from ignorance was a crime graver than premeditated murder, and to doubt the Donation of Constantine

Johann Friedrich, *Geschichte des Vatikanischen Konzils*, vol. 1 (Bonn: Neusser, 1877). This review was published in *The Academy*, 22 September 1877, pp. 281–282.

was to play with fire. Even to reckon among the means by which ecclesiastical authority maintained itself the power over life and death, which was the most potent of all, would disturb the conventional grouping of opinions and the distribution of parts. In 1761, when the French Jesuits acknowledged the duty of upholding the Gallican maxims against their General, they alleged that they had pronounced themselves to similar purpose as early as 1626. Dr. Friedrich seems to doubt the allegation. The circumstances alluded to are beyond question, and have been set forth quite lately by Father Carayon in the Memoirs of Garasse, and by Father Prat in his Life of Coton. The declaration is extant. The two most eminent names of the society, Sirmond and Petau, stand beneath it; and the manner of obtaining it, the plea of *timor cadens in constantem virum*, by which the Jesuits soothed their scruples, might well raise a suspicion that there was something hollow in the Gallican structure. Prof. Friedrich imputes the misfortunes of religion to Baronius, Bellarmine, and writers of their stamp, and seldom vexes with censure the divines of Constance, Bossuet, or the Church of France. But the Council of Constance is conspicuous among Councils for having stifled opposition in blood; Bossuet wrote: "Ceux qui ne veulent pas souffrir que le prince use de rigueur en matière de religion, parce que la religion doit être libre, sont dans une erreur impie"; the French clergy promoted persecution almost down to the eve of the Revolution; and the penalty of death, revived in France many years after the last heretic suffered at Tor di Nona, and the last priest at Tyburn, was inflicted on Huguenot ministers as late as 1762. French theology hardly produced a more vigorous and independent intellect than Arnauld; yet that champion of rigid morals acted on a principle which Guy Fawkes would have owned, when he excused compulsory conversions by observing that insincere converts had little reason to complain, as they were already assured of damnation for their heresy. These facts probably explain the somewhat technical treatment of an exceedingly complex and manifold process, and the author's willingness to leave untouched some of the broader human interests over which it ranges. It has been his purpose to avoid controversy; and it is evident that he must become more polemical the deeper he probes for motives, beneath the surface, and the farther he extends the area of his judgments. Thus, in his description of apocryphal divinity and its influence on religion, the graver problem would be to know by what arguments men were so persuaded that fraud is meritorious, that the first scholar who detected the great forgeries added that the exposure did not destroy their authority. But Dr. Friedrich's business is with the nineteenth century, and with public events that are not shrouded in psychological obscurity.

He points out that Pius IV was obliged to withdraw a canon he had proposed to the Council of Trent, assigning to the Holy See *plena potestas gubernandi Ecclesiam universalem*; and, to complete the statement, it might be added that the passage was modified before the attempt to carry it was abandoned, and that the Pope suggested to substitute the words *Ecclesiam Dei,* for *Ecclesiam universalem.* But it would be a mistake to regard the incident as a sign of the spirit that prevailed at Trent, for the resisting force was not so much among the prelates as at the Court of France. The ambassadors made known that their instructions obliged them to oppose the intended definition; and the Cardinal of Lorraine, who was the leading French statesman, after accusing his adversaries of atheism, threatened them with the loss of France, and of the whole Church with it, if more was done to repel the heretics. The first religious war was raging, with doubtful fortune, at the time; and the Government dreaded whatever might have obstructed the pacification of the kingdom, just as, twenty years later, while professing their readiness to adopt the discipline of the Council, they refused its dogmatic decrees. Cardinal Borromeo, who knew well from what quarter the blow came, wrote to France:

"Nostro Signore è risolutissimo di non voler comportar che gli si faccia un si grande affronto e pregiudicio; né havemo a maravigliarci dei flagelli che Dio manda a quello regno, poiché mentre procuriamo di darli rimedio opportuno, de là nascono tutti gli impedimenti di venire a questa santa risolutione."

The most studious prelate of the French Opposition at the last Council was willing to accept the canon drawn up by Pius IV, on the ground that the bishops would have agreed to it, provided, at the same time, their own claims had been adequately secured. These tactics are indicated by one of the legates, in a letter which shows that the accepted formula was not the same that was originally proposed:

"Io sarei di parere che si proponesse la dottrina con i canoni dell' ordine secondo la conclusione che ne è stata presa da tutti li deputati in presenza mia, tra quali non è stato un minimo disparere, et contiene, secondo me, la verità della dignità et potestà della sede apostolica. Ma con questo non pare che si possa fuggire di proporre ancora il Decreto della Residenza sotto quella forma, che fu già concluso nella deputatione della quale fu capo Monsignor Illustrissimo di Lorena."

Prof. Friedrich dates the era when the Papal system was put into working order from the appearance of a volume better known among literary curiosities than as a landmark of religious history. Twenty-five distinct editions of the Roman Index, published *Summi Pontificis jussu*, attest the literary policy of Rome; but the *Index Librorum Expurgandorum*, which appeared in 1607, is a work of different character and inferior significance. The first Tridentine Index, of 1564, introduced the prohibition of books *donec corrigantur*; and, in 1596, Clement VIII invited bishops and inquisitors to draw up lists of necessary corrections. The Spaniards did this on such a scale that one of their Indexes filled two folio volumes; but the Roman Court and congregations avoided the indication of censured passages. Besides the *Censura in glossas,* and the famous *Monitum* of 1620, authorising the study of Copernicus, they made scarcely an exception to their rule. Guangelli, of Brisighella, whom Clement placed at the head of the censorship, published an expurgatorial volume of Errata for fifty works that were then in request, making up half of it with a reprint of the corrections to the canon law, and a curious critique of the *Bibliotheca Patrum,* by Malvenda. It was soon found, in the cases of Becanus and Sa, that Rome incurred a perilous responsibility by the partial approbation thus indirectly given to incriminated works. Guangelli's volume was put on the shelf—*suppressus modeste,* as Papebroch says—and he himself was promoted from his office. The wisdom of this course appeared when vehement and pugnacious scholars, like Raynaud and Alexandre, having ascertained the passages for which they had been censured, published them with comments of their own. The Index of 1607, therefore, was not official; it was disavowed; and it was an act of relaxation rather than of rigour.

Coming to more recent times, Prof. Friedrich exhibits, in the most significant light, and with vast research, every detail in the ecclesiastical history of Germany and France that could illustrate the propensity and the progress to centralisation; and events most unlike each other, such as the dealings of Rome with Wessenberg, Hirscher, and the *Petite Église,* enforce the same moral. He turns away from politics, partly, no doubt, because the writings of Friedberg, Golther, Sicherer, and especially of Mejer, have made his readers familiar with the course of negotiations between Church and State. He does not speak of the

Constitution Civile, which was the grave of the Gallican Church; and although one of his twenty-eight chapters is entirely devoted to the vain declamations of Lamennais, and another, which is well worth reading, to the microscopic communities which cluster round the Lake of Lucerne, he never alludes to the temporal power, which was prominent among the generating causes of the Council. It was the touchstone that divided Catholic Italy, forced Liberals and Ultramontanes to face the reality of their antagonism, and brought the Pope to choose irrevocably between them. Since the revolutions of 1776 and 1789 put the adherents of civil and religious liberty in opposition with the accepted policy of Rome, they avoided actual collision, because of the advantage which religion derived from those principles, and because the Catholics who held them did not recognise the accident, the exception, or the expedient in emergency as the constant and consistent practice of their Church. Cardinal Chiaramonti justified democracy by the New Testament; Cardinal de Bonnechose discovered the Rights of Man in the Syllabus; and the most distinguished and devoted of Irish bishops wrote: "Let the Church perish that thrives by oppression, and visits by temporal penalties the consciences of men!" But the Italian Revolution forced the people of Rome and Bologna to make up their minds whether they possessed the same rights as those of Palermo and Milan. Two priests were the guides of Italy in the movement of those days—Gioberti, who was Minister at Turin, and Rosmini, whom he sent as ambassador to Rome, and whom the Pope wished to make the President of his Ministry. Technically they were both Ultramontanes, and, apart from their theology, if they had had their will, they would, like Leibnitz, have exalted the Papacy to an influence over men that would almost have realised the mediaeval dream. They were, at the same time, strenuous Liberals, and reformers of Church and State more profound and original than the Frenchmen who occupy so much of Dr. Friedrich's space. Their vast popularity, their sudden failure, the repudiation of their teaching, ought not to have escaped his notice, for the reaction against them determined the later position of Pius IX. In January, 1861, when France and Austria had suffered his army to be dispersed, and while the Piedmontese were besieging Gaeta, a cardinal, advised by Passaglia, approached him with proposals from Cavour. He was to have absolute control over the clergy, and the property of the clergy, with securities for his own independence, if he would allow his dominions to be governed for him.

There were passages in the chequered records of his life that made it seem conceivable that, in the language of the day, he might consent to betray Legitimacy to Revolution. He had striven to be a liberal and patriotic Pope; he had seemed to Metternich almost a revolutionist, and to Ventura almost a rationalist, and his views touching the salvation of Protestants have been quoted with admiration by Lutheran divines. The Piedmontese consul telegraphed to Cavour: "Le Cardinal Santucci lui a parlé de la perte inévitable du temporel, et des propositions reçues amicalement. Le pape a montré se résigner à tout." In the words of the Italian Foreign Office, the Pope, "selon le témoignage du Cardinal, s'en montra frappé et convaincu." But the Liberal party could offer nothing to compensate for a breach with those who had been associated, in prosperity and adversity, with the Papal cause. It admitted the temporal power only if exercised in conformity with its own principles; and it was sure, in the long run, to prove irreconcileable with the whole system of privileges, the immunity of the clergy, and the Dead Hand. When the King of Naples became his guest, the Pope announced that he would not treat, and Rome became the Archimedian point of the European reaction. The Papacy relied thenceforth on straining the energy of the forces that were in harmony with its claims, and were most opposed to the Liberal doctrine. In those days the Syllabus began to ripen, and men accustomed themselves to vague talk of a coming Council. The plan was disclosed in the autumn of the year 1864, when the Convention of September gave warning that the temporal power must depend on spiritual resources.

That men should have expected that a Council would strengthen the position, especially the political position, of the Holy See may seem a paradox. Soon after the opening, Antonelli said: "Io temo che sarà una seconda edizione dell'amnistia"; and Minghetti, who had concerted with Cavour and Passaglia the scheme for the independence of Church and State, visited Rome in January 1870, and came away convinced that Italy would not have long to wait for its capital. Some months later the same belief gained ground in the Council itself. The Bishop of Rotenburg spoke mysteriously of "magna et gravissima pericula, immo, non solum pericula, sed certissima damna, ecclesiae inde oritura." The Archbishop of Paris spoke in terms more definite and ominous:

"Nemo non videt si politicae gnarus, quae semina dissensionum

Schema nostrum contineat, et quibus periculis exponatur ipsa temporalis Sanctae Sedis potestas. Sed haec exponere longum foret, forsan indiscretum; vel certe omnia quae in promptu sunt argumenta hic non possem praebere, quin in plura inciderem quae prudentia dicere dissuadet."

But these speeches were delivered in May, when the resignation of Daru and Ollivier's impatient despatch had made the peril of the hour visible to all. At the inception of the Council the distance was not so clear. There were doubts whether the monarchy could survive the king; whether Garibaldi would not contrive, as he said, to destroy the nation he himself had made; whether Italy would not go to pieces against the Quadrilateral, or against a deficit of sixteen millions. Down to the eve of the Council there were keen eyes that saw no rocks ahead. Although the programme had been proclaimed to France by the *Univers*, on February 13, one of the ablest Frenchmen, an opponent of Papal infallibility, but a paladin of Papal sovereignty, wrote, in May, "Il faut espérer et attendre beaucoup de la future assemblée." Two months later Gratry saw no reason to expect anything but "un coup d'épée dans l'eau." When, at the eleventh hour, Montalembert roused the alarm of the Bishop of Orleans, he declared that it was too late:

"Il a attendu beaucoup trop tard, il a tiré ses deux coups de canon coup sur coup, de manière à en affaiblir l'effet et l'écho, et surtout il n'est pas défendu, parce qu'il a prêché lui-même le silence et l'inaction depuis la convocation du Concile."

The last chapter describes the attitude of indifference assumed by the European Powers until the production of the *Schema de Ecclesia*. Dr. Friedrich writes of these things with his usual reserve, and neither treats the rejection of the Hohenlohe scheme as a decoy, nor repeats the reproaches which one of his most distinguished predecessors has addressed especially to this country. Friendly counsel, indeed, was not spared; but Lord Clarendon, the Foreign Secretary, did not breathe freely in the atmosphere of the schools. Fenianism was at its height; he remembered his viceroyalty of 1848, and differed from other public men in thinking it desirable to have spiritual aid from Rome in our domestic trouble. He therefore fortified himself with a statement of reasons why our intervention might be received with suspicion; and he kept aloof until, at Easter, he joined France in her remonstrance.

PERSPECTIVES ON HISTORY, RELIGION, AND MORALITY

[19]
Human Sacrifice

Theses

I

Permultum attulisse ad systema Epicuri contemnendum, quod corrupta modo et paucissima scripta hujus philosophi nobis tradita sint.

II

Satius esse, singulorum Stoicorum opiniones historice adumbrare, quam omnia totius scholae placita velut unum systema et bene elaboratum explicare.

III

Mechanicam contemplationem universi nunquam nobis satisfacere posse.

In the recent volume of his *Miscellanies* Lord Stanhope has published a correspondence between himself, Sir Robert Peel, and Lord Macaulay, on human sacrifice among the Romans. The letters had for some time been privately circulated, and had attracted much attention to this singular phenomenon in the history of humanity; but the most remarkable fact about them is, that two of the writers regard human sacrifice as so conclusive a sign of a barbarous society that, in defiance of the strongest and most abundant evidence, they endeavour to prove that it had no existence among the civilised Romans. That Sir Robert Peel and Lord Macaulay were in error in this strange opinion, will

Privately printed (London: Robson, Levey, and Franklyn, 1863).

hardly be questioned by any student of antiquity; and our object, therefore, in this paper is not so much to refute their arguments as to trace in different ages, different countries, and different systems, the religious idea and the varying forms of the rite which was the subject of their discussion.

Human sacrifice is an institution which may be the outward sign of contrary religious ideas, and of opposite extremes of civilisation and barbarism. But instead of distinguishing its local causes and circumstances, the different writers on the subject have tried to generalise all the instances of it into a single law, advocating each his one view of the meaning of the rite, and consequently giving contradictory explanations. But in reality different nations have approached it by different paths; and it is therefore a symptom sometimes of one, sometimes of another phase of cultivation, reacting in different ways on the national character.

By human sacrifice we do not understand every act of putting a man to death with religious forms, or in obedience to a religious idea. When a nation of fanatics wages a war of extermination against those who do not worship its gods, and piles up pyramids of bodies, the idea of honouring the divinity does but dimly tinge the savage thirst for blood. When a traveller cast on an inhospitable shore, like that of Tauris, is murdered by the inhabitants to appease the god whose land his foot has defiled, it is the act of barbarians, who imagine that their gods, like themselves, look on every stranger as a foe:

> Sacrifici genus est, sic instituere priores
> Advena virgineo caesus ut ense cadat.

Or when an unwary wanderer trespasses on the consecrated grove, or witnesses the secrets of an unnatural worship, his murder, even at the altar, is rather the punishment of sacrilege than a real sacrifice. In the German armies the priests alone could inflict punishment: "ne verberare quidem nisi sacerdotibus permissum, non quasi in poenam nec ducis jussu, sed velut Deo imperante."[1] In Iceland the judgment-seat was close to the altar where the condemned were slain. Here the gods were avenged by the punishment of the criminal, and civil justice received a religious sanction. When the wife or slave was burnt or buried with the chief, it was to console the departed spirit; and when slaves or prisoners were slaughtered at his tomb, it was in homage to him, not

---

[1] Tacitus, Germania, 7.

to honour the gods. So in our day wretches are wantonly put to death on the slave-coast to celebrate some great occasion. The arrival of a distinguished traveller must be notified to the departed spirits; but the victim who carries the news is not properly sacrificed. In Russia there are great pits black with smoke and the charred bones of men; but the sect whose votaries have perished there never dreams of offering men in sacrifice to God, but believes that death is better than life, and suicide an atonement for guilt, and the crown of a well-spent life.[2]

Again, cannibals who believe that their gods delight in human flesh, or savages who slay all their prisoners, will set apart a portion of their victims for the share of the gods. Or those who, instead of killing, reserve the prisoner as a chattel of no more value than so many sheep or oxen, will sacrifice men, not as things different in kind from cattle, but as representing a certain amount of property. The pious owner will immolate so many sheep, or so many bullocks, or so many slaves, according to the solemnity of the occasion, or the convenience of his establishment, not through the idea that the slave, as being like his master, is different from the beasts offered with him.[3] No distinct religious significance is attributed to the nature of the victim. The cannibal offers human flesh to his cannibal god; and in this the celebrated Wolf imagined that he had discovered the origin of all human sacrifices.[4] The savage slave-owner sacrifices the slave with other animals, without a thought of his humanity, without a scruple about killing, torturing, or defiling him, because he is taught that the slave has no moral existence, and can have no moral value in the sight of the gods when he has no rights among men.

Such acts, though like sacrifice in externals, must rather be classed under the heads of religious intolerance, wholesale massacre, military execution, criminal law sanctioned by religion, the penalty of sacrilege, the funeral rites of a people whose hades is only a continuation of this life, and the effects of cannibalism and slavery. They are all compatible with the disavowal, or even the abhorrence, of human sacrifice; and

---

[2] When the imperial commissary came to inspect their colony, thirty-eight of their number shut themselves up in a hovel, and burnt themselves to death in his presence. But this idea of baptism by fire does not always result in suicide. The sect of the *Dietooubiizi* burn their children in order to send their immaculate souls to heaven. In this form, therefore, it may be said that human sacrifice continues to be practised among the European nations.

[3] "Men are our oxen," said a Fiji. Bastian, *Der Mensch in der Geschichte*, iii. 104.

[4] *Ueber den Ursprung der Opfer—Vermischte Schriften*, p. 243.

yet, as acts of immolation tinged with superstition, they indicate habits on which that institution could be grafted, and with which it could easily coalesce. Yet there is an essential distinction to be made between those cases in which a religious idea has been superadded to a barbarous custom, giving it an outward hypocritical varnish, and those in which the inhuman rite can be directly traced to a theological idea. Without this distinction the subject will remain obscure, and its discussion will only lead into profitless generalities.

In the one case, the sufferer is a victim of the ignorance and ferocity of savages, who, in degrading their gods to their own level, and looking on their captives as no better than beasts, betray the most material conception of divinity, and the lowest idea of the worth of human life. The practice grows up in some of the deepest stages of degeneracy, and tends still further to debase man, and corrupt the idea of God. It is not consistent with a thoughtful theology or an advanced culture, and therefore disappears with the progress of civilisation, and is unable to coexist or combine with rites which, though perhaps equally sanguinary, proceed from the most subtle and logical developments of pagan belief. Thus the same act, which in the one case displays the ferocity of the savage, his vindictiveness, and his godless ignorance of divine things, may in the other case exhibit the ripest fruit of gentile theology and morality, speculation and worship, and the most lofty protest against the cowardice and selfishness with which men elude the legitimate consequences of their convictions.[5]

Sacrifice is either propitiatory, to add strength and perfection to prayer—for αἱ μὲν χωρὶς θυσίων εὐχαὶ λόγοι μόνον εἰσίν, καὶ δὲ μετὰ θυσίων ἔμψυχοι λόγοι[6]—or expiatory, to atone for sin. The former is the most natural;[7] and the classical writers agree that the original sacrifices were of that kind, and there is no trace of expiatory sacrifice in Scripture previous to the Mosaic law. Yet even propitiatory sacrifice admits of human victims. The best or first of its kind was chosen for the altar; and then, as need pressed more sorely, and the true idea of God waxed dim, the child, as the most prized possession,

---

[5] Wuttke, Geschichte des Heidenthums, i. 136. This profound historian, the first to explain the moral character of human sacrifice, has unfortunately abandoned the pursuit in which he eminently excelled.

[6] Sallustius, De Diis et Mundo, 16, ap. Gale, Opusc. Mythol. p. 272.

[7] On the naturalness of sacrifice see St. Thomas, as cited note 9, below, De Maistre has a pointed saying, "Ni la raison, ni la folie n'ont pu inventer cette idée."

was given up. Sacrifice was a bargain, in which the things prayed for were purchased; and the disposition of the sacrificer became less and less an element, till at last the intrinsic value of the thing offered was the only measure of the efficacy of the sacrifice. Thus would arise the notion of sacrificing the child or the slave as the most valuable, and therefore most acceptable, of gifts—for *omnium seminum optimum est genus humanum.*[8] But before this step could be taken, idolatry must have prevailed, and extirpated the memory of the curse of Adam and the idea of the hereditary sinfulness of mankind. For the belief in original sin—for the remission of which, as St. Gregory and St. Thomas say, the patriarchal sacrifices were the provision[9]—seems inconsistent with what probably was the original form of human sacrifice, the immolation of infants.[10]

Human sacrifice, however, is more properly expiatory. In the Jewish law the offerings for sins of ignorance, which included ceremonial mistakes and unconscious defilements,[11] involved the idea that satisfaction had to be made even for acts in which the will had no part; while for conscious transgressions not only repentance, but an atoning offering was exacted. Among the heathen the same feeling may have grown up, till the accumulated sense of guilt drove them to seek a means of expiating it. A new idea was introduced into the sacrificial rites, and a victim was sought whose death might have an atoning power, to satisfy the justice which was the sovereign attribute of the gods that ruled the world. There was no ministry of grace and mercy in pagan mythology, nothing to teach mankind that the sorrow and amendment of the offender might gain the remission of the penalty of his sin.[12]

This idea of a penalty inexorably exacted, without respect for repentance and conversion, is the basis of a system of Christian theology. For Christianity, says Lasaulx, as the universal religion, comprehends all that was true in earlier systems; and there are few truths explicitly proclaimed in it which are not in substance to be discovered in the pre-Christian world.[13] The famous argument of the

---

[8] Aug. de Civ. Dei, vii. 19. See also Bähr, Symbolik des Mosaischen Cultus, ii. 333.

[9] Sum. 2ª 2ᵃᵉ, q. 85, art. 1 ad 2.

[10] Hence we regard De Maistre's derivation of human sacrifice from the *réité originelle* (Éclaircissement sur les Sacrifices, in the Soirées de S. P. ii. 352) as untenable.

[11] Lev. iv. v.

[12] See Nägelsbach, Die nachhomerische Theologie, p. 362.

[13] Lasaulx, Academische Abhandlungen, p. 233. This is also the leading idea of his

Cur Deus homo of St. Anselm is founded on this theory of satisfaction. The dishonour which sin does to God is not made good by repentance alone. We owe Him something more than the return to virtue; but we have nothing to give but what is previously due to Him. Yet His honour must be avenged, and His justice vindicated. And this expiation cannot be made by anything else than the death of the God-man, without annulling the eternal justice of God.[14] Yet even then, adds St. Thomas, He cannot forego inflicting the temporal punishment due to sin; so that even when we have returned to the state of grace, a penalty still remains due.[15] The Catholic doctrine of Indulgences is generally based upon that theory of satisfaction which was philosophically systematised by St. Anselm.

The same truth was vaguely present to the heathen conscience. It is expressed in the Aeschylean aphorism, πάθει μάθος—"nothing suffer, nothing learn";[16] and still more strongly in the lines,

μίμνει δὲ μίμνοντος ἐν θρόνῳ Διὸς
παθεῖν τὸν ἔρξαντα· θέσμιον γάρ[17]

"while Zeus sits on his throne, the law that the doer shall suffer must stand." The honour of the gods was engaged; mankind would cease to believe in them, ἔρρει τὰ θεῖα, if they allowed sin to go unpunished, or accepted unseen contrition as a substitute for the visible penalty. It was not merely a speculative or symbolical, but a juridical truth, that "the wages of sin was death." There was no other expiation. And human sacrifice, the last and remotest growth of propitiation, was the first and most natural step in expiation. No ordinary sacrifice can redeem the forfeited life of the sinner, or stay the vengeance which his crime may have called down on his family, his city, or his country. His own death will not do it, for his life has become worthless. He and the community whom his guilt has involved must be ransomed by a victim more pure than he would be. The innocent must die for the guilty, in order that society may escape the just anger of the offended gods. Hence expiation could not be originally made with less

---

beautiful essay, Die Sühnopfer der Griechen and Römer, und ihr Verhältnis zu dem einen auf Golgotha. It is the most complete treatise that exists on ancient sacrifices; but the author's definition of expiation is so comprehensive as to be indistinct and confused.

[14] Anselm, Cur Deus homo, i. 11, 12, 20.
[15] St. Thomas, Summa contra Gentiles, iii. 158.
[16] Agamemnon, 177, 231.
[17] Ib. 1494.

than a human victim, for whom animals, or even mere symbols and tokens, were subsequently substituted.

The victim most naturally selected to ransom the guilt of the individual is the child. In the East the child is also the oldest victim known within the historical period who had to expiate the guilt contracted by the State. Infant sacrifice was a later introduction into Europe. The idea that children have to bear their parents' guilt, and that the punishment which does not overtake the sinner falls on his descendants, was unknown to Homer. In Greece it first found expression in Solon.[18] The value of children as victims was that, while they justly suffered for their parent, it was considered that their innocence could at the same time atone for him. If the criminal was to escape, it could only be at the expense of his descendants. To ensure his escape, he must forestall his own punishment, by substituting them for himself. Either he or they must suffer for his sin.

The myth of the Phenician Moloch shows that the original cause of the national infant-sacrifice was not the guilt of the individual, but the consequent danger to the State. It is chiefly in this aspect that it is found in Greece, where it never became usual, but was only employed to avert some public calamity or expiate some private crime, the guilt of which had rendered the whole city odious to the gods. Here, as the guilt of one was imputed to all, so might the sacrifice of one atone for all. This was only the European idea: *Unum pro multis dabitur caput.*[19] The Asiatic idea was not one for many, but one for one. In the words of Macrobius: "Praeceptum est ut pro capitibus capitibus supplicaretur: idque aliquandiu observatum ut pro familiarum sospitate pueri mactarentur." As in the family the child atoned for the father, so in the monarchical state the king or his daughter was the victim who had to die for the people. Early mythical history is full of such sacrifices.

---

[18]   ἀλλ' ὁ μὲν αὐτίκ' ἔτισεν, ὁ δ' ὕστερον· οἱ δὲ φύγωσιν
        αὐτοί, μηδὲ φεῶν μοῖρ' ἐπιοῦσα κίχῃ
        ἤλυθε πάντως αὖθις· ἀναίτιοι ἔργα τίνουσιν
        ἢ παῖδες τούτων, ἢ γένος ἐξοπίσω.

Solon, apud Bergk, Poetae Lyrici Gr. ed. alt. p. 340. So Lycurgus c. Leocratem, 79: τοὺς δὲ θεοὺς οὔτ' ἂν ἐπιορκήσας τις λάθοι, οὔτ' ἂν ἐκφύγοι τὴν ἀπ' αὐτῶν τιμωρίαν, ἀλλ' εἰ μὴ αὐτός, οἱ παιδές γε καὶ τὸ γένος ἅπαν τὸ του ἐπιορκήσαντος μεγάλοις ἀτυχήμασι περιπίπτει.

[19] The well-known lines of Ovid—

        Cor pro corde precor, pro fibris sumite fibras,
        Hanc animam vobis pro meliore damus (*Fasti*, vi. 161)—

have no reference whatever to expiation.

Later on, in republics, a youth or maid was chosen to die for the rest. Thus, in very early times, the more civilised pagans had instituted a sacrifice which, like that of Isaac,[20] was the profoundest sign of the need of a Redeemer, and the most solemn and earnest effort which, in default of better knowledge, mankind could make to satisfy that need. Satisfaction was necessary: death was the just punishment of sin, and the only satisfaction man could make; yet a life already forfeited could not be given in ransom.[21] Crushed by the sense of actual guilt, and ignorant of original sin, men substituted the innocent child for their own guilty selves. Thus the deepest ideas of religion possible to the ages of pagan ignorance gave birth to a rite, the more tremendous and apparently efficacious character of which made even the Jews crave after it, in spite of the elements of better knowledge which their law contained.

All that we have said on the moral elevation of the practisers of human sacrifice must be understood only of those heathens who still retained a belief in a personal and supreme God. Wherever polytheism had corrupted that belief into pantheism, the rite necessarily had another significance. Where God is identified with the animating spirit of the universe, dispersed through infinite space (the macrocosm), and where man is supposed to be a concentrated portion of the same spirit (the microcosm), surpassing the infinite in intensity of mental power, but inferior to it in force and pervasiveness, the idea of prayer and sacrifice, of propitiation and expiation, necessarily becomes changed. Instead of a moral end, its aim becomes cosmical; instead of religious, it becomes magical. Instead of perfecting prayer, it supersedes prayer; it becomes compulsory and imperative, instead of propitiatory and impetrative; it is the "blacker charm" which "compels," when the "spell" of prayer has failed.[22] Instead of expiatory, it becomes medicinal and restorative, like the liver of the murdered child used by Canidia to revive the quenched fires of age.[23] It is the craft whereby man, wiser but weaker than the brute powers of matter, compels them to serve him—compels the moon to shed its vigour-giving influence, the earth to bring forth its fruits, the winds and weather to moderate themselves, and all things to cooperate to human uses.

[20] See Windischmann, Die Philosophie im Fortgang der Weltgeschichte, p. 1266.
[21] See Möhler, Neue Untersuchungen, p. 517.
[22] See Coleridge's drama, Remorse, act iii. sc. 1.
[23] Hor. Epod. v. 37.

The belief in the sovereign and creative power of sacrifice to influence the powers of the universe reacted on the doctrine of creation, and caused it to be mythically represented as a sacrifice. The cosmogonical doctrine of many races was that the world owed its origin to the sacrifice of a primitive living creature, generally represented as human, the different parts of whose body were fashioned by the sacrificing powers into the corresponding portions of the universe. Thus, in the Edda, the three sons of Bör slew Ymir, dragged his body into the midst of the abyss, and of it formed the world. His blood became the waters, his flesh the land, his bones the mountains, and his skull the heavens. In the Vedas, the Rishis formed the world in the same way out of the divided body of Purusha (the primeval man). In Berosus, the woman Omoroca served the same purpose. The same belief is found in races which have no connection with the Aryan stock. In Mexico the primitive man, who was himself formed from a bone sprinkled with the blood of the heroes, threw himself into a fire and became the sun; the moon was afterwards formed in the same way. The mysteries of Greece, Egypt, and Asia, represented the cosmogony, or at least the restoration of the world in spring, as the mutilation and new birth of Zagreus, Osiris, Adonis, or Attys. The Persians derived the world from the mutilation of the primitive ox Abudad. The Finns and the Japanese represent the creation as the breaking of an egg, out of the various portions of which the universe is formed. The New-Zealanders have a myth about the creation arising from the forcible and painful separation of heaven and earth, which is not unlike the Hesiodic myth of the mutilation of Uranus. All these myths express the belief that the rite of sacrifice had a demiurgic force over the mundane elements, which were compelled by it to serve the needs of man.

Now that the victim in this sacrifice was originally man we have the strongest proof. In two places of the Rig Veda there are hymns which assert not only the cosmogonical character of the original human sacrifice, but the derivation of all the other Vedantic sacrifices from this, and their merely representative and substitutive character.[24] They describe the sacrifice of Purusha, the primeval man, who is identified with the world, by the Rishis. From this sacrifice come Soma, the

[24] Rig Veda, lib. viii. cap. iv. hymns 17, 18, 19, and lib. x. c. xi. hymn 2. The former may be found in Burnouf's preface to the Bhagavata, and in the Asiatic Researches, vii. p. 251; the latter in Asiatic Researches, viii. p. 393. The former hymn is also repeated in the White Jajur-Veda, cap. xxxi.

curdled milk, the butter, the animals, and the Vedantic hymns. That is to say, the materials and ritual of the Vedantic sacrifice are derived from and substituted for the materials and ritual of the Purusha sacrifice. From the parts into which the body of Purusha was divided sprang the four castes, that is to say, the political organisation of the Brahmins. Also from the same division came the different portions of the universe—the moon from his heart, the sun from his eyes, fire from his mouth, the wind from his breath, the heaven from his skull, the earth from his feet. "Thus did the Rishis form the world." "Such," concludes one of the hymns, "were the primeval rites. [The Rishis] made great by this ceremony, established the heavens." The other concludes thus: "By that sacrifice sages and men are formed. . . . Viewing with observant mind this oblation, which primeval saints offered, I venerate them. The seven inspired sages (*i.e.* the seven priests of the Vedantic ritual) with prayers and thanksgivings follow the path of these primeval saints, and wisely practise (sacrificing) as charioteers use reins." That is to say, the same thing that was done by the legendary Rishis when they formed the worlds by the primeval human sacrifice, is done by the seven Vedantic priests in their sacrifice of Soma, milk and butter, which are the substitutes for the ancient human victim, and not, as Lassen supposes,[25] the oldest offerings of the Vedantic religion. The horse sacrifice, the mystic power attributed to which is known to English readers by Southey's *Kehama*, had the same cosmogonical significance. In the last chapter of the Black Jajur Veda, it is said that the divided members of the horse are the parts of Time and of the Universe; the horse sacrifice is thus, as Lassen says, a representation of the self-sacrifice of Narajana to Viraj, which is merely another form of the Purusha myth.

Substitution of one victim for another is the fundamental idea of expiatory and of medicinal or restorative sacrifice; after substituting the sufferings of the innocent child for those of the guilty father, or the pure maiden for the defiled community, it was only another step to find substitutes for the child or the maiden. Such substitutes were either animals, living vegetables, or intoxicating liquids (Soma), which were supposed to partake of the same life which man enjoyed; or portions of his life, as contained in his blood; or the food on which his life was supported—cakes, oil, butter, milk, cooked meat, salt, and the

[25] Ind. Alterthumskunde, vol. i. p. 788.

like; or finally, models and symbols of the victim—dolls, wax figures, and tablets or scraps of paper with diagrams on them.

The earliest, most consistent, and most enduring form of human sacrifice concerning which we have definite history is that which was offered to the Assyrian Bel and the Phenician Moloch. The same nation which led the civilisation of Asia, and invented the alphabet, was the first to reach the phase of religious thought through which at some period of its progress all other paganism passed. One of the Fathers ascribes to Chaldaea the invention of heathen sacrifices;[26] and Döllinger[27] considers Babylon to be the real birthplace and ancient metropolis of paganism and idolatry. There, however, the sacrifice of maiden purity had been already substituted in the time of Herodotus for the bloodier rite.[28] Among the Canaanites infant sacrifice was prevalent before the period of the Exodus,[29] and is stated to be the reason why God destroyed them, and gave their land to His people.[30] It was the characteristic of the Syrian cultus:

> Mos fuit in populis quos condidit advena Dido
> Poscere caede Deos veniam, ac flagrantibus aris,
> Infandum dictu, parvos imponere natos.[31]

And it was the purest form of vicarious expiation which nature could suggest. The sinner offers his own flesh and blood, a life of his own life; but, unlike his own, still innocent, and therefore meet to atone for him. The innocence of the victim was the chief requisite; and its healthiness, as the token of innocence, was more indispensable than its blood-relationship to him on whose behalf it was offered. The childless might buy children of the poor to sacrifice.[32] But the victims must be sound—*puras et incorruptas*.[33] An adult victim could not perfectly correspond to these requirements, nor to the mythological purpose of commemorating the act of Kronos (Moloch), the ancient king and then god of the country, who in a moment of public danger immolated his only son.[34] His worshippers could do no less, nor, as Bunsen says,

---

[26] Münter, Der Tempel der himmelischen Göttin zu Paphos, p. 23.
[27] Heidenthum und Judenthum, p. 391.
[28] Münter, Religion der Babylonier, p. 72.
[29] Lev. xviii. 21, xx. 2; Deut. xii. 31.
[30] Wisdom xii. 6.
[31] Silius, iv. 765.
[32] Plutarch, De Superstitione, 13.
[33] Orosius, iv. 6.
[34] Philo, ap. Euseb. Praep. Ev. i. 10.

could "Moloch accept less than this,[35] for he had done the same thing himself deliberately and solemnly." A thoughtful Swiss writer has pointed out the real significance of the rite: "Le seul vrai sacrifice humain est celui de l'enfant par son père; car l'enfant seul est relativement assez pur pour mourir au lieu d'un pécheur, et sa mort seule peut causer, dans l'âme de celui qui veut apaiser Dieu, une douleur assez profonde pour qu'il tremble de l'offenser par de nouveaux péchés qui exigeraient de nouvelles victimes."[36] Accordingly the regular victims were children only. When Gelo made it a condition of peace with the Carthaginians that they should cease to sacrifice their children,[37] he clearly understood these to be the only human victims offered. In the rare cases where men were sacrificed to the Punic gods, the mode of slaughter seems to have been entirely different from that of the children, who were burnt alive in the glowing idol, as described by the Jewish commentators.[38] He who felt the intense significance of the Eastern rite,

> Poeni suos soliti Dîs sacrificare puellos,[39]

must have felt how inadequate was the slaughter of an enemy, or a stranger, or a worthless slave, or to express his craving to give his firstborn for his transgression, the fruit of his body for the sin of his soul.[40]

Among the Greeks human sacrifice was gradually extinguished by the advance of civilisation; among the Phenicians it extended with the progress of enlightenment. Sanchoniathon knows of it only on great occasions, such as that which led to its institution, and only among the royal family.[41] Afterwards the rite became annual;[42] and on great occasions it was performed on a vast scale. At Tyre it had been abolished in very early times; and a proposal to restore it was rejected, even when the mole of Alexander threatened the city with destruction.[43] But at Carthage the custom was never abandoned; and when the

---

[35] Aegyptens Stelle in der Weltgeschichte, v. 382.

[36] M. de Rougemont, Le Peuple primitif, ii. 414.

[37] Plutarch, Reg. et. Imp. Apophthegmata. Script. Mor. 175 A.

[38] Münter, Religion der Karthager, p. 21.

[39] Ennius, Annal. fr. 178.

[40] Mic. vi. 7.

[41] Euseb. Pr. Ev. i. 10; Porphyrius, De Abst. ab Esu Carnium, ii. 56.

[42] Euseb. de Laud. Constantini. 13: καθ' ἕκαστον ἔτος ἔθυον τὰ ἀγαπητὰ καὶ μονογενῆ τῶν τέκνων. Pliny, N. H. xxxvi. 4. 12.

[43] Quintus Curtius, iv. 15.

victorious army of Agathocles stood before its walls, and it was found that many families had secretly bought other children to sacrifice instead of their own, two hundred children of the best houses were immolated at once to expiate the neglect.[44]

But it was necessary that the sacrifice should seem voluntary. As in Sardinia the captives and old men sacrificed to Baal were compelled to meet their fate with smiles—the famous Sardonic grin[45]—so the terror of Moloch's infant victim was soothed by caresses, its cries drowned with music, and its mother forbidden to weep, unless she wished to lose the benefit of the sacrifice. Milton forgot this when he wrote:

> First Moloch, horrid king, besmeared with blood
> Of human sacrifice, and parents' tears;
> Though for the noise of drums and timbrels loud
> The children's cries unheard, that passed through fire
> To his grim idol.[46]

It was a great point in such sacrifices στόματός τε καλλιπρῴρου φυλακὰ κατασχεῖν, φθόγγον ἀραῖον οἴκοις.[47] The voluntary meekness of the victim, going as a lamb to the slaughter, was so essential that such self-devotion rendered even adults fit victims. There is a story of three hundred Carthaginians offering themselves to expiate a crime and ward off a great danger;[48] and it is perhaps from such instances not being very uncommon that Justin was able to say, "Homines ut victimas immolabant et impuberes." [49]

The fiery worship of Moloch was carried by the Phenicians and their colonists to nearly all the coasts of the Mediterranean;[50] but it lost its significance every where except at Carthage, where alone the race remained independent. It could only flourish where astrolatry was supreme, and where the sun was worshipped as the life-giver and the life-destroyer—the god who renewed the earth in spring, burnt it

---

[44] Lactantius, De falsa Religione, 21.

[45] Αἰσχρὸν γὰρ ἡγοῦντο δακρύειν καὶ θρηνεῖν. Zenob., ap. Münter, Rel. der Karthager, p. 27.

[46] Paradise Lost, i. 463.

[47] Agamemnon, 213.

[48] Diodorus, xx. 14.

[49] Justin, xviii. 6.

[50] Böttiger has expended superfluous ingenuity in tracing this transmission. He explains even the story of Cacus by the hypothesis of an image of Moloch. Movers has reduced this idea to its just proportion in the first chapter of his work.

up in summer, and himself suffered in winter, to be restored and to restore the world in spring. These two powers of production and destruction were gathered up in Astarte, the goddess of fertility, and Kronos, the devourer of his own offspring.[51] Two modes of sacrifice corresponded to these ideas; and wherever the Phenician influence extended, they may be traced in holocausts of human beings, and the systematic violation of female virtue.[52]

The union of bloodshed and licentiousness had one of its roots in the physical philosophy of the old world, which considered generation and destruction, like night and day, to be the necessary and mutually-produced successions of being, caused by the excentric motion of the *primum mobile* in the ecliptic.[53] Φθορά, the necessary prelude of all production, was used in two meanings—destruction by death, and pollution. The same philosophy is still exemplified in the Indian rites of Siva, Kali, and Juggernath. The notion of the physical productivity of sacrifice may be connected with the idea of Empedocles, that flesh and bone were the simple elements and the universal germs (πανσπερμία) of earth, water, and air.[54] And this idea accounts for the intimate connection between human sacrifice and agriculture.

In another aspect, the passage from the slaughter of the innocent victim to the ruin of the innocence which gave it its value was strictly logical. As the spilling of blood was substituted in so many cases for the sacrifice of the life that was in the blood, so the destruction of innocence was substituted for the sacrifice of the innocent, without any original reference to the hatefulness of the means by which the substitution was made, but simply on the principle that, instead of the victim itself, that which gave it value might be sacrificed.

But there is also an ethical relationship between the two acts expressed by the verb φθειρείν. Leaving the general question to moralists and psychologists, we may observe that, with whatever indifference men might have sacrificed captives, criminals, or slaves, they could not cast their children into the fire without feeling that they

---

[51] The Grecian myth adds cannibalism to the Phenician story; and the author of Wisdom (xii. 5) affirms, what it would be difficult to prove from the classics, that the murderers of their own children in Canaan were eaters of human flesh.

[52] Justin records a vow of the Locrians, which shows how strangely a religious character was attached to this crime: "Voverant, si victores forent, ut die festo Veneris virgines suas prostituerent" (xxi. 3).

[53] Aristotle, De Generatione et Corruptione, ii. 10.

[54] Ib. i. 1.

were tearing out a fibre, as it were, of their own selves, or without awakening an unnatural frenzy, which might easily lead them to gloat over destruction, and to invert the right impulses of humanity, precisely in the same way as the frenzy of sensuality does. The union of the two frenzies is shown in the self-mutilating orgiasts of Cybele and Attys. Immoral rites and inhuman ceremonies are cognate and corresponding caricatures of the true ideas of worship and of love.

Thus human sacrifice was the turning-point at which paganism passed from morality to wickedness. The highest possible effort at expiation became the natural source of unnatural practices and ideas. The human victim was put to death as a substitute for the conversion and purification of the sinner, and a door was opened for rites in which all distinction of virtue and vice was ignored, and sin itself was often made meritorious:

> Saepius illa
> Religio peperit scelerosa atque impia facta.

At this stage even the indistinct and ignorant worship of God which had survived in polytheism was abandoned, and that of other powers usurped its place. It is this distinction between the purer and more corrupt paganism which accounts for the opposite views taken of it by theologians.

The Jews and early Christians, who saw paganism in its last stage of degradation, universally believed that its gods were devils. In the Bible this identity is not distinctly expressed: sometimes the gods are said to have no real existence, sometimes to be demons.[55] The same Hebrew word is translated by the Seventy in three ways—demons,[56] idols,[57] and vanities.[58] St. Paul is careful not to assert the real existence of the gods while he says that the devils receive the homage offered to them.[59] The early Fathers understood that these gods were actual devils; Justin Martyr, who, with all the Antenicene Fathers but one, interprets Gen. vi. 2 of sinful angels, holds that their offspring were the demons who became heathen gods, and actually existed in the form represented by the idols, and perpetrated all the crimes recorded

---

[55] Döllinger, Heidenthum und Jud. p. 825.
[56] Ps. cv. 37.
[57] Ps. xcvi. 7.
[58] Zach. xi. 17: see König, Theologie der Psalmen, pp. 284, 311; Isaiah xli. 29.
[59] I Cor. viii. 4, x. 19.

in mythology.[60] St. Augustine believed that the gods were real devils, who usurped the place of God in order to enjoy the homage due to Him, and intercept the prayers and sacrifices intended for Him.[61] But this opinion in its sweeping universality has not held its ground among Christian philosophers and divines. Yet the character of certain rites is so distinctly diabolical as to confirm the belief that in these cases particular demons both inspired and received the abominable worship.

When paganism had reached this development, all that had mitigated or redeemed its demoralising influence at once disappeared; it could no longer soften manners, uphold the sanctity of laws, tame pride and passion, or inculcate reverence for the past or care for the future. All those social and political influences which distinguished the religions of Greece, Persia, and Rome, were lost, and the degraded worship became the poison of morality and the enemy of civilisation. And every pagan religion exhibited such a phase when the old belief was disintegrated, and when the powers which had gradually led men away from God seemed finally to have usurped His place. This phase has not always coincided with the period of lowest national decline, because in some favoured countries an intellectual reaction has transformed a perishing religion, or scepticism has delivered men from its thraldom; "quum et politiores homines et minus creduli esse coeperunt."[62] But wherever there was no such intellectual revival to produce a conflict between the awakened reason and the degenerating tradition, and wherever error pursued its blindfold course unchecked by great lawgivers like those of India, Persia, and China, or by culture like that of the classic world, there the horrors of paganism developed themselves helplessly, till the only remedy was the strong hand of an imperial administration, as in Gaul; the extermination of the priesthood, as in Britain; or the destruction of the race itself, as in Central America. There is no other natural term; the orgies of the Syrian Venus were revived at fixed intervals in the Lebanon down to the nineteenth century.[63]

Greece presents a contrast to the unvarying East, in the modifications

---

[60] Apol. i. 5, 9, 21, 25; ii. 5.

[61] Cont. Faustum, xx. 18, 21, xxii. 17; De Civ. Dei, x. 19, vii. 33, viii. 23, xv. 16; Sermo de Tempore Barbarico, 5; Epist. cii. 18, 19, 20. The similar statements of the other Fathers are referred to in Usteri, Paulinischer Lehrbegriff, p. 421; and Semisch, Justin der Märtyrer, ii. 388.

[62] Minucius Felix, Octavius, 26.

[63] Movers, Die Phönizier, i. 689, quoting Burckhardt and Buckingham.

which a people of restless temper and sharp intellect introduced into the original idea of human sacrifice, and in the rapidity with which the rite passed through all phases of progress and decline. The stubborn consistence and unreflecting conservatism of the Punic race converted religious earnestness into a demoralising influence, while the unstable indifference, the keen vital enjoyment, and the intellectual liberty of the Greek soon made the rigid ceremonial of expiation conform to the feelings of a civilisation in which religion was not the only, and sometimes not the most powerful, of the influencing forces. Without questioning that human sacrifice was indeed the most efficacious of offerings, the Greek felt that it was connected with a more earnest religion, a more cheerless theology, a more mystical philosophy, than that which belonged to the fantastic and poetical world of Greek mythology. He never lost sight of the foreign and "barbarous" origin of the rite.[64] It was strange and unhallowed, alien from Hellenic manners. Heracles, who represents their influence, suppressed it in Italy. The chorus in Euripides condemns the sacrifice of Iphigenia; and Herodotus calls the sacrifice of two Egyptian boys by Menelaus, to obtain a fair wind, an unholy act—πρῆγμα οὐκ ὅσιον. Aeschylus and Herodotus are the earliest writers who mention it, and from the first it is regarded with fear and aversion. The mythology of Greece knew nothing of propitiatory human sacrifice, in which the victim is offered up as a better kind of animal. The myth of Pelops was referred to Phrygia. Neither legends nor histories know of human victims, except in expiation of offences that had drawn down public calamities;[65] and even then it was desired that the act should be the victim's own, and that he who died for thousands should die cheerfully,[66] and then there was little need of any religious rite.

The Centaur Chiron, whom one authority calls the inventor of sacrifice, was the earliest mythological personage who gave up his life to ransom another, when he resigned his immortality in favour of

---

[64] θυσίαν ξένην, Pausanias, vii. 19; θεσμοῖς ξενίοις. Certamen Hes. et Hom. 323, ed. Göttling.

θυσίας
ἃς ὁ παρ᾽ ἡμῖν νόμος οὐχ ὁσίας
Ἕλλησι διδοὺς ἀναφαίνει.   Eurip. Iph. in T. 463.

[65] See Eurip. Electra, 1024.

[66]

ἀρκεῖν γὰρ οἶμαι κἀντὶ μυρίων μίαν
ψυχὴν, τάδ᾽ ἐκτίνουσαν, ἢν εὔνους παρῇ.

Soph. Oed. Col. 498.

Prometheus.[67] The daughters of Orion volunteered to die when the oracle declared that a pestilence could only be averted from Aonia by the voluntary deaths of two maidens. So Macaria, and the daughters of Erechtheus, and Codrus and Cratinus in historic times, died for Attica. At Thebes the king's son slew himself in obedience to the prophecy of Tiresias. Even the death of Leonidas was counted among voluntary sacrifices. Now in all these cases the responsibility was thrown upon the oracles, or upon the gods; not one is represented as proceeding from the customs of the people.

The rite could not long subsist in this pure form. The dread of it, which at first made the Greeks ascribe it to the direct command of their gods, and require the victim to be a voluntary one, soon led to further changes, which portended its gradual but sure extinction. For when once the rigid consistency of the original Moloch-worship was abandoned, an opening was given for the irresistible influence of civilisation and humanity, of religious scepticism, and the sense of men's social and moral rights. The first amendment was to select the victim by lot; the idea grew naturally from the democratic institutions of Athens, but its earliest victim was the daughter of Aristodemus in the first Messenian war. The next change was to give the victim a chance of escape. The oracle had decreed that, to expiate the violence offered to Cassandra, for a thousand years two Locrian virgins should be sent annually to Troy, where they were sacrificed, unless they could escape into the temple of Pallas. At Athens the rite soon degenerated. Two poor persons were annually sacrificed for the people. The same usage prevailed in other places; but instead of the spotless and voluntary victim, first a slave or a captive, and afterwards an animal, was slaughtered with the consent of the god, or blood was drawn without destruction of life, or the victim was slain in effigy.

Yet, in spite of the horror which devised all these modes of evading the rite, we find traces of it throughout almost the whole Hellenic world, in the cultus of almost every god, and in all periods of their independent history. There is no nation, says Lasaulx, of which more numerous or more various sacrifices of human victims are recorded. Gerhard has classified the instances geographically, and assigned them to their respective myths. In the middle of the fourth century B.C., Plato speaks of the rite as a common custom,[68] and it was not entirely abolished even at the beginning of the Christian era. Yet the Greek

[67] Apollodorus, ii. 5, 6.
[68] Laws, vi. 22, p. 782.

religion could never be thoroughly harmonised with making the present life unhappy to secure enjoyment in the next, and with atoning for all evil actions by voluntary suffering, which is the natural development of the doctrine of expiation by sacrifice. A system, then, which enacts bloody sacrifices without providing for the lower grades by inculcating self-imposed penance, moral discipline, and self-denial, is mutilated and inconsistent. The idea of expiation requires more than a substituted victim. It is but a superficial theology which would exempt the sinner from any effort beyond that of providing a vicarious sufferer. But the Greek idea, at least in historic times, was never properly theological, for the victim did not wash away the guilt of the individual, but only warded off the consequences of sin from the community. And these consequences remained after the guilt was washed away. Orestes, though purified of his mother's blood, was still pursued by the Furies. It was not the conscience of guilt, but the terror of its consequences, which overcame the humanity of the Greeks. Where this terror found no place, there, instead of the human victims which other nations offered, they contented themselves with hecatombs of animals,[69] and with the mysteries which unquestionably satisfied those religious cravings that in other places could only be appeased by human sacrifice.

But in Rome, where religion was more real, the awe of the gods greater, the view of life more earnest and gloomy, and morals more severe, human sacrifice was less hateful to the popular mind. There was no horror of bloodshed in the national character, and no provision for substituting an easier atonement for human victims in the religious ritual. The deification of the State made every sacrifice which it exacted seem as nothing in comparison with the fortune of Rome; and the perils which for centuries menaced it from Carthage or Gaul, Epirus or Pontus, Parthia, Spain, or Germany, each demanded its human victims. There are but few records of the sentiments of the earlier Romans. The bulk of their literature belongs to the age of universal empire, when the people dwelt securely in the capital of the world, thinking only of distant conquest, and when their religion had lost its local and national character. As Prudentius says,

> Roma antiqua sibi non constat, versa per aevum,
> Et mutata sacris, ornatu, legibus, armis:

---

[69] Hence they were obliged to keep larger flocks and herds than even modern civilisation requires. Götte, *Das Delphische Orakel*, p. 101.

Multa colit, quae non coluit sub rege Quirino.
Instituit quaedam melius, nonnulla refugit;
Et morem variare situm non desinit, et quae
Pridem condiderat jura in contraria vertit.
Quid mihi tu ritus solitos, Romane senator,
Objectas, cum scita patrum populique frequenter
Instabilis placiti sententia flexa novarit?

When the fulness of time was at hand, the energy of the old belief was broken, and the decomposition of the national religion was first manifested in its effects on that rite which was its highest and most forcible expression. Those substitutions were adopted which became to after ages the proof of the earlier prevalence of human sacrifice while the Etruscan influence was strong.[70] Resemblances, as Servius says, were taken for realities; the name was held to be as good as the thing. Dolls were flung into the Tiber instead of men; and it was pretended that the animals which were sacrificed were human beings transformed.[71]

Human sacrifices were first prohibited in the Republic B.C. 95; and "for some time," says Pliny, "the open celebration of the monstrous rite was unheard of."[72] But, as Sillig says on the passage, Pliny can only have meant that human sacrifice for magical purposes ceased, as he must have known that men continued to be publicly offered for other causes down to his own times. The few traces that remain prove that the magical rite was still practised, though in secret and with shame, whilst human victims continued to be publicly immolated for other ends, till they also were proscribed by the law. Augustus interdicted all Roman citizens from partaking in the inhuman rites of the Druids, whose sacrifices were suppressed by Claudius in Gaul,[73] and by Suetonius in Britain.[74] In the sentences of Julius Paullus, written in the beginning of the third century, we find a law making it a capital offence to offer a human sacrifice either secretly or in a

---

[70] Müller, Etrusker, ii. 108. It is wonderful that a scholar like Preller should have written that human sacrifice was entirely abolished by Numa, Römische Mythologie, p. 116.

[71] Hartung, Religion der Römer, i. 160.

μορφὴν δ' ἀλλάξαντα πατὴρ φίλον υἱὸν ἀείρας
σφάξειγ ἐπευχόμενοσ μέγα νήπιος.

Empedocles, ap. Plutarch, De Superst. 13.

[72] Pliny, Nat. Hist. xxx. 1, 12.

[73] Suetonius, Claudius, 25.

[74] Tacitus, Ann. xiv. 30.

temple.[75] This must be drawn from the edict of Hadrian, to which many later writers attribute the extinction of the practice.[76] But the belief in the magical or atoning efficacy of human blood grew, under the influence of Oriental priests, with the increasing stringency of the law that forbad it, and human victims perished long after the decree of the year 97 B.C., and in defiance even of the edict of Hadrian.

In the year 63 B.C. Catiline and his accomplices sacrificed a boy, and ratified the oath they had taken over his bleeding body by eating his flesh.[77] Seven years later Cicero publicly accused Vatinius of offering up human victims to the infernal gods.[78] Juvenal speaks of similar practices under the Flavian Caesars;[79] and Justin Martyr under the Antonines.[80] In the times of Marcus Aurelius, Aristides the rhetorician—who had been for many years afflicted with an incurable disease, and, as a priest of Aesculapius, was used to receive in his sleep directions from the god, through which he hoped for a cure—learnt one day, when he felt himself better, that his foster-brother Hermias had just sacrificed his own life to save him.[81] A sister, Philumena, remained, to whom he was affectionately attached; but he was warned by the god, that unless she died he could not live. Casaubon understands Aristides to say that she also was sacrificed.[82] He for whom they died published the facts to the world in his Sacred Orations.

What the Roman people were restrained from by law, and by a horror still more effective, was practised by their rulers without fear or disguise. In every generation of the four centuries from the fall of the Republic to the establishment of Christianity, human victims were sacrificed by the emperors. In the year 46 B.C. Julius Caesar, after suppressing a mutiny, caused one soldier to be *executed*, while at the same time two others were *sacrificed* by the flamen of Mars on the altar

---

[75] Jurisprudentiae Antejustinianae quae supersunt, ed. Huschke, p. 438.

[76] Pallas and Porphyry: Porph. De Abst. ab Esu Anim. ii. 56. Eusebius, Praep. Ev. iv. 15, and De Laud. Constantini, 16. Lactantius, De Falsa Rel. 21, who says, "Apud Cypri Salaminem, humanam hostiam Jovi Teucrus immolavit: idque sacrificium posteris tradidit, quod est nuper Hadriano imperante sublatum." In Cyprus the guest, and not the child, was selected as the most efficacious victim. Ovid, Met. x. 224.

[77] Dio, H. R. xxxvii. 30; Florus, iv. 1; Minucius Felix, Octavius, xxx. 5.

[78] In Vatinium, 14.

[79] vi. 552.

[80] Apol. i. 18, ii. 12.

[81] Aristides, i. 476, ed. Dindorf.

[82] In a note to Spartianus, Hist. Aug. SS. i. 135.

in the Campus Martius.[83] The historian is careful to distinguish the
religious rite from the military execution; and there are many reasons
against supposing that the priest could have been a common execu-
tioner. Five years later, when Perugia was taken, Octavian sacrificed
three hundred senators and knights to his deified predecessor;[84] and
the altars of Perugia became a proverb.[85] In the same age Sextus
Pompeius flung captives into the sea, as a sacrifice to his father
Neptune.[86] Augustus sacrificed a maiden named Gregoria, and buried
her beneath the walls of Ancyra.[87] Another, Antigone, was sacrificed
by Tiberius when he built the theatre of Antioch.[88] When Germanicus
died, his house was found to be lined with charms, images, and bones
of men whom Tiberius had sacrificed to the infernal gods to hasten
his end.[89] Augustus had refused to let a senator offer his life to prolong
the days of the emperor.[90] But Caligula compelled one to die who,
having thus devoted himself, shrank at the last moment from consum-
mating the sacrifice.[91] Nero, by the advice of the astrologers, put many
nobles to death, to avert from himself the evils with which a comet
threatened him.[92] Trajan, when he rebuilt Antioch, sacrificed the
beautiful Calliope, and placed her statue in the theatre.[93] In the next
reign Antinous offered himself up for Hadrian.[94] Commodus sacrificed
a man to Mithra.[95] Didius Julianus offered sacrifices of children;[96] and
Caracalla sacrificed human victims in the temple of Serapis.[97] Helio-
gabalus sacrificed children according to the Syrian rites;[98] and Valerian
in obedience to an Egyptian magician.[99] Aurelian, when the frontiers

---

[83] Dio, H. R. xliii. 24.

[84] Suetonius, Augustus, 15, "Scribunt quidam." Dio, H. R. xlviii. 14, λόγος γε ἔχεις.

[85] "Perusinae arae." Seneca, De Clementia, i. 11.

[86] Dio, H. R. xlviii. 48. ὡς γέ τινές φασι.

[87] Malalas, Chron. p. 221. For other instances of this wide-spread superstition see
Bastian, Der Mensch in der Geschichte, iii. 105, 106.

[88] Malalas, Chron. p. 235.

[89] Tacitus, Ann. ii. 69; Dio, H. R. lvii. 18.

[90] Dio, H. R. liii. 20.

[91] Suetonius, C. Caligula, 27.

[92] Suetonius, Nero, 36.

[93] Malalas, Chron. p. 275.

[94] Spartianus, Adrianus, 14; Xiphilinus, p. 356, 21, ed. Sylburg.

[95] Lampridius, Commodus, 9, 11.

[96] Spartianus, Didius Julianus, 7; Dio, H. R. lxxiii. 16.

[97] Dio, H. R. lxxvii. 23.

[98] Ib. lxxix. 11.

[99] Dionysius, ap. Euseb. H. E. vii. 10.

were threatened by the Marcomanni, ordered the sacred books to be opened, and declared that from every nation victims should be supplied for the altars.[100] At the beginning of the fourth century Maxentius divined the future by sacrificing infants, and opening the bodies of pregnant women.[101] The same rites were practised by Julian the Apostate. After his death the body of a woman was found hanging by the hair in a temple at Carrae. He had inspected her entrails to divine the issue of his campaign; and his palace at Antioch was filled with the corpses of human victims.[102] In the year 371 the tribune Pollentianus confessed that he had sacrificed a woman to the infernal gods, in the hope of compassing the destruction of Valens.[103] The instances recur with a uniformity which prove the practice to have been habitual. The un-Roman rite of burying alive a man and woman of the nation with which Rome was at war, described by Livy, survived to the days of the elder Pliny.[104] Children were publicly sacrificed to Moloch in Africa until the middle of the second century. The Romans had crucified the priests on the trees around the temple; but the rite was not extinct in the time of Tertullian.[105] Eusebius, indeed, believed that the edict of Hadrian had effected its purpose; but Porphyry speaks as if human sacrifices lasted until the close of the third century.

But it is unnecessary to prove the Roman practice so circumstantially, when in fact the combats of gladiators were a form of the rite, in which the religious idea still survived beneath the secularity of the spectacle.[106] At first these shows were celebrated for the souls of the dead, like the games which Achilles united with the sacrifice of prisoners at the funeral of Patroclus.[107] At the death of Junius Brutus, the victims furnished by the gentes were so numerous, that they were made to fight together and kill each other; thus converting the rite into a spectacle.[108] The god in whose honour these games were held was the

---

[100] Vopiscus, Aurelianus, 20.

[101] Euseb. H. E. viii. 14.

[102] Theodoret. H. E. iii. 26, 27.

[103] Ammianus, xxix. 2, 17.

[104] "Etiam nostra aetas vidit." Nat. Hist. xxviii. 3.

[105] Apologet. 9.

[106] Tertullian, De Spectac. 12.

[107] Iliad, xxiii. 174, 258.

[108] Servius ad Aen. iii. 67. It was not Brutus the first consul who died on the last day of the year of Tarquin's expulsion, for the event occurred in the first year of the first Punic war, 264. Valerius Max. ii. 4, 7; Liv. Epit. 16.

same who devoured his children.[109] In two places combats distinctly religious in character survived to a very late period. Under Marcus Aurelius the candidates for the priesthood of Diana at Aricia fought at her temple, and the survivor obtained it.[110] And on the same Alban mount a gladiator was annually sacrificed to Jupiter Latiaris until the time of Constantine.[111] But though the Romans were not too civilised to endure the spectacle of wholesale massacres, in which the memory of a religious origin was dimmed by the splendour of the unholy festivity, yet they retained too little of the old spirit to tolerate an inhuman rite the object of which was simply religious. Yet a people in whom unbelief was counterbalanced by superstition, and who were familiar with bloodshed, required no more than the example of their emperors, and the incentives of magic, and of the Phenician and Celtic worship, to confirm them in a taste for sacrifices, for which slavery supplied the victims and secured impunity. The practice defied the laws of the empire, and ceased only with the downfall of paganism. Among the barbarians it survived still longer, and resisted even the preaching of the Christian faith.

The human sacrifices of the Druids may have begun in cannibalism. Strabo says that the Celts of Gaul and Spain were taught by famine to eat human flesh; and he cites a rumour that it was the ordinary practice in Ireland.[112] Diodorus confirms the report.[113] And St. Jerome, in the middle of the fourth century, was an eye-witness of the cannibalism of a British people, who picked out the choice morsels with gluttonous relish.[114] Solinus shows the connection between this unnatural custom and the religious rite, when he speaks of the Irish drinking the blood of their victims.[115] There are indications of the

[109] Auson. Ec. de Feriis Romanis, 33. But the assertion is not sufficiently authenticated, and the evidence of Lactantius, De Vero Cultu, 21, does not prove it.

[110] Pausanias, ii. 27.

[111] Porphyr. De Abstin. ii. 56. Christian and pagan writers agree in considering it a religious rite. The former are quoted by Döllinger, Heidenthum und Judenthum, p. 538, and Lasaulx, Academische Abhandlungen, p. 249.

[112] Strabo, iv. 5, 4.

[113] Bibliotheca Historica, v. 32.

[114] This is one of the passages on which a learned and ingenious writer has constructed the paradox that there were no Druids in Britain, and that the Celts of these islands had nothing in common with the inhabitants of Gaul. Holtzmann, Kelten and Germanen, p. 61.

[115] "Hibernia, inhumana incolarum ritu aspero . . . sanguine interemtorum hausto prius victores vultus suos oblinunt." Polyhist. 22. See Brandes, Das ethnographische

progress in Druidism from an earlier period, when such barbarous customs were widely spread in the race, to its high development in the age of Caesar. The intermediate phase is shown in a practice, out of harmony with the latest form, which had died out not long before the conquest of Gaul—that of burning the clients and slaves of the deceased, together with all that had been most useful to him, at his funeral.[116]

Two centuries before Caesar, the Gauls strove to atone for their offences against the gods by the sacrifice of innocent human victims. Thus, in their war against Antigonus, they offered up their wives and children[117] to "expiate the menaces" of the adverse omens. And Cicero says that any fear led them to offer human sacrifices to avert the peril.[118] On this idea the later Druidic sacrifices, which so horrified the sceptical Romans, were founded. First, the notion was that each man bought himself off by substituting another.[119] And criminals were kept in prison to be thus immolated, for private persons had no right to sacrifice the innocent.[120]

But in the public sacrifices, when the supply of criminals was insufficient, then, in the interest of all, the innocent might be slain. And when the occasion was exceptional, as when the plague visited Marseilles, the atoning victim was not chosen from amongst the criminals; but some poor and harmless man voluntarily offered his life, and on to his head, after he had been maintained for a year at the public expense, the woes of the city were solemnly transferred, and he was thrown into the sea.[121] For the ordinary quinquennial sacrifices,

---

Verhältniss der Kelten und Germanen, p. 44; a work which contains the best refutation of Holtzmann's extravagant views.

[116] De Bello Gallico, vi. 19.

[117] Justin, xxvi. 2.

[118] Pro Fonteio, 10.

[119] "Qui sunt affecti gravioribus morbis, quique in proeliis periculisque versantur, aut pro victimis homines immolant, aut se immolaturos vovent." They would not have gained much if Caesar's words could mean, as Mr. Wright translates them (*The Celt, the Roman, and the Saxon*, p. 45), "When they are seriously ill, or in danger from war or other causes, they either offer up men as victims to the gods, or make a vow to sacrifice themselves."

[120] This must be the meaning of the words, "Supplicia eorum qui in furto aut in latrocinio aut aliqua noxia sint comprehensi gratiora diis immortalibus esse arbitrantur." De Bell. Gal. vi. 16. They could not suppose that the forfeited life of a criminal was more acceptable than that of a spotless victim; but it was forbidden them to murder the innocent.

[121] Lucan, Pharsalia, iii, 399–425. Petronius, Satiricon, ad fin. "Circumducebatur per

however, enemies and criminals were reckoned sufficient. They were massacred in various ways. Some were crucified, some pierced with arrows, and large numbers burnt in one heap with the firstlings of various kinds.[122] These were not expiatory sacrifices, but propitiatory thank-offerings of the earliest and simplest type; and men were offered as the "best victims,"[123] not in kind, but in degree. The divination sometimes connected with the rite was not its primary object.[124] The Druids inspected the victim to augur how the gods had accepted him.

Great authorities have concluded from Lucan's lines—

> Et quibus immitis placatur sanguine diro
> Teutates, horrensque feris altaribus Hesus,
> Et Taranis Scythicae non mitior ara Dianae[125]—

that men were sacrificed to all the principal Celtic gods. This, however, would have been inconsistent with the refining subtlety of the Druidic theology, and we have not sufficient warrant in the Classics for the notion. Tertullian and Minucius Felix[126] know of human sacrifices only to their chief god Mercury (Teutates). Zeuss argues that men must have been sacrificed to Mars (Hesus) if they were offered to Apollo.[127] But Diodorus does not mention it in his account of the cultus of Apollo, and Caesar omits men from his catalogue of the offerings made to Mars.[128] Perhaps, however, the victims slain before battle were offered to Mars, to whom, as well as Mercury, Lactantius says that men were sacrificed.[129]

The Teutonic Odin, whom the Romans identified with the Celtic Teutates, likewise exacted human victims. But the Germans offered such sacrifices before the time when we first hear of Odin. Caesar, who thought they had no personal gods, relates that they thrice

---

totam civitatem cum exsecrationibus, ut in ipsum reciderent mala civitatis; et sic projiciebatur."

[122] De Bell. Gal. vi. 16; Strabo, iv. 4, 5; Diodorus, Bib. Hist. v. 32.

[123] Pomponius Mela, iii. 2; Plutarch, De Superstit. 13.

[124] The testimony of Diodorus to the contrary is of little weight, for he entirely fails to comprehend the real significance of the Druidic sacrifices, v. 31, παράδοξον καὶ ἄπιστον ἔχουσιν νόμιμον.

[125] Phar. i. 444.

[126] Apologeticus, 9; Octavius, 30.

[127] Die Deutschen und die Nachbarstämme, p. 32.

[128] Bib. Hist. ii. 47; De Bell. Gal. vi. 17.

[129] De Fals. Rel. 21. His authority would be greater if he had not written a century later than Tertullian.

determined by lot whether they should sacrifice a Roman prisoner.[130] It seems to have long been their custom to let the gods thus select the victim. Thirty years later, before fighting with Marcus Crassus, the Pannonians vowed they would sacrifice and devour the officers they captured.[131] In their wars with the Cimbri, the Romans believed that the prisoners whom they lost would be sacrificed.[132] The Getae, who deemed death better than life, and mourned their birthday, buried the widow with the husband. So did the Heruli down to the sixth century.[133] In the early times, however, before the struggle with the Empire, the idea of sacrifice was undeveloped in the German mind.[134] But the mythology of the ruthless Odin, which arose during the migrations and expeditions of the Northmen, found in these ancient customs the nucleus of its sanguinary cultus, and elevated the slaughter of captives and widows into a religious rite.

In the times described by Tacitus, the thoughtless barbarity of a nation of warriors coexisted with the religious notions to which it afterwards gave way. The officers of the army of Varus were slain upon the altars;[135] and in the war between the Hermunduri and Chatti, the vanquished were sacrificed to Mercury and Mars.[136] The slaughter of captives was gradually softened down, probably by being more and more assimilated to a religious rite. At first all the officers captured were slain.[137] Later on, the Saxons, the most cruel of the German

[130] De Bell. Gal. vi. 21, i. 53.

[131] Florus, iv. 12.

[132] Strabo, vii. 2, 3.

[133] Mela, ii. 2; Procopius, De Bell. Gothico, ii. 14.

[134] "Neque Druides habent . . . neque sacrificiis student." De Bell. Gal. vi. 21.

[135] Annals, i. 61, xiii. 57.

[136] Germania, 9, 39. Mars cannot be clearly identified with any German god; the Roman historian probably assumed that if any god was invoked in battle, the god of war could not be forgotten, and Mercury had his own human sacrifices at fixed intervals. Jordanes says distinctly that the victims of Mars were enemies captured in battle: De Reb. Get. 5, ap. Muratori, SS. Rer. Ital. i. 195. But the theological idea of these sacrifices appropriated them to Odin, who was the real god of battle, and very inadequately represented by Mercury. "Refert antiquitas . . . quod accedentes Wandali ad Wodan, victoriam de Winilis postulaverint . . . sicque Winilis Wodan victoriam concessisse." Paulus Diaconus, De Gestis Langob. i. 8, ap. Muratori, i. 411. Later writers identify Odin with Mars. Stälin, Wirtembergische Geschichte, i. 111, thinks that the change was probably in some measure due to the influence of the Druids of Gaul; at last Odin absorbed all the human sacrifices of the Germans: as Zeuss, Die Deutschen und die Nachbarstämme, p. 22; Rückert, Culturgeschichte des Deutschen Volkes, i. 3; and Menzel, Odin, p. 135, agree that he did.

[137] Sidonius Apollinaris, Epist. viii. 6.

tribes, decimated their prisoners. The daily sacrifice of a Christian Roman by Rhadagaisus[138] was an unusual act of mingled ferocity and fanaticism. The practice was one of the great obstacles which Christianity had to overcome among the Germans. In the time of St. Boniface, Christians sold their serfs to the pagans of the Baltic for sacrifice.[139] The Saxons must have clung to the rite even after their conversion; for it is punished with death in the very next paragraph of Charlemagne's Capitularies to that which makes the refusal of baptism a capital crime.[140] The Franks practised it long after the death of Clovis: in their Italian invasion of 539 they sacrificed the women and children of the Goths on the bridge of Pavia. Procopius enumerates it among the relics of the paganism which they retained;[141] for, like the Saxons and the Hessians, they were converted, not when their national paganism had become a listless and decrepit form, but while it was in all the energy of expanding vigour. And the resistance of the priests of Odin to the Christian champions, St. Boniface and Charlemagne, left profound impressions on the ideas and forms of the German Church. The gods were too keenly loved and believed in, to be rejected as mere creatures of the imagination; the missionaries did not believe them to be all illusions, and they considered those gods which were worshipped with inhuman rites to be really infernal spirits. This belief of the primitive Church was forced upon the clergy who did battle against the paganism of Northern Europe, by signs which the theology of ancient Rome did not afford. It was admitted then that the German gods were real beings, not divine, however, but devilish. The substance was carefully distinguished from the attributes, and those qualities which were not inconsistent with Christian morality were transferred to the saints. Churches were built on the sites of the heathen sanctuaries,[142] and dedicated to the saint whose legend bore most resemblance to the myth of the dispossessed deity.

A strange fusion ensued. The fallen gods were not believed to be powerless because they were demons; and their anger had been provoked to the utmost by the destruction of their altars. Thus the

---

[138] Orosius, vii. 37; Augustin. De Civ. Dei, v. 23; Sermo, cv. 10; Isidorus, Chron. Gothorum, ad ann. 446; Grimm, Deutsche Mythologie, p. 39.

[139] Epist. 25.

[140] Capit. de partibus Saxoniae, 9.

[141] De Bell. Gothico, ii. 25.

[142] "Ubi fana destruebantur, statim monasteria aut ecclesias construebat," writes the biographer of St. Amandus—Mabillon, Acta SS. O.S.B. ii. 715.

image of Perun at Novgorod broke out into a loud lament for the faithlessness of its ungrateful worshippers, when it was thrown down and dragged to the river.[143] It might still be prudent, therefore, to conciliate the deposed and dishonoured deities, so far as was compatible with the newly-adopted faith. Thus a mass of superstition clustered round the old divinities, and they survived in many a legend of the wild huntsman, or the cave of Venus, or the spirits of mountain and stream, peopling with supernatural figures the minstrelsy of the Middle Ages, and our own fairy- and nursery-tales. But pagan reminiscences not only created and supplied one whole moiety of this dualistic tendency, but also penetrated into the conception of Christianity. Figures in human shape were carried about on certain festivals, in memory of the forbidden victims, and sacrifices were offered, in the eighth century, to the saints.[144] These abuses were rigidly put down by the Church; but she tolerated a species of accommodation, of which two remarkable memorials remain. One is a Saxon poem of the ninth century, in which the Gospel is translated into a kind of Teutonic legend, and our Lord represented as a German warrior-king, surrounded by his faithful liegemen. The other is a poem of Southern Germany, and of the same date, in which the Apocalyptic vision is related with the names and scenery of the Edda.

Long after the worship of Odin was extinct in Germany, it was flourishing enough in Scandinavia to put forth a new theology. For centuries the fierce Northmen were ceaselessly battling against the Christian nations along the ocean coasts, and in the violence of the struggle their religious rites and their social character grew more and more savage. Prodigal of others' blood and reckless of their own, they afforded a congenial soil for the plant of human sacrifice, which put forth some of its rankest shoots just as paganism was about to fail.

The native tradition assigns the origin of the rite to the remotest antiquity, and makes it prevalent among the Northmen from their first appearance among the nations. It was Frey, the second king after Odin, who, in a period antecedent to all chronology, changed the primitive rite, and instituted human sacrifice.[145] Man was the noblest victim; and therefore the first prisoner taken in any expedition was

---

[143] Grimm, Mythologie, p. 957.
[144] Rettberg, Kirchengeschichte Deutschlands, i. 329.
[145] Saxo Grammaticus, Historia Danica, i. 120.

offered up to the god of war.[146] These sacrifices, which were perhaps partly an artifice of the priesthood to mitigate the horrors of war and prevent the general massacre of prisoners,[147] lasted as long as Paganism itself, and in the most various forms. There was a regular form of imprecation to devote the enemy to Odin before the battle.[148] In 893 the Jarl of the Orkneys sacrificed the son of the king of Norway, and offered up his lungs to Odin; and then composed a war-song in memory of his deed.[149] Harold Hildetand, in return for Odin's protection in battle, promised him all the souls that his sword should separate from their bodies.[150] The Swedish regent, Eric, vowed to sacrifice himself to Odin at the end of ten years if he gained the victory over the Danes.[151] In 993 Hakon Jarl, the hero of Oehlenschläger's powerful drama, though he had been baptised, offered all kinds of victims to ensure the success of his arms; but could only propitiate the gods by the sacrifice of his son.[152] The delay of an expedition by contrary winds was occasion enough for the sacrifice; and a Norwegian king was chosen by lot to die for this cause.[153]

It was not unusual to compel the king to die for his people. There was a famine in Sweden in the reign of Domald. In the first year oxen were sacrificed at Upsala; in the second, men; and in the third, the king was immolated, and the altar smeared with his blood.[154] Another

---

[146] Procopius, De Bello Gothico, ii. 15, τῶν δὲ ἱερείων σφίσι τὸ κάλλιστον ἄνθρωπός ἐστιν. Jordanes says the same of the Huns, "Quantoscunque prius in ingressu Scytharum habuere, litavere Victoriae." c. 24, ap. Muratori, i. 203.

[147] So Gagern conjectures, Nationalgeschichte der Deutschen, i. 57; and Münter, Geschichte der Einführung des Christenthums in Dänemark und Norwegen, p. 138.

[148] Ersch und Gruber, Allgemeine Encyclopädie, third section, iv. 95. In this passage Ferdinand Wachter cites several examples of the kind. The article, however, by no means justifies the epithet of excellent bestowed on it by Sepp, who borrows from it his meagre notice of northern sacrifice (Das Heidenthum, ii. 141); as a single instance will show. Dr. Wachter says (p. 105) that the Christian Franks sacrificed the living to the dead, and "the wife of Guntram Boso was buried with many ornaments and much gold;" for which he refers to Gregory of Tours. The words of Gregory are, "Uxor autem ejus cum filiis exsilio data est, resque illius fisco conlatae sunt." Historia Francorum, ix. 10.

[149] Snorre, Heimskringla, ii. 31, ed. Schöning. Torfaeus, Hist. Rerum Norvegicarum, ii. 52, "Exemptosque pulmones Odino pro victoriae perennitate dedicavit."

[150] Saxo, p. 361. "Nec praemii inops beneficium fuit. Animas quippe ei, quas ferro corporibus ejecisset, pollicitus proditur."

[151] Münter, p. 143.

[152] Snorre, Heimskringla, i. 241; Saxo, p. 483; Annales Islandici, p. 25.

[153] Saxo, p. 276.

[154] Snorre, i. 21.

scarcity, under Olave Tretelja, being attributed, like all other evil (or good) to the influence of the king, who was sparing in his sacrifices, his house was surrounded, and he was burnt in it as a sacrifice to Odin.[155] A mythical king of Upsala was promised ten years' additional life for each of his sons that he sacrificed.[156] One Icelander is even related to have offered his son, that he might have grace to find a tree to serve as a column in a temple.[157]

These narratives, though of no value as records of events, prove how familiar was the rite to the Scandinavian mind. For there were certain fixed solemnities at which human victims were sacrificed; and traces of the custom, as Bishop Münter tells us, may still be found in the soil of all the three Scandinavian kingdoms.[158] In Denmark, ninety-nine victims were sacrificed every ninth year, till the beginning of the tenth century.[159] A similar rite existed at Upsala till the middle of the eleventh; and Christians were obliged to purchase exemption by a fine. One of them told Adam of Bremen that he had seen seventy-two bodies hanging at one time.[160] In Iceland, and probably in the other kingdoms, the usual victims were condemned criminals.[161]

Owing to the efforts of the missionaries to save the victims, this horrible rite figures in the history of the planting of the Church in several countries. Sometimes a strange mixture is seen. In the laws of Friesland, after many enactments entirely Christian in character, the code ends with punishing sacrilege by immolation, *immolatur (sacrilegus) diis quorum templa violavit.*[162] Christianity coexisted with Paganism for some time among the Frisians, who were much scandalised at being told by St. Wulfram that they would not meet their ancestors in heaven.[163] While this saint was preaching, a youth named Ovo was once led forth to be sacrificed. Wulfram interceded for him; and was told that the victim should be his slave, if his God would save him. Wulfram prayed; and the rope by which Ovo was hanging broke, and let him fall to the ground. He declared that he had been half asleep,

[155] Snorre, i. 56.
[156] Ib. i. 34.
[157] Münter, p. 144.
[158] Ib. p. 59.
[159] Dithmar, i. 9.
[160] Adam of Bremen, iv. 27.
[161] Historia Olavi Tryggvii Filii, Scripta Hist. Islandorum, ii. 222.
[162] Corpus Juris Germanici antiqui, ed. Walter, i. 374.
[163] Jonas, Vita S. Wulframni, ap. Mabillon, Act. SS. O.S.B. iii. 361.

and felt as if he was held up by the saint's girdle. Upon this great numbers were baptised; and the rescued victim became a priest, and died in 749 at the Abbey of Fontenelle.[164] The demoniacal possessions, so frequent in the Gospels, often broke out with similar frequency and intensity in countries where the Gospel was being preached for the first time. So it was with human sacrifice. In the final conflict of Paganism, it was the most signal proof of the intense tenacity of error, and of the power of the heathen gods over their worshippers, and, at the same time, the most flagrant act of defiance and contradiction to the new teaching. It was, as it were, the demoniacal possession of Paganism. No system, which had once admitted it, ever cast it out by natural and esoteric progress, though it sometimes disappeared with the diminished energy of belief, or by the conquest of another system.

In the reign of king Olave Tryggvason, the Christian skald Hallfred Ottarson narrowly escaped immolation among the heathens of Gothland.[165] In Iceland, the struggle between the new faith and the old was arduous. Olave endeavoured to enforce baptism, and the Pagans insisted that he should sacrifice to the gods, like his predecessors. In 999 he promised the Norwegians to do so; and declared that, to propitiate the gods whom he had deserted, he would offer the most splendid sacrifice ever known, where the victims, instead of slaves and malefactors, should be chosen from the Norwegian chiefs.[166] In 1000 the heathen party in Iceland resolved to sacrifice two men from each province, to defend them against Christianity. The Christians answered the challenge by two men of each province devoting their lives to religion, as nobler victims to obtain the conversion of their country.[167] This is the last instance of human sacrifice among the Northmen; the memory of the barbarous rite long survived among their descendants. Dudo of St. Quentin, and William of Jumièges, and Roger Wace,[168]

[164] Ib. p. 360. The facts were told by the man himself, who was living when Jonas wrote. "Penes nos superstes manet venerabilis vitae presbyter Ovo ex ipsa Fresionum natione oriundus, qui viva voce narrat. . . ." p. 357.

[165] Historia Olavi Tryggvii Filii, ii. 79.

[166] Ib. p. 38.

[167] Müller, Notae uberiores in Hist. Dan. Saxonis Grammatici, p. 116; Finni Johannaei Hist. Eccl. Island. i. 65; Maurer, Die Bekehrung des Norwegischen Stammes zum Christenthume, i. 427.

[168] See Duchesne, Hist. Normann. Scriptores, pp. 62, 218, and the Roman de Rou:
Hommes vis li sacrifioient;
Du sanc de l'homme s'arrosoient.
Mes anchiez s'en desgeunoient.

who borrowed from them the subject of his poem, probably did not know that the ancient rites which they described had been continued almost down to their own time.

Schafarik, the profoundest scholar of the Slavonic world, gives, in his Slavonic Antiquities, an idyllic picture of the primitive manners of the race. They were not barbarians, as the Germans describe them, nor restless warlike adventurers, like the Germans themselves. Their happiness was in the peaceful cultivation of the soil; and it was their expulsion of the Germanic tribes from the rich plains of the Vistula which gave the first impulse to the great migrations. They were civilised, humane, and free, in spite of the Russian writers, who maintain that the natural condition of the people is one of oppression and servitude. In consonance with this cheerful description, Schafarik affirms that human sacrifice was unknown to the great Slavonic race, or only transiently introduced by strangers among some of the northern tribes.[169] His patriotism was incapable of acknowledging that human sacrifice, in various forms, not only prevailed in the race, but continued, in spite of Christianity—perhaps we may say by reason of the conflict with Christianity—down to a period when it had long disappeared throughout the rest of Europe.

One type of it, common to all the nations from the Baltic to the Altaï mountains, is described by Herodotus, in his account of the funeral of a Scythian king.[170] One of his wives and many of his servants were compelled to share his grave, together with his horses, and precious vessels, and the first-fruits of all products. After a year, fifty men and horses were slain and stuffed, and set round the monument as guards. The Scythians gashed and wounded themselves in presence of the royal corpse. The ruling idea was, that the king was deified by death, and that the gods were no other than the dead. They were supplied, therefore, with all that was most needful to them, in order to continue an existence not very different from that which they had lost. The sacrifice of deposition was for use, the anniversary one for honour. This notion of providing the dead monarch with attendants, was capable of an indefinite extension, and led, in a subsequent age, to some of the most appalling scenes in the sanguinary annals of Central Asia. The wounding of the survivors,[171] and the offering of the

---

[169] Slawische Alterthümer, Deutsch von Mosig von Aehrenfeld, i. 538.

[170] Herodotus, iv. 71, 72.

[171] Jordanes affirms that this was only the symbol of a manly sorrow, a substitute for

first-fruits, seem to point to a distinct order of ideas, and indicate a more spiritual conception of divinity and sacrifice.

The earliest notice of similar customs among the Slavonic people, in the Middle Ages, is furnished by St. Boniface,[172] in the year 745. Among the Wends, "foedissimum et deterrimum genus hominum," the widows refused to survive their husbands, but slew themselves, to be burnt with them—"tam magno zelo matrimonii amorem mutuum servant." If the practice had sprung from pure attachment, it would have indicated the existence of sentiments highly favourable to the adoption of Christianity; whereas, being a religious rite, it proved to be a stubborn support of Paganism. Three hundred years later, the Wends, though spoken of very favourably by the Catholic clergy, still shed human blood upon their altars; all their sacrifices were expiatory, and all therefore were bloody. They made no difference in kind between human and animal sacrifices, nor did they understand that bullocks or sheep might be offered up vicariously for human victims. These were selected from Christian captives. One was sacrificed every year; and on great occasions large numbers suffered a lingering death. Dithmar, bishop of Merseburg, who died in 1018, does not particularise the victims as specially Christian: "Hominum ac sanguine pecudum ineffabilis horum (deorum) furor mitigatur." [173] But Helmold, who wrote towards the year 1168, knows only of Christian victims: "mactantque diis suis hostias de bobus et ovibus, plerique etiam de hominibus Christianis . . . annuatim hominem Christicolam . . . litare consueverunt." [174] It seems, therefore, that the original notion of human sacrifice was extinct, and that the practice was kept alive down to the twelfth century only by the antagonism to Christianity.[175]

As practised among the ancient Prussians, human sacrifice exhibits

tears: "Tunc ut gentis illius [Hunnorum] mos est, crinium parte truncata, informes facies cavis turpavere vulneribus, ut proeliator eximius non foemineis lamentationibus et lacrymis, sed sanguine lugeretur virili," De Rebus Geticis, cap. 49, ap. Muratori, i. 215.

[172] S. Bonifacii Epist. 19.

[173] Chronicon, vi. 18.

[174] Chronicon Slavorum, i. 52, apud Leibniz, SS. Brunsvicenses, ii. 582.

[175] War der Einzelne oder die Nation durch irgend eine Schuld, die er wissentlich oder unwissentlich beging, Gegenstand des Zornes der Götter geworden, so konnte die Hingebung des Verhassten keinen Werth haben. Bevor sie annehmbar wurde, musste die Schuld gesühnt sein. Die Sühne forderte Seele für Seele, die Seele aber war im Blut; daher waren alle Opfer blutig. Thier- und Menschenseele wurden nicht als wesentlich verschieden betrachtet; daher konnte eine für die andere als Sühnopfer gelten." Ludwig Giesebrecht, Wendische Geschichten, i. 88. These are the ideas of a highly civilized paganism; and we do not find them in the sources of our knowledge of the Wends.

far higher notions of theology than the ordinary immolation of prisoners and slaves. Not only captives, but children, and the priests themselves, were sacrificed to the god Potrimpos. A perpetual fire burnt before his sacred oak, and the supreme reward of the priests was to perish in its hallowed flames.[176] If it was allowed to go out, the priest who was responsible was burnt as soon as it was lighted again. The priest was mediator between mankind and the gods. When he grew old, he mounted a pyre and exhorted the people to desert their evil ways; and if they professed sorrow, he caused the logs to be set on fire, and offered himself up in satisfaction for their sins.[177] But the rite lost much of its religious significance, and became a mere act of vengeance and ferocity during the long warfare with the Teutonic knights. A Christian who approached the holy places was put to death, in order to appease the outraged gods. Before an expedition, a captive belonging to the hostile nation was slaughtered, in order to ascertain its result—a practice resembling that which, according to Livy and Pliny, prevailed for centuries in Rome. Prisoners taken in battle were put to death with solemn rites, and the swords of the warriors were dipped in their blood. Maidens were crowned with flowers, and slain; commanders were burnt with their horses. A knight of the order was sacrificed in this way in the year 1261, and another so late as 1320. This is the latest instance of the rite in the history of European Paganism, and it is almost entirely stripped of its original religious character.

The Esthonians exhibited the same ferocity against the Christian enemy. In 1221 they sacrificed a Danish captive, and devoured his heart, in order to give themselves courage for the fray.[178] But they were not content with the victims they could obtain in war. A regular trade was carried on, by which Christian slaves were supplied for their altars; and nobles used to sell their serfs for this purpose.[179] The classic historian of Poland[180] tells us that the heathen Poles occasionally sacrificed enemies taken in war; and adds that the rites were accompanied by those acts which in Asia and America, though not in Northern Europe, seem almost inseparable from the sacrifice of human beings.

In Russia it cannot be proved that human sacrifices were known

---

[176] Voigt, Geschichte Preussens, i. 582.
[177] Schwenck, Die Mythologie der Slawen, p. 55.
[178] Peter of Dusburg, Chronicon Prussiae, iii. 86, 331.
[179] Mone, Geschichte des Heidenthums im nördlichen Europa, i. 69.
[180] Johannes Dlugossi, Historiae Polonicae, i. 37.

before the Waragian conquest. But in the tenth century there were many gods to whom parents sacrificed their children.[181] We know no other case in which the rite was practised promiscuously, without distinguishing the deity to whom it was specially grateful. Sacrifices to the dead are described with great fulness by an Arabian writer who was sent by the caliph in the year 921 to convert the Russians to Islam.[182] A man of note having died, his family asked who would die with him. A girl of his house volunteered, and the particulars of her death are remarkable, for they are described by an eyewitness. It is evident that matrimonial affection had as little to do with it as the idea of expiation; for the victim is not the wife, and she exclaims, "My lord calls me, so take me to him," and speaks not a word about the gods, but dies solely to be company to the dead. On the other hand, we are strongly reminded of the Phenician rites when we read that the men beat their shields in order to drown her cries, and that a scene of cold debauchery immediately preceded her death.

On the 12th of July the Russians still commemorate the festival of Theodore and Iwan, the only martyrs of the Church at Kiev. Their legend is connected with the last human sacrifice recorded of the pagan Russians. Five years before their conversion in 983, Wladimir proposed to celebrate his victories in Galicia by offering up the usual human victims to the gods. The lot fell on the son of a Waragian who had been converted at Constantinople. He refused to deliver him up, and denounced the false gods of the people, who thereupon slew both father and son.[183] The Russian Church soon canonised them, and has continued to venerate them ever since. The memory of the blood he had shed haunted Wladimir after his baptism, and great disorders

---

[181] "Il y avait encore le dieu Daschbog, le dieu Stribog, le dieu Smargel et le dieu Mokosch: on leur offrait des sacrifices; ils étaient regardés comme tout-puissans, et les Russes y conduisaient leurs enfans. C'est ainsi qu'ils vénéraient le diable." La Chronique de Nestor, trad. par Louis Paris, i. 119. Strahl imagines that the children were offered up only to the supreme god Perun (Geschichte der Russischen Kirche, i. 29). But the text of the Chronicle is explicit. The passage is remarkable in another way, as it describes five omnipotent gods distinct from each other. The inconsistency of polytheism with omnipotence led the Greeks to that development of the notion of Moira which distinguishes the period subsequent to the trilogy of Prometheus, and to that impersonal monotheism which grows up from the time of Socrates and of Sophocles.

[182] Ibn Foszlan's narrative is given in the appendix to Karamsin's Geschichte des Russischen Reichs, iii. 246, 249.

[183] Nestor, i. 120. Nestor lived within a century after this event, and his story is confirmed in the 13th century by Simon, bishop of Wladimir. Pogodin's Nestor, Beiträge zur Kenntniss des Russischen Reichs, x. 199.

were "caused by the mildness of his later rule. He feared to provoke the anger of God if he destroyed a human life, and the clergy were compelled to admonish him that severity was an important duty of kings.[184]

The conversion of the people did not deliver the soil of Russia from the horrors of human sacrifice. It was universally practised by the Tartars, says Mirkhond,[185] but apparently only at the burial of chieftains, and not in honour of the divinity. Those who dug the grave of Attila were immediately slain, in order that the place might be concealed from the knowledge of mankind.[186] One hundred years later a similar custom prevailed among the Turks, but with a somewhat deeper significance. Terxanthus slew, together with his father's horses, four captive Huns at his grave, bidding them inform him of the state of his affairs.[187] At the death of Gengis Khan forty maidens followed him to the other world; and, in order that the secret might be kept, his followers slew all whom they met while carrying his body from the place where he died on the Hoang-Ho to the sepulchre of the Khans in the Altaï.[188] Marco Polo says that this became the regular practice thenceforward at the funeral of the Khans, and that the victims were told that they must go to serve their master in the other world.[189] When Mengu died, in 1259, many thousand corpses marked the passage of his funeral procession across the plains of Tartary. The favourite wife of Oktai died upon his grave; and maidens covered with jewels were buried with Hulagu.[190]

The long and arduous struggle of the gentler religion of Buddha against this ancient rite has been recorded by one of the descendants of Gengis. In 1578 it was forbidden to destroy even horses or camels at funerals. Nevertheless, when Altan Khaghan lost his only son, the mother of the boy, regardless of the sin, says the Mongol historian, ordered one hundred children to be slaughtered as companions for her

---

[184] Nestor, i. 142.

[185] Hammer-Purgstall, Geschichte der goldenen Horde in Kiptschak, i. 205.

[186] "Ut tot et tantis divitiis humana curiositas arceretur, operi deputatos destestabili mercede trucidarunt, emersitque momentanea mors sepelientibus cum sepulto." Jordanes, ibid. p. 216.

[187] Stritter, Memoriae Populorum olim ad Danubium &c. incolentium, iii. 62.

[188] D'Ohsson, Histoire des Mongols, i. 381.

[189] Il Milione di Messer Marco Polo, ed. Bandelli Boni, ii. 117. The text says 10,000; but the Della Cruscan edition has 20,000. The figures are of course entirely worthless.

[190] Hammer's Goldene Horde, i. 205.

child. More than forty had perished when the threats of the people put an end to the massacre. The guilt of the mother caused strange things to befall when she was dead. The devil would not abandon the corpse, and made it move in horrible imitation of real life. The Bogda Lama invoked the most awful of the gods. The upper garment of the dead was laid in a triangular grave, into which the Bogda Lama also flung as many passing demons as he could catch; whereupon a lizard appeared. The Bogda Lama then discoursed so impressively on inevitable death, that the creature, having bowed its head three times, gave up the ghost. Then the garment and the lizard were consumed by fire, from which proceeded a stench so foul that many of those who were present fainted. But the faith of those who preserved their senses was wonderfully confirmed when they beheld a great white pillar rising out of the smoke, bearing on its summit a heavenly figure.[191]

So great is the force of this superstition, that it survives to the present day among a race which has professed for centuries a religion which condemns it as a monstrous crime. Huc relates that young slaves of both sexes are even now poisoned with quicksilver, and placed around the body of a Mongol prince.[192] There can be no more conclusive proof that the custom can subsist without the slightest reference to the religious idea of sacrifice.

Buddhism encountered human sacrifices of another and far more spiritual kind in India. Hegel has very correctly explained how the pantheism of the Hindoo religion led to the sanctification of suicide. The Hindoos depreciate and despise the life of man. It has no more value, they say, than the life of nature, and it can only acquire dignity by that negation of itself to which all concrete existences are essentially opposed. Hence, in their ritual, men sacrifice themselves, and parents their children, and widows are burnt after their husbands' death; not in satisfaction for guilt incurred, or to expiate a wrong, but only for the purpose of becoming meritorious.[193] Hence these acts must be spontaneous; for the victim dies not for others but for himself; and be he ever so great a sinner, he becomes, by the act of self-sacrifice, pure from sin. In this form the rite is peculiar to India; but it existed there

---

[191] Geschichte der Ostmongolen von Ssanang Ssetsen, ed. J. J. Schmidt, p. 249.

[192] See Neumann, Die Hellenen im Skythenlande, i. 235.

[193] Hegel, Philosophie der Religion, i. 320. When human beings are offered up to the spirit of destruction, self-mutilation and torture follow as subordinate effects of the same cause. See Windischmann, Philosophie im Fortgang der Weltgeschichte, p. 1266.

in many other forms, whether of native growth or as Aryan imports.[194] In later times it was confined to the worship of Kali;[195] but although recognised and regulated in the Vedas, it was discouraged, and prevailed chiefly among the sects.[196]

Ritter, in his great work on the geography of Asia, has collected many instances of human sacrifice, either known by memorials, or still practised early in this century and about the time of Heber's travels.[197] Since those volumes were published, the investigations of English officers have proved that a kind of vicarious sacrifice prevailed very extensively in Southern India. Macpherson and Campbell discovered sects by whom human victims were regularly put to death in incredible numbers. Generally they were bought for the purpose, and were kept in comfort for years until the moment of their doom arrived, when they were slain, in order to secure fine weather and rich crops, but seldom at the dictation of a subtle theology such as that which devotes crowds of voluntary and cheerful victims to Kali.[198]

The most perfect spectacle of the natural development of human sacrifice is afforded by America, where during fifteen centuries after the birth of Christ, and probably for as long a period before, the gods of idolatry retained their authority unmolested by those influences which in the Old World interrupted or altered the progress of paganism—such as the contact of nations not equally civilised, the rise of commerce, philosophy, and political freedom, the presence of a chosen people, and the action of monotheism, polytheism, and pantheism upon each other. The people of the New World, separated from the rest of mankind, lived for ages on their original stock of religious ideas, which they, with persevering consistency, pushed to their extremest consequences. There is no other example of a civilised people whose religion was abandoned entirely to the action of its own laws, without the restraint of literature or speculation, and therefore without any recorded theological reform such as those of Buddha and Zoroaster, or philosophical opposition like that of Socrates or Zeno. Here then the natural history of human sacrifice may be most distinctly traced, from its conjectural origin to a development which is far beyond the

---

[194] Köppen, Die Lamaische Hierarchie, p. 29.
[195] Weber, Indische Literaturgeschichte, pp. 103, 104, 114; Benfey, Indien, p. 186.
[196] Orlich, Allgemeine Geschichte von Indien, p. 3.
[197] Erdkunde von Asien, ii. 762, 1066, iv. 390, v. 595, 623, 821, 933.
[198] Böttger gives an abstract of the Reports—Culturgeschichte Indiens, p. 247.

last extreme ever reached in the religions of the eastern hemisphere. The multitude and variety of phenomena supplied by the universality of the custom, and its tendency to indefinite increase, render the study easy.

So strictly do the essential qualities of American paganism correspond with those of the Old World, that they have been justly quoted as a proof of original unity. They both display the remnants of the same primitive traditions, acting on the same human nature; and the different stages of American civilisation resemble each other far less closely than they resemble the corresponding stages of the civilisation of the other continents. The similarity is not external, imported, or artificial, but the spontaneous fruit of similar principles and a common origin. Those facts which broadly divide the society of America from that of the rest of mankind, and prove how early the separation must have been effected—the absence of domestic animals, and the ignorance of the pastoral life—are the same which most deeply mark the character of their religious worship. This shows that the continent was not peopled by the nomades who inhabit Eastern Asia; for they, from time immemorial, have had flocks and herds, and have known the use of iron, which was first made known in America by the European adventurers.

The conquistadores found some civilised states surrounded by savage tribes of hunters and fishermen, but without the intermediate phase of pastoral life. This is the great feature that gives its peculiar character to their form of worship, as well as to their whole existence. Without the domestication of animals, the tribes of the New World lacked that powerful instrument for softening the wild nature of man, which is not only a division of labour and an economy of strength, but a perpetual occasion for the exercise of self-control and unbought kindness. The Indian knew dumb animals only as food, and pursued them only to destroy them. His wars were as ferocious as his treatment of animals; for he could not learn in the violence of warfare the lesson of humanity which was never taught him in ordinary life. As the Indians had no domestic animals, so they had no slaves. They killed their prisoners just as they killed the beasts they caught. To men whose means of existence were so precarious, every additional mouth to be fed added to their difficulty. Their enemies were put to death for the same reason which made a Pennsylvanian chief, at the end of the last century, foresee their own extinction: "The white man lives on grain, and we on flesh. This flesh takes thirty months to grow, and is often hard to find; but every one of those wonderful seeds that they sow in the earth returns them more than a hundred-fold. The flesh on which we live has four legs to run away upon, and we have only two to catch it with; but the seed remains where it is sown. That is why the white man has more children and lives longer than we. Therefore, I say, before the cedars of our village are dead, and the maple-trees in the valley cease to yield sugar, the little race of the sowers of grain will have exterminated the race of the eaters of meat, unless the hunters begin to sow."[199]

Every war threatened them with starvation. They had no time to spare from the pursuit of game, no idlers who could stay at home and provide them with food, nothing which the women could prepare. When many of them came together to fight an enemy, the places through which they passed did not contain food enough for their number, even if they had had time to catch it. They were therefore compelled to make the war support them, and to live upon what they could get from their enemies. But these were in the same plight, and the conquerors could obtain nothing but the bodies of the captives and the slain. In this extremity, in very early times famine soon taught the hunter, whose food was all flesh, and who deemed all animal flesh eatable, that there was no specific difference between that of man and beast. Thus, in time of war and scarcity, the hunter becomes by easy stages a cannibal. Hunger is, however, but a temporary and local cause of the cannibalism which may be shown to have existed in early times throughout the continent. Other inducements would be required in order to make it a general and permanent custom, even in times of peace and plenty.

The first step was to regard cannibalism as the natural mode of disposing of a slaughtered enemy. After it had been often done when there was reason for it, and done with some solemnity and rejoicing by men flushed with victory and with the excitement of danger and bloodshed, they became unwilling to forego the same festivity when there was no necessity and no provocation but the presence of the captive. The idea of feasting on the body of the enemy was not easily dissociated from success in war; and even in places where there was abundance of vegetable food, captives and strangers were eaten. As

---

[199] Far the greater part of their captives was anciently sacrificed to their vengeance, and it is only since their numbers began to decline fast that they have generally adopted milder maxims. Culturgeschichte Indiens, p. 338.

an act of vengeance and retaliation, it spread from those who had done it from necessity to those whom the splendid vegetation of tropical America preserved from such necessity. Hence we find the practice confined in some cases to prisoners. When the Spaniards, in 1528, driven to extremity by famine, devoured their dead comrades, the natives of Florida were filled with horror at the sight, though they would have rejoiced to eat an enemy. On the other hand, we find it usual among the inhabitants of very fertile countries.[200]

The idea of revenge superseded the condition of hunger, and the idea of sacrifice preserved the custom even in peaceful times. It was natural to give the gods the same food which was eaten by their worshippers. They were supposed to have the same tastes as men; and human flesh had become a luxury to those who had first eaten it from necessity. That which was eaten in moments of victory, and with a sense of triumph, was especially suited for an oblation to the spirits. Thus it became a regular habit to offer to the gods the flesh of slaughtered captives; and this custom is the vast background of the human sacrifices of America. In some cases, as among Caribees, cannibalism long survived the sacrifice of human victims; but even here it is certain that the custom formerly subsisted. In other places— and this is the great fact in the history of human sacrifice in Central America—cannibalism had long been extinct in ordinary life, when it was still preserved as a part of the religious rites.

But if human sacrifice in America sprang from cannibalism, and owed its extension to the scarcity of animals, it did not disappear with the progress of civilisation and wealth. The Pawnees, who, according to Gallatin, were among the gentlest of the Indians, and who never tortured their prisoners, nevertheless offered up a human victim annually at sowing-time to secure a good harvest. We find instances of captives who were killed and eaten without any religious ceremony whatever, but were nevertheless treated with extraordinary kindness down to the moment of a quick and painless death. In Brazil the prisoner was entertained for a year, a wife was given him, and not a word of unkindness was spoken to him till he was killed and eaten.[201] A neighbouring tribe considered this not as an act of enmity, but as an affectionate favour. They abominated those who ate their enemies;

[200] Berghaus, Ethnographie, p. 201.

[201] Histoire de Santa Cruz, par M. de Gandavo, ed. Ternaux-Compans, Relations de l'Amérique, ii. 135.

but they killed and ate their own relations, when they saw that their end was approaching.[202] Among the South-American Indians the temptation to cannibalism was so strong, that the Spanish officers felt obliged to permit even the baptised tribes to kill and devour their enemies.[203]

The human sacrifices of the Americans were various in intention. In its lowest form the rite was meant to supply the dead with the blood for which they thirsted. The torture of captives was intended as an expiation for the slain, and was in some cases a substitute for ancient sacrifices. The gods too had their share of the booty, and of the captives amongst the rest. But the idea of the enjoyment the gods derived from the sacrifice was utterly material and sensual. The Iroquois prayed to Areouski that he would eat the flesh of the victim, and reward them with victory.[204] In Florida the firstborn child was sacrificed to the sun; and one of the Peruvian tribes always immolated the first child of every mother. On the Missouri these sacrifices have occurred even in the present century. In early times this Syrian rite was performed all over Central America. In Chili they sacrificed the favourite child on every urgent occasion.

> Hay otra detestable circunstancia,
> Que muda bien la especie del pecado,
> Y es, que si lo por ellos preguntado
> Es cosa de muchísima importancia,
> Metidos en aquella escura estancia
> Degüellan al hijuelo mas amado,
> O la especiosa niña en sacrificio
> Para tener al ídolo propicio.[205]

The most exalted instance of human sacrifice in the legends of the Indian tribes is that of the American Iphigenia, Hiawatha's daughter, who perished to save the Onondagas.

But the great extension of human sacrifice in America did not take place among ignorant savages, or thriftless hunters, or hungry cannibals. It was the act of the Mexicans, the most humane, the most highly

---

[202] Ib. p. 145.

[203] Commentaires de Cabeça de Vaca, Ternaux-Compans, vi. 461.

[204] Müller, Geschichte der Amerikanischen Urreligionen, p. 142. This excellent work is useful as a corrective to Wuttke, who grossly exaggerates the depth and sanctity of the theological idea associated with human sacrifice even by barbarians, while Müller refers them too exclusively to cannibalism.

[205] Pedro de Oña, Arauco Domado, ii. 58.

civilised, and the most prosperous of all the races that inhabited the continent. It was the result, not of degradation, but of extraordinary moral energy and fidelity to religious conviction. Instead of being an extension of a national cannibalism, it preserved in the service of the temples the practice which the refined and wealthy people had otherwise long discarded. Far from being prompted by revenge, it was a mode of death often chosen as an honour by the noblest of the people. It was not an act of cruelty; for the death was as prompt as possible, and in certain cases the victim was feasted and venerated for months before his death. Almost all the degrading accessories, all the mixture of other than purely spiritual elements, which were inseparable from human sacrifice in the rest of the world, were things unknown to those ceremonials of Central America which have been rightly called the most tremendous religious drama in the whole of Paganism. The scale on which the rite was performed distinguishes it not in proportions merely, but in kind, from all other oblations of human victims. The Mexicans did not sacrifice for the dead, like the Hyperboreans, the Tartars, and the Romans in the circus. They did not merely give their children, like the worshippers of Moloch, or their captives like most savage tribes. The occasion was not, as among the Greeks, some actual guilt to be atoned, or some particular expiation to be commemorated. Their sacrifices included all kinds of human victims—their own children, their nobles, who freely volunteered, and prisoners *en masse*. They were constant and regular, and the number of the victims was the very largest which it was possible to supply. The idea from which they sprang was that of original universal sinfulness—a guilt which the most enormous sacrifices could hardly wipe away, a chasm between man and the divinity which the very utmost efforts would not do more than fill up.[206] This notion of the necessity of a universal atonement for a guilt inherited and not incurred, independent of all actual sin, expiable only in infinite time by the incessant immolation of men, on a scale which must needs always increase, until it must have eventually terminated in a sort of national suicide, was unknown to the paganism of antiquity, and was in one respect a deeper view of religion than the

---

[206] "Die dogmatische Bedeutung des Menschenopfers als Versöhnung, nicht im moralischen und rechtlichen, sondern im metaphysischen Sinne, als Aufhebung des nicht verschuldeten, sondern im Wesen der Sache liegenden Gegensatzes zwischen Gott und dem Menschen—" Wuttke, Die ersten Stufen der Geschichte der Menschheit, p. 273.

Gentiles had hitherto attained. But there was another idea vaguely present in the minds of the ancients, but utterly lost to the Mexicans—the idea that all sacrifice is insufficient, that its merit can only be that it symbolises, or prefigures, or commemorates, a perfect and divine sacrifice, and that it is a sign of spiritual efforts of the soul. Hence the stress and value of their sacrifice was in the ritual alone. It was not a sign, but the actual purchase-money, of human redemption. Its merit was in quantity and accumulation.

In the Mexican sacrifices Paganism exhausted and confounded itself in a way exactly opposite to that by which it reached its end in the ancient world, where religion lost its power over men partly through the intellectual opposition of philosophy, and partly through the moral degradation of society, and was neither believed in nor obeyed. But the Aztecs were a strange contrast to the Greeks and Romans. They united the simple credulity of the Homeric age with the moral strength of the Stoics. So far from abandoning their religion, it continually exacted larger sacrifices which they willingly made. No claims of the gods staggered their faithfulness or their zeal. They did not fall into the extremes of ferocity or sensuality. They still believed in their gods with a primitive sincerity, and testified to their belief with an increasing submissiveness and earnestness; and yet this energetic consistency in their heathen practices would have ended in the depopulation of the country, through maintaining a form of worship more contrary to nature, and more constant with the schemes of hell, than the most infamous aberrations of declining Hellenism. If in the old world Paganism was confuted by the intellectual capacity of the Greeks, it may be said that it was reduced to absurdity in the new world by the moral energy of the Mexicans.

Garcilasso has induced many to believe that the gentle government of the Incas extinguished human sacrifice in Peru; but, in fact, although it was diminished and regulated, it still survived. The mildness of the customs did not mitigate the practice, any more than Saturn's golden reign prevented him from being the special god who was pleased with human victims. The worship of the sun, with which human sacrifice was connected throughout Central America, prevailed also in Peru. At the accession of an Inca, great numbers of children were buried alive. At the death of another, one thousand persons were immolated; and one of the Incas sacrificed his own son, in the hope of recovering his health. Yet unquestionably there was in Peru a restraining and opposing influence; and among the Aztecs alone did human sacrifice flourish without any symptom of fear, or shame, or loathing among the people or the kings.

All the forms of human sacrifice prevailed in Mexico. The innocent were put to death, as the most precious oblation to the idol.[207] Men of rank selected this mode of death, sometimes for the good of the people, sometimes as an honour to themselves.[208] Some victims of great distinction were identified with the god to whom they were to be sacrificed, and represented his death by their own. Decorated with the insignia of the sun, they led a life of luxury and ease, and were invoked by the people as powerful mediators, until with great ceremony they were slain before the idols.[209] The wives and children of the nobles were often buried in their graves.[210] When the victims had no special merit individually, they gained importance by their numbers; and when this principle was once admitted, it followed inevitably that the numbers ever continued to increase. Any diminution in the quantity of victims would be an explanation of the anger of the gods; and the successes of Cortes were actually attributed to a relaxation in the zeal with which victims were supplied by Montezuma. In reality there was no diminution, except from the exhausted supply of captives, of whom his immediate predecessors had made a wasteful slaughter. In ordinary years, at the most probable estimate, 2500 human victims perished at Mexico. The skulls piled up in the temple were found to amount to 136,000; and in a town of moderate size there were near 100,000 skulls. The great temple at Mexico was finished in 1487, and inaugurated in the following year. For a long time captives had been collected for this occasion, and when the time came, 84,000 men were sacrificed, and 16,000 more were added to them before the end of the year.[211] The name of the monarch who perpetrated this unexampled butchery is used to this day in Mexico as a synonym for a scourge.

[207] "Niños inocentes y niñas virgines sacrificadas y abiertas por los pechos para ofrecer los corazones por primicia al idolo." Gomara, Conquista de Mejico, ed. Vedia, p. 350.

[208] Müller, p. 635.

[209] Relation sur la Nouvelle Espagne, par un Gentilhomme de la Suite de Cortès. Ternaux-Compans, x. 82, 86. "De toutes les nations que Dieu a crées, ces gens-là sont les plus stricts observateurs de leur religion, à ce point qu'ils se laissent sacrifier de bon coeur, espérant ainsi sauver leur âme."

[210] Lettre du Père Francesco de Bologne, ib. p. 213.

[211] Histoire des Chichimèques, par Ixtlilxochitl. Ternaux-Compans, xiii. 48. "Le démon fit une grande récolte à cette époque, car le massacre ne fut pas moins grand dans les provinces ennemies de l'empire."

Prescott, who has failed to comprehend the nature of the sanguinary rites of Anahuac, and to whom the very notion of sacrifice seems to be unintelligible, in his anxiety to brand these customs by the most degrading comparison he can conceive, borrows from Voltaire the idea of comparing the Mexican priests to the Dominicans; and their ceremonies to the modern Inquisition.[212] Even if we could admit his supposition of "fiendish passions" as the motive in either case, still no comparison could be more infelicitous than that of a tribunal essentially political, and serving after a fashion the ends of State, with one so entirely and intensely religious that the wealth and prosperity of the country was deliberately sacrificed to it. And yet, long after the last victim had fallen in honour of the sun-god of the Aztecs, the civilised nations of Christian Europe continued to wage wholesale destruction on as vast a scale against persons accused of no crime against the civil order, and not even convicted of the religious guilt which was imputed to them. The parallel phenomenon of trials for witchcraft ought to explain to us the power of superstition to familiarise men with the most inhuman butchery of helpless beings. Here there was no distinction of religion or of calling. Protestants and Catholics, clergy and laity, vied with each other for two hundred years to provide victims, and every refinement of legal ingenuity and torture was used in order to increase their number.[213] In the north of Italy, the great jurist Alciatus saw 100 witches burnt on one day. In a little town of Silesia, 102 witches were executed in the year 1651; and in a village of Hesse, with 540 inhabitants, 30 suffered in four years. At Salzburg, in 1678, a murrain among the cattle cost 97 suspected persons their lives. In the neighbourhood of Werdenfels in Bavaria, nearly all the women were exterminated. In two villages near Treves, all but two were put to death. The Jesuit Spee, whose hair turned prematurely gray in his terrible calling, attended 200 in two years, every one of whom had confessed in order to escape torture. He tells us of a single judge who had sent 500 witches to the flames; and another had caused 700 to be burnt in the course of nineteen years. At Quedlinburg, in the year 1589, on one day 133 witches were put to death. In two villages of the

---

[212] Conquest of Mexico, p. 27.

[213] In 1591, at Nördlingen, a girl was tortured twenty-three times before she confessed. Wächter, Beiträge zur Deutschen Geschichte, p. 108. Three years later, in the same town, a woman suffered torture fifty-six times without confessing that she was a witch. W. Menzel's Geschichte der Deutschen, iii. 401.

diocese of Mentz, the dean condemned 300 persons to die for the crime of witchcraft. A single bishop of Würzburg condemned 219; and the bishop of Bamberg, where the population did not exceed 100,000, caused a report to be published, in 1659, of the death of 600 witches in his episcopate. In England alone, under the Tudors and the Stuarts, the victims of this superstition amounted to 30,000.

Yet, from the appearance of Spee's *Cautio* in 1631 to the burning of the last witch in 1783, all sensible men were persuaded that the victims were innocent of the crime for which they suffered intolerable torments and an agonising death. But those who hunted them out with cunning perseverance, and the inflexible judges who never spared their lives, firmly believed that their execution was pleasing in the sight of God, and that their sin could not be forgiven by men. If this was done amid the civilisation of modern Europe, by experienced jurists and by Christian bishops, from an erroneous interpretation of the precepts of religion, it is surely ridiculous to attribute to unintelligent barbarity, and to treat with a contemptuous horror, the enormous efforts of expiation which were made by the unhappy Mexicans, who for fifteen hundred years were deprived of the Gospel of Redemption, and who sacrificed the most precious thing on earth, because they were ignorant of the death of that Victim who alone could take away the sins of the world.

[20]
Buckle's Philosophy of History

In our last Number we explained the theory which Mr. Buckle's book is written to prove, and estimated his merits as a philosopher. We have now to consider his attainments as a scholar. We have to examine his competency for the task he has undertaken, and the degree of success with which he has executed it. This is the more imperatively necessary, that it would be very unfair to Mr. Buckle to judge him by the merits of his system only; for the system is not his own. We may praise him or blame him for his judgment in adopting it, certainly not for his skill in devising it. His view of "the principles which govern the character and destiny of nations" is borrowed partly from Comte and partly from Quételet, and has already been applied, not indeed by historians, but by natural philosophers. We find it stated, for instance, by the celebrated physiologist Valentin, as follows (*Grundriss der Physiologie*, 1855, p. 10):

> Chance, to which we ascribe the event of an isolated case, must make way for a definite law as soon as we include a greater number of cases in

Henry Thomas Buckle, *History of Civilization in England*, vol. I (London: J. W. Parker, 1857). This review was published in the *Rambler*, n.s. (2d ser.) 10 (August 1858):88–104. It was the second of two articles on Buckle published in the *Rambler*; the first was "Mr. Buckle's Thesis and Method," (July 1858):27–42. Editors and critics of Acton persist in attributing both pieces to Acton; so William McNeil in Acton, *Liberal Interpretation of History*, pp. 3–21 and John Kenyon, *The History Men* (London 1983), p. 113. In fact, only "Mr. Buckle's Philosophy of History," reprinted here, was actually by Lord Acton. The July review was written almost entirely by Richard Simpson, Acton contributing only a short paragraph on the Belgian statistician L.A.J. Quetelet and the concluding paragraph of the article (pp. 317 and 323 in Acton, *Historical Essays*). Simpson's authorship was already pointed out by Figgis and Laurence in their 1908 edition of *Historical Essays*, and the matter is well documented in the editorial correspondence between Simpson and Acton: Acton-Simpson I, pp. 19–28, 30–34, 50, 52, 55, 67. The anonymity of Acton's and Simpson's contributions to their periodicals and their "association plan" of authorship—one supplying the ideas for and one writing an article—present enormous difficulties for the bibliographer of Acton's writings. These problems are discussed in more detail in Acton, *Selected Writings* I, pp. xxiv–xxvii.

our observation. No fixed rule appears to regulate the proportion of the sexes to each other, or the relative number of twins that are born, or the kind of crimes committed within a given period. But if we extend our range of observation over millions of cases certain regular quantities constantly recur. Where this is not the case, the causes of the fluctuation can often be ascertained by the rule of probabilities. Here, as everywhere, chance vanishes as a phantom of superstition,—as a result of that short-sightedness which has burdened the history of human opinion with so many apparently higher, but in reality degrading and erroneous, ideas.

This nearly describes the theory which Mr. Buckle has transferred from the history of nature to the history of man. He can hardly be said to challenge inquiry into its truth. He is at small pains to recommend it to those who are not predisposed in its favour. He is more inclined to dogmatise than to argue; and treats with placid scorn all who may not agree with him, and who are attached to one or other of the creeds and systems which have subsisted amongst men. It is a characteristic of certain diminutive parties to make up by the confidence and doggedness of their language for the small support they are able to command in public opinion. It is the same spirit in which Coleridge used to be worshipped at Highgate, and Jeremy Bentham at Westminster.

Taking a survey of literature from the pinnacle of his self-esteem, Mr. Buckle repeatedly affirms that history had been generally written by very incapable men; that before his time there was no science of history; that "the most celebrated historians are manifestly inferior to the cultivators of physical science" (p. 7), and much more to the same purpose *passim*. He gives us, moreover, to understand that he is as much at home in ethical as in historical literature; and delivers the valuable opinion, "that a man, after reading everything that has been written on moral conduct and moral philosophy, will find himself nearly as much in the dark as when his studies first began" (p. 22). Having thus cleared the way for his own appearance on the neglected fields of history and philosophy, he leaves us to infer that there are very few people capable of appreciating his performance, or for whose judgment he cares a pin. He writes for a school; and uttering its oracles to the world, he may question the competency of any tribunal which does not in some degree admit his premises and consents to judge him out of his own mouth. But if we are unworthy to judge his theories, his facts at least are common property, and are accessible to all men;

and it is important to see what they are worth, and how much Mr. Buckle knew about the matter when he endeavoured to make history subservient to his philosophy.

The attempt to reconcile philosophical speculation with the experience of history, and to harmonise their teachings, is perfectly natural, and, at a certain stage, inevitable. Both are unbounded in their range, and in some sense they may be said to include each other. Neither science is perfect till it obtains the confirmation of the other. "Man," says Jacobi, "requires not only a truth whose creator he is, but a truth also of which he is the creature." Yet the comparison could take place only at an advanced period of the progress of philosophy and of the knowledge of history. Philosophy must be seen by the light of history that the laws of its progress may be understood; and history, which records the thoughts as well as the actions of men, cannot overlook the vicissitudes of philosophic schools. Thus the history of philosophy is a postulate of either science. At the same time, history, unless considered in its philosophic aspect, is devoid of connection and instruction; and philosophy, which naturally tends to embrace all the sciences, necessarily seeks to subject history, amongst the rest, to its law. Hence arose the philosophy of history. "In history," says Krug, "philosophy beholds itself reflected. It is the text to which history supplies the commentary."[1] Both sciences had attained a certain maturity of development before they sought each other. "Philosophy," said Schelling, "ought not to precede the particular sciences, but to follow after them."[2] Generalisation in history was not possible until a great part of its course was run, and the knowledge of its details tolerably complete. Nor could the history of philosophy be written before it had passed through many phases, or before it had attained a considerable development. Thus it naturally happened that the philosophy of history and the history of philosophy, as they proceeded from the same causes, began to be cultivated about the same time. They are scarcely a century old.

The mediaeval philosophy had taken no cognisance of the external world until, in the sixteenth century, a reaction took place. As theology had predominated in the Middle Ages, now physiology prevailed in its stead. The study of nature became the first of sciences, and in the

---

[1] *Handwörterbuch der philosophischen Wissenschaften*, ii. 217.

[2] Salat, *Schelling in München*, i. 60.

age of the supremacy of the Baconian system, Kepler and Galileo and Newton were considered philosophers. To the philosophic investigation of nature was added, in the eighteenth century, the philosophic contemplation of history. The method by which Bacon had revolutionised natural science "ab experientia ad axiomata, et ab axiomatibus ad nova inventa,"[3] came to be tried on history. Since that time a philosophy of history has been attempted upon the principles of almost every system. The result has not always been to the advantage of history, or to the credit of the philosophers. "When things are known and found out, then they can descant upon them; they can knit them into certain causes, they can reduce them to their principles. If any instance of experience stands against them, they can range it in order by some distinctions. But all this is but a web of the wit; it can work nothing."[4]

The first attempt to give unity to universal history by the application of philosophic system was made by Lessing, in his celebrated fragment on the *Education of the Human Race*. It was his last work, "and must be considered the foundation of all modern philosophy, of religion, and the beginning of a more profound appreciation of history."[5] He employs the ideas of Leibnitz's *Théodicée* to explain the government of the world. Condorcet's *Sketch of the Progress of the Human Mind* is inspired, in like manner, by the sensualist doctrines of Condillac. Kant, though perfectly ignorant of the subject, was incited by the French Revolution to draw up a scheme of universal history in unison with his system. It was the entire inadequacy of Kant's philosophy to explain the phenomena of history which led Hegel, "for whom the philosophical problem had converted itself into an historical one,"[6] to break with the system altogether. Thirty years later, when the supremacy of Kant had long passed away, and Hegel was reigning in his stead, he too set up his philosophy of history as the crown and end of his own philosophy, and as the test of its absolute truth.[7] "It is for historical science," says

---

[3] *De Augmentis*, iii. 3: "From experiment to axioms, from axioms to new discoveries."

[4] Bacon, "In Praise of Knowledge," *Works*, ed. Bohn, i, 216.

[5] Schwarz, *Lessing als Theologe*, p. 79.

[6] Haym, *Hegel und seine Zeit*, p. 45.

[7] "Gewissermassen, die Probe des ganzen Systems" (Michelet, *Entwickelungsgeschichte der neuesten deutschen Philos.*, p. 304). "Die Wahrhafte Theodicee, die Probe von der Wahrheit des ganzen Systems" (Huber, *Deutsche Vierteljahrs Schrift*, 1853, ii, 50). "Die unwidersprichlichste Bewährung des Systems" (Haym, *Allgem. Encyclop.*, art. "Philosophie," sect. iii. vol. xxiv. 176).

his latest biographer, "to enjoy the inheritance of Hegel's philosophy."[8] In like manner, the transcendental system of Schelling resulted in a Christian philosophy of history, of which a late able writer says that by it "the antagonism of philosophy and history, proceeding from a defective notion of the first, and an utterly inadequate view of the latter, was removed."[9] So, again, the system of Krause presents a combination of philosophy and history in which their respective methods are blended together.[10] Especially since the publication of Hegel's *Lectures*, history has been generally considered by philosophers as belonging to their legitimate domain. And their dominion is such, that even a moderate acquaintance with the events of the past has ceased to be deemed a necessary or even a useful ingredient in the preparation of a philosophy of history. No system will confess itself so poor that it cannot reconstruct the history of the world without the help of empirical knowledge. A Pole, Cieszkowski (*Prolegomena zur Historiosophie*, 1838), has a physical scheme for the arrangement of historical phenomena. According to him, light is the type of Persia, mechanism of China, Athens represents dynamic electricity, Sparta static electricity. The electro-magnetic system answers to Macedon, the expansive force of heat to the Roman Empire. The dualism of Church and State in the Middle Ages corresponds to the antithesis of acid and alkali, etc. etc. The same ingenious person argues from the analogy of the natural sciences, in which, with the help of an old tooth, you can reconstruct an antediluvian monster, that history has to deal with the future, and cannot submit to be confined to the knowledge of the past. Twenty years ago, the well-known novelist Gutzkow was in prison, and not having books at hand to help him in writing a novel, beguiled the time by writing and publishing a philosophy of history.

These recent examples may serve to show us that it is not to be wondered at that an attempt should be made to obtain for a new system the sanction of history; or that, having been made, it should have furnished the most complete confutation of the system it was meant to confirm. But we have already said that the theory is not the most remarkable part about Mr. Buckle's book. It is by his portentous

---

[8] Haym, *Hegel, etc.*, 466.

[9] Schaarschmidt, *Entwickelungsgang der neuesten Speculation*, p. 194; and Schelling. *Werke*, i. 480, 481

[10] According to his disciples, "der harmonische Haupttheil," "die Blüthenknospe," of the system (Erdmann, *Entwickelung der Speculation seit Kant*, ii, 676).

display of reading that he will impose upon many in whom the principles in their naked deformity would simply excite abhorrence. The theoretical portion is completely overgrown and hidden by the mass of matter which is collected to support it, and on which Mr. Buckle has brought to bear all the reading of a lifetime. The wonderful accumulation of details and extravagance of quotation have the manifest purpose of dazzling and blinding his readers by the mere mass of apparent erudition. "So learned a man cannot be mistaken in his conclusions," is no doubt what they are expected to say. We cannot, therefore, consider the success of Mr. Buckle's work as a fair indication of the extent to which the peculiar form of infidelity which he holds prevails in this country. To accept his conclusions, we must be prepared to say, *Credo quia impium*; but in order to be overawed by his learning, it is enough to have less of it than Mr. Buckle himself.

It is for this reason worth while to inquire briefly whether Mr. Buckle is in this respect so great an authority as he professes to be, and as it is commonly taken for granted he is—whether he really possesses that knowledge of his subject which justifies him in writing upon it, or whether, in a word, he is an impostor.

Apart from the historical excursions of modern philosophers which we have spoken of, and with which Mr. Buckle has not thought fit to make himself acquainted, the great problems of civilisation which he tries to solve have been discussed within the last few years by three eminent men, whose works have some points of similarity with his own. In 1853 a French diplomatist, M. de Gobineau, published the first portion of a work which he has since completed in four volumes, *Essai sur l'Inégalité des Races humaines*. Familiar with all the latest researches of French and German writers, he investigates in great detail the laws which regulate the progress and the decline of civilisation. He finds that it depends entirely on purity of blood. The deterioration produced by the mixture of races is the sole cause of decline: "A people would never die if it remained eternally composed of the same national elements" (i. 53). The fate of nations is unconnected with the land they inhabit; it depends in nothing on good government or purity of morals. Even Christianity has no permanent influence on civilisation: "Le Christianisme n'est pas civilisateur, et il a grandement raison de ne pas l'être" (p. 124). Whether we admit or reject these conclusions, it is unquestionable that they are founded on most various and conscientious research, and an abundance of appropriate learning, strongly contrasting with the dishonest affectation of knowledge by which Mr. Buckle deludes his readers. There is, moreover, a learned appendage to Gobineau's book, in the shape of a pamphlet of 275 pages, by Professor Pott. About the same time an anonymous work appeared at Marburg, in three volumes, bearing the somewhat obscure title, *Anthropognosie, Ethnognosie und Polignosie*, in which also the laws which influence the political and social progress of mankind are explained with uncommon erudition. It was by a well-known political writer, Dr. Vollgraff; and, though disfigured by endless subdivisions and an obscure arrangement, it is undoubtedly one of the most comprehensive and instructive works that have appeared in our time. All the principal points of Mr. Buckle's theory are here discussed and illustrated with infinitely greater fulness of knowledge than in the work of our English author; and although the conclusions to which the German philosopher would lead us are not much better, at least there is much more to be learnt on the road.

The third work to which we allude is very different in style and spirit, and bears a motto which at once deprives it of any considerable resemblance to Mr. Buckle's work: *Lo bueno, si breve, dos vezes bueno.* It is the work of the most eloquent and accomplished philosopher in Germany,[11] and passes in review, in 168 pages, all the great questions which constitute the philosophy of history. The wisest sayings of the ancients, and the latest discoveries of the moderns, are brought together with incomparable taste and learning; since Schlegel, so brilliant a work had not appeared on the same field.

We have drawn attention to these works because they treat of exactly the same questions as Mr. Buckle's *History of Civilisation*, and are all written by men of distinguished abilities—the last by one of the greatest modern scholars; because, moreover, they are the only works which, during the last ten years, have really advanced the study of philosophy of history, and are therefore the first books to which anybody would naturally turn who is employed upon the subject. None of them, we may add, are written from a specifically Catholic point of view, yet Mr. Buckle has never once alluded to any of them.

We may attribute this monstrous neglect of what has been done and is doing in the field which he is cultivating, either to simple ignorance of the present state of learning, or to a wary dislike of whatever might

---

[11] Ernst von Lasaulx, *Neuer Versuch einer alten auf die Wahrheit der Thatsachen gegründeten Philosophie der Geschichte.*

not help to support his own views. There is no other alternative, and either supposition is equally fatal to his credit.

As Mr. Buckle despises the historians, and knows nothing of the principal philosophers, it may be asked, where, then, are his authorities? The answer is given in a note (p. 5), where we are told that Comte is the "writer who has done more than any other to raise the standard of history." This is the key to the whole book, and in general to Mr. Buckle's state of mind. His view seldom extends beyond the bounds of the system of that philosopher, and he has not sought enlightenment in the study of the great metaphysicians of other schools. The limits of his knowledge in this respect are curious. Of Aristotle, though he frequently mentions him, and in one place even places him on a level with the French physician Bichât (p. 812), there is no proof that he knows anything at all. He tells us, for instance, that the chief writers on the influence of climate are Hume, Montesquieu, Guizot, and Comte. It never occurs to him that his favourite theory on this point is to be found in Aristotle (*Problemata*, xiv), or that Hippocrates wrote a work on the subject. Plato, though sometimes quoted, seems hardly better known. Nobody familiar with his works and life would venture upon the statement that it is doubtful whether he ever visited Egypt (p. 81); still less would a scholar with any self-respect have cited Bunsen as an authority on the matter. In reality, the only question is how long he remained there.

This is a fair instance of our author's habit of going to the wrong place for information, and ignoring the obvious authorities. Altogether Mr. Buckle, who does not commonly put his light under a bushel, exhibits acquaintance with scarcely four or five of the most common writers of antiquity.

It is not to be expected that the Christian writers should come off better; there is a good deal said about them, but it is borrowed at second-hand, generally from Neander, sometimes from Mosheim or Milman. For it makes no difference to Mr. Buckle whether a thing is true, or whether somebody has said that it is true. It is enough that it should answer some particular purpose of the moment. Indeed, although his reading appears excessively promiscuous, it is in reality selected with great discrimination. So far as we have observed, the standard work which is the real and acknowledged authority on each particular subject is never by any chance or oversight consulted for the purpose. We have shown how the case stands relatively to the general subject of civilisation. For the history of philosophy we have continual references in Tennemann, who was greatly esteemed at the time of Kant's supremacy in the schools. The progress of learning has long since displaced his works, as well as those which immediately succeeded him. Sometimes we find reference to Ritter's *Ancient Philosophy*, the most antiquated portion of his highly unsatisfactory work. The vast literature on this subject which has arisen within the last few years is never noticed. So, for the history of medicine we have Sprengel and Renouard, whose books were long since superseded by the works of Hecker, Häser, and others. On India, again, we are referred to a number of obsolete publications, and the great work of Lassen is never mentioned. The same ignorance prevails upon almost every branch of learning that is ostentatiously brought forward; but we should be following Mr. Buckle's very bad example if we were to go on giving lists of books which he ought to have consulted.

The title of the sixth chapter, "Origin of History, and State of Historical Literature during the Middle Ages," excited our expectations. To a man of Mr. Buckle's industry, the hundreds of folios in which the historical works of the Middle Ages are contained offer a splendid and inexhaustible field for the exhibition of his powers of research. Here was to be found, in the history of European civilisation for a thousand years, the secret of its subsequent progress. But Mr. Buckle's method is the same here as elsewhere. He shows himself acquainted with just half a dozen of the commonest mediaeval historians; and these, if we remember rightly, with only one exception, all English. On the other hand, whatever is to be found about them in the most ordinary books—Hallam, Warton, Turner, Palgrave, Wright, etc.—is diligently repeated. The vulgar practice of reading the books one is to write about was beneath so great a philosopher. He has read about them, but very little in them. They could not greatly attract him; for the Middle Ages must be a mere blank to one who writes the history of modern civilisation without taking into account the two elements of which it is chiefly composed—the civilisation of antiquity, and the Christian religion. Having to utter a few generalities upon the subject, it was obviously more convenient to know nothing about it, and to take counsel of a few writers who knew very little about it, than to run the risk of finding an imprudent curiosity rewarded by the unexpected discovery of unpalatable and inflexible facts. This safe and timely ignorance, which he has discreetly cherished and preserved, has made him fully competent to declare "that not only was no history written before the end of the sixteenth century, but that the state of society was such as to make it impossible for one to be written" (p. 299).

Agreeably to the materialistic character of his philosophy, Mr. Buckle examines with special predilection the physical causes which influence mankind. His second chapter, which is devoted to this inquiry, is the most interesting and elaborate part of the volume. In these regions he is somewhat more at home. It is but an act of justice, therefore, to give some attention to this chapter. Nowhere do the ignorance and incapacity of the author more visibly appear.

The subject here treated has very recently been raised to the dignity of a separate and distinct science; and it has been cultivated on the Continent with extraordinary zeal and success. In no department was so much assistance to be derived from contemporary writers. Ritter, the founder of the science of comparative geography, began forty years ago the great work of which he has not yet finished even the Asiatic portion. He was the first among the moderns to determine in detail the connection of the material world with the history of man. In his footsteps a numerous school of writers have followed—Rougemont, Mendelssohn, Knapp, etc.—and a variety of able writers have made it a popular study.

As Ritter first established a bridge between history and geography, the link between geology and history was discovered by the Saxon geologist Cotta. Another branch of the same subject—the connection between the vegetable world and the civilisation of man—has been treated by the celebrated botanist, Unger of Vienna.[12] Finally, Professor Volz[13] has produced a most learned work on the influence of the domestic animals and plants on the progress of civilisation. Yet Mr. Buckle is totally ignorant of the writings and discoveries of these men; and he has therefore written a dissertation which not only does not exhaust the subject, but is of no value whatever at the present day.

The proposition that out of Europe civilisation is dependent chiefly upon physical causes, and man subordinate to nature, is proved, among other examples, by that of Egypt (p. 44). The instance is infelicitous, inasmuch as it is cited by Ritter in support of precisely

---

[12] *Botanische Streifzüge auf dem Gebiete der Culturgeschichte.*
[13] *Beiträge zur Culturgeschichte.*

the contrary view.[14] The original inhabitants of the valley of the Nile were not better off or more civilised than their neighbours in the deserts of Libya and Arabia.

It was by the intelligence of the remarkable people who settled there that Egypt became the richest granary of the ancient world. The inundation of the Nile was rendered a source of fertility by the skill of those who made use of it. But when the vigour of the nation died away under the wretched government which succeeded upon the fall of Rome, that fertile valley relapsed in great measure into its old sterility; the Thebais became a desert, and the Mareotis a marsh. Instead of proving Mr. Buckle's case, Egypt is the best instance of the subordination of nature to the intellect and will of man.

Pursuing his idea of the influence of the aspect of nature on man, Mr. Buckle, who has a theory for everything, discovers that the cause of Catholicism lies in earthquakes:

> "The peculiar province of the imagination," he informs us, "being to deal with the unknown, every event which is unexplained as well as important, is a direct stimulus to our imaginative faculties. . . . Earthquakes and volcanic eruptions are more frequent and more destructive in Italy and in the Spanish and Portuguese Peninsula than in any other of the great countries, and it is precisely there that superstition is most rife, and the superstitious classes most powerful. Those were the countries where the clergy first established their authority, where the worst corruptions of Christianity took place, and where superstition has during the longest period retained the firmest hold."

In other words, sequence is cause, as Hume proves; whence *post hoc, ergo propter hoc,* the great logical principle of the positivists. But increase of Popery follows increase of earthquakes; therefore, the consequence is clear. And not only is Christianity extracted out of earthquakes, but also, by a similar chemistry, Providence is derived from the plague.

Our ignorance about another life, he says, is complete:

> On this subject the reason is perfectly silent; the imagination, therefore, is uncontrolled. . . . The vulgar universally ascribe to the intervention of the Deity those diseases which are peculiarly fatal. The opinion that pestilence is a manifestation of the Divine anger, though it has long been dying away, is by no means extinct, even in the most civilised countries. Superstitions of this kind will, of course, be strongest either where medical knowledge is most backward, or where disease is most abundant.

---

[14] "Ueber das historische Element in der geographischen Wissenschaft," 1833, in his *Abhandlungen,* p. 165.

It is in tropical climates that nature is most terrible; and here, says our author, "imagination runs riot, and religion is founded on fear; while in Europe nature is subject to man, and reason rules supreme." This theme he illustrates by the extreme instances of India and Greece; and he generalises his conclusions into the statement that "the tendency of Asiatic civilisation was to widen the distance between men and their deities; the tendency of Greek civilisation was to diminish it." Hence "in Greece we for the first time meet with hero-worship, that is, the deification of mortals"; this could not take place in tropical countries. "It is therefore natural that it should form no part of the ancient Indian religion; neither was it known to the Egyptians, nor to the Persians, nor, so far as I am aware, to the Arabians"; but it was part of the national religion of Greece, and has been found so natural to Europeans, that "the same custom was afterwards renewed with eminent success by the Romish Church."

Perhaps no writer of pretension ever made a more disgraceful exhibition of ignorance and unreason than Mr. Buckle in these passages. Unreason: for if the Catholic cultus of saints is to be identified with the Greek deification of heroes, then certainly this deification is not simply European; it is as natural to the Indian Catholic as to the Italian or German, not to mention the Orientals. Exactly the same thing is found in Mahometanism, wherever it spreads. If Allah alone receives divine honours, anyhow the chief cultus is paid to the tomb of the prophet, and to the graves of the various holy personages with which Moslem countries are so thickly studded. But if this cultus is not what Mr. Buckle meant by the Greek hero-worship, then his mention of the Catholic practice is invidious, impertinent, and utterly irrelevant to his argument. Ignorance: for the "deification of mortals," so far from forming no part of the ancient Indian and Egyptian religions, was their very central idea and foundation. The fearful, terrible gods that Mr. Buckle's imagination is so full of, were only elemental deities, rising and falling with the world, destined to be annihilated; while the human soul was to last forever, and was in its essence superior to all those beings that kept it in a tedious but temporary thraldom. The whole idea of the Vedas is the power of the Brahmin over the elemental deities, exerted by means of the sacrifice. The deities in question, though vast in power and wonderfully large, are by themselves undefined and vague; they want personality, and therefore require personal direction; though they are in some sense universal intellect and soul, yet they are formless and void; they are mere blunderers till they are directed by the more sure intelligence of minds akin to those of man. Hence, in the Vedantic genesis of things, the elemental deities are the matter of forces which compose the universe; while the intelligent agents who conduct the creative process are the seven primeval sages, Rishis, or Manus, whose very name attests their human nature.[15] It is by the sacrifice of these Rishis, and by the metres they chanted, that the mundane deities received their place and office in the world; and, what is more, the sacrifices of the Vedantic religion are all identified with this primitive creative offering. The seven priests who offer the Soma sacrifice, so often mentioned in the hymns, are only the successors of the primitive Rishis or Angiras, whose work they carry on. The Sama Veda was their ritual; and they pretended that this ceremonial was necessary for the preservation of the universe, by continuing the action of the seven creative forces which first formed the world. In the more modern system of the Puranas the same agency is found. The world is successively destroyed and reconstructed; there are seven such revolutions each day of Brahma, and each time the world is restored by a Manu and seven attendant Rishis. Here, instead of the subserviency of man to nature, we have the inferiority of nature to man, and the deification of men in as exaggerated a form as can possibly be conceived. The same may be said of the Buddhist system; the seven human Buddhas are successively the great rulers of the universe. And here the facts are so directly contrary to Mr. Buckle's crude speculations, that in the very country where nature is most intractable, and where natural forces exert the most terrific influence on man—in the great frozen plateau of Thibet—there the deification of man is carried to the farthest extent, and the Grand Llama, or living Buddha, is actually identified with the Supreme God. With regard to the Egyptians, Mr. Buckle founds a hasty conclusion on a few words of Herodotus, and cares nothing for the universal and most ancient worship of Osiris, the human god, with whom every man is identified at death in the ritual. In Egypt the human soul, or man, was superior to the elemental deities. "I am your lord," says the soul to the mundane gods in a monumental inscription:[16] "Come and do homage to me; for you belong to me in right of my

---

[15] See the fable of Purusha, *Rig Veda*, lib. viii. cap. iv., hymns 17, 18, 19; and *Yadjur Veda*, cap. xxxi.

[16] Champollion, *Grammaire*, p. 285.

divine father." The same doctrine may be found in the Egypto-Gnostic lucubrations of the pseudo-Hermes Trismegistus. In the Persian system, Mithra seems to have held a place somewhat similar to that of Osiris in Egypt. At any rate, so far from its being true that the deification of mortals was unknown, the fact is, that the king assumed successively the insignia of each of the seven planets, and was adored by the people as the incarnate presence of each.[17] Of the ancient Arabian religion, Mr. Buckle professes his ignorance; the name, therefore, is only inserted to swell his catalogue to the eye, without any corresponding increase in the value of his induction. As we have shown each of his other assertions to be exactly the contrary of the truth, we need not trouble ourselves with disproving one that he owns to be a mere guess. In a later page he says, that in Central America, as in India, the national religion was "a system of complete and unmitigated terror. Neither there, nor in Mexico, nor in Peru, nor in Egypt, did the people desire to represent their deities in human forms, or ascribe to them human attributes." On the contrary, we can prove, in all these countries, the gods—at least the human-formed gods—are in sculptures only distinguishable from men by the addition of their respective symbols; while, on the other hand, the Egyptian kings and queens are continually represented by the characters of the various gods and goddesses whom they patronised. As to human attributes being ascribed to these gods, it is more difficult to prove this point against Mr. Buckle from the scarcity of poetical legends. But he will find his negative still harder to prove against us. In Mexico, the progenitors of our race, Cihuacohuatl (the woman-serpent, or mother of our flesh) and her husband, are placed among the thirteen great gods; and, as such, take precedence of all the elemental deities, coming next after Tezatlipoca, the creator, and Ometeuctli and his wife, the progenitors of the heroes. In Peru the Aztec sovereign was, as in Egypt, worshipped as the sun. Again, Mr. Buckle's principle is as false as his facts. Religious terrorism is in direct proportion to the humanitarianism of a religion. As among men, according to Mr. Mill, and therefore according to Mr. Buckle, cruelty is in proportion to inequality—as the despot sheds more blood than the constitutional sovereign, and as the despot by divine right, who claims not only the civil homage but the religious veneration of his people, is obliged to be more severe than the mere military adventurer;

---

[17] Dabistan, p. 42.

so, when we go a step further, and raise a living man, or a caste, into the place of God, we are obliged to hedge them round with a fence of the most bloody rites and laws. The real cause of Brahmin and Mexican cruelty was not because the Divine nature was so separated from mankind, but because it was so identified with a certain class of men, that this class was obliged to maintain its position by a system of unmitigated terrorism. The farther we remove God from humanity, the less we care about Him. We could not fancy an Epicurean fighting in defence of his indolent deities. As a general rule, those who persecute are willing to suffer persecution, we cannot fancy anybody willing to suffer in defence of an abstract divinity: hence we suppose that the more abstract, intangible, and unreal a religion is, the less cruelty will be perpetrated in its name. This, it appears to us, is the true account of the cruelties of the religions Mr. Buckle enumerates, and not the mere influence of climate and the aspects of nature.

The origin of Mr. Buckle's mistakes here, as in other subjects, is his learned ignorance. He never goes to the best authorities; he scarcely ever consults the originals. If he had given himself the trouble to read and understand the Vedas, which he so ostentatiously quotes at second-hand, the Puranas, the collections of Egyptian monumental inscriptions, the Zendavesta, and to understand the documents about America by M'Culloch, he might have given a rather more rational account of the religions which he pretends to philosophise upon.

In the same unlucky chapter Mr. Buckle declares, what on his principles was inevitable, that "original distinctions of race are altogether hypothetical" (p. 36); in support of which view that eminent positivist Mr. Mill is very properly quoted. As we have to deal now with Mr. Buckle's false learning rather than with his false theories, we can only glance at this great absurdity. For the same race of men preserves its character, not only in every region of the world, but in every period of history, in spite of moral as well as physical influences. Were not the Semitic races everywhere and always monotheists; whilst Japhetic nations, from Hindostan to Scandinavia, were originally pantheists or polytheists. Epic poetry, again, is distinctive of the Indo-Germanic race alone. The most amusing example of a nation's fidelity to the character which it obtained on its first appearance in history is afforded by France. Lasaulx has collected the judgments of the ancients upon the Gauls: "Gallia," said Cato, "duas res industriosissime persequitur, rem militarem et argute loqui. Mobilitate et levitate animi novis imperiis studebant" (*Caesar, B. G.* ii. I). "Omnes fere Gallos novis rebus studere et ad bellum mobiliter celeriterque excitari" (*Ibid.* iii. 10). "Sunt in consiliis capiendis mobiles, et novis plerumque rebus student" (*Ibid.* iv. 5). "Galli quibus insitum est esse leves" (*Trebellius Pollio Galien.* 4). "Gens hominum inquietissima et avida semper vel faciendi principis vel imperii" (*Flavius Vopiscus Saturninus,* 7).[18]

But we must conclude. We have said quite enough to show that Mr. Buckle's learning is as false as his theory, and that the ostentation of his slovenly erudition is but an artifice of ignorance. In his laborious endeavour to degrade the history of mankind, and of the dealings of God with man, to the level of one of the natural sciences, he has stripped it of its philosophical, of its divine, and even of its human character and interest.

When an able and learned work appears, proclaiming new light and increase of knowledge to the world, the first question is not so much whether it was written in the service of religion, as whether it contains any elements which may be made to serve religion. A book is not necessarily either dangerous or contemptible because it is inspired by hatred of the Church. "Nemo inveniret, quia nemo discuteret, nisi pulsantibus calumniatoribus. Cum enim haeretici calumniantur, parvuli perturbantur. . . . Negligentius enim veritas quaereretur, si mendaces adversarios non haberet"[19] (Augustin, *Sermones ad Populum,* lib. xi). Theodore of Mopsuestia, Julian of Eclanum, Calvin, and Strauss, have not been without their usefulness. An able adversary, sincere in his error and skilful in maintaining it, is in the long-run a boon to the cause of religion. The greatness of the error is the measure of the triumph of truth. The intellectual armour with which the doctrine of the Church is assailed becomes the trophy of her victory. All her battles are defensive, but they all terminate in conquest.

The mental lethargy of the last generation of English Catholics was due perhaps not a little to the very feebleness of their adversaries.

---

[18] "Gaul pursues two things with immense industry,—military matters and neat speaking." "Through instability and levity of mind they were meditating the overthrow of the government." "Almost all men of Gaul are revolutionists, and are easily and quickly excited to war." "In council they are unstable, and generally revolutionary." "The French, to whom levity is natural." "A most restless kind of men, always wanting to set up a king or an empire."

[19] No one would discover, for no one would discuss, unless roused by the blows of misrepresentation. For while heretics misrepresent, the little ones are scandalised. . . . Truth would not be sought so industriously, if it had no enemies to tell lies of it.

When a formidable assailant arose at Oxford, he found an adversary amongst us who was equal to the argument. In like manner, when the Duke of Wellington was the no-popery champion of Toryism, a very sufficient opponent appeared in the person of O'Connell. And now that Mr. Spooner is the representative of anti-Catholic politics, by a similar admirable dispensation and fitness of things he too finds among Catholic statesmen foemen who are worthy of his steel.

It is not, however, on such grounds as these that Mr. Buckle had a claim on our attention. He is neither wise himself, nor likely to be the cause of wisdom in others; and with him

Bella geri placuit nullos habitura triumphos:[20]

for we could not allow a book to pass without notice into general circulation and popularity which is written in an impious and degrading spirit, redeemed by no superiority or modesty of learning, by no earnest love of truth, and by no open dealing with opponents.

We may rejoice that the true character of an infidel philosophy has been brought to light by the monstrous and absurd results to which it has led this writer, who has succeeded in extending its principles to the history of civilisation only at the sacrifice of every quality which makes a history great.

[20] We understand a war where victory is no triumph.

[21]
Review of Cross's
George Eliot's Life

If it is true that the most interesting of George Eliot's characters is her own, it may be said also that the most interesting of her books is her Life. Mr. Cross has made known what is in fact the last work of the great Englishwoman. He possesses that art of concealing the artist which is still the rarest quality of biographers, and, apart from a few necessary pages, gives nothing but letters, journals, and fragmentary memoirs, written partly with a dim vision of publicity. The volumes will be read less for the notes of travel, the emphatic tenderness of the letters to friends, often on a lower plane, and the tonic aphorisms devised for their encouragement, than for the light they shed on the history of a wonderful intellect. The usual attractions of biography are wanting here. We see the heroine, not reflected from other minds, but nearly as she saw herself and cared to be known. Her own skilled hand has drawn her likeness. In books variously attributable to a High Church curate and to a disciple of Comte, the underlying unity of purpose was not apparent. For valid reasons they invite interpretation as much as *Faust* or the *Paradiso*. The drift and sequence of ideas, no longer obscured by irony, no longer veiled under literary precautions or overlaid with the dense drapery of style, is revealed beyond the risk of error now that the author has become her own interpreter.

The Life, while it illustrates the novels, explains what they do not indicate—the influences which produced the novelist. George Eliot

George Eliot's Life as Related in her Letters and Journals, arranged and edited by her husband, J. W. Cross, 3 vols. (London and Edinburgh: William Blackwood and Sons, 1885). This review was first published under the title "J. W. Cross's 'Life of George Eliot' " in the *Nineteenth Century* 17 (March 1885):464–485. Reprinted as "George Eliot's Life" in Acton, *Historical Essays*, pp. 273–304. A German translation by J. Imelmann appeared as a monograph: *George Eliot: Eine biographische Skizze* (Berlin: R. Gaertner, 1886).

was no spontaneous genius, singing unbidden with unpremeditated art. Her talents ripened successively and slowly. No literary reputation of this century has risen so high after having begun so late. The even maturity of her powers, original and acquired, lasted only thirteen years, and the native imagination was fading when observation and reflection were in the fulness of their prime. Mr. Cross's first volume describes the severe discipline of life and thought, the trials and efforts by which her greatness was laboriously achieved.

Marian Evans spent the first thirty years of her life in a rural shire, and received her earliest and most enduring impressions in a region of social stability, among inert forces, away from the changing scenes that attend the making of history. Isolation, the recurring note of her existence, set in early, for her urgent craving for love and praise was repelled by the relations around her, and her childhood was unhappy. We are assured that she was affectionate, proud, and sensitive in the highest degree; and the words are significant, because they bear the concurrent testimony of her brother and her husband. The early letters, written with the ceremonious propriety of Miss Seward, give no sign of more than common understanding. She was just out of her teens when she wrote the following words:

> Men and women are but children of a larger growth; they are still imitative beings. We cannot (at least those who ever read to any purpose at all)—we cannot, I say, help being modified by the ideas that pass through our minds. We hardly wish to lay claim to such elasticity as retains no impress. How deplorably and unaccountably evanescent are our frames of mind, as various as the forms and lines of the summer clouds! A single word is sometimes enough to give an entirely new mould to our thoughts; at least I find myself so constituted, and therefore to me it is pre-eminently important to be anchored within the veil, so that outward things may be unable to send me adrift. Society is a wide nursery of plants, where the hundreds decompose to nourish the future ten, after giving collateral benefits to their contemporaries destined for a fairer garden. The prevalence of misery and want in this boasted nation of prosperity and glory is appalling, and really seems to call us away from mental luxury. Oh, to be doing some little towards the regeneration of this growing travailing creation!

Beneath the pale surface of these sentences, and of one touching "that joyous birdlike enjoyment of things which, though perishable as to their actual existence, will be embalmed to eternity in the precious spices of gratitude," there are germs of sentiments to which the writer clung through the coming years. But the contrast with her developed character is stronger than the resemblance. She is struck at this time with compassion at the spectacle presented by people who go on marrying and giving in marriage. Music seems to her an unholy rite. On a visit to London she buys a Josephus, but refuses to go to the play with her brother. Even Shakespeare is dangerous. She lamented that novels had been supplied to her early, teaching her to live by herself in the midst of an imaginary world; and she had been disturbed at reading in *Devereux* that religion is not a requisite to moral excellence. She concluded that history is better than fiction; and her growing energy, her accuracy, her power of mastering hard books, seemed to promise a rival to Clinton or Long. The first literary enterprise in which she was engaged was a chart of ecclesiastical history, intended to include an application of the Apocalyptic prophecies, "which would merely require a few figures"—the sense of humour was still dormant. The taste for material erudition was soon lost, and turned to bitterness. In her books George Eliot has twice exhibited the vanity of pointless learning, and she looked back gratefully upon the agencies which rescued her from the devious and rugged ways by which history approaches truth.

Evangelical and Baptist teachers had imbued her with practical religion, and she enjoyed the writings proper to the school. In after-years Sydney Smith's account of his occupations about this time must have seemed to her a burlesque of her own: "I console myself with Doddridge's *Exposition* and *The Scholar Armed,* to say nothing of a very popular book, *The Dissenter Tripped Up.*" She was intent on Doddridge, Wilberforce, and Milner, admired Hannah More, and commended *The Infidel Reclaimed.* Respect for the logic of Calvinism survived most of her theology, and it was attended originally by a corresponding aversion for what pertains to Rome. She reads the Oxford tracts, and unconsciously applying a noted saying of St. Thomas, detects the Satanic canker amidst so much learning and devotion.

This seriousness is the most constant element which early education supplied to her after career. She knew, not from hearsay or habit, but from the impress of inward experience, what is meant by conversion, grace, and prayer. Her change was not from external conformity to avowed indifference, but from earnest piety to explicit negation, and the knowledge of many secrets of a devout life accompanied her through all vicissitudes. Writers of equal celebrity and partly analogous career, such as Strauss and Renan, have made the same claim, somewhat confounding theological training with religious insight, and deliberate conviction or devotional feeling with faith. But George Eliot continued to draw the best of her knowledge from her own spiritual memories, not from a library of local divinity, and she treated religion neither with learned analysis nor with a gracious and flexible curiosity, but with a certain grave sympathy and gratitude. Her acquaintance with books had been restricted by the taste or scruples of teachers who could not estimate the true proportions or needs of her mind, and the defect was not remedied by contact with any intelligent divine. Such instruction as she obtained has supported thousands faithfully in the trials of life, but for an inquisitive and ambitious spirit, gifted with exceptional capacity for acquiring knowledge, it was no adequate protection under the wear and tear of study.

In the summer of 1841 the thought quickens, the style improves, and a new interest is awakened in disputed questions. She already aspired after that reconciliation of Locke with Kant which was to be the special boast of one of her most distinguished friends, and she was impressed by Isaac Taylor's *Ancient Christianity*, allowing some drawback for his treatment of the Fathers. At this point, while still a trusted member of the Church, Miss Evans was introduced at Coventry to a family of busy and strenuous freethinkers.

The first visit to their house was early in November 1841, after which she speaks of being absorbed in momentous studies, and on the 13th of the same month she writes to her most intimate friend: "Think! is there any conceivable alteration in me that could prevent your coming to me at Christmas?" The obstacle announced in these words was a vital alteration in her religious principles. The revolution was sudden, but it was complete. For a time she continued to speak of eternal hope and a beneficent Creator; in deference to her father she even consented, uneasily, to go to church. But from that momentous November until her death it would appear that no misgiving favourable to Christianity ever penetrated her mind or shook for an instant its settled unbelief. There was no wavering and no regret. And when George Eliot had become a consummate expert in the pathology of conscience, she abstained from displaying the tortures of doubt and the struggles of expiring faith.

The history of a soul is never fully told, even for edification. We learn that Miss Evans was initiated in the mysteries of scepticism at her first encounter with cultivated society; and her early convictions, artlessly propped upon Young and Hannah More, yielded to the combined influence. Her new friend was the wife of Mr. Bray, who had written *The Philosophy of Necessity*, and sister to Mr. Hennell, the author of *An Enquiry concerning the Origin of Christianity*. The formal country schoolgirl, whose wondering companions called her "Little Mamma," who gathered them for prayer, who knew how to organise and to invigorate district work, and had dismissed her own brother for his High Church propensity, was fascinated and transformed by these surroundings. She pronounced Mrs. Bray the most religious person she knew, and Mr. Hennell a perfect model of manly excellence. She read his *Enquiry* twice through, and found it more interesting than any book she had seen. It represented in its day the antepenultimate stage of Biblical study; and Strauss, swathing his German criticism in politer Latin, said that it was written *Britannis, Britannice*. Mr. Hennell's reading of Gospel history was not the outcome of untried method or hypothesis, and those whom he convinced were tempted to conclude that arguments so specious and acceptable to themselves ought in fairness to satisfy others. They impressed Miss Evans, and at the critical moment she met with some unfavourable specimen of the Christian advocate. "These dear orthodox people talk so simply sometimes, that one cannot help fancying them satirists of their own doctrines and fears." Endowed with many virtues which go to constitute the ideal of the Christian character, with self-knowledge, unflinching sincerity, and an ardent devotion to the good of others, she became impatient of minds that could not keep pace with her own, and learnt during a portion of her life to reckon prejudice, fallacious reasoning, and wilful blindness among the properties of orthodoxy.

Strauss himself never made so important a proselyte. He provoked a reaction which nearly balanced his direct influence, and the *Leben Jesu* had already become, like the *Génie du Christianisme* and the *Sermon on National Apostasy*, the signal of a religious revival. Between Hennell's *Enquiry* and George Eliot's answer there is no proportion. His views need not have implied condemnation of all foreign and American Churches. She was more thorough in her rejection of the Gospels, and she at once rejected far more than the Gospels. For some years her mind travelled in search of rest, and, like most students of German thought before the middle of the century, she paid a passing tribute to pantheism. But from Jonathan Edwards to Spinoza she went over at one step. The abrupt transition may be accounted for by the probable action of Kant, who had not then become a buttress of Christianity. Out of ten Englishmen, if there were ten, who read him in 1841, nine got no further than the *Critique of Pure Reason*, and knew him as the dreaded assailant of popular evidences. When George Eliot stood before his statue at Berlin she was seized with a burst of gratitude, but she hardly became familiar with his later works.

Mr. Bray was a phrenologist who remained faithful to the cause after it had been blighted by Dr. Carpenter; and he soon found out that, if there is truth in phrenology, Miss Evans must be a portent. Mrs. Bray and her sister, the Cara and Sara of the biography, relieved the sadness and the solitude of her life at home, and comforted her in fits of nervous depression, in her fretful introspection, in her despair of ever winning affection or doing work worth living for. She associated with their friends, used their library, and surveyed the world through their windows. Greek and German, and the depths of unconscious energy within, carried her presently beyond their sphere, and she followed her own path in literature. A time came when the correspondence between them fell under constraint. But for ten eventful years, in which her mind was forming and settling upon fixed lines, this family group was able to encourage and to limit her progress, and the letters to Miss Hennell, written under the stress of transition, described her first attempts to steer without the accustomed stars:

Of course I must desire the ultimate downfall of error, for no error is innocuous; but this assuredly will occur without my proselytising aid. I cannot rank among my principles of action a fear of vengeance eternal, gratitude for predestined salvation, or a revelation of future glories as a reward. The mind that feels its value will get large draughts from some source if denied it in the most commonly chosen way. Where is not this same ego? The martyr at the stake seeks its gratification as much as the court sycophant, the difference lying in the comparative dignity and beauty of the two egos. People absurdly talk of self-denial. Why, there is none in virtue to a being of moral excellence. There can be few who more truly feel than I that this is a world of bliss and beauty; that is, that bliss and beauty are the end, the tendency of creation, and evils are its shadows. When the soul is just liberated from the wretched giant's bed of dogmas on which it has been racked and stretched ever since it began to think, there is a feeling of exultation and strong hope. We think we shall run well when we have the full use of our limbs and the bracing air of independence, and we believe that we shall soon obtain something positive which will not only more than compensate us for what we have renounced, but will be so well worth offering to others that we may venture to proselytise as fast as our zeal for

truth may prompt us. But a year or two of reflection, and the experience of
our own miserable weakness, which will ill afford to part even with the
crutch of superstition, must, I think, effect a change. Speculative truth
begins to appear but a shadow of individual minds; agreement between
intellects seems unattainable, and we turn to the truth of feeling as the only
universal bond of union.

We find that the intellectual errors which we once fancied were a mere
incrustation have grown into the living body, and that we cannot, in the
majority of cases, wrench them away without destroying vitality. We begin
to find that, with individuals as with nations, the only safe revolution is one
arising out of the wants which their own progress has generated. It is the
quackery of infidelity to suppose that it has a nostrum for all mankind.

So much of George Eliot's permanent characteristics had taken root
independently of Rousseau, Spinoza, Feuerbach, Goethe, Comte, or
Spencer, and before the dynasty of thinkers began to reign in her
mind. Mrs. Cross would have recognised herself in these confessions
of 1843. The acute crisis was over: a long period of gradual and
consistent growth ensued.

Miss Evans translated the *Leben Jesu* from the fourth edition, in
which Strauss betrayed the feeling roused by the violence of the conflict,
and withdrew the concessions which his ablest opponents had wrung
from him. It was not a labour of love to the translator. In her judgment
the problem was exhausted. She had her own more radical solution,
which the author did not reach for twenty years, and she shared neither
his contentious fervour, his asperity, nor his irresolution. The task was
accomplished under a sense of growing repulsion. One of her friends
even says that she gathered strength to write on the Crucifixion by
gazing on the crucifix, and we may infer from this remark that some
confusion of thought prevailed at Coventry.

When she visited Germany in 1854, the first person she met, at
Cologne, was Strauss. A miniature revolution had driven him from
the career for which he was bred, and he was leading an indeterminate
existence, without an occupation fitted for his powers, and without a
home. Cologne irritated him by want of literature, and by the cathedral
which a Protestant government was proceeding to complete, while
those to whom it belonged had been content that it should stand for
centuries a monument of profuse and miscalculating zeal. Theology
made him sick, and fame did not console him, for he was tired of
being called the author of his book, and was not yet reconciled to
popularity among classes that could neither substitute precept for

dogma nor ideas for facts. The meeting left no agreeable impression. In the life of George Eliot Strauss is an episode, not an epoch. She did not take him up to satisfy doubts or to complete an appointed course. These studies were carried no further, and she was not curious regarding the future of the famous school whose influence extended from Newman and Ritschl to Renan and Keim. But there is no writer on whom she bestowed so large a share of the incessant labour of her life. Two years spent in uncongenial contact with such a mind were an effectual lesson to a woman of twenty-six, unused to strict prosaic method, and averse from the material drudgery of research. She could learn from Strauss to distrust the royal road of cleverness and wit, to neglect no tedious detail, to write so that what is written shall withstand hostile scrutiny.

Five studious years followed, which strengthened the solid qualities of her mind. There had been much docility in complying with the nearest teaching and taking the line of least resistance. There was some risk of falling into worn channels, as men do who keep the colours of school and college, who read for agreement, and privately believe in some sage of Highgate or Westminster, Chelsea or Concord, as chance determines. George Eliot set herself earnestly to get out of the current, to be emancipated from the forces about her, and to secure the largest area of choice for guidance and instruction.

> I say it now, and I say it once for all, that I am influenced in my own conduct at the present time by far higher considerations, and by a nobler idea of duty, than I ever was while I held the evangelical beliefs. It seems as if my affections were quietly sinking down to temperate, and I every day seem more and more to value thought rather than feeling. I do not think this is man's best estate. Now I am set free from the irritating worn-out integument. I am entering on a new period of my life, which makes me look back on the past as something incredibly poor and contemptible. I am beginning to lose respect for the petty acumen that sees difficulties.

> I love the souls that rush along to their goal with a full stream of sentiment, that have too much of the positive to be harassed by the perpetual negatives, which after all are but the disease of the soul, to be expelled by fortifying the principle of vitality. The only ardent hope I have for my future life is to have given to me some woman's duty, some possibility of devoting myself where I may see a daily result of pure calm blessedness in the life of another.

After losing her father and spending several months at Geneva she settled down to a literary career in London. At Geneva she is still remembered with affection. Her days were spent obscurely, in the hard work which was her refuge from loneliness, from despondency, from the absence of a woman's joys and cares. She kept the secret of her authorship, and avoided aggressive speech; but those whom she trusted knew her as a pantheist and a stubborn disputant. She is described as talking well but showily, like one overfed on the French of the days when Quinet and Mickiewicz were eminent. France and the emotional philosophers had their time. She became, and to some extent remained, a devoted advocate of Jean Jacques and George Sand, and she startled Emerson by her taste for the *Confessions*.

Half of the books mentioned at this period are in verse. She knew how to distil working ideas from the obscurest poems; and her decorated prose, artificial with the strain to avoid commonplace, charged with excessive meaning, and resembling the style of no other writer, was formed on the English poets. She preferred Milton, Shelley, Wordsworth, and the early dramatists, specially excluding Marlowe. No one was fitter by intellectual affinity to penetrate the secret of Shakespeare; but the influence of Goethe was deeper, and perhaps near the end the influence of Dante. Goethe's preponderance is explicable by Strauss's reason, that Sirius may be larger than the sun, but ripens no grapes for us. It is recorded that George Eliot thought Shakespeare unjust to women; and we may believe that a mind so carefully poised was repelled by his flagrant insularity, his leaning for obvious characters, his insensibility to the glories of Greece and the mystery of the Renaissance, his indifference to the deeper objects for which his generation contended. The preference for Dante, with all his passion, fanaticism, and poverty of logic, is a symptom of that swerving towards religious sentiments which, in spite of Comte, if not by virtue of Comte, marked the later years.

Beyond the pleasures of literature arose the sterner demand for a certain rule of life in place of the rejected creeds. The sleepless sense that a new code of duty and motive needed to be restored in the midst of the void left by lost sanctions and banished hopes never ceased to stimulate her faculties and to oppress her spirits. After the interrupted development and the breach with the entire past, only her own energy could avail in the pursuit that imparted unity to her remaining life. It was the problem of her age to reconcile the practical ethics of unbelief and of belief, to save virtue and happiness when dogmas and authorities decay. To solve it she swept the realm of knowledge and stored up that large and serious erudition which sustains all her work, and in reality far exceeded what appears on the surface of the novels or in the record of daily reading. For an attentive observer there are many surprises, like that of the mathematician who came to give her lessons and found that she was already in the differential calculus. It is her supreme characteristic in literature that her original genius rested on so broad a foundation of other people's thoughts; and it would be hard to find in her maturer life any parallel to Mr. Spencer's historic inacquaintance with Comte, or to the stranger ignorance of Mr. Spencer's own existence avowed in 1881 by Michelet, the legendary mantle-bearer of Hegel.

George Eliot always read with a purpose before her, and there was no waste and little raw material in her learning. But her acquirements were mainly those of a person who had taught herself, and might not have satisfied University tests. The Latin is dubious in *Romola* and the Italian in *Mr. Gilfil's Love Story*. The Princess of Eboli, who is supposed in the Life to have been a beauty, wore a patch over her eye. A questionable date is assigned to the Platonic anniversary in *Romola*, and the affair of the Appeal is misunderstood. There is a persistent error regarding the age of Pico; and Savonarola, instead of proclaiming that he went straight to heaven, gave his evidence the other way. These and all other mistakes which the patience of readers has detected are immeasurably trivial compared to those which occur in the most famous historical novels, such as *Ivanhoe* and *John Inglesant*.

Caution and vigilance in guarding even the vestige of inaccuracy are apparent in other ways than the trip to Gainsborough and the consultation with Mr. Harrison on the legal obscurities of *Felix Holt*. Ladislaw's fatal allusion to German scholarship, which shattered Dorothea's belief in her husband, was an audacious hyperbole. Comparative mythology was as backward in Germany as elsewhere, besides which the *Aglaophamus* was written in Latin and the *Symbolik* was already appearing in French. But George Eliot takes care to warn us that Ladislaw did not know what he was talking about, and that Casaubon scorned to learn from a German even writing in Latin. Macchiavelli, in *Romola*, blows hot and cold on the Frate, but the inconsistency is faithfully taken from his writings. While the enthusiasts prevailed he went easily with the tide; but after he had been ruined and tortured for the Republic, and had become the officious expounder of Borgian theory to Medicean experts, he spoke as became him of the man who had the blood-feud with Borgias and Medicis. The discovery of a single epithet, of a single letter *(versuto* for *versato)*, has determined his real opinion since George Eliot wrote. The supreme test of the solidity of her work is the character of Savonarola. She possibly underestimates the infusion of artifice in the prophecies, but no historian has held more firmly the not very evident answer to the question how a man who denounced the Pope as fiercely as Luther, who was excommunicated and consigned to death by Rome, should nevertheless have left such a reputation behind him that, within eleven years of his execution, Julius the Second declared him a true martyr, and was willing to canonise him; that Paul the Third suspected any man who should venture to accuse him; that he was honoured among the saints in the liturgy of his Order. The answer is that Savonarola assailed the intruder, not the institution. He was no reformer of the prerogative, and would have committed full powers to a pontiff of his choice. He upheld the Papal authority against the usurper of the Papacy. Three false Popes were once upon a time removed to make way for Clement the Third, for the same reason for which Savonarola deemed Alexander an illegitimate pretender, who ought to be made to yield his place to a better man.

The essential articles of George Eliot's creed were the fruit of so much preceding study that she impresses us less than some other writers by originality in the common sense of invention. She was anxious to make it known that her abiding opinions were formed before she settled in London. Mr. Spencer confirms the claim, and it is proved by her first paper in the *Westminster Review*. The doctrine that neither contrition nor sacrifice can appease Nemesis, or avert the consequences of our wrong-doing from ourselves and others, filled a very large space indeed in her scheme of life and literature. From the bare diagram of *Brother Jacob* to the profound and finished picture of *Middlemarch*, retribution is the constant theme and motive for her art. It helped to determine her religious attitude, for it is only partly true that want of evidence was her only objection to Christianity. She was firmly persuaded that the postponement of the reckoning blunts the edge of remorse, and that repentance which ought to be submission to just punishment, proved by the test of confession, means more commonly the endeavour to elude it. She thought that the world would be indefinitely better and happier if men could be made to feel there is no escape from the inexorable law that we reap what we have sown. When she began to write, this doctrine was of importance as a neutral space, as an altar of the Unknown God, from which she was able to preach her own beliefs without controversy or exposure. For whilst it is the basis of morals under the scientific reign, it is a stimulant and a consolation to many Christians, for whom the line, "The mills of God grind slowly, but they grind exceeding small," expresses an ancient observation sanctioned by religion, whereas the words once spoken at Salerno, "Dilexi justitiam et odi iniquitatem, propterea morior in exilio," are the last cry of a baffled and despairing fanatic.

This fundamental principle, that the wages of sin are paid in ready money, was borne in upon her by all her early environment. Bray had written a book in its defence, and the strength of Dawson's moral teaching was largely ascribed to the firmness with which he held it. Comte had said that obedience to each natural law has its peculiar reward, and disobedience its appropriate punishment; and Emerson stated his theory of compensation in these terms: "The specific stripes may follow late upon the offence, but they follow, because they accompany it. Crime and punishment grow out of one stem. We cannot do wrong without suffering wrong." The same law, that evil ensues of necessity from evil deeds, is the pivot of Spinoza's ethics, and it was the belief of Strauss. George Eliot accepted it, and made it bright with the splendour of genius. Other portions of her system, such as altruism and the reign of the dead, exhibit her power of anticipating and of keeping abreast with the quicker movements of the age. In this she plainly followed, and she followed the lead of those who happened to be near.

She belongs to that family of illustrious thinkers whose progress has been made by the ingenious use of existing materials and respect for those who have gone before. Mr. Herbert Spencer owes seminal ideas to Baer, Professor Bain to Johannes Müller, Helmholtz to Young, Darwin to Malthus, Malthus to Euler, Milne Edwards to Adam Smith, Bentham to Hutcheson. Newton has the demerit of having been preceded in his greatest discovery by three contemporaries, and Helmholtz by five. One of Laplace's theories was in 's Gravesande before him and the other in Kant. Comte, if Mill had not given him a release from the study of German, might have found his law of the three stages anticipated by Fries in 1819. The *Westminster Review* adopted a new and characteristic motto when she joined it. There is another maxim of the same writer, which she would have been willing to make her own: "Alles Gescheidte ist schon gedacht worden; man muss nur versuchen es noch einmal zu denken." Goethe's new commentators track the derivation of his sentences, as we in England know how much Latin and Italian poetry was boiled down in Gray's "Elegy," and from which lines of Coleridge Byron got the "Address to the Ocean." George Eliot's laborious preparation and vast reading have filled her books with reminiscences more or less definite. The suggestion that she borrowed the material of plots from George Sand, Freytag, Heyse, Kraszewski, Disraeli, or Mrs. Gaskell, amounts to nothing; but the quack medicine which is employed to make the Treby congregation ridiculous is inherited from Faust. The resemblance of ideas is often no more than agreement. The politics of Felix Holt may be found in Guizot—"C'est de l'état intérieur de l'homme que dépend l'état visible de la société." A Belgian statesman has said, "Plus on apporte d'éléments personnels, spontanés, humains, dans les institutions, moins elles sont appelées à régler la marche de la société." Probably George Eliot had read neither the one nor the other, though she may have met with the same thoughts constantly. But she had read *Delphine*, and the conclusion of *Delphine* is the conclusion of the story of *Gwendolen*: "On peut encore faire servir au bonheur des autres une vie qui ne nous promet à nous-mêmes que des chagrins, et cette espérance vous la ferait supporter." The passage on the roadside crucifix in *Adam Bede* ends thus: "No wonder man's religion has sorrow in it: no wonder he needs a suffering God!" The sentence reads like a quotation from Chateaubriand, but it is the quintessence of Feuerbach. In the same chapter of *Deronda* the lament of Francesca is quoted with repeated emphasis, and the moon is entangled among trees and houses. The figure occurs in the poem which Musset wrote against those very verses of Dante. A motto before the fifty-seventh chapter of *Daniel Deronda* comes very near the preface to *Fiesco*. Several candidates have felt that Mr. Brooke has purloined their speeches at the hustings. One of his good sayings points to France. "I want that sort of thing—not ideas, you know, but a way of putting them." The speechless deputy in the comedy says, "Ce n'est jamais les idées qui me manquent, c'est le style."

When she left Warwickshire, where Mr. Froude and Miss Martineau had been her friends and Emerson had shone for a moment, she was not dazzled by what she found in London. The discriminating judgment, the sense of proportion were undisturbed by reverence or enthusiasm for the celebrities of the day. The tone towards Macaulay and Mill is generally cold, and she shrinks from avowing the extent of her dislike for Carlyle. Dickens behaved well towards his lofty rival, but she feels his defects as keenly as his merits; and she is barely just to Darwin and Lecky. A long ground-swell followed her breach with Miss Martineau. The admiration expressed for Mr. Ruskin—the Ruskin of 1858—is flavoured with the opposite feeling; and the opposite feeling towards Buckle is not flavoured with admiration; for her artistic temper revolts against the abstraction of the average man and the yoke of statistics, with its attendant reliance on the efficacy of laws. George Eliot highly esteemed both the Newmans. She wished to be within hearing of the pulpit at Edgbaston. The *Apologia* breathed much life into her, and she points out the beauty of one passage; but it is the writer's farewell to friends and no part of his argument. The early vituperation of Disraeli, of his Judaism and the doctrine of race, is a landmark to measure the long procession of her views. In *Deronda* days she judged Lord Beaconsfield more benignly, relishing his disdain for the popular voice and his literary finish beyond the effective qualities of his rival.

Promptness in opening her mind to new influence, and ardour of gratitude and respect had changed into a quiet resolve to keep cool and resist ascendency. There was nobody among her acquaintances to whom she owed such obligations as she acknowledges to Mr. Herbert Spencer. Although she underrated his constructive talent, and did not overrate his emotional gifts, she foresaw very early the position he afterwards attained. He made the sunshine of her desolate life in London; they met every day, and the two minds, strangely unlike each other, worked in a like direction. The friendship with Lewes made slower progress.

George Eliot retired from the management of the *Review* without having found her vocation or struck a vein of ore. She employed herself in translating Spinoza and Feuerbach. The *Essence of Christianity* had been published more than twelve years, and expressed neither a prevailing phase of philosophy nor the last views of the author. More than any other work it had contributed to the downfall of metaphysics, and it contained an ingenious theory of the rise and growth of religion, and of the relation of the soul to God, while denying the existence of either. Feuerbach repudiated Christianity so decisively that Strauss was distanced and stranded for thirty years; and it would have been difficult to introduce to the British public any work of the same kind written with as much ability. It met no demand and was received with cold reserve. A letter of December 1874 shows that Feuerbach's theogony survived in her system longer than his scoffing and destructive spirit. He learnt towards the end of his life that a prominent American politician had been converted from Christianity by his book in the translation of Marian Evans. The news would not have gratified the translator. The book appeared in July 1854, and immediately after she accepted Lewes, who was completing the *Life of Goethe*, and they started for Weimar and Berlin.

Mr. Cross has judged it unnecessary to explain a step which is sufficiently intelligible from the whole tenor of George Eliot's life. The sanctions of religion were indifferent to her after rejecting its doctrines, and she meant to disregard not the moral obligation of marriage, but the social law of England. Neither the law which assigns the conditions of valid marriage, nor that which denied the remedy of divorce, was of absolute and universal authority. Both were unknown in some countries and inapplicable to certain cases, and she deemed that they were no more inwardly binding upon everybody than the royal edicts upon a Huguenot or the penal laws upon a Catholic.

George Eliot can neither be defended on the plea that every man must be tried by canons he assents to, nor censured on the plea that virtue consists in constant submission to variable opinion. The first would absolve fanatics and the other would supersede conscience. It is equally certain that she acted in conformity with that which in 1854 she esteemed right, and in contradiction to that which was the dominant and enduring spirit of her own work. She did not feel that she was detracting from her authority by an act which gave countenance to the thesis that associates rigid ethics with rigid dogma, for she claimed no authority and did not dream of setting an example. The idea of her genius had not dawned. That she possessed boundless possibilities of doing good to men, and of touching hearts that no divine and no philosopher could reach, was still, at thirty-five, a secret to herself. At first she was astonished that anybody who was not superstitious could find fault with her. To deny herself to old friends, to earn with her pen an income for her whose place she took, to pass among strangers by a name which was not her due, all this did not seem too high a price for the happiness of a home. She urged with pathetic gravity that she knew what she was losing. She did not know it. Ostensibly she was resigning a small group of friends and an obscure position in literature. What she really sacrificed was liberty of speech, the foremost rank among the women of her time, and a tomb in Westminster Abbey.

Mr. Cross is loyal to the memory of Lewes, and affords no support to the conjecture that she longed to be extricated from a position which had become intolerable, or ever awoke to the discovery that she had sacrificed herself to an illusion. With a history open to unfriendly telling there were topics difficult to touch upon and views to which she could not well do justice. She endeavoured, when she became an author, to avert celebrity, to conceal her identity, even to disguise her purpose, and to assume an attitude which was not her own. So essential did secrecy seem to success that the revelation compelled by the report that George Eliot was some one else was felt as a serious injury. There was some cause for diffidence, for toleration, and for a veil of irony. But so far was the difficulty of her position from depressing the moral standard that it served in one respect to raise it. Feuerbach thought it affectation to turn away from immodest scenes, and asserted that enjoyment is a duty. Strauss sneered at the text which laid down the law of Christian chastity. The *Westminster Review* praised a wife who had procured a mistress for her husband. Rousseau thought Sophie all the better for her sin. With these writers George Eliot had been associated. Her admiration for Rousseau, for Shelley, for Jacques, the most ignominious of George Sand's stories, her description of the indissolubility of marriage as a diabolical law, indicate that her opinions did not always keep the elevated level of her early religion and her later philosophy. But in her novels the tone is extremely high. It is true that the pure mind of Romola had been fed on *The Decamerone*; but it is also true that Boccaccio, and not Dante, was the favourite classic of the Florentines of the Renaissance. Gwendolen, having been degraded by marriage without love, is rescued and purified by love without marriage; but we are not suffered to forget for a moment that the marriage was criminal and the love was pure. George Eliot determined to write nothing from which it might be inferred that she was pleading for herself. She was scrupulous that no private motive should affect the fidelity of art. To write books, as *Corinne* and *Delphine* were written, in the interest of the writer, would have seemed to her degradation, and she never puts forward her own ideal of character.

Marriage was not the only chapter of social ethics touched by the Feuerbach phase, and it was not the gravest. Mazzini belonged to Lewes's circle, and Mazzini was currently suspected of complicity in practices which were distinctly criminal, practices for which the law prescribes its last and simplest penalty. George Eliot wavered a good deal between her interest in his cause and her distrust of his methods, but she would never have felt it a stigma to be on amicable terms with him. Elizabeth and Mary, James and William, lie under the same ban of imputed murder, and the friends of the republican conspirator had no reason to apprehend the censure of those who admired the heroes of Catholic and Protestant monarchy.

Those who remember George Henry Lewes in his prosperity, when he was the most amusing talker in the town, so well content with his labours as to regret nothing he had written, and running over with mirth and good humour until he could bear contradiction, excuse folly, and even tolerate religion, saw what George Eliot had made him. She knew him first under less genial aspects. Disaster had settled on his domestic life; he had set his hand to too many things to excel in any, and the mark of failure and frustrated effort was upon him. Varnhagen said in 1850 that Lewes's restless endeavours were repulsive, and that he would end badly if he did not mend his ways. His first books did not recommend him; but there were signs in *Ranthorpe* of large undiscriminating knowledge, and he was, with Mill, the earliest propounder of Positivism in England. He was introduced to George Eliot when his fortunes were almost desperate, and two years passed before she discerned that he was not the flippant man he seemed. She helped him to attain a prominent if not quite an important place among men of letters. For twenty years his *Life of Goethe* held its position even in Germany; and the vacant record of incoherent error which he called a *History of Philosophy* is still read with pleasure. Passing with the drift from the discarded illusions of metaphysics to physiology, and in intelligent pursuance of Comte's leading idea, he conceived the noble design of a *History of Science,* which, by displaying the discovery and application of scientific methods, would have fitly crowned the *Positive Philosophy.*

Lewes helped to dispel the gloom and despondency of George Eliot's spirits, and stood manfully between her and all the cares he did not cause. His literary skill must have done her untold service, although the recorded instances of his intervention are contestable, and although his practice of keeping her aloof from all criticism but his own must have profited her comfort more than her art. She deferred to his judgment, but she knew that she could rely on his praise. He admired her essays, her novels, and at last her poetry. He was not quick in detecting her sovereign ability, and must bear the reproach that he under-valued his prize, and never knew until it was too late that she was worthy of better things than the position to which he consigned her. During the years in which she rose to fame she lived in seclusion, with no society but that of Lewes, preferring the country to London, the Continent to England, and Germany to France. In this perfect isolation the man through whose ministry almost alone she kept touch with the wider world exerted much influence. He encouraged her in contempt for metaphysics, in the study of biology, in her taste for French and especially German writers, and in her panoramic largeness of view. The point at which their ways parted and his action ceased most decidedly was religion. She had kept up her early love of the Scriptures, and she contracted a great liking for the solemn services of the Catholic churches. Lewes saw no harm in these tastes, and he even bought her a Bible. But he did not like to hear of it. He was a boisterous iconoclast, with little confidence in disinterested belief and a positive aversion for Christianity. Even Bach, he said, was too Protestant for him. George Eliot's interest in the religious life was therefore kept up under resistance to adverse pressure.

If Lewes did not debase her standard of rectitude, he enlarged her tolerance of error. Having elected to be subject for life to a man still encumbered with his youth, she became indulgent towards sentiments she disapproved, and appreciated the reason and the strength of opinions repugnant to her. Lewes had detached her from the former associations, and she did not accept his views. Step by step, for good or evil, the process of her life had brought her to a supreme point of solitude and neutrality that would have been chilling and fatal to a feebler mind, but gave her the privilege of almost unexampled independence and mental integrity. Her secluded life had important literary consequences. It estranged her from general society and from religious people.

The breach with zealous Churchmen was not new, but it was now irreparable. She knew their ways from the old books and early recollections; but in the active religious work and movement of her time she shows no more concern than in Plato or Leibnitz. There is no trace of solicitude about Christian Socialism, although Parson Lot's letter furnished forth a speech for Felix Holt. Neither Lamennais nor Gioberti is mentioned, although three volumes are occupied with the protomartyr of Liberal Catholicism. The literature of ethics and psychology, so far as it touched religion, dropped out of her sight, and she renounced intercourse with half the talent in the world. The most

eminent of the men who pursued like problems in her lifetime, among
the most eminent who have thought about them at any time, were
Vinet and Rothe. Both were admirable in their lives, and still more in
the presence of death; and neither of them could be taxed with thraldom
to the formulas of preceding divines. George Eliot disregards their
existence. At Heidelberg she passes before Rothe's house without
alluding to his name. Although she knew and highly valued M. Scherer,
she did not remember that he was the friend of Vinet, or that the
history of his opinions is as remarkable as anything to be found in the
Apologia or told in her own biography.

There are marks of a wound inflicted by Warwickshire pride, which
would not heal. She knew how to construct an unseen creature from
scanty materials, but the divination is more true, the touch more sure
in dealing with classes that subsist for profit than with the class that
subsists for pleasure. Having met some friends of Cavour on the Lake
of Geneva, she declares that there is nothing but their language and
their geniality and politeness to distinguish them from the best English
families. The lawyer who on the opening day of the Rugeley trial
pronounced Palmer a dead man, "John Campbell was so infernally
polite," used an argument of which the author of *Romola* would have
admitted the force. Long retirement prepared her to suspect a snare
in conventional gentility, as if company manners concealed a defect of
genuine humanity and served to keep classes apart. She would not
have assented to the definition of a gentleman that he is one who will
bear pain rather than inflict it. This is the angle at which a faint echo
of Carlyle strikes the ear. She pursues with implacable vengeance the
easy and agreeable Tito. Her chosen hero goes bare-necked and treads
on corns. She will not see that Harold Transome is a brute, and salves
over his inconsiderate rudeness by asserting, in parabasis, his generosity
and goodness of heart. Garth, who might have sent in his resignation
by post, prefers an interview which compels a cruel explanation. No
rumours preserved in a family of land agents could justify the picture
of Grandcourt; but his odiousness is requisite in order to contrast the
wife's momentary flash of guilty delectation when he goes overboard
with the ensuing expiation. The same discordant note appears in
Gwendolen's impatience under the burden of gratitude. One of Charles
Reade's characters exclaims, "Vulgar people are ashamed to be grateful,
but you are a born lady," and an Academician, expounding the same
text, has written, "Avant d'obliger un homme, assurez-vous bien

d'abord que cet homme n'est pas un imbécile." The point is almost too subtle for argument, but it is one of the few marks of limitation in George Eliot's field of vision.

Between *Felix Holt* and *Middlemarch* her range expanded and she judged less austerely.

> We have made some new friendships that cheer us with the sense of new admiration of actual living beings whom we know in the flesh, and who are kindly disposed towards us.—Every one of my best blessings, my one perfect love and the sympathy shown towards me for the sake of my works, and the personal regard of a few friends, have become much intensified in these latter days.—I have entirely lost my personal melancholy. I often, of course, have melancholy thoughts about the destinies of my fellow-creatures, but I am never in that mood of sadness which used to be my frequent visitant even in the midst of external happiness.

Reverence for her genius, for the rare elevation of her teaching, bore down the inevitable reluctance to adjust the rule to an exception. Among the first of her new friends were the ladies of Mr. Cross's family, and they were welcomed with fervent gratitude. When George Eliot came to live near Regent's Park her house was crowded with the most remarkable society in London. Poets and philosophers united to honour her who had been great both in poetry and philosophy, and the aristocracy of letters gathered round the gentle lady who, without being memorable by what she said, was justly esteemed the most illustrious figure that has arisen in literature since Goethe died. There might be seen a famous scholar sitting for Casaubon, and two younger men—one with good features, solid white hands, and a cambric pocket-handkerchief, the second with wavy bright hair and a habit of shaking his head backwards, who evoked other memories of the same Midland microcosm, while Tennyson read his own last poem, or Liebreich sang Schumann's "Two Grenadiers," and Lewes himself, with eloquent fingers and catching laugh, described Mazzini's amazement at his first dinner in London, or the lament of the Berlin professor over the sunset of England since Mr. Gladstone had put an Essay-and-Reviewer on the throne of Phillpotts.

The visit to Germany opened out wider horizons. To chat with Varnhagen von Ense, to explore his archives and admire the miniature of Rahel was a function awaiting literary visitors at Berlin, and Lewes, who had reached Weimar in time to see the Teutonic Boswell, Eckermann, had much to say to the man whom the profane Heine called the vicar of Goethe on earth. The chief interpreter of German thought to the travellers was Gruppe, a scholar of many accomplishments, who has since ended extravagantly, but who had vast knowledge of poetry, a keen sense of the exhausted vitality of speculation, and who in the history of cosmology had measured swords with Böckh. George Eliot spent her time in study, seeing little of the intellectual society of the place, and disliking what she saw. She continued to know Germany mainly as it was at the date of initiation in 1855. Even Feuerbach and Strauss remained embalmed in the attitudes of 1841. The aesthetic age, whose veterans still lingered about Dresden and Berlin, was always more present to her mind than the predominant generation between the parliament of Frankfort and the proclamation of Versailles, the Germany of Helmholtz and Mommsen, Jhering and Fischer, Virchow and Rümelin, Roscher and Treitschke. The only master of this stronger and less artistic school who fixed her attention is Riehl, an author worthy of such a commentator, but not faithful to the methods by which his people succeed.

She saw *Nathan der Weise*, not in vain. "Our hearts swelled and the tears came into our eyes as we listened to the noble words of dear Lessing, whose great spirit lives immortally in this crowning work of his." Twenty years later she explained the design of *Deronda* by the reasons given in the preface to the *Juden*. The altered attitude towards the Jews, which gradually prepared her last novel, began at this time, and she must have heard Humboldt's saying that Judaism is more easily reconcilable with science than other religions. The *Hamburgische Briefe* lay open before her at the *table d'hôte*; she pronounces the *Laokoon* the most un-German of German books, and notices nothing between Berlin and Cologne but "the immortal old town of Wolfenbüttel." If Lessing was the favourite, Goethe was the master. Life at Weimar, with the sublime tradition, closed for George Eliot the season of storm and strain. Although she never practised art for its own sake, or submitted to the canon that poetry is aimless song, Goethe's gospel of inviolate serenity was soothing to a spirit disabled by excess of sensibility, and taught her to be less passionately affected either by sympathy or sorrow. The contrast is great between the agonising tones of the earlier life and the self-restraint and composure that succeeded. The conversion was not immediate. A scene is recorded at Berlin which recalls the time when Miss Evans was too clever to succeed at Coventry, and the crude smartness of the Westminster articles (toned in the reprint),[1] the resentment and even misery caused by the impostor Liggins, were below the dignity of so noble a mind. But the change in the later years is unmistakable. Even the genial warmth of affection for persons was tempered by an impartial estimate of their characters and a disinterested neutrality towards their undertakings. A system that denies the hopes and memories which make pain and sadness shrink cannot be rich in consolation; yet she strove not to overdo the tragedy of human life. The pathos of Mrs. Browning is less profound, the pathos of the *Misérables* is less genuine, but they excite more intense emotion. Happiness and success contributed to that majestic calm which is the proper prize of intelligent immersion in Goethe.

George Eliot came back conscious of much affinity with the Germans, and impressed by their methodical energy and massive power. The lack of literary point and grace provoked her; she yawned even over Schiller and Goethe, and the relief she derived from Heine accentuated the favourable estimate of his character in the essay on German wit. She was nowhere so well and so happy; but she described the North as a region of unmannerly pedants, and preferred the cheerful ease and cogent hospitality of the South. International culture had disengaged her patriotism from prejudice, and she felt less for the country between the four seas than for the scenery, the character, and the dialect of the Trent valley.

The Italian journey reveals that weakness of the historic faculty which is a pervading element in her life. Her psychology was extracted from fortuitous experience, from observations made on common people in private life, under the sway of thoughtless habit and inherited stupidity, not from the heroic subjects, the large questions and proportions of history. Italy was little more to her than a vast museum, and Rome, with all the monuments and institutions which link the old

---

[1] Some secrets of style reveal themselves to anybody who compares the articles in the *Review* with the text which she afterwards prepared, and there are many touches and omissions significant of the vast change her mind had undergone. The last essay, which supposes that Young came into the world without a wig, and calls George the First "that royal hog," was composed at the same time as the first novel; and the contrast shows with what effort and constraint the scenes were written. The perfection of language was not reached at once. A single paragraph of the *Mill on the Floss* contains the terms "phiz," "masculinity," "that same Nature." There is a slight mannerism in the formula "which has been observed"; and the perilous word "mutual" is sometimes misapplied. One of her favourite expressions is usual with Comte, and we used to hear another at school in "that central plain, watered at one extremity by the Avon, and at the other by the Trent."

world with the new, interested her less than the galleries of Florence. She surveys the grand array of tombs in St. Peter's, and remarks nothing but some peasants feeling the teeth of Canova's lion.

Travel supplied the later books with the materials which came at first from home. The *Spanish Gypsy* was derived from a Venetian picture. The celestial frescoes in Savonarola's home at San Marco suggested the argument of *Romola*. A Dresden Titian haunted her for years. It became the portrait of her latest hero, whose supposed resemblance to our Lord gives intensity to the contrast between a Jew who sacrificed his people for religion, and a Christian who goes back to Judaism, renouncing his religion in obedience to the hereditary claim of race. When she was writing *Adam Bede* at Munich, a Moldavian Jew came with introduction to her friends, intent on the same vague errand of national redemption upon which Deronda disappears from sight. Liszt, whom they had known at Weimar, became Klesmer; and a young lady over whom George Eliot wept in the gambling rooms at Homburg, and who remembers the meeting, served as the model of Gwendolen.

After many years characterised by mental independence and resistance to control, George Eliot inclined to that system which is popular among men who "yield homage only to external laws." The influence of Comte began early and grew with the successive study of his works, until the revolutionary fervour of 1848 was transformed into the self-suppression of the *Spanish Gypsy,* and the scorn for Liberality and Utilitarianism which appears in *Felix Holt.* It was the second Comte, the dogmatising and emotional author of the *Politique Positive,* that she revered, and she has not a word for the arch-rebel Littré. Positivists deem that she never thoroughly conformed. But she renounced much of her unattached impartial freedom for an attitude of doctrinal observance, and submitted her mind to discipline, if not to authority. She continued to analyse and to illustrate with an increasing fertility and accuracy; but she was in the clasp of the dead hand, and the leading ideas recur with constant sameness. That the yoke was ever shaken does not appear. We learn from the Life that she never became a party politician, and refused to admit that political differences are, what religious differences are not, founded on an ultimate diversity of moral principles.

Comte, who was averse to popular Protestantism, who excluded the reformers from his Calendar, and acknowledged the provisional services rendered to the mediaeval phase of the progress of society by the Church, encouraged the growing favour which she showed to Catholicism. *The Imitation,* which is the most perfectly normal expression of Catholic thought, as it bears the least qualifying impress of time and place, and which Comte never wearied of reading and recommending, prepared the sympathy. It had been in her hands when she translated *Spinoza* and afterwards when she wrote the *Mill on the Floss.* No thought occurs more often in her writings than that of the persecuted Jews; but she spares the persecutors. *Romola* suggests that Catholic life and history is guided by visions; but the stroke is aimed at other religions as well. The man who, for the pure love of holiness, became a brother of the Order of Torquemada, led up to the central problem of Catholicism, how private virtue and public crime could issue from the same root. Comte has extolled De Maistre, the advocate of the Inquisition; and when, in her next work, George Eliot approaches the subject, it was done with reserve, and without advancement of learning. Although she preferred the Protestant Establishment to Sectarianism, Catholicism to Protestantism, and Judaism to Christianity, the margin of liking was narrow, and she was content to say that the highest lot is to have definite beliefs.

George Eliot's work was done before Lewes died. A year and a half after his death she married Mr. Cross, and went abroad for the last time. Her husband's illness at Venice was a severe shock to her; but when she came back to her home, released from the constraint of so many years, a new life began. She was able to indulge her own tastes, choosing retirement, reading the Bible and the *Divina Commedia,* and hearing the Cardinal at Kensington. There was no return to literary composition. The crowding thought had outgrown her control—"E sulle eterne pagine Cadde la stanca man."

Before the summer was over her health gave way. In one of the last letters, written in an interval of recovered strength, she says that she has been cared for with something better than angelic tenderness. "I do not think I shall have many returns of November, but there is every prospect that such as remain to me will be as happy as they can be made by the devoted tenderness which watches over me." During this afterglow of tranquil happiness, George Eliot suddenly fell ill and passed away, silent and unconscious of her approaching end. There has been no deathbed to which the last words of Faust are so appropriate:

> Zum Augenblicke dürft' ich sagen:
> Verweile doch! Du bist so schön!
> Es kann die Spur von meinen Erdentagen

Nicht in Äonen untergehn!
Im Vorgefühl von solchem hohen Glück
Geniess' ich jetzt den höchsten Augenblick.

George Eliot did not believe in the finality of her system, and, near the close of her life, she became uneasy as to the future of her fame. True to the law that the highest merit escapes reward, she had fixed her hope on unborn generations, and she feared to make sure of their gratitude. Though very conscious of power and no longer prone to self-disparagement, she grew less satisfied with the execution of her designs, and when comparing the idea before her with her work in the past, her mind misgave her. She was disconcerted by ignorant applause, and she had not yet poured her full soul. Having seen the four most eloquent French writers of the century outlive their works, and disprove the axiom that style confers immortality, she might well doubt whether writings inspired by distinct views and dedicated to a cause could survive by artistic qualities alone. If the mist that shrouded her horizon should ever rise over definite visions of accepted truth, her doctrine might embarrass her renown. She never attained to the popular pre-eminence of Goethe, or even of Victor Hugo. The name of George Eliot was nearly unknown in France; she had lost ground in America, and at home her triumph did not pass unchallenged, when men like Beaconsfield, Ruskin, Arnold, Swinburne denied her claims. Lewes himself doubted the final estimate, for he announced with some excitement that she had been compared to Wordsworth, and that somebody thought the comparison inadequate. Men very far asunder— the two Scherers, Montégut, Mr. Spencer and Mr. Hutton, Professor Tyndall and Mr. Myers—have declared with singular unanimity that she possessed a union of qualities seldom, if ever, exceeded by man, and not likely to be seen again on earth; that her works are the high-water mark of feminine achievement; that she was as certainly the greatest genius among women known to history as Shakespeare among men. But George Eliot did not live to recognise, in the tribute of admiring friends, the judgment of history.

She has said of herself that her function is that of the aesthetic, not the doctrinal teacher—the rousing of the nobler emotions which make mankind desire the social right, not the prescribing of special measures. The supreme purpose of all her work is ethical. Literary talent did not manifest itself until she was thirty-seven. In her later books the wit and the descriptive power diminish visibly, and the bare didactic granite shows through the cultivated surface. She began as an essayist, and ended as she had begun, having employed meanwhile the channel of fiction to enforce that which, propounded as philosophy, failed to convince. If the doctrine, separate from the art, had no vitality, the art without the doctrine had no significance. There will be more perfect novels and truer systems. But she has little rivalry to apprehend until philosophy inspires finer novels, or novelists teach nobler lessons of duty to the masses of men. If ever science or religion reigns alone over an undivided empire, the books of George Eliot might lose their central and unique importance, but as the emblem of a generation distracted between the intense need of believing and the difficulty of belief, they will live to the last syllable of recorded time. Proceeding from a system which had neglected morals, she became the pioneer in that movement which has produced the *Data of Ethics* and the *Phänomenologie*. Her teaching was the highest within the resources to which Atheism is restricted, as the teaching of the *Fioretti* is the highest within the Christian limits. In spite of all that is omitted, and of specific differences regarding the solemn question of conscience, humility, and death, there are few works in literature whose influence is so ennobling; and there were people divided from her in politics and religion by the widest chasm that exists on earth, who felt at her death what was said of the Greek whom she had most deeply studied—σκότον εἶναι τεθνηκότος.

Many men have compressed their
entire wisdom into portable
aphorisms. Others have had it
done for them.

Lord Acton

SELECTIONS
FROM THE
ACTON
LEGACY

Liberty

How to teach men to wish for liberty, to understand it, to be capable of it.
 Add. Mss. 4941, p. 123.

The theory of liberty is the summit—the supreme law.
 Add. Mss. 4945, p. 184.

Liberty is extremely contagious.
 January 5, 1862. Acton-Simpson II, p. 252.

I
LIBERTY AS THE REIGN
OF CONSCIENCE

Many definitions of Liberty—showing how little people have the same idea before them, in attraction or repulsion.
 Add. Mss. 5399, p. 21.

Definition of Liberty: (1) Security for minorities; (2) Reason reigning over reason, not will over will; (3) Duty to God unhindered by man; (4) Reason before will; (5) Right above might.
 Add. Mss. 5399, p. 3.

Liberty [is the] same cause as the cause of justice and virtue—opposition to liberty is opposition to justice and virtue, and defence of wrong and sin.
 Add. Mss. 5594, p. 13.

Authority and order secure the temporal benefit of man—Liberty secures his spiritual benefit.
 Add. Mss. 5552, p. 19.

489

Liberty enables us to do our duty unhindered by the state, by society, by ignorance and error. We are free in proportion as we are safe from these impediments to fight the battle of life and the conflict with temptation, with nature—the enemy within.

Add. Mss. 4870, p. 1.

It is not only a sense of one's responsibility to God that makes us demand Liberty—but also a sense of others' responsibility, a dread of assuming that, that makes us grant it. No man is truly conscious of his own responsibility, fully fearful who wishes to increase it.

Add. Mss. 5395, p. 27.

Liberty: Power over oneself. Opposite: Power over others.

Add. Mss. 5604, p. 30.

Liberty is the prevention of control by others. This requires self-control and, therefore, religious and spiritual influences: education, knowledge, well-being.

Add. Mss. 4862, p. 126.

If truth is not absolute, then liberty is the condition of truth.

Add. Mss. 4938, p. 174.

Keep liberty as close as possible to morality. If you pursue speculative purposes, you get beyond and out of touch with it.

Add. Mss. 4916, p. 3.

Liberty becomes a question of morals more than of politics.

Add. Mss. 4950, p. 143.

Conservative case: Liberty is a luxury, not a necessity for all men. The poor, ignorant people cannot enjoy it. Give them first all other things. Use your power for their welfare and sacrifice liberty to security, to morality, to prosperity. These have a larger space in the lives of common men, a larger share in their happiness. Their happiness depends, if at all, on the appearance, not the reality. So give them delusive forms, consistent with the strong hand, with guidance from above.

There is no answer to their case, apart from religion. If happiness is the end of society, then liberty is superfluous. It does not make men happy. It depends on the other world. It is the sphere of duty—not of rights. Suffering, sacrifice for an end beyond this life. If there is none, then there is no object to sacrifice to.

Add. Mss. 4945, pp. 232–233.

Liberty is the condition of duty, the guardian of conscience. It grows as conscience grows. The domains of both grow together. Liberty is safety from all hindrances, even sin. So that liberty ends by being Free Will.

Add. Mss. 5006, p. 242.

The center and supreme object of liberty is the reign of conscience. Religion produced this force only in the seventeenth century—just as it redeemed slavery only in the nineteenth century, in the 30 years from 1833 to 1864.

Add. Mss. 5006, p. 252.

Liberty and Morality: How they try to separate them, to found liberty on rights, on enjoyments, not on duties. Insist on their identity. Liberty is the condition which makes it easy for Conscience to govern. Liberty is government of Conscience. Reign of Conscience.

Add. Mss. 4939, p. 326.

Liberty has not subsisted outside of Christianity. Providence, while it summons a larger part of mankind to the enjoyment of truth, which is the blessing of religion, has called a larger part of mankind to the enjoyment of freedom, which is the blessing of the political order—that freedom should be religious, and that religion should be free.

Add. Mss. 5392, p. 140.

Definition: Liberty is the reign of conscience.

Add. Mss. 4941, p. 332.

II
LIBERTY AND THE STATE

Liberty as an idea—as a condition enjoyed—as an established security.

Add. Mss. 4951, p. 280.

All liberty consists in radice in the preservation of an inner sphere exempt from state power. That reverence for conscience is the germ of all civil freedom, and the way in which Christianity served it. That is, liberty has grown out of the distinction (separation is a bad word) of Church and State.

January 5, 1862. Acton-Simpson II, p. 251.

Liberty is the supreme law. Limited only by greater liberty.

Add. Mss. 5611, n.n.

Public interests not to be weighed against private rights.

Add. Mss. 4980, p. 105.

There are no public, as distinct from private objects worthy to be purchased at the expense of souls. Consequently the interest of individuals is above the exclusive interest of the state. The power of the whole is not to be set in the balance for a moment with the freedom—that is, the conscience of the subject and those who act on the other principle are the worst of criminals.

Add. Mss. 4960, p. 278.

Liberty is the harmony between the will and the law.

Add. Mss. 5552, p. 17.

Liberty equals that condition of political life which is not dependent on interests or passions or prejudices or classes.

Add. Mss. 4951, p. 211.

Liberty nothing without security.

Add. Mss. 4943, p. 403.

A right may be abandoned—not a duty. So liberty is less secure as a right than as an obligation.

Add. Mss. 4980, p. 28.

Liberty requires sacrifice. It presupposes the existence of many conditions—It exacts the sacrifice of many competing advantages.

Add. Mss. 4945, p. 87.

As much authority as is wanted to protect the few against the many or the weak against the strong is not contrary to freedom, but the condition of freedom.

Letter to Mary Gladstone, February 19, 1881, in Paul, p. 177.

The test of liberty is the position and security of minorities.

Letter to Mary Gladstone, February 10, 1881, in Paul, p. 169.

Law: The forces that prevail in society tend to control the state. Where one force altogether prevails, there is no way of checking it. For it is by the combination of others that we prevent the predominance of one. Hence liberty requires that all should obtain the due scope, by representation. Business of freedom to prevent that undue predominance, to protect the weak against the strong.

Add. Mss. 5602, p. 14.

Liberty is established by the conflict of powers. Secured by the balance of powers.

Add. Mss. 5552, p. 14.

Equality included one great element of liberty—it implied toleration.

Add. Mss. 4961, p. 30.

Liberty of the press follows liberty of conscience.

Add. Mss. 5594, p. 78.

Corruption is much better than the rack, the thumbscrew or the boot; but it tends to a like end. It undermines liberty.

Add. Mss. 4945, p. 215.

Laws are local and national. Liberty has nothing to do with nationality.

Add. Mss. 4938, p. 165.

The essence of Liberty not to believe in the sanctity of the past.

Add. Mss. 5015, p. 69.

III
HISTORY OF LIBERTY

History of Liberty—a history of the last 200 years. At the end of Charles II's reign, it was extinct in Europe. But although practically beginning then, theoretically 2000 years earlier. Indeed it is the unity, the only unity of the history of the world—and the one principle of a philosophy of history.

    Add. Mss. 4991, p. 198.

Tradition, the argument of long duration, does not favour Liberty. If that which lasts is right, then Liberty is wrong.

    Add. Mss. 5011, p. 296.

We have no thread through the enormous intricacy and complexity of modern politics except the idea of progress towards more perfect and assured freedom, and the divine right of free men.

    Acton, *Lectures on Modern History*, p. 202.

Liberty is the one common topic of ancient and modern history: Every nation, every epoch, every religion, every philosophy, every science.

    Add. Mss. 4941, p. 22.

Progress of Liberty: The conflict for and against it, is the one link between ancient and modern history. That is the one common topic to Athens, Rome, the polity of the migrations, to philosophy and churches, to the conflict of church and state, and between church and church, to the foundation of Christianity, its divisions and its enemies.

    Add. Mss. 4950, p. 332.

The *History of Liberty* should indeed not be a history of the world, but rather a kind of philosophy of history.

    February 11, 1881, translated from the German. Döllinger III, p. 231.

It seems as though liberty, justice, and civilization are three forces constantly struggling, one against the other.

    July 8, 1866, translated from the German. Döllinger I, p. 435.

Liberty is not a gift but an acquisition; not a state of rest but of effort and growth; not a starting point but a result of government; or at least a starting point only as an object—not a datum but an aim. Just as the regular movements of the heavenly bodies produce the music of the spheres, liberty is the result of the principle *suum cuique* in action.

    November 23, 1861. Acton-Simpson II, p. 203.

Liberty is a development, not a survival. A product of advanced civilization, not of nature. The idea that freedom is right does not loom for thousands of years, not until slavery is wrong. For thousands of years man's history is the growth not of freedom but of enslavement.
Add. Mss. 4980, p. 192.

Primitive liberties exist before the notion of the state arises distinctly. As long as it is undefined, those liberties are not real liberty.
Add. Mss. 4980, p. 39.

Theory of primitive liberty leans on the idea that men are free without civilization, the liberty of the noble savage. We mean the slow produce, the highest result of civilization.
Add. Mss. 4951, p. 161.

Original liberty: It is this, that there were primitive forms, before real problems of state arose: land held in common was administered in common—an arrangement compatible with the greatest tyranny— indeed it makes men insensitive to it. But active history begins with the reign of force.
Add. Mss. 4939, p. 2.

Liberty begins only when obedience exists. Until then it is insubordination and anarchy. Therefore we do not reckon as liberty the condition of primitive society. But there are some of its germs. They do not respect rights; they know little of duties.
Add. Mss. 4980, p. 225.

Our present liberties derive partly from the Revolution—partly from earlier sources: 1848, 1830, 1789, 1776, 1688. This, from 1640, that from 1580 and 1517. Liberties of towns, and Representation. Conflicts of Church and state. Germanic polity and Christianity. Roman polity, Greek philosophy, Judaism.
Add. Mss. 4939, p. 289.

Idea of liberty as sacred as life and property not new. Ancient world, classical world, full of it. Therefore we make no great allowance for times.
Add. Mss. 4915, p. 101.

Liberty is not primitive, necessary, or hereditary. It must be acquired. That is, it is not an abstract right, but a privilege. This is the medieval theory. You are free when you prove your claim to freedom.

Add. Mss. 4941, p. 32.

Liberty was medieval—absolutism was modern.

Add. Mss. 4982, p. 127.

Liberty [is] supposed to be connected with popular government. Yet religious liberty was the work of monarchy, in spite of popular government.

Add. Mss. 5594, p. 26.

Monarchy was in many cases an aid to liberty. It protected the nation against the privileged class.

Add. Mss. 4939, p. 288.

National character: Notorious that liberty does not follow talent, original thought, invention, logic, courage, moral culture, thrift. Its home in mixed nations, knowing how and why to obey, patient, tenacious, not united in faith, slow of comprehension, fond of fair play, not zealous for ideas. Liberty in England has long depended on Scots and Irish votes.

Add. Mss. 5011, p. 278.

[The] Reformation broke down continuity, tradition, respect for the past, and for the wisdom of the dead. This undermined one great source of conservatism and made rapid change, independent thought.

Add. Mss. 4960, p. 36.

Penn, a Tory, an adherent of James II, founded the commonwealth of Pennsylvania, hailed by Voltaire as the freest community on earth.

Add. Mss. 4949, p. 228.

Quakers: The last growth of the Protestant principle. Develops the Rights of Man on the grounds of conscience.

Add. Mss. 4952, p. 205.

Rights of man, in Quakers, a product of the Christian religion. So it was handed over to Deism and Scepticism, an inheritance of the religious ages and the latest, ripest product of the Reformation movement.

Add. Mss. 4952, p. 204.

Eighteenth century isolates the individual from society—and from history. Instead of historic facts and forces—abstractions. System is the very crown of the eighteenth century. Negation of history. Essentially revolutionary and unbelieving. Romantic opposes this point. Everything derived from history—no abstract ideal.

Add. Mss. 4952, p. 270.

The theory of the relations between states and churches is bound up with the theory of Toleration, and on that subject the eighteenth century scarcely rose above an intermittent, embarrassed, and unscientific view. For religious liberty is composed of the properties both of religion and of liberty, and one of its factors never became an object of disinterested observation among actual leaders of opinion. They [the thinkers of the eighteenth century] preferred the argument of doubt to the argument of certitude, and sought to defeat intolerance by casting out revelation as they had defeated the persecution of witches by casting out the devil. There remained a flaw in their liberalism, for liberty apart from belief is liberty with a good deal of the substance taken out of it. The problem is less complicated and the solution less radical and less profound. Already, then, there were writers who held somewhat superficially the conviction, which Tocqueville made a corner-stone, that nations that have not the self-governing force of religion within them are unprepared for freedom.

Acton, *Lectures on the French Revolution*, p. 6.

English idea: Every man has a right not to be robbed by a neighbor—an Englishman must not be robbed by the state. Abstract [idea]: Every man has as good a right as an Englishman to be protected against the state as well as against the subject.

Add. Mss. 4945, p. 36.

Liberty depends on so many things besides law—civilisation, morality, knowledge, that the question always is what a country will bear.

Add. Mss. 4943, p. 410.

Freedom belongs to nations flourishing, not to nations unripe or decaying. How do you determine it? By the presence of moral qualities. A nation that does not respect oaths unfit for juries, without education, that does not condemn dishonesty. Does not all this amount to conscience? Where there is an enlightened conscience, there shall be freedom. Where not, not. Mere enjoyment of material pleasures makes men indifferent.

    Add. Mss. 5011, p. 286.

Liberty is a slow growth. It depends on so many things. Nations without god or without a personal god or with infernal gods, obstacles—with caste distinctions, with underdeveloped ideas of property. So political knowledge advanced more slowly than any other science. From Solon to Locke—from the Athenian constitution to the laws of Carolina—the progress is far less than in any branch of human knowledge that was in constant use.

    Add. Mss. 4939, p. 97.

Liberty implies many other things—depends on many conditions. When we say that it is the aim of progress—and essence—we mean that it is the result of other things. It cannot be separated from the things it depends on. There must be independence, culture, prosperity, literature, religion, a healthy public opinion—powerful—a high standard of morality, a long historic training. That is why so many elements contributed.

    Add. Mss. 4951, p. 47.

At certain times liberty makes no progress because society is absorbed in those things which precede liberty and enable it to exist: Religion, social condition, conquest.

    Add. Mss. 4916, p. 13.

Education is not one of the signs of capacity for freedom. See the Swiss Cantons. But what morality does it require? Public opinion in place of law. Sanctity of oaths. Respect for property. NB: Disregard for history made men unable to see that there is this difference between ages and conditions.

    Add. Mss. 4916, p. 61.

Signs of Liberty: Emancipation, Abolition, Free Trade, Free Press, Education, Nationality, Poor Law, Self-Government of Dependencies.
Add. Mss. 5648, p. 21.

Free trade, to improve the condition of the people and fit them for freedom.
Add. Mss. 4945, p. 248.

Very late in human history, Liberty appears, defended for itself all along the line. That can only be when ideas prevail, and not interests or traditions.
Add. Mss. 4945, p. 280.

Obstacles to liberty not only oppression, political and social, but poverty and ignorance.
Add. Mss. 4941, p. 131.

Liberty is part of the same idea that prolongs the life of the aged, rescues sickly children, promotes the survival of the unfit—the maimed and helpless soldier, that endeavors, at great pains and expense, to reform the criminal instead of leaving him to the hangman's cheaper care.
Add. Mss. 5399, p. 28.

What is the way of Providence? Towards Liberty, its security, conception, enjoyment.
Add. Mss. 4895, p. 61.

How the progress of history is often the ruin of freedom: Interest, necessity, passion, ignorance, indolence contribute to it. Only a spiritual redeeming force intervenes and saves us. It has to struggle with the reign of sin, with the dead and the living.
Add. Mss. 4939, p. 316.

The chain of reasoning which went to the making of modern liberty began with the highest spiritual vision of the cause of God and ended in revolution, not because men could not bear poverty and misery and pain, but because they were taught to prefer ruin and death to wrong.
Add. Mss. 4982, p. 4.

Why [liberty] is likely to continue. It is really a modern element in society—belonging to the last two centuries and promoted by the law of Progress, which came in so lately. Besides, if not, then History forfeits the unity of its march. Nothing else links all its parts together. No other principle serves as a basis for a philosophy of history or justifies the ways of God to man [or] displays the design of Providence.

Add. Mss. 5011, p. 213.

IV
THREATS TO LIBERTY

Conflict of liberty with obstacles—and with disguised friends. This comes in moment of victory and robs its fruits: (1) Desire of power; (2) Equality; (3) Communism; (4) Irreligion.

Add. Mss. 5602, p. 5.

Liberty has not only enemies which it conquers, but perfidious friends, who rob the fruits of its victories: Absolute democracy, socialism.

Add. Mss. 5552, p. 18.

Political atheism—End justifies the means. This is still the most widespread of all the opinions inimical to liberty. Utilitarians not the most dangerous because they, especially their greatest writer Mill, were sincerely attached to freedom.

Add. Mss. 5602, p. 45.

Many new enemies of Liberty: Schopenhauer, Hegel, Comte, Fourier, Carey, Prussia, Darwin, Fichte.

Add. Mss. 5551, p. 6.

Opposing Liberty: Spencer, Buckle, Fourier, Nationality, Carey, Darwin, Comte.

Add. Mss. 4941, p. 15.

Spencer's Heredity as an enemy of Liberty: Emancipation from surroundings, the source of progress. Dependence on them, on others, prevents advancement—that is made by listening to God, not to man. That is what produces development, even Revolution.

Add. Mss. 5011, p. 240.

Doctrine of race (Gobineau) one of the many schemes to deny free will, responsibility, and guilt, and to supplant morals by physical forces.

Add. Mss. 4940, p. 81.

They insist on the influence of race—In diminution and denial of freedom. How much of modern history is a protest against Liberty— Buckle, Taine, Mommsen. We to whom it means the reign of conscience.

Add. Mss. 5011, p. 81.

The doctrine of evolution has added new perils [to the progress of liberty] besides nationality, clan, party, sect, interest, school. It adds the subtle inheritance of prejudice.

Add. Mss. 4942, p. 14.

End with the Kingdom of God which is Liberty. How far from the end! Africa not begun—Asia how little. But America and Australia [and] South Africa governed by the ideas of our revolution. The ideas that went out then govern the world. Their reaction on Europe.

Add. Mss. 5504, p. 7.

Conscience

I
THE IDEA OF CONSCIENCE

Idea of one irreducible stronghold, within which a man accomplishes the formation of character and develops the power of resisting the influence of example and the law of multitudes.

> Add. Mss. 4960, p. 284.

Conscience perfect in proportion as independent of outside influences and surroundings.

> Add. Mss. 4960, p. 317.

The sovereignty of conscience destroys the fixed standard. Each man must be judged by his own code.

> Add. Mss. 4901, p. 271.

Men must not be condemned for obeying their conscience. Conscience becomes more and more enlightened by experience and the discipline of history.

> Add. Mss. 4901, p. 258.

Conscience is not absolutely infallible. It is the result of training.

> Add. Mss. 5626, p. 15.

II
CONSCIENCE AND RELIGION

We all know some twenty or thirty predominant currents of thought or attitudes of mind, or system-bearing principles, which jointly or severally weave the web of human history and constitute the civilised

502

opinion of the age. All these, I imagine, a serious man ought to understand, in whatever strength or weakness they possess, in their causes and effects, and in their relations to each other. The majority of them are either religious or substitutes for religion. For instance, Lutheran, Puritan, Anglican, Ultramontane, Socinian, Congregational, Mystic, Rationalist, Utilitarian, Pantheist, Positivist, Pessimist, Materialist, and so on. All understanding of history depends on one's understanding the forces that make it, of which religious forces are the most active, and the most definite. We cannot follow all the variations of a human mind, but when we know the religious motive, that a man was an Anabaptist, an Arminian, a Deist, or a Jansenist, we have the master key, we stand on known ground, we are working a sum that has been, at least partially worked out for us, we follow a computed course, and get rid of guesses and accidents. . . . Religion. . . . without other study [is not enough] for a man living in the world, in constant friction with adversaries, in constant contemplation of religious changes, sensible of the power which is exerted by strange doctrines over minds more perfect, characters that are stronger, lives that are purer than his own. He is bound to know the reason why. First, because if he does not, his faith runs a risk of sudden ruin. Secondly, for a reason which I cannot explain without saying what you may think bad psychology or bad dogma—I think that faith implies sincerity, that it is a gift that does not dwell in dishonest minds. To be sincere a man must battle with the causes of error that beset every mind. He must pour constant streams of electric light into the deep recesses where prejudice dwells and passion, hasty judgements, and wilful blindness deem themselves unseen. He must continually grub up stumps planted by all manner of unrevised influence. The subtlest of all such influences is not family, or college, or country, or party, but religious antagonism. There is much more danger for a high-principled man doing injustice to the adherent of false doctrine, of judging with undeserved sympathy the conspicuous adherent of true doctrine, than of hating a Frenchman or loving a member of Brook's. Many a man who thinks the one disgraceful is ready to think the other more than blameless. To develop and perfect and arm conscience is the greatest achievement of history, the chief business of every life, and the first agent therein is religion or what resembles religion.

Letter to Mary Gladstone, March 31, 1883, in Paul, pp. 278–280.

Liberty of conscience is the first of liberties, because it is the liberty to avoid sin.

Add. Mss. 4870, p. 9.

Conscience [is] the means of emancipation from the servitude of sin.

Add. Mss. 4901, p. 242.

If the conscience has no right to its moral dictates, it has none to its religious dictates. It is not its own master. It owes its light to religion. The conscience is not the judge of religion until it has been the creature of religion.

Add. Mss. 5006, p. 141.

If religion is to Renan a question of science, not of conscience, he never has been touched by religion.

Add. Mss. 4942, p. 18.

III
THE POLITICAL DIMENSION
OF CONSCIENCE

If God speaks to the soul, it must touch politics as well. The idea of law becomes distinct from the insurance of interests.

Add. Mss. 4960, p. 295.

Our conscience exists and acts for ourselves. It exists in each of us. It is limited by the conscience of others. It is enough for oneself, not for another. It respects the conscience of others. Therefore it tends to restrict authority and to enlarge liberty. It is the law of self-government.

Add. Mss. 4901, p. 254.

The more conscience comes to the front, the more we consider not what the state accomplishes, but what it allows to be accomplished. Not the action of the state—its powers of action, and its use of them, but the limitation and division of those powers. The society that is beyond the state—the individual souls that are above it.

Add. Mss. 5011, p. 235.

Conscience: Do I decide, or the community? If I, there is no authority. If they, there is no liberty. Some mediator wanted. That is the Church. Sustains alike liberty and authority.

Add. Mss. 5626, n.n.

Conscience depends on, or is parallel with, clear notions of ethics. Obscure ethics indicate imperfect conscience. Therefore obscure ethics imply imperfect liberty. For liberty comes not with any ethical system but with a very developed one. Therefore liberty was imperfect in the Middle Ages from want of means but also from weakness of conscience, proceeding from a confusion of ethics.

Add. Mss. 5395, p. 40.

Conscience a Basis of liberty. Therefore religion a basis of liberty.

Add. Mss. 4960, p. 101.

[The] theory of conscience brought over religion to the cause of freedom. It was the underlying principle.

Add. Mss. 4901, p. 353.

It is by conscience that religion has served the cause of freedom.

Add. Mss. 4901, p. 357.

Equality from conscience—wherein we are all alike.

Add. Mss. 4960, p. 188.

Theory of Conscience: The main protection against absolutism, the one protection against democracy.

Add. Mss. 4960, p. 318.

Theory of conscience is favorable to monarchy. For a monarch has a conscience, a force within working for good. A body of men has no such force. As the individual responsibility is less, so conscientious influences are less. An association has not got a soul.

Add. Mss. 4945, p. 89.

There is a national conscience as well as an individual. A man's sense of right and wrong depends on others. It is not independent and supreme by nature.

Add. Mss. 5395, p. 49.

IV
THE HISTORY OF
CONSCIENCE

Conscience means also that the individual obtains a larger share of history.

> Add. Mss. 4960, p. 186.

Conscience grows more perfect, both in our lives, and by process of ages.

> Add. Mss. 5395, p. 48.

Apart from demonstration and above it, those ideas have the strongest claim on individual assent which have the largest amount of general assent. The presumption is in favor of any proposition which has not been questioned. An immense volume of men superior to ourselves constitutes an authority for us, in proportion as their opinions are undisputed.

> Add. Mss. 5011, p. 239.

Conscience unknown, unrecognized in the religions of the East. They taught virtue, punishment etc. But they never knew that the test of what is right is within.

> Add. Mss. 5395, p. 5.

In the Old Testament the heart holds the place of conscience. Job XXVII.6, I. Samuel XXV.31. The word is wanting, but not the thing.

> Add. Mss. 5395, pp. 35, 36, 37.

Conscience comes into play in Sophocles, Euripides, Socrates. At the turning of Greek life, at the breakdown of mythology and the rise of democracy.

> Add. Mss. 5395, p. 44.

Greece: First, instead of sacred tradition, present authority, general consent. This led to the extreme of democracy. Reaction against this, in the third stage, conscience or appeal to personal autonomy: Socrates.

> Add. Mss. 5395, p. 46.

When Socrates declared that he would obey god rather than man, he meant god manifest within—with no oracle, no sacred book, no appointed minister.

Add. Mss. 4901, p. 152.

All Greek notions of conscience are negative, warning, never speak of a good conscience.

Add. Mss. 5395, p. 54.

Conscience: It arose at the time when persecution was at its height. Inquisition organized towards 1230. Conscience begins in Alexander of Hales, St. Thomas, St. Bonaventure.

Add. Mss. 4960, p. 262.

The lines of thought most vigorously followed were those on which Christian and classic [thought] independently converged—that is the existence of Conscience and of a Natural Law: Seneca, St. Thomas, St. Bonaventure.

Add. Mss. 4960, p. 282.

Conscience made popular by the writings of Seneca. No other Stoics. Renaissance Humanists supported this process of thought by reviving other philosophers than Aristotle, particularly the Stoics, and among the Stoics the one ancient writer who insists on the authority, and precedence, the perfectibility, the examination of conscience.

Add. Mss. 4960, p. 285.

Conscience was a thing appealed to by the destroyers of church and state, by enthusiasts and fanatics. At the Reformation, it was disparaged and denounced as a plea for revolution and regicide.

Add. Mss. 4901, p. 256.

Hobbes rejects conscience for the sake of arbitrary monarchy. The two went together. So that Butler's restoration of conscience is a preliminary to the establishment of freedom.

Add. Mss. 4901, p. 358.

After Hobbes all liberty resided in the restoration of conscience.

Add. Mss. 4901, p. 362.

It was in the strife for liberty that conscience came to the front. It began to triumph at the end of the seventeenth century.

Add. Mss. 4901, p. 298.

The theory of conscience was full grown. It had assumed in one of the sects, a very peculiar shape: the doctrine of inner light. The Quakers not originally liberals. But the inner light struggled vigorously for freedom. In the very days in which the theory of conscience reached its extreme terms, Penn proclaimed conscience as the teaching of his sect. And it became the basis of Pennsylvania—Voltaire's best government.

Add. Mss. 4901, p. 355.

Conscience understood in this way supplied a new basis for freedom. It carried further the range of Whiggism. The deeper Quakers perceived the consequences. Penn drew the consequences in the Constitution of Pennsylvania. It was the standard of a new party and a new world.

Add. Mss. 4960, p. 299.*

The State

I
THE IDEA OF THE STATE

The state in which freedom would be sufficiently secured against the government, and against the people is ideal.

October 8, 1861. Acton-Simpson II, p. 182.

The right of association is anterior to the actual state. The state has grown out of associations, and can suppress only those directed in some way against itself. To go farther, and to say all societies must get the permission of government to exist, which also implies a certain inspection or control, is to take state absolutism as the starting point in politics, and freedom—or rather liberties, as concessions and compromises of absolutism. Whereas the presumption is in all cases against the state. It has no business where it cannot prove its case. It has no admittance except on business evidently its own.

November 24, 1861. Acton-Simpson II, p. 206.

The object of civil society is justice, not truth, virtue, wealth, knowledge, glory or power. Justice is followed by equality and liberty.

Add. Mss. 5588, p. 27.

All liberty is conditional, limited and therefore unequal. The state can never do what it likes in its own sphere. It is bound by all kinds of law.

November 26, 1861. Acton-Simpson II, p. 209.

We think much more of the rights which protect our duties than for the protection of our enjoyments. They need to be secured as well as proclaimed, and they can be secured only by a complete system of polity.

Add. Mss. 4941, p. 143.

Protection of property: The object of jurisprudence, of laws. Protection of liberty: The object of constitutions.

Add. Mss. 4945, p. 105.

Representation: Taxation and representation. No man's money without his consent so every kind of property must be represented. Much stronger still is the principle *Wehrpflicht und Wahlrecht*. Every man must have a voice in deciding whether he will be killed.

Add. Mss. 4942, p. 6.

Inequality: The Basis of society. We combined and put things in common to protect the weak against the strong.

Add. Mss. 4941, p. 50.

Society constitutes the state as its instrument—pays it, to govern by it. Therefore it forms the state on its own likeness. If it succeeds, then the ruling class governs. If it fails, the ruling class controls the governing class.

Add. Mss. 4942, p. 75.

Government of one, or of a minority [is] not a government of force, but in spite of force, by virtue of some idea. The moral support makes up for inferiority of brute strength. This is authority—which is not equivalent to simple strength.

Add. Mss. 5528, p. 104.

Individualism: Logically it leads to absolute Democracy. It gives to every one an equal share of power. But we mean, not every man, but every interest, every class, every group, every force.

Add. Mss. 4942, p. 7.

Divided, or rather multiplied, authorities are the foundation of good government.

September 25, 1861. Acton-Simpson II, p. 167.

If man has an immortal soul to save, the public interests are subordinate to it. And if he has a conscience, he must not be prevented from obeying it. Therefore the state powers are limited. Strong enough to protect the rights of man—not to oppress. That set up the state against the church—not subordinate to it.

Add. Mss. 4960, p. 1.

The pagan state determines its own purposes and powers. Christianity determines these independently of the state. It fixes the lines and aims for itself. The state submits and accepts them. It is no longer a law for itself—nor assigns its own powers. The state recognizes an authority above its own.

Add. Mss. 5392, p. 95.

In our conviction the true view of the origin and nature of the state, and the only one which must not inevitably succumb to the revolutionary logic, is the one which recognizes in the state the same divine origin and the same ends as in the Church, which holds that it belongs as much to the primitive essence of the nation as its language, and that it unites men together by a moral, not like family and society, by a natural and sensible bond.

Review of James Burton Robertson, *Lectures on Ancient and Modern History*, in the *Rambler* n.s. 2 (March 1860):397. Acton-Simpson II, p. 52.

Every political system requires modification and development, and is meritorious only provided it is capable of bearing it.

Add. Mss. 4862, p. 18.

As to reform agitation, that which is forcibly repressed is more dangerous than that which, however intemperately, makes itself heard.

Add. Mss. 4862, p. 393.

There are many things government can't do—many good purposes it must renounce. It must leave them to the enterprise of others. It cannot feed the people. It cannot enrich the people. It cannot teach the people. It cannot convert the people.

Add. Mss. 4870, p. 35.

The state does not perform the function of conscience—It deals only with the welfare of society, not of individuals. It represses crime, it does not repress sin.

Add. Mss. 5602, p. 53.

Duty [is] not taught by the state.

Add. Mss. 4870, p. 2.

Men cannot be made good by the state, but they can easily be made bad. Morality depends on liberty.

Add. Mss. 4939, p. 3.

II
THE STATE AND ITS
INSTITUTIONS

Institutions [are] not an end but a means.

Add. Mss. 4862, p. 116.

An institution must possess and develop the resources needed for its vitality.

Add. Mss. 4979, p. 89.

Character made by institutions.

Add. Mss. 4895, p. 57.

Change is just because it is inevitable in order to accommodate institutions to the natural alteration of things.

Add. Mss. 4862, p. 393.

Government that is natural, habitual, works more easily. It remains in the hands of average men, that is of men who do not live by ideas. Therefore there is less strain by making government adapt itself to custom. An ideal government much better, perhaps, would have to be maintained by effort, and imposed by force.

Add. Mss. 4953, p. 202.

State has to prevent the oppression of the weak by the strong, the few by the many, the poor by the rich. Theory that the force of society governs the state. Then the state becomes a means of oppression. Monarchy saved you from this. It stood outside. The idea of authority was a bulwark against class government.

Add. Mss. 5011, p. 292.

Concentrate responsibility: That is the idea of imperialism. Responsibility concentrated where it meets conscience. Bring responsibility and conscience together.

Add. Mss. 4942, p. 220.

The authority of history was the negation of personal authority—you defended the spirit of the constitution against the actual king, who could do no wrong.

Add. Mss. 4945, p. 312.

Rationalism [is] in one way opposed to monarchy. It insists on moral, not on religious character. It refuses to play with truth, has no mercy for half truths, for propositions believed without proof, for imaginative truth, for myth or legend. Monarchy cultivates these. Uneducated people cannot distinguish between the office and its occupant. They believe in the virtues of the king—or reject those of the crown. Royalists inclined to cultivate this feeling of awe, this confusion, this illusion. They do not shrink from deceit for the purpose.

Add. Mss. 4942, p. 67.

The whole expanse of the Eastern world proclaimed then as it has not ceased to proclaim until now, the inherent evil of unlimited monarchy.

Add. Mss. 4870, p. 53.

The people—the constituencies, quite incompetent to decide a policy: the balance of power, the colonial trade, the Bank question, the currency question. They are not informed. There is no way to inform them. They must choose their members. Having chosen, they must let them act as they think best.

Add. Mss. 4955, p. 74.

Future bound by the past, example = national debt, treaties.

Add. Mss. 4870, p. 2.

A nation which has no Parliamentary traditions needs to attach to paper constitutions an importance which would be exaggerated in countries where the forms of representation are the expression of the customary life of the people.

"Current Events," *Chronicle* (30 March 1867):3. Ryan, p. 138.

Law is the instrument by which the past holds us. If embodied in a code, it becomes the expression of present will. Therefore they resisted codes, in order to prolong the power of the dead.

> Add. Mss. 4960, p. 135.

It is possible to lose the end in a too technical regard to the means, and to sacrifice liberty by an exaggerated devotion to the forms of law.

> "Current Events," *Chronicle* (30 March 1867):2. Ryan, p. 138.

How little depends on laws compared to spirit. Liberty is the result of laws, of integrity in administering them, of spirit in preserving them. Laws must be not only good, but obeyed; not only obeyed, but willingly obeyed.

> Add. Mss. 5552, p. 15.

Laws [are] preserved by the vitality of the sentiments which produced them. If the convictions and conditions from which they sprang are extinct, the laws follow. That is what Tocqueville means when he says that the condition of opinion is more important than laws.

> Add. Mss. 5552, p. 15.

Laws are local and temporary. It is the idea that survives, propagates, extends.

> Add. Mss. 4951, p. 222.

III
THE MODERN STATE
AND ABSOLUTISM

The first paramount fact with which modern history begins is that the state is above right and wrong, while it pursues its own objects, acquires power, increases territory, promotes prosperity, raises the renown or gratifies the pride of the nation. It is not to be prevented or censured because it employs the basest of crimes, the taking of human life by war, or by the tribunal, or by the assassin. Looks only to the result, to the benefit accruing to the whole.

> Add. Mss. 4982, p. 83.

Venice, which was a republic not of landowners but of shipowners, was the first to revert to the ancient notion of the State, acting for its own purpose, bound to no interest, following the opinion of no majority.

Acton, *Lectures on Modern History*, p.172.

The worst of governments last the longest: Sparta, Venice.

Add. Mss. 4870, p. 55.

[Of the course of the French Revolution] The issue between constitutional monarchy, the richest and most flexible of political forms, and the Republic one and indivisible (that is, not federal), which is the most rigorous and sterile, was decided by the crimes of men, and by errors more inevitably fatal than crime. There is another world for the expiation of guilt; but the wages of folly are payable here below.

Acton, *Lectures on the French Revolution*, p. 239.

Retaining the forms of liberty, Augustus, Lorenzo, Napoleon III were absolute rulers.

Add. Mss. 4870, p. 70.

The idea of a predominant Power in Europe was part of absolutism. It proceeded from the same love of authority, the same pride of greatness, the same disregard for the equal rights of men, the same pretension to superiority and prerogative, international as well as national.

Acton, *Lectures on Modern History*, p. 249.

Wars of conquest and aggrandisement are literally no better in my eyes than murder.

Letter to Mary Gladstone, January 31, 1894, in Acton, *Correspondence*, p. 249.

Absolutism: Sovereignty alone makes war. In war it is free from [the] common law of ethics. You may kill. You may deceive. You may lie. So it is above, the only thing above, morality. Why not in peace also? The object is the same: the public safety.

Add. Mss. 4991, p. 289.

State absolutism, not royal absolutism, is the modern danger against which neither representative government nor democracy can defend us, and which revolution greatly aggravates. If we do not bear this in mind, we shall be led constantly astray by forms to overlook the substance, to confound freedom of speech with freedom of action, to think that right is safer against majorities than against tyrants, that liberty is permanently safer in Belgium, Piedmont, or the United States, than in France, Russia, or Naples.

Review of James Burton Robertson, *Lectures on Ancient and Modern History*, in the *Rambler* n.s. 2 (March 1860):397. Acton-Simpson II, p. 52.

For centuries it was never discovered that education was a function of the State, and the State never attempted to educate. But when modern absolutism arose, it laid claim to every thing on behalf of the sovereign power. Commerce, industry, literature, religion, were all declared to be matters of State, and were appropriated and controlled accordingly. In the same way as all these things education belongs to the civil power, and on the same ground with the rest it claims exemption. When the revolutionary theory of government began to prevail, and Church and State found that they were educating for opposite ends and in a contradictory spirit, it became necessary to remove children entirely from the influence of religion.

"Irish Education," *Rambler* n.s. 3 (September 1860):419. Acton-Simpson II, p. 90.

One who has experienced the tyranny of the partisans of centralisation and universal administration says, with no less feeling than truth, "Whether despotism is exercised in virtue of the principles of 1789 or in virtue of the absolute principle of divine right, it is no less despotism."

Review of G. de Molinari, *Cours d'économie politique*, in the *Home and Foreign Review* 4 (January 1864):314. Acton-Simpson III, p. 132.

Liberty consists in the division of power. Absolutism, in concentration of power.

Add. Mss. 5011, p. 277.

Absolute government must be either despotic or paternal. It is despotic if, as in most continental states, it is used for public or external ends; it is paternal if, as in Rome, it confines itself to private concerns.

"The Roman Question," *Rambler* n.s. 2 (January 1860):147–148. Acton-Simpson II, p. 32.

Bureaucracy is undoubtedly the weapon and sign of a despotic government, inasmuch as it gives whatever government it serves, despotic power.

January 13, 1859. Acton-Simpson I, p. 128.

Bureaucracy tries to establish so many administrative maxims that the minister is as narrowly controlled and guided as the judge.

Add. Mss. 4870, p. 56.

In a bureaucratic state everything that stirs independently of government, and in the mass of the people as such, that is not in their organization, is virtually democratic.

December 6, 1860. Acton-Simpson II, p. 97.

IV
REVOLUTION

The object of Revolution is the prevention of revolution. It supplies a security against the use of violence. Absolute government can only be checked by force. Revolutionary government has a pacific redress.

Add. Mss. 4941, p. 205.

The revolution teaches that a government may be subverted by its subjects, irrespective of its merits. . . . But the revolutionary theory also has an international application, and teaches that a state may be absorbed by its neighbors even if it has not attacked them: when a wish of the kind is presumed on the part of the people, or expressed by insurrection, or ascertained afterwards by vote, or even for rectification of physical boundaries, or for the sake of ethnological boundaries. Therefore (which is a priori necessarily obvious, as it can't contradict itself) the same revolutionary doctrine which puts governments at the mercy of the people, prevents neighbors protecting it against the people. Therefore in an age where the duty of allegiance and even good government are no security, treaties, and international guarantees, and public law, can be no security.

December 20, 1861. Acton-Simpson II, pp. 240–241.

The French Revolution was an attempt to establish in the public law of Europe maxims which had triumphed by the aid of France in

America. By the principles of the Declaration of Independence a government which obstructs liberty forfeits the claim to obedience, and the men who devote their families to ruin and themselves to death in order to destroy it do no more than their duty. The American Revolution was not provoked by tyranny or intolerable wrong, for the colonies were better off than the nations of Europe. They rose in arms against a constructive danger, an evil that might have been borne but for its possible effects. The precept which condemned George III was fatal to Lewis XVI, and the case for the French Revolution was stronger than the case for the American Revolution. But it involved international consequences. It condemned the governments of other countries. If the revolutionary government was legitimate, the conservative governments were not. They necessarily threatened each other. By the law of its existence, France encouraged insurrection against its neighbors, and the existing balance of power would have to be redressed in obedience to a higher law.

Acton, *Lectures on the French Revolution*, p. 317.

Revolution is the greatest enemy of reform—it makes a wise and just reform impossible.

July 9, 1860. Acton-Simpson II, p. 79.

Evolution and Revolution: The one by hearing others; the other by hearing God. If we combine the past with the future, the inward and the outward influences, what follows is Evolution. If we listen within, and reject other influences, that is, if we obey conscience, the result is revolution. That is the only Revolution.

Add. Mss. 5011, p. 234.

No course of obscure planting, of hidden growth, of gradual development, of venerable sanctions, of continuous progress [has] been more creative and constructive, more efficient in controlling events, dictating progress, and moulding the future, than sudden decisions by which men have shaken off their past, have put off the old man and turned their faces to the front.

Add. Mss. 4991, p. 112.

Power

Argument for absolute power: You must put confidence somewhere. You can't escape the conditions of human nature. Put it where responsibility is concentrated.

Add. Mss. 4870, p. 34.

Power tends to corrupt and absolute power corrupts absolutely. Great men are almost always bad men, even when they exercise influence and not authority; still more when you superadd the tendency or the certainty of corruption by authority.

Letter to Mandell Creighton. Add. Mss. 6871, p. 60.

Absolute power demoralizes.

Add. Mss. 5626, p. 10.

History is not a web woven by innocent hands. Among all the causes which degrade and demoralize men, power is the most constant and the most active.

Add. Mss. 5011, p. 111.

Despotic power is always accompanied by corruption of morality.

Add. Mss. 4916, p. 56.

Authority that does not exist for Liberty is not authority but force.

Add. Mss. 4980, p. 31.

Authority exists for the sake of Liberty—a means to an end. But some thought authority good for itself—an end, not a means to something higher—sacred, not by partaking of the reflected sanctity of the thing it exists for. This is divine right. Helped by the Catholic notion of authority.

Add. Mss. 4980, p. 34.

Everybody likes to get as much power as circumstances allow, and nobody will vote for a self-denying ordinance.

December 15, 1863. Acton-Simpson III, p. 151.

Liberty = self-government. Sovereign power is irresponsible power. Irresponsible power must not be irresistible power.

Add. Mss. 4870, p. 28.

Rome discovered—and this constituted the Republic—that power, when it is divided, need not be diminished.

Add. Mss. 4938, p. 234.

Limitation is essential to authority. A government is legitimate only if it is effectively limited.

Add. Mss. 4982, p. 174.

Long before we reach our generation we see that the same issues are always present, that the same fundamental qualities of thought and character are permanently dividing men, that the struggle for the concentration of power and for the limitation and division of power is the mainspring of history.

Add. Mss. 5011, p. 107.

That is the great rhythmic movement of modern history. What we are accustomed to speak of as the rivalry of religion, or of race, or of political forms, is rather the perpetual endeavor of power to increase and to assert itself and of weakness to defend itself. In this way, in resistance to this constant force, liberty has fought, has been saved, and has even extended.

Add. Mss. 4937, p. 130.

Never destroy a force. When it is not dominant, it may serve to check dominion.

Add. Mss. 4949, p. 151.

The triumph and coronation of the Emperor Charles V, when he was superior to all that Europe had beheld since Charlemagne, revived the ancient belief in a supreme authority elevated on alliance with the priesthood, at the expense of the independence and the equipoise of nations. The exploits of Magellan and Cortez, upsetting all habits of perspective, called up vain dreams of the coming immensity of Spain, and roused the phantom of universal empire. The motive of domination became a reigning force in Europe; for it was an idea which monarchy would not willingly let fall after it had received a religious and an international consecration. For centuries it was constantly asserted as a claim of necessity and of right. It was the supreme manifestation of the modern state, according to the image which Machiavelli had set up, the state that suffers neither limit nor equality, and is bound by no duty to nations or to men, that thrives on destruction, and sanctifies whatever things contributed to increase of power. This law of the modern world, that power tends to expand indefinitely, and will transcend all barriers, abroad and at home, until met by superior forces, produces the rhythmic movement of History. Neither race, nor religion, nor political theory has been in the same degree an incentive to the perpetuation of universal enmity and national strife. The threatened interests were compelled to unite for the self-government of nations, the toleration of religions, and the rights of men. And it is by the combined efforts of the weak, made under compulsion, to resist the reign of force and constant wrong, that, in the rapid change but slow progress of four hundred years, liberty has been preserved, and secured, and extended, and finally understood.

Acton, *Lectures on Modern History*, pp. 50–51.

Nothing is more untrue than the famous saying of an ancient historian, that power is retained by the same arts by which it is acquired; untrue at least for men, though truer in the case of nations.

Letter to Mary Gladstone, June 1, 1880, in Paul, p. 108.

Antiquity

Ancients loved liberty. Admitted that the state is bound by a higher law and the rights of man. But failed to accomplish it, when Christianity came. The empire lasted 1000 years from its conversion. Yet it never developed freedom.

Add. Mss. 5436, p. 58.

Greeks fancied that the state was everything. If the state is everything, its power cannot be vested in few hands. The safety lies in making all participate. The power cannot be restrained. It can be diffused. Liberty is greatest, according to the Greek idea, where there are most partners in power. But that also makes the state more irresistible. Increase of liberty is increase of power.

Add. Mss. 5594, p. 80.

Ancient state itself determined duty. Therefore liberty was not from the state but with it. Not absence of authority, but participation in power.

Add. Mss. 4870, p. 23.

The state [in the ancient world] did duty for the church. Combined both functions. This was the great change. Christianity divided the functions. Its distinctive action on politics was to restrict authority.

Add. Mss. 4870, p. 13.

Representation, the real government by the best, unknown to the ancients.

Add. Mss. 4870, p. 1.

The idea of preventing the prevalence of one party is at the bottom of the politics of Aristotle, Polybius, Cicero, the Stoics.

Add. Mss. 4870, p. 20.

Office by lot, in democracies, avoided the predominance of parties.
Add. Mss. 5604, p. 8.

In Greece political thought [was] awakened by actual defects in the government—in Rome by the virtues of the constitution.
Add. Mss. 4860, p. 44.

Philosophy in Greece begins with the beginning of liberty.
Add. Mss. 4860, p. 43.

Before modern times we know the inner mind of scarcely three men: Socrates, Cicero, St. Augustine.
Add. Mss. 4944, p. 218.

Socrates taught a law independent of the state and superior to it.
Add. Mss. 4870, p. 11.

Socrates really died for religion.
Add. Mss. 4870, p. 2.

Polybius was unable to detect a flaw in the marvelous structure [of the Roman constitution]. The harmony appeared complete. The equipoise was perfectly preserved. A better constitution he thought could not be found, and he proclaimed it the type of that mixed constitution which is still the delusive and inaccessible object of civilized nations. But the curse which wrought the destruction of Roman freedom was in full activity—the condition of perpetual war. It brought about those events which subverted the state—the Gracchi, the altered constitution of the army, and the extension of suffrage to the people of Italy.
Add. Mss. 4862, p. 39.

Both Rome and Judaea taught the union of church and state. The normal condition was that the two teachings should agree. No conflict of authority bewildering the people and compelling them to sit in judgement of rival authorities.
Add. Mss. 5393, p. 17.

Roman tolerance not for conscience but absorbed all gods in order to absorb all nations. It was precept of the art of conquest.
Add. Mss. 4980, p. 432.

In Rome . . . the state had arbitrary power to forbid any religion. There was no prerogative that did not derive from the state. Therefore however much religion might be free, it was an exhibition of state power, not a limit [on state power].

Add. Mss. 5006, p. 165.

Roman law also a breach of continuity—prepares absolutism.

Add. Mss. 4981, p. 189.

The political ideas of the Theodosian or Justinian Code are those of a society ground to atoms by the wheel of revolution, consisting no longer of parts, but like sand or water, in which all life and all power are in the sovereign.

November 26, 1861. Acton-Simpson II, p. 208.

Paganism failed where Christianity afterwards failed, to rescue Rome. Neither Emancipation nor Toleration nor Representation. And that is what Rome died of. Without slaves, there would have been a peasantry. With Representation, the provinces would have shared the central power. With Toleration, Christianity would have been equivalent to freedom.

Add. Mss. 5392, p. 98.

We are mistaken generally in attributing to the European nations at the time of their conquest by the Romans and absorption into the empire a very low degree of civilisation, as of barbarous nations at an early age of their progress. On the contrary they were for the most part: (1) very highly cultivated [and] (2) arrived at the close and decline of their civilisation, like the nations of Asia. We know . . . how highly the Gauls were civilized. The same is probable of the Spaniards. Their resistance was longer, and we can trace backwards to a very early period the sign of their civilisation. The civilisation of most of the nations conquered by the Romans was older than theirs. They had a rich history and civilisation, though unlike the countries of the Hellenic world, little literature. Lingard has sought in the Sandwich Islands an analogy for Britain in Caesar's time. Perhaps for Britain, certainly for Gaul and Spain, the Hindoos would be a fairer parallel. The Romans fell before a people of real barbarians, who had not bartered the virtues of barbarism for the advantages of civilisation, whose greatness was to come, and who had not exchanged the future for the past. But the Germans appeared to the Gauls and the Britons as barbarous as to the Romans. In all the countries of western Europe which were successively conquered by the Romans and the Germans, the future progress was attached to the conquering race, and the history is mainly a Teutonic history. Ages after the conquest the Celtic tribes were more civilized than the Teutons, Ireland than England in the ninth century, Wales than England in the thirteenth.

Add. Mss. 5528, p. 155–156.

If we dealt only with institutions, antiquity would be low. It realized no liberty. But in the domain of ideas it ranks high.

Add. Mss. 5686, n.n.

No institutions of paganism survive—influence only by ideas.

Add. Mss. 4870, p. 1.

The intellectual preparation of the world for the teaching of Christ is as specially and exclusively the work of the Hellenic race as the political preparation for the establishment of the Church is the distinctive work of the Romans.

Acton, *Correspondence*, p. 255.

We have lost much of the best literature of later paganism. So that the hymn of Cleanthes seems to us to breathe a spirit strange to paganism. If we possessed Zeno, Chrysippus, etc. we should understand better how the world was made ready for the faith; and how many of the Christian ideas were familiar to the early converts.

Add. Mss. 5392, p. 245.

Philo and Seneca [were] more advanced in politics than any Christian writer for the first twelve centuries.

Add. Mss. 5392, p. 63.

Pagan ideas of society made more progress in five centuries, from Socrates to Epictetus, than Christianity in five centuries, from Constantine to Charlemagne.

Add. Mss. 5392, p. 21.

The Stoics gave Rome her philosophy. First, [the idea] of a higher law, by no means canonizing what exists. Then [the idea that] this law is not bound by religious traditions [nor] by national traditions. [It] has a superior authority in human reason. All men, in this respect, in regard to these rights, are equal. They are brethren, children of God. Conscience teaches us these principles.

Add. Mss. 4862, p. 24.

Christianity extinguished in the Persian empire. Triumphed in the Roman empire. Why? Because in Rome the ruin of the old faith, the need of a better, was prepared by philosophy. For Persia there was an unshaken religion, and no philosophy.

Add. Mss. 4870, p. 12.

What was wanted was to give Greek philosophy the vigour of a religion, to strengthen knowledge with faith. To unite with it the treasures of Judaism, to make Judaism universal.

Add. Mss. 5392, p. 14.

There is this great difference between ancient and modern history: The ancient writers have a value of their own apart from what they teach. The literary treatment of an author is interesting independently of the conclusion deductible from him. He possesses a certain consequence even when he yields nothing.

Add. Mss. 4997, p. 216.

The Middle Ages

Two great principles divide the world, and contend for mastery, antiquity and the Middle Ages. These are the two civilisations that have preceded us, the two elements of which ours is composed. All political as well as religious questions reduce themselves practically to this. This is the great dualism that runs through our society. In the fifteenth and sixteenth century, in the Renaissance and Reformation which followed and agreed with it, as both were a reaction against the medieval ideas, Europe broke with the Middle Ages. They were not misunderstood and condemned. They were forgotten and ignored. All intellectual culture was devoted to antiquity. Politics and literature were attracted exclusively by pagan antiquity, theology addicted itself almost exclusively to Christian antiquity. Both proudly and ignorantly overlooked a thousand years of Christian history. They were abandoned and abjured. In this, Catholics vied with Protestants. Controversy confined itself chiefly to the early ages. To the greatest classical and ecclesiastical scholars, Protestants and Catholics, all that period was nearly a blank, to Grotius as to Bossuet. The result was absolutism and revolution in the state; in the Church Protestantism, Gallicanism, and that aspect of religious things which belongs to the teaching of the Jesuits, which bears so much contrast with the medieval habits of the Church. Indeed in literature as well as theology it has been generally the practice of the order to confine itself to ancient learning and to pay less attention than the Benedictines for instance, to these ages in which it had no existence.

Thus it came to pass that an interest for the Middle Ages was awakened neither among Catholics nor among Protestants, for the one feared, the other hated them, but among Rationalists and infidels. This renaissance of the Christian ages, this discovery of a palimpsest, this renewal of an interrupted continuity is the great work of the nineteenth century. The epoch that was inaugurated by the Renaissance and Reformation had reached its termination and its ruin, in the predominance of unbelief in religion, and of the revolution in politics—when a last determined effort was made to destroy every vestige of the dark, superstitious, or feudal ages, and to saw off the branch upon which all were sitting. Then it came to light that modern Europe had pronounced judgement on itself. The nineteenth century is a period of reaction not merely against the eighteenth century merely, but against all since the fifteenth. But it has this advantage over the Renaissance, that it does not exclude one world in order to adopt another. It does not reject the accumulated progress and treasures of the last three centuries as of old the work of one thousand years was condemned as a failure and wholly worthless. It is not for the sake of the good which is in the Middle Ages only but for the sake of continuity that we require this return. Not because the revival of paganism was wrong in its origins, but because it was wrong in its excess. Nor is the medieval revival of which we speak the enemy of classical culture. The classical world remains one great element of our civilisation as it was already in the Middle Ages. It is inconsistent with the law of continuity to dispense with the ancient as with the medieval world. Antiquity is as indispensable to us as the Middle Ages. But it is not our foundation in the same way, it does not influence us through the same things. It will always be at the bottom of our education. We should otherwise sink into the one-sided partiality of the Middle Ages or into American barbarism. We should lose the memory of human virtues, and the idea of beauty in form. Classical literature will always teach men the form and method of things—not the substance. That is the error and danger of classical education. If it prevails alone, without counterpart or equipoise, we must look to it for substance as well as form. We shall derive our ideas from it. . . . Now the Middle Ages cannot teach us form, cannot affect us literarily. It must give us substance and facts—it must teach us history.

Add. Mss. 5528, pp. 171–172.

This principle of continuity is a principle of conservatism and progress. It demands an historical treatment of all questions. Hence the importance of the historical or genetic method in science, in politics as well as in religion, in philosophy.

Add. Mss. 5528, p. 171.

In politics we desire the development of medieval institutions with the acquirements of modern civilisation, not the substitution of the new for the old. We wish to avoid and to repress revolution whether it come in the form of anarchy or despotism, denying the rights of the people or the rights of the state. But we condemn equally and for the same reason the counterrevolution—we wish in the words of De Maistre, not the counter revolution, but the contrary of revolution.
Add. Mss. 5528, p. 172.

If all the political ideas of the Middle Ages had been combined in a connected series of institutions or a compact body of opinion, there would have been few questions of principle for the modern world to solve.
Add. Mss. 4865, p. 380.

What Christianity without Germans produced, we know from Byzantium. What Germans [produced] without Christianity, we know from Scandinavia.
Add. Mss. 4980, p. 147.

A very liberal modern might be composed of St. Thomas and his antipode Marsilius, taken in equal quantities.
Add. Mss. 4940, p. 293.

Nations are not primitive products. They are the slow produce of History. Nations which are the authors of modern history are the products of medieval history.
Add. Mss. 4960, p. 31.

Towns were the nursery of freedom.
Add. Mss. 4980, p. 6.

What the Middle Ages anticipated: Habeas Corpus; Counsel for prisoners—Venice; Progressive income tax—Florence; Cabinet of responsible ministers—Venice; The judiciary arbiter of legislative and executive—Aragon; Religious toleration; Emancipation; Representation; Political economy.
Add. Mss. 4979, p. 218.

The last two centuries of the Middle Ages developed liberal forms. Yet they did not produce liberty. It was not *lebensfähig*. Why? Why is it that the Middle Ages with such new forms, so many good ideas broke down without bearing fruit. It was not founded on moral principles. The ethical code got worse. [We might speak of the] overclouding, morally, of the later Middle Ages. Thus the towns left nothing behind them nor the parliaments. Decline of medieval society in the fourteenth and fifteenth centuries. That led to Machiavelli.

Add. Mss. 4980, p. 382.

Medieval liberty broke down by medieval Intolerance. Transformation tried by Councils, but failed. They were themselves intolerant— whatever forms of power they encouraged, the substance would be despotic.

Add. Mss. 4980, p. 393.

Savonarola: In the transition from the medieval to the modern life he is to us the most significant figure as the herald and martyr of ideas which began to be powerful more than a century after the Arno had buried his ashes in the sea.

Add. Mss. 4982, p. 23.

The Renaissance

The only branch of literature in which the Renaissance gave birth to real classics, equal to the ancients, was politics. The medieval theory of politics restrained the State in the interest of the moral law, of the Church, and of the individual. Laws are made for the public good, and for the public good, they may be suspended. The public good is not to be considered, if it is to be purchased at the expense of an individual. Authorities are legitimate if they govern well. Whether they do govern well those whom they govern must decide. The unwritten law reigns supreme over the municipal law. Modern sentiments such as these could not be sustained in the presence of indifference to religion, uncertainty as to another world, impatience of the past, and familiarity with Hellenistic thought. As the Church declined the ancient State appeared, a State which knew no Church, and was the greatest force on earth, bound by no code, a law to itself. As there is no such thing as right, politics are an affair of might, a mere struggle for power. Such was the doctrine which Venice practised, in the interest of a glorious and beneficent government, and which two illustrious writers, Machiavelli and Guicciardini, made the law of modern societies.

Acton, *Lectures on Modern History*, pp. 80–81.

Renaissance was not political. It was a class of men of letters, not of statesmen; and it had no philosophy of its own. Nevertheless its greatest achievement was in politics. It substitutes the ancient [concept] of the state without a church for the state under the church. The classics might vary much in their philosophy, in attitudes towards the other world. They might even vary as to personal liberty, but all conceived the state as a thing sui generis, paramount, sharing power with no other institution.

Add. Mss. 4982, p. 136.

They viewed critically the scholastic teaching and the canon law, but they fell under Plato and the civil law. They did not know how to think for themselves—the keenest intellect of them all, Machiavelli, was a slave to Roman examples. Indeed, the Humanists bequeathed to the modern world that passion for exclusive masters, for great names and great authorities, which had made Aristotle a burden on their predecessors. It was Cicero, Plato, Seneca, Plotinus.

Add. Mss. 4960, p. 319.

Machiavelli

The central idea of Machiavelli is that the state power is not bound by the moral law. The law is not above the state, but below it. Is this not a classical notion?

Add. Mss. 4976, p. 12.

Machiavelli: Apart from ideas of the time, it was the classical state, unchecked by anything else, claiming every sacrifice, suffering no limit and no partition. More particularly, admitting no moral code that is not of its own making. No question of rights of property, rights of life, or rights of conscience in any way interfering with its freedom of action. No unwritten law. No submission to God, rather man to man.

Add. Mss. 4982, p. 146.

Machiavelli: First modern utilitarian. He is the direct ancestor of that which has been for a century the most powerful of all modern schools.

Add. Mss. 4976, p. 1.

Machiavelli: Idea of the survival of the fittest actually his theory.

Add. Mss. 5449, p. 3.

Machiavelli: He only knew Roman History. The most successful Romans were the most criminal: Sulla and Octavian. The work of the latter endured like the Church.

Add. Mss. 5449, p. 1.

Machiavelli's immorality good either for monarchy or democracy.

Add. Mss. 5449, p. 49.

Machiavelli: Exposes the practice and theory of his own time, which resembles nothing so much as the theory and practice of ours: mendacity and murder.

Add. Mss. 5449, p. 28.

Whigs

Whig and Tory are elementary divisions, and perpetual.
   Add. Mss. 4949, p. 35.

Definition: A Whig is an Englishman who desires the reign of liberty, alike in a monarchy or a republic, an aristocracy or a democracy.
   Add. Mss. 4949, p. 129.

Whigs were those who wished to preserve Liberty.
   Add. Mss. 4949, p. 115.

Döllinger very much against tyranny. But that did not make a liberal. Men objected to the Bulgarian or Armenian horrors, without being Whig. A Whig was one to whom these horrors made no difference, constituted no additional argument, in an absolute government. He condemned not Nero, Ivan, or Lopez; but Charles V, Lewis XIV, George III. He fights, he stakes his life, his fortune, the existence of his family, not to resist the intolerable reality of oppression, but the remote possibility of wrong, of diminished freedom.
   Add. Mss. 4915, p. 99.

The Whigs made Liberty the party object for the first time. It was not national liberty, not class liberty, not religious liberty, but political.
   Add. Mss. 4949, p. 137.

Whigs: The first party that made liberty its object. Therefore opposed to democracy. There, it shuts a door. It desires the union of elements. That is the division of power. A power not divided is a power not limited. So far then, a lurking tenderness for aristocracy.
   Add. Mss. 4955, p. 2.

The power of Napoleon, administered by Antonine, inherited, confirmed, promoting prosperity, greatness, religion, science, education,

534

security, morality. A Whig would think blood worthily shed to overthrow it.

Add. Mss. 4955, p. 135.

Whigs: Idea that past is wicked—that it is accused, not a defender. That it must justify itself. That the presumption is not for it. That what exists must be made wholesome. Not abolish things that can be tamed—but do not believe in them. That you do not destroy because you may not be able to create. But perpetually correct, remedy, modify, adapt.

Add. Mss. 4955, p. 101.

The Whig did not press his ideas to their consequences. That was to be the work of time. They were in reserve. His compromises were stages and gradations. To insist on principles when you can enforce conclusions is a stoppage. It creates an unnecessary impediment. Leave that to time. The action of time is adopted into their system.

Add. Mss. 4949, p. 32.

The Whigs purchased their long tenure of power by many concessions to conservative principles.

Add. Mss. 4953, p. 77.

The Whig stronghold was not held by men of genius. The theory had been modified by practical men of the ordinary rank of talent, such as every great country produces.

Add. Mss. 4951, p. 115.

Practically the Whigs, Burnet, Halifax, Locke, Somers, Holt, did more for freedom than any body of men who ever appeared on earth. They fell short in theory. The world, seeing their success, their moderation, their resolute conservatism in the midst of revolution, [was] filled with sincere admiration. Montesquieu, Frederic, Voltaire, Leibnitz.

Add. Mss. 4946, p. 232.

Whigs did not invent Whiggism. They discovered it. The system of ideas underlay the several tendencies of their former friends: Selden, Pym, Vane, Harrington. They applied these ideas and gave them the support of a Party. They organized what was dispersed. Their one invention—innovation—was Party government.

Add. Mss. 4949, p. 127.

Selden and Milton, Vane and Harrington had one idea in common. Not for Presbyterianism, not for republic, not for limited monarchy. But for liberty. It was an idea that ripened slowly. It was much darkened by religious passion.

Add. Mss. 4946, p. 237.

A Whig was a reconciled Roundhead. He had learnt by experience to avoid revolution. He had overthrown the monarchy, the Church, the Lords—to see all restored, without a blow, and stronger than before— by operation of natural forces, by no effort of man. The lesson was very clear: The objects of Hampden, Selden, and Vane were not to be attained by the methods of Hampden, Selden, and Vane. They renounced the method and revived the purpose. The throne, the Church, and the Lords might be preserved but tamed and made innocuous. The Republican, Puritan, Democrat became a royalist, a churchman, an aristocrat.

Add. Mss. 4946, p. 248.

Whigs: They were defenders of liberty who defended it for the sake of religion. The union of the two things constituted the Whigs.

Add. Mss. 4946, p. 253.

Whigs: They were not men of original thought—students of the law of Nature or of continental philosophy. But they lived in an atmosphere charged with the legacies of a most active and productive generation. The age which was passing away when these tendencies blended had established by a series of discoveries and theories: The sovereignty of science; international law; government by compact; sovereignty of conscience; religious liberty; the emancipation of the slave; free trade; the condition of property in society; the distribution of wealth determines the distribution of power. They had seen Bacon, Harvey, Descartes, Pascal, Vane, Harrington, Grotius, North, and Penn.

Add. Mss. 4946, p. 258.

They sprang from the conjunctures of the time—influenced by popular currents of thought—but also by deeper currents of law, philosophy, and religion.

Add. Mss. 4955, p. 139.

Whigs: All those preliminary discoveries paved the way for political freedom—Bacon, Descartes, Galileo, Grotius, Sarasa, science, international law, toleration, conscience, progress, emancipation. They were in the air, influencing men here and there, and uniting them. It went to make the Whig party.

Add. Mss. 4946, p. 259.

How all this took visible and concrete shape in men opposing the absolutism of the late Stuarts: Sidney, Burnet, Locke, Halifax, Somers. These men had seen the same thing attempted against Charles I— they had inherited the aspirations of Pym, Hampden, Selden, Vane. They had inherited an experience that went beyond theirs—that it was useless to destroy historic institutions, that you must submit to the conditions of society, that they are paramount in politics and regulate the state. The great doctrine of Harrington illumined them. So they would only impose compromise, conciliation.

Add. Mss. 4946, p. 260.

Whigs: Compromise was the key note. Conciliate opposing interests. Improvement, not destruction. Avoidance of any absolute dogmas, incompatible with mutual tolerance. Admit the Tories to equal terms. No persecution of the vanquished party.

Add. Mss. 4946, p. 261.

Whigs: By their principles America made itself free.

Add. Mss. 4955, p. 293.

The Whig theory pointed to a time when principle would govern. But it did not hasten its advent. In each generation you may find the Whig of the future by the side of the Whig of the past—principle beside compromise—the progressive mind by the quiescent tradition.

Add. Mss. 4949, p. 31.

The age of historical Whiggism is past. The problems coming now are beyond its reach, for it regarded, chiefly, the relations between the subject and the state. They are not a fit motive now to fill man's lives with passion. . . . The juridic phase of Whiggism is gone, and the economic is in full swing, and the social is at hand.

November 19, 1869. Acton-Simpson III, p. 284.

Burke

You can hardly imagine what Burke is for all of us who think about politics, and are not wrapped in the blaze and the whirlwind of Rousseau. Systems of scientific thought have been built up by famous scholars on the fragments that fell from his table. Great literary fortunes have been made by men who traded on the hundredth part of him. Brougham and Lowe lived by the vitality of his ideas. Mackintosh and Macaulay are only Burke trimmed and stripped of all that touched the skies. Montalembert, borrowing a hint from Döllinger, says that Burke and Shakespeare were the two greatest Englishmen.
Letter to Mary Gladstone, December 27, 1880, in Paul, p. 155.

Burke, supreme teacher of conservatism.
Add. Mss. 4948, p. 327.

The Whigs became philosophers after being politicians. Their temporary expedients were transformed into a system for the world. The ideas of one generation were found available for all time. The man who accomplished the change was Burke.
Add. Mss. 4953, p. 238.

Burke is preeminent in the very small number of great political writers, because he refused to concern himself with the sovereignty of the people, divine right, the virginal compact, the law of nature, and all those general principles by which men express the imperfections of their knowledge, and strove only for real securities for substantial freedom, leaving men to hold without contradiction what they pleased. Machiavelli more shrewd; Montesquieu more clever; Rousseau more fervid eloquence; Mirabeau and Hamilton more practical genius; more universal knowledge—Guizot.
Add. Mss. 4965, p. 171.

Burke looked after principles but would not be ruled by them without regard to circumstances. There was room in his capacious mind for opposite principles, subject to different conditions. He would not allow general principles to be absolute and override all considerations. He examined what circumstances required one principle and what another. This is the source of apparent discrepancies. His mind was historical, not systematic. He never forsook theory, but admitted it only in solution, in combination with facts. He studied philosophy but never showed any aptitude for abstract thought. He was rooted in the English system, but in his hands it became a philosophy. He generalized its truth. This was the national habit, to go by precedents—to develop, not to innovate. Still more it was the way of English law. Scots entirely different. He had no system, independent of realities, and never reasoned like Spinoza, Kant, Riccardo, Bentham.

Add. Mss. 4861, p. 151.

Burke right in rejecting the Revolution—an enemy of liberty.

Add. Mss. 4955, p. 247.

[Burke was] master of no science; his knowledge was copious, ready, not complete on any subject.

Add. Mss. 4861, p. 152.

Some are men of action, who act with as little damage to justice as possible. Some are men of justice who avoid damage to interests as much as possible. Burke was between the two.

Add. Mss. 4967, p. 94.

Burke's *Speeches* from 1790 to 1795: They are the law and the prophets.

February 4, 1859. Acton-Simpson I, p. 149.

Burke's public career under American influences. His fame as a public speaker obtained on those questions. The most American of all English statesmen. His sympathy lasted until that question settled. In 1782 that inspiration came to an end.

Add. Mss. 4953, p. 86.

Burke grew more and more liberal from 1770 to 1778 and from 1778 to 1782. Then occurs the ruin of his prospects.

Add. Mss. 4953, p. 239.

Burke: Why not an entire Liberal? How thoroughly he wished for liberty—of conscience, property, trade, in slavery etc. What stood against it? His notion of history, the claims of the past, the authority of time, the will of the dead, continuity. Others held this before, but with other parts of conservatism. Burke was conservative by that alone. And that alone devolved all the rest of his principles, and made the first of liberals, the first of conservatives. That is the element of unity and consistency. He is not consistent, but the element that prevailed at last, existed from the first.

Add. Mss. 4967, p. 76.

There is one doctrine and one only that is taught—impressed by each phase of Burke's career and gives it consistency: That is, that party is above country, as principles are above interests. We cling to our country as a passenger to a ship, whose safety is his own. We cling to our party as to our religion, because we deem it true.

Add. Mss. 4939, p. 367.

Burke understood political economy. But writing about it, in thoughts etc., he is always very careful of exceptions, and more a statesman than a financier. So in other things.

Add. Mss. 4967, p. 72.

Liberalism and Conservatism

The partition is between friends of freedom and others. In principle that is permanent, fundamental, decisive.

Add. Mss. 4949, p. 85.

How to distinguish the Whig from the Liberal: One is practical, gradual, ready for compromise. The other works out a principle, philosophically. One is a policy aiming at a philosophy. The other is a philosophy seeking a policy.

Add. Mss. 4950, p. 280.

A Whig is essentially a government man. He has all the responsibilities, the habits, the tradition. Whereas the Liberal was essentially a man of opposition, who preferred not holding office.

Add. Mss. 4949, p. 130.

The Whig governed by compromise—the Liberal begins the reign of ideas.

Add. Mss. 4949, p. 131.

[The elements of Liberalism]: The idea of the infallible conscience; the supremacy of the individual over the mass, and of eternal interests which belong to the individual, over temporal interests, such as are all those of the state; that legitimate authority depends on the opinion of those for whom it is instituted; that government not justified of its works is government foredoomed to be destroyed; that revolution is part of legitimacy.

Add. Mss. 4982, p. 1.

The elements of Liberalism were developed between the appearance of Aristotle's *Politics* in the West, at the time of Simon de Montfort, and the last medieval publicists, Savonarola and Sir Thomas More, by such thinkers as St. Thomas, Cardinal Zabarella, Archbishop of Florence, who died in the pulpit at Constance while addressing the Council, Gerson, the Chancellor of the University of Paris, and Nicholas, Cardinal of Cusa, the most prophetic intellect of the Renaissance.

Add. Mss. 4982, p. 3.

A Liberal by definition could not exist [in the Renaissance]. It means a man whose polar star is liberty—who deems those things right in politics which, taken all round, promote, increase, perpetuate, freedom, and those things wrong which impede it. Much of modern experience and experiment was requisite before that idea materialized.

Add. Mss. 4982, p. 128.

Liberalism—Term first used about 1707 of Chateaubriand.

Add. Mss. 4955, p. 207.

The true Liberal descries liberty as an end, not a means. To do something for him and others that no other thing can do. Not exchangeable for any amount, however large, of national greatness and glory, of prosperity and wealth, of enlightenment or morality.

Add. Mss. 4949, p. 161.

The Liberal gives to others what he claims. Now many others are disbelievers. He refuses to impose on them his own views. He accepts the situation. He proceeds to govern a community made up partly of believers, partly of disbelievers. He looks for a law common to both, binding on both, acknowledged and evident in both. And he carries more and more his center of gravity from the region of religion to that region where religion has no power. That is, he uses motives admitted by unbelief. So that unbelief prevails. Religion has to plead its cause at an irreligious tribunal. It is deposed. Its place is usurped by its enemy. In this way toleration shifts the balance, makes the enemy not only tolerated but supreme.

Add. Mss. 5006, pp. 262–263.

[It is] the first quality of a Liberal to claim the same thing for others and for oneself, to dislike exception and prerogative, to think of all men and all countries, to acknowledge the right of the individual, derived from nature and universal, in preference to the primitive rights of a country or of a clan, obtained by force and not from heaven.

Add. Mss. 4960, p. 120.

The public good is not to be considered if it is to be purchased at the expense of the individual.

Add. Mss. 4982, p. 16.

A Liberal subjects all authorities to the test of right and wrong. He judges most of all by those principles which change least in the course of centuries. That is, by crime, not by vice or sin.

Add. Mss. 5015, p. 191.

Liberalism is not only a principle of government but a philosophy of history, Progress.

Add. Mss. 4948, p. 177.

Liberalism thinks that you must let God work—not examining His action with fixed barriers. It is the Liberty of Providence they demand. God's chief means of action on man is grace. And grace is individual. Expose the individual to that alone. Do not bury the conscience beneath the ruins of crumbled ages. Snatch the sceptre from the grasp of the dead.

Add. Mss. 4949, p. 83.

Liberalism [is] ultimately founded on [the] idea of conscience. A man must live by the light within—prefer God's voice to man's.

Add. Mss. 4901, p. 20.

This is the Liberal principle: The soul is the end. All else is the means.

Add. Mss. 4939, p. 334.

A liberal feels no reverence for the ancient order. It is a system of murder, organized, defined, proclaimed.

Add. Mss. 4943, p. 404.

Loyalty, authority, tradition, custom, opinion are not decisive in the view of Liberalism—Something above all these.

Add. Mss. 4948, p. 308.

Deliberately set to work to destroy the work of centuries—to destroy what they have painfully built up: This was the triumph of liberal policy, men who yielded themselves to the logic of liberty.

Add. Mss. 5011, p. 254.

The lesson of the past is against the Liberals. What has endured is force, not freedom. Yet so many systems defend the idea that whatever lasts deserves to last. Laws of gravitation don't favor Liberalism. It is an edifice that cannot stand, like cyclopian walls, by mere force of gravity. Its work has passed away. Lasted a century at Athens, six centuries in Rome, one in America. Very little more. Generally, when seen closely, as in Switzerland, it is nothing of the kind.

Add. Mss. 4950, p. 294.

Declaration of Independence and *Wealth of Nations* appeared in the same year. Both were theories of liberty, emancipating from history.

Add. Mss. 5486, n.n.

It is not a question of Past and Future, Stability and Change—but of the Permanent and the Progressive.

Add. Mss. 4950, p. 204.

Time is wanted to overcome friction and to establish a delicate balance. Therefore it is wanted for liberty, not for absolutism. It is the natural cry of Liberalism.

Add. Mss. 4938, p. 180.

A liberal is only a bundle of prejudices until he has mastered, has understood, experienced the philosophy of Conservatism.

Add. Mss. 4945, p. 147.

To European Conservatives Liberalism possesses an answer. It denies that the hand of God's approval rests on things that last. Even if it does not deny His action altogether, like the Deists. Many things succeed and endure and triumph which bear the unmistakable stamp of the Prince of this world. They say that the history of monarchy has proved the prophecy of Samuel: A history of moral degradation—a grand cause of sin. It cannot hold its own against Liberalism.

Add. Mss. 4945, p. 297.

The Conservative principle is egoism. The Liberal is generous. Now a class cannot be generous. It thinks of itself. Therefore Liberalism is not determined by a class. It is the affair of individuals.

Add. Mss. 4949, p. 128.

Conservatism—narrow sphere—limited to national purposes—to the domain of Christianity, to the local, the temporary. Therefore much disposed to promote interests—advantages—and to reject principles and general ideas and conscience. The Liberal derives his views from universal history, and from the succession of nations, churches, philosophers. He extracts from general induction maxims of general application—a wider induction—a larger grasp of principle. A close chain of prejudices and errors, connects the Conservative of today with the Legitimist and the absolutist, with the Royalist of the seventeenth century, the persecutor of the sixteenth century, with the advocate of feudalism, with the party of Sulla.

Add. Mss. 4949, p. 82.

Not absolute contradiction between Liberals and Conservatives. It is a question of time and place and expediency. Liberals admit that men are not always ripe for freedom. Conservatives wish to preserve it lest it be imperilled. But Whig and Tory really near contrary things, excluding each other. One wishes to preserve things for their own sake. The other will sacrifice every institution that does not stand the test of liberality.

Add. Mss. 4955, p. 98.

The Duke of Orleans nearly described my feelings when he spoke, testamentarily, of his religious *flag* and his political *faith*. Politics comes nearer religion with me, a party is more like a church, error more like heresy, prejudice more like sin, than I find it to be with better men. And by these canons I am forced to think ill of Peel, to think, if you won't misunderstand me, that he was not a man of principle. The nature of Toryism is to be entangled in interests, traditions, necessities, difficulties, expedients, to manage as best one may without creating artificial obstacles in the shape of dogma, or superfluous barriers of general principle. "Périssent les colonies plutôt que les principes" . . . expresses the sort of thing Liberalism means and Toryism rejects. Government must be carried on, even if we must tolerate some measure of wrong, use bad reasons, trample on some unlucky men. Other people could recognise the face and sanctity of morality where it penetrated politics, taking the shape of sweeping principle, as in Emancipation, Free Trade, and so many other doctrinaire questions. Peel could not until he was compelled by facts. Because he was reluctant to admit the sovereignty of considerations which were not maxims of state policy, which condemned his own past and the party to which he belonged.

Letter to Mary Gladstone, December 9, 1884, in Paul, pp. 314–315.

What conservatives say: [Liberalism] means confidence in men, denial of original sin, belief in efficacy of conscience. Conservative believes that man is corrupt. Left to himself he goes wrong. He wants help, constraint—all light comes from others. Good and evil the result of a long civilisation.

Add. Mss. 5692, p. 3.

The conservative view: Liberty is the nation weakened, power taken from concentration, given to fluctuation. Attention to interests, which are national, weakened by attention to principles, which are abstract, international, disinterested. Power given to the less educated, the less intelligent, the less moral and taken from the elite. Permanence given up for uncertainty and change.

Add. Mss. 4952, p. 13.

Toryism equals negation of Liberty. In favor of force, of religion, of custom, of property, of authority.

Add. Mss. 4949, p. 110.

Conservatism founded on interests, passions, prejudices, or even superstitions. Only a mental form of disease.

Add. Mss. 4950, p. 195.

Law of continuity, the basis of conservatism. Distinct from absolutism, which is not continuous. It is the reign of the dead.

Add. Mss. 4991, p. 219.

Conservatism: To preserve religion, morality, property, justice. Not to allow any of these things to be endangered. Conservatism of royalists, capitalists, clergy, aristocrats is of no scientific quality. It is not disinterested. Just so, the liberality of poor men, sceptics, democrats. Who are the real Liberals?

Add. Mss. 4939, p. 340.

American conservatives: Hamilton, Webster, Calhoun [are] more valuable for us than the European. European conservatism rests on a basis of history, of religion, of custom. It relies on the theory that God governs the world. He does not cause everything; but He sanctions everything that endures. He shows His approval by success. He confers vitality. If His sanction is not shown in that which succeeds, it is nowhere. History, then, does not proclaim the goodness/gladness of his ways. His works do not praise Him. . . .

Add. Mss. 4897, p. 238.

Democracy

Why democracy? It means liberty given to the mass. Where there is no powerful democracy, freedom does not reign.

Add. Mss. 4945, p. 92.

As to Democracy, it is true that masses of new electors are utterly ignorant, that they are easily deceived by appeals to prejudice and passion, and are consequently unstable, and that the difficulty of explaining economic questions to them, and of linking their interests with those of the State, may become a danger to the public credit, if not to the security of private property. A true Liberal, as distinguished from a Democrat, keeps this peril always before him.

The answer is, that you cannot make an omelette without breaking eggs—that politics are not made up of artifices only, but of truths, and that truths have to be told.

We are forced, in equity, to share the government with the working class by considerations which were made supreme by the awakening of political economy. Adam Smith set up two propositions—that contracts ought to be free between capital and labour, and that labour is the source, he sometimes says the only source, of wealth. If the last sentence, in its exclusive form, was true, it was difficult to resist the conclusion that the class on which national prosperity depends ought to control the wealth it supplies, that is, ought to govern instead of the useless unproductive class, and that the class which earns the increment ought to enjoy it. That is the foreign effect of Adam Smith—French Revolution and Socialism. We, who reject that extreme proposition, cannot resist the logical pressure of the other. If there is a free contract, in open market, between capital and labour, it cannot be right that one of the two contracting parties should have the making of the laws, the management of the conditions, the keeping of the peace, the administration of justice, the distribution of taxes, the control of expenditure, in its own hands exclusively. It is unjust that all these securities, all these advantages, should be on the same side. It is monstrous that they should be all on the side that has least urgent need of them, that has least to lose. Before this argument, the ancient dogma, that power attends on property, broke down. Justice required that property should—not abdicate, but—share its political supremacy. Without this partition, free contract was as illusory as a fair duel in which one man supplies seconds, arms, and ammunition.

That is the flesh and blood argument. That is why Reform, full of questions of expediency and policy in detail, is, in the gross, not a question of expediency or of policy at all; and why some of us regard our opponents as men who should imagine sophisms to avoid keeping promises, paying debts, or speaking truths.

They will admit much of my theory, but then they will say, like practical men, that the ignorant classes cannot understand affairs of state, and are sure to go wrong. But the odd thing is that the most prosperous nations in the world are both governed by the masses— France and America. So there must be a flaw in the argument somewhere. The fact is that education, intelligence, wealth, are a security against certain faults of conduct, not against errors of policy. There is no error so monstrous that it fails to find defenders among the ablest men. Imagine a congress of eminent celebrities, such as More, Bacon, Grotius, Pascal, Cromwell, Bossuet, Montesquieu, Jefferson, Napoleon, Pitt, &c. The result would be an Encyclopaedia of Error. They would assert Slavery, Socialism, Persecution, Divine Right, Military despotism, the reign of force, the supremacy of the executive over legislation and justice, purchase in the magistracy, the abolition of credit, the limitation of laws to nineteen years, &c. If you were to read Walter Scott's pamphlets, Southey's Colloquies, Ellenborough's Diary, Wellington's Despatches—distrust of the select few, of the chosen leaders of the community, would displace the dread of the masses. The danger is not that a particular class is unfit to govern. Every class is unfit to govern. The law of liberty tends to abolish the reign of race over race, of faith over faith, of class over class. It is not the realisation of a political ideal: it is the discharge of a moral obligation. However that may be, the transfer of power to the lower class was not the act of Mr. Gladstone, but of the Conservatives in 1867. It still requires to be rectified and regulated; but I am sure that in his hands, the change would have been less violent.

Nor do I admit the other accusation, of rousing class animosities. The upper class used to enjoy undivided sway, and used it for their own advantage, protecting their interests against those below them, by laws which were selfish and often inhuman. Almost all that has been done for the good of the people has been done since the rich lost the monopoly of power, since the rights of property were discovered to be not quite unlimited. Think not only of the Corn Laws, but of the fact that the State did nothing for primary education fifty years ago. The beneficent legislation of the last half century has been due to the infusion of new elements in the electoral body. Success depended on preventing the upper class from recovering their lost ground, by keeping alive in the masses the sense of their responsibility, of their danger, of the condition from which they had been rescued, of the objects still before them, and the ancient enemy behind. Liberal policy has largely consisted in so promoting this feeling of self-reliance and self-help, that political antagonism should not degenerate into social envy, that the forces which rule society should be separate from the forces which rule the state. No doubt the line has not always been broadly marked between Liberalism where it borders on Radicalism, and Radicalism where it borders on the Charter. Some reproach may visit Bright and Mill, but not Mr. Gladstone. If there were no Tories, I am afraid he would invent them. He has professed himself a decided Inequalitarian. I cannot discover that he has ever caressed the notion of progressive taxation. Until last year I don't think he ever admitted that we have to legislate not quite impartially for the whole nation, but for a class so numerous as to be virtually equal to the whole. He dispels the conflict of classes by cherishing the landed aristocracy, and making the most of it in office. He has granted the Irish landlords an absolution ampler than they deserve. Therefore, though I admit that the condition of English society tends in some measure to make the poor regard the rich as their enemies, and that the one inveterate obstacle to the welfare of the masses is the House of Lords, yet I must add that he whose mission it is to overcome that interested resistance has been scrupulous not to excite passionate resentment, and to preserve what he cannot correct. And I do not say it altogether in his praise.

It is the law of party government that we contend on equal terms, and claim no privilege. We assume the honesty of our opponents, whatever we think or know. Kenealy and Bradlaugh must be treated with consideration, like Wilberforce or Macaulay. We do not use private letters, reported conversations, newspaper gossip, or scandals revealed in trials to damage troublesome politicians. We deal only with responsibility for public acts. But with these we must deal freely. We have to keep the national conscience straight and true, and if we shrink from doing this because we dare not cast obloquy on class or party or institution, then we become accomplices in wrong-doing, and very possibly in crime.

We ought not to employ vulgar imputations, that men cling to office, that they vote against their convictions, that they are not always consistent, &c. All that is unworthy of imperial debate. But where there is a question of unjust war, or annexation, of intrigue, of suppressed information, of mismanagement in matters of life and death, of disregard for suffering, we are bound to gibbet the offender before the people of England, and to make the rude workman understand and share our indignation against the grandee. Whether he ought, after that, to be left to Dean Stanley is another question [for burial in Westminster Abbey].

But I am not surprised at the complaint you heard. To many people the idea is repugnant that there is a moral question at the bottom of politics. They think that it is only by great effort and the employment of every resource that property and religion can be maintained. If you embarrass their defence with unnecessary rules and scruples, you risk defeat, and set up a rather arbitrary and unsanctioned standard above the interest of their class or of their church. Such men are not at their ease with the Prime Minister, especially if he is against them, and even when they are on his side. I am thinking of Argyll in Lytton's first debate; of Kimberley always; of soldiers and diplomatists generally.

Letter to Mary Gladstone, April 24, 1881, in Paul, pp. 193–199.

The working class have much more to lose by an injury to capital than the capitalist. They are more interested in its security. Because what threatens the one with loss of luxury and superfluity, threatens the other with the loss of the necessary.

Add. Mss. 5602, p. 63.

Poverty has its rights as well as property.

Add. Mss. 5602, p. 4.

The whole progress of society is towards the elevation of masses. Centuries have been at work upon it. The theories of progress, of liberty, of equality, are preached and practiced alike by science and religion. And then, new masses of men find themselves unbenefitted by this general law.

Add. Mss. 5487, p. 14.

The essence of democracy: to esteem the rights of others as one's own. [This] was not only Stoic. It received a glorious sanction from Christianity.

Add. Mss. 4939, p. 39.

Democracy [is] not necessarily hostile to monarchy or to aristocracy. Aristocracy retains the influence it has over society by wealth and the natural influence of wealth. America governed by aristocracy until 1861. As long as all aristocrats are allowed to assert their natural superiority, they influence the state.

Add. Mss. 4942, p. 61.

Democracy always succeeds by union of middle class with the poor. Fails, by their division. There were no such classes in Greece.

Add. Mss. 5594, p. 56.

Tocqueville has said that the progress of the world is naturally democratic. Now such generalizations can be safely made only from the nations whose course is wholly before us. We cannot dissect a living body. Doubtless the progress of the ancient nations was democratic, and in the excess of their democracy they perished. It destroyed their political existence and their national existence soon followed.

Add. Mss. 5528, p. 129.

Is not the great delusion of [Tocqueville's] America the belief in the irresistible progress of democracy to predominance through all history? In reality democracy is a part, one of three (or four) elements in the state—which in early, undeveloped societies has no place at all, which it is the business of history to raise to its proper level and proportion, and the effort of the revolution to make sole and supreme. The solution is in self-government which = indifference of monarchy, aristocracy and democracy.

November 23, 1861. Acton-Simpson II, p. 202.

The growth of democracy in a society proceeds from misery and want, and from religious demoralisation. The progress of wealth and happiness destroys it.

Add. Mss. 5528, p. 130.

Democracy tends to despotism, because the old system of authority and liberty did so little for the masses. They left one-half in utter ignorance, in abject poverty; contrived that four poor children should die for one rich; promoted crime; shrank from public works. To alter this a great force was required. Happiness of the people [does] not [lie] in liberty. Liberty, for the masses, [is of] no benefit. [The masses want] progress, wealth, comfort. Liberty [is an] obstacle to progress. For democracy has prevailed in conjunction with social movement in its purpose and its strength.

Add. Mss. 4862, p. 64.

In democracy . . . doctrinal fidelity is neither difficult nor very desirable of attainment. Its disciples embrace a ready-made system that has been thought out like the higher mathematics, beyond the need or the chance of application. The sums have been worked, the answers are known. Their prescriptions are in the books, tabulated and ready for use. We always know what is coming. We know that the doctrine of equality leads by steps not only logical, but almost mechanical, to sacrifice the principle of liberty to the principle of quantity; that, being unable to abdicate responsibility and power, it attacks genuine representation, and, as there is no limit where there is no control, invades, sooner or later, both property and religion.

Letter to Mary Gladstone, December 14, 1880, in Paul, pp. 145–146.

Direct democracy is unrestrained. Representative democracy creates the mutual check. It is therefore higher in principle than Rousseau's theory.

Add. Mss. 4950, p. 254.

The division of sovereignty . . . is the only means hitherto known to political science of setting limits to democracy.

May 12, 1886, translated from the German. Döllinger III, p. 357.

Democracy tends to destroy representative government: Plebiscite, Referendum, Extinction of minorities. [The remedy is] a strong second chamber. This was the American plan.
   Add. Mss. 4862, p. 64.

Division of power would have broken down, if the people had control of the judiciary.
   Add. Mss. 4952, p. 12.

We have made securities for democracy—no securities against it. In that line of thought America is beyond us and beyond our colonies.
   Add. Mss. 5684, n.n.

Universal suffrage has shown itself absolutist and retrograde in France, Germany, Belgium, and Spain.
   Add. Mss. 5602, p. 30.

There should be a law to the People besides its own will.
   Add. Mss. 4862, p. 170.

Democracy admits only liberties applied in general to all. Middle Ages conceived special, personal, particular privileges. All these get swept away. All are possible oppressions, until there is only one oppressor, the state. How to prevent state power from oppressing. By dividing it. Party is an early step in the division of power.
   Add. Mss. 4952, p. 154.

Democracy: Elsewhere institutions protect the mass from the supreme power. But what institution is there that protects the individual from the government when the government represents the whole people and acts in conformity with the will of a vast majority? Therefore the great problem of freedom becomes more difficult.
   Add. Mss. 4870, p. 34.

Intolerance of Democracy: Absolutism more often tolerant [than democracy]. Monarchy possesses means of repression which Democracy has not. It can punish the act without employing prevention. Democracy has no means of putting down opinion. If the opinion of society is corrupt, it cannot punish acts which a body of opinion approves. Its juries would sympathize with the malefactor.
   Add. Mss. 5006, p. 270.

If government is made to express the collective will of the nation, there is nothing that can resist. All obstacles are cleared away. A minority has no refuge or resource but agitation or revolution.

Add. Mss. 5602, p. 4.

Democracy generally monopolizes and concentrates power.

Add. Mss. 5605, p. 4.

Government by law means government by tradition. It means that people shall be subject to laws they know—to laws regulated and recommended by custom. A gradual deposit from custom—ascertained—assimilated. Democracy is government by will, above law. You cannot bind the future. You are not bound by the past. Law is short-lived, uncertain, inconsistent, capricious.

Add. Mss. 4870, p. 35.

Democracy is government of the strongest, just as military despotism is. This is the bond of connexion between the two. They are the brutal forms of government and as strength and authority go together, necessarily arbitrary.

Add. Mss. 5528, p. 104.

Next to the management of dependencies the regulation of foreign policy is the most distressing and incongruous function of a popular government.

"Mr. Grant Duff's Glance over Europe," *Chronicle* (11 January 1868):31. Ryan, p. 390; Döllinger I, p. 494.

The people not the army decide the results of a war. The army only decides in battle.

Add. Mss. 5528, p. 32.

Idea of equality leads to imperialism.

Add. Mss. 5436, p. 185.

Democracy has been known to cherish slavery, imperialism, wars of conquest, religious intolerance, tyranny, equality in ignorance.

Add. Mss. 5684, n.n.

Theocracy: God gives law to man. Democracy: Man gives law to himself. One goes by the past, by tradition. The other by the future, by thought. Intolerant of each other. The intolerance of reason and the intolerance of faith.

Add. Mss. 4870, p. 8.

The more things are left to the people, the more precautions there must be against the triumph of evil influences.

Add. Mss. 5006, p. 286.

The common vice of democracy is disregard for morality.

Add. Mss. 4862, p. 115.

Moral defects lead to the loss of liberty. So we may say that it flourishes jointly with conscience. Decay of the one brings about decay of the other. Democracy undermines conscience by making men prefer what others think best to what they think best themselves. So it demoralizes like excess of authority. It relieves men from the sense of responsibility and the duty of effort.

Add. Mss. 4916, p. 11.

[It is] not always observed [that] sometimes liberty progressed at the expense of democracy. Democracy is not the sole form; it is but one element—qualifying, not absorbing. . . . Democratic government alone is intolerant, takes for its own benefit. Every class uses power for itself. Therefore no one [class] should govern.

Add. Mss. 4862, p. 126.

Federalism

Federalism: It is coordination instead of subordination; association instead of hierarchical order; independent forces curbing each other; balance, therefore, liberty.

Add. Mss. 4895, p. 310.

The essential characteristic of the federal system of government is by dividing and distributing sovereignty, to supply the most perfect check on the excess of power, and the most efficient of all known securities of freedom.

"Mr. Grant Duff's Glance over Europe," *Chronicle* (11 January 1868):31. Ryan, p. 390; Döllinger I, p. 494.

Liberty depends on the division of power. Democracy tends to unity of power. To keep asunder the agents, one must divide the sources; that is, one must maintain, or create separate administrative bodies. In view of increasing democracy, a restricted federalism is the one possible check upon concentration and centralism.

Letter to Mary Gladstone, February 20, 1882, in Paul, p. 230.

Federalism: The only barrier to Democracy.

Add. Mss. 4942, p. 64.

Federalism is the best curb on democracy. [It] assigns limited powers to the central government. Thereby all power is limited. It excludes absolute power of the majority.

Add. Mss. 5504, p. 81.

Failure of Federalism by failure of America. For it is the federal system, not the state system that has failed, and that America is judged by.

Add. Mss. 5602, p. 31.

As one judges the checking power of the church in the Middle Ages, so federalism. Both are much discountenanced now. It is the same central tendency injures both.

Add. Mss. 5415, p. 38.

Centralisation: the counterpart of the compression produced by the centralisation to which great states owe their external power, is that freedom is more easily preserved or established in smaller states.

Add. Mss. 5528, p. 175.

National differences and bureaucratic centralisation are the two opposite poles, and balance each other. Centralisation is needed to bind different nations together in a single empire. National differences again set the strongest barriers against centralisation.

Add. Mss. 5528, p. 183.

Centralisation is the scheme by which the rich part of the country aids the poor. They pay according to their prosperity and receive according to their requirements.

Add. Mss. 4951, p. 41.

Federalism is the greatest check on central power. That of a class may be overcome by other classes. A sovereign state cannot be so overcome. Federalism prevents centralisation. A local government which has to resign so many powers to a central power cannot tyrannize. Federalism allows different nationalities, religions, epochs of civilisation to exist in harmony side by side. Federalism is capable of unlimited extension.

Add. Mss. 4895, p. 284.

Nationality

Nationality: The state absorbs or transcends the will of individuals. They must obey it. Obedience must be made easy. It is easiest when all are of one race and character, formed by the same past. Harmony then more easily preserved, without effort, or repression, or force.
Add. Mss. 4931, p. 28.

Nationality is the great carrier of custom, of unreflecting habit and transmitted ideas that quench individuality. Conscience gives men force to resist and discard all this. Nationality has to be dealt with discriminatingly. It is not always liberal or constructive. It may be as dangerous when its boundary is outside that of the State as salutary when inside.
Letter to Gladstone, February 18, 1888, in Acton, *Correspondence*, p. 182.

Nationality: Originally a truly liberal idea. It made Austria a federation. It produced the federal idea.
Add. Mss. 5436, p. 193.

Socialism

This century has seen the growth of the worst enemy freedom has ever had to encounter: Socialism. Strong, because it solves a problem political economy has, until now, failed to solve: How to provide that the increase of wealth shall not be at the expense of its distribution. Truth, that what the speechless masses of the poor need is not political privilege which they cannot enjoy, but comfort—without which political influence is a mockery or a snare. It has made the common movement of politics contemptible. [It] can only be realized by a tremendous despotism.

Add. Mss. 5487, p. 47.

Socialism: The worst of all enemies of freedom because, if it could fulfil what it promises, it would render such a service to the world that the interests of freedom would pale and mankind would carry over its allegiance to the benefactor who had a higher claim on its gratitude.

Add. Mss. 5847, p. 39.

Do not think ill of the people they call academic Socialists. It is only a nickname for the school that is prevailing now in the German universities, with a branch in France and another in Italy, a school whose most illustrious representative in England, whose most eminent practical teacher in the world, is Mr. Gladstone. In their writings, inspired by the disinterested study of all classic economists, one finds most of the ideas and illustrations of Mr. George, though not, indeed, his argument against Malthus. This makes him less new to one; but nobody writes with that plain, vigorous directness, and I do believe that he has, in a large measure, the ideas of an age that is to come.

Letter to Mary Gladstone, February 9, 1884, in Paul, pp. 287–288.

Democracy and Socialism: Democracy demands that political power shall be shared equally. But it is dangerous to put decisive power in the hands of the ignorant. Therefore it requires universal education. Education is expensive. Therefore it makes the rich pay for educating the poor. It is dangerous that those having nothing should obtain power over those who possess, for they will take their property. Therefore it is desirable that this distinction be weakened, equality promoted, the accumulation of wealth discouraged, and distribution of wealth encouraged. Now Adam Smith does not provide for the distribution, but only for the acquisition of wealth. Therefore it is insufficient for democracies.

Add. Mss. 5594, p. 68.

Government exists for the people—then the rich exist for the poor. Democracy introduced the maxim: All for the people—All by the people. What they want power for is comfort. If the centre of gravity is the masses, in the poorer classes, power will be used for their interest.

Add. Mss. 5487, p. 64.

Political equality destroyed by aristocracy of wealth. It is impossible to deprive wealth of power without depriving men of wealth. In this way equality leads to socialism.

Add. Mss. 5552, p. 5.

Conflict of equality with liberty: The supreme equality of enjoyment. It is from that that communism arose.

Add. Mss. 5847, p. 40.

Socialism easily accepts despotism. It requires the strongest execution of power—power sufficient to interfere with property.

Add. Mss. 5588, p. 28.

The Incas had an exact census, a thing unknown to the Spaniards. It was a system of communistic distribution of land. And the most terrible despotism on earth.

Add. Mss. 5487, p. 58.

The progress of the communistic ideal increases the restrictions on liberty, and as civilisation advances, liberty decreases.

Add. Mss. 5605, p. 47.

The materialistic Socialists will improve history for the poor. Their best writer, Engels, made known the horrors of our factory system.

Add. Mss. 4981, p. 50.

Communism: Proceeding from equality, it was powerless. Now it proceeds from political economy. Thinks less of equality, more of organization and association.

Add. Mss. 5594, p. 50.

Until Adam Smith they misunderstood the claim of Individualism. After Adam Smith it could not be ignored. It was with full knowledge of its strength that socialism acted—not ignoring or misapprehending— but appreciating, developing, and connecting.

Add. Mss. 5487, p. 75.

Communism was not a hollow theory of envious men. It was annointed with the most illustrious names, under the most illustrious sanction of Plato, the pagan who most nearly anticipated Christianity; of the Essenes, the Jews who approached it most; of the Christians in their first fervour; of the Christians of Jerusalem, in the first fervour of their conversion; of the Fathers of the Church, like St. Ambrose; of the canon laws; of the mendicant friars, who predominated in the Middle Ages; Erasmus the most eminent precursor of the Reformation and More, its most illustrious victim; of the Italian monk Campanella; Fénelon the most popular of Christian bishops.

Add. Mss. 5487, p. 61.

Socialism: Old Testament protects the rich; New Testament protects the poor. What one does in favour of property, the other does in favour of poverty.

Add. Mss. 5594, p. 69.

Politics

Ideals in politics—never realized, but the pursuit of them determines history.

March 12, 1860. Acton-Simpson II, p. 53.

Politics like medicine is a science as well as an art. It is treated nowadays as a thing purely empirical, a matter not of theory but of practice only.

Add. Mss. 5528, p. 170.

Politics taught by history as nothing else is.

Add. Mss. 4981, p. 6.

The manner in which politicians commonly try to cure is by small doses that are quickly absorbed and to which the body gets so accustomed that they become powerless.

Add. Mss. 5528, p. 170.

Party

Theory of Party: That the conflict of interests and forces, which are unavoidable in the regime of liberty, be not a conflict between king and people. They must be a conflict between parties in the people. They are permanent as in Rome. Every constitution contains the germ of its destruction. It has a spring, a summer, an autumn, with its enjoyments, a winter. But it has no second spring. Therefore the retarding process is as necessary to vitality, safety, and endurance, as the progressive. Thus the legitimate forms of party are permanent. So they were in Rome, so in England—politically ripest nations. Elsewhere they turn on other things, not so well organized, not bottomed on constant and necessary forces of all political life.

Add. Mss. 4870, pp. 32–33.

The secret of party government is this, that it secures progress and yet secures continuity. It prevents stagnation, and it prevents revolution. That is how the eighteenth century differed from the seventeenth. Its great innovation was gradual advance.

Add. Mss. 4945, p. 214.

Value and importance of party: It constituted Liberty. Founded on principle as distinct from expedients.

Add. Mss. 4947, p. 212.

Party created freedom of speech. It even made attacks on government part of the machinery of government. It absolutely required a free press—and it made the people ready for it.

Add. Mss. 5468, n.n.

Party: Dominion of a class is the dominion of an interest. Party was union on the basis of ideas instead of interests. For a class is never moved except by interests. A party is moved by principles, and capable of sacrificing its interests to them. It is a school of self-denial. A party that will not sacrifice power to principle, is a faction.

Add. Mss. 5468, n.n.

A party is led by ideas, it is not founded on them. The motion comes from the idea. The momentum comes from the interest.

Add. Mss. 4949, p. 128.

A party is strong not by its numbers or its ability so much as by the energy of the idea it represents, and by the fidelity of its members to that idea.

Add. Mss. 5528, p. 131.

There are forces of stability and forces of motion. When they adopt ideas instead of interests, they are parties.

Add. Mss. 4946, p. 243.

Party is not only, not so much, a group of men as a set of ideas and ideal aims.

Letter to Mary Gladstone, June 1, 1880, in Paul, p. 108.

Party: [The] idea that it is better to spare error and let it be free is the triumph of Liberalism. Conservatism tends to suppress error. Liberalism to treat it on equal terms.

Add. Mss. 4947, p. 41.

Party meant not only government by discussion, but government by conflict. It put an end to violence. The adversary, if not outvoted, had a right to power. He could not be punished or excluded for his opinions.

Add. Mss. 4952, p. 200.

Party teaches us the sacredness of opposition. [It] teaches that a man, who is honest, must be prepared to resist his country, his church, his clan, and, by the same principle, his party.

Add. Mss. 5468, n.n.

Party does not mean that one set of men are specially able, always right, virtuous and able. But that the others are profoundly wrong.

Add. Mss. 5468, n.n.

The purpose never concentrated in any individual, or represented by any party. The complete success of any would be injurious. They serve, often unconsciously, always incompletely, the cause of progress. Parties never altogether right. Heroes never perfectly good.

Add. Mss. 4960, p. 128.

Inconsistency is a reproach because men feel that party is a principle and that inconsistent men are unprincipled men.

Add. Mss. 4948, p. 329.

Party—a fortuitous combination of men—taking up opinions or laying them down. . . . One party thrives by the development of its principles—the other, by the abdication of them.

Add. Mss. 4948, p. 176.

Where there is no conflict of principles, there is of interests and persons, and party degenerates into faction.

Add. Mss. 4949, p. 163.

An able man works out ideas of his own apart from those of his party. He remains faithful to it only under constant resistance. He feels very keenly its defects. To smooth this, association, friendship, social communication are required.

Add. Mss. 4949, p. 86.

The theory of compromise mirrored party government.

Add. Mss. 4949, p. 113.

But if party is sacred to me as a body of doctrine, it is not, as an association of men bound together, not by common convictions but by mutual obligations and engagements. In the life of every great man there is a point where fidelity to ideas, which are the justifying cause of party, diverge from fidelity to arrangements and understandings, which are its machinery. And one expects a great man to sacrifice his friends—at least his friendship—to the higher cause.

Letter to Mary Gladstone, December 18, 1884, in Paul, p. 315.

Party government admits that error balances truth. It is exactly opposed to science, which knows nothing of compromise or concession.

Add. Mss. 4865, p. 245.

Party needed to practice true ideas, contrary, to find them.
  Add. Mss. 4870, p. 2.

Party government is demoralizing. A majority—that the government may be carried on—must be obtained. It cannot always be got fairly. Some weak men will be attracted by what government has to give— not mere money [but also] patronage. Measures cannot satisfy all of a party. Then a man must support what he does not approve, help means they think bad.
  Add. Mss. 4870, p. 55.

The result of dogmatic or denominational morals is to abase the standard. Party makes men indulgent to crime—because it has served the cause.
  Add. Mss. 4941, p. 314.

Party: The permanent and universal question is whether the living shall govern, or the dead; past or present; acquired rights or aspired rights; fact or idea; accident or design; the will of man or the will of God; morality or force.
  Add. Mss. 5468, n.n.

Public Opinion

Nobody can be more strongly convinced than I am of the necessity, the practical and moral necessity, of governing nations by consent, national consent being proved both by the vapour of opinion, and by the definite mechanism of representation.

Letter to Mary Gladstone, March 21, 1883, in Paul, p. 275.

Institutions and laws have their roots not in the ingenuity of statesmen, but as much as possible in the opinion of the people. But popular opinion is a plant of slow growth. It is eminently influenced by habit and attached to the past. A statesman is generally far ahead and when he consults an oracle he hears the voice of the last generation.

Add. Mss. 5602, p. 42.

Our great progress has been in the force and light of public opinion. Worst of guides in diplomacy and war. Generally wrong at first— seldom wrong permanently.

Add. Mss. 4993, p. 327.

Opinion governs—always slowly. If genius governed it would be quick and strong. But it takes long to ripen popular convictions. And laws must not be changed until the public is quite clear about them, until the truths have become vulgar.

Add. Mss. 5604, p. 12.

[The] development of nations keeps the reality a little behind the wish and the will. That is, the people live under a rule made by others. Each generation is governed, necessarily, by a former generation. Jefferson's great idea: Let it be governed by its own ideas.

Add. Mss. 4942, p. 219.

Things must be made very plain for public opinion to understand them. Much subtlety is impossible.

Add. Mss. 4870, p. 77.

The people see only those arguments that are very clear. They see resemblances—parallels much more easily than distinctions.

Add. Mss. 5608, n.n.

One view: A nation pursues certain interests—has a policy—what if a question of justice crosses it? Can a national policy be varied as often as facts change? Can you take one side, after the other, according to varying arguments, not according to permanent interests? Public opinion can never be so finely trained as to follow ideas and not things or persons.

Add. Mss. 4942, p. 380.

Party and press, warp and woof of public opinion, did not form it.

Add. Mss. 4870, p. 27.

Everything secret degenerates, even the administration of justice; nothing is safe that does not show it can bear discussion and publicity.

January 23, 1861. Acton-Simpson II, p. 114.

All partisanship depends on concealment. Mere strong language and special pleading take in nobody.

Add. Mss. 5015, p. 80.

Only in our time have men felt the need of knowing. Formerly many were stopped and baffled by the artifices of government, fearful of exposing secrets—men were content to be the sport of a great conspiracy, to conceal, to mislead. [It is] characteristic of this age that this is no longer tolerated.

Add. Mss. 4960, p. 38.

Those nations are happy which do not resent the complexity of life.

Add. Mss. 4870, p. 52.

Military Service

Conscription is not tolerated by a people that understands and loves freedom.

July 9, 1860. Acton-Simpson II, p. 79.

A people that relies on a permanent system of compulsory military service, resembles the statesman, who declared himself ready to sacrifice not only a part, but the whole of the constitution, in order to preserve the remainder. It is a system by which one great liberty is surrendered and all are imperilled, and it is a surrender, not of rights only, but also of power.

"National Defence," *Rambler* n.s. 3 (September 1860):295. Acton-Simpson II, p. 84.

Conscription: I would rather see Englishmen lose their freedom at the hands of a foreign enemy, together with their power, than from an internal enemy, as the price of external greatness. It is no disgrace to fall like Poland, but it is ignominious to be strong of the strength of France or Russia.

Add. Mss. 5528, p. 32.

Jealousy of a standing army has been one of the chief securities of our institutions. Liberty can never be secure in the presence of a large force of mercenaries. The disappearance of the unbought armies of the feudal age, and the introduction of troops who served for pay, led to the establishment of absolute monarchy in Europe. It rendered the sovereign wholly independent of the nation, and separated the people from the state. It would be a dreadful thing, said Burke, if there were any power in this country of strength enough to oppose with effect the general wishes of the people. This is just what an army receiving the pay of the State is intended to do.

"National Defence," *Rambler* n.s. 3 (September 1860):294. Acton-Simpson II, p. 84.

Property

Property, not conscience, is the basis of liberty. For the defence of conscience need not arise. Property is always exposed to interference. It is the constant object of policy.

Add. Mss. 4951, p. 142.

Power goes with property. Three ways of constitutional progress: 1. Property absorbs power. 2. Power adjusted to new forms of property—redistributed. 3. Society protected against engrossing property.

Add. Mss. 4870, p. 48.

Property was instrumental in forming society. But it created unequal laws, partial liberty. This inequality, this partiality, slowly corrected by conscience. The education of political society was made with property. Its perfection, by conscience. One made liberty a privilege; the other, a right. One an acquired and exclusive right—the other, a natural and universal right.

Add. Mss. 4980, p. 36.

Property not the most sacred right. When a rich man becomes poor it is a misfortune, it is not a moral evil. When a poor man becomes destitute, it is a moral evil, teeming with consequences injurious to society and morality. Therefore, in the last resort, the poor have a claim on the wealth of the rich—so far as they may be relieved from immoral, demoralizing effects of poverty.

Add. Mss. 4869, p. 7.

Truth

Truth cannot be confined to formulas.
Add. Mss. 5504, p. 17.

Official truth is not actual truth.
Add. Mss. 5002, p. 120.

Poverty

The permanent force is hunger—that is provision for our own comfort and the comfort of the family.

Add. Mss. 4960, p. 17.

Families multiply and their possessions must increase. That is the great law of hunger. The principle of prosperity. Undercurrent of modern history especially. Increasing demand for wealth.

Add. Mss. 4960, p. 13.

Greed, and pride, and passion extend to public life. The strongest, and the most constant of all passions, is hunger, or the love of life. That no moral influence can ever appease—only food. This physical motive is perpetuated. Hunger has increased while the means of satisfying it have increased. The world grows richer, the poor remain poor, and feel the difference. They know the whole world, and its resources, and the increasing demand on them.

Add. Mss. 4960, p. 45.

The remedy for poverty is not in the material resources of the rich, but in the moral resources of the poor. These, which are lulled and deadened by money-gifts, can be raised and strengthened only by personal influence, sympathy, charity. Money gifts save the poor man who gets them, but give longer life to pauperism in the country.

December 17, 1861. Acton-Simpson II, p. 235.

The avoidance of a Poor Law by means of public works, not actually necessary, is characteristic of a centralized absolutism. It nurses artificially, a proletariat, a classless community, which, instead of being absorbed in its own places, is permanently relying on the state to provide for it, not by barely keeping it alive, and leaving to vice and improvidence all its natural effects, but by raising it up to the level of those who are able to provide for themselves, as far as present profits go, only depriving it of the possibility of becoming independent and normally self-supporting. Thus a constant danger menaces society, and the need of a strong hand perpetually saving society, and converting dictatorship into a regular form of government, is kept always before it, as private individuals cannot constantly go on with this kind of benevolence without ruin, the labourer turns from the proprietor to the state as the protector and refuge, and the antagonism of property and labour is made more irreconcilable, to the great advantage of the civil power.

August 20, 1862. Acton-Simpson III, pp. 9–10.

The men who pay wages ought not to be the political masters of those who earn them, because laws should be adapted to those who have the heaviest stake in the country, for whom misgovernment means not mortified pride or stinted luxury, but want and pain, and degradation and risk to their own lives and to their children's souls.

Letter to Mary Gladstone, December 14, 1880, in Paul, p. 147.

Political Thought

What is political science? The secret of the progress of the world.
Add. Mss. 4941, p. 38.

Behind the man of action, and above him, is the thinker. You must keep to the line where they meet—the history of political ideas.
Add. Mss. 4981, p. 183.

Study politics, both as a national science and as a general science. One set of people will always ask what is the law, others, what ought to be the law. One is to be learnt from constitutional bodies—the other, from books in general.
Add. Mss. 4947, p. 279.

The judgement on political doctrine lies both in the realm of thought and in the realm of fact.
Add. Mss. 4981, p. 137.

Dislike of science in the Middle Ages and in antiquity. Physics and politics were deemed matters of opinion. So in modern times, like physical science, political [science] has had to struggle against generations of alchemists and astrologers.
Add. Mss. 4982, p. 333.

The history of political ideas is essentially associated with that of public events and it receives and combines in a focus all the influences which come from religion, philosophy, jurisprudence and economics.
Add. Mss. 4960, p. 40.

The fruit of philosophies lies not in the system, but in what remains when the system itself is discarded.
Add. Mss. 4979, p. 33.

Luther invented divine right.

    Add. Mss. 4865, p. 290.

The earlier philosophical systems, Hobbes, Spinoza, were dogmatically unbelieving. So they were intolerant, illiberal. It was only scepticism that produced liberality—Bayle, Locke, Shaftesbury.

    Add. Mss. 4954, p. 3 bis.

Locke founds power on property, not on election. His theory of contract implies that power is not delegated, that the rulers are not servants of the people.

    Add. Mss. 4952, p. 69.

Locke satisfied the liberal sentiment of England so well that men of great ability, [such as] Hume, went little beyond him and political thought made little progress until Burke, whose transforming influence was felt 1770.

    Add. Mss. 4954, p. 112.

Monarchy made sovereignty as indivisible as a point. Locke divided it, and thus made it innocuous.

    Add. Mss. 4943, p. 230.

In the history of thought, especially of thought bearing on action, Locke is, not the greatest certainly, but the largest of all Englishmen, looming tremendously, and filling an immense space. The *Lettres sur les anglais,* which put England into continental circulation, deal most with him and Newton, and he is the master of Voltaire and Condillac. As the—unscientific—inventor of the division of power, he is the master of Montesquieu. By his theory of Education and the Social Contract, he is the master of Rousseau, the most powerful political writer that ever lived. By his political economy he is the master of Adam Smith, and, in a sense, of Turgot. He gave to Whiggism whatever general ideas it mixed with the specific national elements, and he is the theorist of government by the great families. Lastly, in the Catena of tradition on Toleration, he is very nearly the principal classic.

    Letter to Gladstone, in Acton, *Correspondence,* p. 230.

Descartes serves Whiggism by his theory of conscience. No certitude until causes of doubt are removed. Consequently, freedom of thought and writing.

Add. Mss. 4953, p. 242.

Leibnitz: The clearest, the most open, the most unprejudiced of minds.

Add. Mss. 4965, p. 245.

Theory that the state does not depend on private virtue. That it depends on institutions, and these form men. Bentham, A. Smith, Sieyès.

Add. Mss. 4952, p. 49.

The best political thinkers are often very poor politicians. Compare Turgot, Radowitz, Burke, Webster with Metternich, Talleyrand, Thiers, Van Buren, Mazarin.

Add. Mss. 4938, p. 72.

Political Economy

[Political economy is] a subject necessary for an enlarged political knowledge, but not so necessary as our modern statesmen seem to suppose. Political economy, when regarded as the basis of political science, leads only to the French system, which seems to have no eye but for the formal distributions of power and wealth, without a moment's consideration of the moral basis which should underlie every constitution, political and social. Better is it to consider the moral basis as every thing, than to attribute too much to the formal distribution; cutting and shuffling the cards is of little use when all the trumps are withdrawn. As the late Duchess of Orleans well remarked, a constitution is something more than a political system ably and dextrously framed; it is also a combination of reciprocal duties, freely and cordially accepted on both sides. Our great political dangers all seem to proceed from the side of the Benthamite system of mechanical morality.

Review of Richard Jones, *Literary Remains; consisting of Lectures and Tracts on Political Economy*, in *Rambler* n.s. 1 (July 1859):249. *Wellesley* II, p. 778.

Political economy cannot be supreme arbiter in politics. Else you might defend slavery where it is economically sound and reject it where the economic argument applies against it.

Add. Mss. 4953, p. 209.

There is . . . no ground for the pretense that in order to maintain equilibrium between production and demand, we must employ the foresight of an army of administrators and surveyors, whose duty it should be to prescribe what every producer should provide, and consequently how much each consumer should enjoy. Inhabitants of our metropolis see every morning an ample but not excessive provision made for its 3,000,000 inhabitants, and this without any previous direction or settled plan; the utmost order and regularity result from the natural economic law of the supply and demand finding their equilibrium spontaneously; whereas we might look for chaos tenfold more chaotic than that of Balaclava, if the problems were left to the arrangement of administrators or directors of social labour and consumption.

Review of G. de Molinari, *Cours d'économie politique*, in the *Home and Foreign Review* 4 (January 1864):314. Acton-Simpson III, p. 132.

Every doctrine to become popular, must be made superficial, exaggerated, untrue. We must always distinguish the real essence from the conveyance, especially in political economy.

Add. Mss. 4955, p. 73.

Political economy brought a new demonstration of the value of liberty. Its value in labour became a strong-hold of liberty altogether.

Add. Mss. 5486, n.n.

Adam Smith's political ideas: Essentially liberal, because directed against despotic state. But not ultimately liberal, for it teaches only what makes a country rich. That wealth must be sacrificed to liberty, that the moral purpose of liberty is superior to the material purpose of wealth, he cannot admit. He would be glad of an absolute government like Turgot, a liberal and intelligent minister of absolute monarchy, strong enough to overcome prejudices and interests in the way, rather than one which presented no guarantee for wealth except liberty.

Add. Mss. 5486, n.n.

Adam Smith disregarded actual facts—history—and made his science universal, general, abstract. Yet he was not thinking of man in general, but of men as he saw them, as circumstances then made them. He started the common idea of Liberalism: Disinterested state; No care for religion, morality, education, poor relief, health; Laissez-faire. We have been correcting this extreme ever since then.

Add. Mss. 5486, n.n.

Smithian state: An association for private purposes, wealth, happiness, and an easy life. While pursuing these ends in the way that is best in our eyes, we pay men in blue to protect our houses, men in red to scare our enemies, one man in black to hang culprits, and another in purple and gold to keep up appearances and dot our i's.

Add. Mss. 5602, p. 46.

Religion and political economy rule the world. That is, what men think best for them in this world and in the next.

Add. Mss. 4870, p. 20.

Self-preservation and self-denial, the basis of all political economy.

Add. Mss. 4870, p. 61.

The moral foundation of political economy is not the satisfaction of appetite, but the fulfillment of duties. Labour, patience, justice, peace, and self-denial are the mainsprings of economical production, and the metaphysical basis of the science is not in a philosophy which reduces religion and science to mere satisfaction of an appetite, like eating or drinking, but in the verification of the promise, "Seek ye first the kingdom of God and His justice and all these things"—the necessaries of life—"shall be added unto you."

Review of G. de Molinari, *Cours d'économie politique*, in the *Home and Foreign Review* 4 (January 1864):315. Acton-Simpson III, p. 132.

England and English Institutions

I wish England to preserve that dignified and courageous attitude which has given her the foremost place among the nations. Never forgetting that she alone influences by means of her moral power and that thus her influence is the great support throughout Europe of the freedom which is the result of good government. Her influence should ever be exercised in conjunction—in conformity—with her example. Her support [should] be extended to those who like herself cling to the traditions of legitimate freedom, distinguished alike from revolutionary absolutism and from those spurious constitutions which disgrace—mock—the model they pretend to imitate.

Add. Mss. 4862, p. 19.

Our government must be adapted to the wants and circumstances of the age by reflecting and representing its conditions and interests—but it upholds the principles not of one age but of all our political history.

Add. Mss. 4862, p. 18.

England: In judging our national merits we must allow much for our national hypocrisy. Where ever we went, we were the best colonists in the world—but we exterminated the natives where ever we went. We despised conquest, but annexed with the greed of Russia. Our government of Ireland, of India—opium in China.

Add. Mss. 4954, p. 23.

Our institutions are part and parcel of the nation itself, not a garment that can be imitated by a skillful workman. What they can teach foreign statesmen is, to cling in every political change to the traditions and character of their own people, and to distinguish between the institutions which are accidental and transient and those which are national and unchangeable. The essence of monarchy does not consist in a citizen king, who reigns but does not govern; nor is its true character diminished or imperilled when each order of the state shares the power.

"The Count de Montalembert," *Rambler* n.s. 10 (December 1858):424–425. Acton-Simpson I, p. 82; Döllinger I, p. 155.

Preserve not existing things but existing forces. Abandon none of those forces that have made England great—for they are her identity, her security for the future. And preserve institutions, when they embody those permanent forces. For to give up what is permanent is to submit to what is changeable. Do not put new forces in the place of the old, for they have no security in them. Correct the errors, don't destroy the force. Be always ready to reform results—never to destroy the product of them. Primogeniture, Establishment—the two secrets are not sacred. But they make up the two great historic forces.

Add. Mss. 5604, p. 12.

Constitutional—the sum of indirect influences which restrain the action of the crown.

Add. Mss. 4950, p. 65.

Not certain that successor will be wiser than his predecessor. But certain that next generation will be wiser. The seat of progress is in the nation, not on the throne. Therefore the monarch adjusts himself to the people, not the people to the monarch.

Add. Mss. 4870, p. 33.

The security for the British constitution resides in the democratic leaven in the House of Peers, and the aristocratic element in the House of Commons.

Add. Mss. 5528, p. 32.

The very essence of the English system was liberty founded on inequality. The essence of the French ideal was democracy, that is, as in America, liberty founded on equality.

Acton, *Lectures on the French Revolution*, p. 97.

The House of Commons lost America—but it did not conquer India, found the colonies, defeat Napoleon, rescue Spain. Many of those things were done in spite of it. We look to its debates for the arts which lost America, not for those that conquered Napoleon. The evil of our legislation originates in parliament—reforms originate outside. Its debates are not as useful, for politics, as those of other states that began afresh, exposed the foundations of politics: Spain, America, France, Switzerland, Belgium, Frankfurt, Berlin.

    Add. Mss. 4947, p. 40.

Aristocracy is the product of inequality, as inequality is the product of liberty. The security for the continuity of law and the stability of political institutions is the permanence of influential families. Influence can only be made permanent by property, and property by primogeniture. This consecration of inequality creates the only force capable of resisting the impulses of the moment, and of protecting institutions from wanton change and perpetual reactions. Laws which express the will of the people for the time being are written on water. The people as well as the king require a check in the exercise of sovereign power lest it become despotic. The check on monarchy is Representation. The check on democracy is primogeniture. It is the condition of unpaid self-government.

    "Mr. Goldwin Smith on the Political History of England," *Chronicle* (31 August 1867):543. Ryan, p. 390.

Nobility is properly an element of progress, for it subsists only on condition of moving in the front rank. Where it feels unable to keep the lead, it tries to maintain itself by impeding the general advance. Aristocracy, says Chateaubriand, has three successive ages: the age of superiority, the age of privileges, the age of vanities; proceeding from the first, it degenerates in the second and expires in the third. Ours is still in the first age.

    "National Defence," *Rambler* n.s. 3 (September 1860):293. Acton-Simpson II, p. 84.

Primogeniture embodies the confusion between authority and property which constitutes modern Legitimacy. Legitimacy has, in this century, acted as an obstacle to free institutions.

    Letter to Mary Gladstone, January 17, 1882, in Paul p. 225.

The most free of all nations in early times were the Germans: No absolute monarchy, no privileged aristocracy. Liberty and equality. This was disturbed by conquest and by Roman institutions of the

conquered race [and] afterwards by Roman law. England has preserved this best because the native Britons, with their Roman customs, were driven away.
Add. Mss. 4980, p. 240.

It is by circumstances, not by race, that we thrive.
Add. Mss. 4868, p. 26.

Burke stops in 1783. England, thenceforth, lost the lead. We turn towards France. The reign of conservatism began in that year. Half a century before Free Trade, Relief of Dissenters, Emancipation, Self-government of dependencies, Catholic Relief, Reform, Peace. England became the enemy of liberty: Wellington in Spain, Castlereagh at Vienna.
Add. Mss. 4953, pp. 94, 96.

England has not been liberal. Only the weight of Scotland and Ireland. Only since Emancipation is Parliament on the road to liberty. NB Catholics—apart from that, it was fear that carried emancipation.
Add. Mss. 4954, p. 184.

[On the Irish Question] I believe that a nation which has been historically formed, which has been conquered and often oppressed has a real right to autonomy, particularly in so far as it is willing to strive to obtain this autonomy by the use of legal and constitutional means. . . . Therefore Ireland's demand for autonomy seems to me in general to be morally, historically, and politically justified. . . . We English took from the Irish what was their property, their land and fields. England's rule over Ireland rests upon robbery. The families that were robbed are still there. The Irish nation is merely reclaiming its own property. In this day of aroused public opinion, in a time when all relationships involving property are being reexamined, when both in theory and in practice attacks are made upon legitimate rights of property, how can such a clearly justified claim be silenced?
May 12, 1886, translated from the German. Döllinger III, pp. 356–358.

[Disraeli], at least if he had no principles or scruples, had no prejudices or superstitions or fanaticism. You have heard it said of _____ that he would have been a good fellow, if he had not been a drunkard, a liar,

and a thief. With a few allowances . . . a good deal may be said for
the Tory leader who made England a Democracy.

Letter to Mary Gladstone, April 2, 1881, in Paul, p. 187.

The Monument is a homage paid by the nation, demanding more
than parliamentary or other intellectual distinction, and implying
public service of some exceptional merit and amount. This is wanting
in Disraeli. And we deem not only that the good was absent, but that
the bad, the injurious, the immoral, the disgraceful, was present on a
large scale. Let us praise his genius, his wit, his courage, his patience
and constancy in adversity, his strength of will, his originality and
independence of mind, the art with which he learned to be eloquent,
his occasional largess of conception, his frequent good nature and
fidelity to friends, his readiness of resource, his considerable literary
culture, his skill in the management of a divided and reluctant party,
even his superiority to the greed of office; let us even call him the
greatest Jewish minister since Joseph—but if we say that he deserved
the gratitude of the nation and might claim his reward from every
part of it, I am afraid we condemn ourselves.

Letter to Mary Gladstone, April 30, 1881, in Paul, p. 201.

[On Gladstone] When our descendants shall stand before the slab that
is not yet laid among the monuments of famous Englishmen, they will
say that Chatham knew how to inspire a nation with his energy, but
was poorly furnished with knowledge and ideas; that the capacity of
Fox was never proved in office, though he was the first of debaters;
that Pitt, the strongest of ministers, was among the weakest of legisla-
tors; that no Foreign Secretary has equalled Channing, but that he
showed no other administrative ability; that Peel, who excelled as an
administrator, a debater, and a tactician, fell everywhere short of
genius; and that the highest merits of the five without their drawbacks
were united in Mr. Gladstone. . . . Looking abroad, beyond the walls
of Westminster, for objects worthy of comparison, they will say that
other men, such as Hamilton and Cavour, accomplished work as great;
that Turgot and Roon were unsurpassed in administrative craft; that
Clay and Thiers were as dexterous in parliamentary management;
that Berryer and Webster resembled him in gifts of speech, Guizot
and Radowitz in fulness of thought; but that in the three elements of

greatness combined, the man, the power, and the result—character, genius, and success—none reached his level.

Letter to Mary Gladstone, December 14, 1880, in Paul, pp. 142, 146–147.

In a famous and characteristic passage, Mommsen declares that Rome reigned over the barbarian West by virtue of superior culture, and over the cultured East by superior organization. The same title by which England reigns over the splendor of Delhi and the desolation of Saskatchewan.

Add. Mss. 4956, p. 157.

English philosophy: Faraday used to say that he went no farther than that water wets and fire burns.

Add. Mss. 4954, p. 3 bis.

America

I
REVOLUTION

All through America meant: Escape from History. They started fresh, unencumbered with the political past and religious.
Add. Mss. 4898, p. 391.

The *nexus* in Europe had to burst the bonds of centuries. Set down apart from medieval remains, and it worked at once for freedom. The faculty was there, only repressed. American colonisation removed the repressing forces. Then it appeared natural to the Englishman to govern himself like a free man. Undo the work of history, remove the civilising influence of centuries, and you found—a free man.
Add. Mss. 4898, p. 184.

1776: The saddest day in English history. Abstract rights as there are duties. Rights not dependent upon positive law.
Add. Mss. 4945, p. 284.

America: At first they strove to preserve the rights of Englishmen. This failed, and they declared their rights as human beings. This had never been done so largely. England had scrupulously avoided it.
Add. Mss. 4895, p. 51.

America started with the habit of abstract ideas. Rhode Island, Pennsylvania. It came to them from religion and the Puritan struggle. So they went beyond conservation of national rights. The rights of man grew out of English toleration. It was the link between tradition and abstraction.
Add. Mss. 4897, p. 130.

Americans were free, prosperous, secure, lightly taxed. Practically [they were] better off than any other people. Yet they rebelled. They were ready to sacrifice life and wealth. They impressed the world with the righteousness of their cause. [They] appealed to general principle, to be applied to all. If they were right, it was high time for other states to set their houses in order.

Add. Mss. 4898, p. 182.

American Revolution: The great point is that the letter of the law was against them. The absence of real oppression likewise. It was definitely an appeal to unwritten law, unchartered rights. There was no religious motive in it. And there was no enthusiasm, no readiness to make sacrifices. The leaders carried the country with them, by great efforts. They would have failed, but for the alliance with France.

Add. Mss. 4895, p. 36.

American Revolution for so little. [The Americans were] more free than any country. Yet they rose in arms, sacrificing everything for an idea.

Add. Mss. 4898, p. 184.

American Revolution: It was the first purely political revolution. As long as liberal movements were caused [by] a religion, when the religion was secured, liberty was disregarded. Liberty was safe only when it was the direct aim of action.

Add. Mss. 4895, p. 39.

There could never be a revolution less provoked by oppression than America. Thenceforth the right of a nation to judge for itself could not be denied.

Add. Mss. 4945, p. 250.

America first established the idea that absolutism is wrong. Till then it had been inconvenient, injurious, a burden and a drawback to prosperity etc. It was a privilege to be free from it. But liberty was an acquired privilege, not a universal right. Aristotle had allowed absolute power; S. Augustine likewise. In the Middle Ages, the idea that the heterodox are equal, that rights belong to individuals, apart from their land, their faith, their colour, was not known. . . . Indeed, it would

have overthrown every throne in Europe. It arose in America. It arose after Rationalism had made way—after Bayle, Montesquieu, Voltaire.
Add. Mss. 4895, p. 289.

The immense effect of American independence—not the work of one man—of a Bacon or a Caesar. The breach was not accomplished by innovators, by men of heroic inventiveness. They were, overall, men of the second rank, without originality or intellectual grandeur. And their work was done by men who looked back, who regretted monarchy, did not aspire to Independence. Jefferson hailed from Magna Charta. Adams, nothing in common with French Revolution.
Add. Mss. 4945, p. 168.

America transformed the English Whigs. Burke, whose capacious mind included every conservative instinct, and who, in his earlier career, avoided general principles and propositions receptive of bilateral application, ended by adopting their extreme doctrine of revolution. How much more in France, men who had served with [the Americans], by whose aid [the American] cause had triumphed.
Add. Mss. 4898, p. 260.

II
CONSTITUTION

The Americans, having broken the thread in 1776, spliced it together again. They became eminently conservative in 1787. Not one new principle but what was derived from their own colonial experience. No fundamental, characteristic principle—except the Supreme Court, election of president.
Add. Mss. 4897, p. 158.

Those Americans had nothing old, traditional, involuntary to maintain. Their institutions were deliberately devised for practical ends. They were the result of living thought and will. They did not reach back to the obscure age of barbarians or of demigods. Practically a Liberal opposition never arose. The real opposition was Absolutism and Nullification.
Add. Mss. 4898, p. 165.

Americans dreaded democracy and contrived their constitution against it.

Add. Mss. 4895, p. 49.

The Americans were aware that democracy might be weak and unintelligent, but also that it might be despotic and oppressive. And they found out the way to limit it, by the federal system, which suffers it to exist nowhere in its plenitude. They deprived their state governments of the powers that were enumerated, and the central government of the powers that were reserved. As the Romans knew how monarchy would become innocuous, by being divided, the Americans solved the more artful problem of dividing democracy in two.

Acton, *Lectures on the French Revolution*, p. 104.

The federal constitution was a system of compromises. No one opinion or system prevailed. At first there were innumerable checks on Democracy. At last they all gave way. Then the federal check became the supreme guarantee. It was the shape in which the dogma survived, that the nation cannot do what it likes.

Add. Mss. 4895, p. 172.

What were the American checks? Instead of monarchy, aristocracy, established church, standing army, colonial empire, primogeniture, ancient tradition, customary law, [the Americans had] Presidential veto, Supreme Court, Nullification.

Add. Mss. 4897, p. 237.

Written constitution—a compact between Americans. Therefore not changeable by them, like other laws. So they set limits to their power.

Add. Mss. 4897, p. 97.

The great novelty of the American Constitution was that it imposed checks on the representatives of the people.

Add. Mss. 4895, p. 288.

In England Parliament is above the law. In America the law is above Congress. The House of Commons is stronger than the judges. In America the Supreme Court defends the Constitution against any act of Congress.

Add. Mss. 4897, p. 72.

In the U.S. Constitution, the executive negotiates but the legislature declares war. Therefore all diplomatic negotiations, if they end in war, must be submitted to the legislature and so to the public.

Add. Mss. 4895, p. 17.

What is a free people? Massachusetts: equal wealth, education, share of power, minorities, good laws, representation, no army, no privileges, high level of knowledge and cultivation. All this could only grow by degrees.

Add. Mss. 4895, p. 46.

America: Greatest amount of liberty ever enjoyed in this world. But there were drawbacks: no real check on the multitude, slavery, irreligion, decomposition of democracy.

Add. Mss. 4895, p. 170.

III
CIVIL WAR

Secession: S. Carolina had nullified first, on the question of tariff. The union had purchased surrender by concession. So the idea was a powerful political engine, an immense security. It got mixed up with slavery, with cruel laws, inhuman cultivation of ignorance, impediments to religion and morality. . . . This cost the federal principle the sympathy of Europe. Neither Russia nor Germany would go with them.

Add. Mss. 4895, p. 173.

American abolitionists and secessionists both admitted a higher principle than the maintenance of the union. [Both would have] sacrificed the national government to a higher purpose.

Add. Mss. 4897, p. 142.

Confederates would prefer emancipation and independence to union with slavery.

Add. Mss. 5692, p. 3.

Lee, who led the armies of the South during three years of warfare more terrible than Napoleon's, was an opponent of slavery.

Add. Mss. 4942, p. 396.

America: Show its increasing defects—Southern attempt to remedy. It would have been a strength to the republican theory. No army, no socialism, local government, safety of minorities, second chamber, universal education, religious liberty, liberty to leave as one liked. Great collective. All this spoilt by slavery. The generals were against slavery. They wished for the arming of the slaves. But the bulk of the south clung to slavery. The arming came too late. The model republic got a great army, debt, immense central power, corruption, socialism, injured credit.

Add. Mss. 5594, p. 82.

Garrison called the Constitution "a league with death and a covenant with hell." NB The Americans sacrificed temporal goods to liberty in Franklin's time. Gave up the national government in absolutism.

Add. Mss. 4897, p. 160.

IV
POLITICAL THOUGHT
IN AMERICA

Fifty Americans deserve to be studied with any of our writers of the second rank—and three are of the first. All politicians. Hamilton, Jefferson, Webster, Calhoun, Franklin, Clay, Madison, Seward, Sumner, Legaré, Adams, Bancroft, Hildreth, Prescott, Ticknor, Motley, Curtis, Story. [The three writers "of first rank" were evidently Madison, Hamilton, and Calhoun. Madison's *Debates of the Congress of Confederation*, Hamilton's *The Federalist*, and Calhoun's *Essay on Government* are the only American works listed in "Lord Acton's Hundred Best Books" in *The Pall Mall Magazine* 36 (July 1905):5–7. J.R.F.]

Add. Mss. 4897, p. 175.

Arguments of Otis, Adams, Franklin, Jefferson, Hamilton incorporated in the Declaration of Independence. Set up a new theory of government. The governed have to decide on grounds universally applicable. This is not grown on English pastures. It is the pure theory of Revolution. It is Rousseau and Tom Paine. It is the absolute condemnation of European politics.

Add. Mss. 4953, p. 84.

Madison's great merit. He was not a man of theories. He examined things practically thinking what will work. Hamilton, Jefferson, even Adams were more doctrinaire. His reason for each opinion is not taken from theory but from life.

Add. Mss. 4895, p. 48.

Jefferson wished individuals to surrender as little power as possible. Above all, never surrender the power of changing their minds and their institutions. Least possible control of individual will. Therefore, nothing permanent; Constitution can be dissolved just as king can be deposed.

Add. Mss. 4895, p. 34.

That there is no absolute power in a state is a dogma much insisted on by the Adams family.

Add. Mss. 4895, p. 84.

The first four presidents were the most eminent men of their time. Afterwards the presidents were inferior men. . . . So that the power increased while the capacity diminished.

Add. Mss. 4895, p. 31.

V
THE FUTURE

Americans [are] selfish and insubordinate—yet capable of sacrifices such as no European nation has made. Austria sued for peace after one great defeat. France after five weeks of war. How different is America. We [British] thought it exhausting to carry 25,000 men to fight the Russian empire, [we] could not bring 30,000 together in 1864, when we wished to defend Denmark—while Grant asked Wellington how many men his father commanded. Their wealth would exceed our own. [The] resources and population [of America] are double our own. [America can be] either a most formidable enemy on our flank, disabling us in Europe, when Belgium or Holland has to be defended, or [a] still more dangerous influence within it, by example—a more populous Ireland—more prosperous. Therefore in 1860, the danger, the threatening crisis, came from America. If they persisted in their absolutism, with greater strength, they would either become the most terrible enemy of England or would drag us over to their doctrine. A view not without its basis here: the omnipotence of the Past, the pride of Asiatic empire, impatience of our stupid unenlightenment, ideas of Manchester, ideas of Bentham. A people as energetic and more inventive than our own. Well able to bear defeat and to repair it. Capable, had defeated English fleets, and put our armies to flight. Federalism was breaking down in Europe: Italy, Switzerland, Germany. Was that to be a power for good or evil. An overwhelming power on the flank of England—was it to be friendly and liberal or deceptive, pressing under disguises the doctrine of popular absolutism, like the Roman republic of Caesar or the French of Carnot. Plainly America was progressing to a degree of wealth and power beyond all nations. By the rate of progress, a hundred millions before the end of the century—surpass us in wealth this year. For the great migration had given the impulse which is wanting in America. A time would come when the thousand mile frontier could not be held—when European wars would throw the ocean trade into American hands.

Add. Mss. 4895, pp. 314–318.

My American notebook [of Acton's 1853 visit] is at Aldenham, but my impressions are clear, and are strengthened by the many Americans I have seen of late years, Ticknor, Sumner, Motley etc. Their notion of liberty is not = security, nor self-government, but participation in government of others, power, not independence, aggression, not safety— that is, always the contrary to what ought to be. Their state is absolute, their sovereign despotic, and irresistible. There is no immunity, no exemption from supreme control, no corner of the pie in which the state has not got a finger. All this is the clean opposite of our ideas of independence, jealousy of interference, of certain spheres and relations of life being beyond public inquiry. Not so much afraid of control as eager to exercise it.

February 16, 1861. Acton-Simpson II, p. 122.

I find a singular resemblance on many points between Russia and the United States, and could make something of an article showing the analogy between them and their equal incompatibility with good government and the true principles both of liberty and authority.

February 16, 1858. Acton-Simpson I, pp. 8–9.

America has not solved the problem of reconciling democracy with freedom, for it has not reconciled power with law—or will with duty, which is the moral aspect of the same thing.

November 23, 1861. Acton-Simpson II, p. 203.

Prussia and Germany

The great growth of intellectual life is in Germany, and nearly all that has been done in France or in England for science is inspired by the Germans.

Add. Mss. 5528, p. 57.

The unity of Italy was the work of favorable circumstances, the unity of Germany of unfavorable.

Add. Mss. 4862, p. 182.

Frankfort: The Professors' Parliament. The professors who there failed to create an empire by votes proceeded to do it by creating opinion. They worked, for the first time, for a cause. History began to be written for a purpose. That purpose was to repress sympathy with Austria, with the smaller states, with Catholicism, with Democracy, and to make men feel the need of shelter and concentration under the most vigorous and the most intelligent of monarchical governments.

Add. Mss. 4956, p. 171.

Modern Germany looked not to its roots in the past, to the Empire, but to Prussia which is modern.

Add. Mss. 4929, p. 76.

History has been one of the chief forces making Germany, especially Droysen. The phalanx of historians at Berlin.

Add. Mss. 4929, p. 130.

Prussia lets the state govern society. Authority not opinion governs. In the South, the objects of the public are above those of the state—it is the servant, not the master.

Add. Mss. 4929, p. 70.

Prussia: the first tolerant state. Holland was tolerant from anarchy, Prussia from authority. The state was strong enough to impose toleration.

Add. Ms. 4956, p. 10.

The Prussian state was created by the arts of its rulers, not formed on a national or a natural basis. The unity of its history, like the cause of its growth, is in its policy.

Review of J. G. Droysen, *Geschichte der preussischen Politik: Friedrich I, König von Preussen*, in the *Chronicle* (7 September 1867):572. Döllinger I, pp. 490–491.

Prussian idea of the state: Not insurance but training. Control opinion by newspapers and the future by schools. The state is a contrivance by which just men judge and intelligent men govern [and] learned men teach. Its purposes are its own. The masses are not the end but the means. The passenger exists for the sake of the ship.

Add. Mss. 4929, p. 69.

As the impulse to expand in Germany has increased, the immorality of the means has become more flagrant, and the liberties of the Prussians themselves have been sacrificed to the one overriding cause. The servile Parliament, which admits that the interest of the State is supreme over the rights of others, cannot vindicate its own. . . . The power of assimilation which dwells in the Prussian system is very great, and . . . the constant direction of forces towards the purposes of aggression has endowed the machinery of state with an almost unexampled elasticity and rapidity of motion.

Review of O. Klopp, *Die preussische Politik des Fridericianismus nach Friedrich II*, in the *Chronicle* (5 October 1867):669. Ryan, p. 391.

[Frederic the Great] so eclipsed Frederic William that the latter became an obscure memory, and was spoken of with contempt and disgust by his own people. Carlyle discovered in him his own ideal, the strong man, and set him on his legs. And when the army which he had created, which had been remodelled by Friederic, Scharnhorst, Roon, and Moltke, became the greatest of armies, Germany remembered its founder and was grateful for his militarism.

They have made their choice, as we must do. Those who remember with honour men like Hampden and Washington, regard with a corresponding aversion Peter the Great and Frederic William I. But without the first Europe might be French, and without the other it might be Russian. That which arose in Northern Europe about the time of our revolution settlement was a new form of practical absolutism. Theological monarchy had done its time, and was now followed by military monarchy. Church and State had oppressed mankind together; henceforth the State oppressed for its own sake. And this was the genuine idea which came in with the Renaissance, according to which the State alone governs, and all other things obey. Reformation and Counter-Reformation had pushed religion to the front: but after two centuries the original theory, that government must be undivided and uncontrolled, began to prevail. It is a new type, not to be confounded with that of Henry VIII, Philip II, or Lewis XIV, and better adapted to a more rational and economic age. Government so understood is the intellectual guide of the nation, the promoter of wealth, the teacher of knowledge, the guardian of morality, the mainspring of the ascending movement of man. That is the tremendous power, supported by millions of bayonets, which grew up in the days of which I have been speaking at Petersburg, and was developed, by much abler minds, chiefly at Berlin; and it is the greatest danger that remains to be encountered by the Anglo-Saxon race.

Acton, *Lectures on Modern History*, p. 289.

France

There is twice as much sound political wisdom in French books than in all the literature of the world together. Yet they cannot make fixed institutions.
Add. Mss. 4929, p. 110.

Political imbecility of the French nation: France deficient in the moral qualities requisite for liberty—Russia in the intellectual qualities.
Add. Mss. 5528, p. 43.

The servitude of the whole nation [of France under Napoleon III] is justified by the servility of the majority. The long duration of a despotism exercised by a man of no conspicuous virtues and of no conspicuous ability, bespeaks a nation singularly fitted for such a yoke. Against the resistance of moral forces the material force of imperial bayonets could not permanently prevail: "Nor stony tower, nor walls of beaten brass, nor airless dungeon, nor strong links of iron, can be retentive to the strength of spirit." The victims of the imperial despotism are for the most part its instruments.
"The Count de Montalembert," *Rambler* n.s. 10 (December 1858):427. Acton-Simpson I, p. 82; Döllinger I, p. 155.

Germans familiar with complex ideas, the French love simplicity. That has more to do with their obscurity than defects of expression.
Add. Mss. 4944, p. 21.

The French historians of the last century were addicted to unscrupulous calumny, and those who have succeeded are for the most part afflicted with a contemptuous indifference to the distinction between fact and invention.
Review of J. F. A. Peyré, *Histoire de la Première Croisade*, in the *Rambler* n.s. 5 (September 1861):403. *Wellesley* II, p. 783.

History in Germany is a science, in France it is pursued as an art.
   Add. Mss. 5528, p. 37.

It is an example of those defects which make the French, who are the
best writers of history in the world, the worst possible historians. It is
written without passion and with a very extensive knowledge of the
medieval writers, but absolutely without the least idea of criticism or
scientific investigation.
   Review of J. F. A. Peyré, *Histoire de la Première Croisade*, in the *Rambler* n.s.
5 (September 1861):403. *Wellesley.*

Church

I
RELIGION

Religion sufficient for death, insufficient for life.
Add. Mss. 4950, p. 296.

Religion becomes gradually a theology, passes from history into system—grows scientific. Not at first—then more and more completely. This is the first element of change, transformation, progress, from confusion and vagueness to definitiveness, from fact to theory, from beginning to system. And thus growing fixed, determined and limited, it left little room for innovation or arbitrary action.
Add. Mss. 4939, p. 91.

We understand religion because of symbolism.
Add. Mss. 4943, p. 65.

Influence of religion. It is the home of general propositions. It is essentially alien to place and time. Adaptable to many races. So it accustoms men to sweeping theories, theories applicable to man as man, no matter what sex or colour or age. So it promoted doctrinaire thinking in politics.
Add. Mss. 4960, p. 12.

There is no wrong men have not been ready to commit when they thought it could serve religious purposes.
Add. Mss. 4869, p. 3.

Every religion has some political tendency or influence.
Add. Mss. 4860, p. 42.

602

II
CHURCH HISTORY

A. General Thoughts

But there are as yet those who know that the progress of historical knowledge can alone cure the wrongs which the perversion of facts has wrought; that a good conscience courts publicity; and that our religion will be better loved the more its character and history are understood.

"Father Theiner's Publications," *Rambler* n.s. 10 (October 1858):267. Acton-Simpson I, p. 78.

Church history is to universal history as the soul to the body. It gives connection and importance to the events of universal history. Without it history could only occupy the memory, not the higher faculties of the mind.

Add. Mss. 4860, p. 1.

Church as model: Invites us to pass through her own discipline, to follow her own course of thought—to live back in the apostolic age, and to realize the phases of thought, the steps of knowledge, in successive ages—to put before us, successively, the same succeeding problems and to consider them from several stand points, with the same resources. This is the method of history. A mind so trained would have a subtle means of dealing with all questions, avoiding systems, distrusting its own fancies, consenting to renounce producing, and only to reproduce, to avoid ideals, and independent speculation.

Add. Mss. 4941, p. 348.

Every effort has been made to accommodate the church to the degenerate nature of man, and these attempts are [a] great part of history.

Add. Mss. 4860, p. 1.

A Christian understands Christianity when Christianity has transformed him. It is his experience, his own growth that discloses the doctrine. So with mankind: The church, transforming the world, taught it the doctrine.

Add. Mss. 5392, p. 44.

Even the apostles had not the full insight into moral truths which did not then exist in the consciousness of the church.
Add. Mss. 4860, p. 43.

B. The Early Church

Religion is more intimately bound up with the whole fabric of society, and with the spirit of a government, than those who take a superficial and external view of religion and society can comprehend. In many ways it is a creating force; and in others it is an element of cohesion; in every way its influence is marvellously subtle and extensive. It is the deepest source and foundation of laws; it gives an essential sanction to government; and it is the soul of innumerable social habits. Whatever may be the circumstances, a change in the religion of a nation involves such a change in its character, its customs, and its laws, as is almost equal to a loss of identity in the nation itself and in the state; and it is impossible in the lower stages of civilisation, for a part of the inhabitants of a country to alter their religion, without putting themselves into a new position towards the laws, or bringing on serious conflicts. Only a very highly developed form of civil society can admit a variety of religions without peril to its existence. For political thought must have been matured before laws can retain their power when their moral and religious sanction, security, and support, have been removed by a schism in the dogmatic ideas which are the basis of the moral code. Up to the moment of such maturity, conversion is revolution; a new faith is ruin to the old polity; and its introduction is resisted with all that vehemence which is natural to a community struggling for existence. The contest, therefore, is not merely between a higher and a lower faith, between truth and superstition, or between priests of the true God and priests of false gods; it is a contest in which the missionary religion encounters a resistance more powerful and more legitimate than that of religious error, a resistance which is sustained by the best and noblest social virtues—reverence for a venerable antiquity, obedience for an established code of morals, allegiance to authority, and the patriotism of a nation threatened in its vital parts. When Christianity came to the Roman empire, the history of the world for thousands of years had been so guided as to prevent those natural obstacles from arresting its progress. Politically and intellectually, the progress of the gentile world had prepared the way for the new faith. The force of national feeling had been destroyed by the arms of Macedon and Rome; and the force of pagan mythology had been undermined by philosophy and unbelief. Where this preparation had not been made, where an old religion and an old polity retained their vigour, as in Persia, the missionary creed was expelled. Even in the Roman Empire, where the necessary conditions of its acceptance existed, the resistance was long and fierce; and Christianity triumphed only when the vitality of the empire was exhausted. The Church could not reconstruct society with the old materials. Degeneracy and corruption prevailed against her efforts; and the new religion was carried forward by new nations, who created a new society, a new civilisation, and a new political system.

"Venn's Life of St. Francis Xavier," *Home and Foreign Review* II (January 1863):186–187. Döllinger I, p. 287.

Christianity: Revolutionary element: It overthrew very ancient authorities. It destroyed the theory that a power must be obeyed because of its antiquity, of its beneficence, of the greatness it has assisted, of the divine sanction it has enjoyed. It taught men to enquire, not of their country, but of themselves. It required them to believe that they had lived and prospered for thousands of years under an imposture, that their people had grown great, had conquered its enemies, under the protection of wickedness—that all their prayers, their sacrifices, their heroic deeds had been offered up to an unclean spirit.

Add. Mss. 5605, p. 47.

Why early Christianity did so little for ethics. Pagan ethics—pagan and Jewish—were almost sufficient. No new idea of morality in the New Testament—only adoption of the best. When we take the ideas of Philo and Seneca, what is there more for society. But they did little even for private, personal, domestic morality. What they brought was the spirit to execute, to enforce what was right. Not better knowledge, but a stronger will.

Add. Mss. 5392, p. 60.

The great lesson of early Christianity was the liberty of conscience.

Add. Mss. 4870, p. 7.

Christianity made its way not by the aid of authorities, but in spite of them, and in defiance of the laws—not by the protection of monarchs but by the voice of poor men. It came in through the rights of conscience. The Fathers appealed to the principle of freedom. And what had been written by Tertullian when the Christians were persecuted, was repeated by Lactantius when they were masters. St. Athanasius declared that truth is not promoted by the sword and javelin and that no man whose faith is sincere can promote it by violence. St. Hilary warned the bishop that if he made converts by compulsion, the bishops themselves would protest against him. And when certain men were put to death for heresy, the bishop who had procured it was deposed, and the most famous prelates of the West, St. Ambrose and St. Martin, looked on it as a crime. The pope agreed with them, and the bishop was deposed from his see. The emperors, indeed, with the exception of Valentinian, were less tolerant than the bishops, and, after the invasion of the barbarians the precept of charity and liberty was attained with difficulty where the conquerors differed in religion from the conquered. They could not possibly maintain themselves. It was politically necessary that one religion or the other should prevail. At first the Arrian kings of Spain tried to force their religion on the Spaniards; and having failed, they forced the Catholic religion on the Goths. It became an axiom of Teutonic statecraft in those half barbarous communities, that the government required all the support that a united clergy could give as a center of influence in every town. Religion had to do most of the work of civilisation and much of the work of government. During many centuries religious unity fulfilled this object and was preserved with little hardship. There was no discordant minority to be coerced, and no great persecutions needed to be taken against it. But this age of comparative tranquillity was brought to an end by the revival of one of the early sects, of a sect that accepted two supreme beings, a good and a bad one, that is, that believed in a god who was worshipped by works of sin. The terror of being among devil worshippers drove one half of churches into that system of intolerance which did much to break down medieval freedom by arming governments with the arms of arbitrary imprisonment, torture, and death by fire.

Add. Mss. 5006, pp. 74–78.

Christianity did not promote freedom in the fifth century, for the poor preferred slavery to freedom and ran away to the Goths. St. Augustine, at last, made non-liberty a theory: a people should be free in proportion

to its moral quality. Under the dominion of sin, they are not free, nor fit to be. What you give them is not freedom but increased oppression.
Add. Mss. 5392, p. 147.

C. The Medieval Church

The contribution of the papacy [in the Middle Ages] was this principle: That power should be checked—that the nation should not be omnipotent—that the governing power should be distinct from the controlling power.
Add. Mss. 4979, p. 9.

The church was, in the Middle Ages, after the Carolingian epoch, the great divider of power.
Add. Mss. 4942, p. 415.

Early and later Church: At first a rude but efficient protection against arbitrary taxation. Afterwards a system of its own taxation largely developed. At first a channel transferring property from rich to poor. Afterwards, by mendicant orders, a competition with the poor.
Add. Mss. 4982, p. 280.

Guelf and Ghibelline are names which changed their meaning as much as Whig and Tory. For at last the Guelfs, who had been defenders of the freedom of the church, became defenders of the power of the pope, a regular court party, postponing the rights and welfare of the church to the interests of the papacy—separating the two in fact, whilst pretending to make them identical. So while I hate the Ghibellines of the twelfth century I don't like the Guelfs of the fourteenth century and Dante is condemned for saying in his time what I would say in ours. He did not stop at the consideration of what would suit the popes, but went on to think of the good of religion, and of certain moral rights and duties, beyond certain religious or rather ecclesiastical interests. The papacy had forfeited the leadership, and the life of the church beat more warmly in other places than at the head. Have we not lived to see the same thing? The revival of faith in this century has left the papacy behind, as far, almost, as in those old days.
March 20, 1861. Acton-Simpson II, p. 136.

There is much to deduct from the praise of the Church in protecting marriage, abolishing slavery and human sacrifice, preventing war, and helping the poor. No deduction can be made from her evil-doing toward unbelievers, heretics, savages, and witches. Here her responsibility is more undivided, her initiative and achievement more complete. . . . It was the negation not only of religious liberty which is the mainspring of civil, but equally of civil liberty, because a government armed with the machinery of the Inquisition is necessarily absolute. So that, if Liberalism has a desperate foe it is the Church, as it was in the West, between 1200 and 1600 or 1700. The philosophy of Liberal history which has to acknowledge the invaluable services of early Christianity, feels at the same time rather more strongly the anti-liberal and anti-social action of later Christianity, before the rise of the sects which rejected, some the divinity of Christ, others, the institutions of the Church erected upon it. Liberalism, if it admits these things as adiaphora, surrenders its own *raison d'être*, and ceases to strive for an ethical cause. . . . If the doctrine of Torquemada makes us condone his morality, there can be no public right or wrong, no political sin, no secular cause to die for, no damnation lurking in affairs of state.

Letter to Gladstone, May 2, 1888, in Acton, *Correspondence*, pp. 217–218.

D. The Inquisition

The Inquisition is peculiarly the weapon and peculiarly the work of the Popes. It stands out from all those things in which they co-operated, followed, or assented as the distinctive feature of papal Rome. It was set up, renewed, and perfected by a long series of acts emanating from the supreme authority in the Church. No other institution, no doctrine, no ceremony, is so distinctly the individual creation of the papacy, except the Dispensing power. It is the principal thing with which the papacy is identified, and by which it must be judged.

Letter to Mary Gladstone, June 19, 1884, in Paul, pp. 298–299.

Papacy: It was an aristocracy of intelligence, morality, knowledge. That is why so much depended on its morality. Such power in bad hands was intolerable. It needed to be justified not only by the sacraments but by character. It was a frightful tyranny when abused.

Add. Mss. 4979, p. 177.

Victories of the church over paganism by persuasion, over heresy, always by violence, and by the resources not of religion but of the state. [Since heresy was] only defeated by force, it seemed that liberty was the resource and safeguard of Hell. [It seemed] that men, left to themselves, instructed but not coerced, would choose errors appealing to passion or sloth.

Add. Mss. 5006, pp. 9,11.

Idea that heresy leads sooner or later to immorality. So that the moral basis of society required the discipline of the church to maintain it.

Add. Mss. 5006, p. 70.

The heresy against which the Inquisition was directed was mainly the heresy of religious liberty.

Add. Mss. 4959, p. 142.

The Inquisition flourished at a time when the right of conscience, the duty of obeying it, was not admitted. It was considered that a man ought, under circumstances, to do what he believed, or even, knew to be wrong. He might be punished for what was avowedly right. The decision as to truth and error, right and wrong, was taken from him, and transferred, with the responsibility, to a living authority.

Add. Mss. 5006, p. 63.

The Inquisition, having achieved its immediate purpose, the destruction of the A[lbigensians], had fallen into disuse, and the fires had gone down for want of fuel. Sorcery was however added to its sphere of action, and the effect was a rapid increase in the number of witches. They had been discovered, sporadically, here and there. From about 1400 it became an epidemic. It was not only heresy but a sect.

Add. Mss. 4963, p. 133.

The decline of heresy made the Inquisition extend its hand: Sorcery, Sodomy, Usury. It was a machinery seeking occupation. Long before 1500 it embraced those other things.

Add. Mss. 4963, p. 349.

Inquisition is a question of government, of obedience, of submission, not of doctrine or ideas. That is how it comes, at last, to be a mere instrument of power.

Add. Mss. 4959, p. 209.

[Of the Inquisition] There were observers who suspected very early that the glare of lightning, the roll of thunder, the rush of the torrent conveniently sheltered hollow convictions and the logic of ignorance.

Add. Mss. 4959, p. 43.

Why did not Inquisition improve morals? For we find the clergy as bad at the end of the thirteenth century as at the beginning. Because they lived in sin. The sacraments did them no good—were not a means of grace but of perdition. If you appeal to force, you cannot also appeal to conscience.

Add. Mss. 4959, p. 152.

[The] object of the Inquisition [was] not to combat sin—for sin was not judged by it unless accompanied by error. Nor even to put down error. For it punished untimely or unseemly remarks the same as blasphemy. Only unity. This became an outward, fictitious, hypocritical unity. The gravest sin was pardoned, but it was death to deny the Donation of Constantine. So men learnt that outward submission must be given. All this to promote authority more than faith. When ideas were punished more severely than actions (for all this time the Church was softening the criminal law, and saving men from the consequences of crime) and the Donation was put on a level with God's own law, men understood that authority went before sincerity.

Add. Mss. 5536, n.n.

III
CHURCH AND STATE

The view of society entirely different if you believe in Christianity or do not. If God sent his son to redeem mankind and found a church, and if the church continues among men to fulfill its mission, its claims and rights must be considered and protected. The system of society must be arranged consistently with that. If it is the presumption that there is no such church then its rights cannot be sacred.

Add. Mss. 5434, p. 32.

It was Rome, not Jerusalem, that determined the political action of Christianity.

Add. Mss. 5392, p. 183.

The church necessarily tends to extend herself without any limits. She has no choice, but her very nature is to do so, and her enemies are forced to aid in the work.

Add. Mss. 4860, p. 1.

It is the union of Church and State that has caused all persecution. A Church cannot persecute except by controlling the State. All established Churches have persecuted—and the establishment in Ireland has been the occasion of the most atrocious persecution that ever disgraced the Protestant religion in my country or in the world.

Add. Mss. 4869, p. 20.

Real liberty depends, not on the separation, but on the distinct and appropriate, but continuous action and reaction, of Church and State. The defined and regulated influence of the Church in the State protects a special sphere and germ of political freedom, and supplies a separate and powerful sanction for law. On the other hand, the restricted and defined action of the state in Ecclesiastical affairs gives security to the canon law, and prevents wanton innovation and the arbitrary confiscation of rights.

"The Roman Question," *Chronicle* (2 November 1867):746. Ryan, pp. 141–142.

Liberty of the Church in the State involves authority of the Church in her own sphere—all liberty means the free exercise of authority in whatever is its right sphere.

October 6, 1862. Acton-Simpson III, p. 25.

Catholicism: The one political idea is that there is a power beyond the state and not coterminous with it. How great is this power? That increased later, until it destroyed the original idea. It absorbed power instead of checking it. Down to the Gregorian age it only checked it, never absorbed it. So that is the genuine Catholic action: a church inside and outside—vaster than the state, bringing genuine influence to bear—a force of public opinion, of international law, of arbitration.

Add. Mss. 4979, p. 19.

Church influence: Force must be met by force. Now the force that can resist the power of government is opinion. The church supplied that force, guided it, and made it independent of the state. It acted for formation of opinion. It was the only power, in the West, that could produce it. There was no press, no popular education. No man spoke to the people except the priest. No other influences reached them. Also it supplied organs—otherwise there were none. So that the force lived in the Church until public opinion itself was formed.

Add. Mss. 4980, p. 26.

Church as a political model: Nearly all the elements of modern Liberty prefigured in her: Election, Representation, Equality, Tradition, Absence of arbitrary power, Local self-government, Money for the poor, Humanity in punishment, Deliverance of slaves, No legislator, Trial by one's peers.

Add. Mss. 4980, p. 76.

A kind of collective infallibility in the state corresponds to that of the church. The sense of original natural right cannot be lost among Christians. The infallibility of the church is the centre and support of this.

Add. Mss. 4860, p. 43.

Religion developed liberty—by the balance of power.

Add. Mss. 4960, p. 5.

The limitation of authority in the state by the immunity of a corporation strong enough for resistance, permanent in its organization, constant in its maxims, and superior to national boundaries, has been the source of modern freedom. It is true that the disinterested love of liberty did not, like the love of humanity, animate the prelates of the Church. The authority which they wished to establish was as absolute as the authority they opposed, and they at one time sought to substitute a despotism of priests for the tyranny of kings. But although unable to gain their own ends, they forced the feudal state to admit exceptions and therefore bounds, to its authority, and thereby accomplished more for political progress than had been done by the wisdom of the ancients, or by the precepts of Christianity.

"M. Littré on the Middle Ages," *Chronicle* (3 August 1867): 443. Ryan, p. 198.

You cannot separate church and state. Religion is the domain of the church. Duty belongs to the domain of religion. The idea of the church will govern unless 1. the people discard religion or 2. there are several religions or 3. the state defines its own rights.

Add. Mss. 4870, p. 20

IV
THE CHURCH IN THE
MODERN WORLD

There is a wide divergence, an irreconcilable disagreement, between the political notions of the modern world and that which is essentially the system of the Catholic Church. It manifests itself particularly in their contradictory views of liberty, and of the functions of the civil power. The Catholic notion, defining liberty not as the power of doing what we like, but the right of being able to do what we ought, denies that general interests can supersede individual rights. It condemns, therefore, the theory of the ancient as well as of the modern state. It is founded on the divine origin and nature of authority. According to the prevailing doctrine, which derives power from the people, and deposits it ultimately in their hands, the state is omnipotent over the individual, whose only remnant of freedom is then the participation in the exercise of supreme power; while the general will is binding on him. Christian liberty is lost where this system prevails: whether in the form of the utmost diffusion of power, as in America, or of the utmost concentration of power, as in France; whether, that is to say, it is exercised by the majority, or by the delegate of the majority—it is always a delusive freedom, founded on a servitude more or less disguised. In one form and under one pretext or another, the state has been absolute on the continent of Europe for the last three hundred years. In the sixteenth century absolutism was founded on religious zeal, and was expressed in the formula *cujus regio, illius religio*. In the seventeenth century it assumed the garb of legitimacy and divine right, and the king was believed when he said, "L'état c'est moi." In the eighteenth century arbitrary government found a new and stronger basis in the theory of the public good, of the greatest happiness of the greatest number, and justified every act of tyranny by the maxim, *the king is the first servant of the people*. All these principles of despotism are incompatible with the Catholic ideas, and with the system by which the Pope, on pain of being in contradiction with himself, and with the spirit and practice of the Church, is compelled to govern. They are condemned by the traditions, and by the moral obligations, of the Court of Rome, whose system is one of charity and liberty, and which knows no public consideration which is superior to the salvation of souls.

"The Roman Question," *Rambler* n.s. 2 (January 1860):146–147. Acton-Simpson II, p. 32.

[The temporal power of the popes] is founded on the most sacred of human institutions, on the rights both of property and of sovereignty. It arose, as the necessary foundation of the liberty and independence of the Church, in ages when property was the indispensable condition of liberty, and sovereignty the only security for independence. For the Church requires that her head should be independent among other princes, that her ministers may be free among the subjects of princes. . . . The temporal authority of the Holy See . . . is not absolutely essential to the nature and ends of the Church; it has its source in causes which are external to her, in the temporary condition of the world, not the spiritual aims of the Church; and as the world becomes impregnated with her ideas, the necessity of the temporal power would probably disappear. It is her protection against the State, and a monument of her imperfect victory over the ideas of the outer world. It is not so much an advantage as a necessity, not so much desirable as inevitable. It is required in order to save her from the political designs and combinations of a system in whose name she is now required to surrender it. It appears to us that the temporal dominion over the Roman people may pass away when the spiritual dominion is acknowledged by all nations.

"The Roman Question," *Rambler* n.s. 2 (January 1860):149.

The *right* of liberty is a *claim*, not always admitted. The Church's right is denied by the pagan state which denies distinction between religious and civil society, and by the modern absolute state. The temporal sovereignty is the only plan we can devise to secure liberty for the pope, but it is a means, subsidiary; in fact it is a negative idea, the not being governed—not the right of governing—though governing is the only way to avoid being governed—derivative. It is wanted as a basis, an acknowledgement of independence—not as a means of defence or a source of political power.

October 8, 1861. Acton-Simpson II, p. 183.

There is a growing up of other powers, setting a thicket—limit to the action of church authority. So that as the authority increased, the domain shrinked: Political authority, scientific, popular, sectarian.

Add. Mss. 4939, p. 92.

[The] political character of false religions [is] due to their national character. So . . . Christianity can only acknowledge principle above all national difference. . . . The church is without political influence from want of political doctrine. But the strong development of national feeling makes it very hard for the church to adopt any fixed principles. Science must prepare the way for her to recover her just influence in civil society.

Add. Mss. 4860, p. 43.

It is beyond doubt that absolute power has an innate tendency to brush aside all restrictions upon it. The defenders of absolutism tend to forget justice in the same way that radical supporters of freedom forget duty. The renunciation of conscience is as much a requirement of absolutism as it is of revolution. This striving for absolutism is an integral part of the papal system. Indeed, it is the *nisus formativus* of the modern papacy. We are dealing with an immoral force. It does not possess the same character of brutality as the contending factions in the French Revolution, because it is not attempting to achieve power from below. But it has the same sinful character. It wishes to use evil as a means of achieving good. . . .

1881/1882, translated from the German. Döllinger III, pp. 266–267.

In politics as in science the church need not seek her own ends—she will obtain them if she encourages the pursuit of the ends of science, which are truth—and of the state, which are liberty.

November 12, 1861. Acton-Simpson II, p. 195.

The Christianity of a science consists in its own real, free, healthy and consistent progress and development. Real science and Christianity cannot come into conflict.

Add. Mss. 5528, p. 53.

In the experimental sciences, where the insufficiency of our knowledge produces a corresponding incompleteness in our perception of the harmony between science and religion, we are compelled to proceed on the admission that, though there can be no discrepancy between God's words and His works, the harmony is not always fully apparent. But this separation cannot be admitted in life, or in those kinds of thought which directly affect practice. All those ideas which influence our actions must necessarily be brought into harmony with religion, which is the supreme guide of our actions.

"The Roman Question," *Rambler* n.s. 2 (January 1860):138. Acton-Simpson II, p. 32.

Innocent XI, the only pontiff in three centuries who has been run for beatification. His action, in the decline of papal power, foreshadowed how much might one day be done by joining the ascending party. If the papacy separated itself from the cause of authorities and joined the rising, ascending cause of freedom.

Add. Mss. 4953, p. 79.

Christianity does not promise new ideas, but a new efficacy and energy.

Add. Mss. 5392, p. 166.

Christianity is the gospel of the poor. Civilization is the gospel of the rich. Christianity leads us to think most of the masses, most of the poor. To think more of distributing the benefits of culture than of centralizing.

Add. Mss. 4960, p. 103.

Church: once for equality—now for the greatest inequality; once for toleration, for milder punishment, for liberty, now for despotism by herself.

Add. Mss. 4980, p. 57.

The example of our Lord, more eloquent than his words, impressed men with the glory of voluntary poverty. Consider, in [the] spirit of Christianity, how much comes from the life of our Lord. To many it is everything—to the millions that cannot read, that have no sense of metaphysics, that are confused by controversy, it has been everything.

Add. Mss. 5847, p. 21.

Liberal Catholics may be defined as those who demand freedom not only *for* the Church but also *in* the Church, those who wish to see the arbitrary authority of both Church and State in religious matters made subordinate to the rule of law and tradition. This alone defines the goal and hope of Liberal Catholicism, but not its principle and not its method. This is a question which concerns the constitution of the Church rather than its dogma; it is a question of law rather than of theology. It is an important point in the present controversy within the Church; but it is not the decisive issue. It is not the relationship to authority, but rather the relationship to science, not freedom but truth which forms the real core of the issue.

April 13, 1870. Döllinger II, p. 314.

V
TOLERATION

Persecution can only be avoided—Liberty can only be secured—by liberality in religion.

Add. Mss. 4991, p. 128.

Separation of church and state necessary for Liberty. If united the state is intolerant. If quite separated, the church is intolerant. Their influence on each other is required.

Add. Mss. 5006, p. 344.

Early Christianity claimed only one liberty—the mother of all—religious liberty.

Add. Mss. 5006, p. 23.

The Edict of Nantes forms an epoch in the progress of toleration, that is, in the history of liberty, which is the marrow of all modern History.

Acton, *Lectures on Modern History*, p. 171.

Toleration could not be claimed by law or custom. Therefore it introduced the new element of abstract right.

Add. Mss. 5007, p. 63.

Religious liberty does not advance with civil [liberty].

Add. Mss. 5006, p. 286.

Persecution is immoral if it compels conformity. For compulsory religion is powerless as a moral motive. But oppressed religion is not powerless.

On the contrary, it is more efficient than religion triumphant and sustained by states.

Add. Mss. 5006, p. 114.

Every religion may be sincerely held. But the man who deprives another of his legitimate freedom cannot be sincere. Hence violence of passions in the strife between liberty and power.

Add. Mss. 5602, p. 3.

Compulsory conformity is contrary to the notion of liberty, but liberty is not essential to every actual state. It is the highest fruit of political cultivation, and the rare reward of political virtue. . . . Its characteristic sign and manifestation is self-government; and it is only as a fruit and result of self-government, that religious liberty necessarily follows. Lower down in the scale of progress, liberty is impossible and toleration ruinous; and when this is the case, religious compulsion is entirely natural and unavoidable.

"Venn's Life of St. Francis Xavier," *Home and Foreign Review* II (January 1863):188–189. Döllinger I, p. 287.

No epoch in Christian history when religious liberty was an innovation. It was from early times a familiar principle. It was deliberately rejected. Invincible ignorance does not protect persecutors. The other idea was always present—was deliberately rejected.

Add. Mss. 4963, p. 217.

Men have not a right to be tolerated. It is conditional. If they are persecutors, they can be tolerated only because there is no danger from them. If they were numerous enough to give trouble, to make life unsafe, they would not be left free. Therefore men are tolerated not because they are flesh and blood but because they are not dangerous to society.

Add. Mss. 5006, p. 254.

Nobody advocates absolute and universal toleration. The people of Canaan who sent their children through fire to Moloch; the Mexicans, who put 80,000 victims to death at a single festival; the Russian sect of suicides, of whom 1700 once burnt themselves to death in a fiery pit; the Thugs, whom, in living memory, the English exterminated in India, [all these] claim no toleration. Evidently these are all opinions on morals inconsistent with the existence of society, and the state has to determine where to draw the line.

Add. Mss. 5006, p. 35.

History

I
THE STUDY OF HISTORY

History is not a master but a teacher. It is full of evil. It is addressed to free men who choose among its examples. Like experimental science—in which many unsuccessful experiments prepare the way to discovery.

Add. Mss. 5648, p. 51.

History ought to be the strongest influence in the formation of character.

Add. Mss. 4942, p. 14.

How is man made superior to prejudice, passion, and interest? By the study of History and the pursuit of the required character.

Add. Mss. 4981, p. 63.

Resist your time—take a foothold outside it—see other times and ask yourself whether the time of our ancestors is fit for us.

Add. Mss. 5011, p. 108.

Knowledge of history means choice of ancestors.

Add. Mss. 4981, p. 53.

To be governed not by the Past, but by knowledge of the Past—Different things.

Add. Mss. 4993, p. 142.

Live both in the future and the past. Who does not live in the past does not live in the future.

Add. Mss. 5608, n.n.

History not only a particular branch of knowledge, but a particular mode and method of knowledge in other branches. Historic thinking is more than historical knowledge.

Add. Mss. 5011, p. 340.

Every generation obtains a new point of view and has a more advanced conception of history.

Add. Mss. 4960, p. 67.

Not what we have come to, but what we have gone through. Each age is an essential of the world's history, and has its influence and its lessons for the future.

Add. Mss. 4960, p. 63.

Each age is worthy of study—to be understood for its own sake, for the way in which it has met its problems, and its share in the suffering of mankind—not as a stepping stone to the present. The wisdom acquired is not carried forward—is not part of the increasing current. It has to be recovered from the place wherein it is buried—from the records of history.

Add. Mss. 4960, p. 65.

Influence of History complex and manifold. It is a combination of many elements, many forces, negation of a single principle—faggot of many combined. That is what the contemplation of history teaches first of all: The most distinct and evident lesson is that the machine is worked by many forces and that the dominion of a single one is against experience.

Add. Mss. 4993, p. 214.

The value of history is its certainty—against which opinion is broken up.

Add. Mss. 4942, p. 3.

History a school of politics away from home where there may be family tradition, class interest, individual passion. Induction requires to be drawn from a large area, and tested by many examples.

Add. Mss. 4981, p. 35.

History, by its abundance, its variety, its unity, delivering men from the authority of men and substituting ideas for systems.
>   Add. Mss. 5436, n.n.

History had never been made the oracle of politics. Montesquieu, with airy pedantry, had taken from it whatever it gave to sustain him. Smith, supposed to be the model of deduction, used its examples with discrimination. Burke used it fully—but Burke ended by confessing that it was but a reed to lean on. Nobody even knew how history serves the science. It serves it by teaching it to know itself. How very late this idea, not of a literary history, but a doctrinal history, awoke amongst us. Savigny was always pointing the way.
>   Add. Mss. 5011, p. 15.

History convinces more people than philosophy—appeals to a larger circle. Its proofs only apparent, its superiority only real, when they are not colored so as to cause suspicion.
>   Add. Mss. 5011, p. 20.

Men turn to history because their memory is stronger than their power of reasoning—not from a historic spirit.
>   Add. Mss. 4993, p. 242.

Idea that there is something greater and more durable than men— making of history.
>   Add. Mss. 4929, p. 118.

History governed when the knowledge of history did not exist. When the knowledge of history came, the power of history departed.
>   Add. Mss. 5011, p. 238.

Wherein history is liberal: Teaches disrespect, shows up horrors, follies, errors, crimes of the ablest and the best. Slowness of all progress.
>   Add. Mss. 5011, p. 14.

Science not Liberal. Only History a security.
>   Add. Mss. 5608, n.n.

History is a hardy plant that does not flourish in the midst of peace and plenty. Truth is best known when it is most assailed.

"Father Theiner's Publications," *Rambler* n.s. 10 (October 1858):266. Acton-Simpson I, p. 78.

Everyone knows the gaps and weaknesses of his own system. History teaches him the strength and reason of others.

Add. Mss. 4993, p. 303.

There is nothing more necessary to the men of science than its history—and the logic of discovery. The way in which truths are predicted, repressed, recovered, disputed, acknowledged—victorious. The way error is detected, the use of hypothesis, of imagination, the mode of testing—great examples, great maxims. The instructions derived from the errors of great men. In all these ways the Past is a teacher, even in mechanics.

Add. Mss. 5011, p. 266.

History gives its due place to religion. Science moves in a world without it. That is why on the whole, history is the refuge of religion in a scientific age.

Add. Mss. 5689, n.n.

Knowledge of the past is knowledge of religious forces—knowledge of the present is study of forces that are not religious. One sails without gas—the other without ballast.

Add. Mss. 4941, p. 106.

Study of history better than writing of history. The writer sacrifices so much for effect. This is to fix images on men's mind. And the image conceals the reality.

Add. Mss. 4943, p. 311.

II
THE WRITING OF HISTORY

Each generation detects new problems in the vast book and adds some of its own.

Add. Mss. 5011, p. 362.

Pursue the main chain—from generation to generation the scene changes, as the lighted torch is passed from hand to hand.

 Add. Mss. 5011, p. 369.

History not only a voyage of discovery, but a struggle with enemies. The enemy has been men in authority. Strong desire to hide the truth.

 Add. Mss. 4931, p. 48.

All modern history, as learnt and taught and accepted, is purely conventional. For sufficient reasons, all persons in authority combined, by a happy union of deceit and concealment, to promote falsehood.

 Add. Mss. 4931, p. 209.

History as Emancipator: It is the examiner, sifter, questioner of Tradition. Receives not for acceptance but for examination what the wisdom of ancestors has handed down. Large experience of the artifice with which that historical literature has been a vast conspiracy against truth. Falsehood has taken many forms—lies, misrepresentations, concealment, distortion, poetry, legend, myth, forgery. Many forms, but only one substance.

 Add. Mss. 5011, p. 276.

By going from book to manuscript, and from library to archive, we exchange doubt for certainty, and become our own masters. We explore a new heaven and a new earth, and at each step forward, the world moves with us.

 "Notes on Archival Researches 1864–1868," in McElrath, p. 140.

History advances perpetually, by increase of material, by experience, and by perfect methods [and] additional problems.

 Add. Mss. 4981, p. 99.

The character of the present day is much more strongly marked by the discoveries in moral than in physical science. The science of history and the science of language, and the philosophical study of jurisprudence, are all new discoveries of this century. Before this, historical controversy was nonsense, for the materials were imperfect and the method did not exist. There is as great a difference between history now and in Gibbon's time as between the astronomy before Copernicus and after him.

September 3, 1861. Acton-Simpson II, p. 161.

The progress is so rapid, that the materials used quite lately are insecure. Very little indeed remains of books which were classics a generation ago. The epochs, part of which have been thoroughly examined, are very few. The second century; early history; gradual recovery of Egypt and of Assyria; the later centuries of the Middle Ages; and even the time between the English and the French Revolution.

Add. Mss. 5011, p. 269.

Escape from the milieu, from heredity. Twentieth century will pretty well complete material—and establish science of laws in History.

Add. Mss. 5406, p. 18.

The Historian, responsible for facts, not for the inductions. Therefore his work is done when the facts are determined. He has not got to bridge every chasm, to stop every hole.

Add. Mss. 5436, n.n.

Historians offend if they work their ideas out too much. They must lay no constraint on the reader. They must allow largely for difference of opinion. They only press the purely historical point—not any other.

Add. Mss. 5011, p. 55.

It is the professional curse of historians, that they shall grope through many dark paths and read many worthless books.

Add. Mss. 5608, n.n.

A historian has no standard or organ for minds greater than his own. He reduces them to the level of his comprehension, if not of his capacity. . . . There are characters in history that wait long before a historian appears capable of understanding, appreciating, sympathising with them.

Add. Mss. 5528, p. 70.

Many men have compressed their entire wisdom into portable aphorisms. Others have had it done for them.

Add. Mss. 5692, n.n.

The best men spend the best part of their lives as editors.

Add. Mss. 4942, p. 39.

My theory is that in history the historian has to disappear and leave the facts and ideas objectively to produce their own effect.

January 19, 1861. Acton-Simpson II, p. 111.

Definitions and formulas dangerous in history—unfit to express its abundance and variety.

Add. Mss. 5608, n.n.

The more a character approaches an epigram or a definition, the more it gratifies the author and deceives the reader.

Add. Mss. 4993, p. 244.

Character not to be designated by epithet or epigram, but complex and varying.

Add. Mss. 4960, p. 309.

History to become a science must not depend on something which is unscientific. It has to be so written that Royalist and Republican shall not differ on the character of Washington—French and English on the character of Napoleon—Christian and Pagan on the character of Julian. To this sort of writing, which is equally valuable to men, whatever way of thinking, Treitschke contributes little.

Add. Mss. 4956, p. 178.

History never loses touch with earth, never gives up contact with fact—nor loses its contemplation of ideas and principles.

Add. Mss. 5011, p. 243.

A man may be measured by his power of understanding others, of entering into systems of ideas not his own. That is the union that history teaches. That is the perpetual lesson of history. Unknown in the Middle Ages.

Add. Mss. 4982, p. 247.

We enlarge history. We do not abandon one sort of it for another. Affairs of state continue to prevail. Not abandon public events for sociology, or the state, for the condition of society.

Add. Mss. 4981, p. 71.

Tendency is towards sociology. Reduction of the personal element and of the range of providence. So, against religion.

Add. Mss. 4981, p. 66.

Not go much into private concerns, in public life or in history, which, as distinct from biography, is a record of public life.

Add. Mss. 5011, p. 29.

A reason for abstinence and reserve in judging. Keep away from private life. Until they enter visibly into publicity, it is best to make little of them. It is too generally unfair, otherwise to examine the private life of Washington or Pitt.

Add. Mss. 5002, p. 24.

Not to insist, as a rule, on things relating to private life. We often know nothing about them—and it gives too great an advantage to those who have not been found out.

Add. Mss. 5011, p. 251.

National character: Nobody doubts it who knows schools or armies.

Add. Mss. 4939, p. 84.

It is a sound maxim to employ the indefinable arbitrary factor of national character with caution as a cause of constant effects.

Add. Mss. 4959, p. 137.

History deals with ideas—facts alone useless.

Add. Mss. 4943, p. 311.

Distrust the verdict of history and do not let your judgement merge in public opinion—often wrong, because preferring literary merit to substance.

Add. Mss. 5011, p. 56.

Historians do not fear to be in contradiction with themselves. Take facts when proved even if hard to reconcile with facts equally proved. He must accept imperfections of knowledge.

Add. Mss. 5608, n.n.

The idea that what is clear is certain is absurd to the eye of the historian.

Add. Mss. 5608, n.n.

The great secret of method: Combination of different sciences and their lessons.

Add. Mss. 4931, p. 60.

A historian, like a philosopher, becomes noxious and dangerous, by exclusion.

Add. Mss. 5015, p. 60.

Everything systematic is anti-historical.

November 28, 1861. Acton-Simpson II, p. 213.

Kritik = the secret of history.

Add. Mss. 5654, n.n.

How much is History influenced by literature? Politics made by political books. History made by works on History. French Revolution largely the result of books—not facts.

Add. Mss. 4991, p. 182.

Imaginary facts exercise a real power over the thoughts and deeds of men. . . . Those fictitious events which, by imperceptible degrees, have established themselves in unquestioned belief, actually control and modify, and sometimes even form, opinions on matters both of theory and practice. Among the different elements which go to make up the body of opinion in a given age, there is scarcely one which has been so little investigated as this belief in fables. The interests and passions of each age, its ruling ideas, the degree of its enlightenment, and the extent of its knowledge, have often been carefully studied by historians who have cast aside, as unconnected with the investigation of truth, and as only likely to mislead, ideas which are proved to be absolute and universal delusions. . . . Men are influenced directly by traditions which they understand to be their own. A thoroughly fictitious idea of French history had much to do with the Revolution; and a living writer, justly arguing that the results of Niebuhr's researches have not impaired the value of the legendary records of early Rome, because it behoves us to know not only the true course of events, but that impression of it which was a living force in the Roman mind, has rehearsed with erudite solemnity the poetic fables of Picus and Evander.

"Medieval Fables of the Popes," *Home and Foreign Review* III (October 1863): 610. Acton-Simpson III, p. 115.

The best of all history is recent history.

Add. Mss. 5684, n.n.

Modern history real—we see the infinite complexity of political calculation, the variety of motives. Unlike Plutarch or Procopius.

Add. Mss. 5655, n.n.

Modern History more dependent on great men: custom and imitation are collective—but initiative, invention are personal—influence of personality therefore greater.

Add. Mss. 5011, p. 268.

III
THE ETHICS OF HISTORY

The first thing is morality, and the morality of history consists in a just severity in public life.

Add. Mss. 4981, p. 8.

History is the record of divine judgements—a limit and a law to man.

Add. Mss. 4931, p. 31.

The emergencies of practical politics have introduced a false morality— and it is the mission of history to expose it.

Add. Mss. 5011, p. 80.

There is no cause which history does not damage or which is not the ruin of history to serve. The writer must put aside his private convictions.

Add. Mss. 5653, p. 49.

History cannot accept the ethics of churches—has its own. Tests applied to ascertain truth belong to its methods, that is, tests of veracity. Its prohibitions concern whatever impedes veracity.

Add. Mss. 4866, p. 121.

We owe the greatest veneration and most entire obedience to the Pontiff under whom we live. We have neither the means nor the duty of judging his actions. But, with respect to the past, it is very different. The historian has a judicial office to fulfill; and if Catholics were bound to approve or excuse whatever the Popes have done, they would be obliged often to do violence to their reason and conscience. Such a necessity would be an insurmountable obstacle to the conversion of those who are out of the Church.

Letter to the Editor, *Weekly Register* (9 June 1855); reprinted in Döllinger III, p. 429.

Scientific treatment requires to be pursued sine acceptione personarum. Only a Jansenist can say that the pope or a Saint was not liable to sin and error, or that the church has the same infallibility in government as in faith. Where such personages appear in a history they cannot be treated as subject to different laws from other men. . . .

June 9, 1861. Newman XIX, p. 510.

To judge—try—the cause of history and politics, which is living history, not by physical or metaphysical, but by a moral standard.

Add. Mss. 4956, p. 114.

A wise man governs his life by plain maxims, still more a historian. He applies those tests that all know, that all understand, and all can apply.

Add. Mss. 5015, p. 154.

To commit murder is the work of a moment—exceptional. To defend it is a constant and shows a more perverted conscience.

Add. Mss. 4939, p. 74.

The strong man with the dagger is followed by the weaker man with the sponge. First, the criminal who slays; then the sophist who defends the slayer.

Acton, *Lectures on the French Revolution*, p. 92.

The honest historian begins by telling the worst that can be truly told of the just cause, which is sacred to him—and the best of the unjust.

Add. Mss. 5015, p. 56.

History demands sympathy for those we do not love, and detachment from those we do.

Add. Mss. 5011, p. 106.

The sincerity of a writer, in moral quality, is tested more by his treatment of friends than of enemies.

Add. Mss. 4931, p. 189.

Praise is the peril of historians. It depresses the moral standard. To be severe, may sometimes be an injustice but it preserves the integrity and sovereignty of the moral code.

Add. Mss. 5011, p. 100.

History undermines heroes.

Add. Mss. 5002, p. 39.

Take care that no reputation is important to you. Do not seek to defend them. It always depresses the moral code.

Add. Mss. 5608, p. 9.

Impartial history does full justice to the enemy, to the vanquished— and gives means of judging one's friends. The reader looking at the particular fact, has the means of forming his own independent opinion on it.

Add. Mss. 4981, p. 72.

History is truly the school of Liberality. It is at once the destroyer of respect. You have to treat the greatest power, antiquity, and fame as unemotionally as a dismissed waiter or a saucy apprentice.

Add. Mss. 4993, p. 217.

Letters . . . give the means of knowing character, as a man is not better than his word, and generally betrays low-water mark in his undraped private correspondence.

Letter to Gladstone, May 23, 1890, in Acton, *Correspondence*, p. 233.

History has done much to encourage the delight in war. The motive has been to make men willing to fight, and to dissimulate the discouraging facts: The night after the battle; the scenes in the hospital;

the horrible wounds; the ruined homes; the devastation; the suffering and misery; the terror of sudden death; the horrors of captured towns. All kept out of sight.

Add. Mss. 4981, p. 64.

Understand what the historian refuses to tell: The degrading misery of the poor; the horror of the battlefield; the scenes in the hospital; the smallness, selfishness, and cowardice of great men; the depravity of wealth.

Add. Mss. 4960, p. 87.

You cannot judge until you have said the worst. You cannot estimate historic phenomena by the most striking fact, or by the best, or by the average. You must be careful to determine the very worst—to be sure there is no deeper depth, before you enunciate an opinion.

Add. Mss. 5011, p. 99.

History is the only immortality known to unbelief, the only reward beyond the grave.

Add. Mss. 5011, p. 95.

The experience of history teaches that the uncounted majority of those who get a place in its pages are bad. We have to deal chiefly, in life, with people who have no place in history, and escape the temptations that are on the road to it. But most assuredly, now as heretofore, the Men of the Time are, in most cases, unprincipled, and act from motives of interest, of passion, of prejudice cherished and unchecked, of selfish hope or unworthy fear.

Letter to Mary Gladstone, January 25, 1882, in Paul, p. 228.

In history there is folly from passion, but no stupidity. It deals with men who were wicked, but seldom stupid.

Add. Mss. 4929, p. 97.

Crimes are not always punished in this life, but folly, always.

Add. Mss. 5011, p. 95.

History prevents men from shutting themselves up in congenial company.

Add. Mss. 4993, p. 312.

My theory weakens interest in character. A certain proportion of courage, hopefulness, veracity is common. In normal quantities they do not determine character. And these variations of mixture do not make progress. They exist in all ages. They add nothing. Peter the Great was wonderful; but so was William the Conqueror. What characterizes, what adds force and denotes progress is not what a man is, but what he has and does. His legacy to mankind is not his personality, but his idea. So S. Francis, S. Augustine, Socrates, Gracchus, Zeno. That Shakespeare was drunk, that More joked, that Turgot put all his irons in the fire—matters not.

Add. Mss. 5407, p. 52.

You can prove geometry to every man, not history. You can only prove history to men of good will.

Add. Mss. 5011, p. 364.

For between two honest men there ought to be no serious differences of opinion in history.

Add. Mss. 5648, p. 17.

By an honest historian we mean one who pleads no cause, who keeps no shelter for a friend, no pillory for a foe—who does the same justice to that which he loathes and to that which he loves.

Add. Mss. 4981, p. 192.

We write history for those who disagree with us.

Add. Mss. 4960, p. 119.

We might wait long if we watched for the man who knows the whole truth and has the courage to speak it, who is careful of other interests besides his own, and labours to satisfy opponents, who can be liberal towards those who have erred, who have sinned, who have failed, and deal evenly with friend and foe—assuming that it would be possible for an honest historian to have a friend.

Acton, *Lectures on the French Revolution*, p. 373.

IV
HISTORY AND PROGRESS

History may be used to subjugate or to emancipate—to close enquiry or to promote it.

Add. Mss. 4931, p. 32.

That is what history does for us. It gives us the line of progress, the condition of progress, the demonstration of error.

Add. Mss. 4960, p. 47.

As a record of progress, history is our emancipation from the Past.

Add. Mss. 5011, p. 70.

History is always moving towards emancipation. Substitutes knowledge of the past for blind submission to the past. One makes us superior and teaches us to judge. The other makes us inferior and teaches us to accept.

Add. Mss. 4960, p. 109.

With the growth of ideas, and their power, the reign of the past, of facts, is not absolute. History ceases to be a master who governs, who commands—and becomes a teacher who instructs and can only instruct by being complete. It has a new function, a function that only operates by being understood, taken or left, as a guide or a warning.

Add. Mss. 4960, p. 88.

If it enables us to govern the future, not live blind—and helpless—by disclosing the secret of progress and the course sailed, the nation that knows the course best and possesses the most perfect chart will have an advantage over others in shaping the destiny of man. So 1870 changed France into a nation of historians.

Add. Mss. 4981, p. 86.

The march of civilization is from the dominion of force to that of ideas—from the reign of will to the reign of law—towards the substitution of divine for human reason.

Add. Mss. 5602, p. 18.

[We] see in the laws of history the sign of wisdom of divine Providence. We recognize it in the striking fact of the advance of mankind through force—through the reign of will to the reign of law.

Add. Mss. 5602, p. 17.

God in Nature more manifest than God in History. Yet History leads to him, and Nature away from him.

Add. Mss. 5011, p. 298.

History is a great innovator and breaker of idols.
Add. Mss. 5011, p. 280.

History is often made by energetic men, steadfastly following ideas, mostly wrong, that determine events.
Acton, *Lectures on Modern History*, p. 70.

Not to believe that certain things, which have been constant, will always continue—one man of genius will alter everything. A single accident—or stray shot—will upset everything.
Add. Mss. 4960, p. 139.

Each age denies and disparages its predecessors.
Add. Mss. 4960, p. 111.

The lesson of modern history: Most religions enjoy the prerogative of perpetual youth, while philosophical systems seldom last a generation.
Add. Mss. 4929, p. 97.

The progress of history tends, not to reconcile opinions, but to make the distinction even greater between them, and to bring out in more naked contrast the antagonism of good and evil.
"The Count de Montalembert," *Rambler* n.s. 10 (December 1858):425. Acton-Simpson I, p. 82; Döllinger I, p. 155.

Is it the law of progress that man, governed mainly by passions and needs, then by inherited prejudices and interests, at last follows knowledge and ideas.
Add. Mss. 4950, p. 121.

The strongest of all obstacles to progress, the reign of the dead.
Add. Mss. 4950, p. 123.

The main events of modern history are endeavors to take a new departure—the main theme of modern history is away from continuity with the past, and the dominion of the dead.
Add. Mss. 4960, p. 29.

All modern history resists government by the past. It endeavors to know the past in order to determine what is good to retain. Not what is consequent, as Roman law or Catholicism. But what is best.
Add. Mss. 4960, p. 28.

Science: Its power to emancipate minds from religion, because it gives a certainty apart from religion. Then it constantly weakened religion as it was. In antiquity deliverance of mankind from religion was progress. NB It was the work of Democracy.
Add. Mss. 4939, p. 330.

Notion of progress: Civilisation produces the survival of the unfittest. The worst elements, and the weakest, are assiduously preserved and propagated.
Add. Mss. 4939, p. 266.

Progress is by contact, by influence, by combination—not by isolation.
Add. Mss. 4960, p. 8.

Not all progress is improvement—no perfection.
Add. Mss. 4960, p. 19.

Progress, if not organic, is nothing but change.
Add. Mss. 4952, p. 221.

Progress, the religion of those who have none.
Add. Mss. 5011, p. 253.

Progress part of the Whig scheme. And Progress essential to Christianity. Christ did not die in vain. Continued his work among men. His action increasing in power. New organs—bent the world to it.
Add. Mss. 4948, p. 326.

Conscience, perception of evil and desire of improvement, that is, what ought to be rather than what is. The disposition to seek makes for progress.
Add. Mss. 4960, p. 33.

How little progress morality has made in 2000 years, though Christianity has intervened, and science, and the accumulations of history.
Add. Mss. 4916, p. 91.

Virtues pass away, but truths remain. Progress lies not in the best men, but in knowledge of what is right—and wrong—in the refinement of the public conscience.

Add. Mss. 4993, p. 315.

Why the antagonism is profound. What Progress has to overcome is crime—the persecution, the tortures, the slaves, the authors of the negro code, the jurists and judges who tormented and burnt witches.

Add. Mss. 5011, p. 209.

Progress is the direction of overcoming natural forces. So the national fades before the universal.

Add. Mss. 4981, p. 140.

Progress consists in this: that men should be governed by authority rather than by force, by opinion rather than by authority, by conscience rather than by opinion.

Add. Mss. 5605, p. 27.

Progress of civilization increases the enlightenment of the will—as it is more enlightened, it is more free.

Add. Mss. 5552, p. 15.

Providence means progress—notion that God is active in history—that Christ pursues His work among men—that His action is not wasted. Grace granted to individuals in vain. But Providence watching over history not in vain. Now Liberty supposes progress. It is an overcoming of what exists, development of potential, destruction of actual. Progress, practically, a modern idea. It comes in with science.

Add Mss. 5011, p. 208.

Progress [is] the work of the individual against authority and majority—otherwise Copernicus, Galileo, Kepler would have been put down. History would have become extinct. Conscience would have been burnt out. Columbus would never have discovered America. The history of progress is the history of the hard won, dearly bought victories of single handed individuals over the resistance of organized and established powers.

Add. Mss. 5602, p. 42.

Modern History tells how the last four hundred years have modified the medieval conditions of life and thought. In comparison with them, the Middle Ages were the domain of stability, and continuity, and instinctive evolution, seldom interrupted by such originators as Gregory VII or St. Francis of Assisi. Ignorant of History, they allowed themselves to be governed by the unknown Past; ignorant of Science, they never believed in hidden forces working onwards to a happier future. The sense of decay was upon them; and each generation seemed so inferior to the last, in ancient wisdom and ancestral virtue, that they found comfort in the assurance that the end of the world was at hand.

Yet the most profound and penetrating of the causes that have transformed society is a medieval inheritance. It was late in the thirteenth century that the psychology of Conscience was closely studied for the first time, and men began to speak of it as the audible voice of God, that never misleads or fails, and that ought to be obeyed always, whether enlightened or darkened, right or wrong. The notion was restrained, on its appearance, by the practice of regarding opposition to Church power as equivalent to specific heresy, which depressed the secret monitor below the public and visible authority. With the decline of coercion the claim of Conscience rose, and the ground abandoned by the inquisitor was gained by the individual. There was less reason then for men to be cast of the same type; there was a more vigorous growth of independent character, and a conscious control over its formation. The knowledge of good and evil was not an exclusive and sublime prerogative assigned to states, or nations, or majorities. When it had been defined and recognised as something divine in human nature, its action was to limit power by causing the sovereign voice within to be heard above the expressed will and settled custom of surrounding men. By that hypothesis, the soul became more sacred than the state, because it receives light from above, as well as because its concerns are eternal, and out of all proportion with the common interests of government. That is the root from which liberty of Conscience was developed, and all other liberty needed to confine the sphere of power, in order that it may not challenge the supremacy of that which is highest and best in man.

The securities by which this purpose has been attempted compose the problem of all later history, and centuries were spent in ascertaining and constructing them. If in the main the direction has been upward, the movement has been tardy, the conflict intense, the balance often uncertain. The passion for power over others can never cease to threaten mankind, and is always sure of finding new and unforeseen allies in continuing its martyrology. Therefore, the method of modern progress was revolution. By a series of violent shocks the nations in succession have struggled to shake off the Past, to reverse the action of Time and the verdict of success, and to rescue the world from the reign of the dead. They have been due less to provocation by actual wrong than to the attraction of ideal right, and the claims that inspired them were universal and detached. Progress has imposed increasing sacrifices on society, in behalf of those who can make no return, from whose welfare it derives no equivalent benefit, whose existence is a burden, an evil, eventually a peril to the community. The mean duration of life, the compendious test of improvement, is prolonged by all the chief agents of civilisation, moral and material, religious and scientific, working together, and depends on preserving, at infinite cost, which is infinite loss, the crippled child and the victim of accident, the idiot and the madman, the pauper and the culprit, the old and infirm, curable and incurable. This growing dominion of disinterested motive, this liberality towards the weak, in social life, corresponds to that respect for the minority, in political life, which is the essence of freedom. It is an application of the same principle of self-denial, and of the higher law.

Taking long periods, we perceive the advance of moral over material influence, the triumph of general ideas, the gradual amendment. The line of march will prove, on the whole, to have been from force and cruelty to consent and association, to humanity, rational persuasion, and the persistent appeal to common, simple, and evident maxims. We have dethroned necessity, in the shape both of hunger and of fear, by extending the scene from Western Europe to the whole world, so that all shall contribute to the treasure of civilisation, and by taking into partnership in the enjoyment of its rewards those who are far off as well as those who are below. We shall give our attention to much that has failed and passed away, as well as to the phenomena of progress, which help to build up the world in which we live. For History must be our deliverer not only from the undue influence of other times, but from the undue influence of our own, from the tyranny of environment and the pressure of the air we breathe. It requires all historic forces to produce their record and submit to judgment, and it promotes the faculty of resistance to contemporary surroundings by familiarity with other ages and other orbits of thought.

In these latter days the sum of differences in international character has been appreciably bound down by the constant process of adaptation and adjustment, and by exposure to like influences. The people of various countries are swayed by identical interests, they are absorbed in the same problems, and thrill with the same emotions; their classics are interchangeable, authorities in science are nearly alike for all, and they readily combine to make experiments and researches in common. Towards 1500, European nations, having been fashioned and composed out of simple elements during the thousand years between the fall of the Roman Empire and that of its successor in the East, had reached full measure of differentiation. They were estranged from each other, and were inclined to treat the foreigner as the foe. Ancient links were loosened, the Pope was no longer an accepted peacemaker; and the idea of an international code, overriding the will of nations and the authority of sovereigns, had not dawned upon philosophy. Between the old order that was changing and the new that was unborn, Europe had an inorganic interval to go through.

Acton, *Lectures on Modern History,* pp. 31–34.

V
THE PHILOSOPHY OF HISTORY

There is as much difference in the old and new notions of God before and since the discovery of the laws of history as before and since the discovery of law in nature. And the science which describes it is the philosophy of History.

Add. Mss. 4916, p. 7.

Only as philosophy of history does history become instructive.

Add. Mss. 4991, p. 56.

Philosophy of history: There must be many, not one. Therefore we must have the history of it, not the thing itself.

Add. Mss. 5002, p. 123.

Hegel—the greatest force ever applied to the theory of History.

Add. Mss. 5011, p. 281.

VI
HISTORIANS

The great point is the history of history.
   Add. Mss. 5436, p. 38.

[History] was, before 1848, the work of men away from public life. Eager for things remote. The triumphs, the controversies referred to Athens or Merovingians. So long it had little purchase to move society. Except Strauss, no writer of history attained anywhere like the influence of Schleiermacher or Hegel or Humboldt. It kept purposely away from the great question that divided mankind—Reformation and Revolution.
   Add. Mss. 4942, p. 40.

History issues from the Romantic school.
   Add. Mss. 5437, p. 18.

There are historians, like Thiers and Ranke, whose cleverness won't allow them to recognize the union of greatness and genius with goodness.
   January 10, 1864. Acton-Simpson III, p. 160.

Niebuhr was always thinking of his own time when he spoke of others— and nobody ever perceived more vividly the unity of Past and Present. In his Roman History he speaks of Ireland.
   Add. Mss. 5015, p. 238.

The discovery of truth a graver matter than attraction of readers. Mommsen, no doubt, began a new epoch. He wrote for scholars, himself the first of scholars. He wrote for students. He won the ear of the public—neglecting proof—by incomparable qualities and by those defects which provoked George Long to confute him in so many volumes.
   Add. Mss. 4956, p. 179.

When you sit down to Macaulay, remember that the Essays are really flashy and superficial. He was not above par in literary criticism; his Indian articles will not hold water; and his two most famous reviews, on Bacon and Ranke, show his incompetence. The essays are only pleasant reading, and a key to half the prejudices of our age. It is the History (with one or two speeches) that is wonderful. He knew nothing respectably before the seventeenth century, he knew nothing of foreign history, of religion, of philosophy, science or art. His account of debates has been thrown into the shade by Ranke, his account of diplomatic affairs by Klopp. He is, I am persuaded, grossly, basely, unfair. Read him therefore to find out how it comes that the most unsympathetic of critics can think him very nearly the greatest of English writers.

Letter to Mary Gladstone, September 1, 1883, in Paul, p. 285.

Excepting Froude, I think [Carlyle] the most detestable of historians. The doctrine of heroes, the doctrine that will is above law, comes next in atrocity to the doctrine that the flag covers the goods, that the cause justifies its agents, which is what Froude lives for. Carlyle's robust mental independence is not the same as originality. The Germans love him because he is an echo of the voices of their own classic age. He lived on the thought of Germany when it was not at its best, between Herder and Richter, before the age of discipline and science. Germany since 1840 is very different from that which inspired him; and his conception of its teaching was a grotesque anachronism. It gave him his most valuable faculty, that of standing aside from the current of contemporary English ideas, and looking at it from an Archimedean point, but it gave him no rule for judging, no test of truth, no definite conviction, no certain method and no sure conclusion. But he had historic grasp—which is a rare quality—some sympathy with things which are not evident, and a vague, fluctuating notion of the work of impersonal forces. There is a flash of genius in "Past and Present," and in the "French Revolution," though it is wretched history. And he invented Oliver Cromwell. That is the positive result of him, and his personal influence over many considerable minds—a stimulating, not a guiding influence.

Letter to Mary Gladstone, February 10, 1881, in Paul, pp. 170–171.

Ideas as Historical Forces

What chiefly distinguishes the modern historical art from that of the ancients is, that the history of ideas is now understood in its bearing on the history of events. . . . To exhibit the course of ideas and the course of events in their parallel progress, and their action on each other is a principal function of the modern historian. . . . If history is to be understood as an intellectual and not as a natural progress, it must be studied as the history of the mind. The accidental will disappear, what seems episodical and isolated will be absorbed and ranged in the harmonious course of history, in proportion as we understand the ideas which have influenced each separate country and each successive age.

Review of Schmidt-Weissenfels, *Geschichte der französischen Revolutionsliteratur,* in the *Rambler* n.s. 2 (November 1859):105–106. Acton-Simpson I, p. 211.

The great object, in trying to understand history, political, religious, literary, or scientific, is to get behind men and to grasp ideas. Ideas have a radiation and development, an ancestry and posterity of their own, in which men play the part of godfathers and godmothers more than of legitimate parents.

Letter to Mary Gladstone, March 15, 1880, in Paul, p. 99.

Progress in ideas, not in institutions. For the world gains by its failures. There is as much to learn from the experience of the nations that have failed, as from the discoveries of truths.

Add. Mss. 5594, p. 45.

There is no unity in the history of institutions, unless one deals with particular countries. But there is a grand unity in the history of ideas— of conscience, or morality, and of the means of securing it. I venture to say that the secret of the philosophy of History lies there: It is the only point of view from which one discovers a constant progress, the only one therefore which justifies the ways of God to man.

September 22, 1882. Döllinger III, p. 312.

Why not institutions. Only in ideas can we see the progress of liberty. It is the great form of progress.

Add. Mss. 5436, p. 7.

We insist on the history of ideas. It is that which rescues history from the grasp of matter, from the struggle for existence, from the reign of hunger and of passion.

Add. Mss. 5015, p. 118.

Ideas mainly govern the world. That is the reason of progress. If they alone governed, progress would be constant, because demonstration is irresistible. But it is partly governed by habit, conditions, interests, passion.

Add. Mss. 4941, p. 207.

An epoch [begins] not [with] a new man, but a new idea or a new force.

Add. Mss. 5692, n.n.

The more ideas dominate, the more they supply the text of history over prejudice, passion, and interest. Therefore ideas, not civilizations, are the object. Ideas are international—make history international: A. Smith, Burke, Bentham, Darwin, Hegel, Comte, Helmholtz. Ideas furnish the missing link with the past—men act from their own ideas, not those of ancestors.

Add. Mss. 4981, p. 70.

Ideas are extraterritorial, and pay no duty as they pass from land to land.

Add. Mss. 4981, p. 77.

New ideas are powerless unless they are proved. Tradition needs no argument beyond custom.

Add. Mss. 4941, p. 44.

Middle Ages governed by institutions and customs. Modern times acknowledge the superior power of ideas and the character and genius of single men.

Add. Mss. 4960, p. 9.

Government by idea tends to take in everything—to make the whole of society obedient to the idea. Spaces not so governed are unconquered—beyond the border—unconverted—unconvinced—a future danger.

Add. Mss. 4941, p. 44.

No certainty of the advent of great men strong enough to cause great changes according to ideas. But it is certain that the conditions of an age tend to change by slow degrees, as evils are discovered.

Add. Mss. 4952, p. 220.

The permanent deposit of History, not laid by politicians and soldiers whose work passes away. But by the men of ideas—constructive layers of truth and knowledge and suggestive error.

Add. Mss. 4993, p. 238.

Representative men walk in grooves, speak as others do, and tell us nothing. Original men break new ground and carry the world forward. Universities deal chiefly with the former, with the acknowledged. We must look out for the unacknowledged masters of thought.

Add. Mss. 5011, p. 22.

[Of Christopher Columbus]: His fallacies were worth more than the science of all the universities in Christendom.

Add. Mss. 4902, p. 140.

The training of men is traditional. They go with the currents. They are borne on by their surroundings, and determined by the accidents of contact. They undergo influences, they do not resist or control them. They generally represent their time, by which is meant the time of their youth, the years of formation. They seldom get an Archimedian point.

Add. Mss. 4977, p. 277.

How much a man is the product of time and place and race. Culture emancipates him, gives him the world to choose from for his governing ideas. By the predominance of mind over matter [it] releases him from his nation in the past, and by the predominance of moral over intellectual matters, releases him from his countrymen at the present.

Add. Mss. 4981, p. 23.

It is dangerous to take your ideas from others. You must take your information from them. But ideas, like experience, must be your own.

Add. Mss. 5011, p. 23.

How necessary it is for people to have an ideal object which excites their energies beyond any material thing though the ideal is never realized—luckily perhaps in general.

March 12, 1860. Acton-Simpson II, pp. 52–53.

Deeds as well as words are the signs of thoughts, and if we consider only external events, without following the course of ideas of which they are the expression and the result, we shall have but a lame notion of history and shall overlook an alternate link in the chain of human progress. The taking of the Bastille, for instance, was a great sign; the appearance of Sieyès pamphlet, *What is the Third Estate?* was a greater fact.

Review of Schmidt-Weissenfels, *Geschichte der französischen Revolutionsliteratur,* in the *Rambler* n.s. 2 (November 1859):107. Acton-Simpson I, p. 211.

The great constant influence of the Middle Ages on the modern age was not in institutions or customs, but in ideas. It was done by books, and by individual writers of books, many of whom found no audience in their time.

Add. Mss. 4960, p. 205.

Government rules the present. Literature rules the future.

Add. Mss. 4982, p. 131.

The world is governed by ideas. Also by facts. They represent the past, ideas, the future.

Add. Mss. 4960, p. 141.

Those books which have most often influenced men—the polemical writings of divines, and the political speculations of philosophers and statesmen—rarely possess that sort of merit which secures renown.

But to the historian they are more important than works of great genius. He is more interested in the *New Atlantis* than in the *Advancement of Learning*, in the *Areopagitica* than in *Paradise Lost*.

Review of Schmidt-Weissenfels, *Geschichte der französischen Revolutionsliteratur*, in the *Rambler* n.s. 2 (November 1859):106. Acton-Simpson I, p. 211.

It was by method that Bacon and Descartes renewed the world.

Add. Mss. 4978, p. 20.

Hegel's philosophy is, in many shapes, the subtlest pervading influence of the present day.

March 15, 1864. Acton-Simpson III, pp. 189–190.

Vice of historians: Care for facts more than ideas. Therefore living on the outside of things—not feeding their minds with wisdom.

Add. Mss. 5692, n.n.

The Ethics of Public Life

.

Politics = the ethics of public life.
Add. Mss. 4897, p. 190.

Every man [is] the best, the most responsive judge of his own advantage. Therefore don't let some one else interfere.
Add. Mss. 4939, p. 196.

It is easier to find people fit to govern themselves than people fit to govern others.
Add. Mss. 4941, p. 109.

Character should be the result of design and effort—not of tradition or accidental surroundings.
Add. Mss. 4960, p. 108.

Whether a man devotes himself to the study of politics, to public life, or to the literature of his age, or to history, the result is nearly the same. One must master much the same topics of learning and cultivate the same faculties.
Add. Mss. 4941, p. 282.

Moral precepts are constant through the ages and not obedient to circumstances.
Add. Mss. 4982, p. 24.

Right and wrong are not contiguous. Politics interpose and occupy the space between.
Add. Mss. 5434, p. 14.

To get rid of needless ballast is a main precept of wisdom.
Add. Mss. 5406, p. 65.

648

The people who foresee, who weigh, who prepare for obstacles, go to work with the most power.
Add. Mss. 5692, n.n.

If our actions are determined by the benefit to our neighbors, we may tell lies. Many untruths are distinctly beneficial. Often we should be sorry not to be deceived. We should resent being made to hear unpleasant truths—as in the case of illness, of misfortune, of disgrace. The doctrine of salutary falsehood would prevail, and with that doctrine, justice could not be administered without the practical use of torture.
Add. Mss. 4939, p. 109.

The notion of sin and repentance waned with the belief in authority. Men thought they could make good the evil they did.
Add. Mss. 4861, p. 103.

Morals exist only in the form of religion for uneducated races. Politics, then, cannot be separated from one without giving up the other. The only way to bring untutored conscience to bear on public duties is to connect them with religion.
Add. Mss. 5006, p. 168.

Putting up a moral standard which was not a religious one undermined religion. It gave the advantage to the lowest dogmatic types, that had no history, had no power to abuse. Promoted, at least, Rationalism, or Scepticism.
Add. Mss. 5434, p. 23.

Morality must be set up apart from religion; for every religion in its turn has promoted its own cause by crimes. As, in time of need, it goes wrong about morality, so about politics.
Add. Mss. 5588, p. 45.

Classics: Religion alone is no safety for morality. Classical philosophy, giving an independent morality, prevents men from falling under such teachers as Knox and Suarez.
Add. Mss. 5594, p. 69.

Those who judge morality by the intention have been less shocked at the crimes of power, where the temptation is so strong and the danger so slight, than at those committed by men resisting oppression. Assuredly, the best things that are loved and sought by men are religion and liberty—they, I mean, and not pleasure or prosperity, not knowledge or power. Yet the paths of both are stained with infinite blood; both have been often a plea for assassination, and the worst of men have been among those who claimed to promote each sacred cause.

Acton, *Lectures on the French Revolution*, p. 93.

Duty kept up by the gift of prayer, and prayer does not exist without religion.

Add. Mss. 5588, p. 45.

No country can be free without religion. It creates and strengthens the notion of duty. If men are not kept straight by duty, they must be by fear. The more they are kept by fear, the less they are free. The greater the strength of duty, the greater the liberty.

Add. Mss. 5588, p. 44.

If moral instead of religious points of view prevail in politics, they will prevail in religion.

Add. Mss. 4929, p. 81.

Gift of reasoning, of logical demonstration, moves truth forward by a constant pressure. If there is a like force of ethical perception, good increases at the expense of evil.

Add. Mss. 4960, p. 61.

Every system of doctrine applies itself to life in its own way. Every dogmatic system creates its own ethical system.

Add. Mss. 5434, p. 50.

If the state says this is obligatory, that is not, the obligatory will appear more sacred than the voluntary. Then, what a religion claims, such as the tithe, is inferior to the tax etc. A new order of sacredness established.

Add. Mss. 5434, p. 28.

Many men can no more be kept straight by spiritual motives than we can live without policemen.

Letter to Mary Gladstone, January 25, 1882, in Paul, p. 228.

You may govern by force, but you cannot at the same time hold by both physical and moral means.

Add. Mss. 4869, p. 13.

There is a very numerous class of politicians who occupy a position closely similar to that of the alchemists and the astrologers in the history of chemistry and astronomy, who imagine politics to be a merely empirical art, and stoutly deny that it corresponds to other sciences, such as political economy and jurisprudence, and is made up of scientific truths and ethical obligations.

"Mr. Grant Duff's Glance over Europe," *Chronicle* (11 January 1868):31. Ryan, p. 390; Döllinger I, p. 494.

No man was richer in sagacious maxims, or in experience of mankind [than was Cardinal Richelieu]; but he was destitute of principle—I mean of political principles, which are the guide of public life as moral principles are the guide of our private lives.

Acton, *Lectures on Modern History*, p. 176.

It seems to me equivalent to a falsehood to vote against the merit of a question, only from general sympathy or resentment towards a party.

June 29, 1861. Newman XIX, p. 522.

You shoot a general who shows cowardice in the field. What punishment is there for the ministers who in the cabinet crouch in terror before the foe, and demoralize the spirit of the people.

Add. Mss. 4862, p. 14.

Public men are stewards of all the interests admitted by the state. We are bound to cherish as carefully the interests of the minority who opposed as of the majority who elected us. Otherwise he is a traitor to his trust.

Add. Mss. 4869, p. 16.

A public man has no right to let his actions be determined by particular interests. He does the same thing as a judge who accepts a bribe. Like a judge he must consider what is right, not what is advantageous to a party or class.

Add. Mss. 4869, p. 2.

We have to live and deal with men of diverse religions and of no religion—of different philosophy and of different combination of philosophy and religion. With men whose knowledge of religion and philosophy is second hand, inaccurate, loose, uncertain, vague. For this situation we require a system of ethics.

Mss. 5692, n.n.

Political life is based on questions of morals. When a man seems to go wrong, not in judgement, but in principle, his friends feel as if they had caught him telling a lie, or cheating at cards, or visiting a brothel.

Add. Mss. 4940, p. 335.

A man without political principles, an unprincipled public man.

Add. Mss. 4944, p. 11.

Whilst you never lose your insight into facts, so you never lose your grasp of principles.

Add. Mss. 5011, p. 112.

You are consistent as long as you change your contrivances and sacrifice them to your principles.

Add. Mss. 4941, p. 295.

That a man is strong by adaptation to surroundings—by following the current—that is a measure of force, not a measure of character.

Add. Mss. 5011, p. 108.

A man does well to rank with the forces of his time. But not to spread his sails to every changing wind.

Add. Mss. 4943, p. 293.

We require that a man shall renounce authorities and majorities, the customs of his country and the ideas of his kindred. [We require] that he shall retain, cultivate, strengthen the resolve. Else we condemn. Socrates, St. Paul, Luther, Jefferson.

Add. Mss. 4942, p. 13.

A convinced man differs from a prejudiced man as an honest man from a liar.

Add. Mss. 4912, p. 98.

The man who never dares to stem the current of the age or to resist the masses is not only a coward but a sophist. And it is the part of great men to stand alone.

Add. Mss. 5648, p. 50.

We require in an honest man, not submission, but resistance and independence.

Add. Mss. 4960, p. 26.

[A] man owes it to his children, to his neighbors, to secure their future and rescue their lives from impediments to holiness and happiness. Therefore he has no right to acquiesce in tyrannical and immoral government.

Add. Mss. 4945, p. 314.

Some believe that men act by interest and passion, cupidity, ambition. Others that they are ready to sacrifice interests to ideas, to give their lives and their property, to a higher cause.

Add. Mss. 4950, p. 191.

The great intellectual and moral defect of the present day . . . [is] the habit of dwelling on appearances, not on realities, of preferring the report to the bullet, and the echo to the report. To spend and lose a majority in some great cause, to be abused and ridiculed and calumniated, seems to the writer a misfortune so great that it is worth while to haul down one's flag rather than incur the risk of it. This is the power of journalism, of salons and club life, which teaches people to depend on popularity and success and not on the guide within, to act not from knowledge, but from opinion, and to be led by opinion of others rather than by knowledge which is their own. . . . Nearly everybody yields up his conscience, his practical judgement, into the keeping of others.

Letter to Mary Gladstone, June 1, 1880, in Paul, p. 108.

Men do not feel enthusiasm for an idea or sacrifice to it. The idea must take a human form. They will do it for a man—or for an institution, or for a body of men. . . . So men care not for a dogma as they do for a church, or political principles as for a party. The doctrine may even disappear behind the body, the idea behind the visible, tangible reality—fact.

Add. Mss. 4944, p. 16.

The idea supersedes the state. A man is more bound to promote it than his country's good. He must rather sacrifice his country than his idea. He must sacrifice his country to his idea. So the Whigs rejoiced over the success of the Americans. The French deplored the conquest of Algiers.

Add. Mss. 5434, p. 21.

Men are always divided on more points than they know of. Time brings on occasions that bring out their differences. Every colleague of today is a future opponent if he only lived a few years. In public life there are no permanent attachments. If private friendship depended on public agreement, it would not be very lasting.

Add. Mss. 4939, p. 254.

If we consider the mass of mankind opposed to good on grounds of moral failure, we make the conflict with them the principal thing, and become indifferent to struggles in which there may fairly be two opinions, and regard a sincere opponent as an opponent not worth powder and shot.

Add. Mss. 5434, p. 19.

A man is lost if he fears to give weapons to adversaries.

Add. Mss. 5608, n.n.

Because you despise a man, you take care not to insult him.

Add. Mss. 5015, p. 55.

If you look for men with international feelings, who can think with many parties, who can feel for what they know to be an error and are solicitous for the foe and the superiority of the adversary as well as the defects of friends—you will lose time and opportunity.

Add. Mss. 4981, p. 190.

False opinions work more mischief than bad men and the most dangerous are those which have not been tested practically in different countries.

Add. Mss. 5011, p. 247.

Every effort at improvement is deemed by its adversaries an injustice to existing merits.
Add. Mss. 5528, p. 55.

It is dangerous as well as revolting to be opposed to adversaries whom one cannot respect. Such contests are to be carried on with scorn and sarcasm.
Add. Mss. 5528, p. 58.

There are two things which cannot be attacked in front, ignorance and narrow mindedness. They can only be shaken by the simple development of the contrary qualities. They will not bear discussion.
January 23, 1861. Acton-Simpson II, p. 116.

I have always considered the polite hypocrite a formidable type of adversary.
"Notes on Archival Researches 1864–1868," in McElrath, p. 131.

It takes a gentleman to live on terms of hearty friendship and kindness and intimacy with men whose ideas and conduct he abhors and when he well knows that they view with contempt and horror the principles on which he shapes his own character and life.
Add. Mss. 4945, p. 188.

Half truths [are] no better than falsehoods. It is always better to speak out candidly.
Add. Mss. 4862, p. 5.

Prejudice to conviction as pride to dignity.
Add. Mss. 4943, p. 308.

An idea not thought out, is not a light, but a will of the wisp. A principle not pursued as far as it will go, is a prejudice.
Add. Mss. 4916, p. 18.

Life's experience dispels prejudice, and so brings opponents together.
Add. Mss. 5468, n.n.

A man's familiar friends should be carefully chosen—and cannot often be chosen by himself.
Add. Mss. 5608, n.n.

An educated man makes a point of avoiding newspapers of his own opinion. The uneducated man seeks them.

    Add. Mss. 4941, p. 294.

The man of culture sees his own circle in its due proportion and in its proper place.

    Add. Mss. 4943, p. 97.

A sense of boredom is a product of luxury, like the gout, and a real epicure tries to escape both, not by avoiding bores only, but by avoiding the sense of their being bored.

    October 13, 1859. Acton-Simpson II, p. 23.

The morality of the periodical press depends on its anonymous character. A high tone of morality can there be maintained by men in whose lips, in private life, it would be a mockery.

    Add. Mss. 5528, p. 32.

A review is not the exponent of other men's ideas. It has a double duty: to bring out the character of the work reviewed, and the importance of the subject—to tell the truth on both. The book reviewed furnishes materials for the former, the reviewer himself must supply the latter.

    Add. Mss. 5528, p. 38.

There is not a more perilous or immoral habit of mind than the sanctifying of success.

    Acton, *Lectures on Modern History*, p. 204.

The idea that Almighty God is not always on the side of the majority, that what succeeds in this world has not always the blessing of the next, that the divine will is weighted in other scales than the scales of numbers.

    Add. Mss. 5602, p. 43.

We contemplate our ideas in the sunlight of heaven, and apply them in the darkness of earth.

    Add. Mss. 4950, p. 263.

Acton on Himself

Nothing is so unclear to me as my own unclarity, no enigma so mysterious as the enigma which my own personality poses for those who know me.

May 12, 1886, translated from the German. Döllinger III, p. 361.

[My story] is the story of a man who started in life believing himself a sincere Catholic and a sincere Liberal; who therefore renounced everything in Catholicism which was not compatible with Liberty, and everything in Politics which was not compatible with Catholicity. As an English Liberal, I judged that of the two parties—of the two doctrines—which have governed England for 200 years, that one was most fitted to the divine purpose which upheld civil and religious liberty. Therefore I was among those who think less of what is than of what ought to be, who sacrifice the real to the ideal, interest to duty, authority to morality.

To speak quite plainly, as this is a confession, not an apology, I carried farther than others the Doctrinaire belief in mere Liberalism, identifying it altogether with morality, and holding the ethical standard and purpose to be supreme and sovereign.

I carried this principle into the study of history when I had the means of getting beyond the common limit of printed books.

There I presently found that there had been a grievous evil in the Church consisting of a practice sanctioned by the theory that much wrong may be done for the sake of saving souls. Men became what we should otherwise call demons, in so good a cause. And this tendency overspread Christendom from the twelfth century, and was associated with the papacy, which sanctioned, encouraged, and employed it. Associated, not exactly identified, for I do not find that Gallicans were better than Ultramontanes. But they had not quite the same retrospective interest or moral solidarity. The Ultramontane, desiring to

657

defend the papacy, had to condone and justify its acts and laws. He was worse than the accomplices of the Old Man of the Mountain, for they picked off individual victims. But the papacy contrived murder and massacre on the largest and also the most cruel and inhuman scale. They were not only wholesale assassins, but they made the principle of assassination a law of the Christian Church and a condition of salvation.

Was it better to renounce the papacy out of horror for its acts, or to condone the acts out of reverence for the papacy? The Papal party preferred the latter alternative. It appeared to me that such men are infamous in the last degree. I do not accuse them of error, as I might impute it to Grotius or Channing, but of crime. I thought that a person who imitated them for political or other motives worthy of death. But those whose motive was religious seemed to me worse than the others, because that which is in others the last resource of conversion was with them the source of guilt. The spring of repentance is broken, the conscience is not only weakened but warped. Their prayers and sacrifices appeared to me the most awful sacrilege.

The idea of putting on the same level an Ultramontane priest and a priest of licentious life was to me not only monstrous but unintelligible. I understood the movement for the glorification of the papacy as a scheme for the promotion of sin. Arbues and Liguori seemed to me the normal and appropriate associates of the Syllabus and the Council; and I was uneasy and perplexed when I saw the honours paid to them were regarded as special, additional facts with a significance of their own.

I heralded the Council by pointing out that the Popes had, after long endeavors, nearly succeeded in getting all the Calvinists murdered. It meant: give them any authority or credit that may be their due, but let it be always subject to that limit and condition. Let everything be conceded to them that is compatible with their avowed character and traditions; but see that you do nothing that could shelter them from the scorn and execration of mankind.

It is well that an enthusiast for monarchy be forced to bear in mind the story of Nero and Ivan, of Louis XIV and Napoleon; that an enthusiast for democracy be reminded of St. Just and Mazzini. It is more essential that an enthusiast of the papacy be made to contemplate its crimes, because its influence is nearer the Conscience; and the spiritual danger of perverted morals is greater than the evil of perverted politics. It is an agency constantly active, pervading life, penetrating the soul by many channels, in almost every sermon and in almost every prayer book. It is the fiend skulking behind the Crucifix. The corruption which comes from revolutionary or absolutist sympathies is far less subtle and expansive. It reaches the lowest regions of the mind and does not poison that which is noblest.

This is my entire capital. It is no reminiscence of Gallicanism. I do not prefer the Sorbonne to the Congregations or the Councils to the Popes. It is no reminiscence of Liberal Catholicism. Rosmini and Lacordaire, Hefele and Falloux seem to me no better than De Maistre, Veuillot, or Perrone. It is nothing but the mere adjustment of religious history to the ethics of Whiggism.

It seems to me that this is very plain sailing, that each step of the process is easy and natural, that those who think it utterly wrong must admit the unity and consistency and simplicity of the exposition; that they may think it a *reductio ad absurdum* of Liberalism more easily than an obscure, a difficult, and unintelligible argument. That is why, hitherto, I have had much difficulty in believing that my doctrine required comment or explanation. I have not felt that it required defence, because I have never really perceived that it was attacked. My impression has rather been that people thought it inconvenient and likely to lead to trouble, and, of course, solitary and new.

Letter to Lady Blennerhassett, February 1879, in Acton, *Correspondence*, pp. 54–57.

I think that there is a philosophy of politics to be derived from Catholicism on the one hand and from the principles of our Constitution of the other, a system as remote from the absolutism of one set of Catholics as from the doctrinaire Constitutionalism of another (the *Correspondant* etc.) [i.e., from continental liberalism].

February 16, 1858. Acton-Simpson I, p. 6.

The one supreme object of all my thoughts is the good of the Church; and I wish to arrange all things so that this may be accomplished as well as my means allow. The greatest good that I can do is by means of literature, for there I have resources greater than any other person, and have collected materials of immense extent. The time has come when I ought to make something of these collections, and it is impossible while I am in Parliament. The good that I can do in the House of

Commons is not greater than that which is in the power of several other Catholic members. I should therefore be sacrificing one sort of activity in which I have advantages such as no other person enjoys, for another in which I should not do anything which is beyond the reach of others. Political influence, and that of a very valuable kind, I shall always continue to possess, while my friendship with Gladstone lasts—for in Catholic matters he trusts me more than anybody. Therefore the question of my own importance is settled; but in fact we must not think of that, but of the means of serving religion; and for the next few years at least I am sure that I am better out of Parliament.

Letter to his wife, May 1865, in McElrath, p. 64.

I cannot bear that Protestants should say the Church cannot be reconciled with the truths or precepts of science, or that Catholics should fear the legitimate and natural progress of the scientific spirit.

July 8, 1861. Newman XX, p. 6.

We must adapt ourselves to this. To be useful to all historically minded people of our tongue.

Add. Mss. 5690, n.n.

The good that men write lives after them, but it is only by patience and prolongation and perseverance that it is to be done at all, with the pen. I hope we shall have patience and fortitude to go on sowing what we shall not reap, although that is a sort of labour which is not its own reward.

December 6, 1860. Acton-Simpson II, p. 98.

I shall never obtain in the *Rambler* any sort of real influence, and the hurry and haste of writing monthly articles harasses and disgusts me. The things I have accumulated in the course of my studies can find no place in it, and whatever I write in a review of such a popular character seems pedantic.

December 20, 1858. Newman XVIII, p. 551.

In the House [of Commons] I find that I am perfectly isolated, and without hopes of obtaining any influence for my principles. I am sure I can do better in another sphere.

June 4, 1861. Newman XIX, p. 504.

We ourselves have in the course of our career met with much obloquy and provoked much censure. And we are sure to meet with it in the future. We have spoken in the sense of no one of the divisions or parties into which our body is divided, and have at various times angered each of them, sometimes nearly all. We regret only if we have given pain to individuals. That we have offended susceptibilities, hurt prejudice, and contradicted many cherished opinions, is merely to say that we have labored earnestly and uncompromisingly.

Add. Mss. 5528, p. 54.

We are not made angry by foolish criticism, and I have less right to than others. Think how unsympathetic my teaching must be to the philistine, the sordid, the technical, the faddist, the coward, the man of prejudice and passion, the zealot etc. This makes more than half the world. So I am always surprised at praise, and wonder only at blame, and especially misinterpretation, in particular places.

Letter of October 30, 1895 to his daughter Annie. Add. Mss. 8121, box 20.

I find that people disagree with me either because they hold that Liberalism is not true, or that Catholicism is not true, or that both cannot be true together.

Add. Mss. 6871, p. 52.

For many years my view of Catholic controversy has been governed by the following chain of reasoning. (1) A crime does not become a good deed by being committed for the good of a church. (2) The theorist who approves the act is no better than the culprit who commits it. (3) That the divine or historian who defends the theorist incurs the same blame.

Add. Mss. 5631, n.n.

Pius the Fifth held that it was sound Catholic doctrine that any man may stab a heretic condemned by Rome, and that every man is a heretic who attacks the papal prerogatives. Borromeo wrote a letter for the purpose of causing a few Protestants to be murdered. Newman is an avowed admirer of Saint Pius and Saint Charles, and of the pontiffs who canonised them. This, and the like of this, is the reason of my deep aversion for him.

Letter to Mary Gladstone, March 21, 1882, in Paul, pp. 242–243.

What I reject and abhor in Catholicism is the godless suppression of morality in favour of dogma, the support of authority through methods that are evil, the corruption of conscience through belief. For me the central issue is not one of dogma, but rather of ethics. The accusation is not error, but rather crime. The question of mass murder absorbs or neutralizes for me the question of power. When mass murder is the issue I can not see bad logic, or erroneous criticism. The poor logician, the baseless critic, who rejects from the heart the teaching of murder, is my comrade, my brother in faith.

    May 1886, translated from the German. Döllinger III, p. 353.

I hoped I was a good whig, and yet had a universal view.

    Letter to his wife, July 10, 1877, in Döllinger III, p. 180.

The whole collection [of my library] was made with a single view to understanding the public life of the time and the world I live in.

    Letter to Gladstone, May 23, 1890, in Acton, *Correspondence*, p. 232.

The source of our ideas is not in us. They pour in from all sides and springs. It takes time to assimilate them. The principle of selection, the point of contact, the link, is what a man finds in himself—and he must be mature before it has done its work and given unity to the whole.

    Add. Mss. 4940, p. 82.

Not to consider books obsolete—they are often restudied.

    Add. Mss. 4941, p. 292.

My life is spent in endless striving to make out the inner point of view, the *raison d'être*, the secret of fascination for powerful minds, of systems of religion and philosophy, and of politics, the offspring of the others, and one finds that the deepest historians know how to display their origin and defects, but do not know how to think or feel as men do who live in the grasp of the various systems.

    Letter to Mary Gladstone, January 21, 1881, in Paul, pp. 158–159.

[Of Augustin Theiner, Papal archivist] That any man should spend years in acquiring many thousands of documents, for nobody's use but his own, and with no better purpose than to form a defined and certain judgement on the problems of controverted history that bear on the living world, was a form of mental infirmity not dreamed of in his pedestrian philosophy.

"Notes on Archival Researches 1864–1868," in McElrath, p. 135.

Being refused at Cambridge, and driven to foreign universities, I never had any contemporaries, but spent years in looking for men wise enough to solve the problems that puzzled me, not in religion or politics so much as along the wavy line between the two. So I was always associated with men a generation older than myself, most of whom died early—for me—and all of whom impressed me with the same moral, that one must do one's own learning and thinking for oneself, without expecting short cuts or relying on other men. And that led to the elaborate detachment, the unamiable isolation, the dread of personal influences, which you justly censure.

Letter to Mary Gladstone, June 3, 1881, in Paul, pp. 208–209.

[Of Ranke] There is no man whose books I have so much read, of whose footsteps I have so constantly followed. I do not owe to him the formation of my opinions, for there is some want of original *Gehalt* in his thought. But he has been my guide to all the original sources of modern history. He has been very much less to me than Döllinger or Roscher, or than Baader and Rothe, for ideas and education; but it is by his means that I became *mündig* in historical study, so that my debt has been great.

Letter to his wife, July 10, 1877, in Döllinger III, p. 179.

[Of Roscher] Assuredly no man on earth has thought my thoughts, and followed out my train of reading as this man has. On every topic we remembered the same books, and reminded each other of the same passages, and corrected each other's quotations. We have the same heroes, the same judgements on the great problems of history, the same favorite writers. I was astonished to find how deep and lasting had been the impression he made on me in the years when my mind was forming, and how strongly his works have influenced my studies. . . . I fancy that I detected in him greater dread of the people, greater reliance on the wisdom of governments, greater admiration for the aristocratic race of statesmen, than I myself feel. . . . The marvelous quality about him is the variety and activity of his mind. He always goes to plays when they act Shakespeare and says that he studies politics in his plays. . . . The secret of [Roscher's] greatness is that, with an immense variety of knowledge, he has always the power of seeing distant things in the same moment, putting them near each other, so that a great light ensues. In that, I think, he excells all men. But I do not find that he binds successive things together by a strong chain of causes. There is an immense deal of illustrations; but not much development. Every step one takes with him is a surprise, because of the striking effect of some unexpected rapprochement of distant facts. I would rather avoid surprises, and proceed by steps so short as to be not only easy, but almost inevitable, softly preparing all that is to come. Mme. Roscher said to me once, what a lot you have read! I answered: I read only the works of Professor Roscher.

The important result [of this visit with Roscher] for me is this: that I have got the measure of my own means and resources. I have seen what the best man knows and thinks. I find that we think nearly the same, and that, in some points, I know nearly the same, as much as he does. I conclude from this test, that whatever may be bad in my book, the book itself will be up to the mark. And so I only want to get back to my books.

Letter to his wife, July 7, 1877, in Döllinger III, pp. 176–178.

As to my tiresome book [*The History of Liberty*], please to remember that I can only say things which people do not agree with, that I have neither disciple nor sympathiser, that this is no encouragement to production and confidence, that grizzled men—except [George Otto] Trevelyan—grow appalled at the gaps in their knowledge, and that I have no other gift but that which you pleasantly describe, of sticking eternal bits of paper into innumerable books and putting larger papers into black boxes.

Letter to Mary Gladstone, February 9, 1884, in Paul, p. 287. Paul omits the name of Trevelyan.

Acton and Döllinger

St. Martin June 16, 1882
[Acton to Döllinger]
My last letter brings me into the midst of the questions we discussed last year. The heavy care which then distracted me perhaps made me less able to express my real meaning, and no doubt my habit of talking German contributed to the failure. Allow me for once to try my chance in English.

It has been suggested that things I have said struck you unfavorably because I seemed to be aiming at some hidden object. There is nothing hidden or untold, and I will do my best to define the view which in the last three years has brought me into collision with your own. For I date my consciousness of divergence from the article on Dupanloup in the XIX Century.

There is an inclination, about the world, to defend one's cause by unfair or illicit means. Much reading of histories with the object of reviewing them long ago made me familiar with this vice and keen in detecting it. The one question I came to ask was this: Is the man honest or dishonest in the use of materials? At the same time I took great pains to consult eminent men who, I thought, could guide me to shortcuts and certain conclusions. With infinite credulity and trust I frequented such authorities as I could find in the chief countries of Europe, and laid in a store of their wisdom. My opportunities were good and my experience a very wide one. For I knew, more or less intimately, and questioned, and tested such men as—Eckstein, Newman, Montalembert, Ventura, Faber, Cullen, Wiseman, Passaglia, Gratry, Dupanloup, De Luca, De Rossi, Brownson, Russell, De Buck, Maret, Darboy, Mermillod, Ketteler, Theiner, Veuillot, Windischmann.

But when I came to study and judge for myself I found that what they told me and preached and wrote was, on many decisive questions,

665

false. I saw that the vice I commonly detected in average writers was usual among great Catholic notabilities. I came, very slowly and reluctantly indeed to the conclusion that they were dishonest. And I found out a special reason for their dishonesty in the desire to keep up the credit of authority in the Church; as the authority of to-day is solidaire with same in the past, and so it is impossible honestly to apply a moral standard to history without discrediting the Church in her collective action. When I got to understand history from the sources, especially from unpublished sources, the reason of all this became obvious. There was a conspiracy to deceive, and this conspiracy was identical with the desire to uphold the hierarchy. Respect for the hierarchy could not stand without disrespect for the law of God. That men might believe the Pope it was resolved to make them believe that vice is virtue and falsehood truth.

I did not in the least observe that this infirmity was associated with ignorance or want of talent. I perceived it in the ablest, in the most learned, in the most plausible and imposing men I knew—for instance in Theiner, Newman, Hefele, Falloux. The question I used to ask in reviewing new books came back with increased force in judging the notabilities of the Church. It was a question, not of less or greater literary credit, but of religious merit. First, because it cannot be faith in the true sense, which a man defends by immoral means. Second, because belief is not sincere when the believer is not sincere. Thirdly, because the things to be excused or recommended are not mere laxities, but the worst of all crimes. Therefore, men who were outwardly defenders of religion appeared to me in reality advocates of deceit and murder. In those days a good test was put by the late Pope. He covered with the white skull cap of the Syllabus the overt acts of his predecessors, and invited the sanction of the Church for them at the Council. To me that was a mere detail. The great point was that these men justified the things to which in the past the papacy stood committed. They wished men to think that those things had not happened, or that they were good. They preached falsehood and murder.

To me they were not as other liars or other murderers. The theorist who, under no instant pressure, puts the idea of assassination into ignorant minds, seems to me worse than the ignorant criminal who acts upon it. The theorist who goes astray for the sake of religion, and of religion only, is worse than another. Corruptio optimi pessima. Other men go wrong from human passion: their religion may still work, in extremis, to convert and to save them. They may be criminals, but yet retain a conscience. The door of repentance is not closed to them. There is a spring unbroken that may react, even in the worst culprit. But in the Churchman there is no resource left. He is dragged down by the best thing in him. What redeems others leads him to destruction. It is at his best, when he is swept and garnished that he takes the devil into his soul. He never repents. His conscience is at rest; and his conscience is what he has made it. I must here repeat what I have often said to you: I am taking the finest specimens. I do not deal with common, obscure, incapable men, victims of a bad training, of a narrow sphere, of a backward age. I am thinking of men with whom I should not venture for an instant to compare myself, in knowledge, or talent, or yet greater gifts of God.

Speaking of such men in general, we cannot excuse them as we do inferiors. They are not sincere if they do not watch themselves and battle with all the familiar influences that lead men to error. With them prejudice is dishonesty.

Seeing this wickedness in the present, in men apparently excellent, I cannot doubt its existence in the past. And therefore I am very unwilling, in morals, and in discussing great men, to make allowances for their times. I allow for what they could not know. I do not allow for what they might have known. I insist upon the greater guilt of greater men for a special reason. A common writer of the grosser kind lies downright, deceives nobody, is found out, and despised. A clever writer dazzles and deceives without a downright lie. He insinuates a doubt, he takes advantage of somebody's error, exposes it, and so raises a prejudice; or he says Tu quoque; judges friends and enemies in different scales, etc. Now the last seems to me much the worse of the two. De Maistre says, no priest ever sent a heretic to death. Newman says, no heretic was ever put to death in Rome, excepting one mentioned in the life of S. Philip, an exception that proves the rule. Here is the brutal liar, and the artful deceiver, who seems so scrupulous, and certainly does his work, the devil's work, best.

I mean then, that this method, or opinion, or vice, exists; that it exists, for special reasons, among Catholics, especially among the defenders of the papacy; that it is substantially or essentially a scheme to make good Catholics by making bad Christians; that it is a doctrine of mendacity and nothing else; that its advocates are refined criminals, who would be infamous if their motive was not religion, and who are more infamous because their motive is religion—and this is what I understand by Ultramontanism, or Vaticanism. Between such men and innocent dupes or enthusiasts the distance is immense; and of the last I do not speak. I mean that we have to deal with a criminal conspiracy, with men who are neither enthusiasts, nor dupes, nor ignorant; but who know much more than I do, and know particularly what they are about.

It is a spirit that has taken many shapes in successive ages. The Crusaders who slaughtered the Jews, Conrad of Marburg, Simon de Montfort, Torquemada, Caraffa, Philip II, Gregory XIII, Suarez, the Cardinal of Guise, Pius V, Borromeo, and later under altered constellations, with other conditions, the men who, unable to imitate these, have praised them and shielded them from the execration which belongs to Marat—whether they be coarse and crude like De Maistre and Veuillot, or artful and shrewd, like Newman and Dupanloup—all these seem to me to manifest the same spirit of evil, to be links in the same tradition and symptoms of one disease. I should never think of reasoning with them. But I should never think of imputing the same roguery for any profane motive. I am persuaded that they have many good qualities, and as I heard you praise Möhler and Haneberg, I have known others enumerate the virtues of Suarez and Sir Everard Digby. Only I think that Suarez and Digby fully deserved to hang from the same beam.

Fully recognizing great qualities in the individuals, just as I recognise them in Carnot or Danton, I do not know how, because their error is theory, not practice, and founded on religion, not on selfishness, to regard them with a favour I am not to extend to political criminals.

Religion cannot excuse them, unless the end justifies the means. Instead of excusing, it aggravates the fault.

If I have made my meaning clear, several things will at once explain themselves: Why the various errors and absurdities of Ultramontanes fail to interest me, because they are but tiny diversions for men whose consciences are familiar with guilt such as that which marks them off from other men; why the dogmatic issues disappear for me behind the question of life or death; why books like those of Huber and Friedrich seem to me weapons borrowed from the enemy's arsenal; why I feel no surprise or indignation at the anticlerical policy in France; why Pius VII is more offensive to me than Pius IX; why I was so bewildered by your tenderness to Dupanloup, and still more by what you told me of Möhler. For I do not know how to assign degrees of guilt to the several Ultramontanes. The papacy sanctions murder; the avowed defender of the papacy is necessarily involved in that sanction. He cannot say, I defend the teacher but not the teaching, the culprit but not the deed. He must either deny or approve the doctrine. That is, he must be guilty of falsehood or of murder, neither more nor less than an advocate of Marat or St. Just. No man defends the papacy who has not accommodated his conscience to the idea of assassination. The thing is neither psychologically nor logically possible.

This wholesale condemnation of very religious, very able, very amiable men, is not at all singular, when one considers how very weak the conscience of this age is in respect of murder. It inspires less horror among men than many other things. Those who admire Mary Stuart, or Elizabeth, or Cromwell, or Lewis XIV, or James II, or William III, or Napoleon, or Mazzini, or Carnot, that is much more than half the educated world, have to go through a similar defilement.

And if it is right, in these things, to resist the current as Burke did in 1790, to fix the anchor of one's ethics in something apart from liquid opinion, it is right to do so in religion. Just as the people of the Commune seem to me altogether odious, so do the people of the Vatican.

As often as I have endeavoured to state these views you have rejected them by a series of objections which I think I should be able to weaken if I could ask you to go minutely over such weary ground. My real difficulty is not to answer your points, but to explain the reason of your disagreements with what seems to me so plain.

When you say that if I was older I should judge differently, you forget that I have long since outgrown the follies of youth, that I have devoted all my life to these questions, and have come to them with a great advantage. For, being your disciple, I started without any evil purposes or prejudice, or any idea at all but that religion is morality and truth, absolutely without any weak point. And this is not an effect of youth and inexperience, but of years of study and observation—as much study and observation, probably, as any man in my position has enjoyed. I began by thinking exactly the contrary. I looked up to men I have learnt to look down upon, and I have had to overcome a strong tendency to hero-worship and reverence. When you say that I speak without knowledge, as of Arnauld, that is hard to answer; but there is something to say. It has so often happened that you have dismissed some statement so positively as to make it difficult to pursue the subject without persistency, and so I have appeared to say more than I could prove. I remember, for instance, stating that the Hussites had in 1429 anticipated the Toleration of the Utopia. When you denied it, I really did not know whether I ought to fetch the passage I alluded to or not.

You urge that I am too uncharitable. But in reality I am severe in certain things; while in others I see that I judge more favourably than you do. I could cite many examples; but I only want to assure you that I do not start with any wish to condemn people. The real distinction is that you admit redeeming qualities and extenuating circumstances whereas I think it essential to be very particular in applying the same canons to all, so as to leave room for indulgence to friends or severity to foes. Absolute power is the only reproach I remember on which we differ. It is true that you have an indulgence for Marcus Aurelius, Frederic II, Frederic the Great, Bismarck, which a wooden-headed Whig finds it hard to share.

You often say that people err from ignorance. I do most decidedly disagree with the use you make of that argument. Omissis omittendis, I have never found that people go wrong from ignorance, but from want of consciousness. Even the ignorant are ignorant because they wish to be—an ignorant in bad faith. The argument falls to the ground if you apply it in the past. Baronius, Bellarmin, Suarez, Liguori, Pallavicini, Becanus, were not by any means ignorant. It is not by superior knowledge that we, many of us, differ from them. Moreover, we have all of us very often observed that you think people more stupid than they are, and in common conversation interpret what they say by the assumption that it is nonsense. And I have long convinced myself that it is a parti pris by which you avoid uncharitableness.

Then you separate past and present. Bossuet seems to you far better than Bellarmin; Möhler better than Bossuet. And you say, if I had lived then I might have been as blind as they; if they lived now they might be better than I. To this I reply, the same spirit is at work under altered conditions. Conrad of Marburg would now-a-days burn nobody. He would only go as near it as the times allow. He would calumniate where he could not burn: he would praise those who burnt. That is the only way in which our contemporaries can follow and canonize, and become responsible for the fanatics of other days. Newman or De Maistre would have been Mariana or Keller, if not

Clement or Gerard. There is no solution of continuity. There is nothing to distinguish Lacordaire from Torquemada but the spirit of the age around him. By becoming a Dominican he accepted the solidarity of the record of his order, as a man would who became a Jacobin.

Sometimes you object that I have not always spoken in this way. That is most true. I have always respected men until I found them out. Until last year I always spoke with reverence of Möhler. Indeed I might reply that I have spoken differently when I have spoken under your influence, and that what I have seen for myself compels me to speak otherwise. All this has been borne in upon me with a force and a consistency not to be resisted; and the great marvel to me is your vigorous and quite uncompromising contradiction. You have found out no theologian telling lies, conniving at murder, praising Borromeo or Pius V, defending Ximenes, esteeming Philip II, justifying the Inquisition, the Revocation, the Catholic reaction, the Catholic massacres, the Syllabus which covered these things. I have met nothing else wherever I have met Catholics of any distinction.

I have been tempted to attribute something to your friendship for Möhler. Yet I remember that you would not reprint his early writings (though reprinting some which scientifically were quite as bad); and that you were uneasy in his last days about the state of his soul. Or it may be early impressions of your own. But if St. Paul condemned his own conduct in his unregenerate days, surely we may do the same. Besides I do not think you tried to exalt the papacy, and it is by the papacy that our hands are soiled.

Forgive this long exposition, and do not allow any looseness of expression or any questionable instance to put out of sight the real drift of my statement. I may put it in a nutshell as follows:

You would not deem a Septembriseur, on the day of his crime, to be in a state of grace. Not until he repents. So long as he thinks his action right he will not repent. I apply this to St. Bartholomew. The assassins were not in a state of grace until they repented. If they were now living, they would not have repented, for they would always find priests to say that the Pope had judged that it was no sin. Now take an Ultramontane back to Paris in those days. The Pope, the judge of his conscience, decides that the Protestants must be killed. The Bulls of the Inquisition add that whoever protects them from their just fate shall incur the same penalty here and hereafter. If he says that the Pope is a bad guide in morals, that the Inquisition is a foul nest of criminals, he is no Ultramontane. If he is one, he will obey the injunction of the Holy Father, and will kill. Therefore I define as Ultramontane one whose opinions make him an assassin in 1572, an accomplice and abettor of assassination in 1882. The two are not separable. The guilt, the infamy, are the same. I cannot separate Möhler from the authority he wished to uphold, or the authority from the things it authorized. Sala, who says that Borromeo was right to get Protestants murdered, is the genuine type of Ultramontane. The same spirit produced the assassin, the Pope that canonized and the biographer or editor who approves him.

That spirit is the one thing we have to contend with. I trouble you with all this useless explanation because it is for me a very vital question. I find that I am alone. I do not see that this is decisive because I cannot obey any conscience but my own. But I not only cannot cite authorities on my side—I find that I have misunderstood the very teaching from which I start, and that my canons have become inconsistent with yours. Apart from dogma, I should feel myself, at heart, nearer to Rothe or Vinet or Martensen or Thiersch than to a Church in which nobody agrees with me in the fundamental question of the conditions of Grace.

Most faithfully yours

Acton

Döllinger III, pp. 283–291.

When, in reply to Gladstone, I said there is no indictment short of wilful murder: You must either hang or absolve—I became aware that the Professor [Döllinger] was not in harmony. It did not make a deep impression on me—I know not why. Two or three years later [in 1879], you [Lady Blennerhassett] published your paper on Dupanloup. You asked me for reminiscences, and afterward told me that you had made no use of them. I concluded that it was because I was hard upon him, and such views could not be worked into your own. And I imagined that your judgement on him was more favourable, treating him perhaps as a man who was mistaken, but not as a common rogue and impostor.

I told you that you were right to say that I lived in a world of illusions. The illusion I meant was the belief that the Professor and I objected to the Papacy, its crimes and in its adherents their indulgence to crime. It began to appear that he saw error where I saw crime, that his objection was academic, scientific, theoretic, almost professional, as I might object to a Protectionist or to a Conservative, to Thiers or Stein or Burke, not as we all object to Marat or Ravaillac or Carey.

Every summer since I have spent all my time and energy trying to discover whether we [Döllinger and Acton] really differ so widely. The response was not always the same or even consistent nor always clear. I made very little way, and had to meet *des fins de non recevoir*—as when you are older or, if you mean to bring a new doctrine of Christianity into the Church or consider the advantages of your position or what should we have done in like circumstances or men must have men to look up to.

The result has been to confuse. In all these years no fact and no conviction has been put forward which disturbs my conviction. And I have seen that my facts and points were generally evaded or put aside. It is incredible, if any valid argument exists, that I should never have discovered it myself, or heard it in five years of minute and searching discourse from him. In a great number of men . . . he sees virtue where I see vice: Gerson, Arnauld, Luther, Bossuet, Pius VII, St. Bernard, Lacordaire.

The difference is fundamental and as wide as the firmament. The Professor's position would then not be very far from Gallican. It is no progress at all. He follows no new light. He takes ground taken long before, and he takes it when it is weakened by the decision of a Council. He remains in sympathy with French institutions and teachers as odious to me as the Italians. And he affords no instrument for the reform and purification of the Church. He thinks that an Ultramontane may be saved. He thinks they have a right to toleration. He thinks that they carry with them, weakened and impaired but still efficacious, the sacramental gifts.

I do not suppose that the Professor approves these things. But to me it comes to the same thing if he excuses them and denies their criminality.

To me it is a question of morality and nothing else.

Often it appeared to me that the Professor did not give me of his best; but rather put me off with imperfect statements of fact. Very often he was disposed to treat my points not as the results of many years incessant study and varied observations, but as a harsh paradox or prejudice, not worthy of very serious treatment. The general effect was that the thing became disturbing to him the more definite I became, and at last, in 1883, he made it very clear that it was time for our conversations to cease, for this world.

As he spoke to my wife and her sister otherwise as not being so far apart I made a slight attempt this year in writing; and received an answer which to me is ambiguous and contradictory. As now advised, I must think that he does not like me to know his real mind, or that he is really of the opinion which I reject. For if we really agree, we should not have taken five years to find it out.

Therefore, so far as I can see, I have thoroughly misunderstood the Professor, have been in opposition when I thought myself his disciple and have had to spend five years in merely trying to find out his real sentiments.

1. First I must say that I have probably mistaken many other people, whom I had fewer opportunities of knowing and questioning.

2. Others also may have misunderstood him.

3. I have deceived people by sailing under false colours.

4. I have renounced public life and a position favourable to influence in my own country, to pursue an object I cannot obtain.

5. I am absolutely alone in my essential ethical position, and therefore useless. Not because one wants support or encouragement, but because anyone who asks who agrees with me will learn that no one agrees— and that no one disputes my view with anything like the energy with which the Professor disputes it.

6. No other person can ever be so favourably situated as the Professor. He seeks nothing—knows more, and had, assuredly, a prejudice in my favour. People whose prejudices are the other way, who know less, who are less perfectly independent, will certainly not listen to me better than he.

The probability of doing good by writings so isolated and repulsive, of obtaining influence for views so _____, is so small that I have no right to sacrifice to it my own tranquility, and my duty of educating my children. My time can be better employed than by waging a hopeless war. And the more my life has been thrown away, the more necessary to turn now and employ better what remains.

Add. Mss. 5403, pp. 29, 32, 26, 22, 23, 31, 27, 35, 25, 24, 21, 20, 19.

The *Cambridge Modern History*

I submit the following observations in reply to the question proposed by the Syndics.

The idea of a Universal Modern History has been executed with success already, both in France and in Germany.

I do not allude to Duncker or to Weiss, for Duncker's 24 volumes form a series of independent works, without any attempt to fuse the materials together, and Weiss addresses an exclusive public.

Our competing predecessors would be Weber of Heidelberg, and the authors of the General History which appears under the direction of Lavisse and Rambaud.

Both of these have mastered the difficulties of the task which is before us.

Weber covers in about 4000 pages from the XVth century to the Revolution, and to the present day in as many more. The Frenchmen, who have got down to 1800, observe nearly the same proportion.

Therefore, twelve volumes, each with 650 pages of text, and 550 words to a page, would have a slight advantage, in quantity, over the only rivals that occupy the ground.

In 1896, Lord Acton, as Regis Professor of History, was invited by the Syndics of the Cambridge University Press to undertake the planning and direction of a multi-volume history of the world. In October of that year, he submitted his plan for a universal, modern history. Acton died in 1902 before the first volume of the *Cambridge Modern History* was ready for publication and before his own chapters could be written. However, his insights and editorial labors securely laid the foundation for that great enterprise in the collaborative writing of history. In their introduction, the editors of the *Cambridge Modern History*, A.W. Ward, G.W. Protheroe, and Stanley Leathes, paid eloquent testimony to the influence which Acton's original conception, as it appeared in his "strictly private and confidential" report to the Syndics, exercised on the final product. That report, which is printed here, was published in 1969 in a facsimile edition by the Cambridge University Press under the title *Longitude 30 West*. Acton also expressed some of his views on a work of universal history in the letter he wrote to contributors to the *Cambridge Modern History*, reprinted in Acton, *Lectures on Modern History*, pp. 315–318.

Weber's Weltgeschichte, lately revised by his friends, is a useful compilation, and the Histoire Générale, written almost entirely by experts, is a superlative work of reference.

The University of Cambridge, with its resources and prestige, is in a position to aim higher, and to accomplish more.

I propose to divide the history of the last 400 years into short chapters, averaging 30 pages, each complete in itself, and dealing with one topic, or a single group of events, accurately defined, and I would distribute them among the largest number of available writers, inviting every English historian who is competent, to contribute at least a chapter.

It would be history not as it appears to the generality of instructed men, and is taught all the world over, but as each of the several parts is known to the man who knows it best.

There would be a clean text, without footnotes, or foreign quotations, or reference to particular authorities.

The name of the author would be the reader's security for obtaining without discussion or parade, the most perfect narrative that any English or American scholar can supply, in the appointed space.

It will be necessary to prescribe exact limits and conditions, and to explain clearly what we desire to obtain, and to avoid.

We shall avoid the needless utterance of opinion, and the service of a cause.

Contributors will understand that we are established, not under the meridian of Greenwich, but in longitude 30 West; that our Waterloo must be one that satisfies French and English, Germans and Dutch alike; that nobody can tell, without examining the list of authors, where the Bishop of Oxford laid down the pen, and whether Fairbairn or Gasquet, Liebermann or Harrison, took it up.

It is a unique opportunity of recording, in the way most useful to the greatest number, the fulness of the knowledge which the nineteenth century is about to bequeathe.

A mere reproduction of accepted facts would fall below the occasion and behind the memorable data.

In some instances where there is nothing new to tell, we shall adopt the words of Thiers: ou est déjà bien assez nouveau par cela seul qu'ou est vrai. Nobody, with 30 pages to do it in, can aspire to improve on Pastor's Popes of the Renaissance, Ritter's Counter-Reformation, Holst's Constitutional History of Slavery, Treitschke's Germany During the Peace, or Brückner's and Vandal's volumes on Russia.

Where all accessible information has been thoroughly absorbed, where the work is new and, for the moment, final, intelligent boiling down will be sometimes enough for our purpose. But we shall not often be left to this resource, and I hope that almost every page will be a light to every reader. We must raise the whole to the level of our best men, and discourage second-hand studies.

It used to be meritorious to compose history, as Hallam did, without any original master beyond the usual authorities. Raumer, at the height of his credit, renounced the easy quest of the unknown, and based his Modern History on the assumption that all requisite knowledge may be had from common books. The new material in Ranke's Reformation appeared so scanty as to create an impression that there was nothing more to discover, and Lingard was glad that Macaulay's narrative compelled but few changes in his own. Macaulay would hardly apply Lingard's words to himself, if he could see what his successors have made of the subject on which he satisfied the demand of his contemporaries; and Ranke's book seems to us divided by more than half a century from the Reformation as it is known to Kawerau.

There has been not only progress but subversion and renewal, since manuscripts have come into use almost without limit, since crowds of scholars are on the watch for them, and the supply of documents exceeds the supply of histories. The policy of concealment abandoned in so many places, as neither Italy nor Prussia was interested in keeping the secrets of fallen governments whose records were in their hands, has broken down altogether, and at last the Vatican discloses the guarded treasures of Galileo's tower.

The printing of archives has gone on parallel with the admission of enquirers, and the Master of the Rolls alone has made public 500 volumes of sources. Other countries are as profuse. While the Camden Club has produced 75 volumes, one Spanish Collection, the Documentos Ineditos, extends to half as many more. The Historical MSS. Commission is proud of its 46 volumes; but a single Russian family, the Vorontsovs, have issued about as many from their own family papers. At Vienna there is one series in 48 volumes, another in 83, and a third in 126; at Berlin, one in 65, and a much larger one at Florence.

The example is followed in every province of Italy, France, and Germany. Even Croatia has reached the 28th volume of its records. The Venetian dispatches from Austria, those of the Nuncios from Germany, those from all parts regarding critical stages in Bavarian history are being methodically edited. At Rome, in 1857 Döllinger drew up a remonstrance against the suppression of the Acta Tridentina and urged that there were no means of deciding between Pallavicini and Father Paul. The Council of Trent is known to us now, not through those rivals, but from the evidence that was before them, and from much besides. Between 200 and 300 of Calvin's letters were known when Dyer wrote his Life; ten times as many are in print today. Above 20 volumes of Frederic's correspondence have appeared since Carlyle.

The entire bulk of new matter which the last 40 years have supplied amounts to many thousands of volumes.

The honest student finds himself continually diverted, retarded, misled by the classics of historical literature, and has to hew his own way through multitudinous transactions, periodicals, and official publications, where it is difficult to sweep the horizon or to keep abreast. By the judicious division of labour, we should be able to do it, and to bring home to every man the last document, and the ripest conditions of international research.

Ultimate history we cannot have in this generation; but we can dispose of conventional history, and show the point we have reached on the road from the one to the other, now that all information is within reach, and every problem has become capable of solution.

All this does not apply to our own time, and the last volumes will be concerned with secrets that cannot be learned from books, but from men. Although so much has been done for Cavour and Bismarck, we have little authentic literature about Napoleon III, and less about Thiers. After Sir Theodore Martin, Windsor is silent; Lord Rowton covered one part of our story; Spencer Walpole has left half told another; and much more is buried in a tower at Hawarden.

If we employ the right men, and establish a claim to confidence, we may hope to give a good account even of the Victorian era.

Certain privately printed memoirs, such as Lord Broughton's, may not be absolutely inaccessible; the papers of one Prime Minister are in type, and part is in my custody, and there are elderly men about town gorged with esoteric knowledge. For the unwritten history of later times, as for the unprinted history of earlier times, all will depend on the successful selection of writers.

A true scholar, who is asked to contribute to a monumental work a couple of sheets on the one subject that most occupies his thoughts, and who has several years allowed him for the purpose, can hardly plead want of time. The Encyclopaedia, the National Biography, the Historical Review, and especially Smith's Dictionary of Ecclesiastical Biography, obtained the best work of the best men for little remuneration or for none at all.

I have a hypothetical list of about 120 men whom I should be glad to secure. At close quarters, some will turn out to be men in buckram; but when we have consulted the best advice about contributors, at Oxford, in the North, in Ireland and America, at the Museum and the Rolls, and the Public Offices, for India, the Colonies, and War, among the clergy, the lawyers and the Jews, we shall have as many new suggestions as there will be names to expunge, and we shall still have before us a conjectural 120. Assuming that one half are sure to decline or to fail us, I would undertake the task, as I conceive it, with the remainder.

The French General History, from the Renaissance to the Revolution, is the work of 42 contributors. Our six volumes for the same time would, by that precedent, require 7 writers each.

It is very desirable, at our first public announcement, to start with inspiring names; but it is not necessary at once to appropriate every position, down to the end.

Only 4 volumes can appear in the present century; and it will be enough if we begin by seeing every step of our way clear for full four years ahead, and complete so much of our arrangements this autumn, before we advertise—the rest to follow successively.

In that case, our present need of men is only 20. By issuing the last six volumes parallel with the first six, year by year, 1 and 7, 2 and 8, and so on, we shall interest more readers from the beginning, and shall make good our footing in America. Volumes 1 and 2 would be Renaissance and Reformation; but 7 would be the United States, and 8, the French Revolution.

Both the American volume and the Revolution volume ought, in the main, to be the work of one man. Allowing three for each, instead of one, on account of odd chapters, we could produce the 4 volumes which are first in order of publication with the assistance of 20 writers at the outside.

I subjoin some of the names that occur to me:

Bp. Creighton: Popes of the Renaissance

Harrisse or Winsor: Discovery of America

Burd (ed. of the *Prince*): Florence

Brown: Venice
Gairdner: Henry VIII
Bp. Stubbs: Elizabethan Reformation
Pocock: Edward VI
Hume: Elizabeth
Law: Mary Stuart
Laughton: Armada and Dutch Wars
Armstrong: France
Ward: Germany
Fairbairn: Puritans
Gardiner: 30 Years' War
Firth: The Stuarts
Mackinnon: The Jacobites
Sir F. Pollock: International Law
Goldwin Smith: Oceanic Empire
Bryce: Eastern Question
Douglas: China and Spain
Coolidge: Switzerland
C. Eliot Norton: Intellect of America
Lecky: French Revolution
Lord Wolseley: Bonaparte in Egypt
Captain Mahan: Nelson
Lord Rosebery: Napoleon
Prothero   Dicey   Courtney   Morley   Harrison   Walpole
Lord E. Fitzmaurice   G. Russell   Sir Mountstuart Grant Duff
Thursfield   Brett   Ransome: Recent English History
I say nothing now of the help I look for from Cambridge, but here
are some Oxford equivalents:
York Powell   Poole   Sir W. Anson   Plummer   Edwardes
Hassal   Wakeman   Lodge   Little   Johnson   Oman   Fletcher
Rashdall   Bright
besides more already mentioned.

We must feel our way about the United States. Bryce could write
the volume, but an American would answer better. Nobody knows the
details better than Holst; but he is not superior to party, and does not
write English well. Rhodes, the soundest and most impartial of
Americans, would be my first choice, if he is not inseparable from his
present work. Next to these, Adams, Fiske, Winsor, Cabot Lodge, or
Andrew White.

The Cambridge Modern History ought to be the composition of

English, American, and Colonial pens. But in an emergency we must take a capable foreigner rather than an inferior countryman. I can hardly imagine anybody among ourselves who could do, for instance, South America, or the Kulturkampf.

There are efficient foreigners, Brentano, Liebermann, Bunsen, Gregory, Friedmann, Balzani, who write English; and the chapters will, I hope, be very rare indeed where we have to depend on men who cannot. Perhaps a moderate sum might be allowed for translations. These would of course undergo the closest editorial revision. Indeed, every part of the work must be planed down and made flush, and we shall be obliged to negotiate a good deal, touching the rightful books to employ and the matters which the economy of the whole work requires to be included under each particular head. For the chapter Don John in the Mediterranean ought to cover not only Lepanto and Farragusta, but the Knights of Malta, and the Barbary Pirates. The Maritime Power should include the Levant trade, the East and West Indies, and the Buccaneers. At the Fall of the Jesuits, we must describe their missions, the government of Paraguay, the attempted conversion of China. "Catholic Relief" will bring down Irish history from Sarsfield to O'Connell.

If we fail to enforce this arrangement, then we must divide our chapters into sections and fill in the supplementary information at Headquarters. If we treat history as a progressive science, and lean specially on that side of it, the question will arise, how we justify our departure from ancient ways and how we satisfy the world that there is reason and method in our innovations. If our Wallenstein is very unlike Ranke's; if our Burke is neither the Burke of Morley nor of Lecky; if we differ both from Taine and Sorel in the Revolution, our verba magistri will not avail against greater masters.

To meet this difficulty we must provide a copious, accurate, and well-digested catalogue of authorities; Lavisse and Rambaud have done it most successfuly. They divide 30 or 40 pages to their bibliography, and give at least 1500 titles in each volume. Even with less space, and severer choice, we might make this feature a most valuable aid to historical studies. Our principle would be to supply help to students, not material to historians. But in critical places we must indicate minutely the sources we follow, and must refer not only to the important books, but to articles in periodical works, and even to original documents, and to transcripts in libraries.

The result would amount to an ordinary volume, presenting a

conspectus of historical literature and enumerating all the better books, the newly acquired sources, and the last discoveries. It would exhibit in the clearest light the vast difference between history, original and authentic, and history antiquated and lower than the highwater mark of present learning.

Besides the 20 or 25 pages of literary instruction in small type at the end of the volume, we must have a very full table of contents at the beginning, so as to dispense with an index, with headlines, and with the leaded titles to every paragraph which we find in the Histoire Générale. Contents as ample as Lecky's and a catalogue raisonné of primary and auxiliary authorities, sufficient to compensate for the absence of notes, will add 30 or 38 pages to the 650 of our text. I hope that these dimensions will not be exceeded, as the fixed limit of the whole will enable us to restrict each part to its due proportion, and a heavier bulk would repel.

I imagine each volume complete, procurable separately, provided with a second titlepage of its own, which would bear no number.

The first titlepage would of course be numbered, and might be something like this:

The Cambridge Modern History

I

The Renaissance

Edited

for the Syndics of the University Press

By Lord Acton, Regius Professor

I trust that I shall be authorized to tell people that I am directed by the Syndicate to write to them; and that there will be a short statement in Vol. I describing the whole, and signed by the Syndics. The question of a general index, and a revising supplement, may be considered later. Although the volumes appear in two divisions, they had better be numbered successively, without mention of divisions.

They would begin in 1899, and would be completed in six years, by the end of 1904.

We may find it difficult to get the American volume ready in time, if it is written almost all by one man. Negotiations and corrections will take longer, the Atlantic intervening.

By universal history I understand that which is distinct from the combined history of all countries, which is not a rope of sand but a continuous development, and is not a burden on the memory, but an illumination of the soul. It moves in a succession to which the nations are subsidiary. Their story will be told not for their own sake, but in reference and subordination to a higher series according to the time and the degree in which they contribute to the common fortunes of mankind.

Secondary states appear, in perspective, when they carry flame or fuel, not when they are isolated, irrelevant, stagnant, inarticulate, sterile, passive, when they lend nothing to the forward progress or the upward growth, and offer no aid in solving the perpetual problem of the future.

Renaissance and the Epoch of Discovery, Reformation and Wars of Religion, Turkish Crusade and Western Colonization, European Absolutism, Dutch, English, American, French Revolution, and its derivatives, the constitutional, democratic, national, social, liberal, federal movement of the world—that is the great argument of the epic that we are to expose.

These things are extraterritorial, having their home in the sky, and no more confined to race or frontier than a rainbow or a storm.

I would keep to the main line attending to the byways at the junctions only, and direct our thought on the common effort, the central action of men, by which the landmarks of civilization have been extended, and the moving force renewed.

I would tell all we know of Solyman, Sixtus, Warren Hastings, not of every Sultan, Pope, or Governor General. Geneva would be prominent under Calvin, Portugal under Pombal, Corsica under Paoli; but they would otherwise retire into obscurity. Switzerland slumbers from the Reformation to the Revolution; Denmark, from 1660 to 1770; Venice, from the beginning of the seventeenth century; Holland, from the beginning of the eighteenth.

We should give a retrospect of the history of Russia when it emerges, under Peter the Great, thereby following the natural order of cause, not that of fortuitious juxtaposition.

I think Taine is right when he says: Pour expliquer les événements, il suffit de les disposer dans l'ordre convenable. C'est dire leur cause que leur donner leur place.

Whilst we give general history and not national, unless as tributary, so also we give general history, not that of religion and philosophy, of literature, science and art.

They too appear at many points and influence the course of public events from time to time; but when they do not then we are not concerned with them, and have not to describe their orbit when there is no conjunction.

It may be said that these are vulgar and retrograde notions, contracting the sphere and degrading the level of history; that we might enrich it with what men have thought as well as wrought; that the true mark and measure of the age would be a work combining the method and the wisdom of Buckle and Draper, Whewell and Leslie Stephen, Burckhardt and Lamprecht, Harnack and Haym, Ihering, and Gierke, and Sohm.

I wish I knew how all these strains could be blended; but it is certain that we must present history in the way most widely accepted.

I would meet the objection and unite the moral and intellectual realm with that of political force, on the following plan.

There would be a chapter, at intervals, on each branch of literature when it attains supremacy, and impresses its character on the age:

1. European thought under the predominant influence of theology, from Erasmus to Arminius—

2. of scholarship, and the erudition of the past, from Sigonius and Scaliger to Usher and Saumaise.

3. of philosophy, from Bacon and Descartes, to Leibnitz and Malebranche.

4. of politics and economics, before the American and the French Revolution.

5. In the historic age, from Burke onwards; and

6. In the scientific age, of today.

These are accumulating influences, and their epochs overlap. The six chapters will necessarily be very long ones; several of them can only be written at Cambridge—the last, by more than one hand.

This portion of the plan will be the most difficult to execute, and it is impossible, without much detail, to explain how I hope to conquer the obvious dangers, and to make it practical and scientific.

Certain significant headings of chapters indicate the manner in which I would make further and fuller provision, and will prove that I do not wish to reduce all history to a mere narrative of political transactions.

If history is often called the teacher and the guide that regulates public life, which, to individuals as to societies is as important as private, this is the time and the place to prove the title. The recent past contains the key to present time. All forms of thought that influence it come before us in their turn, and we have to describe the ruling currents, to interpret the sovereign forces, that still govern and divide the world. There are, I suppose, at least a score of them, in politics, economics, philosophy and religion, and our treatment cannot be complex, or systematic, or made to scale.

But if we carry history down to the last syllable of recorded time, and leave the reader at the point where study passes into action, we must explain to him the cause, and the growth, and the power of every great intellectual movement, and equip him for many encounters of life.

The part thus assigned to our later volumes is a thing that no other work has attempted, and that no other work could do so well.

Therefore the essential elements of the plan I propose for consideration are these:

> Division of subjects among many specially
>   qualified writers;
> Highest pitch of knowledge without the display;
> Distinction between the organic unity of general
>   history and the sum of national histories,
>   as the principle for selecting and
>   distributing matter;
> Proportion between historic thought and historic
>   fact;
> Chart and compass for the coming century.

I append a scheme of titles for volume and chapter. It may be convenient to have the entire field mapped out, even tentatively. It will show in what manner I would group events and trace ideas, and in what measure history might be made to afford the basis for a true philosophy of life.

Assuming a chapter to be 30 or 35 pages, England, with about 40 chapters would obtain 1200 or 1400 pages—much more than the longer text of Green. The French Revolution would about equal Carlyle, or the French part of Sybel; America would be double the volume of Goldwyn Smith; and Napoleon, three times the length of Seeley's. France, apart from the quarter of a century where it makes history for the world, would have about 30 chapters, Germany 35, and the rest in proportion.

With this allowance, omitting scenic and biographical detail, and all discussion that is not required for definiteness, clearness and accuracy, everything can be told that men need to know of all that gives permanent value to history.

Besides 5 chapters on the principal treaties, from Westphalia to Vienna, I would have a sixth (Alabama) on the results that the law of nations has achieved for humanity.

Sixteen chapters would be devoted to the problems of Church and State, besides six specially occupied with ecclesiastical history—that is: Eve of Reformation, Indulgences, European opinion, Edward VI, Reforms of Trent, the Jesuits.

Twelve or fourteen are concerned with the history of thought, apart from politics and religion; and near 40 deal with the forms and the development of political doctrines.

In all, about 80 of our chapters, or one third of the twelve volumes, would give history of ideas, not as theoretical truths, but as operative forms.

I propose to conclude with a chapter on socialism and economic conditions; with one on the science of the present day; and with a last chapter, treating of later views on the philosophy of history.

The last topic is not an organic necessity. If Flint will not undertake it, we must do without it. But if he will, it might form a suitable termination to a work which, on the whole, will be aloof from speculation and system; and would probably show convincing reason for our impartial reserve.

Acton

October 1896

Index

687

The typeface for the text of this book is *Baskerville*. Its creator, John Baskerville (1706–1775), broke with tradition to reflect in his type the rounder, yet more sharply cut lettering of eighteenth-century stone inscriptions and copy books. The type foreshadows modern design in such novel characteristics as the increase in contrast between thick and thin strokes and the shifting of stress from the diagonal to the vertical strokes. Realizing that this new style of letter would be most effective if cleanly printed on smooth paper with genuinely black ink, he built his own presses, developed a method of hot-pressing the printed sheet to a smooth, glossy finish, and experimented with special inks. However, Baskerville did not enter into general commercial use in England until 1923.

Book design by Hermann Strohbach, New York, New York
Editorial service and index by Harkavy Publishing Service,
New York, New York
Typography by Monotype Composition Co., Inc., Baltimore, Maryland
Printed and bound by Worzalla Publishing Company,
Stevens Point, Wisconsin